World Scientific Proceedings Series on
Computer Engineering and Information Science 9

Decision Making
and Soft Computing

Proceedings of the 11th International FLINS Conference

World Scientific Proceedings Series on Computer Engineering and Information Science

Series Founding Editor: Da Ruan
Series Editor: Jie Lu, University of Technology Sydney

World Scientific Proceedings Series on
Computer Engineering and Information Science 9

Decision Making
and Soft Computing

Proceedings of the 11th International FLINS Conference

João Pessoa (Paraíba), Brazil   17 – 20 August 2014

editors

Ronei Marcos de Moraes
Federal University of Paraíba, Brazil

Etienne E Kerre
Ghent University, Belgium

Liliane dos Santos Machado
Federal University of Paraíba, Brazil

Jie Lu
University of Technology, Sydney, Australia

World Scientific

NEW JERSEY · LONDON · SINGAPORE · BEIJING · SHANGHAI · HONG KONG · TAIPEI · CHENNAI

Published by

World Scientific Publishing Co. Pte. Ltd.

5 Toh Tuck Link, Singapore 596224

USA office: 27 Warren Street, Suite 401-402, Hackensack, NJ 07601

UK office: 57 Shelton Street, Covent Garden, London WC2H 9HE

British Library Cataloguing-in-Publication Data
A catalogue record for this book is available from the British Library.

World Scientific Proceedings Series on Computer Engineering and Information Science — Vol. 9
DECISION MAKING AND SOFT COMPUTING
Proceedings of the 11th International FLINS Conference (FLINS 2014)

Copyright © 2014 by World Scientific Publishing Co. Pte. Ltd.

ISBN 978-981-4619-96-7

Printed in Singapore

FOREWORD

FLINS, originally an acronym for Fuzzy Logic and Intelligent Technologies in Nuclear Science (1994), was first launched in the Belgian Nuclear Research Centre (SCK•CEN). FLINS was later extended to include the theoretical and practical aspects of fuzzy logic as well as other topics of computational intelligence. The principal mission of FLINS is to bridge the gap between machine intelligence and real complex systems via joint research between universities, research institutions, and industries; encouraging interdisciplinary research and bringing multidisciplinary researchers together.

Following the successful FLINS1994 (Mol, Belgium), FLINS1996 (Mol, Belgium), FLINS1998 (Antwerp, Belgium), FLINS2000 (Bruges, Belgium), FLINS2002 (Gent, Belgium), FLINS2004 (Blankenberge, Belgium), FLINS2006 (Genova, Italy), FLINS2008 (Madrid, Spain), FLINS2010 (Chengdu, China) and FLINS2012 (Istanbul, Turkey), the 11th International FLINS Conference (FLINS2014) is held in João Pessoa, Brazil. This decision was initiated by Professor Da Ruan in 2010 and supported by the FLINS Steering Committee in 2012, and it is the first time a FLINS conference has been held in the Americas. This is a good opportunity to expand the FLINS conference and enhance its standing worldwide.

FLINS2014 focuses on Decision Making and Soft Computing, and aims to provide an international forum for researchers to come together to report on up-to-date innovations and developments in all aspects of those areas.

FLINS2014 is co-organized by the Laboratory of Technologies for Virtual Teaching and Statistics (LabTEVE) and the Laboratory of Applied Statistics to Image Processing and Geoprocessing (LEAPIG), both of which are part of the Department of Statistics and the Graduate Program in Decision Models and Health, the Federal University of Paraíba, João Pessoa, Brazil. The conference is co-sponsored by the Brazilian Federal Agency for the Support and Evaluation of Graduate Education (CAPES), the National Council for Scientific and Technological Development (CNPq), and the Belgian Nuclear Research Centre, as well as the European Society for Fuzzy Logic and Technology (EUSFLAT), Tropical Hotels & Resorts (Brazil) and Waine Formiga Brand Design (Brazil).

FLINS2014 is being held jointly with The 9th International Conference on Intelligent Systems and Knowledge Engineering (ISKE2014) and both conferences will publish papers in the proceedings. The ISKE conference series obtained great success in ISKE2006 (Shanghai, China), ISKE2007 (Chengdu, China), ISKE2008 (Xiamen, China), ISKE2009 (Hasselt, Belgium), ISKE2010 (Hangzhou, China), ISKE2011 (Shanghai, China), ISKE2012 (Beijing, China), and ISKE2013 (Shenzhen, China), and the connection with FLINS2014 will be mutually beneficial. ISKE2014 is particularly sponsored by the Federal University of Paraíba, Brazil, and is technically co-sponsored by Southwest Jiaotong University (China), the University of Technology, Sydney (Australia), and the University of Gent (Belgium). ISKE2014 emphasizes current practice, experience and promising new ideas in the broad area of intelligent systems and knowledge engineering.

A Doctoral Consortium on Soft Computing and Decision-Making has been organized in the conference to provide PhD students with the opportunity to present and discuss their current research and receive feedback from established researchers.

The proceedings consist of a series of invited distinguished professors and individual presentations. In total, 117 papers from 31 countries were accepted for publications in the proceedings following a peer review process. The three invited lectures are: 1) The Contribution of Fuzzy Sets in Decision Sciences by Prof. Didier Dubois (Université de Toulouse, France), 2) Granular Fuzzy Systems: A New Direction in Soft Computing and Human-Centric Decision-Making by Prof. Witold Pedrycz (University of Alberta, Canada), and 3) Some Approaches Towards Lattice Computing in Mathematical Morphology and Computational Intelligence by Prof. Peter Sussner (University of Campinas, Brazil).

The accepted papers have been divided into the following seven parts: 1) Decision Making and Decision Support Systems; 2) Statistics, Data Analysis and Data Mining; 3) Foundations of Computational Intelligence; 4) Soft Computing and Applied Research; 5) Intelligent Systems and Knowledge Engineering; 6) Uncertainty Modeling; and 7) Intelligent Information Processing.

We would like to thank the FLINS steering committee, all contributors, reviewers, regular and invited session chairs and program committee members of FLINS2014 and ISKE2014 for their kind cooperation and enthusiasm for the conference. We also thank Chelsea Chin (Editor, World Scientific) for her kind advice and help in publishing this volume.

Editors
Prof. Ronei Marcos de Moraes, Federal University of Paraíba, Brazil
Prof. Etienne E. Kerre, Gent University, Belgium
Prof. Liliane dos Santos Machado, Federal University of Paraíba, Brazil
Prof. Jie Lu, University of Technology Sydney, Australia

April 2014

CONTENTS

PART 6. UNCERTAINTY MODELING   582

INVITED LECTURES

THE CONTRIBUTION OF FUZZY SETS TO DECISION SCIENCES

D. DUBOIS

CNRS-IRIT,
Université de Toulouse, France
E-mail: dubois@irit.fr
www.irit.fr/ Didier.Dubois

We try to provide a tentative assessment of the role of fuzzy sets in decision analysis. We discuss membership functions, aggregation operations, linguistic variables, fuzzy intervals and valued preference relations. The importance of the notion of bipolarity and the potential of qualitative evaluation methods are also pointed out. We take a critical standpoint on the state of the art, in order to highlight the actual achievements and point out research directions for the future.

Keywords: Decision, qualitative value scales, aggregation, linguistic variables, preference relations, fuzzy intervals, ranking methods.

1. Decision in a fuzzy environment: the state of the art

The idea of using fuzzy sets in decision sciences is not surprising since decision analysis is a field where human-originated information is pervasive. The seminal paper in this area was written by Bellman and Zadeh[1] in 1970, highlighting the role of fuzzy set connectives in criteria aggregation. That pioneering paper made three main points:

- Membership functions can be viewed as a variant of utility functions or rescaled objective functions.
- Combining membership functions, especially using the minimum, can be one approach to criteria aggregation. It claimed that in some situations, criteria can be viewed as flexible constraints. It highlights a max-min paradigm for optimisation, on a par with the usual additive criteria aggregation.
- Multiple-stage decision-making problems based on the minimum aggregation connective can then be stated and solved by means of dynamic programming.

While there is an early literature on the third item,[2] it is the second one that has been extensively developed as witnessed by the numerous papers and books on aggregation functions.[3-5] As to the first issue, not so many scholars studied membership functions in connection with measurement theory (if we except Turksen[6]), nor did they take the connection with utility functions seriously. Fuzzy set theory has been applied to decision sciences in the form of fuzzy ordering relations, linguistic variables and fuzzy intervals. We can especially point out the following:

(1) *Gradual or valued preference relations*, with two streams, one stemming from Zadeh's *fuzzy orderings* dating back to 1971,[7] and more recently studied by Fodor, Roubens, Bodenhofer and colleagues, the other being *reciprocal valued relations*, recently studied by De Baets and colleagues,[8] where the natural understanding is often probabilistic since the preference degrees between two opposite pairwise comparisons sum to 1.

(2) *Linguistic variables*[9] have been used to model preference information, so as to get decision methods hopefully closer to the user cognition.

(3) *Fuzzy interval computations and comparison techniques*[10,11] can cope with epistemic uncertainty in numerical aggregation schemes. Especially, extensions of the weighted average with ill-known weights have been proposed.[12]

What has been the contribution of fuzzy sets to decision sciences? Following the terminology of the original Bellman-Zadeh paper, fuzzy decision analysis (FDA) is supposed to take place *in a fuzzy environment*, in contrast with probabilistic decision analysis, taking place *under uncertainty*. But, what is a fuzzy environment? It seems that many authors take it as an environment where the major source of information is linguistic, so that linguistic variables are used, which does not correspond to Bellman and Zadeh's proposal. One should nevertheless not oppose "fuzzy environment" to "uncertain environment": the former in fact often means "using fuzzy sets", while 'uncertain environment' refers to an actual decision situation: there is epistemic uncertainty due to missing information, not always related to linguistic imprecision. Actually, for many decision theory specialists, it is not clear that fuzzy sets have ever led to a new decision paradigm. Indeed, one may argue that some techniques already existed under a different terminology, and that some fuzzy decision methods are fuzzifications of standard decision techniques.

In several cases indeed, fuzzy sets have just been added to existing techniques (fuzzy AHP methods, fuzzy weighted averages, fuzzy extensions of ELECTRE-style Multiple Criteria Decision Making (MCDM) methods) with no clear benefits (especially when fuzzy information is changed into precise numbers prior to further processing, via defuzzification, which can be observed sometimes). Likewise, fuzzy preference modelling is an extension of standard preference modelling; it would benefit from a comparison to probabilistic or measurement-based preference modeling. In fact, contrary to what is often claimed in fuzzy decision analysis papers, it is not always the case that adding fuzzy sets to an existing method improves it in a significant way. Too often, these papers contain a method described step by step, with some fuzzy sets involved, but no comparison with existing methods, no formal study of the properties of the method are given. Sometimes fuzzy ratings are modelled by complex entities such as higher order fuzzy sets, which become very difficult to understand by decision-makers, as if moving to more complex rating representations could address difficulties already existing in the numerical measurement of abstract features.

2.   Some prospective issues in fuzzy decision analysis

In fact, we have argued in a recent paper[14] that fuzzy decision analysis could benefit from a critical assessment of its achievements and its limitations. There are several points that would deserve specific investigations in the future.

The choice of a membership scale : do we need numerical ratings or can we live with qualitative ones? Do we need a bipolar scale[15] where the two ends refer to the idea of *good* and *bad* and a special value inside corresponds to the idea of indifference? On the contrary one may use two opposite unipolar scales. The latter choice comes close to papers using interval-valued or so-called intuitionistic fuzzy sets. However, these approaches are often unclear because a pair of values can either represent an ill-known precise one, or can stand as evaluating pros and cons.[17] Some authors have modelled multifactorial evaluations by means of fuzzy linguistic rules and applied fuzzy logic control methods to compute global ratings. This technique is debatable because if the local rating scales are not measurable attributes, linguistic variables with triangular fuzzy intervals make no sense.[13] Perhaps in many cases a finite totally ordered scale is expressive enough. In any case, a prerequisite for a proper use of fuzzy sets in decision analysis is to have a clear intuition of what is the meaning of fuzzy membership grades in a given application,[16] and what kind of scale is appropriate. The issue of measuring membership grades[18] has recently received too sparse attention.

Fuzzy preference modelling : A number of works have been published on fuzzy preference relations. They are valued relations and there are, as recalled, above, two settings: the *reciprocal relations*, and the *valued outranking relation* (the latter often decomposed in a strict part, an equivalence part and an incomparability part[21]) which is the direct extension of reflexive Boolean relations. There is a need for a measurement approach to degrees of preference that parallels the probabilistic understanding of reciprocal relations.[19] A degree of preference in the latter case is often viewed as measuring the probability of strict preference on a bipolar scale (hence not generalizing the usual model of reflexivity), while valued outranking relations express the idea of intensity of preference on a negative scale (the top value meaning indifference[20]). Interestingly, the latter non-probabilistic view can also refer to the idea of *possibility* of preference stemming from the comparison of fuzzy intervals. Some works exist on the representation of fuzzy outranking relations in terms of fuzzy interval orderings, but the full landscape of fuzzy preference relations is far from being laid bare.

Qualitative possibility theory in decision analysis : the idea is that possibility distributions on qualitative scales can play a role similar to probability distributions, but the former explicitly accounts for incomplete information in a more faithful way than subjective probabilities. In this spirit, there exists a fuzzy counterpart of Savage theory, in a purely qualitative setting, justifying max-min and min-max aggregation schemes for decision under uncertainty and multiple-criteria decision-making.[23] More general forms of uncertainty modeling or criteria weighting schemes can be considered, using fuzzy integrals of various kinds.[24] Multiple-stage extensions, such as qualitative decision networks, have been studied,[25] and more recently partially observable possibilistic Markov decision networks.[26]

Uncertainty management in numerical decision methods : Fuzzy sets understood as possibility distributions can be useful to perform a kind of sensitivity analysis on existing decision analysis methods (for instance the AHP technique of Saaty, and all kinds of numerical aggregation schemes). However, it means that we should then not consider fuzzy-valued ratings as an alternative kind of rating, but as flexible constraints on ill-known precise values. Then extensions of compositional schemes (generalized fuzzy set operations) cannot be used without care. For instance, rather than trying to directly define fuzzy eigen-values of fuzzy set-valued preference matrices, as if they were just another kind of matrix, it makes more sense to compute the range of the eigen-values of the usual preference matrices compatible with the fuzzy specification.[27] Nevertheless, the use of fuzzy sets does not circumvent the limitations of the usual AHP method.[13] Likewise, it makes little sense to require that the sum of ill-known weights in a weighted arithmetic mean be equal to 1; what can be required is that the set of normalized weight vectors compatible with fuzzy intervals be not empty.[28] Generally speaking, before solving a decision problem with fuzzy intervals, it is better to solve it in a meaningful way using crisp intervals. If the proposed solution makes no sense with crisp intervals, it will not be better off with fuzzy intervals.

Ranking fuzzy intervals : The same considerations apply to the issue of ranking fuzzy intervals. First, defuzzification is not always the way to go, as it does away with the uncertainty and comes down to working with precise values. Then why modeling uncertainty in the first place? It is clear that if decision evaluations take the form of fuzzy intervals, the advantage of a ranking method is to lay bare the situations where an actual ranking looks difficult to reach. In fact, ranking methods for fuzzy intervals should borrow from interval ordering techniques and the comparison of random numbers (probabilistic preference, stochastic dominance) taking advantage of the fact that in the numerical setting, a fuzzy interval encodes a family of probability measures in the form of nested confidence intervals.[29]

The issues raised in this short note are more fully described in the papers listed below, especially some surveys[14,30] where extensive bibliographies can be found.

References

1. R. E. Bellman and L. A. Zadeh, Decision making in a fuzzy environment, *Management Science*, **17**, B141-B164C (1970).
2. J. Kacprzyk, A. O. Esogbue, Fuzzy dynamic programming: Main developments and applications. Fuzzy Sets and Systems **81**(1), 31-45 (1996).
3. V. Torra, Y. Narukawa, *Modeling Decisions: Information Fusion and Aggregation Operators* (Springer, 2007).
4. G. Beliakov, A. Pradera, T. Calvo, *Aggregation Functions: A Guide for Practitioners* Studies in Fuzziness and Soft Computing, Vol. 221 (Springer, 2008).
5. M. Grabisch, J.-L. Marichal, R. Mesiar, E. Pap, *Aggregation Functions* (Cambridge University Press, 2009).

6. I.B. Türksen , T. Bilgic, Measurement of membership functions: Theoretical and empirical work, *Fundamentals of Fuzzy Sets* (D. Dubois and H. Prade, eds.) The Handbooks of Fuzzy Sets, 195–230, (Kluwer Publ. Comp., 2000).

7. L.A. Zadeh, Similarity relations and fuzzy orderings, *Information Sciences*, **3**177-200 (1971).

8. J.M. Blin A. B. Whinston, Fuzzy sets and social choice, *J. Cybernetics*, **3(4)**, 17-22 (1973).

9. L.A. Zadeh, The concept of a linguistic variable and its application to approximate reasoning, *Information Sciences*, Part 1, **8**, 199-249; Part 2, **8**, 301-357; Part 3, **9**, 43-80 (1975).

10. D. Dubois, E. Kerre, R. Mesiar, H. Prade, Fuzzy interval analysis, *Fundamentals of Fuzzy Sets* (D. Dubois, H. Prade, Eds) The Handbooks of Fuzzy Sets Series, 483-581 (Kluwer, Boston, Mass., 2000).

11. X. Wang and E. Kerre, Reasonable properties for the ordering of fuzzy quantities (2 parts), *Fuzzy Sets and Systems*, **118**, 375-406 (2001).

12. Y.-M. Wang, Y. Luo, Generalised fuzzy weighted mean and its applications *Int. J. of General Systems*, **38**, 533 – 546 (2009).

13. D. Bouyssou, T. Marchant, M. Pirlot, P. Perny, A. Tsoukias, P. Vincke, *Evaluation Models: a Critical Perspective.* (Kluwer Acad. Pub. Boston, 2000).

14. D. Dubois, The role of fuzzy sets in decision sciences: Old techniques and new directions. Fuzzy Sets and Systems **184**(1), 3-28 (2011).

15. D. Dubois, H. Prade, An introduction to bipolar representations of information and preference. *Int. J. Intell. Syst.* **23**(8), 866-877 (2008).

16. D. Dubois, H. Prade, The three semantics of fuzzy sets. *Fuzzy Sets and Systems*, **90**, 141-150 (1997).

17. D. Dubois, H. Prade, Gradualness, uncertainty and bipolarity: Making sense of fuzzy sets, *Fuzzy Sets and Systems*, **192**, 3-24 (2012).

18. C. Desimpelaere T. Marchant, An empirical test of some measurement-theoretic axioms for fuzzy sets *Fuzzy Sets and Systems*, **158**, 1348-1359 (2009).

19. B. De Baets, H. De Meyer (2005) Transitivity frameworks for reciprocal relations: cycle-transitivity versus FG-transitivity, *Fuzzy Sets and Systems,* **152**, 249-270 (2005).

20. U. Bodenhofer, B. De Baets, J. C. Fodor A compendium of fuzzy weak orders: Representations and constructions. *Fuzzy Sets and Systems* **158**(8), 811-829 (2007).

21. J. Fodor and M. Roubens, *Fuzzy preference modelling and multicriteria decision support* (Kluwer Academic Publishers, 1994).

22. M. Roubens, P. Vincke, Fuzzy possibility graphs and their application to ranking fuzzy numbers, In *Non-Conventional Preference Relations in Decision Making* (Kacprzyk J. and. Roubens M., eds.), 119-128 (Springer-Verlag, 1988).

23. D. Dubois, H. Fargier, H. Prade, R. Sabbadin. A survey of qualitative decision rules under uncertainty. *Decision-making Process- Concepts and Methods* (D. Bouyssou, D. Dubois, M. Pirlot, H. Prade, Eds.) Chap. 11, 435-473 (ISTE London & Wiley, 2009).

24. D. Dubois, H. Prade, A. Rico, Qualitative integrals and desintegrals: how to handle positive and negative scales in evaluation. *IPMU (3)* (S. Greco, Ed.) Communications in Computer and Information Science, vol. 299, 306-316 (Springer, 2012).

25. R. Sabbadin, H. Fargier, J. Lang Towards qualitative approaches to multi-stage decision making *Int. J. of Approximate Reasoning*, **19**(3-4), 441-471 (1998).

26. N. Drougard, F. Teichteil-Konigsbuch, J.-L. Farges, D. Dubois. Qualitative Possibilistic Mixed-Observable MDPs. *Proc. Conference on Uncertainty in Artificial Intelligence (UAI 2013)*, 192-201(AUAI Press, Corvalis, Or. USA, 2013).

27. S. Ohnishi, D. Dubois, H. Prade T. Yamanoi, A Fuzzy Constraint-Based Approach to the Analytic Hierarchy Process, *Uncertainty and Intelligent Information Systems* (B. Bouchon-Meunier *et al.* Eds.) 217-228 (World Scientific, Singapore, 2008).

28. O. Pavlačka Note on the lack of equality between fuzzy weighted average and fuzzy convex sum, *Fuzzy Sets and Systems*, **213**,102-105 (2013).

29. I. Couso and D. Dubois, An imprecise probability approach to joint extensions of stochastic and interval orderings *IPMU (3)* (S. Greco, Ed.) Communications in Computer and Information Science, vol. 299 (Springer, 2012).

30. D. Dubois, P. Perny, A review of fuzzy sets in decision sciences: achievements, limitations and perspectives, *MCDA- State of the Art Surveys,* (M. Ehrgott, S. Greco, Eds.) 2d Ed., Springer, to appear.

GRANULAR FUZZY SYSTEMS: A NEW DIRECTION IN SOFT COMPUTING AND HUMAN CENTRIC DECISION-MAKING*

WITOLD PEDRYCZ

Department of Electrical & Computer Engineering
University of Alberta, Edmonton Canada
Department of Electrical & Computer Engineering
King Abdulaziz University
Jeddah, 21589, Saudi Arabia
and
Systems Research Institute, Polish Academy of Sciences
Warsaw, Poland
e-mail: wpedrycz@ualberta.ca

In numerous real-world problems including a broad range of decision-making tasks, we are faced with a diversity of locally available distributed sources of data and expert knowledge, with which one has to interact, reconcile and form a global and user-oriented model of the system under consideration. While the technology of Soft Computing has been playing a vital and highly visible role with this regard, there are still a number of challenges inherently manifesting in these problems when dealing with collaboration, reconciliation, and efficient fusion of various sources of knowledge. To prudently address these problems, in this study, we introduce a concept of *granular* fuzzy systems forming an essential generalization of fuzzy systems pursued in Soft Computing. Information granularity of fuzzy sets used in these models is formalized in the framework of Granular Computing. We briefly elaborate on the fundamentals of Granular Computing including (i) a principle of justifiable granularity, (ii) an allocation of information granularity being sought as an essential design asset, and (iii) an emergence of higher type and higher order information granules in investigations of hierarchical architectures of systems. We show the roles of these principles in the analysis and synthesis of granular fuzzy systems. A class of group decision-making problems is studied in detail. We investigate granular AHP models and demonstrate a pivotal role of information granularity in the generalization of these constructs.

1. Introduction

Information granules are omnipresent. They form an integral ingredient of natural language. They support our abilities to comprehend complex phenomena, help describe and organize knowledge about the external world and facilitate a way we communicate our findings. Information granules support our

---

* This work is supported by Natural sciences and engineering research Council of Canada (NSERC) and Canada Research Chair (CRC) Program.

abilities to develop some helpful levels of abstraction. Forming information granules, establishing their formal computational models, and processing information granules fall under the domain of Granular Computing. Interestingly, by looking at the discipline of Granular Computing, one can express quite distinct views. On the one hand, one can stress that Granular Computing is a new and original endeavor. On the other hand, one may argue that a number of its underlying conceptual pursuits and associated methodologies (such as those delivered by rough sets, fuzzy set, interval analysis) forming essentials of Granular Computing have been around for several decades. Along this line, we have also witnessed an emergence of a significant number of generalized granular constructs such as type-2 [4][5][6] or interval-valued fuzzy sets, rough sets [7], rough fuzzy sets [8], probabilistic sets [2][3], and alike.

One has to be cognizant that (and this point needs to be underlined) a research agenda of Granular Computing focuses on building a coherent, unified and comprehensive framework which abstracts from individual granular constructs and their underlying methodologies and strives to establish some overarching principles that apply equally well across various formalisms and lay down methodological and algorithmic foundations.

From this perspective, Granular Computing is still in *statu nascendi*. Having this in mind, in this study we put forward the three fundamentals of Granular Computing, namely (i) a principle of justifiable granularity (which supports a construction of information granules, and fuzzy sets, in particular), (ii) an allocation of information granularity where granularity is sought as an important modeling asset making the fuzzy model to become more in rapport with reality, and (iii) a hierarchical mode of processing which gives rise to information granules of higher type and higher order. A thorough elaboration on these pillars of Granular Computing is one of the objectives of this study (covered in Sections 2-4). We show how these principles help augment our view at fuzzy decision-making scenarios – with this regard we study a series of constructs bringing a necessary and intuitively appealing granular generalizations and supporting concepts of granular fuzzy sets. Decision-making models engaging information granules are discussed in Section 5.The backbone of this study links with the concepts, methodologies, and algorithms of Granular Computing and is covered in more detail in the recent comprehensive treatise of the subject [10]. One may also refer to some seminal thoughts delivered in [16] and further considerations conveyed in [1].

2. Towards building information granules - the principle of justifiable granularity

In what follows, we briefly highlight the concept of justifiable information granularity [10]. In essence, information granules as certain abstract entities require two fundamental reasons for their emergence. They have to be *justified* by some experimental evidence (either numeric in terms of measurements or as a collection of human-delivered judgments), viz. there must be some sound justification why a concept – information granule is brought into existence. In other words, we envision that such an information granule embraces (represents) a significant portion of the available pieces of evidence we have started from. Furthermore a constructed information granule should be *semantically sound* – it has to be specific enough to exhibit a well- understood meaning.

In the sequel, for illustrative purposes, we concentrate on the detailed computational aspects investigated in case of interval and fuzzy set-based formalisms of information granules.

The requirement of strong experimental evidence is quantified by counting the number of data falling within the bounds of a certain numeric interval Ω. More generally, we may consider an increasing function of this cardinality, say $f_1(\text{card}\{x_k \mid x_k \in \Omega\})$ where f_1 is any increasing function of its argument. In the simplest case, we can consider a function in the form $f_1(u)=u$. The specificity of the information granule Ω associated with its well-defined semantics (meaning) can be articulated in terms of the length of the interval. In case of $\Omega= [a, b]$, any continuous non-increasing function f_2 of the length of this interval, say $f_2(m(\Omega))$ where $m(\Omega) = |b-a|$ serves as a sound indicator of the specificity of the information granule. The narrower the interval (the higher the value of $f_2(m(\Omega))$), the better the satisfaction of the specificity requirement. It is evident that the two requirements identified above are in conflict: the increase in the values of the criterion of experimental evidence (justifiability) comes at an expense of a deterioration (lowering) of the specificity of the information granule. As usual, we are interested in forming a sound compromise between these requirements.

Having these two criteria in mind, let us proceed with the detailed formation of the interval information granule. We start with a numeric representative of the set of data **D** around which the information granule Ω is created. A sound numeric representative of the data is its median, med(**D**). Recall that the median is a robust estimator of the sample and typically comes as one of the elements of **D**. Once the median has been determined, Ω (the interval [a,b]) is formed by specifying its lower and upper bounds, denoted here by "a" and "b", respectively. The determination of these bounds is realized independently. Let us concentrate on the optimization of the upper bound (b). The optimization of the lower bound (a) is carried out in an analogous fashion. For this portion of the interval, the length of Ω or its non-increasing function, as noted above is considered. In the calculations of the cardinality of the information granule, we take into consideration the elements of **D** positioned to the right from the median, that is card $\{x_k \in \mathbf{D} \mid \text{med}(\mathbf{D}) \le x_k \le b\}$. As the requirements of experimental evidence (*justifiable granularity*) and specificity (*semantics*) are in conflict, we resort ourselves to a maximization of a certain multiplicative form of the optimization criterion

$$V(b)=f_1(card\{x_k \in \mathbf{D}| \ med(\mathbf{D}) \le x_k \le b\})_* f_2(|med(\mathbf{D})-b|). \quad (1)$$

We obtain the optimal upper bound b_{opt}, by maximizing the value of V(b), namely

$$V(b_{opt}) = max_{b>med(\mathbf{D})}V(b). \quad (2)$$

An important design aspect of the discussed concept is concerned with the formation of the information granule in the presence of weighted experimental evidence or inhibitory experimental evidence.

weighted experimental evidence

Here, we have the data x_k associated with some weighting coefficients f_k assuming values in the unit interval. Thus we have a collection of pairs of data (x_1, f_1), (x_2, f_2),...,(x_N, f_N). The higher the value of the weight is, the more substantial a contribution of the data to the resulting information granule becomes. The underlying optimization process is arranged as follows. We start with a numeric representative. The weighted median, med, is a viable alternative. It is constructed by determining a value of "med" for which the following sum attains its minimum

$$Min_{\xi} \sum_{k=1}^{M} f_k|z_k - \xi| = \sum_{k=1}^{M} f_k|z_k - med| \quad (3)$$

Subsequently, the detailed calculations of (3) are slightly modified by incorporating the values of the weights f_k associated with the corresponding data. This leads to the corresponding sums of f_ks.

inhibitory experimental evidence We may encounter some experimental evidence that must be excluded from the information granule to be constructed. To reinforce this requirement, we revisit the original expression (3) in its part dealing with the cardinality. Let us consider that some data z_1, z_2, ..., z_K are of inhibitory nature meaning that their inclusion in the interval [m, b] negatively impacts (reduces) experimental evidence. The modified performance index augmenting (3) comes now in the following form,

$$V(b)=max[0, card\{x_k \in \mathbf{D}| \ med(\mathbf{D}) \le x_k \le b\} - card\{z_k \in \mathbf{D}| \ med(\mathbf{D}) \le z_k \le b\}]_*$$
$$_* f_2(|med(\mathbf{D})-b|) \quad (4)$$

This way of forming information granules could be beneficial in problems of data description when we are interested in describing data belonging to some class and at the same time one has to avoid including data that do not belong to this class (viz. they could be outliers or anomalies).

3. Allocation of information granularity- an emergence of granular fuzzy models

The problem of allocation of granularity across the parameters of some function $f(\mathbf{x}, \mathbf{a})$ is regarded as a way of assigning a given level of information granularity $\varepsilon \in [0,1]$ being viewed as a design asset. It transforms the vector of numeric parameters $\mathbf{a}$ into a vector whose coordinates are information granules $\mathbf{A} = [A_1\ A_2\ \dots\ A_p\ ]$ such that the level of admissible granularity ε is allocated to A_is in such a way a balance of levels of information granularity (with $\varepsilon_1\ \varepsilon_2\ \dots\ \varepsilon_p$ being the levels of information granularity) becomes, namely $\sum_{i=1}^{p} \varepsilon_i = p\varepsilon$ i.e., $\varepsilon = \sum_{i=1}^{p} \varepsilon_i /p$. Concisely, we can articulate this process of granularity allocation as follows

$$f(\mathbf{x}, \mathbf{a}) \rightarrow \text{granularity allocation } (\varepsilon) \rightarrow f(\mathbf{x}, \mathbf{A}) = f(\mathbf{x}, G(\mathbf{a})) \qquad (5)$$
$$\text{numeric mapping} \qquad\qquad\qquad \text{granular mapping}$$

that is $A_i = G(a_i)$ with $G(.)$ denoting a transformation of the numeric parameter a_i to a certain granular counterpart A_i. Note that this expression is general and we are not confined to any particular formalism of information granules used here [10]. The mapping itself can be realized in various ways depending upon its original realization and a way in which information granules are represented. As a result, we come up with a plethora of modeling constructs such as granular linear regression (with detailed instances of fuzzy linear regression, rough linear regression, interval-valued linear regression, and probabilistic linear regression), granular rule-based models (fuzzy rule-based models, rough rule-based models, interval-valued rule-based models, probabilistic rule-based models, etc.), granular fuzzy models (fuzzy fuzzy models or fuzzy^2 models, rough fuzzy models, interval-valued fuzzy models, probabilistic fuzzy models).

4. Allocation of information granularity- an emergence of granular fuzzy models

A two-level hierarchy of processing where at the lowest level we have started with fuzzy sets leads to emergence of granular (interval) fuzzy sets. This means that as a result of reconciliation or aggregation, the emerging information granules are made more abstract. More specifically, we observe that the type of the fuzzy sets has to be elevated. Once working with type-1 fuzzy sets (with numeric membership grades), the result formed at the higher level of hierarchy is expressed as a type-2 (interval) fuzzy set. The emergence of higher types of fuzzy sets is a consequence of processing information granules positioned at the lower level of hierarchy and being of lower type.

Intuitively, we can anticipate that the level of fuzzy set increases when moving up along the levels of the hierarchy; in case of interval information granules we visualize this symbolically as the following sequence: [....] [.....] [[.,.] [.,.].... [.,.]] ... In other words, an aggregation of the bounds of the intervals of membership grades, say $a_i[1]$, i=1, 2, ..., c gives rise to a certain interval formed again in the unit interval (more precisely, the subinterval of the [0,1] with the lower and upper bound expressed as $\min_{ii}a_i[ii]$ and $\max_{ii}a_i[ii]$. More descriptively, in contrast to type-2 (interval) fuzzy set where membership bounds are numbers, here the bounds are intervals. This construct relates in a convincing way to shadowed sets [12][13] or rough sets [7]. In both constructs we deal with boundary regions of the information granules and their description.

Along with the emergence of information granules of higher type, in hierarchical processing there is also an emergence of information granules of higher order, viz. information granules defined in a space of information granules themselves.

5. Allocation of information granularity- an emergence of granular fuzzy models

Information granularity plays an important role in processes of decision-making. Here we show how the underlying principles of Granular Computing can be used effectively in improving the quality of a solution both in case of an individual decision-making as well as its group version. As a class of models we consider the well-known Analytic Hierarchy Process (AHP) [15]. In this model, we are aimed at forming a vector of preferences for a finite set of "n" alternatives. These preferences are formed on a basis of a reciprocal matrix R, R=[r_{ij}], i, j=1, 2, ..., n whose entries are a result of pairwise comparisons of alternatives being provided by a decision-maker. The quality of the result (reflecting the consistency of the judgment of the decision-maker) is expressed in terms of the following inconsistency index

$$v = \frac{\lambda_{max} - n}{n-1} \qquad (6)$$

where λ_{max} is the largest eigenvalue associated with the reciprocal matrix. The larger the value of this index is, the more significant the level of inconsistency associated with the preferences collected in the reciprocal matrix becomes. In what follows, we distinguish here two main categories of design scenarios: a single decision-maker is involved or we are concerned with a group decision-making where there is a collection of reciprocal matrices provided by each of the member of the group. Several representative scenarios are envisioned.

single decision-maker scenario. The results of pairwise comparisons usually exhibit a certain level of inconsistency. The inconsistency index presented above quantifies this phenomenon. One of the reasons behind this inconsistency is that the judgments of the decision-maker are expressed in the numeric form and the transitivity property is not satisfied at the numeric level. To alleviate this issue, we allow for granular entries of the reciprocal matrix to reflect a lack of a precise numeric mapping of results of pairwise comparison. We allocate admissible level of granularity to the individual entries of the matrix. Formally, the process can be schematically described in the following form

$$R \xrightarrow{\varepsilon} G(R) \qquad (7)$$

where $G(R)$ stands for the granular version of the reciprocal matrix R. A certain predetermined level of information granularity ε is then distributed among elements of the reciprocal matrix R. This is realized by optimizing an allocation of the information granularity across the entries of R.

Group decision making scenarios When dealing with a group of decision-makers, several options are considered:

<u>Building a granular reciprocal matrix</u>. Here we consider a number of decision-makers where each of them comes with his/her own reciprocal matrix R_1, R_2, ... R_p and an overall global reciprocal matrix is formed by using the principle of justifiable granularity with the weights w_i (expressed as $w_i = 1 - v_i$) that are used to quantify the relevance of the individual matrices involved in the construction of the granular reciprocal matrix. The final result becomes a granular reciprocal matrix $G(R)$. The quality of the reciprocal matrix is assessed in the same way as described above by computing the expected value $E(v)$. Furthermore the values of $E(v)$ can be associated with the values of the parameter used in the realization of the principle of justifiable granularity.

<u>Building a vector of granular preferences</u> In contrast to the previous approach, for each reciprocal matrix determined is a vector of preferences e_1, e_2, ... e_p along with their inconsistency indexes v_1, v_2, ... v_p. The principle of justifiable granularity is now invoked for the weighted data $(e_1, 1-v_1)$, $(e_2, 1-v_2)$,..., $(e_p, 1-v_p)$ to construct a granular (for instance interval-valued) vector of preferences $G(e)$.

<u>Construction of granular² reciprocal matrix</u> Here the overall process consists of two processing layers. First, the granular reciprocal matrices are formed for the matrices provided by decision-makers. We obtain $G(R_1)$, $G(R_2)$,..., $G(R_p)$. Next these matrices are aggregated yielding $G(G(R)) = G^2(R)$, viz. a granular construct of the second type. We note that in this development we take advantage of the principle of justifiable granularity as well as treat information granularity as an important design asset.

Some related studies involving an active way of building granular models of decision-making in the AHP setting are reported in [9]; refer also to [14].

6. Conclusions

Granular fuzzy models support a new direction of system modeling. Information granularity plays a pivotal role in augmenting fuzzy models with a substantial level of conceptual flexibility, which directly translates into interesting algorithmic alternatives. It is essential to stress that information granules can be realized in various formal frameworks and this in addition enhances the flexibility of the resulting granular models. It has been shown that the emergence of information granules of higher order and higher type (which per se could be treated as an important and interesting direction of fundamental research), comes with strong compelling and practically viable arguments.

References

1. A. Bargiela and W. Pedrycz, *Granular Computing: An Introduction*, Kluwer Academic Publishers, Dordrecht (2003).
2. K. Hirota, *Fuzzy Sets and Systems*, **5**, 31 (1981).
3. K. Hirota and W. Pedrycz, *Pattern Recognition Letters*, **2**, 213 (1984).
4. E. Hisdal, Int. Journal of Man-Machine Studies **15**, 385 (1981).
5. N.M. Karnik and J. M. Mendel, Q. Liang, *IEEE Transactions on Fuzzy Systems,* **7**, 643 (1999).
6. J. Mendel, *Uncertain Rule-Based Fuzzy Logic Systems: Introduction and New Directions.* Prentice Hall Upper Saddle River, NJ (2001).
7. Z. Pawlak, *Rough Sets: Theoretical Aspects of Reasoning about Data, System Theory*, Kluwer Academic Publishers, Dordrecht (1991).
8. Z. Pawlak, *Fuzzy Sets and Systems*, **17**, 99 (1985).
9. W. Pedrycz and M.L. Song, *IEEE Transaction on Fuzzy Systems*, **19**, 527 (2011).
10. W. Pedrycz, *Granular Computing: Analysis and Design of Intelligent Systems*, CRC Press/Francis Taylor, Boca Raton (2013).
11. W. Pedrycz and F. Gomide, *Fuzzy Systems Engineering: Toward Human- Centric Computing*, J. Wiley, Hoboken, NJ, 2007
12. W. Pedrycz, *IEEE Trans. on Systems, Man, and Cybernetics, Part B*, **28**, 103 (1998).
13. W. Pedrycz, *Pattern Recognition Letters*, **26**, 2439 (2005).
14. W. Pedrycz and P. Rai, *Fuzzy Sets and Systems*, **159**, 2399 (2008).
15. T.L. Saaty, *The Analytic Network Process: Decision-Making with Dependence and Feedback*, 2nd ed, RWS Publ, Pittsburg (2001).
16. L.A. Zadeh, *Fuzzy Sets and Systems*, **90**, 111 (1997).

SOME APPROACHES TOWARDS LATTICE COMPUTING IN MATHEMATICAL MORPHOLOGY AND COMPUTATIONAL INTELLIGENCE

PETER SUSSNER

Dept. of Applied Mathematics, IMECC, University of Campinas,
Campinas, So Paulo - Brazil
E-mail: sussner@ime.unicamp.br

Abstract

The technical term "lattice computing" was recently coined to refer to an evolving collection of tools and mathematical models for processing lattice ordered data such as numbers, intervals, possibility and probability distributions, (fuzzy) sets, extensions of fuzzy sets as well as other types of information granules. In this context, note that many classes of information granules such as the classes of the extended integers, the extended reals, intervals, as well as classes of fuzzy sets and several of their extensions represent complete lattices that have played important roles in mathematical morphology and fuzzy set theory since many years.

In the 1990's, several researchers have started transferring operators, ideas, and concepts of mathematical morphology into the area of computational intelligence and morphological neural networks emerged as a new paradigm for computing with artificial neural networks. Other lattice computing approaches towards computational intelligence were inspired by the fuzzy ART model. Since the latter approaches towards computational intelligence rely heavily on the use of inclusion measures or fuzzy partial orders in a general lattice setting, they can also be related to mathematical morphology. We believe that lattice computing approaches will benefit from recent extensions of fuzzy mathematical morphology since type-2, interval-valued, bipolar, and intuitionistic fuzzy sets have become increasingly important in image processing/computer vision, in rule-based systems for applications in engineering and computing with words, and in approximate reasoning.

PART 1

DECISION MAKING AND DECISION SUPPORT SYSTEMS

SOFTWARE ARCHITECTURAL STYLE FOR DECISION SUPPORT SYSTEMS

ZAKARYA A. ALZAMIL

Software Engineering Department, King Saud University,
Riyadh, Saudi Arabia
zakarya@ksu.edu.sa

The decision support system is a software system that aims to facilitate and/or enhance the process of decision making activities at any organizational level. Decision support system has moved from the traditional role of supporting traditional business process into supporting intelligent decision making. Most of the proposed software architectures for decision support system are domain-specific software architecture. We have proposed simplified software architecture for decision support systems that is suitable as a generic software architectural style for decision support systems. We believe that the proposed software architectural style can work for many different domain problems for decision support systems.

1. Introduction

Software architecture deals with the design and implementation of the high-level structure of the software. It is the result of assembling a certain number of architectural elements in some well-chosen forms to satisfy the major functionality and performance requirements of the system, as well as some other non-functional requirements such as reliability, scalability, portability, and availability [3]. Perry and Wolf [1] define the software architecture in terms of building blocks that is concerned with the selection of architectural elements, their interactions, and the constraints on those elements and their interactions necessary to provide a framework that satisfies the requirements and serves as a basis for the design. A set of systems or subsystems may have some common architecture in which an architectural style or pattern may be used for designing such systems. In [2] the architectural style or pattern is determined by set of element types, topological layout of the elements indicating their interrelationships, set of semantic constraints, and set of interaction mechanisms that determine how the elements coordinate through the allowed topology.

The decision support system (DSS) has evolved from a broader concept of management information system that focuses on information gathering and management to focus more on decision making. The decision support system is a software system that aims to facilitate and/or enhance the process of decision making activities at any organizational level to make it more productive, greater agility, innovative, reputable, and satisfactory [8]. Although the decision making might be structured i.e., deterministic and well-defined with recurring routine that involves a definite procedure for handling certain situation, most of the organizations use an unstructured decision making [9], which requires a human interaction with the DSS system. The motivation of this paper is to present a simplified architectural style for decision support systems that provides a general purpose software architectural style for decision support systems. This paper is organized as follows, the related works are presented in section 2, our proposed approach is presented in section 3, and the conclusions are presented in section 4.

2. Related Works

The architectures of decision support systems have been recognized in early eighty e.g., [4, 5, 6, 7]. In the literatures, there are several software architecture proposals for decision support systems for specific domains, however, due to the paper size limitation; we present few research studies. For instance, in [10] software architecture for an intelligent instructor pilot decision support system has been proposed to help instructors during simulated missions instruction, post-flight debriefing, and performance evaluation. A distributed architecture has been used to propose distributed decision support system to help radiologists in the diagnosis of soft tissue tumors. The proposed architecture consists of three specialized nodes: radiologist visual interface, information system, and decision support web-services [11]. Information architecture of a clinical decision support system has been presented in [12] to facilitate the decision making within medical processes. In [20] another clinical decision support system (CDSS) approach has been proposed to support clinical decision making by supporting a complete knowledge-driven CDSS architecture via a rule-based guideline knowledge repository and multi-agent system architecture. Software architecture for environmental decision support systems has been presented in [13] to help in managing hydraulic of the ecosystem of Camargue, a French region. Another proposal of software architecture for event-driven traffic management system has been described in [14] that enables the analysis and processing of complex event streams in real-time, in which it may be suitable for decision support in sensor-based traffic control systems. In [15] a distributed architecture for e-business environment based on web technology was introduced. The proposed framework is based on the J2EE platform by using Internet-based web technologies. A decision support system has been proposed in [19] for selecting the solar power plant site based upon the qualitative and quantitative five criteria under cost and environmental factors including climate, geographical, transportation, environmental and cost criteria. Hybrid reasoning approach has been presented in [16] for the purpose of designing a decision support system. Rule-based reasoning and case-based reasoning are used to design knowledge-based decision support systems. In [17] agent technology has been used to propose an open DSS model based on the agent grid to enhance the openness, dynamics and complexity of DSS in grid circumstance. Based on our research in the literatures, available online, we found that, most of the proposed approaches of the decision support systems are domain-specific software architectures. In addition most of these approaches do not support design reusability. In this paper we are proposing a simplified and general purpose architectural style that is suitable as a generic software architectural style for decision support systems.

3. Decision Support System Architectural Style

The decision support system aims to aid in automating the decision making process that considers all factors influencing the decision making as well as the clarity about the decision alternatives, preferences, and decision uncertainty. Uncertainty of a decision making originates from incompleteness of information, imprecision, and model approximations made for the sake of simplicity. The DSS should contain the following major components; data and information streaming management, business model management, and interface management [18]. In addition the knowledge base management, which might be considered as the machine learning, should be integrated within the DSS [4]. A good user interface should support model construction and model analysis, and should be transparent to the user. The decision making process goes through three phases, first the intelligence which identifies the problem that requires decision and collection of information relevant to decision; second design, which involve creating, developing, and analyzing alternative course of actions, third choices, that select a course of action from those available.

In the following paragraphs we describe the proposed approach in designing an architectural style for decision support system that facilitates the design of such software system. Figure 1 depicts the proposed decision support system's architectural style, which consists of four layers; interface layer, business model layer, knowledge base layer, and data warehouse layer. In addition, we have defined the specification of the proposed DSS architectural style in Table 1. In the following paragraphs we describe the integrated layers of the proposed architectural style. In layered approach each layer is independent from other layers which may provide some non-functional properties such as reliability, scalability, and availability.

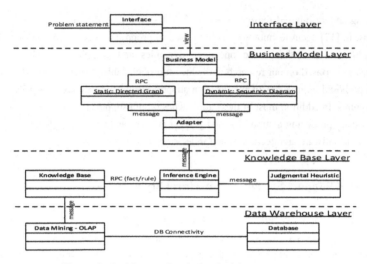

Figure 1: Architectural style for decision support system

Table 1. Specification of the DSS architectural style

Item	Description
Element types	Standalone subsystems or components
Connectors	Typically procedure call/Message passing.
Topology layout	Hierarchical and API interface between layers.
Semantic constraints	Layer interaction by protocols connectors Standardized layer interfaces to maintain layer independence
Interaction mechanisms	Each layer acts as a service provider to layers above and service consumer of layer below

The interface layer consists of the interface component that interacts with system users. This layer represents the interaction between the DSS system and the users (human or machines), which understands the problem statement to identify and extract or develop a list of choices/alternatives (options). The statement problem may be interpreted in two views; simple view or sophisticated view. In the simple view; the interface reads lists of alternatives or options to make a decision, however, in the sophisticated view; the interface reads the problem statement and constructs a list of alternatives by developing a list of choices/options.

The business model layer is responsible for building the business model based on the view of the statement problem interpreted by interface. The business model is constructed as static model (directed graph) or dynamic model (sequence diagram), in which the decision problem may be decomposed into simpler components/pieces (well-define/well understood problem). The problem may be abstracted in an abstract representation of the real-world problem by omitting the details of the problem. The problem is transferred into a set of problems or domains. The business model consists of set of variables and specification of interaction among variables. In order to have a better decision making options or alternatives, the business model measures the preferences over decision objectives which should be presented as numerical, identifies the available decision options/alternatives, and measures of uncertainty over variables influencing the decisions and the outcomes. As stated earlier, the domain in which a decision making may be applied can be static or dynamic (customized) in which the DSS may be work in a static domain model or dynamic (customized) domain model. The static model is built based on the given data as a directed graph, and the static domain is similar to rule-base system. The dynamic/customized model is built based on an interaction between the DSS and the decision-maker on case-by-case basis to build a sequence diagram. A hybrid approach may be used as a learning system that learns a model from data, in which a graphical model may be built from the existing data for a certain domain.

The knowledge base layer aims to look for the fact or rule that is applicable for such case, in which a selected approach is used, e.g., mathematical method, the problem is identified as certain or uncertain, uncertainty originates from incompleteness of information, imprecision, and model approximations made for the sake of simplicity. It should be noticed that most of the decision-making comes under the uncertainty category. The certain choices may require the use of mathematical programming, scenario analysis, flow analysis, or some ad hoc algorithm. The uncertain choices may use statistical approaches, reliability analysis, simulations, or statistical decision making. The inference engine applies rules/facts to the knowledge base and deduced new knowledge or do some query for an option/alternatives. The DSS system makes a decision analysis that aims to provide insight into a decision (analysis of all relevant factors, their uncertainty, critical nature of some assumptions etc.). The decision analysis could be an equation-based model e.g., statistical equation model. Because of the fact that decision making in most cases is unstructured or semi-structured decision, there is a need for a human interferences to collect some information from human experts. Therefore, the system may use judgmental heuristics in which a normative approach that aims to support the human in combing many factors into an optimal decision may be used to apply the principles of decision theory and probability theory into the decision analysis. The normative system is based on graphical probabilistic models, i.e., probability distribution over model variables in terms of directed graph, which also, known as influence diagram.

The data warehouse layer consists of two components, the data mining/OLAP subsystem and the databases. In this layer the data is extracted from the data warehouse and manipulated or passed to the knowledge base layer for additional data manipulation for the purpose of knowledge discovery. The database at this layer can be a traditional database, relational database, or multidimensional database. As stated earlier, the database structure i.e., the blackboard as well as the components operating on it, is managed by a BDMS, such sub-system is controlled by the blackboard state. Online analytical processing (OLAP), as a business intelligence technique, helps in discovering some knowledge by extracting data from the data warehouse and viewing it from

Table 2. Comparison between our proposed approach and related approaches

Related approach	Generality	Independency/Reusability
FAD [7]	General purpose	Based on blackboard and requires central database
IP [10]	Domain-specific	Based on Hazard Monitor subsystem
STT-DDSS [11]	Domain-specific	More than one connector as a point of connectivity between components which complicates their reusability
AGBODSS [17]	Domain-specific	Layered style in which each layer may be independent
EDSS [13]	Domain-specific	Requires wrappers and mediator for reusability
RBR-CBR [16]	General purpose	More than one connector as a point of connectivity between components which complicates their reusability
C-DSS [12]	Domain-specific	Reusable within same domain
EDA [14]	Domain-specific	Component are dependable on each other which complicates their reusability
DA-DSS [15]	Domain-specific	More than one connector as a point of connectivity between components which complicates their reusability
SPPL-DSS [19]	Domain-specific	Reusable within the same domain
FD-DSS [4]	General purpose	Component are dependable on each other which complicates their reusability
CAG-DSS [5]	General purpose	Component are dependable on each other which complicates their reusability
C-DSS [20]	Domain-specific	Reusable within the same domain

different points-of-view. The data mining discovers a new knowledge by extracting information from a database, analyzing it from different perspectives, and transforms it into an understandable structure of knowledge for further use.

To understand the advantages of our proposed approach over the related ones, we have conducted a simple comparison between our proposed software architectural style and the existing approaches with respect to the generality and independency/reusability of the approach. Table 2 shows the comparison, in which we have abbreviated the names of the related approaches for the purpose of presentation.

As can be seen in Table 2, most of the existing DSS software architectural approaches are domain-specific approach and/or have some limitation related to the independency and/or reusability. In contrast, and as stated earlier, our proposed approach is a general purpose DSS software architectural style, simple to adapt, and more flexible for reusability.

4. Conclusions

In this paper we have proposed a software architectural style for decision support system that facilitates the design of such software system. The existing software architectures of decision support systems are domain-specific software architecture and some of which are not flexible for the reusability. The proposed architectural style is simplified approach and we believe that it can be used for most of the problem domains for decision making software systems. Our approach consists of four layers; interface layer, business model layer, knowledge base layer, and data warehouse layer. As stated earlier, this approach is a generic and flexible software architectural style that fits most of the problem domains. In addition, the proposed approach aims to simplify the design of the DSS system and avoid any complexity in the design, in which each layer is independent from other layers. To better understand the advantages as well as the limitation of the proposed approach, we plan to investigate the applicability of such software architectural style on some of the commercial decision support systems software tools such as Oracle BI, Sybase Spoornet management, IBM Cognos, or SAP BI.

References

1. D. Perry and A. Wolf, "Foundations for the Study of Software Architecture", ACM SIGSOFT Software Engineering Notes, Vol. 17, No. 4, pp. 40-52, October (1992).
2. L. Bass, P. Clements, and R. Kazman, Software Architecture in Practice, SEI series in Software Engineering, 2nd Edition, Addison-Wesley, (2003).
3. P. Kruchten, "Architectural Blueprints - The "4+1" View Model of Software Architecture", IEEE Software 12 (6), pp. 42-50 November (1995).
4. R.H. Sprague Jr., "A Framework for the Development of Decision Support Systems", MIS Quarterly, Vol. 4, No. 4, pp. 1-26, Dec. (1980),
5. M. S-Y Wang and J.F. JR Courtney, "A Conceptual Architecture for Generalized Decision Support System Software", IEEE Transactions on Systems, Man, and Cybernetics, Vol. smc.14, No.5, pp. 701-711, Sept./Oct. (1984).

6. R. Wheeler and K. Narendra, "Learning Models for Decentralized Decision Making", Automatica, vol. 21, No. 4, pp. 479-484, (1985).
7. E. Tropper and S. Beland, "A New Expert System Architecture For Decision Support", IEEE International Workshop on Artificial Intelligence for Industrial Applications, pp. 251-257, (1988).
8. F. Burstein and C. Holsapple, Handbook on Decision Support Systems 1, Basic Themes, Ch. 9, (2008), Springer.
9. M. Tonelli, *Unstructured Strategic Decision-Making Processes: CRE Decision-Making in the Italian Consulting Industry*, PhD Dissertation, School of Management, Faculty of Business, Queensland University, (2009).
10. E. Bass, "Architecture for an Intelligent Instructor Pilot Decision Support System", IEEE proceedings of International Conference on Systems, Man, and Cybernetics, pp. 891-896, (1998).
11. J. Garcia-Gomez, C. Vidal, J. Vicente, L. Marti-Bonmati, and M. Robles, "Medical Decision Support System for Diagnosis of Soft Tissue Tumors based on Distributed Architecture", IEEE Proceedings of the 26th Annual International Conference of the Engineering in Medicine and Biology Society (EMBS), pp. 3225-3228, (2004).
12. D. Robbins, V. Gurupur, and J. Tanik, "Information Architecture of a Clinical Decision Support System", IEEE Proceedings of 2011 Southeastcon, pp. 374-378, (2011).
13. J. Serment, B. Espinasse, and E. Tranvouez, "Environmental Decision Support System for Hydraulic Management of the Camargue: Functionalities and Software Architecture", IEEE Proceedings of the First international Symposium on Environment Identities and Mediterranean Area, ISEIMA '06, pp. 308-313, (2006).
14. J. Dunkel, A. Fernández, R. Ortiz, and S. Ossowski, "Event-Driven Architecture for Decision Support in Traffic Management Systems", IEEE Proceedings of the 11th International Conference on Intelligent Transportation Systems, pp. 7-13, (2008).
15. Y. Qiongwei, Q. Renjun, L. Yumei, and S. Guangxing, "Distributed Architecture of Decision Support System (DSS) and its Implementation in E-Business Environment", IEEE Proceedings of the 3rd International Conference on Information Management, Innovation Management and Industrial Engineering, pp. 48-52, (2010).
16. X. Zhang, H. Xia, and S. Cai, "An Decision-Support System based on Hybrid Reasoning Architecture", IEEE Proceedings of the 2nd International Conference on Information Management and Engineering (ICIME 2010), pp. 335-339, (2010).
17. J-Y. Chi, L. Sun, X-G. Chen, and J-L. Zhang, "Architecture and Design of Distributed Decision Support System Based on Agent Grid", IEEE Proceedings of the Fourth International Conference on Machine Learning and Cybernetics, pp. 321-327, (2005).
18. R.H. Sprague Jr. and E.D. Carlson, *Building Effective Decision Support Systems*, Prentice-Hall, (1982).
19. A. Kengpol, P. Rontlaong, and M. Tuominen, "A Decision Support System for Selection of Solar Power Plant Locations by Applying Fuzzy AHP and TOPSIS: An Empirical Study", Journal of Software Engineering and Applications, Vol. 6 No. 9, pp. 470-481, (2013).
20. L. Xiao, G. Cousins, T. Fahey, B. Dimitrov, and L. Hederman, "Developing a Rule-Driven Clinical Decision Support System with an Extensive and Adaptative Architecture", IEEE Proceedings of the 14th International Conference on e-Health Networking, Applications and Services (Healthcom), pp.250-254, (2012).

EARLY COLLECTION SYSTEM DESIGN USING FUZZY RULE BASED INFERENCE

SEZI CEVIK ONAR

Industrial Engineering Dept., Istanbul Technical University,
34367, Istanbul, Turkey
cevikse@itu.edu.tr

BASAR OZTAYSI

Industrial Engineering Dept., Istanbul Technical University,
34367, Istanbul, Turkey
oztaysib@itu.edu.tr

CENGIZ KAHRAMAN

Industrial Engineering Dept., Istanbul Technical University,
34367, Istanbul, Turkey.
kahramanc@itu.edu.tr

Early debt collection systems aim at collecting payments from the creditors with a minimum cost before the legal procedure. Our study develops a fuzzy inference system for early debt collection problems including the inputs amount of loan, wealth of debtor, past history of debtor, and amount of other debts and the output possibility of repaying the debt and the way of communication. Thus maximum collection of debts before legal process with minimum cots can be achieved.

1. Introduction

Unfortunately in the current global recessionary climate unpaid invoices and unpaid credits are becoming more and more common. Companies may have sold goods/services and invoiced to their customers but left waiting for the payment, or banks may have given credits but couldn't get the imbursements. These kinds of situations can seriously affect cash flow, turnover, credit ratings and even business' reputation. Debt collection processes take in case of unpaid invoices or credit imbursements to gather the unpaid amount.

During the recent years Turkey's credit and credit card applications are increased whereas interest rates are decreased; also competition among banks has increased which caused lower profitability. According to Turkish Banking Regulation and Supervision agency as of March 2013 total amount of issued credits in Turkey is around 420 billion dollars and the total amount of past due payments are around 13 billion dollars. Collecting payments from the creditors with a minimum cost before the legal procedure is crucial for the banks since legal procedure is not only costly but also damages the customer relations. On the other hand due to the inconvenient debt collection systems there are debtors who directly face with legal processes without any warning and they have to compensate high interest rates. As a result banks are trying to reach and collect the debts before legal process and for this purpose they're sending e-mails and text messages via phone or calling the debtors. Collection in litigation starts after 90 days of past due. The collection systems that are trying to collect before 0-90 day are called early collection systems. In Turkey currently there are some approaches that support early debt collection systems (0-90 days) but they are generally primitive and efficiencies are rather low. Consequently banks need effective debt collection systems. On the other hand in literature only several studies focused on early collection systems thus an intelligent early collection system will be beneficial both for banks and academicians. This study proposes an effective fuzzy rule based early collection system by considering the complexity and the vagueness of the system.

2. Debt Collection Systems

Companies and banks may try to handle debt collection processes by themselves or may outsource the work to a debt collection agency. A recent market research report on debt collection agencies in USA indicate that 9,599 agencies exist in USA market making an 13 billion dollars revenue [1]. Howard [2], after a research on debt collectors, highlights the major problems of debt collection as (i) it takes taking more people/resources to collect (ii) confirm debt is costing companies more than ever before (iii) the costs are escalating because debt collection is taking longer to retrieve. The results indicate that handling debt collection is a very important for companies and should be handled very carefully.

Besides, the legislations about debt collection such as fair debt collection practices act [3] in USA, and policies designed by Member States of European Union [4], the collectors should also be very careful about their behaviors to the customer since the communication can damage the relationship with the customer. Lund, [5] identifies the term Soft Debt Collection (SDC) as a process of understanding your customer's business and their reasons for not paying, and choosing the appropriate course of action. From the debt collectors perspective, if the debtor is in trouble it's vital not to be the last one in the queue, but, pushing too hard when they might only have short-term cash-flow problems could lose a customer in whom a lot of time and money is invested for acquisition and development. Pushing too hard can also tip a customer over the edge into insolvency, in which case you may receive nothing, whereas understanding their problems and getting proper actions may put the collector in a much better position.

With the emergence of information age the collectors are using many information sources to get information about and to reach to debtors, such as internet, mobile phones, telephones, emails, voice messages [6]. Each one of these technologies has different levels of atomization and thus causes different amounts of costs. The selection of the most proper communication type directly affects the costs of the collector.

3. Rule Based Systems

Fuzzy rule based systems are composed of fuzzy rules with linguistic inputs and outputs to obtain a decision based on all the rules. There are two types of fuzzy inference systems (FISs): Sugeno and Mamdani inference systems. When the inputs are given there are six steps to compute the output of this FIS [7]: (1) determine a set of fuzzy rules, (2) fuzzify the inputs using the input membership functions, (3) combine the fuzzified inputs according to the fuzzy rules to establish a rule strength, (4) find the consequence of the rule by combining the rule strength and the output membership function, (5) combine the consequences to get an output distribution, and (6) defuzzify the output distribution (this step is only if a crisp output is needed).

4. A Real Case Study

A debt collection agency in Turkey wants to develop an intelligent early collection system. This firm is expert on problematic debts and is one of Turkey's leading debt collection agencies. 9 out of 13 major banks and all GSM operators, electricity providers are the customers of this firm.

The inputs of our inference systems will be amount of loan, wealth of debtor, past history of debtor, and amount of other debts. Each input has a membership function composed of linguistic variables. We defined these membership functions intuitively. The membership functions of the inputs are given in

Figures 1-4. The membership function for amount of loan is defined by seven linguistic terms. We use exactly the same membership function for amount of other debts.

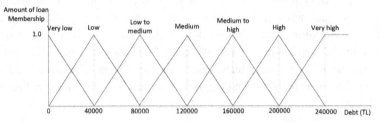

Figure 1. Linguistic Terms for Amount of Loan

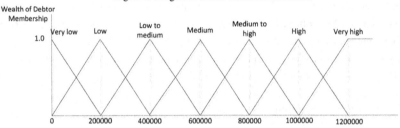

Figure 2. Linguistic Terms for Wealth of Debtor

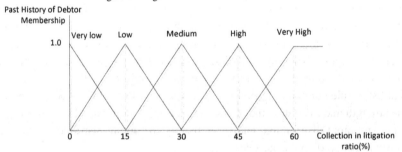

Figure 3. Linguistic Terms for Past History of Debtor

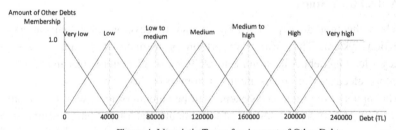

Figure 4. Linguistic Terms for Amount of Other Debts

Flow chart of the fuzzy rule based inference system is given in Figure 5.

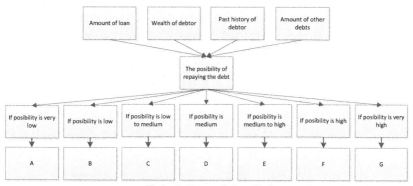

Figure 5. Fuzzy rule based inference system

Since Figure 5 is a very extensive figure we only give the details of part A in Figure 7. A sample of two rules from our fuzzy inference system is shown in Figure 6.

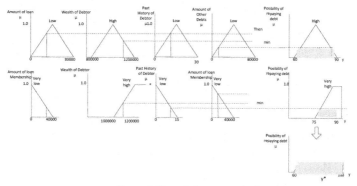

Figure 6. Fuzzy Inference method

5. Conclusion

Debt collection systems are vague and complex systems since they try to predict human behaviors. Therefore fuzzy rule based inference systems are excellent tools to model such problems. We developed an efficient early debt collection system model. With this model communication way with debtors and possibility of repaying the debt can be determined. For further research the model can be enhanced through ANFIS (Adaptive Neuro Fuzzy Inference Systems) to generate new rules by improving the existing rules.

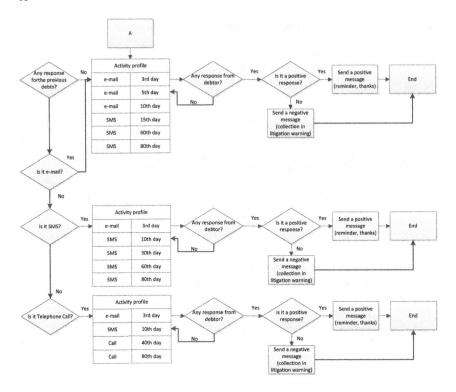

Figure 7. Flow Chart Part A

References

1. IBISworld, Debt Collection Agencies Market Research Report, accessed on 17.01.2014, http://www.ibisworld.com/industry/default.aspx?indid=1474
2. E. Howard, Survey Forecasts Debt Collection Crisis: Big Issues and Increase in Debt Cases – and No Clear Remedy, Credit Control. Vol. 33 Issue 7/8, p63-67, (2012)
3. FDSPA, Fair Debt Collection Practices Act, accesed 17.01.2014, http://www.federalreserve.gov/boarddocs/supmanual/cch/fairdebt.pdf
4. N. Huls, J Consum Policy, 35:497–508, (2012)
5. S. Lund, Soft debt collection – collecting money without alienating your customer, In Busines Guide to Credit Management, Ed. Reuvid J., pages 119-125, kogen page limited Great Britain, (2010)
6. C. Hector Debt Collection in the Information Age: New Technologies and the Fair Debt Collection Practices Act, Cal. L. Rev. 1601 (2011)
7. T.J.Ross, Fuzzy Logic with Engineering Applications, Addison Wesley, (1995)

A NEW ARCHITECTURE FOR A SPATIO-TEMPORAL DECISION SUPPORT SYSTEM FOR EPIDEMIOLOGICAL PURPOSES

RONEI M. MORAES, JORDANA A. NOGUEIRA, ANA C. A. SOUSA

Laboratory of Applied Statistics to Image Processing and Geoprocessing, Department of Statistics, Federal University of Paraíba, João Pessoa/PB, Brazil

This paper presents a new architecture for a Spatio-Temporal Decision Support System. It was designed taking into account epidemiological aspects for decision making in public health management. The main goal is analyze the spatial and spatio-temporal features of a geographic area and make decisions about prevention and control of a disease dissemination on that area. An example of application of this architecture is presented to construct a system for real aids data is presented, as well as the results obtained from it.

1. Introduction

A Decision-Making (DM) process involves to choose the best decision according to a specific problem, a goal to be reached, possible decisions to make and some kind of intelligence to make the best choice [8]. Although there is no consensus on a definition for Spatial Decision-Making (SDM) process, is possible to say it is a DM process in which spatial information should be take into account for the final decision [15]. Similarly, the term Spatial Decision Support System (SDSS) does not have an universally accepted definition, but it can be understood as a computational technology which provides support for decision-making on problems in which there is a geographic or spatial component that affects the final decision [10].

In the last decades, SDSS have been applied with success on several kinds of problems, such as: urban flood risk [1], service accessibility [4], land use allocation [11], health care [6][13][14] and water management [7], among others. These systems can be used stand alone, in a collaborative way or by Web.

However, despite the great potential of SDSS applications in public health, few publications related to this subject can be found in the literature [15]. A large amount of papers found in this area used tools for spatial analysis and several of them provide only descriptive statistics or maps, and did not use inferential methods [3][5][6][14]. In general, the SDSS architectures developed for epidemiological applications are generic and are not oriented to the specific problems of decision making in this area. A classical example in epidemiological decision making is the identification of priority sub-areas for intervention in a geographical region to control or prevent some kind of disease. This mapping provides the basis for public health managers (decision makers) in order to define specific health policies.

In this paper, we propose a new architecture for SDSS, which is designed taking into account epidemiological aspects for decision making in public health management. This architecture is able to provide statistical, spatial and spatio-temporal analysis of a geographic area and to support decision-making about control of a disease dissemination on that area.

2. Methodology

Initially, some concepts are provided and after the SDSS architecture is presented and discussed. A geographical region G is the geographical area of interest, in which the epidemiological study is conducted. From the perspective of public health surveillance, if the region G is a municipality, it can be split into sub-regions, which may be their neighborhoods, the health districts or the areas covered by the Family Health Centers. From the viewpoint of geoprocessing, these entities are distinct and identifiable objects belonging to the geographical region G and they are called geo-objects [9]. In this case, the intention is to understand the epidemiological behavior of each sub-region Gi in G, where i = {1, ..., n}, and n is the total number of sub-regions in G.

In general, spatial epidemiological data can be represented as point elements (the exact geographical position of the epidemiological event is known) or as area elements (the geographical position is unknown, but can be determined the total value of occurrences in each area belonging to G) [2]. The architecture proposed in this paper is able to treat data represented by area elements. This kind of data is very common in epidemiological studies due to ethical restrictions (or even laws in some countries), which deny or difficult access to personally identifiable information.

The architecture proposed is presented in the Figure 1. Relative Risk is calculated in order to allow comparative statistics of epidemiological events. In order to evaluate the correct form of spatial and statistical analysis of epidemiological features, non-spatial and spatial data is checked by normality tests. Correlation and Classification Analysis help to discover association among variables and cluster of them. Spatial Analysis, as spatial conglomerate analysis, identify significant geographical clusters and Spatio-Temporal identity significant geographical clusters over time. Both analysis are able to produce specific maps, but Spatio-temporal analysis can provide two additional information: time of conglomerates (how recent is the conglomerate found) and their persistence (how long each conglomerate has existed). All information is used as input of a fuzzy rule-based system, whose rules can be provided by experts or extracted from historical records of epidemiological data.

The results provided by this SDSS architecture are decision maps in which are pointed out priority sub-areas with different priority levels. For example, analyzing temporal aspects (time and persistence of conglomerates) combined with correlation analysis, it is possible to evaluate localities (geo-objects) with different tendencies, as such as they will become to priority, or not-priority, if this tendency is sustained. The maps provided by this architecture can identify priority sub-areas for intervention in a studied geographical region. They can provide support to decision makers to define specific health policies, which can be different according the priority level of a locality.

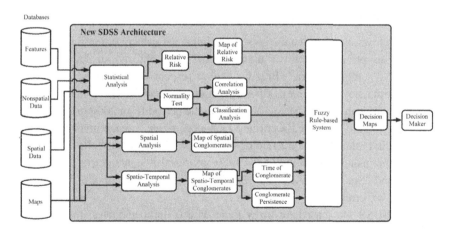

Figure 1. The new SDSS Architecture proposed.

This SDSS architecture provides a new approach oriented to epidemiological problems solving. Several kind of statistical methodologies can be insert in "Statistical Analysis" module in order to provide an eclectic way of analysis. The same can be done with Spatial and Spatio-Temporal Analysis Modules. Different ways of analysis can be inserted in order to the decision makers can choose that one is most appropriate to their problem. Therefore, the Fuzzy Rule-based System should also be able to treat those different kinds of previous analysis and provide corresponding decision maps. Using statistical analyzes cited above, for each geo-object in G, four decisions (or four priority levels) are possible to be assigned: Priority, With a Tendency to Priority, With Tendency to Non-priority and Non-priority

It is worth mentioning that this architecture is modular and oriented to epidemiological problem solving. Therefore, for some kinds of problems, all modules should be used, while for other, some modules can be not necessary.

In comparison with some system found in the literature, this architecture is different from the [12], because the relation analysis among sub-areas in G use statistical methods of spatial analysis. The architecture proposed here is not a Web-based architecture, as that one proposed by [16]. However, it can be adapted to work on Web through a simple client-server architecture. This architecture is specialized to treat data represented by area elements. However, it is possible to change it to treat data represented by point elements, as proposed by [6]. Obviously, several methods inside many modules should be changed in order to allow that specific analysis.

3. Application and Results

In what follows, the architecture presented above was used in order to implement a SDSS on priority levels of municipalities (geo-objects) of Paraíba state (geographic region), in Brazil, with respect to AIDS (acquired immunodeficiency syndrome). All AIDS cases registered in the database of the Secretary of Health of the State of Paraíba in the period from 2000 to 2010 were used and spatially localized according their occurrence in each municipality. It was verified that the epidemiological variables did not follow Normal distributions using Normality Tests. So, it was used nonparametric options for Spatial and Statistical Analysis: Spatial Scan, Spatio-temporal Scan and Spearman´s Correlation.

The SDSS was based on fuzzy logic with 6 input variables: the maps of Relative Risk (Figure 2a), Spatial Scan (Figure 2b) and Spatio-temporal Scan (Figure 3a), Time of Conglomerates, Conglomerates Persistence and Spearman´s Correlation; one output variable: the map of Municipalities with four levels of priority (Figure 3b); and 472 rules. In this case, it was not used the Classification Analysis. Linguistic terms were defined for each variable, as follows:

- Relative Risk: Very High, High, Medium, Low and Very Low Risks;
- Spatial Scan (crisp variable): Significant and Not Significant;
- Spatio-temporal Scan (crisp variable): Significant and Not Significant;
- Time of Conglomerates: Very Recent, Recent and Not Recent.
- Conglomerates Persistence: Not Persistence, Persistence of Approximately

One Year, Persistence of Approximately Two Years, Persistence of Approximately Three Years, Persistence of Approximately Four Years, Persistence of Approximately Five Years and Persistence of More Than Five Years.

- Spearman´s Correlation: High Positive Correlation, Positive Correlation Moderate, Weak Correlation, Negative Correlation Moderate and High Negative Correlation.
- Municipality: Priority, With a Tendency to Priority, With Tendency to Non-priority and Non-priority.

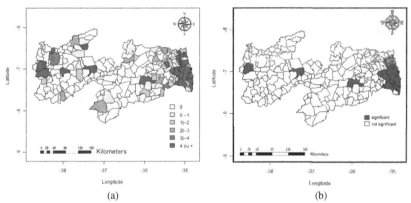

(a)   (b)

Figure 2. (a) Map of Relative Risk; (b) Map of Scan Spatial Statistic with p-value < 0,05.

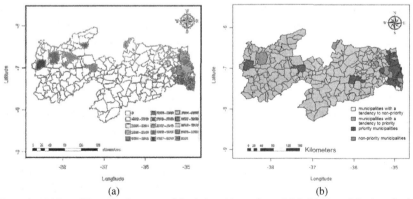

(a)   (b)

Figure 3. (a) Map of Scan Spatio-temporal Statistic with p-value < 0,05; (b) Map of final result: the four degrees of priority to support decision maker.

Some example of fuzzy rules used in the SDSS are presented bellow:

Example 1: IF (Spatial Scan is Not Significant) AND (Relative Risk is LowRisk) AND (Spearman´s Correlation is High Negative Correlation) AND

(Spatio-temporal Scan is Not Significant) THEN (Municipality is Non-priority).

Example 2: IF (Spatial Scan is Significant) AND (Time of Conglomerates is Very Recent) AND (Relative Risk is Very High Risk) AND (Spearman´s Correlation is High Positive Correlation) AND (Spatio-temporal Scan is Significant) AND (Conglomerates Persistence is Persistência5anos) THEN (Municipality is Priority).

Example 3: IF (Spatial Scan is Not Significant) AND (Relative Risk is High Risk) AND (Spearman´s Correlation is High Positive Correlation) AND (Spatio-temporal Scan is Not Significant) THEN (Municipality is With a Tendency to Priority).

Example 4: IF (Spatial Scan is Significant) AND (Time of Conglomerates is Recent) AND (Relative Risk is High Risk) AND (Spearman´s Correlation is High Negative Correlation) AND (Spatio-temporal Scan is Significant) AND (Conglomerates Persistence is Persistência2anos) THEN (Municipality is With Tendency to Non-priority).

According to SDSS, the municipalities of Paraíba state were identified as: priority: 14 (6,27%); with a tendency to priority: 10 (4,48%); with a tendency to non-priority: 4 (1,81%); and non-priority: 195 (87,44%), as showed in the map presented in the Figure 3b. It is worth noting that the Secretary of Health of the State of Paraíba identified just 6 municipalities as priority ones. The SDSS provided these 6 municipalities and pointed out 8 more municipalities as priority, by the use of statistical criteria which were not used by the Health Secretary. The SDSS also pointed out two new categories of priority: With Tendency to Priority and With Tendency to Non-priority. These new categories can help to prevent situations to public health managers, identifying future problems with specific municipalities and also pointing out municipalities where actual policies are working well.

So, the SDSS reached the goal proposed, identifying the municipalities of Paraíba state in accordance with the priority for the control of AIDS, helping public health managers in reducing and prevention of AIDS in Paraíba municipalities.

4. Conclusions

In this paper was proposed a new architecture for Spatio-Temporal Decision Support System. It was designed taking into account epidemiological aspects for decision making in public health management. Spatial and spatio-temporal features of a geographic area, as well as statistical results are used in order to support decision making about prevention and control of a disease on an area.

An example of application using this architecture to implement a SDSS for real data of AIDS ocurrences was presented. Results from implementation showed advantages of using of this architecture with respect to classical epidemiological approach.

This architecture was designed to solve epidemiological problems which can be represented by area elements. However, as it is generic, it can be applied in similar problems in other areas. In the same way, it is possible to change it to treat data represented by point elements, and it will be a goal in a further researches.

References

1. [Ahmad, 2013] S. Ahmad, and S. Simonovic, *Urban Water J.*, **10**, 26 (2013).
2. [Aronoff, 1989] S. Aronoff, *Geographical Information Systems: A Management Perspective* (WDL Publications, Ottawa. 1989).
3. [AvRuskin, 2004] G.A. AvRuskin, *et al.*, Int J. Health Geog. **3**, 26 (2004).
4. [Burdziej, 2012] J. Burdziej, *Appl Geomat*, **4**, 75 (2012).
5. [Chung, 2004] K. Chung, D-H. Yang and R. Bell, *J. of Med. Syst.*, **28**, 349 (2004).
6. [Delmelle, 2011] E. Delmelle, *et al.*, App. Spat. Anal. Policy, **4**, 113 (2011).
7. [Dhore, 2005] K. Dhore, *et al.*, Spatial Decision Support System Architecture: Evolution and Application for Watershed Planning and Management, in *Proc. Int. Conf. Exhib. in Field of GIS and Rem. Sens. 2005* (New Delhi, India 2005).
8. [Feeney, 2002] M.E. Feeney and I. Williamson, *Cartog. J.*, **312**, 21 (2002).
9. [Goodchild, 1992]. M. Goodchild, *Computers & Geosciences*, **18**, 401 (1992)
10. [Keenan, 2003] P.B. Keenan, Spatial Decision Support Systems in *Decision Making Support Systems: Achievements and challenges for the New Decade* eds. M. Mora, G. Forgionne and J.N.D. Gupta (Idea Group, 2003) pp. 28-39.
11. [Main, 2009] H.H. Main, and M.S. Mesgari, *J. of App. Sci.*, **9**, 1758 (2009).
12. [Schockaert, 2011] S. Schockaert, M. de Cock, E. Kerre, *Reasoning about Fuzzy Temporal and Spatial Information from the Web* (World Scientific, 2011).
13. [Schuurman, 2011] N. Schuurman, E. Randall, and M. Berube, *Health Infor. J.*, **17**, 277 (2011).
14. [Scotch, 2006] M. Scotch and B. Parmanto, *J. Med. Inform.*, **75**, 771 (2006).
15. [Sugumaran, 2011] R. Sugumaran and J. DeGroote, *Spatial Decision Support Systems* (CRC Press, 2011).
16. [Sugumaran, 2007] V. Sugumaran and R. Sugumaran, *Comm. Assoc. Infor. Syst.*, **19**, 40 (2007)

DETERMINING AND PRIORITIZING MAIN FACTORS OF SUPPLIER RELIABILITY

BEHICE MELTEM KAYHAN

Department of Industrial Engineering, Karadeniz Technical University
Trabzon, 61080, Turkey

SELCUK CEBI[1]

Department of Industrial Engineering, Karadeniz Technical University
Trabzon, 61080, Turkey

In this study, supplier reliability is considered as a criterion for selecting the suppliers. Although, there are dozens of studies in the literature that use different models on supplier performance evaluation, only in a few of these studies supplier's reliability is taken as a parameter of the evaluation. The goal of this study is to determine the factors which play important role on the reliability of suppliers and analyze the importance degrees of these factors. For this purpose, fuzzy DEMATEL method which is frequently preferred in the literature is used in order to analyze interaction among the factors.

1. Introduction

Business environment changes rapidly due to the globalization, increasing variety of customer needs, competitive pricing, shorter product life cycles, advanced information systems and environmental consciousness [1]. To become competitive and stable in this changing environment firms concentrate on such activities which termed as supply chain management

One of the most important issues in supply chain management is the selection of the suppliers because it directly affects the overall performance of a supply chain system [2]. In other words, a supplier has a lasting effect on the competitiveness of the entire supply chain and the success of the supply chain depends on the appropriate selection of suppliers. Therefore, supply chain management and supplier selection process have received considerable attention

---

[1] Corresponding author e-mail address: scebi@ktu.edu.tr

in the business management during recent years and supplier selection problem has become one of the most important issues for establishing an effective supply chain system [3]. In contemporary supply chain management, choosing the right suppliers depends on a wide range of quantitative and qualitative factors [4]. Delivery, flexibility, cost, quality, and reliability have been consistently identified as being important determinants of supplier selection in many studies [5].

Since the suppliers are the basic components of the production cycle one of the most important items in the evaluation of the supplier's performance is the reliability of the suppliers. Therefore, one of the objectives of every company is to be reliable to its suppliers. The reliability of any business depends on the reliability of its upstream business partners [6]. There are various effects of supplier reliability in an organization. Poor reliability cause delivery and quality problem, disruption in operation, and low customer satisfaction [7-8].

Therefore, in the scope of this study, factors which play an important role on supplier reliability are considered and then, the importance degrees of these factors are determined by utilizing fuzzy DEMATEL technique since it is accepted as an effective procedure for analyzing structure and relationships between components of a system.

2. Literature Review

Selnes and Gonhaug [8] address the important issue of how supplier behavior in terms of reliability and benevolence creates positive and negative effects on customer satisfaction, and subsequently behave oral intentions to be loyal to the supplier. Building on prior work, five items are used to capture reliability: ability to deliver according to contracts; provision of enough and relevant information; trust in provided information; trustworthiness (expertise); and overall reliability of the supplier. As a result, low supplier reliability was found to create negative effect, while high supplier benevolence created positive affect. Supplier reliability showed a strong positive effect on satisfaction with the supplier, which subsequently increased loyalty.

Li et al. [9] investigated the impacts of market conditions, suppliers' wholesale prices and their reliabilities on the optimal sourcing decisions of price-setting and price-taking firms; also they examined how a firm's pricing power affects these impacts. Supplier's reliability was defined in terms of the "size" or the "variability" of its random capacity using the concepts of stochastic dominance. In this study it is found that the supplier reliability affects the optimal sourcing decisions differently for price-setting and price-taking firms.

Specifically, with a price-setting firm, a supplier can win a larger order by increasing its reliability, however it is not always the same with a price-taking firm.

Pinto et al. [10] addressed the problem of the scarcity of quantitative data by considering and extending the human-in-the-loop DSS concept, which accounts for an expert's knowledge and experience. In this concept, a human expert was involved in making and revising data provided by a computational model, with the aim of supporting companies in making decisions when dealing with unreliable suppliers to minimize the costs related to the external discontinuities. To deal with scant quantitative data, a distribution-free model was developed. Findings positively supported the distribution-free approach as an effective tool to be used when only a limited and perhaps unstructured base of data is available.

Benito and Dale [11] reported some empirical observations of the way in which the Spanish auto components industry is implementing supplier quality and reliability practices. It was found that suppliers more advanced in the use of quality practices are achieving better operational performance in terms of quality, reliability, cost, flexibility and design.

Walton and Marucheck [12] researched EDI usage patterns and supplier reliability in a sample of 30 companies that transmit purchase orders to their suppliers via EDI. The study found that the quality of delivered products and materials, as well as the delivery of the correct item/mix, is related significantly to the buyer's experience using EDI as a tool in supplier management; the willingness of both the buyer and the supplier to share sensitive production and capacity information; the acquisition of the EDI system; and the level of EDI integration with other computer applications.

Levary [13] presented a realistic case study in which a manufacturer evaluates and ranks its current foreign supplier against two other potential foreign suppliers based on several criteria of supply reliability.

3. Reliability Factors

Supplier reliability is defined as the supplier's ability to keep their promises. The reliability factors obtained from literature is given in Table 1.

Table 1. Reliability Factors

Factors	Explanation
Timing	Supplier's loyalty to delivery time
Quantity	Supplier's ability to provide expected quantity
Quality	Supplier's ability to provide expected quality
Price	The consistency of the prices offered by the supplier
Flexibility	Supplier's ability to respond timely to changing requirements of the customer
Experience	The experience of the supplier in the business sector in terms of year
Sustainability	Sustainability of the service/product which is proposed by supplier

4. The Method

In order to determine importance degrees of the factors, fuzzy Decision-making trial and evaluation laboratory (DEMATEL) method is used. DEMATEL was introduced to the literature to analyze the relationship between the causes and effects of criteria into an intelligible structure [14]. It is commonly used to extract the interrelationship among factors. So, DEMATEL method presents importance degrees of factors based on cause and effect relations [15]. Any criterion which has more effect on another is assumed to have higher priority and assigned as cause criterion. Otherwise, since the criterion is more affected from other criteria, it is assumed to have lower priority and named effect criteria [16, 17]. In this study, because of the evaluation procedure of the handled problem, Fuzzy DEMATEL method is used. The steps of the method will be presented in   Section 5.

5. Application

In this application, reliability factors are evaluated by stationery products marketer which is one of the biggest in Black Sea Region.

Step 1. The pairwise comparison matrix ($\tilde{M}^k$) which puts forward interactions between reliability factors is constructed by each expert in linguistic form (No influence "N", Very Weak influence "VW", Weak influence "W", Strong influence "S", and   Extreme strong influence "E") [18].

Step 2. In this step, experts' preferences for direct relation are aggregated by applying the fuzzy weighted averaging operator.

Step 3. The normalized direct-relation matrix $\tilde{Z}_{ij}$ is obtained by Eq. (1) [19-21].

$$\tilde{Z} = \min_{i,j} \left[\frac{1}{\max_{1 \le i \le n} \sum_{j=1}^{n} m_{ij}^u}, \frac{1}{\max_{1 \le j \le n} \sum_{i=1}^{n} m_{ij}^u} \right] \times \tilde{M} \tag{1}$$

Step 4. The total relation matrix $\tilde{T}$ is calculated by following formula
$$\tilde{T} = \tilde{Z} \times (I - \tilde{Z})^{-1} \qquad (2)$$
where I is identity matrix [19].

Step 5. $\tilde{R}$ and $\tilde{C}$ *are* $n \times 1$ and $1 \times n$ vectors representing the sum of rows and sum of columns of the total relation matrix $\tilde{T}$, respectively. While $\tilde{r}_i$ presents both direct and indirect effects given by i^{th} factor to the other factors, $\tilde{c}_j$ shows both direct and indirect effects by j^{th} factor from the other factors. If $j = i$, the sum ($\tilde{S} = \tilde{R} + \tilde{C}$) shows the total effects given and received by i^{th} factor. The sum indicates importance of ith factor in the entire system in terms of relation [22, 23]. On the contrary, the difference ($\tilde{D} = \tilde{R} - \tilde{C}$) depicts the net effect that i^{th} factor contributes to the system where $\tilde{D}(d_i^l, d_i^m, d_i^u)$. Based on the difference values, factors are classified as follows [24]:

(i) if the difference is positive ($r_i^l \geq c_j^u$, $\tilde{d}_i \geq 0$),i^{th} factor is a net cause (*NC*),
(ii) if the difference is weak positive $\left(d_i^m \geq 0\right)$, i^{th} factor is a weak cause (*WC*),
(iii) if the difference is negative ($c_i^l \geq r_j^u$, $\tilde{d}_i < 0$) i^{th} factor is a net receiver (*NR*),
(iv) if the difference is weak negative $\left(d_i^m < 0\right)$ i^{th} factor is a weak receiver (*WR*),
(v) otherwise the factor is inconsistent.

According to the results given in Table 2, there are not any factors neither *NC* nor *NR*. The factors, *Timing, Quantity, Experience,* and *Sustainability*, are *WC* and the others, *Quality, Flexibility,* and *Price* are *WR*. Based on the interactions among factors, the priorities of these factors are as follows; *Flexibility> Experience> Quality> Quantity> Price> Sustainability> Timing*.

Table 2. The importance degrees of factors

Factors	R	C	R+C	R-C
Timing	(0.32,0.66,3.49)	(0.14,0.46,2.94)	(0.46,1.12,6.43)	(0.18,0.2,0.55)
Quantity	(0.31,0.83,3.95)	(0.26,0.61,3.35)	(0.57,1.44,7.3)	(0.05,0.22,0.59)
Quality	(0.26,0.7,3.6)	(0.38,0.82,3.92)	(0.64,1.52,7.52)	(-0.12,-0.11,-0.31)
Flexibility	(0.25,0.58,3.28)	(0.45,1.1,4.68)	(0.7,1.68,7.96)	(-0.2,-0.52,-1.41)
Experience	(0.48,1.09,4.64)	(0.19,0.43,2.88)	(0.67,1.52,7.52)	(0.29,0.65,1.76)
Sustainability	(0.36,0.77,3.79)	(0.14,0.53,3.15)	(0.49,1.3,6.94)	(0.22,0.24,0.64)
Price	(0.07,0.35,2.65)	(0.49,1.03,4.48)	(0.56,1.38,7.13)	(-0.42,-0.68,-1.83)

6. Conclusion

One of the most important components of the supply chain is supplier reliability. In the literature, there are lots of papers considering performance of suppliers' and reliability is generally considered as one of the performance factors.

However, none of the studies consider interactions among performance factors all of these factors affect the reliability. Therefore, this paper addresses to determine and prioritize factors of supplier reliability. For this purpose, fuzzy DEMATEL method is used and the most important factor is obtained as flexibility based on the interactions among factors.

For the further study, a method which measures reliability of the supplier can be developed based on fuzzy inference methods.

References

1. M.Tracey and C.L. Tan, *Supply Chain Manag*,**6**,174-188 (2001).
2. S.I.Omurca, *Appl Soft Comput*, **13**, 690-697 (2013).
3. W.Ho, X.Xu, P.K.Dey, *Eur J Oper Res*, **202**, 16-24 (2009).
4. F.T.S.Chan, H.K.Chan, *Int J Adv Manuf Technol*,**51**, 1195 (2010).
5. T.Sawik, *Omega*, **43**, 83-95 (2014).
6. A.Gunasekaran,C.Patel,R.E.Mcgaughey,*Int.J.Production Economics*, **87**, 333-347 (2004).
7. S.P.Venkatesan, S.Kumanan, *Int J Adv Manuf Technol*,**61**, 325-337 (2009).
8. F.Selnes,K.Gonhaug, J Busn Res,**49**, 259-271 (2000)
9. T.Li, and S.Sethi, and J. Zhang, http://ssrn.com/abstract=1673541 (2011)
10. R.Pinto, T.Mettler, M.Taisch, *Dec Sup Sys*,**54**, 1084 (2013).
11. J.G.Benito, B.Dale, *Eur J Purch Supp Manag*,**7**,187-196 (2007).
12. S.V.Walton, A.S.Marucheck, *Int J Purch Mat* , (1997).
13. R.R.Levary, *Comput Ind Eng* ,**55**, 535-542 (2008).
14. Fontela E, and Gabus A..*Futures* **6**(4):361-363, (1974).
15. KHChang, and CH Cheng, *J Intell Manuf,* **22**(2):113-129 (2011)
16. Tseng ML, Lin YH, *Environ Monit Assess*, **158**(1-4):519-533, (2009).
17. Tzeng GH, Chen FH, Hsu TS, *Int J Hosp Manag,* **30**(4):908-932 (2011).
18. Tzeng G-H, Chen W-H, Yu R, Shih M-L, *Soft Comput* **14**(11):1141-1150 (2010).
19. F.Mohamadnejad, J. Jassbi, H.Nasrollahzadeh, *Expert Syst Appl* **38**(5): 5967-5973, (2011).
20. Wu, W.-W. and Lee Y.-T. *Expert Syst Appl* **32,** 499–507, (2007)
21. Lin, C.-L., Tzeng G-H, *Expert Syst Appl* **36** (6) 9683-9697 (2009)
22. Wu H-H, Chen H-K, Shieh J-I *Expert Syst Appl* 37(7):5219-5223 (2010).
23. Wu HH, Tsai YN, *Appl Math Comput* 218(5):2334-2342, (2011).
24. Cebi S, *Elect Com Res and Appl*, **12** (2), 124-135 (2013).

FUZZY LAPLACE DISTRIBUTION WITH VaR APPLIED IN INVESTMENT PORTFOLIO

M. P. C. ROCHA* and L. M. COSTA

*Institute of Exact and Natural Sciences of Federal University of Para,
Belem, Para 66075/110, Brazil
* E-mail: mrocha@ufpa.br
www.ufpa.br*

B.R.C. BEDREGAL

*Department of Informatics and Applied Mathematics, Federal University of Rio
Grande do Norte, Natal, Rio Grande do Norte 59078/970, Brazil
E-mail: brcbedregal@gmail.com*

We present a new possibilistic mean-variance model using the Fuzzy Laplace distribution (PMVFL). We generated a sequence of results and concluded that results showed an expected behavior of model of possibilistic mean-variance. When we increase the VaR (Value at Risk), in other words, when we consider further loss of market value, we mean that the risk rate will be higher, i.e., larger return rate, higher will be risk rate, this fact has been demonstrated in model.

Keywords: Fuzzy; VaR; Portfolio selection; Risk

1. Introduction

Carlsson[1] introduced the notations of upper and lower possibilistic mean values, and introduced the notation of crisp possibilistic mean values and crisp possibilistic variance of continuous distributions. Zhang[4] extended the concepts of possibilistic mean and possibilistic variance of proposed by Carlsson,[1] and introduced the concepts of upper and lower possibilistic variances and covariances of fuzzy numbers.

Li[2] proposed a model portfolio of possibilistic investment restrictions under the VaR and risk-free. This model shows that risk-averse investors want to not only achieve the expected return rate on your actual investment but also ensure that the maximum of their potential future risk is lower than the VaR. With the assumption that returns of assets are fuzzy variables with normal distribution, and derived a crisp equivalent form of portfolio investment restrictions under possibilistic VaR and risk-free.

Based on Li[2] , we propose that assets returns are fuzzy with Laplace distribution, and a theorem with solution to this distribution, considering a portfolio of investment restrictions on possibilistic VaR and risk-free.

2. Possibilistic Variance and Mean Value

In this section, we introduce some concepts that will be needed in the next sections. A fuzzy number $\tilde{A}$ is a fuzzy set of the real line $\mathbb{R}$ with a normal, convex and continuous membership function with a limited support and γ-level set $[\tilde{A}]^\gamma = [a_1(\gamma), a_2(\gamma)]$.

Carlsson[1] defined the upper and lower possibilistic means of a fuzzy number $\tilde{A}$, denoted by $M_U(\tilde{A})$ and $M_L(\tilde{A})$. The possibilistic mean value of $\tilde{A}$ is the arithmetic mean of its lower and upper possibilistic mean values as follows:

$$\overline{M}(\tilde{A}) = \frac{M_U(\tilde{A}) + M_L(\tilde{A})}{2} = \int_0^1 \gamma a_2(\gamma)d\gamma + \int_0^1 \gamma a_1(\gamma)d\gamma \qquad (1)$$

The possibilistic covariance between the fuzzy numbers $\tilde{A}$ and $\tilde{B}$ is defined as:

$$\overline{Cov}(\tilde{A}, \tilde{B}) = \frac{Cov_U(\tilde{A}, \tilde{B}) + Cov_L(\tilde{A}, \tilde{B})}{2}. \qquad (2)$$

3. Portfolio Model under Constraints of VaR and Risk Free Investment

Suppose there are n risk assets and one risk-free assets available for investment. Let $\tilde{\varphi}_i$ be the return rate of asset $i, i = 1, 2, .., n$, which is a fuzzy number. Let x_i represent the proportion invested in asset i, and r_f is the risk-free asset return, defined by

$$\tilde{r}_p = \sum_{i=1}^n x_i \tilde{\varphi}_i + r_f \left(1 - \sum_{i=1}^n x_i \right), \qquad (3)$$

since $\tilde{\varphi}_i$ is a fuzzy membership $\tilde{r}_p$ also is a fuzzy number. The possibilistic mean of the portfolio return $\tilde{r}_p$ is given by

$$\overline{M}(\widetilde{r}_p) = \sum_{i=1}^{n} x_i \frac{M_U(\widetilde{\varphi}_i) + M_L(\widetilde{\varphi}_i)}{2} + r_f \left(1 - \sum_{i=1}^{n} x_i\right). \tag{4}$$

According Carlsson[1], it is known that the possibilistic variance of $\widetilde{r}_p$ is given by

$$\overline{\sigma^2}\left(\sum_{i=1}^{n} x_i \widetilde{\varphi}_i\right) = \sum_{i=1}^{n} x_i^2 \overline{\sigma_{\widetilde{\varphi}_i}^2} + 2 \sum_{i>j=1}^{n} x_i x_j \overline{Cov}(\widetilde{\varphi}_i, \widetilde{\varphi}_j) \tag{5}$$

Similarly to the possibilistic mean-variance model, in this paper, the possibilistic mean is used to describe the portfolio return, and the possibilistic variance is used to describe the portfolio risk. However, when a value at risk VaR constraint is imposed on our portfolio model. Under this structure, the possibilistic portfolio model under constraint of VaR and risk-free investment can be formulated as:

$$\begin{cases} min & \overline{\sigma^2} = \sum_{i=1}^{n} x_i^2 \overline{\sigma_{\widetilde{\varphi}_i}^2} + 2 \sum_{i>j=1}^{n} x_i x_j \overline{Cov}(\widetilde{\varphi}_i, \widetilde{\varphi}_j) \\ s.t. & \sum_{i=1}^{n} x_i \frac{M_U(\widetilde{\varphi}_i) + M_L(\widetilde{\varphi}_i)}{2} + r_f \left(1 - \sum_{i=1}^{n} x_i\right) \geq \widetilde{r}_p, \\ & pos(\widetilde{\varphi}_i x_i \leq VaR) \leq 1 - \beta, \\ & \sum_{i=1}^{n} x_i \leq 1, \\ & 0 \leq l_i \leq x_i \leq u_i, i = 1, 2, ..., n, \end{cases} \tag{6}$$

where pos denotes the measure of possibilistic, $\widetilde{r}_p$ is the expected rate of return, l_i and u_i represents the lower bound and upper bound on investment in asset i, respectively and VaR is defined as the value at risk by the β-confidence level. The model shows that risk-averse investors wish not only to reach the expected rate of returns in their actual investment, but also to ensure that the maximum of their possible risk is lower than an expected loss.

4. Fuzzy Laplace Distribution

According to Rocha[3] the return rate of asset i is a Laplace distribution fuzzy 'variable expressed as $\widetilde{\varphi}_i \sim FL(\mu_i, \sigma_i)$, and its membership function is

$$A_{\widetilde{\varphi}_i}(t/\mu_i, b) = \frac{1}{2b} exp\left(-\frac{|t - \mu_i|}{b}\right)$$

$$= \frac{1}{2b} \begin{cases} exp\left(\frac{-\mu_i + t}{b}\right) & if\, t < \mu_i \\ exp\left(\frac{-t + \mu_i}{b}\right) & if\, t \geq \mu_i, \end{cases}$$

where $\sigma_i^2 = 2b^2 \Rightarrow b = \frac{\sqrt{2}}{2}\sigma_i$. The γ-level set of $\widetilde{\varphi}_i$ is defined as

$$[\widetilde{\varphi}_i]^\gamma = \left[\mu_i - \frac{\sqrt{2}}{2}\sigma_i \ln \sqrt{2}\sigma_i\gamma, \mu_i + \frac{\sqrt{2}}{2}\sigma_i \ln \sqrt{2}\sigma_i\gamma\right] \tag{7}$$

Rocha[3] demonstrates that the rates of return of the assets are Laplace fuzzy distributions variables expressed as $\widetilde{\varphi}_i \sim FL(\mu_i, \sigma_i)$,, $i = 1, 2, ..., n$. Then

$$\sum_{i=1}^n x_i\widetilde{\varphi}_i \sim FL\left(\sum_{i=1}^n x_i\mu_i, \frac{1}{8}\left(\sum_{i=1}^n x_i\sigma_i\right)^2\right), \tag{8}$$

where $x_i \geq 0, i = 1, 2, ..., n$.

Moreover, for a Laplace fuzzy distribution variable, the portfolio model of VaR restrictions and risk free investment can be formulated as:

$$\begin{cases} min & \overline{\sigma^2} = \frac{1}{8}\left(\sum_{i=1}^n x_i^2\sigma_i^2 + 2\sum_{i>j=1}^n x_ix_j\sigma_i\sigma_j\right) \\ s.t. & \sum_{i=1}^n x_i(\mu_i - r_f) + r_f \geq \widetilde{r} \\ (VaR - \sum_{i=1}^n x_i\mu_i) \leq b\ln[2b(1-\beta)] & p/VaR < \sum_{i=1}^n x_i\mu_i, \\ (\sum_{i=1}^n x_i\mu_i - VaR) \leq b\ln[2b(1-\beta)] & p/VaR \geq \sum_{i=1}^n x_i\mu_i, \\ where & b = \frac{\sqrt{2}}{16}\left(\sum_{i=1}^n x_i\sigma_i\right)^2 \\ & \sum_{i=1}^n x_i \leq 1 \\ & 0 \leq l_i \leq x_i \leq u_i, i = 1, 2, ..., n, \end{cases} \tag{9}$$

5. Numerical Example

To facilitate analysis we denote PMVFL to the mean-variance model of possibilistic for a Laplace distribution Fuzzy and PMVFN for mean-variance of possibilistic for a Normal distribution fuzzy model. To analyze the proposed model we used the same actual data used by Li[3] . It was selected by Li[2] five portfolios from Shanghai Stock Exchange, from period between January and December of 2008, Table 1. In this study the return rate of each asset $\widetilde{\varphi}_i \sim FL(\mu_i, \sigma_i)$, is calculated from the frequency distribution of monthly returns of five portfolios, Table 1.

In addition, the γ- level set $\widetilde{\varphi}_i$ ($i = 1, .., 5$) is obtained from the average and the standard deviation of each portfolio, obtained by Eq. (7). Therefore, we obtain the lower bound of investment ratio x_i is

Table 1. The possibilistic distributions of returns of five stocks.

	Stock 1	Stock 2	Stock 3	Stock 4	Stock 5
μ	0.118	0.167	0.223	0.268	0.322
σ	0.05	0.1	0.18	0.26	0.35

$l = \begin{bmatrix} 0.016 & 0.011 & 0.015 & 0.033 & 0.185 \end{bmatrix}$ and the upper bound is $u = \begin{bmatrix} 0.083 & 0.188 & 0.344 & 0.486 & 0.669 \end{bmatrix}$.

Suppose $\beta = 0.95$ and $Var = 0.05$ by solving the model (11), the possibilistic efficient portfolios for the different objective value r are obtained as shown the Table 2 and Figure 1. The Figure 2, we show the relationship between the capital invested in risky assets and risky free assets, it means that 26.2% of capital are invested in risky assets and the remaining 73.8% are invested in risk free assets.

Table 2. Results Using the Fuzzy Laplace Distribution

	01	03	06	09	12	13	21	26	31
$\bar{r}(\%)$	8.366	9.051	10.080	11.108	12.137	16.235	17.011	21.049	22.763
$\sigma^2(\%)$	7.205	8.479	10.584	12.924	15.496	44.232	47.575	48.561	55.736
x_1	0.016	0.016	0.016	0.016	0.016	0.076	0.076	0.076	0.016
x_2	0.011	0.011	0.011	0.011	0.011	0.181	0.181	0.011	0.011
x_3	0.016	0.016	0.016	0.016	0.016	0.336	0.336	0.016	0.016
x_4	0.033	0.033	0.033	0.033	0.033	0.053	0.043	0.033	0.033
x_5	0.186	0.206	0.236	0.266	0.296	0.186	0.216	0.556	0.606
$\sum x_i$	0.262	0.282	0.312	0.342	0.372	0.832	0.852	0.632	0.682
$1 - \sum x_i$	0.738	0.718	0.688	0.658	0.628	0.168	0.148	0.368	0.318

6. Conclusion

We present a new possibilistic mean-variance model using the Fuzzy Laplace distribution (PMVFL). We generated a sequence of results and concluded that results showed an expected behavior of model of possibilistic mean-variance. When we increase the VaR (Value at Risk), in other words, when we consider further loss of market value, we mean that the risk rate will be higher, i.e., larger return rate, higher will be risk rate, this fact has been demonstrated in model.

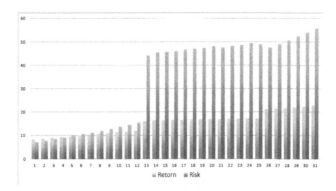

Fig. 1. Results of PMVLZ (Laplace) model with $VaR = 0.05$ and $\beta = 0.95$, we have risk rate and return rate of Portfofio for PMVLZ model.

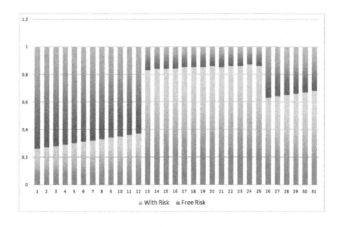

Fig. 2. We show the relationship between the capital invested in risky assets and risky free assets.

References

1. C. Carlsson and Fuller R.. On possibilistic mean value and variance of fuzzy numbers. *Fuzzy Sets and Systems*, **122**, 315-326 (2001).
2. Li, T. and Zhang, W.,Xu, W. Fuzzy possibilistic portfolio selection model with VaR constraint and risk-free investiment. *Economic Modeling*, **31**, 12-17 (2013).
3. M. P. C. Rocha, L. L. Costa and B. C. Bedegral.. On possibilistic variance of fuzzy numbers. *Submitted to Applied Mathematics Modelling.* (2014).
4. Zhang, W. G., Nie, Z. K.. On possibilistic variance of fuzzy numbers. *Lecture Notes in Artificial Intelligence*, **2639**, 398-402 (201).

A MULTICRITERIA SUPPLIER SELECTION MODEL USING HESITANT FUZZY LINGUISTIC TERM SETS

CENGIZ KAHRAMAN   BAŞAR ÖZTAYŞI   SEZI ÇEVIK ONAR

Istanbul Technical University, Department of Industrial Engineering, 34367 Macka Istanbul Turkey

Hesitant fuzzy sets have been developed to handle the situations where a set of values are possible in the definition process of the membership of an element. Hesitant fuzzy linguistic term sets provide a linguistic and computational basis to increase the richness of linguistic elicitation based on the fuzzy linguistic approach and the use of context-free grammars by using comparative terms. In this paper, we propose a multicriteria method based on hesitant fuzzy linguistic term sets and apply it to a supplier selection problem.

1. Introduction

Supplier selection is a crucial process since it is one of the main determinants of the survival of an organization. The supplier selection is complex and uncertain since it involves both different selection criteria with quantitative and qualitative aspects and several decision makers with different perspectives (Hammami et al., 2014). Quality of the products, delivery performance; and service performance are the examples of the criteria that are considered in supplier selection problems. Therefore many researchers utilized multi-criteria decision making techniques in supplier selection (Chai et al., 2013) but there are several limitations of these studies. One of the limitations of such studies is the inconsistencies occurred due to the subjective judgments of the experts on different criteria (Ho et al., 2010). Linguistic expressions are widely used but experts usually hesitant on selecting one of the linguistic terms and prefer a more flexible way for expressing themselves but the current studies in the literature necessitate a single linguistic expression from judgments which may cause inconsistencies. Rodriguez et al. (2013) proposed a methodology in order to deal with such hesitant linguistic expressions but their study is not capable of dealing with multicriteria problems. In this study a multi-criteria hesitant decision making tool is utilized in order to overcome the supplier selection problem.

The rest of the paper is organized as follows. Section 2 gives the basics of hesitant fuzzy linguistic term sets (HFLTS). Section 3 presents our proposed multicriteria method based on HFLTS. Section 4 gives an application of the proposed method to the supplier selection problem. The last section concludes the paper and gives our recommendations for further research.

2. Hesitant Fuzzy Linguistic Term Sets

A group decision making problem is defined as a problem including two more experts and a finite set of alternatives to obtain a solution set. Let experts set be represented by $E = \{e_1, e_2, \dots, e_m\}$ where $m \geq 2$ and alternative sets be $X = \{x_1, x_2, \dots, x_n\}$ where $n \geq 2$. While determining a membership function, it may occur that experts may hesitate among several values to assess a linguistic variable. Torra (2010) introduced the concept of Hesitant Fuzzy Sets (HFS) to manage the hesitant situations where several values are possible for the definition of a membership function of a fuzzy set.

Rodriguez et al. (2012) presented the concept of hesitant fuzzy linguistic term sets based on the fuzzy linguistic approach and hesitant fuzzy sets. Hesitant fuzzy linguistic term sets (HFLTS) improves the existing linguistic approaches to provide experts a greater flexibility in eliciting linguistic preferences through the use of context-free grammars that fix the rules to build flexible linguistic expressions to express preferences. The details of HFLTS can be found in Rodriguez et al. (2013).

3. Multicriteria Hesitant Fuzzy Sets Method

A multicriteria decision making problem includes many criteria and some of them are conflicting criteria. This type of problems can be handled by a hierarchy to divide it into sub-problems and then to combine the solutions of sub-problems.
Rodriguez et al. (2013) proposed a hesitant linguistic group decision making model. This model is based on n alternatives ad m experts and does not include multicriteria. We extend Rodriguez et al.'s algorithm to be able to consider a multicriteria decision making problem.

The steps of the proposed algorithm:

Let the number of any criterion be represented by $z \in \{1, 2, \dots, \tau\}$

Start: with respect to Criterion z
Step 1. Define the semantics and syntax of the linguistic term set S.

Step 2. Define the context-free grammar G_H, where $G_H = \{V_N, V_T, I, P\}$.

$$V_N = \left\{ \begin{matrix} \langle\text{primary term}\rangle, \langle\text{composite term}\rangle, \langle\text{unary relation}\rangle, \langle\text{binary relation}\rangle, \\ \langle\text{conjunction}\rangle \end{matrix} \right\}$$

$V_T = \{\text{lower than, greater than, at least, at most, between, and}, s_0, s_1, \ldots, s_g\}$

$I \epsilon V_N$

Step 3. Gather the preference relations p^k provided by experts $k \in \{1, 2, \ldots, m\}$

Step 4. Transform the preference relations into HFLTS by using the transformation function E_{G_H}.

Step 5. Obtain an envelope $[p_{ij}^{k-}, p_{ij}^{k+}]$ for each HFLTS.

Step 6. Select two linguistic aggregation operators φ and $\emptyset$, which might be the same.

Step 7. Obtain the pessimistic and optimistic collective preference relations P_C^- and P_C^+ by using the linguistic aggregation operator φ.

Step 8. Compute a pessimistic and optimistic collective preference for each alternative by linguistic aggregation operator φ. The 2-tuple set associated with S is defined as $\langle S \rangle = S \times [0.5, 0.5]$. The function $\Delta: [0, g] \rightarrow \langle S \rangle$ is given by

$$\Delta(\beta) = (s_i, \alpha) \; with \; \begin{cases} i = round(\beta) \\ \alpha = \beta - i \end{cases} \tag{1}$$

where round assigns to β the integer number $i \in \{0, 1, \ldots, g\}$ closest to β and $\Delta^{-1}: \langle S \rangle \rightarrow [0, g]$ is defined by

$$\Delta^{-1}(s_i, \alpha) = i + \alpha \tag{2}$$

Step 9. Build a vector of intervals $V^R = (p_1^R, p_2^R, \ldots, p_n^R)$ of collective preferences for the alternatives $p_i^R = [p_i^-, p_i^+]$.

Step 10. Normalize the obtained interval utilities.

Rodriguez et al. (2013) use the following preference degree equations. However these preference degrees are not capable to rank the criteria or alternatives

Let $A = [a_1, a_2]$ and $B = [b_1, b_2]$ be two interval utilities, the preference degree of A over B (or A>B) is defined as:

$$P(A > B) = p_{AB}^s = \frac{max(0, a_2 - b_1) - max(0, a_1 - b_2)}{(a_2 - a_1) + (b_2 - b_1)} \tag{3}$$

Instead, we propose the normalization of the obtained interval utilities.

Go to Start: with respect to Criterion $z+1$

Step 11. Rank the set of alternatives and select the best one.

4. Application

There are three supplier alternatives, which we want to select the best one among them using three criteria *delivery*, *quality*, and *service*. Three experts assess the alternatives with respect to the three independent criteria. The hierarchy of the problem is given in Figure 1.

Figure 1. The hierarchy of supplier selection problem

We will apply the steps of the algorithm given above. For the sake of space limits, we only give some examples from calculations below.

Step 1. Define the semantics and syntax of the linguistic term set S:

$$S = \left\{ \begin{array}{c} no\ importance\ (ni),\ very\ low\ importance\ (vli),\ low\ importance\ (li),\ medium \\ importance\ (mi),\ high\ importance\ (hi),\ very\ high\ importance\ (vhi), \\ absolute\ importance\ (ai) \end{array} \right\}$$

Step 2 and **Step 3**. Define the context-free grammar and Gather the preferences provided by the experts.

Expert 1's assessment for the criteria with respect to the goal:

	Delivery	*Quality*	*Service*
Delivery	–	at most li	at most mi
Quality	at least hi	–	at least hi
Service	at least mi	at most li	–

Step 4. Transform the preference relations into HFLTS.
Expert 1's assessment for the criteria with respect to the goal:

	Delivery	*Quality*	*Service*
Delivery	–	{ni, vli, li}	{ni, vli, li, mi}
Quality	{hi, vhi, ai}	–	{hi, vhi, ai}
Service	{mi, hi, vhi, ai}	{ni, vli, li}	–

Step 5. Obtain its envelope for each HFLTS.

Expert 1's assessment for the criteria with respect to the goal:

	Delivery	Quality	Service
Delivery	–	$[ni, li]$	$[ni, mi]$
Quality	$[hi, ai]$	–	$[hi, ai]$
Service	$[mi, ai]$	$[ni, li]$	–

Step 6. Obtain the pessimistic and optimistic collective preference relations.

We first assign the scale in Table 1 to the linguistic terms:

Table 1. The scale for the linguistic terms

ni	vli	li	mi	hi	vhi	ai
0	1	2	3	4	5	6

The obtained optimistic preference values are given all together in the following matrix:

$$P_c^+ = \begin{bmatrix} & Delivery & Quality & Service \\ Delivery & - & (li, -0.33) & (mi, 0) \\ Quality & (ai, 0) & - & (ai, -0.33) \\ Service & (vhi, 0.33) & (li, -0.33) & - \end{bmatrix}$$

The obtained pessimistic preference values are given all together in the following matrix:

$$P_c^- = \begin{bmatrix} & Delivery & Quality & Service \\ Delivery & - & (ni, 0) & (vli, -0.33) \\ Quality & (hi, 0.33) & - & (hi, 0.33) \\ Service & (mi, 0) & (ni, 0.33) & - \end{bmatrix}$$

Step 7. Compute a pessimistic and optimistic collective preference for each criterion.

Table 2 presents the pessimistic and optimistic collective preferences for the criteria.

Table 2. Pessimistic and optimistic collective preference for each criterion

	Delivery	Quality	Service
Pessimistic	(ni, 0.34)	(hi, 0.33)	(li, -0.33)
Optimistic	(li, 0.34)	(ai, -0.16)	(mi, 0.5)

Step 8. Build a vector of intervals $V^R = (p_1^R, p_2^R, p_3^R)$ for the criteria.

Table 3 gives the linguistic intervals for the criteria.

Table 3. Linguistic interval for each criterion

Delivery	Quality	Service
p_1^R	p_2^R	p_3^R
$[(ni, 0.34), (li, 0.34)]$ $= (0.34, 2.34)$	$[(hi, 0,33), (ai, -0.16)]$ $= (4.33, 5.84)$	$[(li, -0.33), (mi, 0.5)]$ $= (1.67, 3.5)$

Step 9. Build a preference relation P_D.

We propose the following solution. We first calculate the midpoint of each interval: $(0.67, 1.34) \rightarrow 1.005$, $(4.33, 5.84) \rightarrow 5.085$, $(1.67, 3.5) \rightarrow 2.585$. Later we normalize these values by dividing each value with their sum. The

normalized weights are 0.116 for delivery; 0.298 for quality; and 0.586 for service.
Table 4 presents the combination of the obtained weights above and the determination of the weighted scores for alternatives. According to the last column in Table 6, the best supplier is Supplier 2. The second order belongs to Supplier 3 and the worst one is Supplier 1.

Table 4. Determination of weighted scores for alternatives

	Delivery	Quality	Service	Weighted Scores
Criteria Weights	0.15	0.56	0.29	
Supplier 1	0.14	0.14	0.13	**0.137**
Supplier 2	0.54	0.34	0.56	**0.434**
Supplier 3	0.32	0.52	0.31	**0.429**

5. Conclusion

The proposed method has been successfully applied to a supplier selection problem. The obtained results exactly meet the experts' linguistic opinions since HFLTS provide this flexibility. For further research, we recommend the use of a different preference relation or a new preference relation to be developed. We used a normalization approach in our method since Rodriguez et al.'s (2013) preference degree equations do not sufficiently distinguish the small differences among the considered elements.

References

V. Torra, Hesitant fuzzy sets, International Journal of Intelligent Systems 25 (6) (2010) 529–539.

R.M. Rodriguez, L. Martinez, F. Herrera, Hesitant fuzzy linguistic term sets for decision making, IEEE Transactions on Fuzzy Systems 20 (1) (2012) 109–119.

Ramzi Hammami, Cecilia Temponi, Yannick Frein (2014) A scenario-based stochastic model for supplier selection in global context with multiple buyers, currency fluctuation uncertainties, and price discounts European Journal of Operational Research 233 (2014) 159–170

Junyi Chai, James N.K. Liu, Eric W.T. Ngai (2013)Application of decision-making techniques in supplier selection: A systematic review of literature Expert Systems with Applications 40 (2013) 3872–3885

William Ho, Xiaowei Xu, Prasanta K. Dey Multi-criteria decision making approaches for supplier evaluation and selection: A literature review European Journal of Operational Research 202 (2010) 16–24

Rosa M. Rodriguez, Luis Martinez, Francisco Herrera A group decision making model dealing with comparative linguistic expressions based on hesitant fuzzy linguistic term sets. Information Sciences 241 (2013) 28–42.

A WEIGHT DETERMINATION METHOD OF SUBJECTIVE SCORE IN GROUP DECISION[*]

TIEFENG ZHANG, XIN LV

School of Electrical and Electronic Engineering, North China Electric Power University, Baoding, China

JIANWEI GU

Hangzhou Power Supply Company, Hangzhou, China

To weaken the effects of those experts' weights that far away from the center of opinions in decision-making approach for assessing the performances of candidates in many major competitions, this paper proposes a weight determination method of experts in group decision based on the difference value, which can effectively weaken the effects of extreme scores in group decision making and centralize the experts' opinions for achieving consensus. A case study is demonstrated to illustrate this method and the results indicate the effectiveness.

1. Introduction

Most major competitions' assessment is based on subjective score of expert. It is a typical multi-attribute group decision making that multiple experts give each candidate a score on his/her performance [1]. In group decision, the gathering of group's opinions is the key in the whole decision making process [2], and it is also involved in the problem of competition fairness [3]. In order to make the experts' opinions achieve consensus, we should weaken the effects of those experts' weights that far away from the center of opinions. Such as the trimmed mean [2], with removing one of the highest and one of the lowest scores, takes the average of the rest of scores, which is an aggregation method of experts' opinions. In addition, the Ordered Weighted Averaging (OWA) operator is also a kind of common aggregation method [4]. The former can't completely weaken the effects of those experts' weights that far away from the center of opinions, and the latter has a need of further selection for decision making. Therefore, the above methods can't fully solve the problem of avoiding the effects of extreme scores in evaluation process.

---

[*] This work is supported by the Fundamental Research Funds for Central University.

In solving the problem of expert's weight determination in group decision, reference [5] presented a gray relation-based weight determination algorithm with the subjective weight of expert. Reference [6] presented a weight determination method with the idea of maximizing the distance between subjective score and the average. In [7] an entropy theory-based multi-attribute group decision making for weight determination of expert method is presented. Reference [8] presented an adaptive weight determination method in multi-attribute group decision making. Reference [9] presented a weight determination method of expert group and decision makers' preference. Reference [10] used the feedback of difference value of experts' scores for weight determination to solve the problem of consistency, but its weight function is not ideal, for example, there is little difference between the farthest and the closest from the center of weight score. Reference [11] developed a subjective weighting method based on group decision making for ranking and measuring criteria values through considering different situations.

All above methods are proposed to solve the problem of weight determination, but none of them is simple and able to comprehensively express the consistency (or the degree of consensus) of group decision. So, to solve the problem of weight determination for subjective score in group decision, this paper proposes a weight determination method of expert based on the difference value between subjective score and the average, and uses a case study to illustrate this method.

2. Weight Determination Method Based on Distance between Subjective Score and the Average

In the proposed method, the experts' weights are determined based on the distance between subjective score and the average. The distance is closer, the weight will be larger. When subjective score is equal to the average, the weight reaches the maximum (the weight value is 1).The distance is farther, the weight will be smaller. When the distance is the largest of all distance values, the weight reaches the minimum (the weight value is 0).The other weight values are between 0 and 1 according to a linear function. The method and steps of weighting function's set are described as follows.

2.1. *Weight Determination*

We suppose that there are M experts, N candidates, and C criteria. Then for the n-th candidate under the c-th criterion, the scores of these M experts are

$$X_{ncm}, m = 1, 2, L, M,$$

The highest score under the c-th criterion of these M experts is

$$X_{ncH} = max(x_{ncm}, m = 1, 2, L, M),$$

The lowest score is $X_{ncL} = min(x_{ncm}, m = 1, 2, L, M)$,

The average score is $X_{ncA} = avg(x_{ncm}, m = 1, 2, L, M)$,

Then, the score weight for each expert is

$$W_{ncm} = 1 - \frac{|x_{ncm} - x_{ncA}|}{max(x_{ncH} - x_{ncA}, x_{ncA} - x_{ncL})} \tag{1}$$

That is, the score closer to the average gets a larger weight.

The sum of these weights is defined by $S_{nc} = \sum_{m=1}^{M} w_{ncm}$

The normalized weight is defined by $g_{ncm} = w_{ncm}/s_{nc}$ $\qquad$ (2)

2.2. Calculation of Weighted Score

The total score of all experts under each criterion is $x_{nc} = \sum_{m=1}^{M} x_{ncm} * g_{ncm}$ $\qquad$ (3)

The total score of each candidate can be calculated by $x_n = \sum_{c=1}^{C} x_{nc} * c_c$ (4)

C_c is the weight of each criterion, $c = 1, 2, \cdots, C$.

3. Case Study

A competition of graduate course lecture is used to demonstrate the proposed method. There are 6 candidates and 8 experts in the competition. Five criteria are described as follows.

Integrity of Content (IC): Content with Methods and discussions described clearly, sufficient example and accurate summary.

Difficulty of Topic (DT): Topic with relatively complex theory, profound model and time-consuming preparation.

Vitality of Case (VC): Using suitable example with a popular and easy to understand.

Beauty of Courseware (BC): Courseware with well-organized slide, relatively modest amount of words and more appropriate outline.

Clarity of Expression (CE): Expression with clear, coherent and understandable language.

A weight equal to one is assigned to each criterion. Each score is from 5 to 10. For each candidate, the scores of experts are shown in Table 1 (a)-(f). With

Eq.(1)-(3), we calculate the total score of all the experts under the proposed method.

Table 1 (a) Candidate 1

Criteria Experts	IC	DT	VC	BC	CE
Expert1	8.5	8.5	9	10	9
Expert2	9	9	9	9	10
Expert3	10	9	9	9	9
Expert4	8	9	9	7	9
Expert5	10	10	10	10	9
Expert6	8	8	7	7	9
Expert7	8	8	8	8	8
Expert8	9	9	9	9	9
Trimmed mean method	8.75	8.75	8.83	8.66	9
The proposed method	8.60	8.79	8.94	8.90	9

Table 1 (b) Candidate 2

Criteria Experts	IC	DT	VC	BC	CE
Expert1	9	9	9	10	9
Expert2	9	9	9	10	9
Expert3	10	9	9	9	9
Expert4	8	7	7	7	8
Expert5	10	10	9	10	10
Expert6	8	8	7	7	8
Expert7	7	7	7	7	7
Expert8	9	8.5	8.5	8.5	9
Trimmed mean method	8.83	8.42	8.25	8.58	8.67
The proposed method	8.87	8.60	8.82	8.88	8.76

Table 1 (c) Candidate 3

Criteria Experts	IC	DT	VC	BC	CE
Expert1	9	8.5	8.5	9.5	7.5
Expert2	9	8	8	8.5	8.5
Expert3	9	9	8	9	8
Expert4	9	9	9	8	8
Expert5	9	9	9	8	8
Expert6	8	8	7	7	7
Expert7	9	8.5	8.5	10	8
Expert8	8.5	9	8	7	7
Trimmed mean method	8.92	8.67	8.33	8.33	7.75
The proposed method	8.94	8.75	8.33	8.33	7.9

Table 1 (d) Candidate 4

Criteria Experts	IC	DT	VC	BC	CE
Expert1	9	9	9	8.5	8.5
Expert2	9	9	9	8	9
Expert3	9	8	8	6	8
Expert4	9	9	8	8	8
Expert5	8.5	9	8	8.5	10
Expert6	8	8	7	7	8
Expert7	8	8	8	8	8
Expert8	9	8	8	8	8
Trimmed mean method	8.75	8.5	8.17	7.92	8.25
The proposed method	8.89	8.5	8.09	8	8.22

Table 1 (e) Candidate 5

Criteria Experts	IC	DT	VC	BC	CE
Expert1	10	9	10	10	9.5
Expert2	9	9	9	9	9
Expert3	9.5	8.5	9	8	9.5
Expert4	9	9	8	9	9
Expert5	9	9	9	9	10
Expert6	8	8	8	8	8
Expert7	10	9	9	10	10
Expert8	10	9	9	9	9
Trimmed mean method	9.42	8.92	8.83	9	9.33
The proposed method	9.41	8.94	8.91	9	9.33

Table 1 (f) Candidate 6

Criteria Experts	IC	DT	VC	BC	CE
Expert1	10	9	10	9	9
Expert2	9	9	9	10	9
Expert3	9	9	9	10	9
Expert4	9	9	8	7	8
Expert5	10	10	10	9	10
Expert6	8	9	8	7	9
Expert7	7	7	7	7	7
Expert8	9	9	9	10	9
Trimmed mean method	9	9	8.83	8.67	8.83
The proposed method	9.05	9.07	8.87	9.23	8.94

According to the weight of each criterion in Table 1, the total score can be obtained by weighted the single scores for each candidate. The calculation is carried by Eq.(4), where C_c=1,c=1, 2, $\cdots$, 5.

With the similar way, the calculation result of average and trimmed mean are shown in Table 2.

Table 2. Comparison results of different methods

Criteria Candidates	Average (The sum score)	Trimmed Mean (The sum score)	Paper's Method (The sum score)
Candidate1	44.00(2)	44.00(3)	44.25(3)
Candidate 2	42.56(4)	42.75(4)	43.91(4)
Candidate 3	41.81(5)	42.00(5)	42.26(5)
Candidate 4	41.50(6)	41.58(6)	41.70(6)
Candidate 5	45.25(1)	45.50(1)	45.59(1)
Candidate 6	43.88(3)	44.33(2)	45.16(2)

Note: the number in the bracket is the candidate's rank.

According to Table 2, the ranking order is different between "average" and "trimmed mean" according to candidate's sum score, that is, using different decision methods may lead to different results. Because of the trimmed mean method is helpful to the fairness of the competition, we consider the trimmed mean method is better than the average method on the whole. Table 2 shows that the ranking order of candidates with the proposed method is same to that with the trimmed mean method, but the proposed method is more comprehensive, and it can comprehensively express the idea that the farther from "the center", the lower importance of the opinion. This method can effectively avoid the flaw that experts who can't evaluate objectively and ensure the result of the competition with fairness and justice. At the same time, this method is of great significance in the other group decision process involving subjective scores of experts, such as decision-making evaluation of distribution network planning[12].

4. Conclusion

In the group decision method based on subjective scores of experts, it is expected that the effects of extreme opinions is minimized to ensure the fairness of decision result. Usual methods such as the average, trimmed mean and OWA are not able to comprehensively express the consistency (or the degree of consensus) of group decision.

In order to solve this problem, this paper proposes a weight determination method of expert in group decision based on the difference value between subjective score and the average. This method uses the distance between expert evaluation value and the average as a base for constructing weight function. In this method, the distance is closer, the weight is larger. The importance of opinion center is expressed by the weight function, at the same time the objectivity and fairness of decision result are ensured. Case study shows that the proposed method is effective, and it is more helpful to fairness than that of the trimmed mean method.

Acknowledgment

This research was financially supported by the Fundamental Research Funds for Central University.

References

1. Z. S. Xu, "Uncertain multiple attribute decision-making: methods and applications," *Beijing: Tsinghua University Press*, 2004.
2. J. X. Yuan, "A study on group decision-making mechanism in the games of subjective scoring," *China Soft Science*, no. 2, pp. 173-176,192, 2009.
3. P. P. Li, "The fairness analysis in match," *Journal of Tianjin Institute of Technology*, vol. 19, no. 3,pp. 64-69, 2003.
4. Y. Wang, Z. S. Xu. "A new method of giving OWA weights," *Mathematicas in Practice and Theory*, vol. 38, no. 3, pp. 51-65, 2008.
5. Y. N. Zhou, Y. A. Zhu, "Algorithm for adjusting weights of decision-makers in multi-attribute group decision-making based on grey system theory," *Control and Decision*, vol. 27, no. 7, pp. 1113-1116, 2012.
6. Y. H. Ma, R. X. Zhou, Z. G. Li, "The method of determining the weights of decision-makers based on the maximizing deviation," *Journal of Beijing University of Chemical Technology*, vol. 34, no. 2, pp. 177-180, 2007.
7. J. Wan, H. G. Xing, X H Zhang, "Algorithm of adjusting weights of decision-makers in multi-attribute group decision-making based on entropy theory," *Control and Decision*, vol. 25, no. 6, 907-910, 2010.
8. Y. Z. Liu, D. P. Xu, Y. C. Jiang, "Method of adaptive adjustment weights in multi-attribute group decision making," *Systems Engineering and Electronics*, vol. 29, no. 1, pp. 45-48, 2007.
9. P. Cheng ,W. Liu, "Method of determining attributes weights based on subjective preference in multi-attribute group decision-making," *Control and Decision*, vol. 25, no. 11, pp. 1645-1650, 1656, 2010.
10. J. Zhang," A feedback algorithm of experts' weight for system estimate in the process of group decision," *Journal of WUT(Information & Management Engineering)*, vol.24, no. 6, pp. 145-146, 150, 2002.
11. T.E. Abbas, H. Mahdi, A. Masoumeh, A. Pouneh,"A Subjective Weighting Method Based on Group Decision Making For Ranking and Measuring Criteria Values," *Australian Journal of Basic & Applied Sciences*, vol. 5 , no. 12, pp. 2034-2040, 2011.
12. T. F. Zhang, G. Q. Zhang, M. Jun, et al, "Power distribution system planning evaluation by a fuzzy multi-criteria group decision support system," *International Journal of Computational Intelligence Systems*, vol. 3, no. 4, pp. 474-485, 2010.

EVALUATION OF MEDICAL DEVICES USING FUZZY TOPSIS WITH TYPE-2 FUZZY NUMBERS

ISMAIL BURAK PARLAK[*]

Department of Computer Engineering, Galatasaray University,
34357, Ortakoy, Istanbul, Turkey
bparlak@gsu.edu.tr

A.CAGRI TOLGA

Department of Industrial Engineering, Galatasaray University,
34357, Ortakoy, Istanbul, Turkey
ctolga@gsu.edu.tr

The evaluation of medical imaging devices is a critical issue for both biomedical engineers and health-care investors. This study proposes a new technique to assess common medical imaging devices using type-2 fuzzy multi-criteria decision making approach. The evaluation criteria were characterized by the interviews with the experts. A Gaussian type-2 Fuzzy membership function was assigned for each interval of the evaluation. TOPSIS algorithm was applied to our system using type-2 Fuzzy numbers. The results were classified with the Wu and Mendel's ranking method. The ranking of device alternatives highlighted the accurate order of future imaging technologies with the fuzzy behavior of medical investments in conjunction with the requirements of the clinicians and the engineers.

Keywords: Biomedical Engineering; Medical Imaging; Multi-Criteria; Fuzzy; TOPSIS; Type-2, NPV, Economics.

1. Introduction

The selection of medical imaging devices is a challenging problem for both budget planning and medical decision making. The clinicians require new generation devices to perform reliable diagnosis whereas the investors try to invest medical devices with some priorities depending on both the hospital requirements and specifications. The selection of a medical device has several features regarding both technological and financial aspects.

Financial aspects of medical devices were evaluated in several studies. Torres et al. proposed a methodology to adapt the Bayesian methods for their application to directly support investment decisions in a commercial setting

[*] Corresponding author; e-mail: bparlak@gsu.edu.tr Tel:+902122274480-, Fax: +902122595557.

from early stages of the development of new medical devices [1]. Gilard et al. held a round table, then they noted and proposed the methodology of scientific evaluation of medical devices and the associated procedures with a view to their pricing and financing by the French National Health Insurance system [2].

As noted in the first paragraph, multiple-criteria decision making in device selection is one of the hardest problems in hospital engineering. A flexible and intelligent manner provides an accurate distribution of budget between different devices through priorities and budget planning.

Taghipour et al. presented a multi-criteria decision-making model to prioritize medical devices according to their criticality. Devices with lower criticality scores can be assigned a lower priority in a maintenance management program [3]. Cho and Kim showed how the analytic hierarchy process (AHP) can be used in assessing selected medical devices and materials for grants by the Korean Ministry of Health and Welfare [4]. Pecchia et al. offered AHP to design a hierarchy of 12 needs for a new Computed Tomography scanner, grouped into 4 homogenous categories, and to prepare a paper questionnaire to investigate the relative priorities of these [5].

In this study, we focused on the medical imaging devices which are commonly in use for clinicians and in conjunction with the health-care investors and hospital engineers. Our proposed approach was based on one of the multi-criteria fuzzy decision making methods –TOPSIS- to evaluate the selection of these devices. Due to the growing impact factor of complex systems, technological investments require more realistic approaches within fuzzy systems. Interval Type-2 Fuzzy Sets (IT2 FSs) were found feasible to offer better selection and ranking approaches [6].

The device selection within our approach was integrated with type-2 fuzzy ranking priorities. We remarked that type-2 fuzzy interpretation would fit better in our case to describe real world problems [7].

The organization of this paper is as follows: In section 2 a literature review for type-2 fuzzy numbers and fuzzy multi-criteria decision making is given. The following section provides theory of type-2 fuzzy numbers and their ranking. The fourth section consists of the proposed algorithm for type-2 fuzzy TOPSIS with the alternative ranking procedure. Criteria for selecting medical devices and application are proposed in section 5. Finally in section 6 the conclusions of this study are discussed.

2. Literature Review: Type-2 Fuzzy Numbers and Fuzzy Multi-Criteria Decision Making

Type-2 FS topic is newly introduced at the last decade. In his article, Ngan [8] extended the probabilistic linguistic framework to type-2 linguistic sets and he performed arithmetic operations on type-2 linguistic numbers concerning multi-criteria decision making. Hu et al. proposed another approach for multi criteria decision making problem in which the criteria value takes the form of interval type-2 fuzzy number [9]. They defined a new expected value function at first and constructed an optimal model based on maximizing deviation method to obtain weight coefficients when criteria weight information is partially known. TOPSIS method is mostly used among these evaluation methods by reason of its efficient and accurate nature. Fuzzy TOPSIS method based on interval type-2 fuzzy numbers is first enhanced by Chen and Lee [7]. The authors claimed that the proposed method provides them with a useful way to handle fuzzy multiple attributes group decision-making problems in a more flexible and more intelligent manner.

3. Type-2 Fuzzy Numbers and Ranking

Type-2 fuzzy numbers are complex representation of fuzziness which is characterized by interval valued type-2; a special form and generalized type-2 values.

For type-2 FS we used the following Gaussian membership function where m is the mean and k is the standard deviation;

$$\mu_A(x) = e^{\frac{(x-m)}{2k}} \tag{1}$$

A type-2 fuzzy set $\tilde{I}$ is defined by a type-2 membership function $\mu_{\tilde{I}}(x,a)$ where $x \in X$ and $a \in I_x \subseteq [0,1]$ as it follows;

$$\tilde{I} = \left\{ \left((x,a), \mu_{\tilde{I}}(x,a) \right) \middle| \forall x \in X, \forall a \in I_x \subseteq [0,1] \right\} \tag{2}$$

where; $0 \leq \mu_{\tilde{I}}(x,a) \leq 1$.

In order to represent a type-2 fuzzy set, constructing the upper and lower membership degrees would be preferred to build up the footprint of uncertainty. This representation is given by;

$$\tilde{I} = \{(x, \mu_U(x), \mu_L(x)) | \forall x \in X, \mu_L(x) \leq \mu(x) \leq \mu_U(x), \mu \in [0,1]\} \tag{3}$$

In our study, we adopted the *Wu and Mendel's new ranking method* which was found better than several ranking methods for type-2 FSs [6]. The centroid $C(\tilde{I})$, of an IT2 FS $\tilde{I}$ is the union of the centroid of all its embedded T1 FSs I_e, i.e.;

$$C(\tilde{I}) \equiv \bigcup_{\forall l_e} c(I_e) = [c_l(\tilde{I}), c_r(\tilde{I})], \tag{4}$$

where $c_l(\tilde{I}) = \min_{\forall l_e} c(I_e)$, $c_r(\tilde{I}) = \max_{\forall l_e} c(I_e)$, and $c(I_e) = \frac{\sum_{i=1}^{N} x_i \mu_{l_e}(x_i)}{\sum_{i=1}^{N} \mu_{l_e}(x_i)}$.

4. Proposed Fuzzy TOPSIS Methodology

For our article we adapted a similar approach of Type-2 TOPSIS algorithm [7]. Furthermore, we proposed a new methodology for the selection of medical devices using interval type-2 fuzzy sets combined with *Wu and Mendel's centroid ranking method* as depicted in Figure 1.

Table 1. Linguistic terms and their corresponding Gaussian type-2 fuzzy sets [17]

Linguistic terms for the weights of the attributes	Linguistic terms for the ratings	Interval type-2 fuzzy sets
Very Low (VL)	Very Poor (VP)	$(x, N(0.125,0.035),0.8 * N(0.125,0.01))$
Low (L)	Fairly Poor (FP)	$(x, N(0.25,0.035),0.8 * N(0.25,0.01))$
Medium Low (ML)	Poor (P)	$(x, N(0.375,0.035),0.8 * N(0.375,0.01))$
Medium (M)	Moderate (M)	$(x, N(0.5,0.035),0.8 * N(0.5,0.01))$
Medium High (MH)	Good (G)	$(x, N(0.625,0.035),0.8 * N(0.625,0.01))$
High (H)	Fairly Good (FG)	$(x, N(0.75,0.035),0.8 * N(0.75,0.01))$
Very High (VH)	Very Good (VG)	$(x, N(0.875,0.035),0.8 * N(0.875,0.01))$

Although the general form of type-2 fuzzy sets is represented as in Eq. (3), according the reference [10] one can depict the Gaussian type-2 fuzzy number as shown in the third column of Table 1.

5. Criteria for Selection of Medical Equipments and Application

In hospital engineering, medical devices and diagnostic facilities are the most expensive investments to achieve health standards and perform reliable decision making. However this expensive investment requires a better understanding within a fuzzy state-of-art due to the broad range of medical devices: 1-Hardware Specifications: 1.1 Resolution, 1.2 Physical Properties (Size-Weight), Portability, 1.3 Power Standards and Patient Conformability, 1.4 Acquisition Properties, 2-Imaging Specifications: 2.1 Monitoring 2.2 Digital Standards 2.3 Integrability, 3-Recording and Archiving: 3.1 Support for Digital and Analog Radiology 3.2 Digital radiology features 3.3 PACS-Telemedicine, 4-Software Specifications: 4.1 Signal/Noise Ratio, 4.2 Multidimensional view 4.3 Artificial enhancements-Augmented Reality, 5-Annual worth (AW) of alternatives.

In this paper six different medical imaging devices were determined as alternatives; Echocardiography, X-Ray Imaging, Computerized Tomography, Magnetic Resonance (MR) Imaging, Single-Photon Emission Computed Tomography, Positron Emission Tomography. They are evaluated by the experts according to the scale depicted in Table 1.

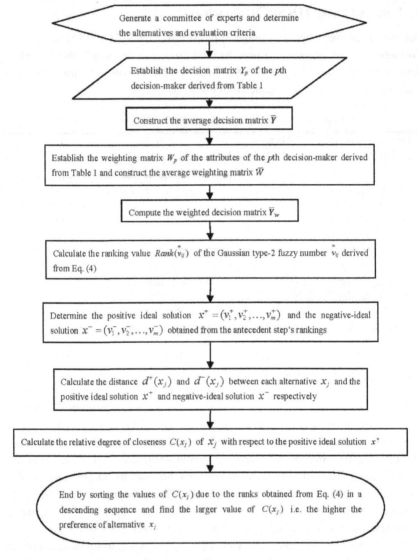

Figure 1. Flow chart of the proposed model.

The proposed fuzzy TOPSIS methodology given in Figure 1 is used for selection among these alternatives. The economic data are gathered from experts working in the healthcare, and at the same time these experts are utilized as decision makers for the steps of the proposed methodology.

Table 2. Ranking values of $Rank(\tilde{v}_{ij})$ obtained from Eq. (4).

	A	B	C	D	E	F
Resolution	1.94767	0.90314	1.744901	2.1504472	1.744901	1.74490
Physical Properties	1.75511	0.01023	0.659445	0.8622106	0.446450	0.02046
Power Standards	1.52167	0.89291	0.892912	1.5216617	1.308668	1.09566
Patient Comfort	2.16065	2.16065	1.562595	1.9476277	0.061381	0.03069
Acquisition Properties	2.75876	2.34301	2.758765	2.9513284	1.957884	1.73469
Monitoring	1.724416	1.53189	1.511424	1.7346541	0.882674	1.12637
Digital Standards	0.903142	2.16065	1.105914	0.4566776	1.329126	1.54210
Integrability	0.456677	1.53190	0.466907	0.2436845	1.329136	1.10590
Support for A&D Radiology	0.040921	0.92359	1.126343	1.0854660	1.126372	1.12636
Digital Radiology Properties	3.528970	0.75150	2.373685	2.9513284	0.984952	2.37368
PACS-Telemedicine	1.744901	1.95788	1.744901	1.5421292	1.947674	1.93746
SNR Ratio	1.906723	2.71777	0.923599	0.4566797	0.649211	0.61852
Multidimensionality	2.951328	0.4975	2.951328	2.7587653	1.43305	1.43305
Augmented Reality- Special Features	2.34294	1.2984	1.095666	1.5011971	2.47408	0.61852

Due to field restriction in this paper, only the $Rank(\tilde{v}_{ij})$ values those are the Gaussian type-2 fuzzy number $\tilde{v}_{ij}$ derived from Eq. (4) are given in Table 2.

Table 3. Ranking of $C(x_i)$ values.

$C(x_1)$	0.8421	ECHOCARDIOGRAPHY	A
$C(x_2)$	0.7254	X_RAY	B
$C(x_3)$	0.5853	COMPUTERIZED TOMOGRAPHY	C
$C(x_4)$	0.7536	MAGNETIC RESONANCE IMAGING	D
$C(x_5)$	0.4755	SINGLE PHOTON EMISSION COMPUTED TOMOGRAPHY	E
$C(x_6)$	0.6738	POSITRON EMISSION TOMOGRAPHY	F

Finally, from Table-3 Echocardiography was found as the best alternative based on the Type-2 TOPSIS algorithm.

6. Conclusions

In hospital engineering, medical device selection is one of the hardest problems for feasible investment to ensure reliable diagnosis and benefit the necessity and the integration of clinicians. The priority selection is the key point for the medical investments. In our study, we focused on the medical imaging facilities which are considered as the backbone of medical decision making. We conclude that T2 FS are robust representations for the problem of medical investments where the fuzziness is relatively higher than other applications. For future studies comparison of the fuzzy type-2 numbers with Wu and Mendel's ranking method could be integrated to the other multi criteria decision making problems, hence they explicate the vagueness better.

Acknowledgments

This work is financially supported by Galatasaray University scientific research project funds.

References

1. L. V. Torres, L. M. G. Steuten, M. J. Buxton, A. L. Girling, R. J. Lilford, T. Young, *International Journal of Technology Assessment in Health Care*, **24**(2008), 459–464.
2. M. Gilard, F. Debroucker, C. Dubray, *Thérapie*, **4**(2013), 201–208.
3. S. Taghipour, D. Banjevic, A. K. S. Jardine, *Journal of the Operational Research Society*, **62** (2011), 1666–1687.
4. S. M. Chen, L. W. Lee, *Expert Systems with Applications*, **37**(2010), 824-833.
5. L. Pecchia, J. L. Martin, A. Ragozzino, C. Vanzanella, A. Scognamiglio, L. Mirarchi, S.P Morgan, *BMC Med Inform Decis Mak.*, **13**(2013).
6. D. Wu, J. M. Mendel, *Information Sciences*, **179**(2009), 1169-1192.
7. S. M. Chen, L. W. Lee, *Expert Systems with Applications*, **37**(2010), 2790-2798.
8. S. C. Ngan, *Computers and Industrial Engineering* , **64**(2013), 721-730.
9. J. Hu, Y. Zhang, X. Chen, Y. Liu, *Knowledge-Based Systems*, **43**(2013), 21-29.
10. J. M. Mendel, R. I. B. John , *IEEE Transactions on Fuzzy Systems*, **(10)** 2002, 117-127

EMPLOYING AN INTERVAL TYPE-2 FUZZY TOPSIS METHOD FOR KNOWLEDGE MANAGEMENT TOOL EVALUATION

GULCIN BUYUKOZKAN[*]

*Department of Industrial Engineering, Galatasaray University,
34357, Ortakoy, Istanbul, Turkey*

ISMAIL BURAK PARLAK

Department of Computer Engineering, Galatasaray University,
34357, Ortakoy, Istanbul, Turkey

A.CAGRI TOLGA

*Department of Industrial Engineering, Galatasaray University,
34357, Ortakoy, Istanbul, Turkey*

In the knowledge economy, a key source of sustainable competitive advantage relies on the way to create, share, and utilize knowledge. This paper presents an application of the interval type-2 TOPSIS method used to select the most appropriate tool to support knowledge management (KM) activities in a healthcare system. The method provides us with a useful way to handle fuzzy multiple attributes group decision-making problems in a more flexible and more intelligent manner to analyze and compare KM tools in the software market. A case study is given to demonstrate the potential of the methodology.

Keywords: Interval type-2 fuzzy sets, Fuzzy multiple attributes group decision making, TOPSIS, KM tools selection.

1. Introduction

Since a successful knowledge management (KM) can provide sustainable competitive advantage [1-3], interest from both industry and academy to KM has been growing rapidly. KM tools are information technology based systems developed to support and enhance the organizational processes of knowledge creation, storage/retrieval, transfer, and application [4]. KM tools make it possible to deliver knowledge to all departments within an organization. They also integrate various knowledge processes to solve one or more business

[*] Corresponding author; e-mail: gulcin.buyukozkan@gmail.com Tel:+902122274480-,
Fax: +902122595557.

problems as an organizational information system. KM tools are then used as enablers to supply chain management to build dynamic communities connecting the enterprise with customers and suppliers. Tightly integrated processes applying collaborative technologies represent a shared value chain that delivers increased efficiency in the design and execution, and that leads to reduced costs and greater customer satisfaction [5]. Unfortunately, limited studies [6-9] exist and this paper presents an enhanced method to assess such tools. The utilized method handles fuzzy multiple attributes group decision-making problems in a more flexible and more intelligent manner due to the fact that it uses interval type-2 fuzzy sets rather than traditional type-1 fuzzy sets to represent the evaluating values and the weights of attributes.

The paper is organized as follows. Next section presents the identified evaluation criteria for KM tools. Section 3 introduces the details of the utilized method. In section 4, the method is applied through a case study. And in the last section a brief conclusion of the whole paper is made.

2. Evaluation Criteria to Assess Knowledge Management Tools

The KM tool evaluation criteria have been identified after a careful study of literature [9-16], examination of commercial vendor surveys, public product briefings and demos. We have also held some discussions with KM consultants. In order to fulfill the expected outcome, the following ten main evaluation criteria are identified.

- *Software enhancement possibilities (C1):* KM systems need integration with a wide range of other daily applications. The system should provide a platform whereby additional development can easily be made.
- *Compliance with company standards (C2):* Standardization of information technology applications in a global company with wide range of products in several locations is crucial.
- *Document management (C3):* Comprehensive authorization, good search mechanism, versioning, document discussions and alerts are inevitable aspects of a document management system.
- *Collaboration (C4):* Collaboration is the backbone of KM. Collaborative problem solving, conversation and teamwork generate a significant proportion of knowledge assets.
- *Portal functions (C5):* Portals provide an easy to use entry point to knowledge domain of a global company.

- *Workflow facilities (C6):* Workflow management is one of the main interfaces between process management and document management. Workflow facilities speed up the document flow through processes in a company.
- *Ease of use (C7):* A tool that is easy to use is more likely to be accepted by users.
- *Capital expenditure (C8):* Capital costs are non recurring expenditures involved in setting up the KM system product, licenses and training costs are of this definition.
- *Operating expenditure (C9):* Operating expenditures are recurring costs based on day to day operations of the system.
- *Vendor reputation (C10):* The vendor as a business partner should care about the quality of services and support given to the customer.

3. Interval Type-2 Fuzzy TOPSIS Method in a Group Decision Making Setting

In this paper, a modified model of Chen and Lee's [17] interval Type-2 TOPSIS algorithm will be used. The steps of the applied approach are given in Figure 1.

4. Case Study

The evaluation framework is applied to a real case with the purpose of assisting decision-makers in the local branch (briefly called XYZ) of an internationally recognized corporation in the healthcare sector.

An evaluation process was performed by five different experts. As the participation and support of top managers significantly influences the success of KM tool adoption, one member of the committee was a top manager. Two other members of the committee were from the information technology department, each having considerable experience in corporate projects involving change management. The last two members were senior representatives and potential users of the KM tools. All experts were treated equally. Three determined alternatives (A, B, C) are to be evaluated versus ten evaluation criteria given in Section 2. The experts expressed their preference for criteria weights and alternatives linguistically by using the linguistic terms shown in Table 1 as given in Tables 2-5.

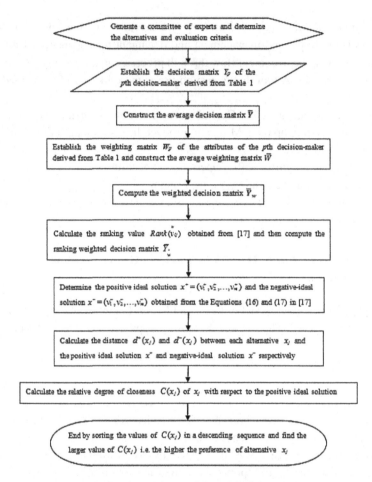

Figure 1. Flowchart of the type-2 fuzzy TOPSIS methodology.

Table 1. Linguistic terms and their corresponding interval type-2 fuzzy sets [17]

Linguistic terms for the weights of the attributes	Linguistic terms for the ratings	Interval type-2 fuzzy sets
Very Low (VL)	Very Poor (VP)	((0, 0, 0, 0.1; 1, 1), (0, 0, 0, 0.05; 0.9, 0.9))
Low (L)	Fairly Poor (FP)	((0, 0.1, 0.1, 0.3; 1, 1), (0.05, 0.1, 0.1, 0.2; 0.9, 0.9))
Medium Low (ML)	Poor (P)	((0.1, 0.3, 0.3, 0.5; 1, 1), (0.2, 0.3, 0.3, 0.4; 0.9, 0.9))
Medium (M)	Moderate (M)	((0.3, 0.5, 0.5, 0.7; 1, 1), (0.4, 0.5, 0.5, 0.6; 0.9, 0.9))
Medium High (MH)	Good (G)	((0.5, 0.7, 0.7, 0.9; 1, 1), (0.6, 0.7, 0.7, 0.8; 0.9, 0.9))
High (H)	Fairly Good (FG)	((0.7, 0.9, 0.9, 1; 1, 1), (0.8, 0.9, 0.9, 0.95; 0.9, 0.9))
Very High (VH)	Very Good (VG)	((0.9, 1, 1, 1; 1, 1), (0.95, 1, 1, 1; 0.9, 0.9))

Table 2. The linguistic evaluation of criteria importance

	Decision makers				
	1	2	3	4	5
C1	VL	L	L	VL	L
C2	H	VH	H	VH	VH
C3	H	H	M	H	H
C4	M	L	M	M	H
C5	M	M	M	H	M
C6	L	VL	VL	VL	VL
C7	H	M	M	M	H
C8	L	L	H	M	L
C9	M	H	M	M	H
C10	VH	H	VH	VH	H

Table 3. The linguistic evaluation of alternative A

	Decision makers				
	1	2	3	4	5
C1	G	M	M	M	G
C2	VG	VG	VG	G	VG
C3	FG	G	M	M	G
C4	FG	VG	G	G	M
C5	FP	P	P	VP	FP
C6	M	G	M	FP	P
C7	P	FP	P	P	FP
C8	VG	VG	G	VG	G
C9	G	G	FG	M	M
C10	M	G	M	G	G

Table 4. The linguistic evaluation of alternative B

	Decision makers				
	1	2	3	4	5
C1	P	FP	P	VP	FP
C2	VP	FP	P	VP	VP
C3	FP	VP	FP	VP	VP
C4	FP	VP	FP	FP	VP
C5	M	G	FG	M	G
C6	M	G	P	M	P
C7	FG	G	G	VG	M
C8	VP	FP	P	VP	P
C9	FP	FP	VP	P	P
C10	G	VG	FG	M	G

Table 5. The linguistic evaluation of alternative C

	Decision makers				
	1	2	3	4	5
C1	M	M	FG	G	G
C2	FP	VP	VP	P	VP
C3	G	FG	G	M	M
C4	G	G	M	G	M
C5	G	G	P	M	G
C6	FG	G	M	M	G
C7	M	G	P	FP	P
C8	P	FP	P	P	VP
C9	G	M	G	M	M
C10	FP	P	P	VP	VP

In order to calculate the best alternative, the procedure described in Figure 1 was applied. We started by constructing the decision matrix $\mathbf{Y}p$. Then, the weighting matrix Wp of the attributes of the pth decision maker and the average weighting matrix $\widetilde{W}$ were calculated. Thus, the weighted decision matrix $\overline{Y}_w$ was determined. Then, the ranking value $Rank(v_{ij})$ of the interval type-2 fuzzy set was calculated and the ranking weighted decision matrix $\overline{Y}_w$ was constructed as shown in Table 6. Furthermore, the positive and negative ideal solutions were calculated. The distances $d^+(x_j)$ and $d^-(x_j)$ were found and the relative degree of closeness to $C(x_j)$ was calculated as given in Table 7. Finally, as seen in Table 7, the obtained values were: $d^+(A)=1.33$, $d^-(A)=3.05$, $d^+(B)=2.86$, $d^-(B)=1.72$, $d^+(C)=1.98$ and $d^-(C)=2.43$. When we sorted the results using $C(x_i)$ values, we found that the first alternative (Alternative A) was the best choice. (We only provide the final results of the study due to space limitation).

Table 6. Ranking of v_{ij} values of alternatives A,B,C and calculation of positive and negative ideals.

STEP5							
	A	B	C				
Soft	4,3665	4,0887	4,4025	x+	4,4025	x-	4,0887
Comp	5,9137	4,6701	4,6701		5,9137		4,6701
Doc	6,0089	4,3024	6,0089		6,0089		4,3024
Collo	5,7912	4,3243	5,6426		5,7912		4,3243
Port	4,8093	5,793	5,6991		5,793		4,8093
Work	4,0338	4,0454	4,0994		4,0994		4,0338
EOU	5,0681	5,9727	5,4704		5,9727		5,0681
CAP	5,6206	4,5176	4,6662		5,6206		4,5176
OPE	5,8829	5,3346	5,7934		5,8829		5,3346
VEN	6,0545	6,0776	4,9938		6,0776		4,9938

Table 7. Ranking of $C(x_i)$ values.

STEP6	A	B	C
dij+	1,338693	2,868642	1,980721
dij-	3,054501	1,720675	2,437006
STEP7			
c(x1)	0,69528		
c(x2)	0,374931		
c(x3)	0,551642		

5. Conclusions

Due to the difficulties that a decision maker faces in the precise assessment, this study suggests an interval type-2 fuzzy TOPSIS method within the context of KM system selection which involves an important decision for any enterprise to achieve competitive advantage. The criteria of the selection process are extracted with an in-depth analysis and the existing KM systems are evaluated based on those criteria. Type-2 fuzzy sets involve more flexibilities than type-1 fuzzy sets. They provide with additional degrees of freedom to represent the uncertainty and the fuzziness of the real world.

Although an interval type-2 fuzzy TOPSIS method presented in this paper is applied to the KM tool evaluation problem of healthcare system, it can also be used in many software evaluation problems. In future, we aim to apply other type-2 fuzzy sets based MCDM methods for this problem and compare the obtained results.

Acknowledgements

The authors would like to express their gratitude to the industrial experts for their support in evaluation of the framework. The authors acknowledge also the financial support of the Galatasaray University Research Fund.

References

1. P.F. Drucker, Management challenges for the 21st century. Harper Business (1999).
2. L. Edvinsson, Corporate longitude. Prentice Hall, London (2002).
3. I. Nonaka and H. Takeuchi, The knowledge creating company. Oxford University Press, New York (1995).
4. M. Alavi and D.E. Leidner, MIS Quartely. 25, 107-136 (2001).
5. Y. A. Pollalis and N. K. Dimitriou, International Journal of Information Management 28, 305–321 (2008).
6. P. Tyndale, Evaluation and Program Planning 25, 183–190 (2002).
7. R. Ruggles, Knowledge management tools, Butterworth-Heinemann, Oxford, (1997).
8. G. Buyukozkan, O. Feyzioglu, G. Cifci, International Journal of Computational Intelligence Systems, 4(2), 184 - 195, (2011).
9. E. W. T. Ngai and E. W. C. Chan, Expert Systems with Applications 29, 889–899 (2005).
10. C. G. Şen and Hayri Baraçlı, Expert Systems with Applications 37(4), 3415–3426 (2010).
11. V. S. Lai, R. P. Trueblood and B. K. Wong, Information & Management 36, 221–232 (1999).
12. J. Sarkis and R. P. Sundarraj, International Journal of Physical Distribution and Logistics Management 30, 196–220 (2000).
13. M. C. Y. Tam and V. M. R. Tummala, Omega 29, 171–182 (2001).
14. A. Tiwana and B. Ramesh, IEEE Internet Computing 5, 2–9 (2001).
15. J. Sarkis and S. Talluri, European Journal of Operational Research 159, 318–329 (2004).
16. C. G. Şen, H. Baraçlı, S. Şen and H. Başlıgil, Expert Systems with Applications, 36, 5272–5283 (2009).
17. S. M. Chen and L. W. Lee, Expert Systems with Applications, 37, 2790–2798, (2010).

EXPERT SYSTEM FOR EVALUATION OF SATISFACTION OF EMPLOYEES[*]

BOGDAN WALEK

*Institute for Research and Applications of Fuzzy Modeling, NSC IT4Innovations,
University of Ostrava, 30.dubna 22, Ostrava, 701 03, Czech Republic*

JIŘÍ BARTOŠ

*Department of Informatics and Computers, University of Ostrava, 30. dubna 22, Ostrava,
701 03, Czech Republic*

Today, most companies monitor the satisfaction of their employees. Companies are trying to measure the satisfaction of their employees and with this aspect they are making efforts to increase workload and work quality, which is beneficial for the company itself. This article proposes a fuzzy tool for assessing the employee's satisfaction within the company. A part of the fuzzy expert system is a tool for evaluating satisfaction questionnaires. All the parts of the system are introduced and verified on a specific example.

1. Introduction

Nowadays, most companies require not only the hard work of their employees, but also their loyalty. The company then invests into its staff development and training and the employees are also financially motivated accordingly. For each company it is therefore very important that the employees in the company are satisfied [1] [2] [3].

In the area of IT companies this aspect is compounded by the fact that development in the IT industry is faster and demands on staff increases accordingly. Companies that in the course of employment are investing a lot of money in the development of their employees do not want to lose such employees, so the companies seek to provide its employees with adequate and

[*] This work was supported by the European Regional Development Fund in the IT4Innovations Centre of Excellence project (CZ.1.05/1.1.00/02.0070)

motivating conditions. Therefore, for most IT companies, the satisfaction of the employees is one of the priorities.

2. Problem formulation

As already mentioned in the introduction, most companies are trying to keep their employees in the company satisfied [4] [5]. The employees are thus highly likely to present a good work performance and will be beneficial for the company.

One of the main methods for determining the employee's satisfaction is a questionnaire method. The questionnaire mostly consists of questions and answers, which are given in the form of selecting one or more responses and the questionnaire is in the form of a survey sent or made available to employees who fill it in. The completed questionnaires, which should obviously be anonymous, are then evaluated.

An example of the satisfaction questionnaire is depicted in the following table:

Table 1. An example of the satisfaction questionnaire

	Answer n. 1	Answer n. 2	Answer n. 3	Answer n. 4
Question n. 1	yes	probably yes	probably not	no
Question n. 2	yes	probably yes	probably not	no
Question n. 3	yes	probably yes	probably not	no

The evaluation of the questionnaire is then carried out manually or by using a simple tool that evaluates the answers using a simple graph. What is lacking is a comprehensive evaluation of the level of the satisfaction of the employees, which would give the company director a way to simply determine how many company employees are satisfied or dissatisfied.

Another disadvantage is the absence of ability to identify the issues and topics more or less important for the employees. Each employee subjectively perceives various aspects and conditions in the company. For one employee, a good atmosphere within the team may be important, for another it is the way of communication with the management or the scope for further benefits or the number of the days of leave. The importance of different aspects and the bound responses may affect the responses of the employees and their resulting satisfaction with the company.

3. Problem solution

For the above reasons, this paper proposes a fuzzy tool with an expert system for evaluating of the satisfaction of employees within a company.

In the proposed fuzzy tool the theory of Natural Fuzzy Logic is applied. For this theory, the characteristic term is the linguistic description. The linguistic description is understood as a special text of a natural language. It requires a special inference method, namely Perception-based Logical Deduction (PbLD), which is a specific inference method working with the genuine meaning of evaluative linguistic expressions (such as "very small, more or less good, roughly medium", etc.) and is based on formal properties of a mathematical fuzzy logic. It was described in several papers [8] [9]. For this inference, it is specific that it is based on the local properties of the linguistic description. Consequently, a difference can be made between the rules but at the same time they can be dealt with as the vague expressions of a natural language. To obtain a specific conclusion, a special defuzzification method DEE (Defuzzification of Evaluative Expressions) must be used.

The fuzzy tool consists of several parts; the basis of the expert system knowledge base is then composed of IF-THEN rules. The diagram of the tool and method is shown in the following figure:

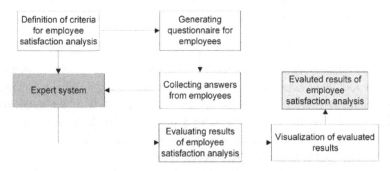

Figure 1. The proposed fuzzy tool

3.1. *Definition of criteria for employee satisfaction analysis*

In the first step, it is necessary to define the criteria by which the employee's satisfaction will be evaluated – with properly selected criteria, a comprehensive assessment of the employee's satisfaction will be possible.

Each criterion represents a range of questions (topics) to which the employee will respond. The criterion will be the basis for selecting appropriate questions within the satisfaction questionnaire. The examples of possible criteria are listed below:

The atmosphere within the company, the potential of employee's development, the offered benefits, the salary, the communication with the management, the setting of the company processes.

3.2. *Generating questionnaire for employees*

The next step is based on criteria from the previous step and generates the satisfaction questionnaire. The questionnaire contains questions that are grouped by the criteria defined in the previous step. To save the questions and answers of the questionnaire, the XML format was chosen. The structure of the proposed XML file was proposed in the article [6] and is shown below:

- *question* – represents the specific question of the questionnaire
- *answer* – represents the answer for the question
- *importancy_q* – represents the importance of the specific set of the questions (topic) for employee
- *importancy_a* – represents the importance of the answer

3.3. *Collecting answers from employees*

In this step, the responses are collected and stored. The easiest way is to publish the proposed satisfaction questionnaire as a web form linked to a database. The replies are stored in the database ready for a later use for a subsequent evaluation.

3.4. *Creating the knowledge base of the expert system*

Furthermore, the knowledge base of the expert system is created. The knowledge base consists of the relevant IF-THEN rules. Each question represents one input linguistic variable of the IF-THEN rules.

The questions and answers about the importance of each topic will not be included in the expert system, as it is a subjective evaluation of each employee. They will be marked in the resulting visualization, where the manager or the HR manager will be able to assess the level of the importance that the recruiting staff put to each of the criteria (area).

The output linguistic variable of the IF-THEN rules then determines the aggregate level of the satisfaction of the employees in the company in the field (criterion). Consequently, the IF-THEN rules are created for each of the criteria (region) of the satisfaction questionnaire. The example of the output linguistic variables of the IF-THEN rules can be:

Satisfaction with the atmosphere within the company, satisfaction with the potential development of the employee, satisfaction with the offered benefits, satisfaction with the salary, satisfaction with communication with the management, satisfaction with the setting of the company processes.

The examples of several IF-THEN rules for individual areas:

```
IF (ATMOSPHERE DEGREE IS HIGH) AND
(TEAM WORK DEGREE IS VERY HIGH) AND
(EMPLOYEES BEHAVIOR IS GOOD) THEN
(ATMOSPHERE_SATISFACTION IS HIGH)

IF (ATMOSPHERE DEGREE IS LOW) AND
(TEAM WORK DEGREE IS VERY LOW) AND
(EMPLOYEES BEHAVIOR IS VERY BAD) THEN
(ATMOSPHERE_SATISFACTION IS VERY LOW)
```

For the expert system knowledge base the LFL Controller was used. Linguistic Fuzzy Logic Controller is more described in [7].

3.5. *Evaluating results of employee satisfaction analysis*

After creating the knowledge base of the expert system, the evaluation of the results of the satisfaction questionnaires follows. Each area (topic) is separately evaluated by the expert system.

3.6. *Visualization of evaluated results*

Finally, the evaluated results are visualized in the form of a general model, which is shown below:

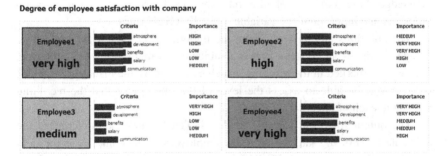

Figure 2. Visualization of evaluated results

Acknowledgments

This work was supported by the European Regional Development Fund in the IT4Innovations Centre of Excellence project (CZ.1.05/1.1.00/02.0070)

Conclusion

In this article a fuzzy tool for assessing of employee's satisfaction within a company was proposed and designed. The individual steps of the proposed tool were introduced along with the examples of their uses. The evaluation of the results of employee's satisfaction analysis was described and visualized.

In subsequent work, the proposed instrument to company specific ratings for the satisfaction of their employees will be verified. The expert system will be also generalized.

References

1. D. J. Koys, *The effects of employee satisfaction, organizational citizenship behavior, and turnover on organizational effectiveness: A unit-level, longitudinal study,* Personnel Psychology, Vol. 54, No. 1, pp. 101–114 (2001).
2. T. S. Bateman, D. W. Organ, *Job Satisfaction and the Good Soldier: The Relationship Between Affect and Employee "Citizenship",* Academy of Management, Vol. 26, No. 4, pp. 587-595 (1983).
3. R. Hoppock, *Job satisfaction,* Oxford, England: Harper (1935).
4. A. Brayfield, H. Rothe, F. Harold, *An index of job satisfaction,* Journal of Applied Psychology, Vol 35, No. 5, pp. 307-311 (1951).
5. L. W. Porter, R. M. Steers, R. T. Mowday, Paul V. Boulian, *Organizational commitment, job satisfaction, and turnover among psychiatric technicians,* Journal of Applied Psychology, Vol. 59, No. 5, pp. 603-609 (1974).
6. B. Walek, *Fuzzy tool for customer satisfaction analysis in CRM systems,* 36th International Conference on Telecommunications and Signal Processing, Rome, pp. 11-14 (2013).
7. H. Habiballa, V. Novák, A. Dvořák, V. Pavliska, *Using software package LFLC 2000,* 2nd International Conference Aplimat 2003, Bratislava, pp. 355-358 (2003).
8. V. Novák, M. Štěpnička, J. Kupka, *Linguistic descriptions: their structure and applications,* International Conference FQAS 2013, Granada, pp. 209-220 (2013).
9. V. Novák, *On modeling with words,* International Journal of General Systems, Vol. 42, No. 1, pp. 21-40 (2013).

EXPERT SYSTEM FOR SELECTION OF SUITABLE JOB APPLICANTS[*]

BOGDAN WALEK

*Institute for Research and Applications of Fuzzy Modeling, NSC IT4Innovations,
University of Ostrava, 30.dubna 22, Ostrava, 701 03, Czech Republic*

JIŘÍ BARTOŠ

*Department of Informatics and Computers, University of Ostrava, 30. dubna 22, Ostrava,
701 03, Czech Republic*

Every company occasionally deals with the problem of hiring new staff. The issue of selecting of a suitable candidate for a job is often very complicated and many criteria enter the selection and hiring process. This paper proposes an expert system for the selection of the most suitable applicants for employment. A part of the proposed approach is the definition of criteria for selection of suitable applicants and lining to the database of all applicants. Furthermore, this paper introduces each part of the proposed expert system and all the steps are verified on a specific example.

1. Introduction

Hiring of new staff is usually solved by the HR department. This paper will focus mainly on the area of medium and big companies, where the HR manager is responsible for the hiring process.

The paper will propose an expert system for the selection of suitable applicants, involving the most possible inputs which are entering the selection and afterwards the hiring process.

2. Problem formulation

As mentioned above, the HR manager has an uneasy role in the process of the selection of the most appropriate applicant [1] [2]. HR departments in medium-large and big companies have a summary database of all applicants available. The method of storing the data of applicants may be different, but in the case of

---

[*] This work was supported by the European Regional Development Fund in the IT4Innovations Centre of Excellence project (CZ.1.05/1.1.00/02.0070)

finding a suitable candidate for the position, the HR department has it available. The applicant database is continuously updated with information on new applicants that are applying for a position in the course of the selection procedure or in response to a job offer.

The most difficult task of an HR manager is the selection of a suitable candidate regarding both of his hard and soft skills [3] [4]. The selecting of a suitable candidate depends on a large number of selection criteria in combination with the properties and behavior of a particular candidate. The problem can then be neglecting any of the criteria or characteristics of the applicant, in the event of a greater number of the applicants or a multi-round tender, the neglecting of any criteria is even a bigger issue. Another problem is the manager's subjective assessment of candidates, where the candidate can be prioritized because of his impression on the HR manager and not his skills/expertise. The HR manager can also make mistakes during the selection process due to time pressure or the miscalculations of an employee contribution to the company.

3. Problem solution

For the above reasons, an expert system for the selection of the most suitable candidates for employment is proposed. The proposed expert system contains important criteria for selecting of a suitable candidate and is connected to the database of all registered candidates in a given company. The expert system can help to reduce the occurrence of certain risks involved in the selection of a suitable candidate for the particular position and can help the HR manager to eliminate mistakes in such selection.

In the proposed expert system, the theory of Natural Fuzzy Logic is applied. For this theory, the characteristic term is the linguistic description. The linguistic description is understood as a special text of a natural language. It requires a special inference method, namely Perception-based Logical Deduction (PbLD), which is a specific inference method working with the genuine meaning of evaluative linguistic expressions (such as "very small, more or less good, roughly medium", etc.) and is based on formal properties of a mathematical fuzzy logic. It was described in several papers [6] [7]. For this inference, it is specific that it is based on local properties of the linguistic description. Consequently, a difference can be made between the rules but at the same time they can be dealt with as the vague expressions of a natural language. To obtain a conclusion, a special defuzzification method DEE (Defuzzification of Evaluative Expressions) must be used.

The knowledge base of the proposed expert system contains a set of IF-THEN rules, which is filled using an expert on human resources. The expert system is schematically shown in the following figure:

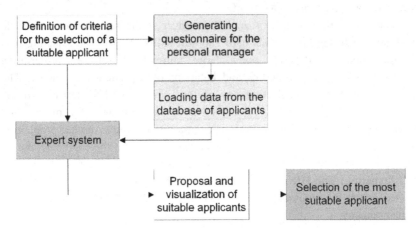

Figure 1. Proposed expert system

As shown in Figure 1, the system is divided into several steps that are introduced in the following sections.

3.1. Definition of criteria for the selection of a suitable applicant

In the first step, it is necessary that the personnel manager define the main criteria for the selection of a suitable candidate for the position. These criteria may be the same for most positions, however, some may vary. Therefore, this step comes first. Following this step, a questionnaire is generated for the HR manager, the appropriate information from the database is loaded and the knowledge base of the expert system is proposed. The selection of the appropriate criteria should logically affect other follow-up steps. The examples of the criteria for the selection of the most suitable candidates may include the following:

- Level of education
- Length of practice
- The required level of salary
- Knowledge of a foreign language
- Ability to communicate
- Ability to work in a team
- Ability to work under pressure
- The level of loyalty

3.2. *Generating questionnaire for the personal manager*

This step is based on criteria from the previous step and generates the questionnaire with which the HR manager will then determine which values of the individual criteria for assessing the candidates. This will define the criteria for the selection of the most suitable candidates, and ideally the most suitable candidate should meet all these criteria. The XML format is used to save the criteria and their possible values.

3.3. *Loading data from the database of applicants*

This step is based on the retrieval of the selected criteria information from the database of all applicants. Only the applicants who meet at least one of the required criteria are selected. For each candidate, in the event of compliance with at least one criterion, the values of all other criteria are retrieved. This will ensure that a complete profile of each applicant is created and some profiles will conform to the defined criteria more, some less.

3.4. *Creating the knowledge base of the expert system*

The knowledge base consists of the individual IF-THEN rules that are all based on the required criteria. For different positions and thus different criteria, different sets of rules exist, but only the necessary set of rules that corresponds to the selected criteria is loaded each time.

The individual criteria correspond to the input linguistic variables of the IF-THEN rules. The output linguistic variable then determines the degree of suitability of the candidates. An example of several IF-THEN rules is shown below:

```
IF (LEVEL OF EDUCATION IS HIGH) AND
(REQUIRED SALARY IS MEDIUM) AND
(COMMUNICATION LEVEL IS GOOD) AND
(TEAM WORK LEVEL IS VERY GOOD) AND
(LOYALTY IS VERY GOOD) THEN
(DEGREE OF SUITABILITY IS VERY HIGH)

IF (LEVEL OF EDUCATION IS HIGH) AND
(REQUIRED SALARY IS HIGH) AND
(COMMUNICATION LEVEL IS GOOD) AND
(TEAM WORK LEVEL IS GOOD) AND
(LOYALTY IS VERY GOOD) THEN
(DEGREE OF SUITABILITY IS HIGH)
```

72

For the expert system knowledge base the LFL Controller was used. Linguistic Fuzzy Logic Controller is more described in [5].

3.5. Proposal and visualization of suitable applicants

This step is the evaluation of suitable candidates by using the expert system. The output is an ordered list of the candidates according to the degree of suitability for the position. This list is displayed in a visual form to the HR manager. For each candidate criteria, the resulting values are displayed along with the required values. Furthermore, supplementing information which can affect the final decision is displayed. The visualization of suitable candidates is shown in the following figure:

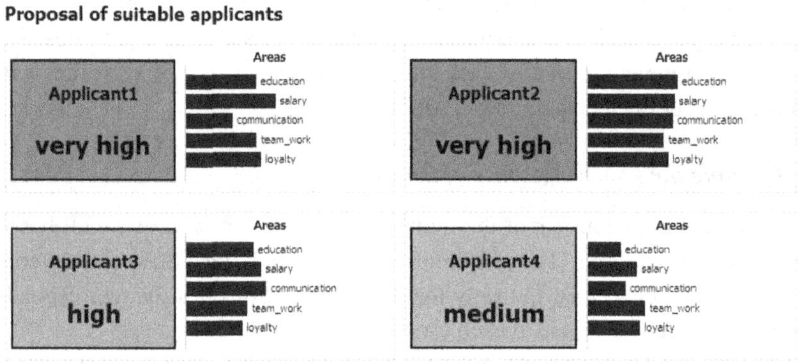

Proposal of suitable applicants

Figure 2. Visualization of suitable applicants

3.6. Selection of the most suitable applicant

In the last step, the HR manager selects the most suitable candidate for the particular position. The expert system thus only proposes suitable candidates for the position, based on the grounds of the selected criteria and loaded candidate profiles. It is therefore a helpful tool for the human resources manager who will make the final selection of the most suitable candidate.

Acknowledgments

This work was supported by the European Regional Development Fund in the IT4Innovations Centre of Excellence project (CZ.1.05/1.1.00/02.0070)

Conclusion

This article proposed the expert system for the selection of the most appropriate applicant on any position within the company. The proposed expert system works with the selected criteria and the database of all applicants and is utilized for choosing the most appropriate applicant. Based on this information and the knowledge base, the expert system suggests the most suitable candidates for employment. The individual steps of the proposed system were introduced along with the examples of their uses.

In future work, attention will be focused on the verification of the proposed expert system on specific companies. And next, a new approach to the selection of the most appropriate applicant using fuzzy logic will be proposed.

References

1. J. L. Farr, B. S. O'Leary, C. J. Bartlett, *Effect of work sample test upon self-selection and turnover of job applicants*, Journal of Applied Psychology, Vol. 58, No. 2, pp. 283-285 (1973).
2. R. E. Steinpreis, K. A. Anders, D. Ritzke, *The Impact of Gender on the Review of the Curricula Vitae of Job Applicants and Tenure Candidates: A National Empirical Study*, Sex Roles, Vol. 41, No. 7-8, pp. 509-528 (1999).
3. K. Puram, G. Sadagopal, *Consultant matching system and method for selecting candidates from a candidate pool by adjusting skill values*, US 6289340 B1 (2001).
4. J. D. Werbel, S. W. Gilliland, G. R. Ferris, *Person–environment fit in the selection process,* Research in human resources management, Vol. 17, pp. 209-243 (1999).
5. H. Habiballa, V. Novák, A. Dvořák, V. Pavliska, *Using software package LFLC 2000*, 2nd International Conference Aplimat 2003, Bratislava, pp. 355-358 (2003).
6. V. Novák, M. Štěpnička, J. Kupka, *Linguistic descriptions: their structure and applications,* International Conference FQAS 2013, Granada, pp. 209-220 (2013).
7. V. Novák, *On modeling with words*, International Journal of General Systems, Vol. 42, No. 1, pp. 21-40 (2013).

DYNAMIC SIMULATION OF ENTREPRENEURIAL PROJECT ENVIRONMENTAL ASSESSMENT

ZHIYAN XU

Economics and Management School, Southwest Jiaotong University
Chengdu, China

KAIJUN XU

Department of air navigation, School of flight technology, CAFUC Guanghan, Sichuan,
618307, P. R. China, E-mail: k_j_xu@163.com

Environmental factors are the difficulties of entrepreneurs when facing in the whole process of entrepreneurship. Due to the dynamic complexity of environmental factors and the limitations of entrepreneurial recognition, an entrepreneur will find it difficult to comprehend the business environment. The analysis of entrepreneurial environment assessment is born based on the necessity, effectiveness of the proposed model, giving a pioneering project environmental assessment, establishing venture project dynamic environmental evaluation algorithm, which application will be approved by examples.

1. Introduction

Entrepreneurship is an investment behavior attractive to many young people. In order to increase the success rate of entrepreneurship, government and scholars have a common concern to promote entrepreneurial success factors, such as the government formulates preferential policies to encourage and promote entrepreneurship, entrepreneurs strives to successful enterprises and entrepreneurs learn to imitate, scholars created various theory, paths and model providing the basis and methods to support this matter.

Fuzzy comprehensive evaluation is a multi factor comprehensive evaluation method commonly used treatment fuzzy content, which has been applied widely in many fields successfully. At first, effectiveness is used to improve the entrepreneur evaluation of entrepreneurial environment, according to the market transaction relationship, entrepreneurial environment assessment from the entrepreneurial perspective. Then in order to improve the effectiveness of entrepreneurship environment assessment, third evaluation process model based on the establishment of Fuzzy Comprehensive evaluation applying to pioneering project environmental assessment algorithm. At last, the application examples shows the entrepreneurial project environmental assessment model.

2. Necessity of entrepreneurial project environmental assessment

Pioneering project is a special investment project, according to the project life cycle theory; entrepreneurial project is divided into the definition, design, execution and completion. Figure 1 shows the general characteristics of entrepreneurial projects in the life cycle of abandonment probability and the proportion of investment with the investment project.

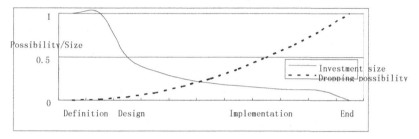

Figure 1. Dropping possibility and investment size

To investing certain projects, the definition phase abandonment probability relates to minimum (close to 0), the investment size relates to its maximum (close to 1), dropping probability is still smaller, the investment size is relatively larger in the design stage, in the implementation stage as the project moves up step by step, probability gradually increased as investment ratio decreases, at the end of stage gives up the probability approaches 1, the proportion of investment tends to zero.

3. Availability of entrepreneurial project environmental assessment

In order to improve the environmental assessment of the relative effectiveness of entrepreneurial projects, based on the life cycle theory, we put forward the venture project environmental assessment model validity, as shown in Figure 2.

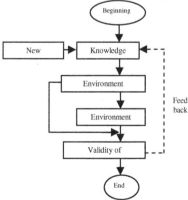

Figure 2. Investment project of Environment Assessment of Validity Model

Figure 2 shows the adapted model of entrepreneurial projects:

1. Data base: Building a date base is the foundation to carry out the work of pioneering project environmental assessment, which requires entrepreneurs usually long-term accumulation, learning and constantly updated.

2. New knowledge: The first discovery of entrepreneurs to venture project environmental assessment relates to the incident, cause and the destruction of background conditions, and the formation of new events relates professional learning and research or practical work experience.

3. The environment that is conducive to business opportunities: Through different dimension reflect to the advantage of entrepreneurial projects on the environmental assessment.

4. Threats: Through different dimensions reflect the disadvantage of entrepreneurial projects in environmental assessment. Environmental threat study is the main reason of entrepreneurial projects to give up, or is the pioneering project definition or transferred to the main resistance of the next stage, entrepreneurs effective environment threat is to abandon the project as a key factor for the effective treatment of entrepreneurial projects.

5. Environmental feasibilities study: It means a study of comprehensive environmental opportunities and threats to the environment assessment results to predict the influence of environment on entrepreneurial project work.

4. The discretization method of entrepreneurial project dynamic environmental assessment

As the change of effective evaluation entrepreneurial projects on the environment in the life period of the factors and their influence on the success or failure of the projec. This paper will venture project dynamic environment assessment is divided into three stage assessment, respectively is the definition phase of environmental assessment (S0), the design phase of environmental assessment (S1) and the stage of implementation of environmental assessment (S2), as shown in Figure 3.

These three stages of environmental assessment are determined by satisfaction criterion, in S0 and S1, if not through the satisfaction criterion to judge, it should be chosen to give up the entrepreneurial projects; in S2, if not through the satisfaction criterion to judge, is the preferred plan environmental assessment results to adjust the phase of S1 and project, if the adjustment is still not satisfactory criterion, then sooner rather than give up the project.

Figure 3 can be simplified into a model for the assessment of three stage context, as shown in Figure 4. In Figure 4, the first stage (S0) is a necessary condition for entrepreneurial project environmental assessment. In the environmental evaluation and decision of entrepreneurial projects, so the S0 assessment is a necessary condition; only when the evaluation results satisfies, can it enter the second stage (S1), at the same time, a certain degree will be on the effects of third stage (S2 evaluation) results.

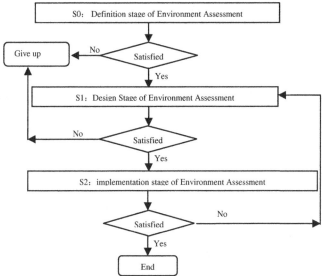

Figure 3. The discretization model of entrepreneurial project dynamic environmental assessment

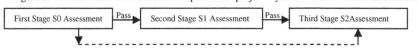

Figure 4. Three stages of Assessment Model

The second stage (S1) is a sufficient condition of pioneering project environmental assessment. In the environmental evaluation and decision making of entrepreneurial projects, the S1 assessment is a sufficient condition, the evaluation results do not meet the requirements of the project shows abandonment, when evaluating the results, it is possible to get the third stage (S2) with satisfactory results.

The third stage (S2) to predict environmental effectiveness assessment of entrepreneurial environment projects. In the environmental evaluation and decision making of entrepreneurial projects, the third stage (S2) prediction results of dynamic change, mainly with the second stage (S1 evaluation) evaluation result and fluctuation. The third stage (S2 evaluation) evaluation result according to main factors (the second stage) and secondary factors (the first stage) prediction.

In summary, evaluation of the venture project dynamic environment based on Fuzzy three stage algorithm:

Suppose U is a multistage fuzzy attribute evaluation objects with m indexes and 3 stages ($s=0,1,2$). In the sth stage, there are p_s evaluation indexes y_j, $r_{ij}(s)$ is the degree of the ith ($i=1,2,\cdots,p_s$) index belongs to the jth ($j=1,2,\cdots,m$) object, the fuzzy evaluation matrix $\tilde{B}(s)$ in the sth stage is given as follows:

$$\tilde{B}(s) = \begin{bmatrix} r_{11}(s) & r_{12}(s) & \cdots & r_{1m}(s) \\ r_{21}(s) & r_{22}(s) & \cdots & r_{2m}(s) \\ \vdots & \vdots & & \vdots \\ r_{p_s 1}(s) & r_{p_s 2}(s) & \cdots & r_{p_s m}(s) \end{bmatrix} = (r_{ij}(s))_{p_s \times m}, \qquad (1)$$

where $0 \le r_{ij}(s) \le 1$, $s=0,1,2$.

Set $R(s)$ as an assessment consequence of the sth stage, then we have:

$$R(s) = W_{p_s} \circ \tilde{B}(s) = \begin{bmatrix} r_{s1} & r_{s2} & \cdots & r_{sm} \end{bmatrix} \qquad (2)$$

where W_{p_s} is the weight vector, $\circ$ is the matrix operator.

With the normalization method, $R(s)$ can be normalized, then set:

$$C(s) = R(s) \wedge A(s) = \left((r_{sj} \wedge a_{sj}) \right)_{1 \times m} = \begin{bmatrix} C_{s1} & C_{s2} & \cdots & C_{sM} \end{bmatrix} \qquad (3)$$

where $A(s)$ is the insurance coefficient matrix, a_{sj} is the insurance coefficient,

$$A(s) = \begin{bmatrix} a_{s1} & a_{s2} & \cdots & a_{sm} \end{bmatrix} \qquad (4)$$

where $a_{sj} = \begin{cases} 1 & if & r_{sj} \ge \alpha \\ 0 & otherwise \end{cases}$.

Set the consequence of integral assessment of U as Ω and we have:

$$\Omega = C(s) \circ W = \begin{bmatrix} c_{11} & c_{12} & \cdots & c_{1m} \\ c_{21} & c_{22} & \cdots & c_{2m} \\ \vdots & \vdots & & \vdots \\ c_{s1} & c_{s2} & \cdots & c_{sm} \end{bmatrix} \circ \begin{bmatrix} w_1 \\ w_2 \\ \vdots \\ w_s \end{bmatrix} = \begin{bmatrix} c_1 \\ c_2 \\ \vdots \\ c_m \end{bmatrix}. \qquad (5)$$

According to the maximum membership degree principle or weighted average operator to make the result determination.

5. Case study

After comprehensive entrepreneur evaluation opinions, the fuzzy evaluation matrix are given as $\tilde{B}(0)$、$\tilde{B}(1)$ and $\tilde{B}(2)$。suppose $\alpha = 0.66$, the weight vectors in each stage are $W_{p_1} = W_{p_2} = W_{p_3} = \{0.2, 0.2, 0.2, 0.2, 0.2\}$, the weight vectorof stages is $W = \{0.2, 0.3, 0.5\}$.

$$\tilde{B}(0) = \begin{bmatrix} 0.6 & 0.4 & 0 & 0 & 0 \\ 0.6 & 0.4 & 0 & 0 & 0 \\ 0.7 & 0.3 & 0 & 0 & 0 \\ 0.7 & 0.3 & 0 & 0 & 0 \\ 0.7 & 0.3 & 0 & 0 & 0 \end{bmatrix} \quad \tilde{B}(1) = \begin{bmatrix} 0.7 & 0.3 & 0 & 0 & 0 \\ 0.7 & 0.3 & 0 & 0 & 0 \\ 0.8 & 0.2 & 0 & 0 & 0 \\ 0.8 & 0.2 & 0 & 0 & 0 \\ 0.8 & 0.2 & 0 & 0 & 0 \end{bmatrix} \quad \tilde{B}(2) = \begin{bmatrix} 0.75 & 0.25 & 0 & 0 & 0 \\ 0.75 & 0.25 & 0 & 0 & 0 \\ 0.75 & 0.25 & 0 & 0 & 0 \\ 0.75 & 0.25 & 0 & 0 & 0 \\ 0.75 & 0.25 & 0 & 0 & 0 \end{bmatrix}$$

To choose fuzzy operator as $(\cdot, +)$, According to (2) we have:

$R(0)=[0.66\ 0.34\ 0\ 0\ 0]$, because $r_{11} \geq \alpha=0.66$, so this innovation project of environmental assessment pass the S0 assessment.

$R(1)=[0.76\ 0.24\ 0\ 0\ 0]$, because $r_{21} \geq \alpha=0.66$, so this innovation project of environmental assessment pass the S1 assessment.

$R(2)=[0.75\ 0.25\ 0\ 0\ 0]$, because $r_{31} \geq \alpha=0.66$, so this innovation project of environmental assessment pass the S2 assessment.

According to(3), (4) and (5) we have:

$$C = \begin{bmatrix} 0.66 & 0 & 0 & 0 & 0 \\ 0.66 & 0 & 0 & 0 & 0 \\ 0.66 & 0 & 0 & 0 & 0 \end{bmatrix}.$$

To choose matrix operations with $(\cdot, \ +)$, According to (5) we have:

$$\Omega = W \circ C = \begin{bmatrix} 0.2 & 0.3 & 0.5 \end{bmatrix} \circ \begin{bmatrix} 0.66 & 0 & 0 & 0 & 0 \\ 0.66 & 0 & 0 & 0 & 0 \\ 0.66 & 0 & 0 & 0 & 0 \end{bmatrix} = \begin{bmatrix} 0.66 & 0 & 0 & 0 & 0 \end{bmatrix}.$$

Based on the maximum membership degree principle, environment effectiveness of the project environmental assessment is satisfied.

6. Conclusion

In this paper, that is, the entrepreneur only from the rational angle consideration of environmental assessment is not good enough, because entrepreneurs will quickly adapt to the changes of environmental factors is the ultimate goal of environmental assessment, and some factors affect the entrepreneurial ability of adapting the environment occasionally and unpredictably, so we need to further enhance the entrepreneur in the environmental assessment strain ability.

References

1. Peter F. Drucker. Management challenges for the 21st century. Boston: Harvard Business School Press, 1999
2. Paul Westhead, Gerard McElwee, Mike Wright. Entrepreneurship: Perspectives and Cases. Financial Times Prentice Hall, 2011
3. David J., Ketchen Jr., R. Duane Ireland, Charles C. Snow. Strategic entrepreneurship, collaborative innovation, and wealth creation. Strategic Entrepreneurship Journal, 2007, 1(3-4): 371-385
4. Xiaohong Liu, Xianyi Zeng. A model of selecting expert in sensory evaluation. The 7th Intelligent System and Knowledge Engineering (ISKE 2012), Springer Press, 2012
5. Yongjian Wang, Weihong Xie, Hailin Lan. An Empirical Study on the Relationship among Entrepreneurial Orientation, Human System Flexibility and Firm Performance. Chinese Journal of Management, 2013, 10(10): 1485-1491
6. Huatao Peng. Second startup social network feedback mechanism: A literature review. Review of economic research, 2013(48): 47-53

USING DUAL-ADAPTIVE NEURO-FUZZY INFERENCE SYSTEM IN PILOT'S RISK ASSESSMENT[*]

KAIJUN XU[†]

Department of air navigation, School of flight technology, CAFUC
Guanghan, Sichuan, 618307, P. R. China, E-mail: k_j_xu@163.com

Risk assessment is one of the most important skills that pilots are expected to acquire to ensure the safe and successful management of flight. The traditional approach to the development of these skills requires pilots to directly engage with potentially hazardous events. This paper develops dual adaptive neuro-fuzzy inference system (D-ANFIS) in civil aviation as context for pilot's risk assessment, which can help reduce the risk to the aircraft aviation flight, while maintaining operational performance. It was concluded that exposure to hazards within a simulated environment could provide the basis for the development of risk assessment skills amongst less experienced pilots.

1. Introduction

Approach and landing are critical flight phases that require formalized sequences of actions (e.g. to lower the gear down, to extend the flaps) and to follow an arrival procedure through several waypoints. Uncertainty, a worsening factor since it generates psychological stress, deleterious to piloting activity [1], can be high during landing. According to the legislation, hazardous conditions (e.g. un-stabilized approach, vehicles on the runway, strong crosswind or wind shear) require to go-around to perform a new safe attempt or to divert to another airport. The go-around decision-making rules follow legal guidelines that are adapted by aircraft manufacturers in their operating manual and airport authorities. In addition, pilots should use their own judgment and may decide to perform a go-around at any time. A study conducted by MIT [2] has demonstrated that in 2000 cases of approaches under thunderstorm conditions, two aircrews out of three keep on landing in spite of adverse meteorological conditions. This phenomenon called plan continuation error (PCE) [3] also exists in general aviation. Indeed, the BEA (the French Accident Investigation Bureau) revealed that this pilots'

[*] This work is supported by the Open Foundation of Civil Aviation Flight University of China (Grant No. F2012KF02).
[†] Work partially supported by grant 61175055 of the National Natural Science Foundation of P.R. China.

trend to land (the get-home- it is syndrome) have been responsible for more than 41.5% of casualties in general aviation [4].

Risk is defined as the possibility of loss when a known hazard is encountered, and it represents an inherent part of human engagement with the environment [5]. The assessment of risk involves a process where operators attempt to determine, to the best of their ability, the anticipated consequences associated with an event and the likelihood of exposure to the conditions under which those consequences are likely to occur [6]. In the context of the present study, risk assessment is regarded as a complex process that involves the identification of potential hazards, an estimation of the extent to which the impact of such hazards can be controlled, and a consideration of the potential costs in achieving the operational goals. Adaptive neuro-fuzzy inference system (ANFIS), which has been widely used for different purposes such as prediction [8]-[10], knowledge discovery [11], medical decision making and disease diagnosis [12], has not been tested yet. In this paper, we test ANFIS and use two same ANFIS to compare its performances with those of Dual-ANFIS in modeling aviation flight risks. This will provide more methodological comparisons for pilot's risk assessment.

The paper is organized as follows: Section 2 provides a brief description of ANFIS. Section 3 develops a dual ANFIS model and then using it in aviation flight pilot's risk assessment and use D-ANFIS model to do some simulation in Section 4. Conclusions and Future works are presented in the last Section.

2. Adaptive Neuro-fuzzy Inference System (ANFIS)

ANFIS is a multilayer feed-forward network which uses neural network learning algorithms and fuzzy reasoning to map inputs into an output. It is a fuzzy inference system (FIS) implemented in the framework of adaptive neural networks. Fig. 1 shows the architecture of a typical ANFIS with two inputs, four rules and one output for the first-order Sugeno fuzzy model, where each input is assumed to have two associated membership functions (MFs).

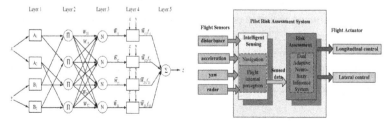

Figure 1. ANFIS structure for a two input Sugeno model with four rules

Figure 2. Block-diagram of the disturbance Pilot's risk assessment system

For a first-order Sugeno fuzzy model [13], a typical rule set with four fuzzy if–then rules can be expressed as:

Rule 1: if x is A1 and y is B1, then f11 = p11x + q11y + r11,

Rule 2: if x is A1 and y is B2, then f12 = p12x + q12y + r12,

Rule 3: if x is A2 and y is B1, then f21 = p21x + q21y + r21,

Rule 4: if x is A2 and y is B2, then f22 = p22x + q22y + r22,

where A1, A2, B1 and B2 are the MFs for the inputs x and y, respectively, pij, qij and rij (i, j = 1,2) are consequent parameters [14].

3. Sample Mathematical Text Description of Dual-adaptive Neuro-fuzzy Inference System (D-ANFIS)

The disturbance parameters of environments have to be known in order to control the pilot's risk assessment system with conventional control techniques since the disturbance affects the whole system.

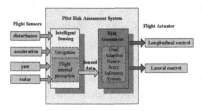 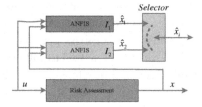

Figure 3. Block-diagram of the disturbance risk assessment system

Figure 4. The structure of dual-ANFIS Pilot's assessment system

Research on Pilot's risk assessment system mainly focused on risk prediction, risk tolerance and the learning process that enhanced comfort and lowered fuel consumption by moderating the aircraft's fight actuator. In the risk assessment part, we designed the dual neuro-fuzzy inference system which used the sensed data to help pilot make a choice.

The pilot's risk assessment system is comprised of the system identifier and two adaptive neuro-fuzzy inference systems. The system identifier inspect the assessment strategy which is not satisfied the real system after a while, it changes two ANFIS function. The learning ANFIS which has suitable strategy became to provide risk assessment to pilot in the adaptive aviation flight. The former assessed ANFIS became to learning the new strategy. The identifier combines two parts: performance index and selector.

4. Modeling Pilot's Risk Assessment using D-ANFIS

This section presents the development of an D-ANFIS for pilot's risk assessment and tests its performance. The dataset used for developing a D-ANFIS was provided by the Cessna-172 in Civil Aviation Flight University of China in Fig. 4 and 5. The dataset contains 510 approaching and landing missions and is randomly split into two sample sets: training dataset with 390 missions and testing dataset with 120 missions. Both the training and testing datasets cover all levels and types of flight risks.

Figure 5. Cessna-172 in CAFUC

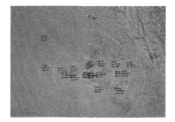

Figure 6. The dataset contains approaching and landing missions in ADS-B

Inputs to the D-ANFIS are the safety risk rating (SRR), functionality risk rating (FRR), sustainability risk rating (SURR), and environment risk rating (ERR) of the 510 approaching and landing missions, which all range from 0 to 3 with 0 representing no risk, 1 low risk, 2 medium risk and 3 high risk. Output to the D-ANFIS is the risk scores (RSs) of the 510 flight missions, which range from 5 to 99, as shown in Fig. 6.

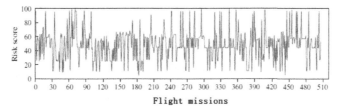

Figure 7. The flight risk score of 510 missions

Figs. 8 and 9 show the initial and final MFs before and after 500 epochs of training (Epoch is set as 500 in this study), from which it can be seen that significant modifications have been done to the shapes of initial MFs through the learning process. The trained if–then rules are presented

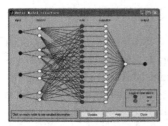

Figure 8. The model structure of ANFIS in
pilot's risk assessment

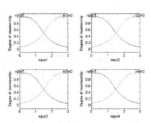

Figure 9. The membership functions before training

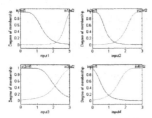

Figure 10. The membership functions after training

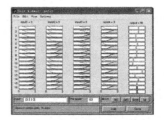

Figure 11. If-then rule after training

In Fig. 10, which can be used for prediction. For example, if we change the values of the four inputs from 1.5 to 3, then we immediately get the new output value of the ANFIS as 99.

5. Conclusions and Future Works

In the absence of appropriate training, less experienced practitioners are often faced with the dilemma of engaging hazards in order to acquire the very skills necessary to assess the risks of those hazards in the future. Using D-ANFIS model as a context, the present study was designed to test whether active involvement in a simulated training flight, and personalized feedback concerning performance, impacted the risk-oriented behavior of pilots during subsequent flights. In the case of the present study, the results indicated that active involvement in the training flight, rather than the provision of feedback concerning performance per se, resulted in behavior that reduced the risk of flight mission performance. This suggests that, amongst pilots, behavior consistent with a more conservative assessment of risks may be acquired and generalized to relatively novel tasks, through engagement with hazards within a simulated environment.

References

1. Katsis, C., Goletsis, Y., Rigas, G., Fotiadis, D., A wearable system for the affective monitoring of car racing drivers during simulated conditions. *Transportation Research Part C: Emerging Technologies* 19 (3), 541–551. (2010)
2. Rhoda, D., Pawlak, M., An Assessment of Thunderstorm Penetrations and Deviations by Commercial Aircraft in the Terminal Area. *Massachusetts Institute of Technology*, Lincoln Laboratory, Project Report NASA/A-2, 3 (1999)
3. Orasanu, J., Ames, N., Martin, L., Davison, J., Factors in aviation accidents: decision errors. In: Salas, E., Klein, G.A. (Eds.), *Linking Expertise and Naturalistic Decision Making*. Lawrence Erlbaum Associates, Mahwah, NJ, pp. 209–225 (2001)
4. BEA, Objectif: Destination. Technical Report, *Bureau Enquête Analyse.*(2000)
5. Hunter, D.R., Risk Perception and Risk Tolerance in Aircraft Pilots. *Federal Aviation Administration*, Washington, DC (DOT/FAA/AM- 02/17). (2002)
6. Faber, M.H., Stewart, M.G., Risk assessment for civil engineering facilities: critical overview and discussion. *Reliab. Eng. Syst. Safety* 80, 173–184.(2003)
7. Deery, H.A., Hazard and risk perception among young novice drivers. J. Safety Res. 30, 225–236.(1999)
8. Bateni, S. M., & Jeng, D. S. Estimation of pile group scour using adaptive neuro-fuzzy approach. *Ocean Engineering*, 34, 1344–1354. (2007).
9. Bateni, S. M., Borghei, S. M., & Jeng, D.-S. Neural network and neuro-fuzzy assessments for scour depth around bridge piers. *Engineering Applications of Artificial Intelligence*, 20, 401–414. (2007).
10. Chang, F. J., & Chang, Y. T. Adaptive neuro-fuzzy inference system for prediction of water level in reservoir. *Advances in Water Resources*, 29, 1–10. (2006).
11. Huang, M. J., Tsou, Y. L., & Lee, S. C. Integrating fuzzy data mining and fuzzy artificial neural networks for discovering implicit knowledge. *Knowledge-Based Systems*, 19, 396–403. (2006).
12. Huang, M. L., Chen, H. Y., & Huang, J. J. Glaucoma detection using adaptive neuro-fuzzy inference system. *Expert Systems with Applications*, 32, 458–468. (2007).
13. Sugeno, M. Industrial applications of fuzzy control. *Amsterdam*: Elsevier. (1985).
14. Jang, J. S. R. ANFIS: Adaptive-network-based fuzzy inference systems. IEEE Transactions on Systems Man and Cybernetics, 23, 665–685(1993).

α-PARAMODULATION FOR LATTICE-VALUED LOGIC WITH EQUALITY

Xingxing He [1], Yang Xu [1], Jun Liu [2], Xiaomei Zhong [1]

[1] *Intelligent Control Development Center, Southwest Jiaotong University, Chengdu 610031, Sichuan, PR China*
[2] *School of Computing and Mathematics, University of Ulster, Northern Ireland, UK*
E-mail: x.he@home.swjtu.edu.cn

Aiming to handle logical formulae with equality in lattice-valued logic, this paper focuses on α-paramodulation for lattice-valued logic with equality. Firstly, the axioms of equality and their related properties in lattice-valued logic are presented. Then the concept of α-paramodulation is given, which is the essential rule for processing logical formulae with equality. Finally, the soundness of α-paramodulation is established.

Keywords: Lattice-valued logic; Equality; α-Paramodulation; Automated reasoning

1. Introduction

In mathematics equality is a relationship between two quantities or, more generally two mathematical expressions, asserting that the quantities have the same value or that the expressions represent the same mathematical object. Reasoning with equality is very common and well known to be useful in mathematics, logic and computer science, hence the study of equality predicate has been particularly important. As a development of resolution principle, paramodulation[1-5,10,12] is one of the main computational methods and reasoning rules for deal with logical formulae with equality in classical first-order logic. Robinson[11] showed that resolution together with factoring is refutation complete, that is, the empty clause will eventually be inferred by systematically enumerating all consequences of an unsatisfiable set of clauses by binary resolution. Compared with resolution method,[6] equality predicate should be extended and satisfied congruence axioms such as reflexivity, symmetry, transitivity and monotonicity.

To deal with uncertainty especially for incomparability in intelligent information processing from a symbolism point of view, Xu et al. extended the classical logic in many ways such as the truth-valued field, the implication connective and language, and proposed lattice implication algebra (LIA),[13] lattice-valued logic[16] based on LIA, uncertainty reasoning and automated reasoning[7-9,14,15] in lattice-valued logic based on LIA. For judging the α-unsatisfiability of logical formulae with different levels, α-resolution principle has been proposed for lattice-valued logic.

Similar to classical logic, for judging the α-unsatisfiability of logical formula S with equality, two main methods exist for chosen. The equality is an important and special predicate symbol, if we only treat equation as a ordinary one, and use the α-resolution method to judge the α-unsatisfiability of S, then it may not get an α-refutation if S is α-unsatisfiable. One is adding the equality axioms to the original clauses set S, and get a new clauses set S_1. Then the α-unsatisfiability of S is equivalent to S_1, and the α-unsatisfiability of S_1 can be gotten by α-resolution principle. However, this method can increase the complexity of S by adding the equality axioms set, and the clauses set becomes too large if S includes too many different predicate symbols or functional symbols. The other is dealing with the logical formula S directly. Of course, only using α-resolution principle is incomplete, so we should extend α-resolution method and develop some complete automated reasoning method for handling the logical formula with equality. In this paper, by combining α-resolution and paramodulation, α-paramodulation is proposed to handle equality logical formulae directly. Some properties of equality predicate and α-paramodulation are also discussed.

2. Equality relation in lattice-valued logic based on LIA

In this section, we only recall some elementary definitions and properties needed in the following discussions, more detailed notations and results about lattice-valued logics based on LIA and α-resolution principle can be seen in the related references.[13-16]

Definition 2.1.[13,16] Let $(L, \vee, \wedge, O, I)$ be a bounded lattice with an order-reversing involution "'", I and O the greatest and the smallest element of L, respectively, and $\rightarrow: L \times L \longrightarrow L$ be a mapping. $\mathcal{L} = (L, \vee, \wedge, ', \rightarrow, O, I)$ is called a lattice implication algebra (LIA) if the following conditions hold for any $x, y, z \in L$:

(I_1) $x \rightarrow (y \rightarrow z) = y \rightarrow (x \rightarrow z)$,
(I_2) $x \rightarrow x = I$,
(I_3) $x \rightarrow y = y' \rightarrow x'$,
(I_4) $x \rightarrow y = y \rightarrow x = I$ implies $x = y$,

(I_5) $(x \to y) \to y = (y \to x) \to x$,
(L_1) $(x \lor y) \to z = (x \to z) \land (y \to z)$,
(L_2) $(x \land y) \to z = (x \to z) \lor (y \to z)$.

Definition 2.2.[16] Let X be the set of propositional variables, $(L, \lor, \land, ', \to, O, I)$ be an LIA, $T = L \cup \{', \to\}$ be a type with $ar(') = 1$, $ar(\to) = 2$ and $ar(a) = 0$ for any $a \in L$. The proposition algebra of the lattice-valued proposition calculus on the set X of propositional variables is the free T algebra on X and denoted by LP(X).

Definition 2.3.[14] Let p be a logical formula in LP(X), $\alpha \in L$. If there exists a valuation γ_0 of LP(X) such that $\gamma_0(p) \geq \alpha$, p is satisfiable by a truth-value level α, in short, α-satisfiable. If $\gamma(p) \geq \alpha$ for every valuation γ of LP(X), p is valid by the truth-value level α, in short, α-valid. If $\gamma(p) \leq \alpha$ for every valuation γ of LP(X), p is always false by the truth-value level α, in short, α-false.

The truth-value domain of lattice-valued first-order logic LF(X) is an LIA. This logic system can be used to deal with propositions with quantifiers.[14,16]

Definition 2.4. Let S be a set of g-clauses in LF(X), $\alpha \in L$, W be the set of all the interpretations of S, $Q \subseteq W$ ($Q \neq \emptyset$). S is α_Q-false if and only if S is α-false under the interpretation Q.

In the following, $s = t$ is denoted by $E(s, t)$ for convenient, where s and t are terms.

Definition 2.5. Let S be a set of g-clauses in LF(X), $\alpha \in L$. K_α is an α-equality axioms set of S if it satisfies:

(E_1) $E(x, x) > \alpha$, for any term $x \in S$.
(E_2) $E(x, y)' \lor E(y, x) > \alpha$, for any terms $x, y \in S$.
(E_3) $E(x, y)' \lor E(y, z)' \lor E(x, z) > \alpha$, for any terms $x, y, z \in S$.
(E_4) $E(x_j, x_0)' \lor P(x_1, x_2, \ldots, x_j, \ldots, x_n)' \lor P(x_1, x_2, \ldots, x_0, \ldots, x_n) > \alpha$,
for any terms $x_0, x_1, \ldots, x_n \in S$, $j = 1, 2, \ldots, n$, P is a predicate symbol in S.
(E_5) $E(x_j, x_0)' \lor E(f(x_1, x_2, \ldots, x_j, \ldots, x_n))' \lor E(f(x_1, x_2, \ldots, x_0, \ldots, x_n))$
$> \alpha$, for any terms $x_0, x_1, \ldots, x_n \in S$, $j = 1, 2, \ldots, n$, f is a function symbol in S.

Definition 2.6. Let S be a set of g-clauses in LF(X), K_α an α-equality axioms set of S, $\alpha \in L$. I_E is an E_α-interpretation if I_E satisfies K_α.

Definition 2.7. Let S be a set of g-clauses in LF(X). S is α_E-false if for any interpretation I_E such that $I_E(S) \leq \alpha$. S is α_E-true if for any interpretation I_E such that $I_E(S) > \alpha$.

Theorem 2.1. Let S be a set of g-clauses in LF(X), K_α be an α-equality axioms set of S. I_E is an E_α-interpretation if and only if for any I_E such that $I_E(K_\alpha) > \alpha$.

Theorem 2.2. Let S be a set of g-clauses in LF(X), K_α be an α-equality axioms set of S. S is α_E-false if and only if $(S \cup K_\alpha) \leq \alpha$.

Theorem 2.3. Let S be a set of g-clauses in LF(X), $|S| < +\infty$. S is α_E-false if and only if there exists a set of finite ground instances S_1 of S in LP(X), such that S_1 is α_E-false.

3. α-Paramodulation for lattice-valued logic with equality

Definition 3.1. Let C_1, C_2 be g-clauses without the same variables in LF(X), $C_1 = L[t] \vee C_1^0$, $C_2 = E(r, s) \vee C_2^0$, where $L[t]$ is the literal including term t, C_1^0 and C_2^0 are g-clauses. If t and s have an mgu σ, then

$$PR_\alpha(C_1, C_2) = L^\sigma[s^\sigma] \vee C_1^{0\sigma} \vee C_2^{0\sigma}$$

is called an α-paramodulation of C_1 and C_2, where $L^\sigma[s^\sigma]$ denotes that t^σ in L^σ is substituted by s^σ.

Definition 3.2. Let C_1, C_2 be g-clauses in LF(X). C_1 α_E-implies C_2 if $C_1 \to C_2$ is α_E-true, denoted by $C_1 \Rightarrow_{\alpha_E} C_2$.

Theorem 3.1. Let C_1, C_2 be generalized clauses in LP(X), then $C_1 \wedge C_2 \Rightarrow_{\alpha_E} PR_\alpha(C_1, C_2)$.

Theorem 3.2. Let C_1, C_2 be g-clauses in LF(X), then $C_1 \wedge C_2 \Rightarrow_{\alpha_E} PR_\alpha(C_1, C_2)$.

Obviously, the soundness of α-paramodulation in LF(X) follows according to Theorem 3.2.

4. Conclusion

This paper proposed α-paramodulation in lattice-valued logic for dealing with logical formulae with equality. Some properties of equality predicate were discussed, and the soundness of α-paramodulation was also given. The further research will be concentrated on completeness of α-paramodulation, its restricted α-paramodulation methods and their efficient algorithms.

Acknowledgments

This work is partially supported by the National Natural Science Foundation of China (Grant No. 61305074, 61175055 and 61100046), and the Fundamental Research Funds for the Central Universities of China (Grant No. A0920502051305-24).

References

1. L. Bachmair, H. Ganzinger, C. Lynch, W. Snyder, Basic paramodulation. Inf Comput, 121, pp. 172–192 (1995).
2. D. Brand, Proving theorems with the modification method. SIAM J Comput, 4, pp. 412–430 (1975).
3. J. P. Bridge, S. B. Holden, L. C. Paulson, Machine learning for first-order theorem proving, Journal of Automated Reasoning, DOI: 10.1007/s10817-014-9301-5 (2014).
4. M. Bofill, A. Rubio, Paramodulation with non-monotonic orderings and simplification. Journal of automated reasoning, 50(1), pp. 51–98 (2013).
5. M. Echenim, N. Peltier, S. Tourret, An Approach to Abductive Reasoning in Equational Logic, Proceedings of the 23rd International Joint Conference on Artificial Intelligence (IJCAI'13), Beijing, China, pp. 531–537 (2013).
6. D. Guller, Binary resolution over complete residuated stone lattices, Fuzzy Sets and Systems 159, pp. 1031–1041 (2008).
7. X.X. He, J. Liu, Y. Xu, L. Martínez, D. Ruan, On α-satisfiability and its α-lock resolution in a finite lattice-valued propositional logic, Logic Journal of IGPL, 20(3): 579–588 (2012).
8. X.X. He, Y. Xu, J. Liu, D. Ruan, α-Lock resolution method for a lattice-valued first-order logic, Engineering Applications of Artificial Intelligence, 24(7): 1274–1280 (2011).
9. J. Liu, D. Ruan, Y. Xu, Z.M. Song, A resolution-like strategy based on a lattice-valued logic, IEEE Transactions on Fuzzy Systems, 11(4), pp. 560–567 (2003).
10. R. Nieuwenhuis, A. Rubio, Paramodulation-based theorem proving. In: Robinson A, Voronkov A, eds. Handbook of Automated Reasoning, vol. I Chapter 7. Amsterdam: Elsevier Science, pp. 371–443 (2001).
11. J.P. Robinson, A machine-oriented logic based on the resolution principle, J. ACM 12, pp. 23–41 (1965).
12. G. Robinson, L. Wos, Paramodulation and theorem proving in first order theories with equality. In: Machine Intelligence, vol. 4. Edinburgh, Scotland: Edinburgh University Press, pp. 135–150 (1969).
13. Y. Xu, Lattice implication algebras, J. Southwest Jiaotong University, 89(1), pp. 20–27 (1993) (in Chinese).
14. Y. Xu, D. Ruan, E.E. Kerre, J. Liu, α-Resolution principle based on lattice-valued propositional logic LP(X). Information Sciences 130, pp. 195–223 (2000).

15. Y. Xu, D. Ruan, E.E. Kerre, J. Liu, α-Resolution principle based on lattice-valued first-order lattice-valued logic LF(X), Information Sciences 132, pp. 221–239 (2001).
16. Y. Xu, D. Ruan, K.Y. Qin, J. Liu, Lattice-Valued Logic: An alternative approach to treat fuzziness and incomparability, Springer-Verlag, Berlin, 2003.

APPROXIMATE REASONING METHOD IN LINGUISTIC TRUTH-VALUED FIRST-ORDER LOGIC SYSTEM

Xiaosong Cui[1], Di Liu[1], Xin Wen[1] Li Zou[1,2]

[1]*School of Computer and Information Technology, Liaoning Normal University, Dalian 116081*

[2]*State Key Laboratory for Novel Software Technology, Nanjing University, Nanjing 210093*

Based on 6-elements linguistic truth-valued lattice implication algebras this paper discusses 6-elements linguistic truth-valued first-order logic system. We give some equivalent formal of 6-elements linguistic truth-valued first-order logic system is given. We provide 6-elements linguistic truth-valued first-order logic of general implications formula and the law of negative transformation.

1. Introduction

Artificial Intelligence, as an active research domain, devotes to developing programs that enable computers to display behavior that can be characterized as intelligent. Words and languages are important aspects for embodying human intelligence. Human beings usually express world knowledge by using natural language with full of vague and imprecise concepts. Lattice-valued logic system is an important case of multi-valued logic[1]. It can be used to describe uncertain information that may be comparable or incomparable.Lattice-valued propositional logic LP(X) and gradational Lattice-valued propositional Logic Lvpl based on lattice implication algebra have been proposed Xu [2-3].

L. Zou proposed a new resolution method in $L_6P(X)$, and then proposed linguistic truth-valued propositional logic based on LIA[4]. Meng, D. gave some necessary preliminaries, and discussed resolution principle in $L_6F(X)$ and proved theorem is soundness and completeness[5]. Y. Xu gave a-resolution automated reasoning algorithms, established their soundness and completeness in LF(X), which can directly apply to $L_{n\times2}F(X)$[6]. Y. Xu discussed the completeness of α-resolution in $L_{n\times2}F(X)$, and gave the equivalence of transformation for a-resolution between $L_{n\times2}F(X)$ and $L_{n\times2}P(X)$, and further to that of $L_nP(X)$[7]. L. Zou discussed the satisfiability problem of linguistic truth-valued intuitionistic prepositional logic[8-10]. W. T. Xu discussed the structure of generalized literals in linguistic truth-valued prepositional logic systems[11]. Xu wei-tao proposed ideal-based resolution principle for lattice-valued first-order logic system LF(X), which is an extension of α-resolution principle in lattice-valued logic system based on lattice implication algebra [12].

This paper will be based on 6-elements linguistic truth-valued lattice implication algebras to discuss 6-elements linguistic truth-valued first-order logic system. Definition and nature of 6-elements linguistic truth-valued first-order logic system is given. We provide 6-elements linguistic truth-valued first-order logic of general implications formula and the law of negative transformation.

2. Preliminaries

Definition 1 [4].Qualitative linguistic hedge variable set is obtained from the partition of linguistic hedge operator set due to the effect of the linguistic hedge operators to the proposition. We can get three classes of the linguistic hedge operators:{strengthen operators, none, weaken operators}.Denote the set of qualitative values by symbol $\{h_+, h_0, h_-\}$. Let h is a qualitative linguistic hedge variable, its qualitative value $[h]$ is defined as follows:

$$[h] = \begin{cases} h_+, & \text{if } h \text{ is a strengthen operator;} \\ h_0, & \text{if } h \text{ has no effect to the truth or there is not hedge} \\ & \text{operator;} \\ h_-, & \text{if } h \text{ is a weaken operator.} \end{cases}$$

The operation " $\oplus$ "," $\otimes$ "and " ' "of qualitative linguistic hedge value is defined as follows:

Tab. 2-1 Operation " $\oplus$ "   Tab. 2-2 Operation " $\otimes$ "   Tab. 2-3 Negative Operation

$\oplus$	h_+	h_0	h_-
h_+	h_+	h_+	h_0
h_0	h_+	h_0	h_-
h_-	h_0	h_-	h_-

$\otimes$	h_+	h_0	h_-
h_+	h_+	h_0	h_-
h_0	h_0	h_0	h_0
h_-	h_-	h_0	h_+

$[x]$	$[x]'$
h_+	h_-
h_0	h_0
h_-	h_+

Definition 2[4]. Let $L = (V, \vee, \wedge, O, I)$ be a bounded lattice with an order-reversing involution" ' ", I and O the greatest and the smallest element of L respectively, and $\rightarrow: L \times L \rightarrow L$ be a mapping. $L = (V, \vee, \wedge, O, I)$ is called a lattice implication algebra if the following conditions hold for any $x, y, z \in L$:

(I_1) $x \rightarrow (y \rightarrow z) = y \rightarrow (x \rightarrow z)$;

(I_2) $x \rightarrow x = I$;

(I_3) $x \rightarrow y = y' \rightarrow x'$;

(I_4) $x \rightarrow y = y \rightarrow x = I$, implies $x = y$;

$$(I_5) \quad (x \rightarrow y) \rightarrow y = (y \rightarrow x) \rightarrow x;$$
$$(I_6) \quad (x \vee y) \rightarrow z = (x \rightarrow z) \wedge (y \rightarrow z);$$
$$(I_7) \quad (x \wedge y) \rightarrow z = (x \rightarrow z) \vee (y \rightarrow z).$$

Let $V = \{h_+T,\ h_0T,\ h_-T,\ h_+F,\ h_0F,\ h_-F\}$, $L_6 = (V,\vee,\wedge,\rightarrow)$
its "$\vee$", "$\wedge$" operation are shown in the Hasse diagram of L_6 defined as fig 2-1
and its " $'$ ", "$\rightarrow$" operation are defined as table 2-4 and table 2-5 respectively.
Then $L_6 = (V,\vee,\wedge,\rightarrow)$ is a lattice implication algebra.

Tab. 2-4 Complementary operator of $L = (V,\vee,\wedge,',\rightarrow)$

V	h_+F	h_0F	h_-F	h_-T	h_0T	h_+T
V'	h_+T	h_0T	h_-T	h_-F	h_0F	h_+F

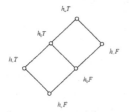

Fig . 2-1 Hasse diagram of L_6

Tab. 2-5 Implication operator of $L = (V,\vee,\wedge,',\rightarrow)$

$\rightarrow$	h_+F	h_0F	h_-F	h_-T	h_0T	h_+T
h_+F	h_+T	h_+T	h_+T	h_+T	h_+T	h_+T
h_0F	h_0T	h_+T	h_0T	h_0T	h_+T	h_+T
h_-F	h_-T	h_0T	h_+T	h_-T	h_0T	h_+T
h_-T	h_-F	h_-F	h_-F	h_+T	h_+T	h_+T
h_0T	h_0F	h_-F	h_-F	h_0T	h_+T	h_+T
h_+T	h_+F	h_0F	h_-F	h_-T	h_0T	h_+T

Definition 3[4].The formula of $6LTVP$ is defined as follows:
1. $6LTVP$ atom hP is a formula where $h \in H$;
2. If A is $6LTVP$ formula then $(hA), (\neg A)$ are $6LTVP$ formulas too;
3. If A,B are $6LTVP$ formulas then $\neg A$, $(A \vee B)$, $(A \wedge B)$ and $(A \rightarrow B)$ are
   $6LTVP$ formulas too;
4. All the formulas are the symbolic strings which use (1) to (3) with finite
   times.

Definition 4[4].A valuation of $6LTVP$ is a propositional algebra homomorphism
$\gamma: 6LTVP \rightarrow L_6$.

3. 6-elements linguistic truth-valued first-order logic

Definition 5.The formal language of 6-elements linguistic truth-valued
first-order logic is made up of the following symbols:
1. Individual constants: a, b, c, ...;
2. Individual variables: x, y, z, ...;

3. Function of symbols: f, g, h, ...;
4. The first-order languages: F, G, H, ...;
5. Conjunction symbols: ¬, ∧, ∨, →, ↔, ...;
6. Quantifier symbols: ∀, ∃;
7. Punctuations: ,, （,）.

Definition 6. Let x be a individual variable and $P(x)$ be a formula of atom, $v((\forall x)P(x))$ and $v((\exists x)P(x))$ are called $Lvfl_6$ atom where $v \in L_6$.

Definition 7. The formula of $Lvfl_6$ is defined as follows:

1. Lvfl6 atom $hP(x)$ is a formula where $h \in H$;
2. If $A(x)$ is a Lvfl6 formula then $(hA(x)), (\neg A(x))$ are $Lvfl_6$ formulas too;
3. If $A(x), B(x)$ are $Lvfl_6$ formulas then $\neg A(x), (A(x) \vee B(x))$、$(A(x) \wedge B(x))$ and $(A(x) \to B(x))$ are $Lvfl_6$ formulas too;
4. If $A(x)$ is a $Lvfl_6$ formula and x is a individual variable then $(\forall x)A(x)$ and $(\exists x)B(x)$ are $Lvfl_6$ formulas too;
5. All the formulas are the symbolic strings which use (1) to (4) with finite times.

Definition 8. A valuation of $Lvfl_6$ is a propositional algebra homomorphism $\gamma : Lvfl_6 \to L_6$.

Definition 9. Let P(x) be a fomular in $Lvfl_6$,

1. For its any valuation γ, if the truth value of fomular P(x) is h_+T, then this formula is strong valid type or strong tautologies.
2. For its any valuation γ, a formula $P(x)$ is generally valid type or generally tautologies if its true value satisfies the condition as follows:
   ① $\gamma(P(x)) = h_0T$
   ② $\gamma(P(x)) = h_0T (or\ h_+T)$
   says that this formula is .
3. If there is a formula $P(x)$ for its any valuation γ its true value as follows:
   ① $\gamma(P(x)) = h_-T$
   ② $\gamma(P(x)) = h_-T (or\ h_+T)$
   ③ $\gamma(P(x)) = h_-T (or\ h_0T)$
   ④ $\gamma(P(x)) = h_-T (or\ h_0T, h_+T)$
   says that this formula is weak valid type or weak tautologies.
   If there is a formula for its any valuation γ its true value for h_+F, says that this formula is strong contradiction.
   If there is a formula $P(x)$ for its any valuation γ its true value as follows:
   ① $\gamma(P(x)) = h_0F$
   ② $\gamma(P(x)) = h_0F (or\ h_+F)$
   says that this formula is generally valid type or generally contradiction.

If there is a formula $P(x)$ for its any valuation γ its true value as follows:

③ $\gamma(P(x)) = h_-F$

④ $\gamma(P(x)) = h_-F(or\ h_+F)$

⑤ $\gamma(P(x)) = h_-F(or\ h_0F)$

⑥ $\gamma(P(x)) = h_-F(or\ h_0F, h_+F)$

says that this formula is weak contradiction.

Theorem 1 Let $P(x)$ is contains the variable x of first-order logic formula, then the negation equivalent type as follows:

$\qquad$ 1. $\neg(\forall x)P(x) \Leftrightarrow (\exists x)\neg P(x)$ $\hfill (1)$

$\qquad$ 2. $\neg(\exists x)P(x) \Leftrightarrow (\forall x)\neg P(x)$ $\hfill (2)$

Proof. (1) Let E is a domain of individual.

If the true value of $\neg(\forall x)P(x)$ under the valuation γ respectively are h_+T、h_0T、h_-T、h_+F、h_0F、h_-F, then the true value of $(\forall x)P(x)$ are respectively corresponding as h_+F、h_0F、h_-F、h_+T、h_0T、h_-T,（as table 2-4）, i.e., for any $x \in E$, let the true values of $P(x)$ are h_+F、h_0F、h_-F、h_+T、h_0T、h_-T. So we can get $\neg P(x)$ is corresponding as h_+T、h_0T、h_-T、h_+F、h_0F、h_-F. That is to say, there is a x_0 for the truth value of $\neg P(x_0)$ are respectively as h_+T、h_0T、h_-T、h_+F、h_0F、h_-F,i.e., the true values of $(\exists x)\neg P(x)$ are respectively corresponding as h_+T、h_0T、h_-T、h_+F、h_0F、h_-F.That is to say, if the true value of $\neg(\forall x)P(x)$ are h_+T、h_0T、h_-T、h_+F、h_0F、h_-F, there must be have the true value of $(\exists x)\neg P(x)$ are also respectively corresponding as h_+T、h_0T、h_-T、h_+F、h_0F、h_-F.

If the true value of $(\exists x)\neg P(x)$ under the valuation γ respectively are h_+T、h_0T、h_-T、h_+F、h_0F、h_-F,i.e., there is a $x_0 \in E$,for the true values of $\neg P(x_0)$ are respectively corresponding as h_+T、h_0T、h_-T、h_+F、h_0F、h_-F,then the true value of $P(x_0)$ are h_+F、h_0F、h_-F、h_+T、h_0T、h_-T.So we can get for any x , there has the truth value of $P(x)$ are respectively as h_+T、h_0T、h_-T、h_+F、h_0F、h_-F, i.e., the true value of $(\forall x)P(x)$ is corresponding as h_+T、h_0T、h_-T、h_+F、h_0F、h_-F. Therefor, the true value of $\neg(\forall x)P(x)$ are respectively corresponding as h_+T、h_0T、h_-T、h_+F、h_0F、h_-F.That is to say if the true value of $(\exists x)\neg P(x)$ are h_+T、h_0T、h_-T、h_+F、h_0F、h_-F, there must be have the true value of $\neg(\forall x)P(x)$ are also respectively corresponding as h_+T、h_0T、h_-T、h_+F、h_0F、h_-F.

4.   Conclusions

This paper based on 6-elements linguistic truth-valued lattice implication algebra to discuss 6-elements linguistic truth-valued first-order logic. Definition and nature of 6-elements linguistic truth-valued first-order logic system is given.

we provide 6-elements linguistic truth-valued first-order logic of general implications formula and the law of negative transformation.Discuss about the approximate reasoning rule of the 6-elements linguistic truth-valued first-order logic is also further work.

Acknowledgments

This work is partly supported by the National Natural Science oundation of China (Grant no. 61105059, 61175055, 61372187and 61173100).

References

1. Y. Xu. Lattice implication algebras, *J.Southwest Jiaotong Univ*, vol.89-1, pp. 20-27, (1993).
2. Y. Xu, K.Y. Qin. Lattice-value proposition logic(I), *J.Southwest Jiaotong Univ*, vol. 1-2, pp. 123-128, (1993).
3. Y. Xu, D. Ruan, K.Y. Qin, J. Liu.Lattice-valued logic: an alternative approach to treat fuzziness and incomparability, *Berlin: Springer-Verlag*, (2003).
4. L. Zou, X. Liu and Y. Xu. Resolution Method of Linguistic Truth-valued Propositional Logic, *in Proc. 2005 Neural Networks and Brain, 2005, ICNN&B '05.International Conference on*, pp. 1996-1999,(2005).
5. Meng, D., Xu, Y., Jia, H.D. Resolution Principle Based on Six Lattice-Valued First-Order Logic L6F(X), *Proceedings of 2005 IEEE Networking, Sensing and Control Conference*, pp838-843, (2005).
6. Y. Xu, J. Liu, D. Ruan and T. T. Lee. On the Consistency of Rule Bases Based on Lattice-valued First-order Logic LF(X), *International Journal of Intelligent Systems*,vol.21, pp. 399-424, (2006).
7. Y. Xu, X. B. Li, J. Liu and D. Ruan. Determination of a-Resolution for Lattice-Valued First-Order Logic Based on Lattice Implication, *in Proc, 2007 Proc. 2007 International Conference on Intelligent Systems and Knowledge Engineering (ISKE2007)*, pp. 1567-1574(2007).
8. L. Zou,S. Fang and X. Yang. Resolution method of six-element linguistic truth-valued intuitionistic propositional logic, *in Proc. 2008 Intelligent System and Knowledge Engineering, 2008, 3rdInternational Conference on*, pp. 141-145(2008).
9. L. Zou, L. Jinglong, K. Xu and Y. Xu. A Kind of Resolution Method of Linguistic Truth-Valued Propositional Logic Based on LIA, *in Proc. 2007 Fuzzy Systems and Knowledge Discovery, 2007. Fourth International Conference on*, pp. 32—36(2007).
10. L. Zou and W. Li. Satisfiability Problem of Linguistic Truth-Valued Intuitionistic Propositional Logic, *in Proc. 2008 Innovative Computing Information and Control,2008. ICICIC '08. 3rdInternational Conference on*, pp. 301—305(2008).
11. W. T. Xu, α -Generalized linear resolution method for linguistic truth-valued lattice-valued logic system based on lattice implication algebras, *PhD dissertation, Southwest Jiaotong University*, Chengdu, （2011）.
12. Xu wei-Tao,Xu Yang, Ideal resolution principle for lattice-valued first-order logic based on lattice implication algebra Journal of Shanghai Jiaotong University (Science), vol.17(2), p 178-181,(2012).

PART 2

STATISTICS, DATA ANALYSIS AND DATA MINING

NASH-PARTICLE SWARM OPTIMIZATION APPLIED TO THE ANALYSIS OF TIMBER MARKETS IN THE AMAZON FOREST

ANDERSON ALVARENGA DE MOURA MENESES AND MARCOS XIMENES PONTE

Instituto de Engenharia e Geociências, Universidade Federal do Oeste do Pará
Av. Vera Paz, s/n – Salé, Santarém, PA, 68005-110, Brazil

In the present work, we assess the application of the Nash-Particle Swarm Optimization (Nash-PSO) algorithm to the analysis of timber markets in the Amazon forest within a game theoretical framework. The usage of the PSO algorithm and the game theory's best response concept are the bases of the Nash-PSO algorithm, implemented for such analysis. With the Nash-PSO algorithm it is possible to analyze the interactions of players in a continuous space of strategies, for non-linear objective functions with a fast and accurate convergence. The results also demonstrate the viability of the Nash-PSO algorithm in the estimation of real values for government investment in forest areas.

1. Introduction

In the present work, conflicting objectives and the competitive relationship between government and the timber industry are modeled according to the Game Theory [1], [2] with the application of Particle Swarm Optimization (PSO) [3] for the analysis of the timber market in the Amazon forest. The timber industry wants to maximize its revenues, whereas, according to a green economy perspective, the government wants to implement sustainable policies for the timber extraction and is able to provide financial support to sustainable activities as well as enforcement and penalties to illegal logging.

Literature on real-world game theory problems solved with metaheuristics is scarce. Sefrioui and Periaux [4] proposed the application of Nash-Genetic Algorithms (Nash-GA) to the problem of the nozzle reconstruction with multiple criteria. In our research the GA is substituted by the PSO algorithm, which presents outstanding performance in various scientific and engineering fields, outperforming several optimization algorithms.

2. Theoretical Background

2.1. *Economic Models*

The government controls the variable investment (in governance, which comprises social investment, financial support as well as law enforcement) and the timber industry controls the variable extraction (which may comprise sustainable or predatory extraction, or both mixed). Once the timber industry selects its extraction strategy guided by the maximization of its revenues, the government selects its response strategy based on the extraction of the Timber Industry. The behavior of both agents, as stated earlier, is modeled with the Nash-PSO: Each agent optimizes its own objective function disregarding the other party's objective, yet receiving fixed values for the decision variables not controlled by them. Table 1 exhibits indices, parameters and decision variables for the timber industries' economic model, based upon previous works [5], [6].

Table 1. Indices, parameters and variables of the economic model.

	Indices	
i	Cell number (area of 500 ha)	$i = 1, 2$
k	Type of wood	$k = 1, 2, 3$
s	Extraction strategy	$s = 1, 2$
	Parameters	
c_1	Cost of extraction	US\$ 7.59/m^3
c_2	Cost of transportation	US\$ 0.11/m^3
c_3	Cost of processing	US\$ 24.58/m^3
τ	Taxes (%)	0.1465
p_k	Price of the wood according to its type	(1)
ϕ	Coefficient of conversion from log to lumber (%)	0.4
ω	Apprehension fine	US\$ 174.73/m^3
tx	Coefficient for the average time for fine execution	1
σ	Total ecosystem value [7]	US\$ 448.40/ha
	Decision variables	
X_{iks}	Volume of extracted timber (2)	Controlled by the industry
l	Investment per cell	Controlled by the government

(1) In US\$/m^3 : 1 – high value (280.00); 2 – medium value: (239.00); 3 – low value (158.00) [5].
(2) Industry's monthly timber extraction average capacity: 333 m^3 [5].

2.1.1. *Timber industry's economic model*

The timber industry's expected revenue Π_e is described by

$$\Pi_e = \sum_i \sum_k \sum_s X_{iks} \{ [\phi(p_k(1-\tau)-c_3)] - c_1 - c_2 \} \ . \tag{1}$$

Eq. (2) describes the expected return rate ρ_e

$$\rho_e = \frac{\Pi_e}{\sum_i \sum_k \sum_s X_{iks}(c_1 + c_2 + \varphi c_3)} \ . \tag{2}$$

The equation (3) describes the expected illegality cost λ_e

$$\lambda_e = \left\{ \gamma(c_1 + c_2) + \frac{\omega}{(1+\rho_e)^{tx}} \right\} \sum_i \sum_k X_{ik2} \ , \tag{3}$$

where $\gamma = \iota_T/50000$ is the coefficient of governance, used to estimate industry's losses due to apprehension of timber extracted illegally ($\iota_T = \iota + \iota_b$, where ι is the government's investment, that is, the decision variable controlled by the government, and ι_b = US$ 190.80 per cell is the estimated basic investment). The term $\omega/(1 + \rho_e)^{tx}$ represents the actual payment of fines over time (fine execution), with $tx = 1$ in our experiments (in other words, since the application of a fine is not immediate, the industry takes into account the profitability of the illegal activity over time).

Finally, the utility function u_{ind} for the timber industry is given by

$$u_{ind} = \Pi_e - \lambda_e \ , \tag{4}$$

which is the objective function to be maximized by the timber industry's swarm.

2.1.2. Government's economic model

In order to estimate environmental losses, a deforested area is firstly estimated based on the volume of timber predatorily extracted. The estimated area α_{iks} (in ha) is given by

$$\alpha_{iks} = \frac{\sum_i X_{iks}}{d_k} \tag{5}$$

where d_k is a timber density for each type of wood k. According to Rivero [5], for high value timber d_1 = 14.62 m^3/ha, for medium value timber d_2 = 29.81 m^3/ha and for low value timber d_3 = 29.90 m^3/ha.

Thus, the estimated virtual value $\xi_{s=1}$ (in US$) for sustainable timber extraction and the virtual value $\xi_{s=2}$ (also in US$) for predatory extraction are given by

$$\xi_s = \sigma \sum_{ik} \alpha_{iks} \qquad (6)$$

The virtual return rate r is then given by

$$r = \frac{\xi_{s=1} - \xi_{s=2}}{\iota_T} \quad . \qquad (7)$$

The government is modeled as a risk-averse investor with a quadratic utility function u_{gov} given by

$$u_{gov} = -r^2 + r \qquad (8)$$

which is the objective function to be maximized by the government's swarm.

2.2. *Nash-Particle Swarm Optimization (Nash-PSO)*

According to the Game Theory's concept of best response [8], for a given strategy of Player II, Player I's best response maximizes the expected payoff, and vice-versa. This is the core idea that enables the usage of optimization metaheuristics such as the PSO algorithm for solving such game theory problems. Let's suppose two players A and B, with the payoff functions (or objective functions) $f_A(x, y)$ and $f_B(x, y)$, with the Player A controlling x and the Player B controlling y. Player A's metaheuristic process searches for the best x for a fixed value of y. Once such value of x is found, Player A's search temporarily stops, the value of x is fixed and then Player B's metaheuristic search for the best value of y begins. Once Player B's metaheuritic process finds a new value y that maximizes its objective function, representing a best response for x, Player B's search temporarily stops and then the process starts over. In the present case, the use of an optimization metaheuristic, namely the PSO, is justified since the economic model is based on non-linear equations. Besides, the PSO presents a fast and accurate convergence in several cases such as the problem discussed herein.

3. Computational Experimental Results

Each experiment was performed 50 times, that is, with 50 independent random initialization of the swarms (50 tests). Therefore, in the charts, the dots represent average results over 50 tests and the bars represent the confidence interval of the mean (Student's t distribution; n = 50; α = 0.05).

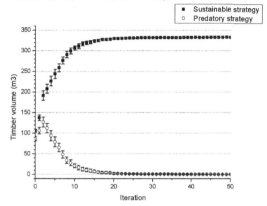

Figure 1. *Timber volume extracted with sustainable and predatory strategies over 50 iterations of the Nash-PSO algorithm. The governmental action is able to induce the timber industry to increase the volume of timber extracted using sustainable strategy.*

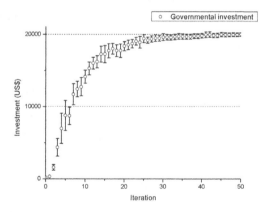

Figure 2. *Governmental investment over 50 iterations of the Nash-PSO algorithm.*

4. Discussion

In the Nash-PSO each swarm tries to optimize its own objective function according to the Game Theory's best response concept. As depicted in Fig. 1, the government's actions, represented by fine application, law enforcement and governance, led the industry to change its strategies from a balanced mixed strategy of sustainable and illegal extraction in the beginning of the execution of the algorithm to almost total sustainable extraction, reaching a convergence for the 50 tests performed. In the first two iterations, one can notice in Fig. 1 an increasing value of timber volume with illegal strategy. In the first iterations, in Fig. 2, as a result of the interaction between the players, the government quickly raises its level of investment, attempting to combat the industry's decision of extracting timber within an unsustainable strategy. The governmental investment (Fig. 2) keeps rising until an equilibrium is reached. Besides, such equilibrium is formed despite the stochastic nature of the Nash-PSO algorithm.

Thus with the Nash-PSO algorithm it is possible to analyze the interactions of players in a continuous space of strategies for non-linear objective functions, therefore it is possible to estimate values of investment according to fine values and execution times using optimization metaheuristics.

5. Conclusion

In the present work, the Nash-PSO algorithm is applied to the analysis of timber markets in the Amazon forest. With the application of the Nash-PSO, a fast and robust convergence was achieved, allowing the estimation of investment government values as public policy strategy of governance. Current research comprises the analysis of different values of fines and execution times in order to determine optimal values of local investment as well as to determine optimal public policies.

References

1. J. von Neumann, O. Morgenstern, Theory of Games and Economic Behavior, Princeton University Press, USA (1944).
2. J.F. Nash, Equilibrium Points in N-Person Games, PNAS 36, 48-49 (1950).
3. J. Kennedy, R.C. Eberhart, Swarm Intelligence, Morgan Kaufmann Publishers, California, USA (2001).
4. M. Sefrioui, J. Periaux, Nash Genetic Algorithms: Examples and Applications, in: Proceedings of the 2000 Congress on Evolutionary Computation, California, USA, 509-516 (2000).
5. S. Rivero, O Nó da Madeira: Modelagem e Simulação Multiagentes da Exploração Madeireira em Rondônia, PhD thesis, Federal University of Pará, Brazil (2004).
6. S.W. Stone, Growth of the Timber Industry in the Eastern Amazon: Economic Trends and Implications for Policy, PhD thesis, Cornell University, New York, USA (1997).
7. R. Naidoo, T.H. Ricketts, Mapping the Economic Costs and Benefits of Deforestation, PLoS Biol. 4, 2153-2164 (2006).
8. E.N. Barron, Game Theory – An Introduction, John Wiley & Sons, New Jersey, USA (2008).

BOOTSTRAPPING DEA SCORES FOR TRAFFIC FATALITY RISK ASSESSMENT IN BRAZIL

JORGE TIAGO BASTOS[1,2], YONGJUN SHEN[1], ELKE HERMANS[1], TOM BRIJS[1], GEERT WETS[1], ANTONIO CLÓVIS PINTO FERRAZ[2]

[1]*Transportation Research Institute, Hasselt University, Wetenschapspark 5 Diepenbeek, Limburg 3590, Belgium*
[2]*School of Engineering of São Carlos, University of São Paulo, Trab. Sãocarlense 400 São Carlos, São Paulo 13ZIP/Zone, Country*

In this paper, three risk indicators on road safety (i.e., traffic fatalities per vehicle, per traveled kilometer and per inhabitants) are combined into a composite indicator in order to assess the overall fatality risk for the 27 Brazilian states. The so-called multiple layer data envelopment analysis (DEA) model is used in this respect. Given their remarkable diversity in terms of road safety context, the states are first clustered (into four clusters) and next, a range of bootstrapped scores is generated to manifest the estimated variability in the road safety performance of each state. Bootstrapping the original DEA scores showed to be a useful strategy to assess the robustness of the states' ranking, which is subjected to uncertainties in input information and DEA model determinism.

1. Introduction

In macro-level road safety research, country/states comparisons are used to evaluate the road safety situation. Most commonly, three indicators are studied: traffic fatalities per inhabitants, traffic fatalities per vehicle and traffic fatalities per traveled kilometer. Although any of these indicators is useful to classify the road safety level of a place, it is possible that different conclusions are drawn depending on the adopted indicator. To overcome this difficulty, the Data Envelopment Analysis (DEA) methodology is a convenient tool to combine these three indicators into a single index or composite indicator capable to express the road safety performance in a more adequate perspective.

However, the application of a deterministic-nature technique, such as DEA, to a non-deterministic problem, such as road safety, requires the index values to be submitted to a sensitivity analysis procedure (bootstrapping), after which DEA scores are expressed throughout a range of possible values, instead of a single number. Therefore, the objective of this paper is to demonstrate the aforementioned methodological process using the road safety indicator data of the 27 Brazilian states (BR-27).

2. Data envelopment analysis in road safety research

2.1. *Computing a composite indicator*

DEA is a term designating a "data oriented" approach in which mathematical programming methods are applied to handle large numbers of variables and relations; that way, it has become an attractive instrument to deal with complex problems (1). In the road safety framework, this technique has been applied for composite index investigations, e.g. (2), through the application of a minimization model (since traffic fatality indicators are undesirable outcomes intended to be minimized), as expressed in Equation 1:

$$OIS_s = \min \sum_{i=1}^{p} w_i y_{i,s} \tag{1}$$

$$subject \quad to \quad \sum_{i=1}^{p} w_i y_{i,s} \geq 1, \quad s=1,\rightleftharpoons,n \quad w_i \geq 0, \quad i=1,\rightleftharpoons,p$$

OIS_s is the optimum index score (or composite indicator − CI) of the *s-th* DMU, $y_{i,s}$ is the *i-th* indicator of the *s-th* DMU (Decision Making Unit) or state, w_i is the weight attributed to indicator y, n is the total number of DMUs and p the total number of indicators. The scores indicating the best performers will present an OIS value equal to one, and underperforming DMUs will present a score larger than one. Subsequential needs of expressing a hierarchy in the set of selected indicators motivated the development of the Multiple Layer DEA-based Composite Indicator model (ML DEA-CI) (2). By solving Equation 2, the composite indicator based on a K-layered hierarchy of p indicators can be calculated for each state s, where u_{fK} is the weight given to the *f-th* category in the *K-th* layer and $w_{fK}^{(K)}$ denotes the non negative internal weights associated with the indicators of the *f-th* category in the *K-th* layer; the sum of all $w_{fK}^{(K)}$ within a particular category is equal to one.

$$OIS_s = \max \sum_{f_K=1}^{p^{(K)}} u_{f_K} \left(\sum_{f_{K-1} \in A_K^{(K)}} w_{K-1}^{(K-1)} \left(\rightleftharpoons \sum_{f_k \in A_{k+1}^{(k+1)}} w_k^{(k)} \left(\rightleftharpoons \sum_{f_{k-1} \in A_{f_3}^{(3)}} w_2^{(2)} \left(\sum_{f_1 \in A_{f_2}^{(2)}} w_{f_1}^{(1)} y_{f_1 s} \right) \right) \right) \right) \tag{2}$$

However, the flexibility in selecting the most favorable weights for each DMU forbids the comparison on a common basis (3). To allow direct comparisons, the cross-index score (CIS) should be computed by applying Equation 3, where CIS_s is the cross-index score of the s-th DMU, $y_{i,s}$ is the *i-th* indicator of the *j-th* DMU which CIS is to be computed, w_i is the weight attributed to indicator $y_{i,s}$, n is the total number of DMUs and p the total number of indicators:

$$CIS_s = \left(1/n\right)\sum_{s=1}^{n}\sum_{i=1}^{p}\left(w_i y_{i,s}\right) \tag{3}$$

2.2. *Sensitivity analysis of DEA scores*

The obtained OIS from the DEA model might represent a very particular combination of parameters and weights that may be unlikely to be found in realistic circumstances. In this context, the general criticism relies on the deterministic nature of DEA estimators, centered on the argument that the technique does not account for uncertainties in the data (due to reporting problems) – being merely a point estimator from which no statistical inference can be derived (4,5)

The suggested procedure to tackle these vulnerabilities and to test the sensitivity of the obtained DEA scores with respect to sampling variations is to bootstrap the DEA estimators (6). The key idea of bootstrapping is to resample from the original data to create replicate datasets, which will mimic the original unknown sampling distribution; in other words, an empirical distribution is artificially constructed (7). In the flowchart of Figure 1, the steps to bootstrap the index scores are summarized.

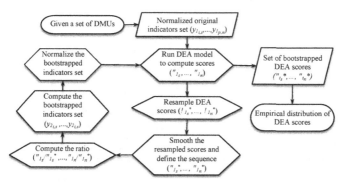

Figure 1. Flowchart containing the steps of the bootstrapping procedure.

Smoothening is the term attributed to the process of incorporating the properties of the original set of index scores into the resampled set, through the use of reflection methods (4,5), represented by the application of Equations 4 to

6, in which:

- h is the smoothing parameter defined by the number of indicators p, the number of outputs q and the number of DMUs N presenting the set of original optimum scores $(\hat{\theta}_{1s},...,\hat{\theta}_{1n})$;
- ε_i^* is a random drawn from a standard normal distribution;
- $\tilde{\theta}_i^*$ is the smoothed sampled score $(\tilde{\theta}_{1s}^*,...,\tilde{\theta}_{1n}^*)$ adjusted to be ≥ 1.0;
- $\hat{\sigma}_\theta^2$ is the plug in estimator of the variance of the original scores $(\hat{\theta}_{1s},...,\hat{\theta}_{1n})$;
- β_i^* is the average of the resampled score $(\beta_{1s}^*,...,\beta_{1n}^*)$;
- θ_i^* is the variance corrected bootstrapped score $(\theta_{1s}^*,...,\theta_{1n}^*)$.

$$h = \left[\frac{4}{(p+q+2)}\right]^{[1/(p+q+4)]} * N^{[-1/(p+q+4)]} \tag{4}$$

$$\tilde{\theta}_i^* = \begin{cases} \beta_i^* + h.\varepsilon_i^* & if \ \beta_i^* + h.\varepsilon_i^* \geq 1 \\ 2 - \beta_i^* - h.\varepsilon_i^* & otherwise \end{cases} \tag{5}$$

$$\theta_i^* = \bar{\beta}^* + \frac{(\tilde{\theta}_i^* - \bar{\beta}^*)}{\sqrt{\left(1+\frac{h^2}{\hat{\sigma}_{\hat{\theta}}^2}\right)}}, \ in \ which \ \ \hat{\sigma}_\theta^2 = \left(\frac{1}{n}\right)\sum_{i=1}^{n}\left(\hat{\theta}_i - \hat{\bar{\theta}}\right)^2 \tag{6}$$

By running the DEA model for the second time, the first loop (constituted by the steps described in the hexagonal forms) is completed and it is repeated t times until an adequate set of bootstrapped scores $\theta_{ts}^*,..., \theta_{tn}^*$ is obtained.

In order to provide more realistic comparisons among the states, the bootstrapping was conducted separately for the defined clusters. A combination of six available parameters was used for the clusters construction of the BR-27: GDP *per capita*, motorization rate, fatalities per vehicle rate, fatalities per traveled kilometer rate, highway density, and a regional parameter. Hierarchical clusters were constructed using Wards method, leading to four main clusters.

3. Application and results

The ML DEA-CI was computed with the software *Lingo* (developed by *Lindo Systems*) for a set of indicators using average values between 2009 and 2011 for the 27 Brazilian states (BR-27). The indicators were combined through a hierarchic structure, in which traffic fatalities per vehicle (FR1) and traffic fatalities per traveled kilometer (FR2) were combined into a single indicator (FR), which was combined with traffic fatalities per inhabitants (MR).

In order to avoid a unilateral weight distribution, but at the same time still preserving adequate flexibility to the model, the shares w_1*MR and w_2*FR were limited in the model definition to vary between 10 and 90% of the index value. Likewise, to control the weight distribution on FR and avoid an exaggerated weight attribution to either FR1 or FR2, the weights $w_{2,1}$ and $w_{2,2}$ were limited to vary within a 20% maximum range. The adoption of such procedure is founded on the assumption that there is no reason to attribute much more weight on any FR indicator, since they are supposed to present high association.

Following a calibration process, additional weight restrictions were inserted on the shares w_1*MR and w_2*FR, being that w_2*FR must be larger than or equal to $1.5*w_1*MR$. The intention of this intervention is to reduce the importance attributed to a somewhat biased indicator (the MR). Before running the model, the data were normalized using the distance to a reference method. The boxplot diagrams in Figure 2 offer an overview of the distribution of the computed CISs.

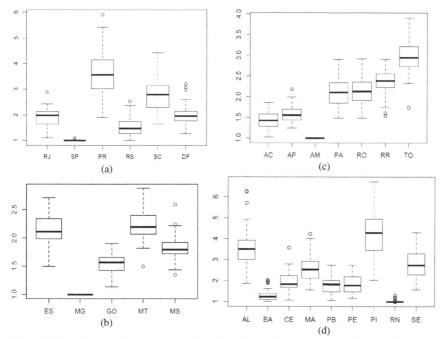

Figure 2. (a) Cluster 1 bootstrapped CISs; (b) Cluster 2 bootstrapped CISs; (c) Cluster 3 bootstrapped CISs; (d) Cluster 4 bootstrapped CISs.

The boxplot diagrams suggest SP, MG, AM and RN as good examples in their regional contexts, instead of the vague and predictable indication of SP as the only model state. On the other hand, PR, TO, MT and PI appear as the most underperforming states in their clusters. The availability of a range of scores instead of a merely point estimate provides a more clear classification and the identification of non-obvious performance differences between states from the same cluster; this is, best performing DMUs had their top position endorsed and underperforming ones had their ineptitude on controlling traffic fatalities emphasized.

4. Conclusions

This paper described a set of procedures aiming to complement and improve the application of DEA research on ranking DMUs with respect to road safety. This analysis was motivated by the absence of such model application for evaluating developing areas such as Brazil. The application of DEA techniques in association with cluster analysis and bootstrapping procedures brought singular and valuable insights for diagnosing the traffic fatality situation in a "per state" perspective. DEA research allowed the use of combined road safety indicators, which were traditionally considered individually, telling only one part of the story. Clustering is important to provide more realistic comparison; in other words, one state can better learn from another's performance if they have similar contexts. Last but not least, the bootstrapping permitted the road safety assessment with the consideration of uncertainties probably present on the indicator data for the country, manifested by the delivered values' ranges.

References

1. W. W. Cooper, L. M. Seiford LM and K. Tone. *Springer*; **21** (2000).
2. Y. Shen, E. Hermans, T. Brijs and G. Wets. *Soc Indic Res.* **114**, 739 (2013).
3. J. Doyle and R. Green. *J Oper Res Soc.* **45**, 567 (1994).
4. L. Simar and P. W. Wilson. *Core Disc. Pap.* **9543** (1998).
5. J. B. Walden. *Mar Resour Econ.* **21**, 181 (2006).
6. L. Simar and P. W. Wilson. *J Appl Stat.* **27**, 779 (2000).
7. B. Efron. *Ann Stat.* **7**, 569 (1992).

FORECASTING HIGH FREQUENCY DATA: AN ARMA-SOFT RBF NETWORK MODEL FOR TIME SERIES

DUSAN MARCEK

Research Institute of the IT4Innovations Centre of Excellence
The Silesian University Bezruc. Sq. 13
746 01 Opava, Czech Republic

In the article we alternatively develop forecasting models based on the Box-Jenkins methodology and on the neural approach based on classic and fuzzy logic radial basis function neural networks. We evaluate statistical and neuronal forecasting models for monthly platinum price time series data. In the direct comparison between statistical and neural models, the experiment shows that the neural approach clearly improve the forecast accuracy. Following fruitful applications of neural networks to predict financial data this work goes on. Both approaches are merged into one output to predict the final forecast values. The proposed novel approach deals with nonlinear estimate of various radial basis function neural networks.

1. Introduction

One of the most important managerial activities is to make the right decisions. The manager as decision-maker uses forecasting models to assist him or her in decision-making process.

Various methods have been developed and applied to forecasting problem. The econometric approach adopted from early days of econometrics is referred to as "AER" or Average Economic Regression [1, 2] and it is concerned with the functional form of the multiple regression or structural model. Economic theory might give some prior view to the relationship between the explanation variable and the independent variables. Using the time series data the model is estimated and checked for the validity.

In many cases economic theory do not give the assumption above the functional form of the model, or the assumption of independent errors and hence independent observations of the explanation variable is frequently unwarranted. If this is the case, forecasting models based on AER may be inappropriate. Box and Jenkins [3] developed a new modeling approach based on time series analysis and derived from the linear filter known as AR or ARMA (AutoRegressive Integrated Moving Average) models. The fundamental aim of time series analysis is to understand the underlying mechanism that generates the observed data and, in turn, to forecast future values of the series. Given the unknowns that affect the observed values in time series, it is natural to suppose that the generating mechanism is probabilistic and to model time series as stochastic processes.

Several new approaches to dynamic modeling in economics have become popular in recent years. One of the most attractive approaches is the neural network. The reasons to use neural networks for forecasting are many [4, 5, 6]. First, neural networks are nonparametric and nonlinear in nature. They do not require any specific assumptions about the underlying model form and are powerful and flexible in modeling real-world phenomena which have more or less nonlinearieties. Second, neural networks are universal functional approximator and they can capture any type of complex relationship. Third, neural networks are data-driven and self-adaptive. They have the capability to learn from experience. All these features of neural networks make them a very useful tool for forecasting tasks.

The paper is organized as follows. In the following section we present the data, describe basic the ARMA/ARCH-GARCH models and characterize the neural-fuzzy logic (soft) modelling approach. In the section "Results and Discussion" we put an empirical comparison. Section four briefly concludes.

2. Data and Development of Forecasting Models

In this section we present the data, introduce the development of statistical (ARCH-GARCH) forecasting models and models based of soft (fuzzy logic) RBF neural network in order to forecast the development of monthly data of platinum price time series. Both types of models will be developed with the same database. Our database is composed of 610 monthly observations of the closing platinum prices (denoted y_t (see Figure 1 left)[a].

2.1. *Construction of an Appropriate ARMA-GARCH Type model*

As we would like to develop a ARMA-GARCH time series model for one month ahead forecast of the platinum price time series, the sample period for analysis from 1960M01 to 2008M12 was defined, i.e. the period over which the forecasting model can be developed and the ex post forecast period from 2009M01to 2010M10 (denoted as validation or testing data set).

In Figure 1 left, we see that the series rises sharply with time with a rising trend, clearly signaling the non-stationary nature of the series, and indicating the need to transform the data to make it stationary. Firstly, we remove trend and then we difference the series to obtain a zero mean series. The time plot of the data after the differencing is depicted in Figure 1 right. In this figure it is seen that the mean appears steady, we assume the series has a constant mean, clearly signaling the stationary nature of the series.

---

[a] You can obtain these files from http://www.kitco.com/charts/historicalplatinum.htm

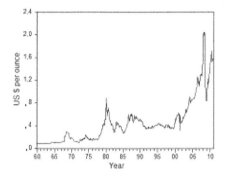 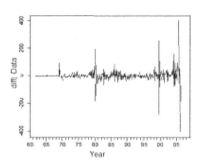

Figure 1. Time series of monthly platinum prices 1960 – 2010 (left), the time plot of the data after the differencing (right).

Input selection is crucial importance to the successful development of an ARCH-GARCH model. Potential inputs were chosen based on traditional statistical analysis: these included the raw data series of the EUR/USD exchange rates and lags thereof. The relevant lag structure of potential inputs was analysed using traditional statistical tools, i.e. using the autocorrelation function (ACF), partial autocorrelation function (PACF) and the Akaike/Bayesian information criterion (AIC/BIC). According to these criterions using the R-system software the final ARMA(1,1)+GARCH(1,1) GED model was specified and fitted in the following form

$$y_t = -2,08398 + 0,8429.y_{t-1} + \varepsilon_t - 0,5328.\varepsilon_{t-1} \qquad (1)$$

and variance equation

$$h_t = 0.104759 + 2.7901\varepsilon^2_{t-1} + 0.3912h_{t-1} \qquad (2)$$

2.2. *Neuronal Approach*

A fully connected feed forward neural network was selected to be used as the forecasting function, due to its conceptual simplicity, and computational efficiency [7]. The neural network used for this research was the network of RBF type [8]. The same data used for ARMA(1,1)+GARCH(1,1) model was also used to train the neural network, i.e. the input variables forming the right hand site of the model (1). This network is one of the most frequently used networks to capture a variety of nonlinear patterns [7]. The transfer function in the hidden layer is the radial basic function (alternatively with the cloud concept [9]), whereas for the output unit a linear transfer function was applied.

The values of centroids were used as initialization values of weight vector w between the input layer and the hidden layer. To find the weights $\mathbf{w}_j$ or centers of activation functions we used the following adaptive (learning) version of K-means clustering algorithm for s clusters:

Step 1. Randomly initialise the centres c_j of RBF neurons

$$c_j^{(t)}, j = 1,2,...,s \tag{3}$$

where s represents the number of chosen RBF neurons (clusters).

Step 2. Apply the new training vector

$$x^{(t)} = (x_1, x_2,...,x_k) \tag{4}$$

Step 3. Find the nearest centre to $x^{(t)}$ and replace its position as follows

$$c_j^{(t+1)} = c_j^{(t)} + \lambda(t) (x^{(t)} - c_j^{(t)}) \tag{5}$$

where $\lambda(t)$ is the learning coefficient and is selected as linearly decreasing function of t by $\lambda(t) = \lambda_0(t) (1 - t/N)$ where $\lambda_0(t)$ is the initial value, t is the present learning cycle and N is number of learning cycles.

Step 4. After chosen epochs number, terminate learning. Otherwise go to step 2.

The synaptic weights between the hidden layer and the output neuron were trained by the Back-Propagation algorithm.

The difference between the structures of classic and fuzzy logic (soft) RBF networks is that in fuzzy approximation the output value from the hidden layer is "normalized" [10] where the normalized output signals from hidden layer neurons signify the output signals whose sum is equal to 1.

We also combined the soft RBF neural network with the statistical ARMA(1,1) model expressed by Eq. (1), in one unified framework. The scheme of such proposed hybrid model is depicted in Figure 2. The thought of this proposal consists in economic theory of co-integrated variables which are related by an error correction model [11]. The simple mean Eq. (1) can be interpreted as the long-run relationship and thus it entails a systematic co-movement between variables y_t and y_{t-1}. If there exists a stable long-run, then error (residual) ε_t from the equation (1) should be a useful additional explanatory variable for the next direction of movement of y_t. According to [11] this mechanism is called as an error correction mechanism.

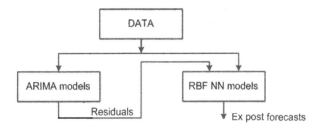

Figure 2. The scheme of proposed hybrid forecasting model (see text for details).

3. Results and Discussion

To evaluate the predictive accuracy we used the Root Mean Squared Errors (RMSE). The benchmarking was performed between latest statistical techniques and neuronal approach used in high frequency financial data. Table 1 presents the accuracy results of 4 prediction methods. As can be also seen from Table 1, all models are very good and they follow the pattern of the actual very closely.

Table 1: Statistical summary measures of model´s ex post forecast accuracy for ARMA(1,1,1) +PGARCH(1,1) model and RBF nets.

Model	RMSE
ARMA(1,1)+GARH(1,1) GED	72.155
RBF NN (classic)	76.206
RBF NN (soft)	67.974
RBF NN (hybrid)	33.601

4. Conclusion

In this paper, we established a statistical model based on Box-Jenkins methodology and as an alternative to that model three models based on Radial Basic Function network (classic, soft and hybrid RBF NN). We showed that the RBF hybrid neural network model outperforms latest statistical models based on ARMA + GARCH approaches. Moreover, RBF networks have such attributes as computational efficiency, simplicity, and ease adjusting to changes in the process being forecast. Thus, neural networks are usually used in the complicated problems of prediction because they minimize the analysis and modeling stages and the resolution time. These models can help managers make better decision-making.

Acknowledgments

This paper has been elaborated in the framework of the IT4Innovations Centre of Excellence project, reg. no. CZ.1.05/1.1.00/02.0070 supported by Operational

Programme 'Research and Development for Innovations' funded by Structural Funds of the European Union and state budget of the Czech Republic.

References

1. P. Kennedy, A Guide to Econometrics. Oxford, Basil, Blackwell (1992).
2. K. Holden, Developments in Dynamic Modelling in Economics. Proceedings of the Mathematical Methods in Economics. International Scientific Conference. VŠB TU Ostrava (1997).
3. G.E.P. Box, and Jenkins, G.M., Time Series Analysis, Forecasting and Control. San Francisco, CA: Holden-Day, (1976).
4. White, H., Consequences and detection of misspecified nonlinear regression models. Artificial Neural Networks: Approximation and Learning Theory, Oxford: UK Blackwell, pp. 224-258 (1992).
5. White, H., Connectionist nonparametric regression: Multilayer feed-forward networks can learn arbitrary mappings. Artificial Neural Networks: Approximation and Learning Theory, Oxford: UK Blackwell, pp. 160-190 (1992).
6. White, H, & Gallant, A.R., Artificial Neural Networks: Approximations and Learning Theory. In There exists a neural network that does not make avoidable mistakes, UK: Blackwell: Oxford, pp. 5-11 (1992).
7. D. Marcek, M. Marcek, Neural Networks and Their Applications, EDIS – ZU, Zilina, (2006).
8. M.J.L. Orr, Introduction to Radial Basis Function Networks, University of Edinburgh, (1996).
9. D. Li, Y. Du, "Artificial intelligence with uncertainty," *Chapman & Hall / CRC, Taylor&Francis Group, Boca Raton* (2008).
10. V. Kecman, Learning and soft computing: support vector machines, neural networks, and fuzzy logic, Massachusetts: The MIT Press (2001).
11. R.F. Engle, C.W. Granger: Cointegration and error correction representation, estimation and testing. Econometrica, 55, pp. 251-276 (1987).

FEATURE SELECTION FOR IMBALANCED DATASETS BASED ON IMPROVED GENETIC ALGORITHM*

LIMIN DU[1,2], YANG XU[1], LIUQIAN JIN[1]

1. Intelligent Control Center, Southwest Jiaotong University, Chengdu 610031, China

2. Pharmacy College of Henan University, Henan Kaifeng 475004, China

This paper presents a feature selection method based on genetic algorithm for unbalanced data. This method improves the fitness function through using the evaluation criterion G-mean for unbalanced data instead of total classification accuracy in order to improve the recognition rate of the minor class. Experimental results on several UCI datasets show that the performance of the proposed method outperforms classic genetic algorithm. It not only reduces the feature dimension effectively, but also improves the precision of the minor class.

1. Introduction

The class imbalance problem refers to the issue that occurs when a data set is dominated by a major class or classes which have more instances than the other rare/small classes in the data. Imbalanced datasets widely exist in real life, such as gene detection, text classification and fault diagnosis [1]. At present there are three kinds of methods to deal with the problem of unbalanced data: re-sampling [2, 3], improvement of classical classification algorithms [4, 5], feature selection [6].

Genetic algorithm is a random search algorithm, using the reference of natural selection and genetic mechanism in living nature. A number of feature selection methods based on genetic algorithm have been proposed [7-11]. But most of them did not consider the imbalance of data categories.

In this paper, a new feature selection method for imbalanced data sets based on genetic algorithm has been proposed through improving fitness function.

This work is supported by National Science Foundation of China (Grant No. 61175055), Sichuan Key Technology Research and Development Program (Grant No. 2011FZ0051), Radio Administration Bureau of MIIT of China (Grant No. [2011] 146), China Institution of Communications (Grant No. [2011] 051).

Email: dulimin@henu.edu.cn, xuyang@home.swjtu.edu.cn, jinliuqian@163.com.

This paper is organized as follows: Section 2 introduces feature selection based on improved genetic algorithm; Section 3 presents the experimental results; Last section is the conclusions.

2. Feature selection based on improved genetic algorithm

Genetic algorithm is a kind of adaptive search algorithm global optimization, which is formed in the proceeding of simulating the genetic and evolution of bios in environment. This algorithm is described from the coding scheme, the design of fitness function and the algorithm scheme respectively.

2.1 The coding scheme

In this paper, classical binary coding method is used, which is simple and very effective. The length of the individual is the number of candidate features for any data set. For example, suppose a data set S has n features. A feature combination can be represented using a n bit string of 0 or 1, where 0 denotes that the corresponding feature has not been selected, on the other hand, 1 denotes that the corresponding feature has been selected.

2.2 The design of fitness function

Some classifier model is adopted to evaluate the chosen feature subset in many feature selection methods based on genetic algorithm and the fitness function is equal to the total classification accuracy. It is not suitable for the unbalanced data sets. High total classification accuracy rate is caused by the classification accuracy of the major class, while the accuracy of the small class is not necessarily high. In order to enhance the accuracy of the small class, it is necessary to select the features which are beneficial to identify the small class.

Table 1 shows the mixed matrix of a two-class data set. The minority class and the majority class are labeled as positive and negative respectively (see Table 1).TP and TN are samples' amount of minority class and majority class respectively under the condition of right classification of classes. FN and FP are samples' amount of minority class and majority class respectively under the condition of wrong classification of classes.

Table 1 The mixed matrix of two classes data set

	Classified Positive	Classified Negative
Positive	TP	FN
Negative	FP	TN

The related concepts of Accuracy and G-mean [12] are introduced as follows:

(1) Accuracy

$$Accuracy = (TP+TN)/(TP+TN+FP+FN)$$ (1)

Accuracy is the common evaluation standard of classification methods, but the classification result of unbalanced data set can't be evaluated reasonably. This is because the samples of majority class are much more than the samples of minority class, if we classify all samples as majority class, the accuracy is still very high, but the recognition rate of minority class is zero.

(2) G-mean [12]

$$G-mean = \sqrt{\frac{TP}{TP+FN} \times \frac{TN}{TN+FP}}$$ (2)

G-mean is the common evaluation standard of unbalanced data set study, it is the square root of the product of minority class's accuracy TP/(TP+FN) and majority class's accuracy TN/(TN+TP),when the value of both are big, G-mean can be big. So, G-mean can reasonably evaluate the total classification performance of unbalanced data set.

So we define the fitness function of genetic algorithm for unbalanced data sets as the following formula (3):

$$f(x) = \alpha \cdot G\text{-}Mean + \beta \cdot \left(-\frac{|X|}{n} \right)$$ (3)

Parameters α, β are used to control the number of features and G-mean, $|X|$ denotes the number of features in the feature subset and n denotes the number of all the features. Uses can set parameters α, β according to different problems and needs, if you hope higher classification accuracy, increase the value of α, or decrease the value of α; if you want bigger dimension reduction, increase the value of β, or reduce the value of β.

2.3 The algorithm scheme

Simple algorithm is described as follows:

(1) Determine the encoding scheme and code;

(2) Initialize the population;

(3) Design the fitness function;

(4) Evaluate the fitness of the individual;

(5) Do genetic operations including selection, crossover and mutation if it does not meet the terminal condition;

(6) Repeat steps (4),(5) until the terminal condition is met.

3. Experiments

In order to verify the validity of the proposed method, we select five unbalanced data sets for testing from the UCI machine learning database [13]. Specific parameters of each data set are shown in Table 2. Features (F) denotes the number of characteristics, Sizes(S) denotes the size of the data set, Min and Max denotes the number of samples in the small class and the number of samples in the large category respectively, Target (T) is the class label of the minority , Ratio (R) denotes the Ratio of the majority class and the minority class.

Table 2 Summary of data sets

Data set	F	S	Min/Max	T	R
Tic-tac-toe	9	958	332/626	Negative	1.89
Pima	8	768	268/500	1	1.87
Ionosphere	34	351	126/225	Bad	1.79
Breast	30	569	212/357	malignant	1.68
Sonar	60	208	97/111	R	1.14

On trail every data set is divided into two parts: training set and testing set the proportion of which is about 4:1, $\alpha = 0.8$, $\beta = 0.2$. Making use of MATLAB language, the paper compiles the genetic algorithm program. Population size is 50, crossover probability is 0.9, mutation probability is 0.05 and termination condition is that fitness function changes little in the recent 10 iterations in this paper. At the same time this paper regards linear SVM in Matlab2012 toolbox as classifier.

In order to prevent the code of the best individual form changing or missing in the process of genetic operation such as crossover and mutation, elite reserved strategy is used.

The experimental results which are means of five tests are shown in table 3 and table 4, where GA denotes that the fitness function of the method is shown as formula (4) and IGA is the method of this paper.

$$f(x) = \alpha \cdot Accuracy + \beta \cdot \left(-\frac{|X|}{n} \right) \tag{4}$$

Where parameters $\alpha, \beta, |X|, n$ are the same as those of formula (3).

Table 3 Number of features selected by different algorithms on data sets

Data set	Full	GA	IGA
Tic-tac-toe	9	5	5
Pima	8	7	4
Ionosphere	34	19	16
Breast	30	17	5
Sonar	60	31	23
Average	28.2	15.8	10.6
Average dimensionality reduction		43.97%	62.41%

Table 4 Minority accuracy of SVM

Data set	GA	IGA
Tic-tac-toe	0.500	0.644
Pima	0.710	0.766
Ionosphere	0.860	0.860
Breast	0.988	1.00
Sonar	0.868	0.947
Average	0.785	0.843

Table 3 shows that average dimensionality reduction of IGA is 62.41%, but average dimensionality reduction of GA is only 43.97%, that is to say, the improved method is better in terms of feature reduction. From Table 4 we can see that the improved method can increase the small class of recognition rate effectively.

4. Conclusions

Aiming at the imbalance data, a feature selection method based on genetic algorithm is proposed through improving the fitness function. Experimental results on five UCI datasets show that the performance of the proposed method outperforms classic genetic algorithm. It not only reduces the feature dimension effectively, but also improves the precision of the minor class on SVM classifier.

Further research is required for discussing the influence of different classifier for the feature selection method.

References

[1] Provost F, Fawcett T. Robust classification for imprecise environments [J]. Machine Learning, 42(3)(2001)203-231.

[2] N. Chawla, K. Bowyer, L. Hall, P. Kegelmeyer, SMOTE: Synthetic Minority Over-sampling Technique, Journal of Artificial Intelligence Research 16 (2002) 321–357.

[3] M. Galar, A. Fernandez, E. Barrenechea, H. Bustince, F. Herrera, A review on ensembles for the class imbalance problem: bagging-, boosting-, and hybrid-based approaches, IEEE Transactions on Systems, Man, and Cybernetics, Part C: Applications and Reviews 99 (2011) 1-22.

[4] L.M. Manevitz, M. Yousef, One-class SVMs for document classification, Journal of Machine Learning Research 2 (2001) 139–154.

[5] H.J. Lee, S. Cho, The novelty detection approach for difference degrees of class imbalance, Lecture Notes in Computer Science 4233 (2006) 21–30.

[6] M. Wasikowski, X. Chen, Combating the small sample class imbalance problem using feature selection, IEEE Transactions on Knowledge and Data Engineering (2009).

[7] Frohlich H, Chapelle O. Feature selection for support vector machines by means of genetic algorithms [C]// Proceedings of the 15th IEEE International Conference on Tools with Artificial Intelligence, Sacramento, CA, USA, (2003)142-148.

[8] Huang Cheng-lung, Wang Chieh-jen. A GA-based feature selection and parameters optimization for support vector machines [J]. Expert Systems with Applications, 31(2006)231-240.

[9] Liu Yuan-ning, Wang Gang, Zhu Xiao-dong etc. Feature selection based on adaptive multi-population genetic algorithm [J]. Journal of Jilin University (Engineering and Technology Edition), 41(6) (2011)1690-1693.

[10] Xuan Zhou, Zheng Pei, Penghui Liu, Sen Zhao and Qiang Li. A new method for feature selection of radio abnormal signal [J].ICIC Express Letters,7(2)(2013)303-309.

[11] JI Zhi-wei, WU Geng-feng, HU Min. Feature Selection Based on Adaptive Genetic Algorithm and SVM [J]. Computer Engineering, 35(14) (2011)200-202.

[12] Lin Zhi-yong, Hao Zhi-feng, Yang Xiao-wei. Effects of Several Evaluation Metrics on Imbalanced Data Learning [J]. Journal of South China University of Technology (Natural Science Edition), 38(4)(2010)147-155.

[13] ASUNCION A, NEWMAN D. UCI repository of machine learning databases [DB/OL]. [2009-04-03]. http: //www. Ics. u ci. edu / ~ mlearn /MLRep-ository. Html.

INFOGRAPHY USAGE IN A SYSTEMATIC MAPPING ABOUT ONLINE SOCIAL NETWORKS ANALYSIS

JARBELE C. DA SILVA, AYSLÂNYA J. WANDERLEY, ED PORTO BEZERRA, ALISSON V. BRITO, ALEXANDRE N. DUARTE

*Informatic Center, Federal University of Paraíba University City,
João Pessoa, Paraíba 58051-900, Brazil*

GIOVANNA ABREU

*College of Communication, Federal University of Paraíba, University City,
João Pessoa, Paraíba 58051-900, Brazil*

The resources and possibilities to reproduce objective information through infography methods are numberless. This article presents interactive infography contributions to represent data as a result of a systematic mapping in the area of online social networks analysis. We tried to evidence how interactive infography resources can synthetize complex information in a simple visual representation.

1. Introduction

To convey a data set in an objective, simple visual information is not an easy task. The increase in demand for resources and strategies to visually simplify the comprehension of a complex data set has been the object of many corporative and academic studies – this specific area of study is best kwon as infography. According to [2] infography is defined as the information's visual engineering. It is not about art but a (cognitive) tool to answer questions.

Systematic mapping is also defined in [8] as a way of taking stock of the researches available in any given area helping us to identify where we have good knowledge, where we need to be cautious, consider commissioning empirical research or reviews.

Gathering all this concepts together, we carried out a systematic mapping about online social networks analysis trying to reach the goal of identifying possible research topics in this field. So, this article intends to introduce some infography contributions to an effective data representation, as a result of this systematic mapping executed.

2. Systematic mapping about online social networks analysis

It is widely known bibliographic research is an important step in the scientific production process. When it comes to the field of online social networks analysis, visualizing and having access to the academic papers could be a pretty hard task, though.

Intending to make this process easier, we proposed to run a systematic mapping about online social networks analysis. Among several methods that systematize the work of searching for data and presenting results, the Systematic Literature Mapping was the one chosen.

To emphasize the choice, according to [6], through a proper systematic literature mapping becomes more likely to identify if an specific field has enough primary studies to make a systematic literature revision possible or if there is any unexplored subtheme in the area.

However, as stated by [7], a systematic literature mapping must include four essential steps. In the first part, all the research questions to be addressed are specified. Then, the primary studies that meet the pre-established requirements are listed. In the third stage, inclusion and exclusion criteria are used to select the set of primary studies that address the research questions. In the last part, a map of the study area is constructed, following the selected categories to classify the studies that were found.

2.1. Systematic Mapping Planning

In the first stage, five questions were defined: i) Which research topics are explored?; ii) Which are the types of publications (conferences, congresses and/or magazines) that have more posts?; iii) Which are the main researchers institutions?; iv) How the evolution of scientific research has been distributed over the years?; v) Where are the researchers who are dedicated to the study of social network analysis?

2.2. Conduction of the Search

The selection of the primary sources occurred by using the search string "Social Network Analysis" AND online, in five different research sources: ACM Digital Library(http://www.acm.org/), Elsevier Scopus (*www.elsevier.com/online-tools/scopus*), IEEExplorer Digital Library (www.ieee.org.br/), Springer Link (*link.springer.com/*) and Science Direct (*www.sciencedirect.com/*).

All those sources were selected according to the availability of the web query, the presence of search engines through keywords, and theirs relevance in the realm of science.

2.3. Selection of the Primary Studies

Criteria for inclusion and exclusion of the studies were established. To include a paper in this research, its relevance to the research questions was determined, considering mainly the assessments of the title, keywords and abstract, but following some conditions: (i) works that, according to the search string, have been found in the five search sources previously determined; (ii) works that were published in conferences, journals, magazines and newspapers in the specific area of social network analysis; (iii) works that are available for access through their own university online library service.

Once applied the inclusion criteria, we started the exclusion step also considering mainly the assessments of the title, keywords, and abstract and following some specific conditions. Thus, papers must be excluded: (i) irrelevant content in relation to the researched areas; (ii) repeated work in more than one source of search; (iii) with content, text or incomplete results; (iv) not written in English; (v) other than primary studies. It is also important to notice that the application of at least one criterion for inclusion or exclusion determined whether the article should be included or excluded, respectively. Table 1 is a succinct representation regarding the evolution of the selection process of the primary studies.

Table 1. The evolution of the selection process of the primary studies

Search Tools	Searching result	1ª Seleccion Excluded				2ª Seleccion Excluded	3ª Seleccion Excluded	FINAL Included
		Irrelevant	Repeated	Incomplete	Not written in english	Irrelevant, Incomplete	Taxonomy	Primary studies
Springer Link	1742	988	52	11	158	454	45	31
Science Direct da Elsevier	1506	832	15	91	70	418	8	74
ACM Digital Library	1254	570	16	76	33	393	17	146
Scopus	1242	348	535	-	20	240	76	23
IEEE Xplore	606	183	6	-	5	238	9	169
Partial Result	6350	2921	624	178	286	1743	155	443
TOTAL	6350	4009				1743	155	443

2.4. *Analysis, Classification and Map Building*

Once the stage of the selection of the primary studies was completed, we performed the analysis and classification of the articles according to the taxonomy proposed by [3], which categorizes the *Social Network Analysis* articles according to the topic addressed by each paper.

3. Generated interactive infographics

Based on the research questions laid out in section 1.1 of this study, interactive infographics that sought to meet the needs of the obtained data in the systematic literature mapping were generated. According to Rodrigues [9], the main characteristics of this specific kind of infographic are interactivity, content personalization and continual updating. The main infographics produced are just represented here.

3.1. *Interactive infographic of the distribution of the researchers*

This interactive infographic (Figure 1) informs the distribution of the online social networks analysis researchers in the world, in a specific year.

By clicking on each country's bubble, another infographic is generated containing a list of institutions, in this country, that have been researching about online social networks analysis, and the number of researchers that each institution contains. In this static version is only possible to visualize the distribution of researchers in a general context.

Figure 1. Infographic of the distribution of the researchers (Available in: http://mappingstudy.wix.com/ mappingstudysna#!distribuicao-dos-pesquisadores/c1p14.)

3.2. *Interactive Infographic of the Publications' Taxonomy*

In this section, the generated infographic (Figure 2) shows the categories under which the publications are classified.

The static display allows only identify the most studied subareas of the published works, which are represented by larger bubbles. On the other hand, the interactive version enables to see, in detail, the number of publications on a particular sub-area of the taxonomy, just by clicking on the desired bubble.

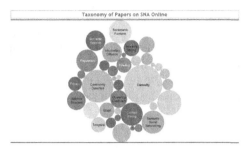

Figure 2. Categorization Taxonomy of Publications (Available in: http://mappingstudy.wix.com/ mappingstudysna#!taxonomia-dos-artigos/cz8)

It is worth saying that in the web (Available in: http://mappingstudy.wix.com/ mappingstudysna#!home/mainPage/) addresses all others infographics generated in this study can be found. There are interactive infographics related to the representation of the information on the annually produced publications, interactive infographics related to the main vehicles of publication and related to the major research institutions in this study area.

4. The Infography contributions to data representation

In a study about well successful projects through the use of data visualization, Kirk [5] emphasizes that the use of clear information such as titles, tutorials, display options (labels), captions and dates are indispensable to project an interactive infographic features. Barbosa et al [1] reported that data representation through interactive infographics assists in the dissemination of scientific data since they are presented in a more dynamic and attractive way, which allows readers to immerse themselves in the content. Isenberg [4] complements the discussion stating that interactivity applied to visualization of scientific data provides various options to data presentation, making the process of active scientific exploration possible.

5. Final considerations

Infographics have been around for many years and recently the proliferation of a number of easy-to-use, free tools have made the creation of infographics available to a large segment of the population. Likewise, the advance of the technology resources has also enabled a new approach to data visualization: the interactive infographics, which facilitates even more the process of analysis.

This study aimed to use the techniques of the interactive infography to represent, in a clear and intuitive way, the results obtained from a systematic literature mapping set in the area of online social networks analysis. We observed that the interaction capabilities applied to infographics allow the user to filter the information he wants according to his own needs, enabling the visualization of details and nuances that could hardly be viewed in static graphs. We concluded that infographics have an essential role in the representation of scientific data, without which the second stage of our article would not be feasible. We intend, therefore, as future work, perform the validation of the generated infographics starting from a comparative study between those generated interactive infographics and those static representation of the data set analyzed.

References

1. G. S. Barbosa, E. C. U. Ribeiro and B. D. Moreira. *Ciência sedutora*: A infografia a serviço da divulgação científica. In: XV Congresso de Comunicação na Região Centro Oeste, 2013, Rio Verde – Go.
2. A. Cairo. *The Functional Art*: an introduction to information graphics and visualization. New Riders, 2013.
3. C. Chelmis, V. K. Prasanna, *Social networking analysis: A state of the art and the effect of semantics*. In: Proceedings of the IEEE Third International Conference on Social Computing (SocialCom), October 2011.
4. T. Isenberg, *Position Paper*: Touch Interaction in Scientific Visualization, Proc. Workshop Data Exploration on Interactive Surfaces (Dexis 11), research report RR-0421, INRIA, May 2012, pp. 24–27.
5. A. Kirk,. *Data Visualization: A Successful Design Process*. Packt Publication, p. 71-116, December 2012.
6. B. Kitchenham, D. Budgen and P. Brereton, *Using mapping studies as the basis for further research—a participant-observer case study*. Inform Softw Technol 53(6):638–651. 2011.
7. E. Y. Nakagawa, D. Feitosa and K. R. Felizardo, *Using Systematic Mapping to Explore Software Architecture Knowledge*. SHARK'10 May 2, 2010, Cape Town, South Africa, pages 29-36, 2010.
8. K. Petersen, et al. *Systematic Mapping Studies in Software Engineering*. In: 12th International Conference on Evaluation and Assessment in Software Engineering, Australia. 2008.
9. A. A. Rodrigues, *A Copa do Mundo em infográfico*: uma discussão sobre interatividade e do uso de base de dados na cobertura on line. In: Encontro Nacional de Pesquisadores em jornalismo (SBPJOR), 2010.

ON INTERVAL FUZZY BAYESIAN GAMES:
PRELIMINARY RESULTS

T. C. ASMUS* and B. R. C. BEDREGAL**

DIMAP, Universidade Federal do Rio Grande do Norte,
Natal, Rio Grande do Norte, Brazil
*E-mail: tiagoasmus@gmail.com, **E-mail: brcbedregal@gmail.com

G. P. DIMURO

PPGMC, PPGCOMP, Universidade Federal do Rio Grande,
Rio Grande, Rio Grande do Sul, Brazil, E-mail: gracaliz@gmail.com

This paper introduces preliminary concepts on interval fuzzy Bayesian games, based on interval-valued fuzzy probabilities for modeling of types of agents involved in the interaction. The interval-valued fuzzy probabilities are given by symmetric triangular interval fuzzy numbers, inspired by Buckley and Eslami, who considered an arithmetic restriction on the interval $[0, 1]$ in their representation of uncertain probabilities by fuzzy numbers.

Keywords: Interval fuzzy Bayesian games, interval-valued fuzzy probabilities

1. Introduction

Game theory is an important basis to simulate several situations where multiple agents (also called players) interact strategically for decision making. In many applications, such as auctions in general, the agents involved in the interaction only know their own types, and must make decisions while having to estimate the characteristics of the other participants of the interaction. This kind of strategic interaction constitutes a Bayesian game.[1] However, there are cases in which it is very difficult to characterize the private information of each agent (e.g., ability, level of effort).[2] In these situations, the payoffs are given as approximate (not probabilistic) values, and the concept of Bayesian Nash equilibrium can not be applied in this context. Fuzzy[3] (interval fuzzy[4]) set theory is an excellent basis for studying this type of game in which the payoffs are represented by (interval) fuzzy numbers[5] that can be modeled in different ways.

In this paper, we introduce the preliminary concepts on Interval Fuzzy Bayesian Games, in which interval-valued fuzzy probabilities of the types of the agents involved in the interaction are given by symmetric triangular interval fuzzy numbers, inspired on work by Buckley and Eslami[6] on fuzzy probabilities.

2. Preliminary Concepts

We consider symmetrical triangular fuzzy numbers $\bar{F}$, denoted by $\bar{F} = (a/u/b)$, where u denotes the core and the α-cuts are given by $\bar{F}[\alpha] = [(u - a)\alpha + a, (u - b)\alpha + b]$. The interval fuzzy numbers can be represented by pairs of fuzzy numbers as $\hat{F} = (\bar{F}_i, \bar{F}_s)$ in which $\bar{F}_i$ and $\bar{F}_s$ define, respectively, the lower and upper fuzzy numbers[5] of $\hat{F}$, called $\hat{F}$'s generator fuzzy numbers. The $[\alpha_1, \alpha_2]$-cuts of $\hat{F}$ can be given by $\hat{F}[\alpha_1, \alpha_2] = \bar{F}_i[\alpha_1] \cap \bar{F}_s[\alpha_2]$. For the ordering of interval fuzzy numbers, we consider the Interval AD-Order.[7]

The definition of interval fuzzy probabilities is inspired by Buckley and Eslami,[6] based on an arithmetic restriction. Let $X = \{x_1, \dots, x_n\}$ be a finite set and $P : \wp(X) \to [0, 1]$ a probability function defined for all subsets of X, with $P(\{x_j\}) = \phi_j, 1 \le j \le n, 0 \le \phi_j \le 1$ and $\sum_{i=1}^{n} \phi_j = 1$, characterizing a discrete and finite probability distribution, denoted by $\Phi = \{\phi_1, \dots, \phi_n\}$. Consider that some of these ϕ_j represent imprecise values, in a way that even its fuzzy modeling is not trivial. Thus, we utilize interval fuzzy numbers substituting each and every ϕ_j for $\hat{\phi}_j$, constituting a new set $\hat{\Phi}$, even if just some of the $\hat{\Phi}$ are imprecise. This leads to an interval fuzzy probability function $\hat{P}$, in a way that the elements of $\hat{\Phi}$ will be represented by symmetric triangular interval fuzzy number as $\hat{P}(x_1) = \hat{\phi}_j = (\bar{\phi}_{j_i}, \bar{\phi}_{j_s})$, for $1 \le j \le n$, in which $\bar{\phi}_{j_i}$ represents the fuzzy modeling with the least imprecision, and $\bar{\phi}_{j_s}$ represents the fuzzy modeling with the greater imprecision, according to the expert opinion.

For $0 \le \alpha_1 \le \alpha_2 \le 1$, choose, from each $[\alpha_1, \alpha_2]$-cut $\hat{\phi}_j[\alpha_1, \alpha_2]$, an e_j such that $\sum_{j=1}^{n} e_j = 1$. Consider the sets $E = \left\{ (e_j, \dots, e_n) \in [0, 1]^n \mid \sum_{j=1}^{n} e_j = 1 \right\}$ of stochastic vectors and $\mathcal{A}_{\hat{\Phi}}^{\alpha_1, \alpha_2} = \mathcal{A}_{\hat{\Phi}}^{\alpha_1, \alpha_2} = \hat{\phi}_1[\alpha_1, \alpha_2] \times \dots \times \hat{\phi}_n[\alpha_1, \alpha_2]$ of the cartesian product of the $[\alpha_1, \alpha_2]$-cuts of the elements of $\hat{\Phi}$. Define $\mathcal{S}_{\hat{\Phi}}^{\alpha_1, \alpha_2} = \mathcal{A}_{\hat{\Phi}}^{\alpha_1, \alpha_2} \cap E$ and consider the set $J_A^X = \{j \in \{1, \dots, n\} \mid x_j \in A\}$ of indexes of $A \subseteq X$. The function that characterizes the arithmetic restriction is defined by $f_{\hat{\Phi}, [\alpha_1, \alpha_2]}^{A} : \mathcal{S}_{\hat{\Phi}}^{\alpha_1, \alpha_2} \to [0, 1]$, with $f_{\hat{\Phi}, [\alpha_1, \alpha_2]}^{A}(e_1, \dots, e_n) = \sum_{j \in J_A} e_j$.

The fuzzy probability of a subset $A \subseteq X$ is defined through its $[\alpha_1, \alpha_2]$-cuts by $\hat{P}(A)[\alpha_1, \alpha_2] = \left\{ f_{\hat{\Phi}, [\alpha_1, \alpha_2]}^{A}(e) \mid e = (e_1, \dots, e_n) \in \mathcal{S}_{\hat{\Phi}}^{\alpha_1, \alpha_2} \right\}$. The interval fuzzy probability $\hat{P}(A)$ may be obtained through its fuzzy generator probabilities $\bar{P}(A)_i$ and $\bar{P}(A)_s$ as $\hat{P}(A)[\alpha_1, \alpha_2] = \bar{P}(A)_i[\alpha_1] \cap \bar{P}(A)_s[\alpha_2]$, for $0 \le \alpha_1 \le \alpha_2 \le 1$.

Define the function $q_{\hat{\Phi}, [\alpha_1, \alpha_2]}^{r} : \mathcal{S}_{\hat{\Phi}}^{\alpha_1, \alpha_2} \to \mathbb{R}$, by $q_{\hat{\Phi}, [\alpha_1, \alpha_2]}^{r}(e_1, \dots, e_n) = \sum_{j=1}^{n} e_j \cdot r_j$, in which $0 \le \alpha_1 \le \alpha_2 \le 1$. The interval fuzzy mean $\hat{\mu}_{\hat{\Phi}}^{r}$, weighting the interval fuzzy probabilities in $\hat{\Phi}$ by real values in $r = (r_1, \ldots, r_n) \in \mathbb{R}^n$ is defined through its $[\alpha_1, \alpha_2]$-cuts, for $0 \leq \alpha_1 \leq \alpha_2 \leq 1$, by:

$$\hat{\mu}_{\hat{\Phi}}^r[\alpha_1, \alpha_2] = \left\{ q_{\hat{\Phi}, [\alpha_1, \alpha_2]}^r(e) \mid e = (e_1, \ldots, e_n) \in \mathcal{S}_{\hat{\Phi}}^{\alpha_1, \alpha_2} \right\}. \tag{1}$$

3. Bayesian Game with Two Players

A simultaneous game in which one or more players are unaware of the type of some other player or even his own type defines a game of *incomplete information*, or *Bayesian game* (BG). Let $L = \{1, \ldots, l\}$ and $M = \{1, \ldots, m\}$ be finite sets of possible types that players $J_\mathbf{A}$ and $J_\mathbf{B}$ can assume, respectively. The players $J_\mathbf{A}$ and $J_\mathbf{B}$ of the specific types $t \in L$ and $t' \in M$, respectively, are denoted by $J_\mathbf{A}^t$ and $J_\mathbf{B}^{t'}$. $J_\mathbf{A}^L$ and $J_\mathbf{B}^M$ are the players $J_\mathbf{A}$ and $J_\mathbf{B}$ whose types vary in L and M, respectively. The players $J_\mathbf{A}^t$ and $J_\mathbf{B}^{t'}$ can choose strategies from the sets $\mathbf{A} = \{A_1, \ldots, A_n\}$ and $\mathbf{B} = \{B_1, \ldots, B_{n'}\}$, respectively. The payoffs depend on the types assumed by $J_\mathbf{A}^L$ and $J_\mathbf{B}^M$, and are determined by payoff functions $h_\mathbf{A}^{tt'} : \mathbf{A} \times \mathbf{B} \to \mathbb{R}$ and $h_\mathbf{B}^{tt'} : \mathbf{A} \times \mathbf{B} \to \mathbb{R}$, for each combination of types $t \in L$, $t' \in M$.

We build a game for each combination of types in L and M, obtaining an $L \times M$ game matrix $G_\mathbf{AB}^{LM} = \left[R_\mathbf{AB}^{tt'} \right]_{t \in L, t' \in M}$, where each entry $R_\mathbf{AB}^{tt'}$, with $t \in L$, $t' \in M$ and $t' \in M$, denotes the payoff matrix of the game between the players $J_\mathbf{A}^t$ and $J_\mathbf{B}^{t'}$. We have that $R_\mathbf{AB}^{tt'} = \left[(h_\mathbf{A}^{tt'}(A_i, B_j), h_\mathbf{B}^{tt'}(A_i, B_j)) \right]_{A_i \in \mathbf{A}, B_j \in \mathbf{B}}$.

Let P and P' be known probabilities functions, with $P(\{t\}) = \phi_t$, $t \in L$, and $P'(\{t'\}) = \phi_{t'}'$, $t' \in M$. Thus, $\Phi = \{\phi_1, \ldots, \phi_l\}$ and $\Phi' = \{\phi_1', \ldots, \phi_m'\}$ are the sought probability distributions. We use these probabilities to build a single probabilistic game from a matrix of deterministic games ($G_\mathbf{AB}^{LM}$). In this game matrix, each cell is a combination of strategies chosen by each players $J_\mathbf{A}^t$ and $J_\mathbf{B}^{t'}$, whose payoff value is given by combining the probabilities ϕ_t and $\phi_{t'}$ assigned to each type with the values of the payoffs contained in the respective matrix $R_\mathbf{AB}^{tt'}$. The payoffs of the BG are obtained through the functions $h_\mathbf{A}^L : \mathbf{A}^l \times \mathbf{B}^m \to \mathbb{R}$ and $h_\mathbf{B}^M : \mathbf{A}^l \times \mathbf{B}^m \to \mathbb{R}$, defined by: $h_\mathbf{A}^L(A^*, B^*) = \sum_{t=1}^l \sum_{t'=1}^m \phi_t \cdot \phi_{t'}' \cdot h_\mathbf{A}^{tt'}(A^t, B^{t'})$ and $h_\mathbf{B}^M(A^*, B^*) = \sum_{t'=1}^m \sum_{t=1}^l \phi_t \cdot \phi_{t'}' \cdot h_\mathbf{B}^{tt'}(A^t, B^{t'})$, in which $A^* = (A^1, \ldots, A^l)$ and $B^* = (B^1, \ldots, B^m)$ represent vectors that have in each position one of the actions of the players $J_\mathbf{A}^L$ and $J_\mathbf{B}^M$, respectively, so that $A^1, \ldots, A^l \in \mathbf{A} = \{A_1, \ldots, A_n\}$ and $B^1, \ldots, B^m \in \mathbf{B} = \{B_1, \ldots, B_{n'}\}$.

We obtain a matrix $Z_\mathbf{AB}$ with order $\{n^l\} \times \{n'^m\}$ which covers all the combinations of strategies and types of each player. With the probability matrix, one may investigate the existence of equilibria as in a regular simultaneous game.

4. Interval Fuzzy Bayesian Game with Two Players

The formulation of interval fuzzy BG is similar to fuzzy BG presented by Asmus and Dimuro.[8] Consider that the crisp version of the BG was already developed for 2 players, J_A^L and J_B^M, and the game matrix $G_{AB}^{LM} = \left[R_{AB}^{tt'} \right]_{t \in L, t' \in M}$ is known. Assume that the interval fuzzy probabilities distributions $\hat{\Phi}$ and $\hat{\Phi}'$ are also known. Let $A^* = (A^1, \ldots, A^l)$ and $B^* = (B^1, \ldots, B^m)$ be the vectors containing combinations of strategies chosen by each player J_A^t and $J_B^{t'}$, respectively. The set $H_{A^*B^*}^A = \{(h_A^{11}(A^1, B^1), \ldots, h_A^{1m}(A^1, B^m)), \ldots, (h_A^{l1}(A^l, B^1), \ldots, h_A^{lm}(A^l, B^m))\}$ contains the vectors whose coordinates constitute the payoffs of a player J_A^t, for $t \in L$, for each combination of vectors A^* and B^* when the player J_B varies his type t' in M, represented by the players $J_B^{t'}$. Such payoffs are expressed by the matrices $R_{AB}^{tt'}$ according to each corresponding t and t'. Let

$$H_{A^*B^*}^A|k = (h_A^{k1}(A^k, B^1), \ldots, h_A^{km}(A^k, B^m)) \in H_{A^*B^*}^A \qquad (2)$$

be the payoff vector of the player J_A^k, with specific type $k \in L$, when J_B varies its type t' in M. Define the following set for $0 \leq \alpha_1 \leq \alpha_2 \leq 1$:

$$V_{A,[\alpha_1,\alpha_2]}^{(A^*B^*)} = \left\{ \left(q_{\hat{\Phi}',[\alpha_1,\alpha_2]}^{H_{A^*B^*}^A|1}(e), \ldots, q_{\hat{\Phi}',[\alpha_1,\alpha_2]}^{H_{A^*B^*}^A|l}(e) \right) \mid e = (e_1, \ldots, e_m) \in S_{\hat{\Phi}'}^{\alpha_1,\alpha_2} \right\}, \qquad (3)$$

where $q_{\hat{\Phi}',[\alpha_1,\alpha_2]}^{H_{A^*B^*}^A|k}$ is as given in Sect. 2, with $\Phi' = \{\phi_1', \ldots, \phi_m'\}$ being the probability distribution of the m possible types for the player J_B^M. The arithmetic restriction is respected in the definition of the set $V_{A,[\alpha_1,\alpha_2]}^{(A^*B^*)}$. From Eq. (3), for each $k \in L$, we compute an interval fuzzy mean related to k, whose $[\alpha_1, \alpha_2]$-cuts for $\alpha_1, \alpha_2 \in [0,1]$, are given by: $\hat{\mu}_{\hat{\Phi}'}^{H_{A^*B^*}^A|k}[\alpha_1, \alpha_2] = \left\{ Proj_k(v) \mid v \in V_{A,[\alpha_1,\alpha_2]}^{(A^*B^*)} \right\}$, where $Proj_k : V_{A,[\alpha_1,\alpha_2]}^{(A^*B^*)} \to \mathbb{R}$ is the projection function of the coordinate of order k of the vector v, and the interval fuzzy mean is in Eq. (1), where $H_{A^*B^*}^A|k$ is given by Eq. (2). The interval fuzzy payoffs of the player J_A^L, for a combination of strategy vectors (A^*, B^*), are obtained, for $0 \leq \alpha_1 \leq \alpha_2 \leq 1$, through its $[\alpha_1, \alpha_2]$-cuts as:

$$\hat{h}_A^L(A^*, B^*)[\alpha_1, \alpha_2] \qquad (4)$$

$$= \left\{ q_{\hat{\Phi},[\alpha_1,\alpha_2]}^v(e) \mid e = (e_1, \ldots, e_l) \in S_{\hat{\Phi}}^{\alpha_1,\alpha_2} \wedge v \in V_{A,[\alpha_1,\alpha_2]}^{(A^*B^*)} \right\} \bigcup_{v \in V_{A,[\alpha_1,\alpha_2]}^{(A^*B^*)}} \hat{\mu}_{\hat{\Phi}}^v[\alpha_1, \alpha_2]$$

where $\Phi = \{\phi_1, \ldots, \phi_l\}$ is the probability distribution of the l possible types for J_A^L, $\hat{\mu}_{\hat{\Phi}}^v[\alpha_1, \alpha_2]$ define the $[\alpha_1, \alpha_2]$-cuts of the interval fuzzy mean (Eq. (1)), $V_{A,[\alpha_1,\alpha_2]}^{(A^*B^*)}$ is given by Eq. (3), $q_{\hat{\Phi},[\alpha_1,\alpha_2]}^v$ and $S_{\hat{\Phi}}^{\alpha_1,\alpha_2}$ are as in Sect. 2. The payoffs of the player J_B^M are computed in a analogous way.

Proposition 4.1. *The payoff $\hat{h}_A^L(A^*, B^*)$ of an interval fuzzy BG can be obtained through its fuzzy payoff generators, for $0 \leq \alpha_1 \leq \alpha_2 \leq 1$, by:*

$$\hat{h}_A^L(A^*, B^*)[\alpha_1, \alpha_2] = \bar{h}_A^L(A^*, B^*)_i[\alpha_1] \cap \bar{h}_A^L(A^*, B^*)_s[\alpha_2]. \qquad (5)$$

Denote the interval fuzzy probabilities $\hat{\phi}$ and $\hat{\phi}'$ by $(\bar{\phi}_i, \bar{\phi}_s)$ and $(\bar{\phi}'_i, \bar{\phi}'_s)$, respectively. From an interval fuzzy BG, we obtain two fuzzy BGs: the first for the

Table 1. Payoffs of the game for $J_{\mathbf{A}}^o$

$R_{\mathbf{A} \circ \mathbf{E}}$	$J_{\mathbf{E}}$	
$J_{\mathbf{A}}^o$	C	NC
CA	$2, -2$	$1, 0$
CM	$-1, 1$	$0, -1$

Table 2. Payoffs of the game for $J_{\mathbf{A}}^c$

$R_{\mathbf{A} c \mathbf{E}}$	$J_{\mathbf{E}}$	
$J_{\mathbf{A}}^c$	C	NC
CA	$-2, 2$	$-1, 0$
CM	$2, 2$	$0, -1$

lower fuzzy probabilities $\bar{\phi}_i$, $\bar{\phi}'_i$ ($\alpha_1 \in [0, 1]$), and the second for the upper fuzzy probabilities $\bar{\phi}_s$, $\bar{\phi}'_s$ ($\alpha_2 \in [0, 1]$). The results of each game, for each pair of vectors (A^*, B^*), constitute the fuzzy payoff generators of the interval fuzzy payoffs of the original game, expressed as $\hat{h}_{\mathbf{A}}^L(A^*, B^*) = (\bar{h}_{\mathbf{A}}^L(A^*, B^*)_i, \bar{h}_{\mathbf{A}}^L(A^*, B^*)_s)$.

To investigate the existence of equilibria, we consider an order relation for interval fuzzy numbers, namely, the Interval AD-Order.[7] An interval fuzzy BG may be treated as a family of fuzzy BGs, covering various payoff fuzzy modelings.

5. An Example of Interval Fuzzy Bayesian Game

This example is the interval fuzzy version of the crisp and fuzzy BGs introduced in previous work.[8] Here, due to the lack of space, we omitted the contextualization of the example, presenting just the numerical data. Consider two players $J_{\mathbf{E}}$ and $J_{\mathbf{A}}$, whose related set of actions are $\mathbf{E} = \{C, NC\}$ and $\mathbf{A} = \{CA, CM\}$, respectively. The player $J_{\mathbf{A}}$ can vary its type in $L = \{o, c\}$, denoted by $J_{\mathbf{A}}^L$. The payoffs for each type that $J_{\mathbf{A}}$ can assume are presented in Tables 1 and 2.

For types o and c, the equilibrium solutions are the combinations (CA, NC) and (CM, C), respectively. The problem is that the player $J_{\mathbf{E}}$ do not know which of the two games he is playing. By assigning probabilities for unknown types of the player $J_{\mathbf{E}}$, we obtain a BG with probabilistic payoffs. Let $p_o = 0.6$ and $p_c = 0.4$ be the probabilities of the player $J_{\mathbf{A}}^L$ to be of type o and c, respectively. We obtain two Bayesian equilibria, in the combinations $((CA, CM), C)$ and $((CA, CM), NC)$. Unless other circumstantial factors are analyzed, the player $J_{\mathbf{E}}$ would not know what action to choose. Considering the uncertainty about the probabilities, we adopt the fuzzy probabilities $\bar{p}_o = (0.5/0.6/0.7)$ and $\bar{p}_c = (0.3/0.4/0.5)$, turning into a fuzzy BG. Analysing the fuzzy payoffs through the AD-order,[7] the equilibrium is in the combination $((CA, CM), NC)$.

Assume that experts do not come into consensus on the modeling of fuzzy numbers for the probabilities, adopting interval fuzzy numbers to represent the probabilities of the types of player $J_{\mathbf{A}}^L$. Suppose that we first choose the interval fuzzy number $\hat{p}_o = (\bar{p}_{oi}, \bar{p}_{os}) = ((0.55/0.6/0.65), (0.45/0.6/0.75))$. Respecting the arithmetic restriction, we have $\hat{p}_c = (\bar{p}_{ci}, \bar{p}_{cs}) = ((0.35/0.4/0.45), (0.25/0.4/0.55))$. Using the interval fuzzy means, we determine the interval fuzzy probabilistic payoffs of the interval fuzzy BG for $J_{\mathbf{A}}$ and $J_{\mathbf{E}}$ (Table 3). As in the fuzzy BG, we obtain an equilibrium in the combination

Table 3. Payoffs of the players J_A^L and J_E for $\hat{p}_o = ((0.55/0.6/0.65), (0.45/0.6/0.75))$

J_A^o, J_A^c	J_A^L	
	C	NC
CA, CA	$((0.2/0.4/0.6), (-0.2/0.4/1))$	$((0.1/0.2/0.3), (-0.1/0.2/0.5))$
CA, CM	2	$((0.55/0.6/0.65), (0.45/0.6/0.75))$
CM, CA	$((-1.45/-1.4/-1.35), (-1.55/-1.4/-1.25))$	$((-0.45/-0.4/-0.35), (-0.55/-0.4/-0.25))$
CM, CM	$((0.05/0.2/0.35), (-0.25/0.2/0.65))$	0

J_A^o, J_A^c	J_E	
	C	NC
CA, CA	$((-0.6/-0.4/-0.2), (-1/-0.4/0.2))$	0
CA, CM	$((-0.6/-0.4/-0.2), (-1/-0.4/0.2))$	$((-0.45/-0.4/-0.35), (-0.55/-0.4/-0.25))$
CM, CA	$((1.35/1.4/1.45), (1.25/1.4/1.55))$	$((-0.65/-0.6/-0.55), (-0.75/-0.6/-0.45))$
CM, CM	$((1.35/1.4/1.45), (1.25/1.4/1.55))$	-1

$((CA, CM), NC)$ by comparing the interval fuzzy payoffs using the interval AD-order relation. Thus, even considering several modeling of fuzzy numbers, we still obtain the same equilibrium solution for this level of interval uncertainty.

6. Conclusion

This paper presented preliminary results on an interval fuzzy approach for BGs, in which interval-valued fuzzy probabilities are used in order to deal with both the uncertainty about the types of the agents involved in the interaction and the difficulty in establish the fuzzy numbers representing such fuzzy probabilities.

Future work is concerned with the modeling of the interval fuzzy Bayesian Prisoner Dilemma, an important approach for dealing with cooperation and regulation of interactions in multiagent systems.[9]

Acknowledgments. Supported by CNPq, Proc. 305131/2010-9, 481283/2013-7, 306970/2013-9, 307681/2012-2.

References

1. Harsanyi, C.: Games with incomplete information. Amer. Ec. Rev. **85** (1999) 291–303
2. Wang, C., Tang, W., Zhao, R.: Static Bayesian games with finite fuzzy types and the existence of equilibrium. Information Sciences **178**(24) (2008) 4688 – 4698
3. Zadeh, L.A.: Fuzzy sets. Information and Control **8**(3) (1965) 338–353
4. Bedregal, B.C., Dimuro, G.P., Santiago, R.H.N., Reiser, R.H.S.: On interval fuzzy S-implications. Information Sciences **180**(8) (2010) 1373 – 1389
5. Dimuro, G.P.: On interval fuzzy numbers. In: 2011 Workshop-School of Theoretical Computer Science (WEIT), Los Alamitos, IEEE (2011) 3–8
6. Buckley, J.J., Eslami, E.: Uncertain probabilities I: the discrete case. Soft Computing - A Fusion of Foundations, Methodologies and Applications **7**(8) (2003) 500–505
7. Asmus, T.C., Dimuro, G.P.: A total order for symmetric triangular (interval) fuzzy numbers. Mathware & Soft Computing Magazine **20**(1) (2013) 76–114
8. Asmus, T.C., Dimuro, G.P.: Uma abordagem para jogos Bayesianos fuzzy com base na probabilidade fuzzy de Buckley. RITA **20**(1) (2013) 180–215.
9. Pereira, D., Gonçalves, L., Dimuro, G.P., Costa, A.R.C.: Towards the self-regulation of personality-based social exchange processes in multiagent systems. In: Advances in Artificial Intelligence. Vol. 5249 of LNCS. Springer, Berlin (2008) 113–123

FUZZY CONDITIONAL ENTROPY BASED FEATURE EVALUATION AND SELECTION

Hua Zhao* and Keyun Qin

School of Mathematics, Southwest JiaoTong University, Chengdu 610031, China
* E-mail: zzh8008@gmail.com

Rough set is an useful tool to characterize uncertain information. It has been widely applied to feature selection. In this paper, we extend the information entropy into the kernel fuzzy rough set. Then, we construct the fast feature selection algorithm based on conditional entropy. Experimental results show that the conditional entropy-based feature selection algorithm can improve the classification performance with few features in most of the cases.

Keywords: Feature selection; Kernel fuzzy similarity relation; Conditional entropy; δ−attribute reduction; Mixed features.

1. Introduction

The high dimensional data are universal in real world, which cause considerable interference as to knowledge discovery, pattern recognition, machine learning and data mining. Irrelevant or redundant features in data sets will result in a battery of issues: increasing the cost of acquiring and storing features; slowing down learning and recognition; confusing the learning algorithm; deteriorating learning and mining performance, etc.

Rough set theory primarily proposed by Pawlak[1] provides an effective tool for dealing with inconsistency and uncertainty information. It has been successfully applied to feature selection.[2–4] With the type, volume and quality of data from practical world has vastly improved and data processing has made dramatic advances, the important thing to recognize is there are more mixed data sets than we can imagine. The mixed data means that a data set includes both numerical and categorical. A series of feature selection algorithms based on rough set and its variant have been proposed. Hu[3] introduced a neighborhood rough set model to reduce numerical and categorical features by assigning different thresholds for different kinds of attributes. Tang[5] proposed a feature selection algorithm for mixed-typed data containing both continuous and nominal features. Dai[6] introduced a new form of conditional entropy to measure the importance of attributes in incomplete decision systems and construct three attribute selection approaches based on proposed conditional entropy.

In this paper, we extend Liang's conditional entropy into kernel fuzzy rough set and discuss some properties concerned. Then we propose the definitions of significance degree of feature and δ-attribute reduction. Additionally, we construct the fast attribute reduction algorithm for mixed data.

2. Preliminaries

In rough set model, a data set is also called an information system, which is formalized $IS = (U, A)$, where $U = \{x_1, x_2, \cdots, x_m\}$ is a nonempty of finite set of samples described as a finite set of attributes $A = \{a_1, a_2, \cdots, a_n\}$. As for arbitrary two samples x and y in U and $B \subseteq A$, if they belong to the same equivalence class, then x and y are indistinguishable, denoted by $IND(B) = \{(x, y) \in U^2 | \forall a_i \in B, a_i(x) = a_i(y)\}$. Then equivalence class of x induced by $IND(B)$ is denoted by $[x]_B$. Hu proposed kernel fuzzy rough set model,[7] which is an extended rough set. In kernel fuzzy rough set model, the fuzzy $T_{\cos}$-equivalence relation matrix induced by $a_j \in C$ is denoted by

$$
R_G^{a_j} = \begin{pmatrix} r_{11} & r_{12} & \cdots & r_{1m} \\ r_{21} & r_{22} & \cdots & r_{2m} \\ \vdots & \vdots & \vdots & \vdots \\ r_{m1} & r_{m2} & \cdots & r_{mm} \end{pmatrix} \tag{1}
$$

The element of the relation $r_{ik} = R_G^{(a_j)}(x_i, x_k) = \exp(-\frac{\|x_{ij} - x_{kj}\|^2}{2\delta^2})$ quantifies the similarity degree between samples x_i and x_j. Here, $[x_i] = \frac{r_{1i}}{x_1} + \frac{r_{2i}}{x_2} + \cdots + \frac{r_{mi}}{x_m}$ and $|[x_i]| = \sum_{l=1}^{m} r_{li}$. Especially, as to a_i and a_j, $R_G^{(a_i) \cup (a_j)} = R_G^{(a_i)} \times R_G^{(a_j)}$. Here, $\times$ denotes algebraic product.

3. Uncertain measurement for kernel fuzzy rough set model

In what follows, we extend Liang's information entropy[8] from equivalent relation into the kernel fuzzy similarity relation and discuss some properties.

Definition 3.1. Given a decision system $\langle U, R_G, C, D \rangle$, R_G is the fuzzy relation induced by Gaussian kernel function, and for arbitrary $B \subseteq C$, the information entropy is defined by

$$E(B) = \frac{1}{n} \sum_{i=1}^{n} \frac{|[x_i]_B^c|}{n} = \frac{1}{n} \sum_{i=1}^{n} (1 - \frac{|[x_i]_B|}{n})$$

According to above definition, we have $0 \leq E(B) \leq 1 - \frac{1}{n}$.

Definition 3.2. Given a fuzzy decision system $\langle U, R_G, C, D \rangle$, R_G is the fuzzy relation induced by Gaussian kernel function, and for arbitrary $B \subseteq C$, the conditional entropy is defined by

$$E(D|B) = \frac{1}{n} \sum_{i=1}^{n} \frac{|[x_i]_B| - |[x_i]_B \times [x_i]_D|}{n}$$

Theorem 3.1. *Given a decision system* $\langle U, C, D \rangle$, B_1, $B_2 \subseteq C$, *kernel matrices* $R_G^{(B_1)}$ *and* $R_G^{(B_2)}$ *are induced by* B_1 *and* B_2, *if* $B_1 \subseteq B_2$, *then we have*

$$(1) E(R_G^{(B_1)}) \leq E(R_G^{(B_2)}) \quad (2) E(D|B_1) \geq E(D|B_2)$$

Proof. Assume that $B_1 \cup a = B_2$, then $R_G^{(B_1)}$, $R_G^{(a)}$ and $R_G^{(B_1)} \times R_G^{(a)}$ are the kernel matrices induced by B_1, a and B_2, respectively. $R_G^{(B_1)} \times R_G^{(a)} \leq 1$ if $R_G^{(B_1)} \leq 1$ and $R_G^{(a)} \leq 1$. Hence, $E(R_G^{(B_1)}) \leq E(R_G^{(B_2)})$. And (2) is straightforward. □

4. Algorithm design for feature selection

In fuzzy rough set, conditional entropy usually be used to evaluate the significant degree of condition attribute relative to decision attribute. Let $\delta \in [0,1]$, if $SIGE(a_1, B, D) \leq \delta$ and $SIGE(a_2, B, D) > \delta$, then we think a_2 is more important than a_1 to decision attribute in the range of δ. Because the uncertainty information relative to decision induced by a_2 is less than a_1's. Next, we introduce the concept of $\delta-$reduct of condition attribute.

Definition 4.1. Given a decision system $\langle U, C, D \rangle$. For arbitrary $B \subseteq C$, $a \in B$ and $\delta \in [0,1]$, $E(D|B - a) - E(D|B) \leq \delta$ if a is $\delta-$superfluous in B relative to D; otherwise a is $\delta-$indispensable. B is called a $\delta-$reduct of C relative to D if B satisfies:

(1) $E(D|B) - E(D|C) \leq \delta$;
(2) $\forall a \in B, E(D|B - a) - E(D|B) > \delta$.

The uncertain information will increase with the reduction of attribute. If $E(D|B) - E(D|B \cup a) < \delta$, that means the degree of uncertain information induced by attribute a relative to decision attribute D is less than δ. While $E(D|B) - E(D|B \cup a) > \delta$, it shows the uncertain information greatly increase after reducing attribute a. That means attribute a is important for decision. It is noted that δ is a threshold of difference of uncertain information. We reduce some attributes at the expend of neglecting additional uncertain information. In what follows, we propose the attribute reduction algorithm based on condition entropy, as shown in Algorithm 4.1.

Algorithm 4.1 Fast mixed feature selection algorithm based on fuzzy conditional entropy(FHFSFCE)

Input: $< U, C, D >$
Output: $redc$;
1: $redc \leftarrow \emptyset$
2: **for** each $a_i \in C - redc$, **do**
3:　compute $E(D|redc \cup a_i))$
4: **end**
5: find the attribute a_k satisfying $E(D|redc \cup a_k) = \min_i E(D|redc \cup a_i)$
6: **if** $SIGE(a_k, redc, D) > \delta$　(δ is the threshold)
7:　$redc \leftarrow redc \cup a_k$
8:　go to step 2
9: **else**
10:　return $redc$
11: **end if**

---

5. Experiment

To prove the effectiveness of the proposed algorithm, we considered 12 data sets from the UCI machine learning data repository.[9] The data sets are illustrated in Table 1.

Based on the discuss in Section 4, it is easy to notice that the uncertain information will increase with the value of δ increase. As a consequence, the value of δ is set to 0.2, 0.3, 0.4, respectively. By modifying the value of δ in interval $[0.2, 0.4]$ with step is 0.1, we compare the proposed *FHFSFCE algorithm* with some classical feature selection techniques: *MFS algorithm*,[5] *DMTQR algorithm*,[2] *NFARNRS algorithm*.[3] The data presented from Table 2 to Table 3, based on 10-fold cross validation, show the classification accuracy by SVM and KNN, respectively.

Table 1. The data sets excerpted from the UCI machine learning repository.

	Data sets	Samples	Numerical	Categorical	Class
1	Heart1	270	7	6	2
2	Liver	345	5	1	2
3	Teaching	151	1	4	5
4	Method	1473	2	7	3
5	Cancer	569	30	0	2
6	Bench	208	60	0	2
7	Ionosphere	351	34	0	2
8	Heart2	267	0	22	2
9	Car	1728	0	6	3
10	Chess2	3196	0	36	2

Table 2. Comparison of classification accuracy of four algorithms with SVM

Data sets	MFS	$DMTQR$	$NFARNRS$	$FHFSFCE$		
				0.2	0.3	0.4
Heart1	81.75± 3.69	84.07± 4.64	84.81± 3.68	89.11± 6.43	88.24± 3.42	88.56± 4.37
Liver	85.76± 5.48	87.76± 3.48	88.54± 5.54	89.49± 3.76	90.69± 2.38	90.65± 2.05
Teaching	88.15± 1.37	89.90± 2.41	88.47± 1.58	91.80± 2.74	90.56± 0.20	89.97± 3.04
Method	89.59± 0.07	90.99± 2.16	91.25± 4.82	90.04± 5.90	93.88± 5.17	95.43± 4.62
Cancer	92.49± 3.42	92.57± 4.65	95.18± 2.93	95.33± 4.27	96.17± 3.94	95.57± 6.27
Bench	91.80± 2.58	94.08± 8.51	96.31± 6.18	96.80± 2.49	98.41± 1.93	97.94± 0.84
Ionosphere	90.83± 4.35	94.23± 5.61	96.76± 0.11	98.48± 0.07	97.25± 1.67	96.81± 1.26
Heart2	82.98± 2.16	88.57± 1.25	89.97± 5.08	90.83± 5.62	92.08± 5.34	92.57± 5.69
Car	91.94± 1.84	92.85± 2.97	94.46± 2.34	92.63± 6.11	94.75± 0.51	95.02± 1.58
Chess2	77.79± 5.96	82.66± 6.32	88.07± 5.08	85.51± 2.34	87.91± 1.36	90.02± 3.89

Table 3. Comparison of classification accuracy of four algorithms with KNN

Data sets	MFS	$DMTQR$	$NFARNRS$	$FHFSFCE$		
				0.2	0.3	0.4
Heart1	80.53± 6.97	85.67± 2.32	86.37± 4.19	89.26± 1.73	88.81± 3.68	87.11± 6.43
Liver	83.94± 2.07	88.46± 3.11	89.90± 2.37	89.94± 2.07	90.54± 5.54	90.12± 3.76
Teaching	79.69± 6.83	85.11± 5.96	88.55± 1.75	90.53± 2.06	89.87± 1.58	89.36± 1.86
Method	85.83± 2.25	90.92± 6.55	93.76± 6.94	90.61± 0.00	92.25± 4.82	94.64± 5.90
Cancer	82.06± 4.72	86.92± 7.04	90.76± 1.55	91.08± 1.57	92.90± 2.37	91.58± 3.59
Bench	90.89± 5.47	91.39± 3.51	96.24± 4.29	96.97± 2.73	97.98± 2.93	96.54± 4.27
Ionosphere	89.22± 4.46	90.84± 4.29	96.38± 2.93	97.97± 3.46	97.25± 5.08	96.77± 5.62
Heart2	80.56± 3.65	86.58± 4.67	88.82± 5.74	89.49± 5.91	90.41± 1.95	90.95± 5.99
Car	82.35± 5.41	87.43± 8.78	90.52± 5.44	89.54± 6.12	91.23± 3.42	94.04± 4.08
Chess2	78.47± 3.61	82.73± 4.18	87.46± 1.21	85.76± 3.68	86.82± 3.27	90.19± 6.65

Table 2 presents the classification results with SVM algorithm, we can find that the proposed algorithm outperforms other algorithms as to the classification accuracy in most cases. However, when $\delta = 0.2$, as to *Method*,

Car, Chess2, the classification results of them are lower than *NFARNRS* algorithm, especially, the accuracy of *Method* is even smaller than *DMTQR*. With the increase of threshold, this situation has improved. When $\delta = 0.3$, the accuracy of *Car* has higher than other three algorithms. In addition, along with δ rises to 0.4, the experimental results of *Method* and *Chess2* can achieve at 95.43 and 90.02, respectively. These records are apparently higher than other methods. One thing to note is that according to Table 3, the experimental results via KNN are roughly consistent with SVM's. That shows that *NFARNRS* can get the best performance in most of cases.

6. Conclusion

In this paper, firstly, we extended conditional entropy into kernel fuzzy rough set and discussed some properties concerned. Then we constructed an attribute reduction algorithm based on conditional entropy for mixed data. To prove the effectiveness of the proposed algorithm, a series of experiments have been conducted. The cross-reference experimental results present the effectiveness of the new algorithm.

Acknowledgements

This work has been supported by the National Natural Science Foundation of China (Grant Nos. 61175044 and 61175055) and the Fundamental Research Funds for the Central Universities of China (Grant No. SWJTU11ZT29).

References

1. Z. Pawlak, *Int. J. Info. Com. Sci* **11**, 341 (1982).
2. N. M. Parthaláin and Q. Shen, *Pat. Rec.* **42**, 655 (2009).
3. Q. Hu, D. Yu, J. Liu and C. Wu, *Inf. Sci.* **178**, 3577 (2008).
4. Q. Hu, Z. Xie and D. Yu, *Pat. Rec.* .
5. W. Tang and K.Z.Mao, *Pat. Rec. Let.* .
6. J. Dai, W. Wang, Q. Xu and H. Tian, *Know. Sys.* **27**, 443 (2012).
7. Q. Hu, L. Zhang, D. Chen, W. Pedrycz and D. Yu, *Int. J. App. Rea.* .
8. J. Liang, K.S.Chin, C. Dang and R. C.M.Yam, *Int. J. Gen. Sys.* **31**, 331 (2002).
9. UCI, machine learning data repository (1997), http://archive.ics.uci.edu/ml/datasets.html.

TIME SERIES GROUPING AND TREND FORECAST USING F^1-TRANSFORM AND FUZZY NATURAL LOGIC

I. PERFILIEVA[a], V. NOVÁK[b]

University of Ostrava
Institute for Research and Applications of Fuzzy Modeling
NSC IT4Innovations
30. dubna 22, 702 00 Ostrava, Czech Republic

E-mail: [a] irina.perfilieva@osu.cz, [b] Vilem.Novak@osu.cz

A. ROMANOV[c] and N. YARUSHKINA[d]

Dept. of Inf. Systems, Ulyanovsk State Technical University, Ulyanovsk, Russia
[c] Email: romanov73@gmail.com, [d] jng@ulstu.ru

We present an idea to group time series according to the course of their local trends that can be well captured by the F^1-transform. On the basis of an adjoint time series consisting of a sequence of F^1-transform components, we form a grouping of time series with closely related trends. This enables us to forecast trend of one selected principal time series and on the basis of it, to forecast trends of the other time series from this grouping. This is realized using the methods of fuzzy natural logic, namely automatic generation of linguistic description from the data and then deriving a conclusion using the perception based logical deduction.

Keywords: F-transform; time series; Fuzzy Natural Logic; evaluative linguistic expressions

1. Introduction

A very effective technique in time series analysis and forecasting is the F-transform. Using it, we can extract trend-cycle (a low-frequency trend component) of the time series with high fidelity. The F-transform provides not only the computed trend-cycle but also also its analytic formula (cf.[1,2]). Moreover, combination of the F-transform with with methods based on the *fuzzy natural logic* (FNL) provides good estimation of the future trend-cycle of the time series.

In,[3] we further developed these techniques and suggested a method for automatic generation of comments in natural language to the local trend of time series. The basic idea is to use linear coefficients of the F^1-transform components that characterize average slope of the time series in a given local area. Then, using the techniques of FNL, we can generate its evaluation using a proper evaluative linguistic expression.

In economic applications of time series we usually deal with many time series that characterize the given economic process. It is clear that they are related, i.e. a dynamic behavior of one influences the other ones. To simplify the forecast, this suggests to select one (basic) time series from a group, forecast its local trend and then apply it for the other ones.

2. First degree F-transform

We recall few basic facts about F-transforms. All the details can be found in.[4,5] Recall that we distinguish F-transform of zero and higher degree. The F-transform is defined for a given (continuous) function $f : [a, b] \longrightarrow [c, d]$ where $[a, b], [c, d]$ are intervals of reals.

The starting point is definition of a *fuzzy partition (with the Ruspini condition)*. This is a set of fuzzy sets $A_0, \ldots, A_n$ defined on $[a, b]$ fulfilling specific conditions on their general shape and interrelation (for the precise definition, see[4] and elsewhere). The direct F^1-*transform* of f with respect to $A_1, \ldots, A_{n-1}$ is a vector $F^1[f] = [F_1^1, \ldots, F_{n-1}^1]$ where the components F_k^1, $k = 1, \ldots, n - 1$ are linear functions

$$F_k^1(x) = \beta_k^0 + \beta_k^1(x - x_k) \tag{1}$$

with the coefficients β_k^0, β_k^1 given by

$$\beta_k^0 = \frac{\int_{x_{k-1}}^{x_{k+1}} f(x)A_k(x)dx}{(\int_{x_{k-1}}^{x_{k+1}} A_k(x)dx)}, \tag{2}$$

$$\beta_k^1 = \frac{\int_{x_{k-1}}^{x_{k+1}} f(x)(x - x_k)A_k(x)}{(\int_{x_{k-1}}^{x_{k+1}} (x - x_k)^2 A_k(x)dx)}. \tag{3}$$

The following holds for the F^1-transform (see[5]): If f is four-times continuously differentiable on $[a, b]$, then for each $k = 1, \ldots, n$

$$\beta_k^0 = f(x_k) + O(h^2), \tag{4}$$

$$\beta_k^1 = f'(x_k) + O(h^2). \tag{5}$$

Thus, the F-transform components provide average value of the function (4) in a given area, and also average slope (5) in the same area.

3. Time series analysis

3.1. *Decomposition of time series*

By a *time series* we understand a stochastic process (see[6]) $X : Q \times \Omega \longrightarrow \mathbb{R}$ where $Q = \{a = 1, \ldots, b = p\} \subset \mathbb{N}$ is a finite set of integers and Ω a set of elementary random events. For each $t \in [a, b]$ the function $X(t, \omega)$ of $\omega \in \Omega$ is a random variable. We assume that $X(t, \omega)$ can be decomposed into components $X(t, \omega) = TC(t) + S(t) + R(t, \omega)$, $t \in [a, b]$, $\omega \in \Omega$ where TC is a *trend-cycle* and S is a seasonal component and R is a noise. Both TC and S are usual (i.e. non-random) functions of a real variable. In[2] we theoretically justified that the F-transform can be effectively applied to estimation of the trend-cycle TC. We can use both F^0 as well as F^1-transform. The latter is more precise but not always convenient as estimation of TC. The F^0-transform is simpler and quite often fully sufficient.

As the name suggests, the trend-cycle includes two subcomponents: *trend T* and *cycle C*. The trend T is a global characteristics of the slope in a given area. Classical time series analysis uses regression analysis. We argue, however, that a stronger and better tool is the F^1-transform because it provides estimation of the average slope (5) that can be well interpreted as a local trend of the time series. Note that the trend may not always be clear even from the graph as can be seen in Fig. 1.

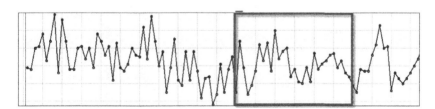

Fig. 1. Example of the local trend of time series in an area marked by a rectangle. The slope is estimated using F^1-transform coefficient (5) and linguistically evaluated as "slight decrease" (we applied the method from[3]).

3.2. *Time series with similar course of local trends*

Let us consider a group of time series $\{X_1, \ldots, X_m\}$ with the same time domain Q and let us specify a fuzzy partition $A_0, \ldots, A_n$ on Q. To each time series X_j, $j = 1, \ldots, m$ we form an adjoint time series

$$B_j = \langle \beta_{1,j}^1, \ldots, \beta_{n-1,j}^1 \rangle \tag{6}$$

where $\beta_{i,j}^1$ are the coefficients of the F^1-transform components (3). Each time series B_j in (6) characterizes course of trend of the corresponding time series X_j. Our goal is to find time series with similar courses (6). For this, we can use the well known Spearman rank correlation coefficient r_{jk}. Note that if this coefficient having been applied to two time series B_j, B_k from (6) is close to $+1$ (or -1) then the corresponding time series X_j, X_k have related courses of their trends (either conformable or opposed).

The next step is to generate a linguistic description that linguistically characterizes dependence between trends of two time series. Hence, if r_{jk} is significant then we generate a linguistic description from the data (6). Using the learning procedure developed in FNL (cf.[1,7]), each couple of values $(\beta_{i,j}^1, \beta_{i,k}^1)$ generates a fuzzy/linguistic rule

$$\mathcal{R}_{jk} := \text{IF } \beta_{i,j}^1 \text{ is } \mathcal{A} \text{ THEN } \beta_{i,k}^1 \text{ is } \mathcal{B} \tag{7}$$

where $\mathcal{A}, \mathcal{B}$ are evaluative linguistic expressions generated using the procedure of *local perception*:

$$LPerc(\beta_{i,j}^1, w_j) = \mathcal{A} \text{ and } LPerc(\beta_{i,k}^1, w_k) = \mathcal{B} \tag{8}$$

with respect to the respective linguistic contexts w_j, w_k[a].

The overall procedure is the following.

(1) Define fuzzy partition $A_0, \ldots, A_n$ on the time domain Q and for each time series X_j compute the adjoint one B_j in (6), $j = 1, \ldots, m$.

(2) Compute the correlation matrix R and determine subgroups of similar time series for all significant correlation coefficients[b].

(3) In each subgroup choose the principal time series X_{j_0} and generate a linguistic description consisting of the rules $\mathcal{R}_{j_0 k}$ for all couples of adjoint time series B_{j_0}, B_k.

(4) Extend the time domain Q to Q' and determine a fuzzy set (basic function) A over $Q' - Q$. Compute forecast of the principle time series X_{j_0} and generate its linguistic evaluation.

(5) Using the generated linguistic descriptions compute estimation of the forecast of each time series X_k over $Q' - Q$ from the forecast of the principle time series X_{j_0} and generate its linguistic evaluation.

---

[a]Recall that by the linguistic context we understand a triple of values $\langle v_L, v_S, v_R \rangle$ where v_L, v_S, v_r are the least, typically medium and the largest values of the variable in concern. For example, when speaking about water boiling temperature then we may set $v_L = 15°C$ (water temperature in the crane), $v_S = 50°C$ and $v_R = 100°C$.

[b]We must be careful because time series X_j, X_k belong to the same subgroup if $r_{jk} \geq r_{crit}$ where r_{crit} is a critical value. But we cannot assume transitivity when delineating these subgroups, i.e., $r_{jk} \geq r_{crit}$ and $r_{kl} \geq r_{crit}$ does not imply that $r_{jl} \geq r_{crit}$.

3.3. Experiment

We tested the above described procedure on a selection of 8 time series (denoted as NN101–NN106, NN110, NN111) from time series chosen for the NN3 competition[c]. All time series are defined on $Q' = \{1, \ldots, 127\}$. First, we shortened the time domain to $Q = \{1, \ldots, 114\}$ and defined on it a fuzzy partition consiting of 20 fuzzy sets. On the basis of that, we computed F^1-transform and from the β^1 coefficients we formed adjoined time series $B_{101}, \ldots, B_{106}, B_{110}, B_{111}$. Then we computed a Spearman correlation matrix (significant r_{jk} are bold):

	NN101	NN102	NN103	NN104	NN105	NN106	NN110	NN111
NN101	1	**0.63**	**0.48**	-0.21	**-0.53**	0.11	-0.24	**0.55**
NN102	**0.63**	1	**0.87**	0.07	**-0.66**	0.24	**-0.48**	**0.74**
NN103	**0.48**	**0.87**	1	0.34	**-0.68**	0.27	**-0.53**	**0.76**
NN104	-0.21	0.07	0.34	1	-0.21	0.01	**-0.45**	0.33
NN105	**-0.53**	**-0.66**	**-0.68**	-0.21	1	-0.23	**0.55**	**-0.56**
NN106	0.11	0.24	0.27	0.01	-0.23	1	-0.01	0.23
NN110	-0.24	**-0.48**	**-0.53**	**-0.45**	**0.55**	-0.01	1	**-0.53**
NN111	**0.55**	**0.74**	**0.76**	0.33	**-0.56**	0.23	**-0.53**	1

and determined three subgroups of time series: {NN101, NN102, NN103, NN110, NN111 }, {NN110, NN104} and {NN106}. After some analysis, we chose NN111 as the principal time series in the first and NN110 in the second subgroup. We estimated trend of NN111 over $Q' - Q = \{115, \ldots, 127\}$. Further, we generated linguistic descriptions characterizing dependencies between trends of NN111 and each of the time series from the first subgroup, and also dependence of NN104 on NN110.

The trend value $\beta^1_{NN111} = -149$ and is linguistically estimated[d] as "clear decrease". The results are summarized in the following table:

time series	real β^1	linguistic evaluation	computed β^1	linguistic evaluation
NN101	-16	clear decrease	-16	clear decrease ($-$ty me)
NN102	-438	clear decrease	-520	clear decrease ($-$vr bi)
NN103	-5216	clear decrease	-5980	clear decrease ($-$ex bi)
NN105	49	clear decrease	64	clear decrease (qr bi)
NN110	163	clear decrease	214	clear decrease (ml me)
NN104	-92	clear decrease	-237	clear decrease ($-$qr sm)

---

[c]http://www.neural-forecasting-competition.com/downloads/NN3/datasets/
[d]All the linguistic estimations must be done w.r.t. a specific context. We ommitted this question in the paper because of the lack of space. The details can be found in.[3]

The real β^1 is the F^1-transform coefficient computed for the time $Q' - Q$ from the real data of the time series and the computed one is obtained from the corresponding learned linguistic description using the PbLD[e] method. The linguistic evaluations are obtained from these values using the procedure of local perception (cf. (8)). Note that the generated linguistic evaluation is the same and that the signs correspond to the above correlation matrix.

4. Conclusion

In this contribution, we developed a new method of forecasting trend of a group of time series with similar course of their local tendencies.

Acknowledgement

The authors acknowledge that this paper was supported by the projects KONTAKT II, LH 12229 "Research and development of methods and means of intelligent analysis of time series for the strategic planing problems", RFFI-10-01-00183 and partially also by the European Regional Development Fund in the IT4Innovations Centre of Excellence project (CZ.1.05/1.1.00/02.0070).

References

1. V. Novák, M. Štěpnička, A. Dvořák, I. Perfilieva, V. Pavliska and L. Vavříčková, *Int. Journal of General Systems* **39**, 305 (2010).
2. V. Novák, I. Perfilieva, M. Holčapek and V. Kreinovich, *Information Sciences* ((to appear)).
3. V. Novák, V. Pavliska, I. Perfilieva and M. Štěpnička, F-transform and fuzzy natural logic in time series analysis, in *Proc. Int. Conference EUSFLAT-LFA'2013*, (Milano, Italy, 2013).
4. I. Perfilieva, *Fuzzy Sets and Systems* **157**, 993 (2006).
5. I. Perfilieva, M. Daňková and B. Bede, *Fuzzy Sets and Systems* **180**, 3 (2011).
6. J. Hamilton, *Time Series Analysis* (Princeton, Princeton University Press, 1994).
7. V. Novák, *Int. J. of General Systems* **42**, 21 (2013).

---

[e]Perception-based Logic Deduction — see.[7]

SYNTHETIC APERTURE RADAR EDGE DETECTION WITH CANNY'S PROCEDURE AND A GRAVITATIONAL APPROACH

G. P. SILVA JUNIOR and S. A. SANDRI

Instituto Nacional de Pesquisas Espaciais – INPE, Av. dos Astronautas, 1758, 12227–010, São José dos Campos, SP – Brazil
E-mails: gp7junior@gmail.com, sandra.sandri@inpe.br

A. C. FRERY

Laboratório de Computação Científica e Análise Numérica, Universidade Federal de Alagoas, Av. Lourival Melo Mota, s/n, 57072-970 Maceió, AL – Brazil
E-mail: acfrery@gmail.com

We address the use of two strategies for edge detection in polarimetric Synthetic Aperture Radar – SAR imagery. Both approaches stem from the realm of optical images: Canny and one inspired by the Law of Universal Gravitation. Images are filtered prior to edge detection by two procedures: Lee and Torres filters. Two types of neighborhoods are employed.

1. Introduction

Edge detection aims at automatically identifying sharp differences in the information associated with adjacent pixels in an image.[1] Edge detection for optical images is traditionally carried out using gradient-based techniques and is nowadays a quite established field.

In synthetic aperture radar (SAR) scenes with no texture, an edge can be defined as an abrupt change in the reflectivity.[2] The observed intensity follows the well-known speckle distribution, the gamma law. Contrary to what happens with optical images, there are still few algorithms specifically dedicated for SAR images.[3] One interesting means to create edge detection algorithms for SAR images is to part from those created for optical images. However, the use of these methods on SAR images is not straightforward, due to a large amount of nongaussian noise. One can either adapt those methods to the meet SAR data properties, or first preprocess the images using filters and then apply the original methods. The two most common ways of preprocessing are in the homomorphic domain, i.e., taking the logarithm of the data, and by speckle filtering.

We investigate the application of an edge detection method based on Computational Intelligence for optical images to synthetic aperture radar imagery. Our approach employs noise-reduction filters. In particular, in this work, we address the use of the well-known Canny method[4] and the gravitational approach proposed by Lopez-Molina et al[5] for edge detection. We make use two different filters, due to Torres et al[6] and to Lee et al,[7] and two different types of neighborhood, the usual 3×3 window and one with a 9×9 support proposed by Fu et al.[3] We apply the methods on a synthetic image, created by Barreto et al,[8] and verify the accuracy of the approaches using the Baddeley Delta metric.[9] The experiments show that the proposal is promising, mainly with the Lopez-Molina method preprocessed using the Fu's 9×9 neighbourhood and no filtering.

2. Related Works

The so-called Lee multiplicative (or sigma) filter introduced in 1983,[7] is still in use today due to its simplicity, effectiveness in speckle reduction, and computational efficiency.[10] It is based on the fact that, under the Gaussian distribution, approximately 95.5% of the probability is concentrated within two standard deviations from the mean. The filter estimates the mean and the standard deviation of samples around each pixel, and only those values within this interval are used to compute the local mean.

Torres et al.[6] recently proposed a nonlocal means approach for PolSAR image speckle reduction based on stochastic distances; the method can be tailored for any distribution, either univariate of multivariate. It consists of, for each pixel, comparing the distributions which describe the central observation and each of the observations which comprise a search region. The comparison is made through a goodness-of-fit test, and the p-value of the test statistic is used to define the convolution matrix which will define the filter: the higher the p-value the larger the confidence and, thus, the importance, each observation will have in the convolution. In their proposal, the tests are derived from h-ϕ divergences between multilook scaled complex Wishart distributions.[11] Their results are competitive with classical and advanced polarimetric filters, wrt the usual quantitative measures. This nonlocal means filter also preserves the polarimetric signature of the targets.

One of the most successful edge detection algorithms for optical images was proposed by Canny,[4] based on the following guidelines: the algorithm should mark as many real edges in the image as possible, the marked edges should be as close as possible to the edge in the real image, a given edge in the image should only be marked only once and image noise should not create false edges. It makes use of numerical optimization to derive optimal operators for ridge and roof edges and the usual implementation of this method uses a 3×3 neighbourhood.

Several methods for edge detection in optical images have also been proposed in the Computational Intelligence field.[5,12,13] In particular, Lopez-Molina et al[5] developed an edge detection method for optical images, based on the Law of Universal Gravitation, an approach that lies in the Computational Intelligence field. The authors propose the use of triangular norms in general in place of the product operation used in the calculation of the gravitational forces. They treat edges as fuzzy sets for which membership degrees are extracted from the resulting gravitational force on each pixel. Several prototypical triangular norms are considered and experimentally show that their features determine the kind of edges detected.

On the other hand, contrary to what happens with optical images, there are still few algorithms specifically dedicated for SAR images.[3]

3. Materials and Methods

We investigate the use in SAR images of edge detection methods developed for optical images using filtering for speckle reduction. We compare the edge detection methods proposed by Canny[4] and by Lopez-Molina et al[5] (gravitational approach), the latter followed by limiarization, with the use of two different filters, due to Torres et al[6] and to Lee et al,[7] as well as two different types of neighbourhood, the usual 3×3 and a particular 9×9 one proposed by Fu et al.[3]

The quality of the binary resulting images are assessed by the Baddeley's Delta Metric (BDM), by comparison with what would be the perfect results. BDM aims at measuring the dissimilarity of the subsets of featured points; smaller values to BDM indicates better edge detection results. Here, pixels in the image boundaries are not taken account in the BDM calculation.

We apply the methods on data derived from a full polarimetric synthetic image, created by Barreto et al[8] using samples from water and different types of vegetation. Figure 1 brings the original synthetic image used in the experiments.

4. Experimental Results

Table 1 brings the BDM results generated by the application of the methods described above; limiarization parameters are indicated by the values inside

Fig. 1.   Original Synthetic Image

brackets. The negative images derived from the methods are depicted in Figures 2 and 3; note that the image boundaries are depicted only for illustration purposes. For Lopez-Molina method we took the limiarization parameter that furnished the best BDM results.

Table 1.   BDM results.

	Original	Torres filter	Lee filter
Canny (3 × 3)	31.66	20.61	22.60
Lopez-Molina (3 × 3)	25.50 (0.20)	27.13 (0.10)	21.91 (0.21)
Lopez-Molina (9 × 9) (Fu)	19.74 (0.07)	20.30 (0.07)	24.26 (0.03)

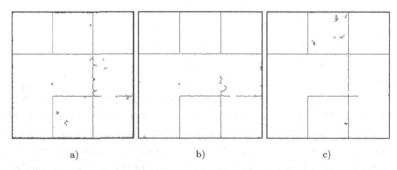

a)   b)   c)

Fig. 2.   Results from Canny algorithm, using a) no filter, b) Torres filter, c) Lee filter.

In Figure 2, we see that Canny's method produced sharp results with some noise, with the filtered images presenting the best results. Figures 3.a), 3.b) and 3.c) respectively show that, using the 3 × 3 neighbourhood, the unfiltered image is very noisy, that Torres filter reduced the noise and separated the regions and that Lee filter detected false edges. In Figures 3.d) and 3.e) and 3.f), we see that Fu's 9 × 9 neighbourhood detected almost

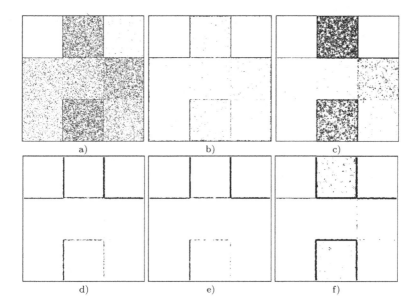

Fig. 3. Results from Lopez-Molina's algorithm, using (i) traditional 3×3 neighbourhood and a) no filter, b) Torres filter and c) Lee filter, and (ii) Fu's 9 × 9 neighbourhood and d) no filter, e) Torres filter and f) Lee filter.

all the edges, but filtering did not improve results (some edges are missing using Torres filter and the edges are too thick using Lee filter).

By visual inspection, we note that Canny's method produced sharp results with some noise and that Lopez-Molina's got a good compromise between edge detection and noise reduction using Fu's neighbourhood and no filter. These main results are consistent with BDM. Note that BDM does not penalize noise as much as missing edges.

5. Conclusions

We address the use of two strategies for edge detection in polarimetric Synthetic Aperture Radar – SAR imagery. Both approaches stem from the realm of optical images: Canny[4] and one inspired by the Law of Universal Gravitation.[5] Images are filtered prior to edge detection by two procedures: Lee[7] and Torres[6] filters. Two types of neighborhoods are employed. The methods were applied on a synthetic image.[8] Using both visual inspection and the Baddeley Delta metric[9] we verify that the combination with the Lopez-Molina technique with the 9×9 neighbourhood proposed by Fu et al[3] and no filtering produces the best results. We also note that the parameter used in binarization process influences the result of BDM.

Future work includes applying other types of neighbourhood such as Nagao-Matsuyama,[14] other types of filtering such as the refined Lee filter,[10] and draw comparisons with the edge detection algorithm proposed by Fu in 2012.[3] Also, we intend to use as other means for comparing the results, such as the one proposed recently by Frery et al.[15]

This work is also a first step towards investigating the use of edge detection methods derived from Computational Intelligence techniques for use of SAR images. In the future we intend to verify the performance of T-norms, other than the product, to calculate the gravitational forces, as well as addressing other methods, such as the one proposed by Lopez-Molina et al in 2011.[13]

Acknowledgements

The authors are grateful for CAPES, CNPq and FAPESP for financial support.

References

1. R. C. Gonzalez and R. E. Woods, *Digital Image Processing (3rd Ed.)* (Prentice-Hall, Inc., Upper Saddle River, NJ, USA, 2006).
2. F. Baselice and G. Ferraioli, *IEEE GRSL* **9**, 185 (2012).
3. X. Fu, H. You and K. Fu, *IEEE GRSL* **9**, 1094 (2012).
4. J. Canny, *IEEE Trans. on PAMI* **8**, 679 (1986).
5. C. Lopez-Molina, H. Bustince, J. Fernandez, P. Couto and B. D. Baets, *Pattern Recognition* **43**, 3730 (2010).
6. L. Torres, S. J. S. Sant'Anna, C. C. Freitas and A. C. Frery, *Pattern Recognition* **47**, 141 (2014).
7. J.-S. Lee, *IEEE Trans. on SMC* **13**, 85 (1983).
8. W. B. da Silva, C. da Costa Freitas, S. J. S. Sant'Anna and A. C. Frery, *IEEE J-STARS* **6**, 1263 (2013).
9. A. J. Baddeley, An error metric for binary images, in *Robust Computer Vision: Quality of Vision Algorithms*, eds. W. Förstner and H. Ruwiedel (Wichmann, Karlsruhe, 1992) pp. 59–78.
10. J.-S. Lee, J.-S. Lee, J.-H. Wen, T. Ainsworth, K.-S. Chen and A. Chen, *IEEE Trans. on GRSL* **47**, 202 (2009).
11. A. C. Frery, A. D. C. Nascimento and R. J. Cintra, *IEEE Trans. on GRS* **52**, 1213 (2014).
12. M. Danková, P. Hodáková, I. Perfilieva and M. Vajgl, Edge detection using f-transform, in *ISDA*, (IEEE, 2011).
13. C. Lopez-Molina, B. D. Baets and H. Bustince, *Computer Vision and Image Understanding* **115**, 1571 (2011).
14. M. Nagao and T. Matsuyama, *J-CGIP* **9**, 394 (1979).
15. M. E. Buemi, A. C. Frery and H. S. Ramos, *PRL* **36**, 281 (2014).

NEW PARAMETERS ESTIMATORS USING EM-LIKE ALGORITHM FOR NAIVE BAYES CLASSIFIER BASED ON BETA DISTRIBUTIONS

Ronei M. Moraes*

*Department of Statistics, Federal University of Paraiba, João Pessoa-PB, Brazil
*E-mail: ronei@de.ufpb.br

Alexandre B. Simas

Department of Mathematics, Federal University of Paraiba, Brazil

Liliane S. Machado

Department of Computer Science, Federal University of Paraiba, Brazil

Andrea V. Rocha

Department of Applied Mathematics, Federal University of Paraiba, Brazil

In this paper we proposed new estimators of parameters for a Naive Bayes Classifier based on Beta Distributions. Equations were obtained for these estimators using an EM-like algorithm and they provide numerical estimates for those parameters. Furthermore, two forms for that Naive Bayes Classifier were presented.

Keywords: Naive Bayes Classifier; Beta Distribution; EM-like algorithm.

1. Introduction

The beta distribution is characterized by two parameters p and q, whose values can completely change the shape of the beta distribution. It is used to model phenomena which are restricted to [0,1], as probabilities, proportions and percentages. If X follows a beta distribtuion, then its probability density function is given by.[3]

$$f_X(x; p, q) = \frac{\Gamma(p+q)}{\Gamma(p)\Gamma(q)} x^{p-1}(1-x)^{q-1}, \quad \text{with } 0 < x < 1, \ p, q > 0,$$

with:

$$E(X) = \frac{p}{p+q}$$

and

$$Var(X) = \frac{pq}{(p+q)^2(p+q+1)}.$$

According to Owen,[10] the methods of Maximum Likelihood (MML) and Moments (MoM) are effective for determining the parameters of the beta distribution. The MML requires a numerical approximation for these parameters.[1] However, the MoM is more interesting, because it has closed form[7] when the mean (first order moment) and variance (second order moment) values are available. Van Dorp and Mazzuchi proposed a numerical solution to estimate the parameters of the beta distribution given quantile constraints.[11]

As the parameters of beta distribution are not easily estimated, Johnson[5] proposed use triangular distribution as a proxy for the beta distribution. Johnson and Kotz[6] also proposed the triangular distribution as an alternative to the beta distribution due to problems with maximum likelihood parameters estimation and their parameters with unclear meaning.

Van Dorp and Kotz[12] showed that the two-sided power (TSP) distribution has several similarities to the beta distribution, as such as their capacities to be symmetrical or asymmetrical unimodal distributions. This distribution is an extension of the triangular three-parameter distribution.[9] In the literature, TSP distribution has been used replacing beta distribution because their parameters can be obtained more easily and have a better interpretation of those ones of beta distribution. Owen[10] proposed the use of the mean and variance estimators of TSP distribution to estimate the parameters of the beta distribution due to similarities between them.

However, we did not found in the scientific literature a proposition for Expectation-Maximization estimators for Beta distribution. Our interest is to find parameters estimators for a naive Bayes classifier based on beta distribution.

2. Mathematical Framework

We begin by briefly reviewing some basic aspects of the beta distribution. The parameters p and q are shape parameters, and thus they are not easy to interpret. Therefore, we will use a reparameterization in terms of the mean of the distribution and a parameter that may be interpreted as a precision parameter. Let $\phi = p + q$ and $\mu = p/\phi$, then density of X is given by:

$$f_X(x; \mu, \phi) = \frac{\Gamma(\phi)}{\Gamma(\mu\phi)\Gamma((1-\mu)\phi)} x^{\mu\phi-1}(1-x)^{(1-\mu)\phi-1},$$

with $0 < x < 1$, $0 < \mu < 1$ and $\phi > 0$, and we say that X follows a $Beta(\mu, \phi)$ distribution, with:

$$E(X) = \mu \ \text{ and } \ Var(X) = \frac{\mu(1-\mu)}{\phi+1}.$$

From the point of view of the Classification Theory,[2] let C be a random variable taking values on the set $\{1, \ldots, k\}$ i.e., we have k classes. So, for a class i, one can sample independent and identically distributed random variables $X_1^i, \ldots, X_n^i$. Assume that, for each i, this sample comes from a distribution $Beta(\mu_i, \phi_i)$, where (μ_i, ϕ_i) is some vector-valued parameter. Initially, our goal is to estimate these parameters $(\mu_1, \phi_1), \ldots, (\mu_k, \phi_k)$ nicely. Afterwards, we want to use these estimates to classify these variables using a naive Bayes scheme. Therefore, we are interested in calculating

$$P(C = i | (X_1, \ldots, X_n) \in A),$$

where A is an event in $\mathbb{R}^n$.

From Bayes' theorem,[4] one knows that:

$$P(C = i | (X_1, \ldots, X_n) \in A) =$$
$$= \frac{P(C = i)P((X_1, \ldots, X_n) \in A | C = i)}{\sum_{j=1}^{k} P(C = j)P((X_1, \ldots, X_n) \in A | C = j)}.$$

Thus, we want to estimate $\theta_i = (\mu_i, \phi_i)$ for $i = 1, \ldots, k$ assuming we have the naive Bayes condition:[8]

$$P(X_1 \leq x_1, \ldots, X_n \leq x_n | C = i) = \prod_{j=1}^{n} P(X_j \leq x_j | C = i),$$

where $P(X_j \leq x_j \mid C = i) = \int_0^{x_j} f(x; \mu_i, \phi_i) dx$, that is, we are assuming that $(X_j \mid C = i)$ follows a $Beta(\mu_i, \phi_i)$ distribution.

3. Estimation Procedures

Notice that we are not under the usual assumption of the EM algorithm. Nevertheless, the naive Bayes condition puts us "almost" in the condition of the EM algorithm and therefore, we are able to adapt this algorithm to our current setup, So, the naive Bayes condition implies that

$$P(X_1 \leq x_1, \ldots, X_n \leq x_n) = E\left[P(X_1 \leq x_1, \ldots, X_n \leq x_n \mid C)\right]$$

$$= \sum_{i=1}^{k} P(C = i)P(X_1 \leq x_1, \ldots, X_n \leq x_n \mid C = i)$$

$$= \sum_{i=1}^{k} P(C = i) \prod_{j=1}^{n} P(X_j \leq x_j \mid C = i)$$

Let $\tau_i = P(C = i)$. From the above expression, and the density of the beta distribution, is easy obtain that the log-likelihood function is given by

$$\ell(\theta; x_1, \ldots, x_n, c) = \sum_{j=1}^{n} \sum_{i=1}^{k} \mathbb{I}(c = i) \left[\log(\tau_i) + \log(f(x_j; \mu_i, \phi_i))\right],$$

where

$$\log(f(x_j; \mu_i, \phi_i)) = \log(\Gamma(\phi_i)) - \log(\Gamma(\mu_i\phi_i)) - \log(\Gamma((1 - \mu_i)\phi_i))$$
$$+ (\mu_i\phi_i - 1)\log(x_j) + ((1 - \mu_i)\phi_i - 1)\log(1 - x_j),$$

$\theta = (\tau_1, \ldots, \tau_k, \mu_1, \ldots, \mu_k, \phi_1, \ldots, \phi_k)$, and $\mathbb{I}$ stands for the indicator function. Suppose an inital guess $\theta^{(0)}$ is given. The EM algorithm is carried in two steps.

3.1. *E step*

Given the current estimate of the parameter $\theta^{(t)}$, it follows from Bayes theorem that

$$T_i^{(t)} = P(C = i \mid X_1 = x_1, \ldots, X_n = x_n; \theta^{(t)}) =$$

$$= \frac{\tau_i^{(t)} \prod_{j=1}^{n} f(x_j; \mu_i^{(t)}, \phi_i^{(t)})}{\sum_{m=1}^{k} \tau_m^{(t)} \prod_{j=1}^{n} f(x_j; \mu_m^{(t)}, \phi_m^{(t)})}.$$

Therefore, the E step gives us the function

$$Q(\theta \mid \theta^{(t)}) = E[\ell(\theta; x_1, \ldots, x_n, C)] =$$

$$= \sum_{i=1}^{k} T_i^{(t)} \left[n \log(\tau_i) + \sum_{j=1}^{n} \log(f(x_j; \mu_i, \phi_i))\right].$$

3.2. *M step*

In this step we obtain the new values $\theta^{(t+1)}$ by determining which values of θ maximizes $Q(\theta \mid \theta^{(t)})$. We begin by obtaining $\tau_j^{(t+1)}$. From a straightforward calculation, and noting that $\tau_1 + \cdots + \tau_k = 1$, we have that

$$\tau^{(t+1)} = \arg\max_\tau Q(\theta \mid \theta^{(t)}) = \arg\max_\tau \left\{ \sum_{i=1}^k T_i^{(t)} \log(\tau_i) \right\},$$

which has the same form as the MLE for the multinomial distribution. Therefore, $\tau_i^{(t+1)} = T_i^{(t)}$. The remaining estimates are obtaining by

$$(\mu^{(t+1)}, \phi^{(t+1)}) = \arg\max_{\mu,\phi} Q\left(\theta \mid \theta^{(t)}\right) =$$

$$= \arg\max_{\mu,\phi} \left\{ \sum_{j=1}^n \sum_{i=1}^k T_{i,j}^{(t)} \log(f(x_j; \mu_i, \phi_i)) \right\},$$

which has no closed-form expression and must be obtained numerically.

4. Bayes Classifier for the EM-like Algorithm

We have two possibilities of classification here. One of them is using the empirical estimator for τ_i, and the other one is using the EM algorithm estimate of τ_i.

Let $\breve{\mu}_i$ and $\breve{\phi}_i$ be the EM algorithm estimates of μ_i and ϕ_i. Then, the Bayes classifier for these estimates is given by

$$\breve{c} = \arg\max_i \hat{\tau}_i \prod_{j=1}^n f(x_j; \breve{\mu}_i, \breve{\phi}_i).$$

Finally, one should notice that during the E step of the EM algorithm, we compute the quantity needed to classify. Therefore, if we want to use the EM estimator for τ_i, the Bayes classifier is given by

$$\tilde{c} = \arg\max_i T_i^{(t)},$$

where t is the last iteration used to obtain the estimator, i.e., we are assuming that at step t the algorithm converged.

5. Conclusions

In this paper we presented a new approach for parameters estimation of beta distribution for a naive Bayes classifier. This approach is based on a previous reparametrization and following EM-like algorithm.

As future works, we intent to compare this new approach with other approach found in the literature, such as Maximum Likelihood and Method of Moments in order to know its properties, advantages and limitations.

References

1. G. Casella and R.L. Berger, *Statistical Inference.* (Cengage Learning, 2nd ed., 2001).
2. R.O. Duda, P.E. Hart and D.G. Stork, *Pattern Classification.* (Wiley, 2nd ed.,2000)
3. A.K. Gupta and S. Nadarajah (Eds) *Handbook of Beta Distribution and Its Applications* (CRC Press, New York, 2004).
4. R. V. Hogg, J.W. McKean and A. Craig (Eds), *Introduction to Mathematical Statistics.* (Pearson, 7th ed., 2012).
5. D. Johnson, *The Statistician,* **46**, 387 (1997).
6. N.L. Johnson and S. Kotz, *The Statistician,* **48**, 179 (1999).
7. K. Pearson, *Tables of the incomplete Beta function.* (University College, Biometriks Office, 1934).
8. R.E. Neapolitan, *Learning Bayesian networks.* (Prentice Hall, 2004).
9. O.E. Oruc and I. Bairamov, *Communications in Statistics: Theory and Methods,* **34**, 1009 (2005).
10. C.B. Owen, Parameter estimation of the beta distribution. Master's thesis, Brigham Young University (2008).
11. J.R. van Dorp and T.A. Mazzuchi, *Journal of Statistical Computation and Simulation,* **67**, 189 (2000).
12. J. R. van Dorp and S. Kotz, *Journal of the Royal Statistical Society, Series D: The Statistician,* **51**, 63 (2002).

ACCURACY EVALUATION OF EVOLVING FUZZY NEURAL NETWORKS IN PATTERN RECOGNITION TASKS USING DATA FROM FOUR DIFFERENT STATISTICAL DISTRIBUTIONS

JODAVID DE ARAÚJO FERREIRA, RONEI MARCOS DE MORAES[1†]

Department of Statistics, Federal University of Paraiba, Cidade Universitária João Pessoa, Paraiba, Brazil

Evolving Fuzzy Neural Networks (EFuNNs) are dynamic connectionist feed forward networks. Several paper can be found in the literature in which EFuNN reach better results than other methods. However, only one paper was found in which EFuNN results were analyzed with respect to some statistical distributions of data. This study has as goal to complement the previous study, evaluating the EFuNN performance using four other statistical distributions. Results of assessment are provided and show different accuracy according to the statistical distribution of data.

1. Introduction

In the last years, the Fuzzy Neural Networks named Evolving Fuzzy Neural Networks (EFuNNs) has been successfully applied to the solution of several kinds of pattern recognition problems. EFuNN was proposed by Kasabov [5], as structures that evolve according ECOS (Evolving Connectionist System) principles [4]: quick learning, open structure for new features and new knowledge, representing space and time and analyze itself of errors. It is known that statistical distributions of training data, affect the final results of any pattern recognition method. In the literature, we found only one paper in which results on EFuNN were analyzed with respect to seven different statistical distributions of data [8]. However, some important statistical distributions were not analyzed.

In this study we performed an accuracy evaluation of EFuNNs in pattern recognition using data from four other statistical distributions, up to 4 dimensions for each distribution. The results allow knowing what is the better kind of statistical distribution of data to be used for better EFuNN performance and what is the minimum dimension of data which allows reaching it.

1 This work is partially supported by the Brazilian Council for Scientific and Technological Development (CNPq): processes 310470/2012-9, 310561/2012-4, PIBIC//UFPB and 181813/2010-6 (INCT-MACC).

2. Evolving Fuzzy Neural Networks

EFuNN is a connectionist feed forward network with five layers of neurons [9], where nodes and connections are created or connected when data examples are presented [5]. The input layer of the network (Figure 1) receive crisp value x. The second layer represents fuzzy quantization of input variables. In this layer, each neuron implements a fuzzy set [11] and its membership function (MF), which can be triangular, gaussian or other [6], with goal to convert input values for membership degrees using some MF available. When an input value does not have membership degree greater than a threshold, new neurons will be created (evolving).

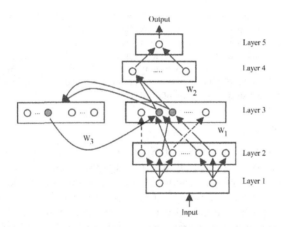

Figure 1. Diagram of an EFuNN. Adapted from [5]

The third layer contains rules nodes (r_j) that evolve through training. The rule nodes represent groups of input-output data associations. The fourth layer represents fuzzy quantization of the output variables from a weighted sum function of inputs and from an activation function. So, the degree to which an output vector belongs to some output MF is computed. The last layer uses an activation function to calculate defuzzified values for output variables y. More details about EFuNN can be found in [5].

3. Methodology

For each statistical distribution we analyzed data from one up to four dimensions. Our goal is to know for what statistical distribution we can use EFuNN and what performance is expected for each statistical distribution. Besides that, we can know for what statistical distribution of data the better performance of EFuNN can be expected. For performance evaluation, we use the Mean Square Error (MSE) computed between the values expected (y) and that one estimated by EFuNN (y') and it is defined as:

$$MSE = \frac{1}{N}\sum_{i=1}^{N}(y_i - y'_i)^2,$$ (1)

where N is total number of elements to be classified [10]. We use also the matrix of classification for performance assessment. From this one, we obtain the percentile of correct classification (relation between sum of values in the diagonal of classification matrix and N [3]), the number of classifications mistakes (sum of the values outside of the diagonal) and Kappa Coefficient [1]. The percentile of correct classification is a measure of easy interpretation [7], but it computes only the correct classifications. Kappa Coefficient is the coefficient widely used in the literature of pattern recognition [2] to take into account not only successes in classification, but also classification mistakes [8]:

$$K = \frac{P_0 - P_c}{1 - P_c}$$ (2)

where:

$$P_0 = \frac{\sum_{i=1}^{M} n_{ii}}{N} ; P_c = \frac{\sum_{i=1}^{M} n_{i+}.n_{+i}}{N^2},$$ (3)

where n_{ii} is element of i line and of i column of matrix classification, n_{i+} is the sum of i line of classification matrix and n_{+i} is the sum of i column of the same matrix. The Kappa variance σ_k^2 is given by [8]:

$$\sigma_k^2 = \frac{P_0(1-P_0)}{N(1-P_c)^2} + \frac{2(1-P_0)+2P_0P_c-\theta_1}{N(1-P_c)^3} + \frac{(1-P_0)^2\theta_2-4P_c^2}{N(1-P_c)^4}$$ (4)

where

$$\theta_1 = \frac{\sum_{i=1}^{M} n_{ii}(n_{i+} + n_{+i})}{N^2} ; \theta_2 = \frac{\sum_{i=1}^{M} n_{ii}(n_{i+} + n_{+i})^2}{N^3}$$ (5)

4. Results

In this section we present the results of the classification of EFuNN model. For the execution of model, 4 dimensions for each statistical distribution studied and two kinds of samples were generated:

1. Random sample for training: A sample with 2000 values, different by 4 classes, which means 500 observations for each class used for training the model.
2. Random sample for testing: A sample used for classification test based on the parameters of the previous sample.

From those samples, we obtained the results, which are presented in the next sections.

4.1. *Negative Binomial Distribution*

The negative binomial distribution is a discrete distribution, for which the same conditions defined for geometric distribution are considered: the experiment consists on an undetermined amount of repeated attempts, the probability of success is the same in each attempt, which are independent.

In the simulation data for Negative Binomial, the parameters used were: Number of MF equal 2, no-prunning, sensitivity threshold value 0.999 and error threshold value 0.001. Using this configuration, we obtained the percentile of correct classification of 87.4%, Kappa Coefficient was 83.4% with variance of 4.83×10^{-5}. With dimension 2, and using the same parameters above, we obtained Kappa Coefficient of 99.87% with variance of 4.4×10^{-7}.

For dimension 3, number of MF equal 2, no-prunning, sensitivity threshold value 0.999 and error threshold value 0.001, the Kappa Coefficient was 100% and variance zero. The same was observed for data with four dimensions.

With these results, it can be seen that the EFuNN is a good classifier for Negative Binomial distribution. When the number of dimensions is 3 or above it, the rating was 100% correct.

4.2. *Logistic Distribution*

For the Logistic distribution we used the following parameters: number of MF equal 2, no-prunning, sensitivity threshold value 0.999 and error threshold value 0.001. For dimension equal one, Kappa Coefficient was 93.3% and variance of 2.1×10^{-5}. For two dimensions, we obtained Kappa Coefficient of 99.93% with variance of 2.2×10^{-7}, with misclassification of only 2 observations. Increasing the dimension to 3, there was obtained Kappa of 100% and variance zero. For Logistics distribution, EFuNN proved to be a good classifier with dimensions small. The rating achieved was 100%, when the dimensions are greater than or equal 3.

4.3. *Log Normal Distribution*

The Log Normal distribution is a continuous distribution, and it can be used for characterizing lifetime of products and materials (metal fatigue, semiconductors, diodes and electrical insulation, etc.). The EFuNN parameters used for this distribution were: MF equal to 2, no-prunning, sensitivity threshold value 0.999 and error threshold value 0.001. For dimension equal one, we obtained correct classification percentage of 82.15%, Kappa Coefficient equal 76.2% and variance of 6.5×10^{-5}. Increasing the dimension for three, the Kappa Coefficient rose to 99.4% and variance 1.9×10^{-6}. When the dimension size was increased to 4, the Kappa Coefficient obtained was 99.8% and variance 6.7×10^{-7}.

4.4. *Gamma Distribution*

Gamma distribution is a continuous probability distribution, which has two parameters, a parameter of shape, and a parameter of scale. It is required that both parameters are greater than zero. Using EFuNN for Gamma distribution, we obtained the following results: for dimension equal one, the number of membership functions (MF) 2, no-prunning, sensitivity threshold value 0.999 and error threshold value 0.001, missed 483 rating values, the Kappa Coefficient of 83.9% and variance of 4.7×10^{-5}. For dimension 2, and the number of membership functions (MF) 2, no-prunning, sensitivity threshold value 0.999 and error threshold value 0.001, Kappa Coefficient was 99.3%, and variance 2.36×10^{-6}.

For three dimensions, MF equal to 2, no-prunning, sensitivity threshold value 0.999 and error threshold value 0.001, the method missed only 4 observations, the percentage of correct classification was 99.9%, Kappa Coefficient was 99.8% and variance 4.44×10^{-7}. For four dimensions, using the same previous parameters, the classification obtained was 100% correct.

4.5. *Summary of Results*

The Table 1 presents a summary of the best results obtained in the classifications, according to all statistical distributions studied in this paper. For the Negative Binomial distribution, Logistic and Gamma, Kappa Coefficient was 100%, i.e. using EFuNN can be obtained 100% correct classification of data. For the Log Normal distribution, the best Kappa Coefficient obtained was 99.85%, for four dimensions.

Table 1. Summary of bests results by statistical distributions, according to the Kappa Coefficient.

Statistical Distribution	MF	N° of dimensions	Kappa Coeficient
Negative Binomial	2	3 or more	100.00%
Logistic	2	3 or more	100.00%
Log Normal	2	4	99.85%
Gamma	2	4	100.00%

5. Conclusions

In this paper, we studied EFuNN performance for four different statistical distributions, which are different those studied by [8]. For each distribution was checked four different dimensions, according to the Mean Square Error (MSE), percentile of correct classification, number of misclassifications, Kappa Coefficient and its variance.

The EFuNN obtained satisfactory results for all four statistical distributions analyzed: Negative Binomial distribution, Gamma distribution, Log Normal distribution and Logistics distribution. In three of them, namely Negative Binomial, Gamma and Logistics, the classification results, according to the Kappa Coefficient were 100% and with zero variance. In the case of Logistics distribution, the Kappa Coefficient obtained was 99.8% and variance 6.7×10^{-7}.

According to the results obtained, it seems advisable to use EFuNN to classification of data for all those four distributions studied. When the dimension of data is increased, EFuNN becomes more accurate.

References

1. J. Cohen, *Educ. and Psych. Measur.*, **20**, 37 (1960).
2. R.O. Duda, P.E. Hart and D.G. Stork, *Pattern Classiffication* (Wiley, 2nd ed, 2000).
3. G.M. Foody, *Rem. Sens. of Environ.*,**80**, 185 (2002).
4. N. Kasabov, *ECOS:* A Framework for Evolving Connectionist System and the ECO Learning Paradigm, in *Proc. ICONIP'98.* **1232** (1998).
5. N. Kasabov, *IEEE Trans. On Man, Mach. Cyber.*, **31**, 902 (2001).
6. G.J. Klir and B. Yuan, *Fuzzy Sets and Fuzzy Logic: Theory and Applications.* (Prentice Hall, 1995).
7. R.M. Moraes, G.J.F. Banon and S.A. Sandri, *Inform. Sci.*, **142**, 7 (2002).
8. R.M. Moraes, *Mathware& Soft Computing*, **v. 20, n.1, p. 63-69,** (2013).
9. Simpson, P., *Artificial Neural Systems.* (Pergamon, 1990).
10. Z. Wang and A.C. Bovik, *IEEE Signal Processing Magazine*, **26**, 98 (2009).
11. L.A. Zadeh, *Inform. Control*, **8**, 338 (1965).

PERFORMANCE EVALUATION OF ONLINE TRAINING ASSESSMENT ON EMBEDDED SYSTEM[1]

ELAINE A.M.G. SOARES, LILIANE S. MACHADO, RONEI M. MORAES

LabTEVE, Federal University of Paraíba, 58051-900, João Pessoa/PB, Brazil

Assessment systems of training based on Virtual Reality are used to measure users' skills when performing a procedure. This kind of systems can demand expressive time of CPU. A solution was pointed out using an architecture for assessment based on embedded systems. The goal of this paper is to analyze the efficiency of hardware architecture in producing good results, using two previously proposed online methods based on fuzzy sets.

1. Introduction

One of the main demands of the services area is the improvement of the skills of employees, with the goal of ensuring the quality of these services. Particularly in the medical area, many applications based on virtual reality (VR) have been developed in order to provide realistic training [1]. In those systems, users are exposed to simulated problems in 3D environments to safely practice and improve their technological and psychological skills. In addition, VR systems demand integration and synchronizations of routines, hardware and techniques [2], what require high processing rates to provide real time responses to users.

Using training based on VR simulators it is possible to monitor user actions and register their movements in the virtual environment. Relevant information as force, position and acceleration, among others performed with interaction devices (as haptics) must be acquired and processed during entire the training session. This information is used to assess and provide feedback about users' skills. A fast feedback (called *online* [1]) demands expressive time of CPU, which can compromise the other tasks of the simulator. As a solution for this problem, Moraes and Machado [3] proposed an architecture for assessment based on embedded systems. In this architecture, an embedded system is connected to the VR simulator to enhance the execution of the assessment tasks

---
[1] This work is partially supported by the Brazilian Council for Scientific and Technological Development (CNPq): processes 310470/2012-9, 310561/2012-4, PIBIC//UFPB and 181813/2010-6 (INCT-MACC).

and release the CPU for other tasks related to the simulation. However, studies need analyze the real efficiency of this architecture, when compared to a CPU based approach. This paper provides an analysis of the results from the implementation for two previously proposed online methods based on fuzzy sets: Possibility and Necessity Measures (PMN) [4] and Weighted Possibility and Necessity Measures (WPMN) [5].

2. Virtual Reality and Training Assessment

An advantage of using VR to simulate real medical problems for training of procedures is avoiding risks and ethical issues [1]. In addition, it is possible to simulate a variety of cases, including rare and atypical occurrences, as well as make it repetitively without risks and degradation of materials. In general, VR systems use special devices to reach high levels of immersion and interactivity, providing for users the feeling of presence by the manipulation of elements in the virtual environment [6]. A kind of those devices is the haptic device, which can capture interaction data in rates between 500 and 1000 Hz. So, the amount of data to be processed in a simulation can be massive.

Interaction data of the training simulation can be collected and used to assess trainees' performance. Online assessment methods can provide real-time feedback and are important since they can provide a more effective learning process for users [1,2,4]. The calibration of an assessment system must be done in order to acquire and label correct and incorrect ways to perform a procedure. It is provided by an expert who executes several times the procedure in different ways in order to generate parameters for each execution. The expert defines previously the number for classes of performance and labels each execution. All interaction and environment parameters are acquired during this process to be used by the assessment method, which is normally based on pattern recognition techniques [1]. As example, a M=3 number of classes can refers to 1: "good performance", 2 - "regular performance", 3 - "bad performance" [4].

3. Assessment Methods and Decision Rule

3.1. *Possibility and Necessity Measures (PMN) Method*

Let A be a fuzzy subset of Ω, with its membership function $\bigcirc_A$, and let X be a variable which assumes values x in Ω. Then, the possibility distribution π is a function associated to X and is defined as:

$$\pi_X(x) = \mu_A(x) \qquad (1)$$

The possibility measure Π and the necessity measure are defined respectively by:

$$\Pi (A) = \sup \{\pi (x) \mid x \in A\} \quad \text{and} \quad N (A) = \inf \{1 - \pi (x) \mid x \notin A\}.$$

The possibility and the necessity measures are dual:

$$\Pi(A) = 1 - N(\bar{A}) \quad \text{and} \quad N(A) = 1 - \Pi(\bar{A}).$$

Let A and B be fuzzy subsets of Ω, with membership functions μ_A and μ_B, respectively. Let X be a variable which assumes values $\omega \in \Omega$. The conditional possibility and necessity measures are given by [8]:

$$\Pi (A \mid B) = \max_{x \in X} \min (\mu_A (x), \pi_B (x)) \text{ and}$$

$$N (A \mid B) = \min_{x \in X} \max (\mu_A (x), 1 - \pi_B (x)). \quad (2)$$

From equation (2) it is possible to construct an interval for the real value of the class of performance ω_i, given each feature X_k, with $k=\{1,...,n\}$, from the training data $X = \{X_1, X_2, ..., X_n\}$ from a user [4]:

$$\mu_{\omega_i} (X_j) \in [N(\omega_i \mid X_k); \Pi(\omega_i \mid X_k)]. \quad (3)$$

The domain of membership function for the class of performance ωi is an interval where the minimum value is the minimum compatibility and the maximum value is the maximum compatibility:

$$\mu_{\omega_i} (\mathbf{X}) \in [compat_{min}; compat_{max}]. \quad (4)$$

As the class of performance ω_i is expressed by a conjunction of features X_j, then this aggregation is performed by a t-norm. In this case, the "min" operator preserves the semantics of possibility and necessity measures [4]:

$$compat_{min} = \min_k (N (\omega_i \mid X_k)) \quad \text{and} \quad compat_{max} = \min_k (\Pi (\omega_i \mid X_k)). \quad (5)$$

The defuzzification process can be done using, for instance, the centroid method, where $C [\mu_{\omega_i} (X)]$ is the centroid between $compat_{min}$ and $compat_{max}$ for the pertinence function of class ω_i, according to X. Then, the decision rule for PNM method is: select performance class ω_i for the vector X if [4]:

$$\omega_i = \arg \max_{1 \le i \le M} C [\mu_{\omega_i} (X)]. \quad (6)$$

3.2. Weighted Possibility and Necessity Measures (WPMN) Method

The WPNM method is an extension of PNM method, in which weights v_j should be introduced to improve compatibility interval. From (3) and (4):

$$\text{compat}_{min} = \min_{1 \le j \le n} [\max (v_j, N_j (\omega_i \mid X_j))] \quad \text{and}$$

$$\text{compat}_{max} = \min_{1 \le j \le n} [\max (v_j, \Pi (\omega_i \mid X_j))], \tag{7}$$

where $\max_j v_j = 1$. After all intervals were obtained, the problem is to provide an answer to training assessment for the user. A possible solution is to provide information about each class of performance and its interval respectively. However, the decision maker may not be prepared to interpret this result and a crisp answer can be more suitable for interpretation. Among several ideas, it is possible to use a defuzzification method as the centroid C of interval and take the maximum one. Thus, for WPNM method, the decision rule is similar to the one presented in (6):

$$\omega_i = \arg \max_{1 \le i \le M} C [\mu_{\omega_i}(X)]. \tag{8}$$

4. Embedded Systems and Implementation

An embedded system is a combination of hardware and software with additional components dedicated to perform a specific function [7]. Its architecture is generally similar to that of a computer system and may be composed by main memory, secondary memory, processor and buses input and output, such as: USB port, VGA port, network adapter and others. The entire project is specifically designed to fulfill requirements of a system making it cheaper. Due to these characteristics, in [3] an architecture was proposed for assessment based on embedded systems in order to meet timing requirements for an online assessment [1].

5. Methodology

The objective of this paper is analyze the efficiency of the architecture proposed by [3] in producing good results, investigating the limits of this architecture in providing online assessments and what are performance relationships between the assessments provided by a PC-only system and the architecture proposed by [3]. Initially, the authors developed computational programs for both assessment methods, a PC-only system and an embedded system, using the programming language C. For the PC-only system, a program was developed for each method that reads the file containing the result of the expert's performances, classifies the data and return the result of the classification. To the FitPC system (embedded system), was made a server application for each method and a client application in order to build a TCP/IP communication. The client app sends the data to the server, which performs the classification corresponding to the method and returns to the client the result of the classification. To simulate the WPMN approach, the weights 1, 0.987 and 1 was used.

The database was composed by 3 variables, each one with 50 observations that corresponds to the data read from the haptic system manipulated by an expert. The Monte Carlo simulation was performed increasing by 100 the quantity of objects per class to be classified by the method at each interaction, starting on 100 and going to 3000 in order to verify how the system answers to a larger amount of data. At each iteration, the program's running time was saved to generate the classification matrix to calculate the Kappa coefficient.

6. Results and Discussions

Through Monte Carlo simulation, the classification matrices were obtained, with no changes in the execution on PC and on FitPC, and the average time of execution for both methods. Tables 1 and 2 show the matrices of the methods WPNM and PNM, respectively, and the main diagonal of the matrices represent the correct classifications. The PC platform was a 2.4GHz AMD Athlon 64 X2 processor, 2GB of DDR2 RAM running Fedora Linux. The embedded system FitPC was a 500 MHz AMD Geode processor, 256 MB of DDR RAM running Gentoo Linux.

A Kappa coefficient equal to 0.9700 was obtained for the WPNM method, with variance 1.468×10^{-4}. Such value was calculated from the classification matrix of the method (Table 1). This method took 1.66×10^{-4} seconds on PC and 17.51×10^{-4} seconds on FitPC. As it can be seen on Table 1, there were 6 errors in the first class, which means that the method has 98% success rate for this specific amount of data, having 100% of success in classes II and III and 94% in class I.

Table 1. Classification matrix for WPNM.

Class of performance according to experts	Class of performance according to Weighted Possibilistic approach		
	I	II	III
I	94	0	6
II	0	100	0
II	0	0	100

For the method PNM, a Kappa coefficient equal to 0.9550 was obtained, with variance 1.468×10^{-4}. Such value was calculated from the classification matrix of the method (Table 2). This method took 1.14×10^{-4} seconds on PC and 16.28×10^{-4} seconds on the embedded system. In Table 2, it can be seen that there were 9 errors in the first class, which means that the method has 97% success rate for this specific amount of data, having 100% of success in classes II and III and 91% in class I.

Table 2. Classification matrix for Possibility and Necessity Measures.

Class of performance according to experts	Class of performance according to Possibilistic approach		
	I	II	III
I	91	0	9
II	0	100	0
II	0	0	100

Both methods satisfied the requirement of time response for online assessment (lower than 1 second) on both the PC system and the embedded system. The WPNM surpassed the 1 second time on the PC platform in 2800 objects per class, while the PNM exceeded in 300 objects per class, which corresponds to 140000 and 150000 observations per execution, respectively. On the FitPC platform, both methods surpassed the threshold in 200 objects per class, the equivalent of 10000 observations.

7. Conclusions

An architecture for assessment based on embedded systems was proposed by [3] some years ago. In the present paper were presented answers for some open questions, as the real efficiency of this architecture, its limitations to provide online assessment and its performance if compared to a CPU based approach. The results obtained shown this assessment architecture can provide the same results as methods implemented for PC-only. When comparing the processing time necessary to perform the assessment task, the PC-only execution was around 10.5 times faster than the FitPC execution, but the last still achieved the requirement for online assessment time (lower than 1 second).

By the results obtained it was possible to confirm the proposal [3] of transferring assessment tasks to an embedded system and leave the main system available to process the tasks related to the VR simulation. It was important to observe that even with a less powerful configuration, the embedded system was able to provide fast answers. Therefore, the use of assessment methodologies, even if computationally expensive, can be considered to be implemented in embedded systems without compromising the simulation performance.

References

1. R.M. Moraes and L.S. Machado, L., Development of a Medical Training System with Integration of Users' Assessment. In: Jae-Jin Kim (Ed.), Virtual Reality, chapter 15. Intech (2011).
2. L.S. Machado, A.N. Mello, R.D. Lopes, V. Odone Fo., M.K. Zuffo, *Studies In Health Technology and Informatics* **81** 293 (2001).
3. J.T. Segundo, E.A. Soares, L.S. Machado, R.M. Moraes, Lecture Notes in Computer Science. **8259**, 158 (2013).
4. L.S. Machado and R.M. Moraes, *Proc. 10th Int. FLINS Conf. (FLINS 2012)*, pp. 339-345. Istanbul, Turkish, (2012).
5. R.M. Moraes and L.S. Machado. *Knowledge-Based Systems* (submitted).
6. L.S. Machado, R.M. Moraes, Intelligent Decision Making in Training Based on Virtual Reality. In: Da Ruan. (Org.). Computational Intelligence in Complex Decision Systems. Amsterdam **85**. Paris: Atlantis Press (2010).
7. M. Barr, *Programming Embedded Systems in C and C++*. O'Reilly, (1999).
8. D. Dubois, H. Prade, *Possibility theory*. Plenum Press, New-York. (1988).

A MODEL FOR FISHERY FORECAST BASED ON CLUSTER ANALYSIS AND NONLINEAR REGRESSION

HONGCHUN YUAN

Shanghai Ocean University, Shanghai 201306, China

MINGXING TAN

Shanghai Ocean University, Shanghai 201306, China

YING CHEN

School of Computing and Information Systems, University of Tasmania, Hobart, Tasmania, Australia

There has been an increasing amount of research in the relationship between environmental factors and fishing yield. This paper adds to the body of knowledge by developing a new model for forecasting fishing yield. The model combines fishery domain expert knowledge, marine environmental factor data such as water temperature, chlorophyll concentration and sea surface level as base data and applies cluster analysis that incorporates function fitting and nonlinear regression for data analysis and processing. The model is tested for forecast accuracy and the test result is compared with those using RBF and SVM, the two methods commonly used for similar purposes. The comparison result reveals this new model increases both the accuracy in fishery forecast and the reliability in guiding fishery production and related activities. It can also help explore and discover the distribution of fishing grounds.

Keywords: pelagic fishing; fisheries forecasting; cluster analysis; nonlinear regression

In the past twenty years, China has experienced steady development in its pelagic fishery. By the end of 2012, the total number of offshore fishing vessels in China reached 2200. Offshore fishing has improved the piscatorial income of the nation and the living standards of its people with an increased supply of aquatic products. It has also contributed to the nation's fishing industry,

Foundation item: This work is supported by Innovation Program of Shanghai Municipal Education Commission(12ZZ162),and is also supported by Shanghai Municipal science and Technology Commission(12510502000)

Corresponding author: Mingxing Tan E-mail:345010018@qq.com Telnumbers: 00862161900620 Fax numbers:00862161900623 protected its inshore fishery resources and promoted the development of other related industries [1]. Illex argentinus takes a very important position in the fishery economy regardless of its output value or yield. Research in Illex argentines covers various aspects [2-6]. Bakun and Csirke[7] studied the impact of marine environmental changes on Illex supplement group resources. Song and Xiong[8] reported the correlation between Illex production distribution and sea surface temperature. In spite of the large population in China, existing data still shows China lagging way behind most developed countries in terms of the amount of offshore fishing per capita share. Even though aquatic operators have accumulated an enormous marine fish catch database over the years yet the data has not been used due to lack of data analysis tools. Consequently, aquatic workers are still relying purely on personal knowledge and experience for tasks such as the delineation of fishing waters and the ascertaining of fishing time, resulting in aimless fishing and an overly high cost of fishing overall. There is an urgent need for a sophisticated and reliable analysis tool to process and analyze the fishery data so that it can assist fishery prediction and support more cost effective and efficient fishing [9-11]. It can also stabilize the further development of China's offshore fishing, enhance China's current status in international fishery and reduce the pressure of China's inshore fishery resources.

1. Materials and Methods

1.1. *Research data sources*

For the purpose of this research, the environmental data of Illex argentinus' fishing include sea surface level, sea surface temperature and chlorophyll concentration in Southwest Atlantic in January-April 2000. This data is downloaded from OceanWatch (http://oceanwatch.pifsc.noaa.gov/las/). The corresponding fishery yield or catch data is provided by Shanghai Ocean University.

1.2. *Data analysis methods and principles of clustering*

The proposed data analysis method is hierarchical clustering which works by grouping data objects into a tree of clusters. Hierarchical clustering methods can be further classified as either agglomerative or divisive, depending on whether the hierarchical decomposition is formed in a bottom-up (merging) or top-down (splitting) fashion. However a pure hierarchical clustering method suffers from its inability to be adjusted if a merge or split decision turns out to be a poor choice, ie, the method does not allow backtracking for any necessary corrections. Recent studies have emphasized on the integration of hierarchical agglomeration with iterative relocation methods.

Four widely used measures for distance between clusters are presented here. Where $|p - p'|$ is the distance between two objects or points, p and p'; m_i is the mean for cluster, C_i; and n_i is the number of objects in C_i.

$$\text{Minimum distance: } d_{\min}(C_i, C_j) = \min_{p \in C_i, p' \in C_j} |p - p'| \qquad (1)$$

$$\text{Maximum distance: } d_{\max}(C_i, C_j) = \max_{p \in C_i, p' \in C_j} |p - p'| \qquad (2)$$

$$\text{Mean distance: } d_{mean}(C_i, C_j) = |m_i - m_j| \qquad (3)$$

$$\text{Average distance: } d_{avg}(C_i, C_j) = \frac{1}{n_i n_j} \sum_{p \in C_i} \sum_{p' \in C_j} |p - p'| \qquad (4)$$

When an algorithm uses the minimum distance, $d_{\min}(C_i, C_j)$, to measure the distance between clusters, it is sometimes called a nearest-neighbor clustering algorithm. Moreover, if the clustering process is terminated when the distance between nearest clusters exceeds an arbitrary threshold, it is called a single-linkage algorithm. If we view the data points as nodes of a graph, with edges forming a path between the nodes in a cluster, then the merging of two clusters, C_i and C_j, corresponds to adding an edge between the nearest pair of nodes in C_i and C_j. Because edges linking clusters always go between distinct clusters, the resulting graph will generate a tree. Thus, an agglomerative hierarchical clustering algorithm that uses the minimum distance measure is also called a minimal spanning tree algorithm.re only one referencing equation number is wanted.

1.3. Data processing

The data of sea surface level, sea surface temperature, chlorophyll concentration and fishing yield is normalized in this analysis. The formula of normalization is defined in (5) to (9).

$$x'_{year} = \frac{x_{year} - 1995}{2050 - 1995} \qquad (5)$$

$$x'_{month} = \frac{x_{month}}{12} \qquad (6)$$

$$x'_{latitude} = \frac{x_{latitude} + 90}{180} \qquad (7)$$

$$x'_{longitude} = \frac{x_{longitude} + 180}{360} \tag{8}$$

$$x'_i = \frac{x_i - x_{i\min}}{x_{i\max} - x_{i\min}} \tag{9}$$

Where x_i is the sea surface level, sea surface temperature and chlorophyll concentration in(9). $x_{i\max}$ represents the maximum value while $x_{i\min}$ represents the minimum value of the month.

A dendrogram of sea surface level, sea surface temperature and chlorophyll concentration data has been created by clustering analysis with MATLAB 7.10. With the clustering analysis in MATLAB, it is revealed that there are five sets of data which are divided into two categories, so that in the range of non-central fishing ground these minimal sets of data points which are relative to the overall data are outliers.

1.4. *Fitting and regression analysis*

Since there is no existing reference for quantitative analysis between fishing yield and environmental factors or functions of the exact relationship, data and fitting function are considered in this paper.

Equations (10), (11) and (12) have been created by function fitting of sea surface temperature, sea surface level or chlorophyll concentration with fishing yield data using a software package called 1stOpt after removing outliers.

$$A = y = \sqrt{\left((0.0413 - 0.0726 * x) \Big/ 1 - 3.421 * x + 2.940 * x^2 \right)} \tag{10}$$

$$B = y = \frac{1}{(31288.2 + 13527.9 * e^x + 83204.8 \big/ Ln(x))} \tag{11}$$

$$C = y = 0.0336 * e^{-62.141 * x} + 0.3380 * e^{-\left((x-0.022)^2 \big/ (-0.001)^2\right)} + 0.0002 * e^{-\left((x-0.1989)^2 \big/ 0.006^2\right)} \tag{12}$$

Where Equation (10) is the function of the relationship between fishing yield and sea surface temperature, Equation (11) is the function of the relationship between yield and sea surface level, and Equation (12) is the function of the relationship between yield and chlorophyll concentration.

The complexity of the model can be reduced with the assumption that these three marine environmental factors are independent of each other. As a result a regression model of the yield (y) and sea surface temperature, x_1, sea surface level, x_2, and chlorophyll concentration, x_3 , can be created through the fitting function of the production and each marine environmental factors. See (13) below.

$$y = a*A + b*B + c*C + d \tag{13}$$

Where a, b, c, d are coefficients which are unknown.

The final non-linear regression model (14) is obtained with a, b, c, d and using formula (13):

$$
\begin{aligned}
y = 0.4539 * &\sqrt{\left(\left(0.0413 - 0.0726 * x_1\right) \middle/ 1 - 3.421 * x_1 + 2.940 * x_1^{2}\right)} \\
&+ 0.8528 * \frac{1}{\left(31288.2 + 13527.9 * e^{x_2} + 83204.8 \middle/ Ln(x_2)\right)} \\
&+ 0.8067 * \left(0.0336 * e^{-62.141 * x_3} + 0.3380 * e^{-(x_3 - 0.022)^2 \middle/ (-0.001)^2} + 0.0002 * e^{-(x_3 - 0.1989)^2 \middle/ 0.006^2}\right) \\
&- 0.006
\end{aligned}
\tag{14}
$$

Finally the actual data and the resulting function point chart, residual plots are shown in Fig. 1 and Fig. 2.

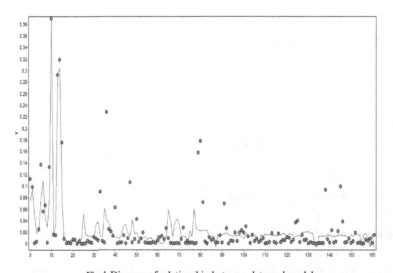

Fig.1 Diagram of relationship between data and model

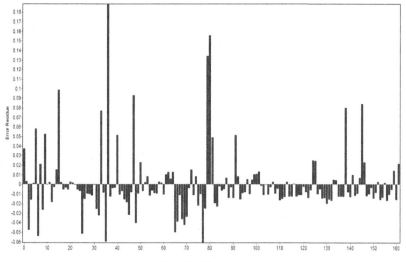

Fig.2 Residual plot

2. Results and discussion

RBF and SVM are two commonly used methods for fishing forecast. It is worth comparing these two methods with the Nonlinear Regression Model (NRM) proposed in this paper. A few sets of environmental data are randomly selected to forecast fishing production using NRM and the resulting forecast data is compared with the actual measured yield data from the existing database hosted in Shanghai Ocean University.

A comparison is conducted involving five methods that have been used in fishing predictions with results in Table 1 and Table 2. This comparison shows NRM contains the lowest mean square error and the highest coefficiency. These comparison results support the conclusion that the NRM method surpasses all other existing methods in making fishing yield forecast.

Tab 1. Mean square error of 5 methods

RBF	SVM	SVM based on priori knowledge	Linear regression	NRM: new proposed method
0.043	0.037	0.035	0.058	0.033

Tab 2. Coefficiency of determination of 5 methods

RBF	SVM	SVM based on priori knowledge	Linear regression	NRM: new proposed method
0.4775	0.5513	0.5838	0.2889	0.6572

3. Conclusion

This paper proposes a non-linear regression model (NRM) for fishing forecast. It employs cluster analysis and nonlinear regression to help forecast fishing yield based on marine environmental data. Measured data of Illex argentinus in Southwest Atlantic has been used for the experiment. The model has been verified for forecast accuracy and its result is compared with those applying the commonly used methods, RBF and SVM. The comparison confirms that NRM is more accurate in fishery prediction. There is speculation that if NRM is adopted it can lead to better efficiency and effectiveness in fishing.

4. Acknowledgments

This work is supported by Innovation Program of Shanghai Municipal Education Commission(12ZZ162), and is also supported by Shanghai Municipal science and Technology Commission(12510502000). Their support is gratefully acknowledged.

References

1. Wei Fan, Xuesen Cui, Xinqiang Shen. Progress in fishing-ground analysis and fishing condition forecasting[J], Journal of Fisheries of China, 2005, 29(5):707-710.
2. Zhengzhi Dong. The world oceans economic cephalopod biology [M]. Jinan: Shandong Science and Technology press, 1991:131-134.
3. Feng Chen, Xinjun Chen, Bilin Liu. Relationship between fishing ground of ommastrephes bartramii and vertical temperature structure in the northwestern Pacific Ocean [J]. Journal of Shanghai Ocean University, 2010, 19(4):495 −504.
4. Xinjun Chen, Bilin Liu, Yuezhong Wang. Study on the distribution of production of Illex Argentinus and its relationship with sea surface temperature in the Southwest Atlantic Ocean in 2000 [J]. Journal of Zhanjiang Ocean University, 2005,25(1):29 −34.

5. Feng Gao, Xinjun Chen, Jiangtao Fan. Implementation and verification of intelligent fishing ground forecasting of Illex Argentinus in the Southwest Atlantic [J]. Journal of Shanghai Ocean University, 2011,20(5):754-758.

6. Rodhouse P G, Barton J, Hatfeld EMC, Symon C. Illexargentinus: life cycle, population structure, and fisher [J]. ICES Mar Sci Symp 1995, 199(1):425-432.

7. Bakun A, Csirke J. Environmental Processes and Recruitment Variability in Squid Recruitment Dynamics [M], Rome: FAO,1998,105-124.

8. Weihua Song, Pengfei Xiong. Research on the developing of argentine shortfin squid-jig fishing in the Southwest Atlantic [J]. Transactions of Oceanology and Limnology, 2002(1):62-68.

9. Xinjun Chen. Fisheries Resources and Fisheries [M]. Beijing: Ocean press, 2004.

10. Global Capture Production. Food and Agriculture Organization of the United Nations [EB/OL]. [2010−12−01].http://www.fao.org /fishery /statistics /global-capture-production /query /en.

11. Yuexia Zhang, Zhongfeng Qiu, Yumei Wu. Predicting central fishing ground of scomber japonica in East China Sea based on case based reasoning [J]. Marine Science, 2009, 33(6):8−11.

AN EFFICIENT ONLINE LEARNING APPROACH FOR SUPPORT VECTOR REGRESSION

JIE LIU

Chair on Systems Science and the Energetic Challenge, European Foundation for New Energy - Électricité de France, CentraleSupelec, France

VALERIA VITELLI

Department of Biostatistics, University of Oslo, Norway

REDOUANE SERAOUI

EDF R&D, Simulation and information TEchnologies for Power generation System (STEPS) Department, 6 quai Waiter, F-78401, Chatou, France

ENRICO ZIO

Energy Department, Politecnico di Milano. Chair on Systems Science and the Energetic challenge, European Foundation for New Energy - Électricité de France, CentraleSupelec, France

In this paper, an efficient online learning approach is proposed for Support Vector Regression (SVR) by combining Feature Vector Selection (FVS) and incremental learning. FVS is used to reduce the size of the training data set and serves as model update criterion. Incremental learning can "adiabatically" add a new Feature Vector (FV) in the model, while retaining the Kuhn-Tucker conditions. The proposed approach can be applied for both online training & learning and offline training & online learning. The results on a real case study concerning data for anomaly prediction in a component of a power generation system show the satisfactory performance and efficiency of this learning paradigm.

1. Introduction

Support Vector Machine (SVM) is capable of estimating nonlinear relations among input-output variables by mapping the data points into a high dimensional Reproducing Kernel Hilbert Space (RKHS) with linear relations between their mapping. Training a SVM model involves solving a Quadratic Programming (QP) problem in a number of coefficients equal to the number of training examples. For very large datasets, this may become infeasible, so that a reduction in the size of the training dataset must be sought. Another problem with SVM (and other data-driven methods) is that when there is a drift of the assumed fixed distribution of the dataset, the model may no longer work well and would need to be updated. As retraining a SVM model from the beginning is time-consuming, a more efficient way is to update the model by adding / removing some Support Vectors (SVs) and / or changing the Lagrange multipliers and hyperparmeters [1].

Some efforts have been made to solve these two problems. Most of these works tackle only one of the previous problems, and some of the solutions proposed do not work well in nonstationary environments. In this paper, we propose an online learning approach for regression using SVM (called SVR), by combining a simplified version of the FVS introduced in [3] with the incremental learning method presented in [4] to give a solution to the two problems mentioned above. The method is called Online Learning approach with FVS and Incremental Learning, and hereafter named OL-FVS-IL for short. FVS aims at reducing the size of the training dataset: only part of the training dataset is chosen (called Feature Vectors) to build the SVR model and the mapping of the other training data points in the RKHS can be expressed by a linear combination of the feature vectors. When adding a new FV in the model, instead of retraining the model, incremental learning constructs the solution recursively, while retaining the Kuhn-Tucker conditions on all previously seen data.

A real case study concerning a component nuclear power plant is carried out within the Probabilistic Support Vector Regression (PSVR) paradigm, which is a Bayesian treatment of SVR with Gaussian priors [2].

The rest of the paper is organized as follows. Section 2 gives some insights about the modified FVS and a brief recall of the incremental learning method; the proposed online learning approach is also detailed in this section. Section 3 describes the real case study and the experiments results. Some conclusions and prospects are presented in Section 4.

2. Online Learning Approach with Feature Vector Selection and Incremental Learning (OL-FVS-IL)

In this paper, an efficient online learning approach is proposed for regression using SVM. The proposed method can reduce the number of data points used in building the model, thus reducing its computational burden with large datasets. It can also incrementally add new FVs in the model to improve its adaptivity and capacity for different patterns.

2.1. *Feature Vector Selection*

In [3], the authors define a global criterion to characterize the feature space in SVM. A number of Feature Vectors (FVs) are selected from a training dataset to represent the useful dimension of RKHS in these data points. Any data can be projected on these FVs and, then, application of classical algorithms for training and prediction can be carried out. Several simplifications and developments are made for this FVS approach proposed in [3], after deliberate derivation. Constrained by the size of this document, sophisticated details of calculation cannot be listed and only important results are presented.

The aim of FVS is to represent all the data points with a linear combination of FVs in RKHS. Suppose (x_i, y_i), for $i = 1, 2, ..., M$ are the training data points, and the mapping $\varphi(x)$ maps each input x_i into RKHS with the mapping φ_i, for $i = 1, 2, ..., M$. $k_{i,j} = k(x_i, x_j)$ is the inner product between φ_i and φ_j.

In order to find a new FV, we just need to verify if the mapping φ_N of a new data point x_N can be represented by a linear combination of the mapping of the existing FVs. Suppose the existing FVs are $\{ x_1, x_2, ..., x_L \}$ and the corresponding mapping are $S = \{\varphi_1, \varphi_2, ..., \varphi_L\}$. The verification of the new FV is to find $\{a_{N,1}, a_{N,2}, ..., a_{N,L}\}$, which gives the minimum of Eq. (1).

$$\delta_N = \frac{\left\| \varphi_N - \sum_{i=1}^{L} a_i \varphi_i \right\|}{\|\varphi_N\|} \tag{1}$$

The minimum of δ_N can be expressed by an inner product, which is calculated by Eq. (2).

$$\min \delta_N = \left| 1 - \frac{K_{S,N}^t K_{S,S}^{-1} K_{S,N}}{k_{N,N}} \right| = J_{S,N} \tag{2}$$

where $K_{S,S} = (k_{i,j}), i, j = 1, 2, ..., L$ is the kernel matrix of S and $K_{S,N} = (k_{i,N}), i = 1, 2, ..., L$ is the vector of the inner product between φ_N and S. $J_{S,N}$ is called the local fitness of data point x_N. If $J_{S,N}$ is 0, the new point is not a new FV, otherwise, it is added to S as new FV. Considering the noise in the data and the reduction of the computational complexity, a small value θ is compared with $J_{S,N}$ instead of 0.

We introduce also the global fitness J_S on the training data set with Eq. (3) for the following illustration.

$$J_S = \sum_{i=1}^{M} J_{S,i} \tag{3}$$

2.2. Incremental learning

The incremental learning method proposed in [4] provides a good solution for online learning SVR, with changing environmental and operational conditions. The key idea is to find the appropriate Kuhn-Tucker conditions for a new data by modifying its influence in the regression function while maintaining consistency in the Kuhn-Tucker conditions for the rest of the data used for learning. This method can "adiabatically" add a new point in the SVR model instead of retraining it from the beginning. Although this method is proposed for classification problems in [4], it can be expanded to regression problems.

In this section, we present the offline training and online learning procedures using FVS and the incremental learning method as shown in Figure 1. To keep within the limits of length of the paper, details on the procedure of computation are not provided; readers who are interested can refer to [4] for more details.

2.3. Online learning procedure

Initialization:
  Training dataset: (x_i, y_i), for $i = 1, 2, ..., M$
  FV space: S = [ ]
  Minimal threshold value of local fitness: θ
Offline Training:
  First FV in S:
    For i = 1 to M calculate
      S = $\{x_i\}$, compute global fitness J_S and the local fitness $J_{S,j}$ of the other points.
    End for.
    Select the point which gives the minimum of the global fitness as the first FV and add it to S as the first FV.
  Second and the other FVs:
    Calculate local fitness for all training data points with the existing FV space S;
    Select the point J which gives the maximum of local fitness;
    If $J_{S,J} > \theta$, this point is a new FV and added to S;
    If $J_{S,J} \leq \theta$, end the process of FVs selection;
    Train the SVR model on the FVs in the FV space S.
Online Prediction and Incremental Learning:
  When a new point becomes available, calculate the local fitness $J_{S,N}$ of this new point with S;
  If $J_{S,N} > \theta$, this point is a new FV; add it to S and add this new point in the model using the incremental learning method.
  If $J_{S,N} \leq \theta$, keep the model unchanged and continue with the online prediction.

Figure 1. Procedure of OL-FVS-IL.

The offline training includes two parts. The first part is selecting the FVs in the available training dataset with FVS. Our aim is to find the feature space S formed by part of the training dataset which gives the minimum of the global fitness J_S on the training dataset. The procedure is an iterative process of sequential forward selection. For the first iteration, the point which gives the minimum of the global fitness J_S is selected as the first FV in the feature space S. The following iterations are the same: the next possible FV is the point which gives the maximum of local fitness with feature space S; if the local fitness for this point is bigger than the predefined threshold value θ, it is added to the feature space S and we move to the next iteration; otherwise, the selection of FVs in the training dataset is finished. The next step is to train a SVR model on the selected FVs with a classical algorithm.

The online learning is adding the new FVs in the model by the verification of the value of the local fitness of the new data with the existing feature space S.

3. Real Case Study

In the case study, a time series dataset from a sensor for measuring the leaking flow of the first seal of the reactor coolant pump in a nuclear power plant is used to test the performance of the proposed OL-FVS-IL approach applied within PSVR.

After the reconstruction of the raw data, the first 200 data points are selected as training dataset and the following 500 data points form the testing dataset.

A PSVR model is trained with FVs in the training dataset using the approach proposed in [5]. There are totally 26 FVs, which reduces greatly the computational burden of training compared to 200 points. The new FVs in the testing dataset are added in the model one by one with the proposed procedure. A total number of 48 new FVs are added in the model to improve the prediction performance on the testing dataset.

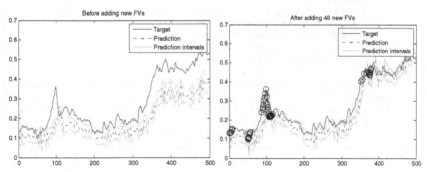

Figure 2. Prediction results before adding any new FVs (left) and after adding 48 new FVs (right).

Figure 2 shows the prediction results before adding any new FVs and after adding 48 new FVs in the testing dataset. It is obvious that the performance is greatly improved with only 10% of all the test data points added to the model. In the right of Figure 2, the circles are the position of the new FVs in the training dataset. It is clear that a new FV is found when there is a change of the ongoing trend. This fact can prove that the proposed online learning approach can efficiently detect and learn the new patterns.

Compared to the prediction results using online learning approaches proposed in [4] and [6], OL-FVS-IL gives better performance on prediction accuracy with less computational complexity (Limited by the length of the paper, details cannot be presented).

4. Conclusions and Prospective

In this paper, an efficient online learning approach called OL-FVS-IL is proposed for reducing the computational burden of offline training and online learning, and for updating the (P)SVR model by incrementally adding one data point in the model each time. The experimental results on a real case study show that the proposed approach can not only reduce significantly the number of data points used for training a (P)SVR model, but also make it appropriate for online prediction and incremental learning: the proposed approach can efficiently learn the new patterns in newly coming data and the prediction performance is improved.

References

1. M. Martin, "On-line support vector machines for function approximation," *tech. rep.*, Software Department, University Politechnica de Catalunya (2002).
2. J. B. Gao, S. R. Gunn, C. J. Harriset and M. Brown, "A Probabilistic Framework for SVM Regression and Error Bar Estimation," *Mach. Learn.,* 46(1-3): 71-89 (2002).
3. G. Baudat and F. Anouar, "Feature Vector Selection and projection using kernels," *Neurocomputing*, 55(1-2): 21-38 (2003).
4. G. Cauwenberghs and T. Poggio, "Incremental and decremental support vector machine learning," *Fourteenth conference on advances in neural information processing systems, NIPS*: 409-415 (2001).
5. J. Liu, R. Seraoui, V. Vitelli and E. Zio, "Nuclear Power Plant Components Condition Monitoring by Probabilistic Support Vector Machine," *Ann. Nucl. Energy*, 56: 23-33 (2013).
6. J. Kivinen, A. J. Smola, R. C. Williamson, "Online learning with kernels," *IEEE Transactions on signal processing*, 52(8): 2165-2176, (2004).

PART 3

FOUNDATIONS OF COMPUTATIONAL INTELLIGENCE

α-ORDERED LINEAR MINIMAL RESOLUTION METHOD IN LATTICE-VALUED PROPOSITIONAL LOGIC SYSTEM LP(X)[*]

HAIRUI JIA[1], HUICONG HE[1], YANG XU[1], YI LIU[1,2]

1. School of Mathematics, Southwest Jiaotong University, Chengdu 610031, China

2. College of Mathematics and Information Science Neijiang Normal University, Neijiang 641112, China

Based on the academic ideas of resolution-based automated reasoning and the previously established research work on general form of α-resolution based automated reasoning schemes in the framework of lattice-valued logic with truth-values in a lattice algebraic structure-lattice implication algebras (LIA), this paper is focused on investigating α-n(t)-ary resolution dynamic automated reasoning method in lattice-valued propositional logic LP(X) based in LIA. In this paper, the definition of α-ordered linear minimal resolution in LP(X) is introduced firstly. Then, its soundness and completeness are proved. One of key issues for α-n(t)-ary resolution dynamic automated reasoning for LP(X) is how to choose generalized literals. It will guide how to choose generalized literals to improve the resolution efficiency in LP(X). This lays the foundation for the further study on α-n(t)-ary resolution automated reasoning.

1. Introduction

Since Robinson presented the resolution principle based on classical logic in 1965 [2], resolution-based automated reasoning has become an active realm and aroused the interest of many scholars [3,4,5,6]. Many classical resolution methods have also been studied. Particularly, there are three typical resolution methods based on Robinson's resolution principle, such as semantic resolution, lock resolution and linear resolution [10]. All these methods are devoted to reducing the redundant clauses and improving the resolution efficiency in the course of resolution.

As an important non-classical logic, lattice-valued logic system based on lattice implication algebra provides a strict and reasonable foundation for automated reasoning [20]. In 2000, Xu et al. [7] established an α-resolution principle in LP(X), as well as its soundness and weak completeness. In 2006, Xu

[*] This work is supported by the National Natural Science Foundation of China (Grant No.61175055, 61100046, 61305074) and the application fundamental research plan project of Sichuan Province(Grant No.2011JY0092). Email: hairuilover@163.com, xuyang@home.swjtu.edu.cn

et al. [8] established a linguistic truth-valued lattice implication algebra $L_{V(n \times 2)}$ by constructing some linguistic truth values frequently used in daily life. In 2007, Xu et al. [9] established the weak completeness of α-resolution in lattice-valued propositional logic $(L_n \times L_2)P(X)$ based on LIA $L_n \times L_2$, and also provided the weak completeness of α-resolution in linguistic truth-valued lattice-valued propositional logic. In 2008, Li et al. [18] studied the properties of α-resolution fields of generalized literals in lattice-valued propositional logic $L_{n \times 2}P(X)$ and the relation between α-resolution in $L_{n \times 2}P(X)$ and that in lattice-valued propositional logic $L_nP(X)$. To further improve the efficiency of α-resolution automated reasoning, in 2010, Xu et al. [1] established the general form of α-resolution principle in LP(X), as well as its soundness and completeness. This lays the foundation for the research of resolution automated reasoning methods. Afterwards, Zhong and Xu established α-group resolution principle in LP(X), and also proved its soundness and completeness theorems [21].

To further improve the resolution efficiency and reduce redundancy clause, α-n(t)-ary dynamic resolution automated reasoning was proposed in the National Natural Science Foundation of China (Grant No. 61175055) by Xu in 2011. In α-n(t)-ary resolution, the number n(t) of resolution generalized literals in the tth resolution is not fixed at some number. In order to research α-n(t)-ary dynamic resolution automated reasoning, α-minimal resolution principle which determines how to choose generalized literals in LP(X), as well as its soundness and completeness are introduced in [24]. It is the theoretical guidance for α-n(t)-ary resolution dynamic automated reasoning. Under the guidance of the theory, the corresponding resolution method in LP(X) is researched in this paper.

This paper is organized as follows: Section 2 reviews some preliminary relevant concepts about LP(X); In Section 3, α-ordered linear minimal resolution method in LP(X) is proposed, and its soundness and completeness are also obtained. Thus, this lays the foundation for researching on α-n(t)-ary resolution dynamic automated reasoning algorithm in the future.

2. Preliminaries

Definition 2.1 [11] Let $(L, \vee, \wedge, O, I)$ be a bounded lattice with an order-reversing involution $'$, I and O the greatest and the smallest element of L respectively, and $\rightarrow: L \times L \rightarrow L$ be a mapping. $(L, \vee, \wedge, ', \rightarrow, O, I)$ is called a lattice implication algebra if the following conditions hold for any x, $y, z \in L$:

$(I_1)\ x \rightarrow (y \rightarrow z) = y \rightarrow (x \rightarrow z)$,

$(I_2)\ x \rightarrow x = I,$

$(I_3)\ x \rightarrow y = y' \rightarrow x',$

$(I_4)\ x \rightarrow y = y \rightarrow x = I$ implies $x = y,$

$(I_5)\ (x \rightarrow y) \rightarrow y = (y \rightarrow x) \rightarrow x,$

$(l_1)\ (x \vee y) \rightarrow z = (x \rightarrow z) \wedge (y \rightarrow z),$

$(l_2)\ (x \wedge y) \rightarrow z = (x \rightarrow z) \vee (y \rightarrow z).$

Definition 2.2 [20] (α-resolution principle) In lattice-valued propositional logic system LP(X), let L be a lattice implication algebra, $\alpha \in L$, G_1 and G_2 two generalized clauses of the form

$$G_1 = g_1 \vee \ldots \vee g_i \vee \ldots \vee g_m, \qquad G_2 = h_1 \vee \ldots \vee h_j \vee \ldots \vee h_n,$$

where g_i (i= 1,2, ...,m) and h_j (j = 1,2, ...,n) are generalized literals in G_1 and G_2 respectively. If $g_i \wedge h_j \leq \alpha$ then

$$g_1 \vee \ldots \vee g_{i-1} \vee g_{i+1} \vee \ldots \vee g_m \vee h_1 \vee \ldots \vee h_{j-1} \vee h_{j+1} \vee \ldots \vee h_n$$

is called an α-resolvent of G_1 and G_2, denoted by $R_\alpha(G_1, G_2)$, and (g_i, h_j) is called an α-resolution pair, denoted by (g_i, h_j)-α.

Definition 2.3 [23] Let C = $g_1 \vee g_2 \vee \ldots \vee g_i \ldots \vee g_n$ be a generalized clause. If there exists some equivalent generalized literals in C, then we remain the leftmost generalized literal and delete the other equivalent generalized literals. The above process is called left-combination rule.

Definition 2.4 [23] A generalized clause C is called an ordered generalized clause if the following criterions hold:

(r1) C has been simplified by using the left-combination rule,

(r2) align by the length of the generalized literals from left to right and put the longest generalized literal on to the leftmost position in C, where the length means the order of the generalized literal (if the order is equivalent, they can be arbitrary arrange),

(r3) especially, put the generalized literals containing the constants in front of the constants in C.

We refer the readers to for more details about the concepts and properties about lattice implication algebra and lattice-valued propositional logic system and α-resolution principle based on LP(X)[11, 20, 22].

3. α-ordered linear minimal resolution method in lattice-valued propositional logic system LP(X)

Definition 3.1 Let $C_i = p_{i1} \vee \ldots \vee p_{in_i}$ be generalized clauses in LP(X), $H_i = \{p_{i1}, \ldots, p_{in_i}\}$ the set of all generalized literals occurring in C_i, $x_i \in H_i$, i=0,1,2,...,n. $\alpha \in L$, and C_0 is an ordered generalized clause. If there exists the leftmost generalized literal x_0 in C_0 such that $x_0 \wedge x_1 \wedge x_2 \wedge \ldots \wedge x_n \leq \alpha$, but for any $j \in \{1, 2, ..., n\}$, $x_0 \wedge x_1 \wedge ... \wedge x_{j-1} \wedge x_{j+1} \wedge ... \wedge x_n \nleq \alpha$, then

$C_0(x_0 = \alpha) \vee C_1(x_1 = \alpha) \vee ... \vee C_n(x_n = \alpha)$ is called α-ordered minimal resolvent of C_0 and $\{C_1, ..., C_n\}$, denoted by

$R_{p(og-\alpha)}{}^m (C_0(x_0), \{C_1(x_1), ..., C_n(x_n)\})$, and x_0, x_1, ..., x_n are called an α-ordered minimal resolution group.

Theorem 3.1 In LP(X), let C_0 be an ordered generalized clause, C_i ($i=1,2,...,n$)be generalized clauses, H_i the set of all generalized literals occurring in C_i, $\alpha \in L$. If there exist the leftmost generalized literal x_0 in C_0 and generalized literals $x_i \in H_i$, $i = 1,2,...,n$, such that $x_0 \wedge x_1 \wedge x_2 \wedge ... \wedge x_n \leq \alpha$, and $R_{p(og-\alpha)}{}^m (C_0(x_0), \{C_1(x_1), ..., C_n(x_n)\})$ is α-ordered minimal resolvent of C_0 and $\{C_1, ..., C_n\}$, then

$C_0 \wedge C_1 \wedge C_2 \wedge ... \wedge C_n \leq R_{p(og-\alpha)}{}^m (C_0(x_0), \{C_1(x_1), ..., C_n(x_n)\})$.

Definition 3.2 Suppose S be a set of generalized clauses in LP(X), an ordered generalized clause $C_0 \in S$, $\alpha \in L$. $\{C_0, \Phi_1, \Phi_2, ..., \Phi_t\}$ is called an α-ordered linear minimal resolution deduction from S to an ordered generalized clause Φ_t (or S can be α-ordered linear minimal resolved into Φ_t), if

(1) C_0 is a top ordered generalized clause, T_i is a set of side generalized clauses with respect to Φ_i, where $i=0, 1, ..., t-1$, $\Phi_0 = C_0$;

(2) $\Phi_i = R_{p(og-\alpha)}{}^m (\Phi_{i-1}, T_{i-1})$, $i=1,..., t$;

(3) For any side generalized clause set T_i, $T_0 \subseteq S - \{C_0\}$, $T_i \subseteq S \cup \{\Phi_0, ..., \Phi_{i-1}\}$, $i=1,..., t$.

Theorem 3.2 (Soundness) In LP(X), Suppose S be a set of generalized clauses, an ordered generalized clause $C_0 \in S$, $\alpha \in L$. $\{C_0, \Phi_1, \Phi_2, ..., \Phi_t\}$ is an α-ordered linear minimal resolution deduction from S to an ordered generalized clause Φ_t with the top generalized clause C_0. If Φ_t is α-$\odot$, then $S \leq \alpha$, i.e., if $\Phi_t \leq \alpha$, then $S \leq \alpha$.

Proof According to theorem 3.1, the soundness theorem holds.

Theorem 3.3 (Completeness) Suppose that $S = C_1 \wedge C_2 \wedge ... \wedge C_m$, where C_1, C_2, ..., C_m are generalized clauses in LP(X) and $\alpha \in L$. If $S \leq \alpha$, then there exists an α-ordered linear minimal resolution deduction from S to α-$\odot$.

Proof According to the proof course of completeness theorem in [1] and [24], it is obvious that the theorem holds.

Example 3.1 Let $C_1 = x \rightarrow y$, $C_2 = (x \rightarrow z)'$, $C_3 = (a_5 \rightarrow q) \vee (y \rightarrow z) \vee (y \rightarrow a_2)$, $C_4 = (p \rightarrow q)'$ be four generalized clauses in lattice-valued propositional logic $L_9P(X)$, where a_2, $a_5 \in L_9$, x, y, z, p, q are propositional variables, written as $S = C_1 \wedge C_2 \wedge C_3 \wedge C_4$. If $\alpha = a_6$, then $S \leq \alpha$ and there exists an α-ordered linear minimal resolution deduction from S to α-$\odot$.

According to Definition 3.2, α-ordered linear minimal resolution deduction as follows:

Step 1. Set a top generalized clause C_3 and a set C_4 of side generalized clauses such that $(a_5 \rightarrow q) \wedge (p \rightarrow q)' \leq \alpha$, then the α-ordered linear minimal resolvent $D_1 = R_{p(og-\alpha)}{}^m (C_3, \{C_4\}) = (y \rightarrow z) \vee (y \rightarrow a_2) \vee \alpha$.

Step 2. Set a center generalized clause D_1 and a set $\{C_1, C_2\}$ of side generalized clauses such that $(y \rightarrow z) \wedge (x \rightarrow y) \wedge (x \rightarrow z)' \leq \alpha$, then the α-ordered linear minimal resolvent

$$D_2 = R_{p(og-\alpha)}{}^m (D_1, \{C_1, C_2\}) = (y \rightarrow a_2) \vee \alpha.$$

Step 3. Set a center generalized clause D_2 and a set $\{C_1, C_2\}$ of side generalized clauses such that $(y \rightarrow a_2) \wedge (x \rightarrow y) \wedge (x \rightarrow z)' \leq \alpha$, then the α-ordered linear minimal resolvent

$$D_3 = R_{p(og-\alpha)}{}^m (D_2, \{C_1, C_2\}) = \alpha.$$

Conclusions

In this paper, α-resolution method for resolution dynamic automated reasoning based on lattice-valued logic system is studied. α-ordered linear minimal resolution method is presented in lattice-valued propositional logic system LP(X) based on lattice implication algebra. In a resolution process, a set of side generalized clauses with respect to a center generalized clause is selected, and their α-ordered linear minimal resolvent is obtained. Both soundness and completeness theorems are established in LP(X). On the basis of the present methods of α-ordered linear minimal resolution method in LP(X), automated reasoning algorithm for α-ordered linear minimal resolution based on lattice-valued logic system can be designed.

References

[1] Yang Xu, Jun Liu, Xiaomei Zhong, Shuwei Chen, Multiary α-Resolution Principle for a Lattice-Valued Logic, IEEE TRANSACTIONS ON FUZZY SYSTEMS, 2013, 21(5): 898-912.

[2] J.A. Robinson (1965), A machine-oriented logic based on the resolution principle, J. ACM, 12(1), 23-41.

[3] C.L. Chang, R.C.T. Lee (1973), Symbolic Logic and Mechanical Theorem Proving, New York: Academic Press.

[4] D.W. Loveland (1978), Automated Theorem Proving: A logical Basis, Amsterdam: North- Holland.

[5] D. Luckham (1970), Refinements in resolution theory, Proc. IRIA Symp.Automatic Demonstration, Versailes, France, Spring-Verlag, 125, 163-190.

[6] Sofronie-Stokkermans V., Ihlemann C. (2007), Automated reasoning in some local extensions of ordered structures, Journal of Multiple-Valued Logic and Soft Computing, 13(4-6), 397-414.

[7] Y. Xu, D. Ruan, E. E. Kerre and J. Liu, α-resolution principle based on lattice-valued propositional logic LP(X), Information Sciences, 130 (2000), 195-223.

196

[8] Y. Xu, S. W. Chen and J. Ma, Linguistic truth-valued lattice implication algebra and its properties, Proc. IMACS MuLticonference on "Computational Engineering in Systems Applications" (CESA2006), Beijing, China, (2006), pp.1413-1418.

[9] Y. Xu, S. W. Chen, J. Liu and D. Ruan, Weak completeness of resolution in a linguistic truth-valued prepositional logic, Proc. IFSA2007: Theoretical Advances and Applications of Fuzzy Logic and Soft Computing, June 18-21, (2007), Cancun, Mexico, pp. 358-366

[10] Xuhua Liu (1994), Resolution-based Automated Reasoning, Beijing: Academic Press of China (in Chinese).

[11] Y. Xu, Lattice implication algebras, J. Southwest Jiaotong University 89(1) (1993) 20-27 (in Chinese).

[12] Yang Xu, Keyun Qin (1993), Lattice-valued propositional logic(I), J. Southwest Jiaotong University, 1(1), 123-128 (English version).

[13] Yang Xu, Keyun Qin (1994), Lattice-valued propositional logic(II), J. Southwest Jiaotong University, 2(1), 22-27 (English version).

[14] Yang Xu, Keyun Qin, Jun Liu, Zhenming Song (1999), L-valued propositional logic Lvpl, Information Sciences, 114, 205-235.

[15] Yang Xu, Jun Liu, Zhenming Song, Keyun Qin (2000), On Semantics of L-Valued First-Order Logic Lvfl, Int. J. General Systems, 29(1), 53-79.

[16] Yang Xu, Keyun Qin, Eun Hwan Roh (2001), A First Order Lattice   Valued Logic System I: Semantics, The Journal of Fuzzy Mathematics, 9(4), 969-976.

[17] Yang Xu, Zhenming Song, Keyun Qin, Jun Liu (2001), Syntax of L-valued First-Order Logic Lvfl, Int. Multi. Val. Logic., 7, 213-257.

[18] X. B. Li, X. P. Qiu, Z. Y. Chang and Y. Xu, The properties of α-resolution and J-resolution based on lattice-valued prepositional logic system, Chinese Quarterly Journal of Mathematics, 6(2008), 262-269 (in Chinese).

[19] Weitao Xu, Yang Xu, Dexian Zhang, General form of α-Linear Resolution Based on Lattice-Valued Propositional Logic LP(X), The 10th International FLINS Conference on Uncertainty Modeling in Knowledge Engineering and Decision Making, Istanbul, Turkey, August 26-29, 2012, 720-725.

[20] Yang Xu, Da Ruan, Keyun Qin and Jun Liu, Lattice-Valued Logic--An Alternative Approach to Treat Fuzziness and Incomparability, Berlin: Springer-Verlag (2003).

[21] X. M. Zhong and Y. Xu, α-group resolution principle based on lattice-valued logic, 2011 Eighth International Conference on Fuzzy Systems and Knowledge Discovery (FSKD), 1418-1422.

[22] Yang Xu, Xiaomei Zhong, Xingxing He, Jun Liu (2012), Research advances on resolution automated reasoning in lattice-valued logic based on lattice implication algebra, The 10th International FLINS Conference on Uncertainty Modeling in Knowledge Engineering and Decision Making (FLINS2012), Istanbul, Turkey, August 26-29, 2012, 714-721.

[23] Weitao Xu, Yang Xu (2012), α-ordered linear resolution for lattice-valued logic system based on lattice implication algebra, Int. J. Applied Management Science, 4(4), 460-479.

[24] HAIRUI JIA, YANG XU, YI LIU, HUICONG HE, α-minimal resolution principle based on lattice-valued propositional logic LP(X), Program for International Conference on 2013 Machine Learning and Cybernetics(ICMLC2013), Tianjin, China, 1729-1734(2013).

NON-CLAUSAL MULTI-ARY α-GENERALIZED RESOLUTION PRINCIPLE FOR A LATTICE-VALUED PROPOSITIONAL LOGIC

Yang Xu[1], Jun Liu[2], Xingxing He[1,*], Xiaomei Zhong[1], and Shuwei Chen[2]

[1] *Intelligent Control Development Center, Southwest Jiaotong University, Chengdu 610031, Sichuan, PR China*
[2] *School of Computing and Mathematics, University of Ulster, Northern Ireland, UK*
E-mail: xuyang@home.swjtu.edu.cn, j.liu@ulster.ac.uk, x.he@home.swjtu.edu.cn, zhongxm2013@home.swjtu.edu.cn, s.chen@ulster.ac.uk

As a continuation and extension of the established work on binary resolution at certain truth-value level (called α-resolution), this paper introduces non-clausal multi-ary α-generalized resolution principle and deduction for lattice-valued propositional logic LP(X) based on lattice implication algebra, which is essentially a non-clausal generalized resolution avoiding the reduction to normal clausal form. Non-clausal multi-ary α-generalized resolution deduction in LP(X) is then proved to be sound and complete.

Keywords: Resolution automated reasoning; Lattice-valued propositional logic; Lattice implication algebra; Non-clausal multi-ary α-generalized resolution

1. Introduction

Automatic theorem proving is mechanization of mathematical inference by means of logical system and inference rules, rather than computation among numbers. The resolution principle, is just one simple inference principle, but is effective, and the resolution deduction is sound and complete in Boolean logic system. Since it is introduced by Robinson in 1965,[6] resolution-based automated reasoning has been extensively studied with the attempt at finding natural and efficient proof systems to support a wide spectrum of computational tasks, and successfully applied into many areas[5] such as artificial intelligence, software model checking and testing, and so on.

The use of many-valued logics[2] becomes increasingly important in computer science and artificial intelligence aiming at establishing the logical foundation for uncertain information processing. Lattice-valued logic[14] ,

---

*The corresponding author

as one of the most important many-valued logics, extends the chain-type truth-valued field to a general lattice in which the truth-values are incompletely comparable with each other. Lattice-valued logic is thus an important and promising research direction that provides an alternative logical approach to dealing with imprecision and incomparability as well. Up to now, many researchers have made some investigation on resolution-based automated reasoning in the framework of many-valued logic, and obtained some important results.[1,8]

Xu et al. developed α-resolution principle and deduction in lattice-valued logic based on lattice implication algebra,[11] and claimed its soundness and completeness.[12,13] Compared with resolution principle in Boolean logic, the α-resolution principle in lattice-valued logic based on lattice implication algebra has some new features.[14] Furthermore, in order to handle more than two generalized clauses simultaneously, Xu et al. extended the α-resolution principle to multi-ary α-resolution principle in lattice-valued logic,[16] which can greatly improve the efficiency of α-resolution automated reasoning. Inspired from motivation of generalized resolution[4,9,10] in Boolean logic and multi-ary resolution[16] in lattice-valued logic, the present paper is a continuation and extension of these work, and proposes non-clausal multi-ary α-generalized resolution principle for lattice-valued propositional logic.

2. Preliminaries

Definition 2.1.[11,14] Let $(L, \vee, \wedge, O, I)$ be a bounded lattice with an order-reversing involution "'", I and O the greatest and the smallest element of L respectively, and $\rightarrow: L \times L \longrightarrow L$ be a mapping. $\mathcal{L} = (L, \vee, \wedge, ', \rightarrow, O, I)$ is called a lattice implication algebra (LIA) if the following conditions hold for any $x, y, z \in L$:

(I_1) $x \rightarrow (y \rightarrow z) = y \rightarrow (x \rightarrow z)$,
(I_2) $x \rightarrow x = I$,
(I_3) $x \rightarrow y = y' \rightarrow x'$,
(I_4) $x \rightarrow y = y \rightarrow x = I$ implies $x = y$,
(I_5) $(x \rightarrow y) \rightarrow y = (y \rightarrow x) \rightarrow x$,
(L_1) $(x \vee y) \rightarrow z = (x \rightarrow z) \wedge (y \rightarrow z)$,
(L_2) $(x \wedge y) \rightarrow z = (x \rightarrow z) \vee (y \rightarrow z)$.

Definition 2.2.[14] Let $L_6 = \{O, a, b, c, d, I\}$, the Hasse diagram of L_6 be defined as Fig. 1 and its implication operator be defined as Fig. 2. Then $(L_6, \vee, \wedge, ', \rightarrow, O, I)$ is an LIA.

→	O	a	b	c	d	I
O	I	I	I	I	I	I
a	c	I	b	c	b	I
b	d	a	I	b	a	I
c	a	a	I	I	a	I
d	b	I	I	b	I	I
I	O	a	b	c	d	I

Fig. 1. Hasse Diagram of L_6 Fig. 2. Implication Operator of L_6

Definition 2.3.[14] Let X be the set of propositional variables, $(L, \vee, \wedge, ', \rightarrow, O, I)$ be an LIA, $T = L \cup \{', \rightarrow\}$ be a type with $ar(') = 1$, $ar(\rightarrow) = 2$ and $ar(a) = 0$ for any $a \in L$. The proposition algebra of the lattice-valued proposition calculus on the set X of propositional variables is the free T algebra on X and denoted by LP(X).

The detail about other important definitions and properties such as logical formula, valuation, generalized literal (g-literal), generalized clause (g-clause) in LP(X) can be found in.[12,14]

Definition 2.4.[12] (α-Resolution). Let $\alpha \in L$, and G_1 and G_2 be two g-clauses in LP(X) of the forms $G_1 = g_1 \vee \ldots \vee g_i \vee \ldots \vee g_m$, $G_2 = h_1 \vee \ldots \vee h_j \vee \ldots \vee h_n$.
If $g_i \wedge h_j \leq \alpha$, then

$$G = g_1 \vee \ldots \vee g_{i-1} \vee g_{i+1} \vee \ldots \vee g_m \vee h_1 \vee \ldots \vee h_{j-1} \vee h_{j+1} \vee \ldots \vee h_n$$

is called an α-resolvent of G_1 and G_2, denoted by $G = R_\alpha(G_1, G_2)$, and g_i and h_j form an α-resolution pair, denoted by (g_i, h_j)-α. Generation of an α-resolvent from two clauses, called as α-resolution, is the sole rule of inference of the α-resolution principle.

Definition 2.5.[12] In LP(X), suppose a generalized conjunctive normal form $S = C_1 \wedge C_2 \wedge \ldots \wedge C_n$, $\alpha \in L$. $w = \{D_1, D_2, \ldots, D_m\}$ is an α-resolution deduction from S to a g-clause D_m, if for any $i \in \{1, 2, \ldots, m\}$

(1) $D_i \in \{C_1, C_2, \ldots, C_n\}$, or
(2) there exist $j, k < i$, such that $D_i = R_\alpha(D_j, D_k)$.

The soundness and completeness[12,14] of α-resolution deduction hold for LP(X).

3. Non-Clausal Multi-ary α-Generalized Resolution Principle for LP(X)

Definition 3.1. Let $g_1, g_2, \ldots, g_n$ be g-literals in LP(X). A lattice-valued propositional logical formula in LP(X) is called a general generalized ground clause (in short, general g^2-clause) if it is a composite formula from the g-literals $g_1, g_2, \ldots, g_n$ connected by logical connectives $\wedge$, or $\vee$, or $\rightarrow$, or $'$ or $\leftrightarrow$, denoted by $\Phi(g_1, g_2, \ldots, g_n)$.

Definition 3.2. A general g^2-clause G in LP(X) is called a constant g^2-clause if all the g-literals in G are all constants. Particularly, if $\gamma(G) = \alpha$ for any valuation γ of LP(X), then G is called an α-constant g^2-clause.

Definition 3.3.[15] Let Φ be a general g^2-clause in LP(X). A g-literal g of Φ is called a local extremely complex form, if

(1) g can't be expanded to a more complex g-literal in Φ by adding $\rightarrow$ and $'$.

(2) If $g = g_1 \leftrightarrow g_2$, g_1 and g_2 are g-literals in LP(X), then g is the local extremely complex form as a whole.

Definition 3.4. (Non-clausal n-ary α-generalized resolution) Let Φ_1, Φ_2, $\ldots$, Φ_n be general g^2-clause in LP(X), H_i be the set of g-literals in Φ_i $(i = 1, 2, \ldots, n)$, $\alpha \in L$. If there exists general literals $g_i \in H_i$, such that $\wedge_{i=1}^{n} g_i \leq \alpha$, then

$$G = \vee_{i=1}^{n} \Phi_i(g_i = \alpha)$$

is called a non-clausal n-ary α-generalized resolvent of Φ_1, Φ_2, $\ldots$, Φ_n, denoted by $G = R_{p(N-n-\alpha)-g}(\Phi_1(g_1), \Phi_2(g_2), \ldots, \Phi_n(g_n))$, here "$p$" means "propositional logic" and "$(N$-n-$\alpha)$-g" means "non-clausal n-ary α-generalized" in "$R_{p(N-n-\alpha)-g}$".

Theorem 3.1. Let $\Phi_1, \Phi_2, \ldots, \Phi_n$ be general g^2-clauses in LP(X), H_i the set of g-literals in $\Phi_i (i = 1, 2, \ldots, n)$, $\alpha \in L$. If there exists $g_i \in H_i$, such that $\wedge_{i=1}^{n} g_i \leq \alpha$, then

$$\wedge_{i=1}^{n} \Phi_i \leq R_{p(N-n-\alpha)-g}(\Phi_1(g_1), \Phi_2(g_2), \ldots, \Phi_n(g_n)).$$

Remark 3.1. If a g-literal which includes many implication connectives is not seen as the local extremely complex form, then Theorem 3.1 may not hold. An example is shown as follows.

Example 3.1. Let Φ_1 and Φ_2 be two general g^2-clauses in $L_6P(X)$, $\Phi_1 = (b \to x)' \to d$, $\Phi_2 = (d \to x)' \to b$, where x is a propositional variable, $b, d \in L_6$, and set $\alpha = a \in L_6$ (see Definition 2.2). Therefore, $\Phi_1 \wedge \Phi_2 = ((b \to x)' \to d) \wedge ((d \to x)' \to b) \geq (b \to d) \wedge (d \to b) = a$. On the other hand, since $(b \to x)' \wedge (d \to x)' \leq b \wedge d = d < a$, if $g_1 = (b \to x)'$, $g_2 = (d \to x)'$, then $R_{p(N-2-\alpha)-g}(\Phi_1(g_1), \Phi_2(g_2)) = (a \to d) \vee (a \to b) = b \vee b = b$. However, $\Phi_1 \wedge \Phi_2 \nleq R_{p(N-2-\alpha)-g}(\Phi_1(g_1), \Phi_2(g_2))$ for $a \nleq b$.

Definition 3.5. Suppose S is a set of general g^2-clauses in LP(X), $\alpha \in L$. Then $w = \{D_1, D_2, \ldots, D_m\}$ is called a non-clausal muti-ary α-generalized resolution deduction from S to a general g^2-clause D_m, if

(1) $D_i \in S(i = 1, 2, \ldots, m)$, or
(2) There exist $r_1, r_2, \ldots, r_{k_i} < i$, such that $R_{p(N-k_i-\alpha)-g}(D_{r_1}, D_{r_2}, \ldots, D_{r_{k_i}}) = D_i$.

Theorem 3.2. *(Soundness) Let S be a set of general g^2-clauses in LP(X), $\alpha \in L$, $\{D_1, D_2, \ldots, D_m\}$ be a non-clausal muti-ary α-generalized resolution deduction from S to a general g^2-clause D_m. If $D_m = \alpha$, then $S \leq \alpha$.*

Theorem 3.3. *(Completeness) Suppose S is a set of general g^2-clauses in LP(X). If $S \leq \alpha$, then there exists a non-clausal muti-ary α-generalized resolution deduction from S to an α-constant g^2-clause.*

4. Conclusion

In this paper, a non-clausal multi-ary α-generalized resolution principle and its resolution deduction for lattice-valued propositional logic based on LIA were proposed. The definitions of the general form of non-clausal multi-ary α-generalized resolution and its resolution deduction in LP(X) were given, along with its soundness and completeness. The further research will be concentrated on extending it to lattice-valued first order logic LF(X), and contriving an algorithm to achieve the efficiency of the non-clausal multi-ary α-generalized resolution.

Acknowledgments

This work is supported by the National Science Foundation of China (Grant No. 60875034, 61175055, 61305074), the project TIN-2009-0828; Sichuan Key Technology Research and Development Program of China (Grant No. 2011FZ0051), the Radio Administration Bureau of MIIT of China (Grant

No. [2011] 146) and China Institution of Communications (Grant No. [2011] 051).

References

1. D. Guller, Binary resolution over complete residuated stone lattices, Fuzzy Sets and Systems 159, pp. 1031–1041 (2008).
2. P. Hajek, Metamathematics of fuzzy logic. Kluwer Academic Publishers - Dordrecht, 2000.
3. J. Liu, D. Ruan, Y. Xu, Z.M. Song, A resolution-like strategy based on a lattice-valued logic, IEEE Transactions on Fuzzy Systems, 11(4), pp. 560–567 (2003).
4. N. Murray, Completely non-clausal theorem proving. Artificial Intelligence, 18, pp. 67–85 (1982).
5. Z. Pei, D. Ruan, J. Liu, Y. Xu, Linguistic values-based intelligent information processing: theory, methods, and applications, Atlantis Press, 2009.
6. J.P. Robinson, A machine-oriented logic based on the resolution principle, J. ACM 12, pp. 23–41 (1965).
7. D. Smutná-Hliněná, P. Vojtáš, Graded many-valued resolution with aggregation, Fuzzy Sets and Systems, 143, 157–168 (2004).
8. V. Sofronie-Stokkermans, C. Ihlemann, Automated reasoning in some local extensions of ordered structures, Journal of Multiple-Valued Logic and Soft Computing, 13(4-6), pp. 397–414 (2007).
9. Z. Stachniak, Non-clausal reasoning with definite theories, Fundamenta Informaticae 48, pp. 1–26 (2001).
10. X.H. Wang, X.H. Liu, Generalized resolution, Chinese journal of computers, 2, pp. 81–92 (1982) (in Chinese).
11. Y. Xu, Lattice implication algebras, J. Southwest Jiaotong University, 89(1), pp. 20–27 (1993) (in Chinese).
12. Y. Xu, D. Ruan, E.E. Kerre, J. Liu, α-Resolution principle based on lattice-valued propositional logic LP(X). Information Sciences 130, pp. 195–223 (2000).
13. Y. Xu, D. Ruan, E.E. Kerre, J. Liu, α-Resolution principle based on lattice-valued first-order lattice-valued logic LF(X), Information Science 132, pp. 221–239 (2001).
14. Y. Xu, D. Ruan, K.Y. Qin, J. Liu, Lattice-Valued Logic: An alternative approach to treat fuzziness and incomparability, Springer-Verlag, Berlin, 2003.
15. Y. Xu, W. T. Xu, X. M. Zhong, X. X. He, α-Generalized resolution principle based on lattice-valued propositional logic system LP(X), In: Proc. 2010 The 9th International FLINS Conference on Foundations and Applications of Computational Intelligence (FLINS2010), pp. 66–71 (2010).
16. Y. Xu, J. Liu, X.M. Zhong, S.W. Chen, Multi-ary α-resolution principle for a lattice-valued logic, IEEE Transactions on Fuzzy Systems, 21(5), pp. 898–912 (2013).

BASES IN $\mathcal{L}$-SEMILINEAR SPACES

Q. Y. SHU*, Q. Q XIONG and X. P. WANG

*College of Mathematics and Software Science, Sichuan Normal University,
Chengdu, Sichuan 610066, People's Republic of China*
E-mail: lsabels@21cn.com

The aim of this contribution is to discuss the characterizations of $\mathcal{L}$-semilinear spaces which are generated by strong linearly independent vectors. We will show that the basis in $\mathcal{L}$-semilinear spaces which are generated by strong linearly independent vectors is also strong linearly independent.

Keywords: Semilinear spaces; Strong linearly independent; Basis.

1. Semilinear Spaces

We recall that a linear (vector) space is a special case of a module over a ring, i.e. a linear space is a unitary module over a field. In this contribution, we will be dealing with a unitary semimodule over a zerosumfree semiring (see e.g.,[5]) which will be called a semilinear space (see also[2,7]). Below, let us recall necessary definitions.

A semiring $\mathcal{L}$ is called zerosumfree if $a + b = 0$ implies that $a = b = 0$ for any $a, b \in L$. It is clear that fuzzy algebra $\langle [0, 1], max, min \rangle$ is a zerosumfree semiring. The following definition is a general version of that of a semilinear space in:[2]

Definition 1.1 (Shu and Wang, 2011). Let $\mathcal{L} = \langle L, +, \cdot, 0, 1 \rangle$ be a semiring. Then a semimodule over $\mathcal{L}$ is called an $\mathcal{L}$-semilinear space.

Note that in Definition 1.1, a semimodule stands for a left $\mathcal{L}$-semimodule or a right $\mathcal{L}$-semimodule as in.[2] Elements of an $\mathcal{L}$-semilinear space will be called vectors and elements of a semiring scalars. The former will be denoted by bold letters to distinguish them from scalars.

Without loss of generality, in what follows, we consider left $\mathcal{L}$-semimodules for convenience of notation. Let $\underline{n} = \{1, \cdots, n\}$. Then we can construct an $\mathcal{L}$-semilinear space as follows.

Example 1.1 (Shu and Wang, 2011). Let $\mathcal{L}=\langle L, +, \cdot, 0, 1\rangle$ be a semiring. For each $n \geqslant 1$, let

$$V_n(L) = \{(a_1, a_2, \cdots, a_n)^T : a_i \in L, i \in \underline{n}\}.$$

Define

$$\mathbf{x} + \mathbf{y} = (x_1 + y_1, x_2 + y_2, \cdots, x_n + y_n)^T,$$

$$r * \mathbf{x} = (r \cdot x_1, r \cdot x_2, \cdots, r \cdot x_n)^T$$

for all $\mathbf{x} = (x_1, x_2, \cdots, x_n)^T, \mathbf{y} = (y_1, y_2, \cdots, y_n)^T \in V_n(L)$ and $r \in L$, where $(x_1, x_2, \cdots, x_n)^T$ denotes the transpose of $(x_1, x_2, \cdots, x_n)$. Then $\mathcal{V}_n = \langle L, +, \cdot, 0, 1; *; V_n(L), +, \mathbf{0}_{n \times 1}\rangle$ is an $\mathcal{L}$-semilinear space with $\mathbf{0}_{n \times 1} = (0, 0, \cdots, 0)^T$.

From now on, without causing confusion we use $r\mathbf{a}$ instead of $r * \mathbf{a}$ for all $r \in L$ and $\mathbf{a} \in A$ in an $\mathcal{L}$-semilinear space $\langle L, +, \cdot, 0, 1; *; A, +_A, 0_A\rangle$.

Definition 1.2 (Di Nola et al., 2007). In $\mathcal{L}$-semilinear space, a single vector $\mathbf{a}$ is linearly independent. Vectors $\mathbf{a}_1, \cdots, \mathbf{a}_n$, $n \geqslant 2$, are linearly independent if none of them can be represented by a linear combination of the others. Otherwise, we say that vectors $\mathbf{a}_1, \cdots, \mathbf{a}_n$ are linearly dependent. An infinite set of vectors is linearly independent if any finite subset of it is linearly independent.

A nonempty subset G of an $\mathcal{L}$-semilinear space is called a set of generators if every element of the $\mathcal{L}$-semilinear space is a linear combination of elements in G (see[1]). Let S be a set of generators of $\mathcal{L}$-semilinear space $\mathcal{A}$. Then denote as $\mathcal{A} = \langle S\rangle$.

Definition 1.3 (Golan, 1999). A linearly independent set of generators of an $\mathcal{L}$-semilinear space $\mathcal{A}$ is called a basis of $\mathcal{A}$.

Definition 1.4 (Golan, 1999). An element $a \in L$ is called invertible in a semiring $\mathcal{L}$ if there exists an element $b \in L$ such that $ab = ba = 1$. Such element b is called an inverse of a, denote it by a^{-1}. Let $U(L)$ denote the set of all invertible elements in a semiring $\mathcal{L}$.

Definition 1.5 (Wang and Shu, 2013). In $\mathcal{V}_n$, vectors $\mathbf{a}_1, \cdots, \mathbf{a}_n$ are semi-linearly dependent if and only if there exist two nonempty disjoint subsets of indices $J_1 \subset \underline{n}$ and $J_2 \subset \underline{n}$ together with $0 \neq \lambda_i \in L, i \in J_1 \cup J_2$, such that $\sum_{j \in J_1} \lambda_j \mathbf{a}_j = \sum_{j \in J_2} \lambda_j \mathbf{a}_j$ with either $\mid J_1 \mid, \mid J_2 \mid \geq 2$ or if $\mid J_i \mid = 1$ for some $i \in \{1, 2\}$ then $\lambda_j \notin U(L)$ for every $j \in J_i$.

Definition 1.6 (Wang and Shu, 2013). In V_n, a single vector $\mathbf{a}$ is strong linearly independent. Vectors $\mathbf{a}_1, \cdots, \mathbf{a}_n$, $n \geqslant 2$, are strong linearly independent if and only if they are linearly independent and not semi-linearly dependent.

2. Bases in $\mathcal{L}$-semilinear spaces which are generated by strong linearly independent vectors

From Definitions 1.5 and 1.6 we know that, every set of linearly independent vectors either strong linearly independent or semi-linearly dependent. And on the other hand, it is clear that a standard orthogonal vectors are strong linearly independent, but the converse is not true (see[8,9]). We know that in $\mathcal{L}$-semilinear space over commutative semirings which are generated by standard orthogonal, the basis is standard orthogonal, which is different with the conclusion in classical algebra. A natural question to ask now is: if the set of generators of an $\mathcal{L}$-semilinear space is strong linearly independent, what about the other bases? In this section, we shall solve this problem under certain condition. In what follows, we always suppose that $\mathcal{L} = \langle L, +, \cdot, 0, 1 \rangle$ is a commutative zerosumfree semiring. And some notations in,[3] such as yorked semiring, entire, generalized diagonal matrix, etc., we omit them.

Definition 2.1 (Golan, 1999). An element a in a semiring $\mathcal{L}$ is said to be cancellable if and only if $a + b = a + c$ implies $b = c$ for every $b, c \in L$. We denote the set of all cancellable elements of L by $K^+(L)$.

Definition 2.2 (Kuntzman, 1972). Let $A \in M_n(L)$. Denote P (resp. Q) the set of even (resp. odd) permutations of the set $\underline{n}$. A bideterminant $det(A)$ of A is an ordered pair

$$det(A) = (det_1(A), det_2(A))$$

such that $det_1(A), det_2(A) \in L$ with

$$det_1(A) = \sum_{\sigma \in P} a_{1,\sigma(1)} a_{2,\sigma(2)} \cdots a_{n,\sigma(n)} \text{ and}$$

$$det_2(A) = \sum_{\sigma \in Q} a_{1,\sigma(1)} a_{2,\sigma(2)} \cdots a_{n,\sigma(n)}.$$

Note that if $det_1(A) = det_2(A)$, then $det(A) \equiv 0$ (see[9]). Otherwise, we use symbols $det(A) \not\equiv 0$.

Lemma 2.1 (Shu and Wang, 2013). In a cancellative, yoked and entire semiring $\mathcal{L}$, let $\mathcal{W} = \langle \mathbf{x}_1, \mathbf{x}_2, \cdots, \mathbf{x}_t \rangle$, where $\mathbf{x}_1, \mathbf{x}_2, \cdots, \mathbf{x}_t$ are strong linearly independent in $\mathcal{V}_n$. Then every $\mathbf{a} \in \mathcal{W}$, can be uniquely represented by a linear combination of $\mathbf{x}_1, \mathbf{x}_2, \cdots, \mathbf{x}_t$.

Lemma 2.2 (Poplin et al., 2004). *If* $A, B \in M_n(L)$, *then*

$$
\begin{aligned}
&det_1(AB) + det_1(A)det_2(B) + det_2(A)det_1(B) \\
&= det_2(AB) + det_1(A)det_1(B) + det_2(A)det_2(B).
\end{aligned}
$$

Lemma 2.3 (Wang and Shu, 2013). *In a cancellative, yoked and entire semiring* $\mathcal{L}$, *let* $A = (a_{ij}) \in M_n(L)$. *Then* $det(A) \equiv 0$ *if and only if the column-vectors of* A *are linearly dependent or semi-linearly dependent.*

Theorem 2.1. *In a cancellative, yoked and entire semiring* $\mathcal{L}$, *let* $\mathcal{W} = \langle \mathbf{x}_1, \mathbf{x}_2, \cdots, \mathbf{x}_s \rangle$ *with* $\{\mathbf{x}_1, \mathbf{x}_2, \cdots, \mathbf{x}_s\}$ *a set of strong linearly independent vectors in* $\mathcal{V}_n$. *If* $\{\mathbf{y}_1, \mathbf{y}_2, \cdots, \mathbf{y}_p\}$ *is a basis of* $\mathcal{W}$, *then* $\mathbf{y}_1, \mathbf{y}_2, \cdots, \mathbf{y}_p$ *are strong linearly independent and* $s = p$.

Proof. By Lemmas 2.1 we can prove that $s = p$. Let $\mathbf{y}_i = \sum_{j=1}^s a_{ij}\mathbf{x}_j$ with $a_{ij} \in L$ for any $i \in \underline{s}$. Thus

$$(\mathbf{y}_1, \mathbf{y}_2, \cdots, \mathbf{y}_s) = (\mathbf{x}_1, \mathbf{x}_2, \cdots, \mathbf{x}_s)A \tag{1}$$

with $A \in M_s(L)$. Since $\mathbf{y}_1, \mathbf{y}_2, \cdots, \mathbf{y}_s$ are linearly independent, then every column of A has nonzero element. In a similar way, we can let

$$(\mathbf{x}_1, \mathbf{x}_2, \cdots, \mathbf{x}_s) = (\mathbf{y}_1, \mathbf{y}_2, \cdots, \mathbf{y}_s)B$$

with $B = (b_{ji}), b_{ji} \in L, i, j \in \underline{s}$, and every row of B has nonzero element. Therefore,

$$(\mathbf{x}_1, \mathbf{x}_2, \cdots, \mathbf{x}_s) = (\mathbf{x}_1, \mathbf{x}_2, \cdots, \mathbf{x}_s)AB. \tag{2}$$

Since $\{\mathbf{y}_1, \mathbf{y}_2, \cdots, \mathbf{y}_s\}$ is linearly independent, then by Definitions 1.5 and 1.6, we know that $\{\mathbf{y}_1, \mathbf{y}_2, \cdots, \mathbf{y}_s\}$ is either strong linearly independent or semi-linearly dependent. If it is semi-linearly dependent, then by Definition 1.5, there exist two disjoint subsets of indices $J_1 \subset \underline{n}$ and $J_2 \subset \underline{n}$ together with $0 \neq \lambda_j \in L, j \in J_1 \cup J_2$, such that $\sum_{j \in J_1} \lambda_j \mathbf{y}_j = \sum_{j \in J_2} \lambda_j \mathbf{y}_j$ with $\mid J_1 \mid, \mid J_2 \mid \geq 2$ or there exists $\mid J_i \mid = 1, i \in \{1, 2\}$ such that if $j \in J_i$, then $\lambda_j \notin U(L)$. Thus

$$\sum_{j \in J_1} \lambda_j (\sum_{k=1}^s a_{jk}\mathbf{x}_k) = \sum_{j \in J_2} \lambda_j (\sum_{k=1}^s a_{jk}\mathbf{x}_k), \tag{3}$$

where $\mid J_1 \mid, \mid J_2 \mid \geq 2$ or if $\mid J_i \mid = 1$ for some $i \in \{1, 2\}$ then $\lambda_j \notin U(L)$ for every $j \in J_i$. In the first case, $\mid J_1 \mid, \mid J_2 \mid \geq 2$, then we have

$$\sum_{j \in J_1} \lambda_j a_{j1}\mathbf{x}_1 + \cdots + \sum_{j \in J_1} \lambda_i a_{js}\mathbf{x}_s = \sum_{j \in J_2} \lambda_j a_{j1}\mathbf{x}_1 + \cdots + \sum_{j \in J_2} \lambda_j a_{js}\mathbf{x}_s.$$

Since $\mathbf{x}_1, \mathbf{x}_2, \cdots, \mathbf{x}_s$ are strong linearly independent, then $\sum_{j \in J_1} \lambda_j a_{jk} = \sum_{j \in J_2} \lambda_j a_{jk}$ with $k \in \underline{s}$. Let $\mathbf{c}_1, \mathbf{c}_2, \cdots, \mathbf{c}_s$ be column-vectors of A. Then it is obvious that $\sum_{j \in J_1} \lambda_j \mathbf{c}_j = \sum_{j \in J_2} \lambda_j \mathbf{c}_j$, i.e.,$\{\mathbf{c}_1, \mathbf{c}_2, \cdots, \mathbf{c}_s\}$ is linearly dependent or semi-linearly dependent. Thus by Lemma 2.3, we have $det(A) \equiv 0$, i.e. $det_1(A) = det_2(A)$. In the other hand, by Lemma 2.2 and Definition 2.2 we have

$$det_1(AB) + det_1(A)det_2(B) + det_2(A)det_1(B)$$
$$= det_2(AB) + det_1(A)det_1(B) + det_2(A)det_2(B)$$
$$= det_2(AB) + det_2(A)det_1(B) + det_1(A)det_2(B).$$

By $K^+(L) = L$, it is clear that $det_1(AB) = det_2(AB)$, i.e. $det(AB) \equiv 0$. But by Eq.(2), Lemma 2.1 we have $AB = I_s$, i.e. $det(AB) \not\equiv 0$, a contradiction. In the second case, there exists $\mid J_i \mid = 1, i \in \{1, 2\}$ such that if $j \in J_i$, then $\lambda_j \notin U(L)$, say $\mid J_1 \mid = 1$. Then in similar to the proof of the first case, we can prove that this case dose not exist. Therefore by the discuss as above, we know that $\{\mathbf{y}_1, \mathbf{y}_2, \cdots, \mathbf{y}_s\}$ is strong linearly independent. $\square$

By Theorem 2.1, we have the following statement

Corollary 2.1. *In a cancellative, yoked and entire semiring $\mathcal{L}$, let $\mathcal{W} = \langle \mathbf{x}_1, \mathbf{x}_2, \cdots, \mathbf{x}_s \rangle$ with $\{\mathbf{x}_1, \mathbf{x}_2, \cdots, \mathbf{x}_s\}$ a set of semi-linearly dependent vectors in $\mathcal{V}_n$. If $\{\mathbf{y}_1, \mathbf{y}_2, \cdots, \mathbf{y}_p\}$ is a basis of $\mathcal{W}$, then $\mathbf{y}_1, \mathbf{y}_2, \cdots, \mathbf{y}_p$ are also semi-linearly dependent.*

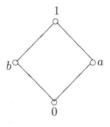

Fig. 1

Note that in Theorem 2.1 the condition of semiring $\mathcal{L}$ is cancellative, yoked and entire can not be deleted generally. For instance, over semiring as Fig. 1, it is obvious that $\mathcal{L}$ is not cancellative, yoked and entire. Then it is easy to see that in $\mathcal{V}_2$, $\{ \begin{pmatrix} 1 \\ 0 \end{pmatrix}, \begin{pmatrix} 0 \\ 1 \end{pmatrix} \}$ and $\{ \begin{pmatrix} a \\ 0 \end{pmatrix}, \begin{pmatrix} b \\ 0 \end{pmatrix}, \begin{pmatrix} 0 \\ a \end{pmatrix}, \begin{pmatrix} 0 \\ b \end{pmatrix} \}$ are equivalent and linearly independent. However, $\{ \begin{pmatrix} 1 \\ 0 \end{pmatrix}, \begin{pmatrix} 0 \\ 1 \end{pmatrix} \}$ is a set of strong linearly independent, but $\{\begin{pmatrix} a \\ 0 \end{pmatrix}, \begin{pmatrix} b \\ 0 \end{pmatrix}, \begin{pmatrix} 0 \\ a \end{pmatrix}, \begin{pmatrix} 0 \\ b \end{pmatrix}\}$ is semi-linearly dependent.

Theorem 2.2. *Let* $A \in M_n(L)$. *If* L *is entire, then* A *is invertible if and only if there exists a permutation matrix* $P \in M_n(L)$ *such that* PA *is an invertible diagonal matrix.*

Theorem 2.3. *In a cancellative, yoked and entire semiring* L, *let* $W = \langle x_1, x_2, \cdots, x_s \rangle$ *with* $\{x_1, x_2, \cdots, x_s\}$ *a set of strong linearly independent vectors in* V_n. *If* $y_1, y_2, \cdots, y_p \in W$, *then the follow statements are equivalent:*

(1) $\{y_1, y_2, \cdots, y_p\}$ *is a basis of* W;

(2) There exists an invertible generalized diagonal matrix $A \in M_n(L)$ *such that* $(y_1, y_2, \cdots, y_p) = (x_1, x_2, \cdots, x_s)A$ *and* $p = s$.

Acknowledgments

The research has been supported by National Natural Science Foundation of China (No.11171242, 11201325), Doctoral Fund of Ministry of Education of China (No.20105134110002), Sichuan Youth Fund (No.2011JQ0055) and Sichuan Education Department Scientific Research Fund (No.13ZB0165)

References

1. R. A. Cuninghame-Green, P. Butkovič, Bases in max-algebra, Linear Algebra and its Applications 389 (2004) 107-120.
2. A. Di Nola, A. Lettieri, I. Perfilieva, V. Novák, Algebraic analysis of fuzzy systems, Fuzzy Sets and Systems 158 (2007) 1-22.
3. J. S. Golan, Semirings and Their Applications, Kluwer Academic Publishers, Dordrecht/Boston/London, 1999.
4. J. Kuntzman, Théorie des réseaaux graphes, Dunod (Libraire), Paris, 1972.
5. I. Perfilieva, Semi-linear spaces, in: H. Noguchi, H. Ishii, et al. (Eds.), Proc. of Seventh Czech-Japanese Seminar on Data Analysis and Decision Making under Uncertainty, Hyogo, Japan, 2004, pp. 127-130.
6. Phillip L. Poplin, Robert E. Hartwig, Determinantal Identities over Commutative semirings, Linear Algebra and its Applications 387 (2007) 99-132.
7. Qian-yu Shu, Xue-ping Wang, Bases in semilinear spaces over zerosumfree semirings, Linear Algebra and its Applications 435 (2011) 2681-2692.
8. Qian-yu Shu, Xue-ping Wang, Dimensions of L-semilinear spaces over zerosumfree semiring, 2013 Joint IFSA World Congress and NAFIPS Annual Meeting (IFSA/NAFIPS), 35-40.
9. Xue-ping Wang, Qian-yu Shu, Bideterminant and rank of matrix, Soft Comfuting (to be available on Springer Online).

TWO TYPES OF PRIME IDEALS ON RESIDUATED LATTICES

Y. LIU*, X. Y. QIN, H. R. JIA and Y. XU

Intelligent Control Development Center, Southwest Jiaotong University, Sichuan province, P.R.China.
E-mail: liuyiyl@126.com

This paper mainly focus on building the prime ideals of non regular residuated lattices. Firstly, two types prime ideals of a residuated lattice are introduced, the relations between the two types ideals are studied, in some special residuated lattices (such as MTL-algebras, lattice implication algebras, BL-algebras), prime ideal and prime ideal of the second kind are coincide. Secondly, the notions of fuzzy prime ideal and fuzzy prime ideal of the second kind on a residuated lattice are introduced, aiming at the relation between prime ideal and prime ideal of the second kind, we mainly investigated the fuzzy prime ideal of the second kind.

Keywords: residuated lattice; (fuzzy) prime ideals; (fuzzy) prime ideals of the second kind.

1. Introduction

Nonclassical logic is closely related to logic algebraic systems. A number of researches have motivated to develop nonclassical logics, and also to enrich the content of algebra.[8,15,16] In modern fuzzy logic theory, residuated lattices and some related algebraic systems play an extremely important role because they provide an algebraic frameworks to fuzzy logic and fuzzy reasoning. By using the theory of residuated lattices, Pavalka has built up a more generalized logic systems, and he has successfully proved the semantical completeness of the Lukasiewicz's axiom system in 1979. From a logical point of view, various filters and ideals correspond to various sets of provable formulae. The sets of provable formulas in the corresponding inference systems from the point of view of uncertain information can be described by fuzzy ideals of those algebraic semantics. In the meantime, ideal theory is a very effectively tool for investigating these various algebraic and logic systems. The notion of ideal has been introduced in many algebraic structure such as lattices, rings, MV-algebras, lattice implication algebras. In these algebraic structure, as filter, the ideal is in the center position. However, in BL-algebras and residuated lattices[4,6] (especially non regular residuated lattice), the focus is shifted to deductive systems or filters.[1,2,5–7,9,10,13,18] The study of residuated lattice have experienced a tremendous growth and the main focus has been on filters. For BL-algebras, C.Lele and J.B.Nganou[12] introduced the notion of ideal in BL-algebras as a natural generalization of that of ideal in MV-algebras. However, non regular residuated lattice as a more general important algebraic structure, the notion of prime ideal is missing. The main goal of this work is to build the prime ideals by introducing the notion of prime ideal and fuzzy prime ideals in a non regular residuated lattice.

2. Basic Results on Residuated Lattices

Definition 2.1 (^{4}). *A residuated lattice is an algebraic structure $\mathcal{L} = (L, \vee, \wedge, \otimes, \rightarrow, 0, 1)$ of type (2,2,2,2,0,0) satisfying the following axioms:*
  (C1) $(L, \vee, \wedge, 0, 1)$ is a bounded lattice.
  (C2) $(L, \otimes, 1)$ is a commutative semigroup (with the unit element 1).
  (C3) $(\otimes, \rightarrow)$ is an adjoint pair.

Proposition 2.1 (^{4}). *A algebraic structure $\mathcal{L} = (L, \vee, \wedge, \otimes, \rightarrow, 0, 1)$ of type (2,2,2,2,0,0) is a residuated lattice if and only if it satisfies the following conditions, for any $x, y, z \in L$:*
  (R1) If $x \leq y$, then $x \otimes z \leq y \otimes z$.
  (R2) if $x \leq y$, then $z \rightarrow x \leq z \rightarrow y$ and $y \rightarrow z \leq x \rightarrow z$.
  (R3) $x \otimes y \leq z$ if and only if $x \rightarrow y \leq z$.
  (R4) $(x \otimes y) \otimes z = x \otimes (y \otimes z)$.
  (R5) $x \otimes y = y \otimes x$.
  (R6) $1 \otimes x = x$.

In what follows, let $\mathcal{L}$ denote a residuated lattice unless otherwise specified.

In a residuated lattice $\mathcal{L}$, denote $x^{'} = x \rightarrow 0$.

Proposition 2.2 (^{4,14}). *In each residuated lattice $\mathcal{L}$, the following properties hold for all $x, y, z \in L$:*

(P1) $(x \otimes y) \rightarrow z = x \rightarrow (y \rightarrow z)$.	(P2) $x \otimes (x \rightarrow y) \leq y$.
(P3) $(x \rightarrow y) \otimes z \leq x$.	(P4) $x \otimes y \leq x \wedge y$.
(P5) $(x \vee y) \otimes z = (x \otimes z) \vee (y \otimes z)$.	(P6) if $x \leq y$, then $y^{'} \leq x^{'}$.
(P7) $y \rightarrow z \leq (x \rightarrow y) \rightarrow (x \rightarrow z)$.	(P8) $(x \otimes y)^{'} = x \rightarrow y^{'}$.

(P9) $x^m \leq x^n$, $m, n \in N$, $m \geq n$.   (P10) $1 \rightarrow x = x, x \rightarrow x = 1$.

(P11) $x \rightarrow (y \rightarrow z) = y \rightarrow (x \rightarrow z)$.   (P12) $x \leq y \Leftrightarrow x \rightarrow y = 1$.

(P13) $0' = 1, 1' = 0, x' = x''', x \leq x''$.   (P14) $x \rightarrow y \leq (x \otimes y')'$.

In a residuated lattice, the binary operation $\oplus$ defined by $x \oplus y = x' \rightarrow y$ for any $x, y \in L$.

3. Prime Ideals

Definition 3.1. Let $\mathcal{L}$ be a residuated lattice and $\emptyset \neq I \subseteq L$. I is said to be an ideal of $\mathcal{L}$, if I satisfies:

(I1) for any $x, y \in L$, if $x \leq y$ and $y \in I$, then $x \in I$;

(I2) for any $x, y \in I$, $x \oplus y \in I$.

Theorem 3.1. *Let $\mathcal{L}$ be a residuated lattice. I is an ideal of $\mathcal{L}$ if and only if I satisfies following conditions:*

(I3) $0 \in I$;

(I4) for any $x, y \in L$, if $x' \otimes y \in I$ and $x \in I$, then $y \in I$.

Definition 3.2. Let I be a proper ideal of a residuated lattice $\mathcal{L}$. I is said to be a prime ideal, if for any $x, y \in L$, $(x \rightarrow y)' \in I$ or $(y \rightarrow x)' \in I$.

Definition 3.3. Let I be a proper ideal of a residuated lattice $\mathcal{L}$. I is said to be a prime ideal of the second kind, if for any $x, y \in L$, $x \wedge y \in I$ implies $x \in I$ or $y \in I$.

In a residuated lattice $\mathcal{L}$, denote $R_l = \{l \in L | l \oplus l = l\}$. Then $I_l = \{x \in L | x \leq l, l \in R_l\}$ is an ideal of $\mathcal{L}$. In fact, if $x, y \in L$ such that $x \leq y$ and $y \in I_l$, we have $x \leq y \leq l$, and so $x \in I_l$; At the meantime, if $x, y \in I_l$, then $x \leq l$ and $y \leq l$, and so $x \oplus y \leq l \oplus l = l$, therefore $x \oplus y \in I_l$.

Theorem 3.2. *Let $\mathcal{L}$ be a residuated lattice. If $l \in R_l$ and l be $\wedge$-irreducible element of $\mathcal{L}$, then I_l is a prime ideal of the second kind of $\mathcal{L}$.*

Theorem 3.3. *Let $\mathcal{L}$ be a residuated lattice. Every prime ideal of $\mathcal{L}$ is also a prime ideal of the second kind. If $\mathcal{L}$ is an MTL-algebra, then every prime ideal of the second kind of $\mathcal{L}$ is also a prime ideal.*

Remark 3.1. For a residuated lattice which satisfies the prelinearity, then the prime ideal of the second kind is the prime ideal. Such as, lattice implication algebras, MTL-algebras, BL-algebras, MV-algebras.

4. Fuzzy Prime Ideals

Let $[0,1]$ be the closed unit interval of reals and $L \neq \emptyset$ be a set. Recall that a fuzzy set $(^{17})$ in L is any function $\mu : L \rightarrow [0,1]$.

Definition 4.1. Let μ be a fuzzy subset of a residuated lattice $\mathcal{L}$. μ is called a fuzzy ideal of $\mathcal{L}$, if μ satisfies the following condition:
    (FI1) for any $x,y \in L$, if $x \leq y$, then $\mu(x) \geq \mu(y)$;
    (FI2) for any $x,y \in L$, $\mu(x \oplus y) \geq min\{\mu(x),\mu(y)\}$.

Theorem 4.1. *Let μ be a fuzzy subset of a residuated lattice $\mathcal{L}$. Then μ is a fuzzy ideal of $\mathcal{L}$ if and only if the level set $\mu_t (\neq \emptyset)$ is an ideal of $\mathcal{L}$.*

Theorem 4.2. *Let μ be a fuzzy subset of a residuated lattice $\mathcal{L}$. μ is a fuzzy ideal of $\mathcal{L}$, if μ satisfies the following condition:*
    (FI3) for any $x \in L$, $\mu(0) \geq \mu(x)$;
    (FI4) for any $x,y \in L$, $\mu(y) \geq min\{\mu(x),\mu(x' \otimes y)\}$.

Theorem 4.3. *Let μ be a fuzzy subset of a residuated lattice $\mathcal{L}$. μ is a fuzzy ideal of $\mathcal{L}$, if μ satisfies the following condition:*
    (FI2) for any $x,y \in L$, $\mu(x \oplus y) \geq min\{\mu(x),\mu(y)\}$,
    (FI6) for any $x,y \in L$, $\mu(x \wedge y) \geq \mu(x)\}$.

Definition 4.2. A fuzzy ideal μ of $\mathcal{L}$ is said to be fuzzy prime if it is non-constant and $\mu((x \rightarrow y)') = \mu(0)$ or $\mu((y \rightarrow x)') = \mu(0)$ for any $x,y \in L$.

Definition 4.3. A fuzzy ideal μ of $\mathcal{L}$ is said to be fuzzy prime of the second kind of $\mathcal{L}$ if it is non-constant and $\mu(x \wedge y) \leq max\{\mu(x),\mu(y)\}$ for any $x,y \in L$.

Remark 4.1. Let μ be a non constant fuzzy ideal of $\mathcal{L}$. Then μ is a fuzzy prime ideal of the second kind if and only if $max\{\mu(x),\mu(y)\} = \mu(x \wedge y)$.

Theorem 4.4. *Let μ be a non constant fuzzy set of $\mathcal{L}$. Then μ is a fuzzy prime ideal of the second kind of $\mathcal{L}$ if and only if μ_t is a prime ideal of the second kind of $\mathcal{L}$, where $\mu_t = \{x \in L | \mu(x) \geq t\}$ for any $t \in [0,1]$.*

Corollary 4.1. *Let I be a proper ideal of $\mathcal{L}$. Then I is a prime ideal of the second kind if and only if its characteristic function χ_I is a fuzzy prime ideal of the second kind of $\mathcal{L}$.*

Corollary 4.2. *Let μ be a non constant fuzzy ideal of $\mathcal{L}$. Then μ is a fuzzy prime ideal of the second kind of $\mathcal{L}$ if and only if $\mu_{\mu(0)}$ is a prime ideal of the second kind of $\mathcal{L}$.*

Theorem 4.5. *Let μ be a fuzzy prime ideal of $\mathcal{L}$. Then μ is a fuzzy prime ideal of the second kind of $\mathcal{L}$. If $\mathcal{L}$ is a MTL-algebras, then every fuzzy prime ideal of the second kind of $\mathcal{L}$ is also a fuzzy prime ideal.*

Remark 4.2. For a residuated lattice which satisfies the prelinearity, then the fuzzy prime ideal of the second kind is the fuzzy prime ideal. Such as, lattice implication algebras, MTL-algebras, BL-algebras. In this section. We mainly focus on the fuzzy prime ideal of the second kind of $\mathcal{L}$.

Theorem 4.6. *Let I be an ideal of $\mathcal{L}$ and μ be a fuzzy set in $\mathcal{L}$. Then I is a prime ideal of the second ideal of $\mathcal{L}$ if and only if μ_I is a fuzzy prime ideal of the second kind of $\mathcal{L}$.*

Theorem 4.7. *Let μ be a fuzzy ideal of $\mathcal{L}$. Then the following conditions are equivalent:*
    (1) μ is a fuzzy prime ideal of the second kind of $\mathcal{L}$;
    (2) for any $x, y \in L$, $\mu(x \wedge y) = \mu(0)$ implies $\mu(x) = \mu(0)$ or $\mu(y) = \mu(0)$.

Theorem 4.8. *Let ν be a fuzzy prime ideal of the second kind of a residuated lattice $\mathcal{L}$ and $\alpha \in [0, \nu(0))$. Then $(\nu \vee \alpha)(x) = \nu(x) \vee \alpha$ is also a fuzzy prime ideal of the second kind of $\mathcal{L}$.*

5. Conclusion

In our future work, we will continue investigating the relation among the prime ideal, prime ideal of the second kind and MTL-prime ideal(i.e., A MTL-prime ideal of a residuated lattice is a filter of $\mathcal{L}$ satisfying, for all $x, y \in L$, $(x \rightarrow y)' \wedge (y \rightarrow x)' \in I$.). Another direction is to investigate some types ideals of a residuated lattice. For more details, we shall give them out in the future paper. It is our hope that this work will settle once and for all the existence of ideals in residuated lattices.

Acknowledgments

This work is supported by National Science Foundation of China (Grant No.61175055,61305074), Sichuan Key Technology Research and Development Program (Grant No.2011FZ0051), Radio Administration Bureau of MIIT of China(Grant No.[2011]146), China Institution of Communications(Grant No.[2011]051).The Speciality Comprehensive Reform of Mathematics and Applied Mathematics of Ministry of Education(ZG0464). The Speciality Comprehensive Reform of Mathematics and Applied Mathematics of Ministry of Education(01249). A Project Supported by Scientific

214

Research Fund of Sichuan Provincial Education Department(14ZA0245). The Scientific Research Research Fund of Neijiang Normal University(No.13ZB05)

References

1. M. Akram and B. Davvaz, *Generalized fuzzy ideals of K-algebras*, Journal of Multiple-valued Logic and Soft Computing, **19** (2012), 475-491.
2. R. A. Borzooei, S. Khosravani Shoar and R. Ameri, *Some types of filters in MTL-algebras*, Fuzzy Sets and Systems, **187** (2012), 92-102.
3. R. Belohlavek, *Some properties of residuated lattices*, Czechoslovak Math. J. **53** (2003), 161-171.
4. R. P. Dilworth, M. Ward, *Residuated lattices*, Trans. Am. Math. Soc., *45* (1939), 335–354.
5. B. Davvaz and V. Leoreanu-Fotea, *Structures of fuzzy Γ-hyperideals in Γ-Semihypergroups*, Journal of Multiple-Valued Logic and Soft Computing, **19** (2012), 519-535.
6. Hadi Farahani, Omid Zahiri, *Algebraic view of MTL-filters*, Annals of the University of Craiova, Mathematics and Computer Science Series, **40(1)**(2013), 34–44.
7. B. Van Gasse, G. Deschrijver, C. Cornelis and E.E. Kerre,*Filters of residuated lattices and triangle algebras*, Information Sciences, **180** (2010), 3006-3020.
8. P. Hájek, *Metamathematics of Fuzzy Logic*, Kluwer Academic Publishers, Dordrecht, 1998.
9. Y. B. Jun, Y. Xu, X. H. Zhang, *Fuzzy filters of MTL-algebras*, Information Sciences, **175** (2005), 120–138.
10. M.Kondo, *Filters on commutative residuated lattices*, Advances in Intelligent and Soft Computing, **68** (2010), 343-347.
11. M.Kondo, E.Turunen, *Prime filters on residuated lattices*, 2012 IEEE 42nd International Symposium on Multiple-Valued Logic, 2012, 89-91.
12. C.Lele and J.B. Nganou, *MV-algebras derived from Ideals in BL-algebras*, Fuzzy Sets and Systems **218**(2013), 103-113.
13. Y. Liu, Y. Xu, X.Y.Qin, *Interval-valued T-fuzzy filters and interval-valued T-fuzzy congruences on residuated lattices*, Journal of Intelligent and Fuzzy Systems, DOI:10.3233/IFS-130879.
14. D. W. Pei, *The characterization of residuated lattices and regular residuated lattices*, Acta Mathematica Sinica, **42(2)**, (2002), 271-278.
15. Y. Xu, D. Ruan, K. Qin, J. Liu, *Lattice-Valued Logic*, Springer-Verlag, Berlin, Heidelberg, 2003.
16. X. H. Zhang, W. H. Li, *On fuzzy logic algebraic system MTL*, Adv. Syst. Sci. Appl. **5** (2005) 475-483.
17. L. A. Zadeh, *Fuzzy sets*, Inform. Control, **8** (1965), 338–353.
18. Y. Q. Zhu, Y. Xu, *On filter theory of residuated lattices*, Information Sciences, **180** (2010), 3614–3632. 99.

THE STRONGLY PRIME RADICAL OF A FUZZY IDEAL

Flaulles B. Bergamaschi and Regivan H.N. Santiago*

Departamento de Informática e Matemática Aplicada
Universidade Federal do Rio Grande do Norte
Natal, Brasil
Email: flaulles@yahoo.com.br, regivan@dimap.ufrn.br

In 2013, Bergamaschi and Santiago[1] proposed **Strongly Prime Fuzzy(SP)** ideals for commutative and noncommutative rings with unity, and investigated their properties. This paper goes a step further since it provides the concept of **Strongly Prime Radical** of a fuzzy ideal and its properties are investigated. It is shown that Zadeh's extension preserves strongly prime radicals. Also, a version of **Theorem of Correspondence** for strongly prime fuzzy ideals is proved.

Keywords: Fuzzy ideal; Strongly prime ideal; Strongly prime radical; Fuzzy radical

1. Introduction

In his pioneering paper, Zadeh[2] introduced the notion of a fuzzy subset A of a set X as a function from X to $[0, 1]$. In 1971, Rosenfeld[3] introduced fuzzy sets in the realm of group theory and formulated the concept of a fuzzy subgroup of a group. Since then, many researchers have been engaged in extending the concepts/results of abstract algebra to a broader framework of the fuzzy setting.

In 1973, Formanek[4] showed that if D is a domain and G is a suitable free product of group, then the group ring DG is primitive. In the same year, Lawrence in his master's thesis showed that a generalization of Formanek's result was possible, in which the domain could be replaced by a prime ring with a finiteness condition called strongly prime. Although, the condition of strongly prime was used for primitive group rings it became more interesting. As a consequence, in 1975, Lawrence and Handelman[5] began to

---

*This research was partially supported by the Brazilian Research Council (CNPq) under the process 306876/2012-4.

study the properties of strongly prime rings and then many results were discovered, for example, every prime ring may be embedded in a strongly prime ring; all strongly prime rings are nonsingular and only the Artinian strongly prime rings have a minimal right ideal.

In 1991, Information Sciences published a paper of Malik and Moderson[6,7] about radicals in the fuzzy setting. They provided a definition for radical of fuzzy ideal and showed a characterization of the Jacobson radical in terms of fuzzy maximal ideals. Thus, the primary ideal could be defined based on radical and many results was proven in the fuzzy environment e.g., if I is a fuzzy primary ideal on a ring R, then $\sqrt{I}$ is a fuzzy prime ideal of R. This work provides the concept of Strongly Prime Radical of a fuzzy ideal based on the ideas developed in.[1] The properties of this radical and its relation with strongly prime fuzzy ideals are investigated. Also, it is proved a fuzzy version of Correspondence Theorem for Strongly Prime fuzzy ideals.

2. Preliminaries

This section explains some definitions and results that will be required in the next section. All rings are associative, with identity and usually denoted R.

Definition 1. [8] A prime ideal in an arbitrary ring R is any proper ideal P of R such that, whenever I, J are ideals of R with[a] $IJ \subseteq P$, either $I \subseteq P$ or $J \subseteq P$. Equivalently P is prime whenever[b] $xRy \subseteq P$ for some $x, y \in R$, then $x \in P$ or $y \in P$. A prime ring is a ring in which (0) is a prime ideal.

Note that a prime ring must be nonzero. Also, in commutative rings, the definition above is equivalent to: if $ab \in P$, then $a \in P$ or $b \in P$. Thus, if P has the latter property, then it is called completely prime. In arbitrary rings, every *completely prime* is prime, but the converse is not true according.[1] In some papers, *completely prime* means *strongly prime*, but these concepts are different if you apply them to noncommutative rings. Every completely prime is strongly prime, but the converse is not true. The next definitions are necessary to build up the concept of strongly prime ideal.

Definition 2. [5] Let A be a subset of a ring R. The right annihilator of A is written as follows $An_r(A) = \{r \in R : Ar = (0)\}$.

---

[a] $IJ = \{x : x = ij, i \in I, j \in J\}$
[b] $xRy = \{xry : r \in R\}$

Definition 3.[9] A ring R is said to be right strongly prime if each nonzero ideal I of R contains a finite subset F which has right annihilator zero. F is called right insulator.

In other words, a right insulator in a ring R is a finite subset $F \subseteq R$ such that $Fr = 0, r \in R$, implies $r = 0$. The ring R is said to be right strongly prime if every nonzero ideal(two-sided) contains an insulator. The left strongly prime is defined analogously. Handelman and Lawrence[5] gave an example to show that these two concepts are distinct. From this point forward, we call right strongly prime shortly strongly prime(SP).

Definition 4. The ideal I of a ring R is strongly prime iff for every $x \in R - I$ there exists a finite subset F of R such that if $r \in R$ and $xFr \subseteq I$, then $r \in I$.

It is not hard to prove that an ideal I of a ring R is strongly prime iff R/I is strongly ring. Let $f : R \longrightarrow S$ be a homomorphism of rings. We set $sp(R)$ the set of all strongly prime ideals of R and $sp_f(R) = \{I \in sp(R) : I \supseteq Ker(f)\}$. The following theorem shows that there is a one to one correspondence between $sp_f(R)$ and $sp(S)$.

Theorem 1.[10] *Let $f : R \longrightarrow S$ be an epimorphism of rings. Then*
(i) $f(I) \in sp(S)$ for any $I \in sp_f(R)$;
(ii) $f^{-1}(I) \in sp_f(R)$ for any $I \in sp(S)$;
(iii) The mapping $\Psi : sp_f(R) \longrightarrow sp(S)$, $\Psi(I) = f(I)$ is bijective.

Definition 5 (Zadeh's Extension). *Let f be a function from set X into Y, and let μ be a fuzzy subset of X. Define the fuzzy subset $f(\mu)$ by $\forall y \in Y$*

$$
f(\mu)(y) = \begin{cases} \vee\{\mu(x) : x \in X, f(x) = y\}, \\ \quad \text{if } f^{-1}(y) \neq \emptyset \\ \\ 0, \quad \text{otherwise.} \end{cases}
$$

If λ is a fuzzy subset of Y, we define the fuzzy subset of X by $f^{-1}(\lambda)$ where $f^{-1}(\lambda)(x) = \lambda(f(x))$.

Let μ be any fuzzy subset of a set S and let $\alpha \in [0, 1]$. The set $\{x \in X : \mu(x) \geq \alpha\}$ is called a *level subset* of μ which is symbolized by μ_α. Clearly, if $t > s$, then $\mu_t \subseteq \mu_s$.

A fuzzy subset I of a ring R is called a fuzzy ideal of R if for all $x, y \in R$ the following requirements are met: 1) $I(x - y) \geq I(x) \wedge I(y)$; 2) $I(xy) \geq I(x) \vee I(y)$. Note that[11] a fuzzy subset I of a ring R is a fuzzy ideal of R iff the level subsets I_α, ($\alpha \in [0, 1]$), are ideals of R.

3. Strongly radical of a fuzzy ideal

The right strongly prime radical of a ring R is defined to be the intersection of all right strongly prime ideals of R. The dual notion of left strongly primeness determines a left strongly prime radical. An example given by Parmenter, Passman and Stewart[12] showed that these two radicals are distinct. In this section we define the concept of right strongly radical(shortly strongly radical) of a fuzzy ideal. Also, it is shown a fuzzy version of Correspondence Theorem and the right strongly prime radical(shortly SP radical) of a fuzzy ideal is defined and investigated. Throughout this section, unless stated otherwise, R has identity.

Proposition 1. *Let $f : R \longrightarrow S$ be a epimorphism of rings such that $f^{-1}(Y)$ is a finite set for all $Y \subseteq S$. If I is a fuzzy set of R and J a fuzzy set of S, then $f(I_\alpha) = f(I)_\alpha$ and $f^{-1}(J_\alpha) = f^{-1}(J)_\alpha$.*

Proof. Consider $f(I_\alpha) = \{y \in S \ : \ y = f(x), x \in I_\alpha\}$ and $f(I)_\alpha = \{y \in S \ : \ f(I)(y) \geq \alpha\}$. Let $y \in f(I_\alpha)$, $y = f(x_0)$ where $I(x_0) \geq \alpha$. Thus, $f(I)(y) = sup\{I(x) \ : \ f(x) = y\} \geq I(x_0) \geq \alpha$ and then $y \in f(I)_\alpha$. On the other side, let $y \in f(I)_\alpha$, i.e. $f(I)(y) = sup\{I(x) \ : \ f(x) = y\} \geq \alpha$. As f is surjective, there exists $x_0 \in R$, where $\alpha \leq I(x_0) \leq sup\{I(x) \ : \ f(x) = y\} = f(I)(y)$. Thus, $x_0 \in I_\alpha$ and then $f(x_0) = y \in f(I_\alpha)$.

To prove $f^{-1}(J_\alpha) = f^{-1}(J)_\alpha$, let $x \in f^{-1}(J_\alpha)$, then $f(x) \in J_\alpha$. Thus, $f^{-1}(J)(x) = J(f(x)) \geq \alpha$ and, therefore, $x \in f^{-1}(J)_\alpha$. Now let $x \in f^{-1}(J)_\alpha$ then $J(f(x)) = f^{-1}(J)(x) \geq \alpha$ and therefore $f(x) \in J_\alpha$. In this case, it is not necessarily used $f^{-1}(Y)$ as a finite set. $\square$

Theorem 2. *Let $f : R \longrightarrow S$ be a epimorphism of rings such that $f^{-1}(Y)$ is a finite set for all $Y \subseteq S$. If I is a SP fuzzy ideal of R such that $Ker(f) \subseteq I_\alpha$ for $I(1) < \alpha \leq I(0)$, then $f(I)$ is SP fuzzy ideal of R.*

Proof. Let I be a SP fuzzy ideal of R, where $I_\alpha \in sp_f(R)$ for $I(1) < \alpha \leq I(0)$. Applying Theorem 1, (i) $f(I_\alpha) \in sp(S)$. By the Proposition 1 $f(I)_\alpha$ is SP fuzzy ideal of S. Thus, $f(I) \in sp(S)$. $\square$

Proposition 2. *Let $f : R \longrightarrow S$ be an epimorphism of rings. If J is a SP fuzzy ideal of S, then $f^{-1}(J)$ is a SP fuzzy ideal of R, where $f^{-1}(J)_\alpha \supseteq Ker(f)$ for $J(1) < \alpha \leq J(0)$.*

Proof. It is a consequence from proposition 1 and theorem 1 (ii). $\square$

For the next result, consider $SP_f(R) = \{I$ is SP fuzzy ideal of R $:$ $I_\alpha \in$ $sp_f, I(1) < \alpha \leq I(0)\}$ and $SP(S)$ is the set of all SP fuzzy ideal of S.

Theorem 3. *(Correspondence Theorem) Let $f : R \longrightarrow S$ be an epimorphism of rings such that $f^{-1}(Y)$ is a finite set for all $Y \subseteq S$. Then, there exists a bijection between $SP_f(R)$ and $SP(S)$.*

Proof. Define $\Psi : SP_f(R) \longrightarrow SP(S)$, $\Psi(I) = f(I)$. Let $I, M \in SP_f(R)$, where $I \neq M$. Thus, there exists $x \in R$, where $I(x) \neq M(x)$, if $\alpha = I(x)$, then $I_\alpha \neq M_\alpha$. According to proposition 1 and Theorem 1, $f(I)_\alpha = f(I_\alpha) \neq f(M_\alpha) = f(M)_\alpha$. Therefore, Ψ is injective. On the other hand, let $J \in SP(S)$. As J_α is SP by Theorem 1, we have $f^{-1}(J_\alpha) \in$ $sp_f(R)$, by Proposition 1, $f^{-1}(J_\alpha) = f^{-1}(J)_\alpha$. Thus, $f^{-1}(J)_\alpha$ is SP and $f^{-1}(J) \in SP_f(R)$. Moreover, $\Psi(f^{-1}(J)) = f(f^{-1}(J)) = J$. Therefore, Ψ is surjective. $\square$

Definition 6. Given a crisp ideal I of a ring R, the strongly radical(or Levitzki radical) of I is $\sqrt[s]{I} = \bigcap\{P \; : \; P \supseteq I, P$ is strongly prime$\}$.

Definition 7. Let I be a fuzzy ideal of R, the strongly radical of I is $\sqrt[s]{I} = \bigcap_{P \in \mathcal{S}_I} P$, where $\mathcal{S}_I$ is the family of all SP fuzzy ideals P of R such that $I \subseteq P$.

Clearly $\sqrt[s]{I}$ is an ideal, and if I is a SP fuzzy ideal, then $\sqrt[s]{I} = I$

Proposition 3. *If I, J are a fuzzy ideal of a ring R, then:*
(i) if $I \subseteq J$, then $\sqrt[s]{I} \subseteq \sqrt[s]{J}$;
(ii) $\sqrt[s]{\sqrt[s]{I}} = \sqrt[s]{I}$;
(iii) $I_\alpha \subseteq (\sqrt[s]{I})_\alpha$;
(iv) If I is SP fuzzy, then $\sqrt[s]{I_\alpha} = (\sqrt[s]{I})_\alpha$;
(v) $\sqrt[s]{I \cap J} \subseteq \sqrt[s]{I} \cap \sqrt[s]{J}$.

Proof. (i) $\sqrt[s]{J} = \bigcap_{P \in \mathcal{S}_J} P \supseteq \bigcap_{P \in \mathcal{S}_I} P = \sqrt[s]{I}$. (ii) It is easy to see that $\sqrt[s]{I} \subseteq$ $\sqrt[s]{\sqrt[s]{I}}$. On the other side, let's show $\mathcal{S}_I \subseteq \mathcal{S}_{\sqrt[s]{I}}$. In fact, let $P \in \mathcal{S}_I$, then $P \supseteq I$ using (i) $P = \sqrt[s]{P} \supseteq \sqrt[s]{I}$. (iii),(iv) and (v) is straightforward. $\square$

Proposition 4. *Let $f : R \longrightarrow S$ be a homomorphism of rings and I a fuzzy ideal of R. Then:*
1) $f(I) \subseteq f(\sqrt[s]{I}) \subseteq \sqrt[s]{f(\sqrt[s]{I})}$;
2) $I \subseteq f^{-1}(\sqrt[s]{f(I)})$.

Proof. 1) Straightforward.

2) As $f(I) \subseteq \sqrt[s]{f(I)}$, then $f^{-1}(f(I)) \subseteq f^{-1}(\sqrt[s]{f(I)})$. Thus, $I \subseteq f^{-1}(f(I)) \subseteq f^{-1}(\sqrt[s]{f(I)})$. □

Proposition 5. *Let* $f : R \longrightarrow S$ *be a homomorphism of rings and* I *a SP fuzzy ideal of* R. *Then,* $f(\sqrt[s]{I}) \subseteq \sqrt[s]{f(I)}$.

Proof. As I is SP fuzzy $\sqrt[s]{I} = I$, then $\sqrt[s]{f(I)} = \sqrt[s]{f(\sqrt[s]{I})}$. Thus, $f(\sqrt[s]{I}) \subseteq \sqrt[s]{f(\sqrt[s]{I})} = \sqrt[s]{f(I)}$. □

Proposition 6. *Let* $f : R \longrightarrow S$ *be an epimorphism of rings and* I *a SP fuzzy ideal of* R, *such that* $Ker(f) \subseteq I_\alpha$ *for* $I(1) < \alpha \leq I(0)$. *Then,* $f(\sqrt[s]{I}) = \sqrt[s]{f(I)}$.

Proof. As I is SP fuzzy ideal, $I = \sqrt[s]{I}$, $f(I) = f(\sqrt[s]{I})$. Using the theorem 2 $f(I)$ is SP fuzzy ideal and then $f(I) = \sqrt[s]{f(I)}$. Thus, $f(\sqrt[s]{I}) = \sqrt[s]{f(I)} = \sqrt[s]{\sqrt[s]{f(I)}}$. □

References

1. F. Boone Bergamaschi and R. Santiago, Strongly prime fuzzy ideals over noncommutative rings, in *Fuzzy Systems (FUZZ), 2013 IEEE International Conference on*, 2013.
2. L. Zadeh, *Information and Control* **8**, 338 (1965).
3. A. Rosenfeld, *Journal of Mathematical Analysis and Applications* **35**, 512 (1971).
4. E. Formanek, *Journal of Algebra* **26**, 508 (1973).
5. D. Handelman and J. Lawrence, *Transactions of the American Mathematical Society* **211**, 209 (1975).
6. D. Malik and J. N. Mordeson, *Information Sciences* **53**, 237 (1991).
7. D. S. Malik and J. N. Mordeson, *Information sciences* **65**, 239 (1992).
8. K. R. Goodearl and R. B. Warfield Jr, *An introduction to noncommutative Noetherian rings* (Cambridge University Press, 2004).
9. M. Parmenter, P. Stewart and R. Wiegandt, *Quaestiones Mathematicae* **7**, 225 (1984).
10. I. Herstein, Abstract algebra (1996).
11. V. Dixit, R. Kumar and N. Ajmal, *Fuzzy Sets and Systems* **49**, 205 (1992).
12. M. Parmenter, D. Passman and P. Stewart, *Communications in Algebra* **12**, 1099 (1984).

SOME RESULTS ON FUZZY SUB POSITIVE IMPLICATIVE FILTERS OF NON-COMMUTATIVE RESIDUATED LATTICE

Wei Wang[1,2]* and Yang Xu[1]

1. College of Electrical Engineering, Southwest Jiaotong University, Chengdu, China
2. College of Sciences, Xi'an Shiyou University, Xi'an, P. R. China
* E-mail: wwmath@xsyu.edu.cn

The theory of filters and fuzzy filters in logical algebras play a vital role in reasoning mechanism in information sciences, computer sciences, theory of control, artificial intelligence and many other important fields. We introduce the concept of fuzzy sub positive implicative filters of residuated lattice and investigate the properties of it, and further characterize the fuzzy sub positive implicative filters by proposing the equivalent conditions that a fuzzy filters to be a fuzzy sub positive implicative filters.

Keywords: Non-classical logics; non-commutative residuated lattice; fuzzy filter; fuzzy sub positive implicative filters.

1. Introduction

Logical algebras are the algebraic foundation of reasoning mechanism in information sciences, computer sciences, theory of control, artificial intelligence and other important fields. The non-commutative logical algebras are the algebraic counterpart of the non-classical logic.

The theory of filters plays a vital role not only in non-classical logic, but also in Computer Science. From logical point of view, various filters correspond to various sets of provable formulae [5]. Hajek introduced the notions of filters and prime filters in BL-algebras and proved the completeness of Basic Logic BL [2]. In[3], Turunen proposed the notions of implicative filters and Boolean filters of BL-algebras, and proved the equivalence of them in BL-algebras. In our research work, we find that the structures of the non-commutative logical algebras can be described by the tools of fuzzy filters. [8] introduce the notions of fuzzy Boolean filters and fuzzy positive implicative filters in BL-algebras and it is proved that every fuzzy Boolean filter is a fuzzy positive implicative filter, but the converse may not be true. Therefore, in this paper the theory of fuzzy sub positive implicative filters in non-commutative residuated lattices are studied, which answer the converse relation between fuzzy Boolean filters and fuzzy positive implicative filters and lays a good foundation for the further research in non-commutative logical algebras.

2. Preliminaries

Here we recall some definitions and results which will be needed later.

Defination 1 [6] A residuated lattice is an algebra $(A, \vee, \wedge, \odot, \rightarrow, \hookrightarrow, 0, 1)$ of type $(2, 2, 2, 2, 2, 0, 0)$ such that

(1) $(A, \vee, \wedge, \odot, \rightarrow, \hookrightarrow, 0, 1)$ is a bounded lattice,

(2) $(A, \odot, 1)$ is a monoid,

(3) $x \odot y \leq z$ iff $x \leq y \rightarrow z$ iff $y \leq x \hookrightarrow z$ for all $x, y, z \in A$.

Proposition 1 [1,4,6] In a non-commutative residuated lattice A, the following properties hold for all $x, y, z \in A$

(1) $(x \odot y) \rightarrow z = x \rightarrow (y \rightarrow z)$,
$(y \odot x) \hookrightarrow z = x \hookrightarrow (y \hookrightarrow z)$,

(2) $x \leq (x \rightarrow y) \hookrightarrow y, x \leq (x \hookrightarrow y) \rightarrow y$,

(3) $x \leq y$ iff $x \rightarrow y = 1$ iff $x \hookrightarrow y = 1$,

(4) $x \odot y \leq x \wedge y \leq x, y, 1 \rightarrow x = x = 1 \hookrightarrow x$,

(5) $x \leq y \Rightarrow y \rightarrow z \leq x \rightarrow z$ and $y \hookrightarrow z \leq x \hookrightarrow z$,

(6) $x \leq y \Rightarrow z \rightarrow x \leq z \rightarrow y$ and $z \hookrightarrow x \leq z \hookrightarrow y$,

(7) $x \rightarrow y \leq (z \rightarrow x) \rightarrow (z \rightarrow y), x \hookrightarrow y \leq (z \hookrightarrow x) \hookrightarrow (z \hookrightarrow y)$,

(8) $x \rightarrow y \leq (y \rightarrow z) \hookrightarrow (x \rightarrow z), x \hookrightarrow y \leq (y \hookrightarrow z) \rightarrow (x \hookrightarrow z)$,

(9) $x \vee y \leq ((x \rightarrow y) \hookrightarrow y) \wedge ((y \rightarrow x) \hookrightarrow x)$

(10) $x \vee y \leq ((x \hookrightarrow y) \rightarrow y) \wedge ((y \hookrightarrow x) \rightarrow x)$.

In the sequel, we shall use A to denote a non-commutative residuated lattice and agree that the operations $\vee, \wedge, \odot$ have priority towards the operations $\rightarrow, \hookrightarrow$ and we define $x^- = x \rightarrow 0, x^\sim = x \hookrightarrow 0$ for any $x \in A$.

Definition 2 [4] A filter of A is a non-empty subset F of A such that for all $x, y \in A$, one of the following holds

(1) if $x, y \in F$, then $x \odot y \in F$ and if $x \in F$ and $x \leq y$, then $y \in F$,

(2) $1 \in F$ and $x, x \rightarrow y \in F$ imply $y \in F$,

(3) $1 \in F$ and $x, x \hookrightarrow y \in F$ imply $y \in F$.

Definition 3 [4] For any $x, y \in A$, a filter F of A is called

(1)normal if $x \rightarrow y \in F$ iff $x \hookrightarrow y \in F$,

(2)Boolean if $x \vee x^- \in F$ and $x \vee x^\sim \in F$,

(3)prime if $x \vee y \in F$, then $x \in F$ or $y \in F$,

(4)ultra if $x \in F$ or $x^- \in F$ and $x^\sim \in F$,

(5)obstinate if $x \overline{\in} F$ and $y \overline{\in} F$ implies $x \rightarrow y \in F$, $x \hookrightarrow y \in F$.

Definition 4 [7] A subset F of A is called a sub positive implicative filter of A if for all $x, y, z \in A$,

(1) $1 \in F$,

(2) $(x \to y) \odot z \hookrightarrow ((y \hookrightarrow x) \to x)$ and $z \in F$ implies $(x \to y) \hookrightarrow y \in F$,

(3) $z \odot (x \hookrightarrow y) \to ((y \to x) \hookrightarrow x)$ and $z \in F$ implies $(x \hookrightarrow y) \to y \in F$.

3. Fuzzy sub positive implicative filters of non-commutative residuated lattice

In this section, we extend the concept of fuzzy filter to non-commutative residuated lattice as an extension work of [5] and introduce fuzzy sub positive implicative filters of non-commutative residuated lattice and further characterize it.

Definition 5 Let f be a fuzzy set of A. f is called a fuzzy filter of A if for all $t \in [0, 1]$, f_t is either empty or a filter of A.

We can easily see that F is a filter of A if and only if χ_F is a fuzzy filter of A, where χ_F is the characteristic function of F.

Definition 6 A fuzzy filter f is called a fuzzy Boolean filter if for all $x \in A$, $f(x \vee x^-) = f(x \vee x^\sim) = f(1)$.

Theorem 1 Let f be a fuzzy filter of A. The following are equivalent:

(1) f is a fuzzy Boolean filter of A,

(2) $f(x \to y) = f(x \to (y^- \hookrightarrow y))$, $f(x \hookrightarrow y) = f(x \hookrightarrow (y^\sim \to y))$ for all $x, y \in A$,

(3) $f(x) = f((x \to y) \hookrightarrow x))$, $f(x) = f((x \hookrightarrow y) \to x)$ for all $x, y \in A$.

Proof. Similar to the proof of [5].

Definition 7 [5] A fuzzy subset f of A is called a fuzzy positive implicative filter of A if for all $x, y, z \in A$,

(1) $f(1) \geq f(x)$,

(2) $f(x \to z) \geq f(x \to (y \to z)) \wedge f(x \to y)$.

Theorem 2 [5] Let f be a fuzzy filter of A. The following are equivalent:

(1) f is a fuzzy positive implicative filter,

(2) $f(y \to x) = f(y \to (y \to x))$ for any $x, y \in A$,

(3) $f(y \to x) \geq f(z \to (y \to (y \to x))) \wedge f(z)$ for any $x, y, z \in A$,

(4) $f(x \to x \odot x) = f(1)$ for all $x \in A$.

Definition 7 A fuzzy subset f of A is called a fuzzy sub positive implicative filter of A if for all $x, y, z \in A$,

(1) $f(1) \geq f(x)$,

(2) $f((x \to y) \hookrightarrow y) \geq f(((x \to y) \odot z) \hookrightarrow ((y \hookrightarrow x) \to x) \wedge f(z)$,

(3) $f((x \hookrightarrow y) \to y) \geq f((z \odot (x \hookrightarrow y)) \to ((y \to x) \hookrightarrow x) \wedge f(z)$.

Theorem 3 Let f be a fuzzy filter of A. f is a fuzzy sub positive implicative filter of A if and only if for each $t \in [0,1]$, f_t is either empty or a sub positive implicative filter of A.

Theorem 4 A fuzzy filter f of A is a fuzzy sub positive implicative filter of A if and only if $f_{f(1)}$ is a sub positive implicative filter of A.

Corollary 1 A nonempty subset F of A is a sub positive implicative filter of A if and only if χ_F is a fuzzy sub positive implicative filter of A.

Theorem 5 Let f be a fuzzy filter of a residuated lattices A. Then the followings are equivalent

(1) f is a fuzzy sub positive implicative filter,

(2) $f((x \to y) \hookrightarrow y) = f(((x \to y) \hookrightarrow ((y \hookrightarrow x) \to x))$ for any $x, y \in A$,

(3) $f((x \hookrightarrow y) \to y) = f(((x \hookrightarrow y) \to ((y \to x) \hookrightarrow x))$ for any $x, y \in A$.

Proof. (1) $\Rightarrow$ (2). Let $f(((x \to y) \hookrightarrow ((y \hookrightarrow x) \to x)) = t$. Then $((x \to y) \hookrightarrow ((y \hookrightarrow x) \to x) \in f_t$. And $1 \in f_t$, $(((x \to y) \odot 1) \hookrightarrow ((y \hookrightarrow x) \to x) \in f_t$, hence $(x \to y) \hookrightarrow y \in f_t$, i.e., $f((x \to y) \hookrightarrow y) \geq t = f(((x \to y) \hookrightarrow ((y \hookrightarrow x) \to x))$. The inverse inequation is obvious since f is isotone and $(x \to y) \hookrightarrow y \leq (x \to y) \hookrightarrow ((y \hookrightarrow x) \to x)$.

(1) $\Rightarrow$ (3). Similar to (1) $\Rightarrow$ (2).

(2) $\Rightarrow$ (1). Let $f(((x \to y) \odot z) \hookrightarrow ((y \hookrightarrow x) \to x) \wedge f(z) = t$ for all $x, y, z \in A$, then $((x \to y) \odot z) \hookrightarrow ((y \hookrightarrow x) \to x, z \in f_t$. Since f_t is a filter, so $(x \to y) \hookrightarrow ((y \hookrightarrow x) \to x \in f_t$, then $(x \to y) \hookrightarrow y \in f_t$, i.e., $f((x \to y) \hookrightarrow y) \geq f(((x \to y) \odot z) \hookrightarrow ((y \hookrightarrow x) \to x) \wedge f(z)$. And we have f is a fuzzy sub positive implicative filter.

(3) $\Rightarrow$ (1). Similar to (2) $\Rightarrow$ (1).

Theorem 6 Every fuzzy sub positive implicative filter of A is a fuzzy filter.

Proof. Let $f(x \hookrightarrow y) \wedge f(x) = t$ for all $x, y \in A$, then $x \hookrightarrow y, x \in f_t$. Since we have $((y \to y) \odot x) \hookrightarrow ((y \hookrightarrow y) \to y) = x \hookrightarrow y \in f_t$, so we have $y = (y \to y) \hookrightarrow y) \in f_t$. Hence $f(y) \geq f(x \hookrightarrow y) \wedge f(x)$ and f is a fuzzy filter.

Theorem 7 Let f be a fuzzy filter of a residuated lattices A. Then the followings are equivalent

(1) f is a fuzzy sub positive implicative filter,

(2) $f(y) \geq f((y \to z) \hookrightarrow (x \to y)) \wedge f(x)$ for any $x, y, z \in A$,

(3) $f(y) \geq f((y \hookrightarrow z) \to (x \hookrightarrow y)) \wedge f(x)$ for any $x, y, z \in A$.

Proof. (1) $\Rightarrow$ (2). Let f be a fuzzy sub positive implicative filter of A and $f((y \to z) \hookrightarrow (x \to y)) \wedge f(x) = t$. Then $(y \to z) \hookrightarrow (x \to y) = x \to ((y \to z) \hookrightarrow y), x \in f_t$. Then we get $(x \to y) \hookrightarrow y \in f_t$. And $z \leq y \to z$, $(x \to z) \hookrightarrow y \leq z \hookrightarrow y \in f_t$. hence $z \hookrightarrow y \in f_t$. And we have $(y \to z) \hookrightarrow y \leq (y \to z) \hookrightarrow ((z \hookrightarrow y) \to y) \in f_t$. Then we get $(y \to z) \hookrightarrow z \in f_t$ since f is a fuzzy sub positive implicative filter of A. And $(y \to z) \hookrightarrow z \le (z \hookrightarrow y) \to ((y \to z) \hookrightarrow y)$, then $(z \hookrightarrow y) \to ((y \to z) \hookrightarrow y) \in f_t$. So $(z \hookrightarrow y) \to y \in f_t$, since $z \hookrightarrow y \in f_t$, then $y \in f_t$, i.e., $f(y) \ge f((y \to z) \hookrightarrow (x \to y)) \wedge f(x)$.

(1) $\Rightarrow$ (3). Similar to (1) $\Rightarrow$ (2).

(2) $\Rightarrow$ (1). Let $f((x \to y) \hookrightarrow ((y \hookrightarrow x) \to x)) = t$ for all $x, y \in A$, then $(x \to y) \hookrightarrow ((y \hookrightarrow x) \to x) \in f_t$. Since $(((x \hookrightarrow y) \hookrightarrow y) \to 1) \hookrightarrow (((x \to y) \hookrightarrow ((y \hookrightarrow x) \to x))) \to ((x \to y) \hookrightarrow y)) = ((x \to y) \hookrightarrow ((y \hookrightarrow x) \to x)) \to (((x \to y) \hookrightarrow y) \hookrightarrow ((x \to y) \hookrightarrow y)) = (x \to y) \hookrightarrow ((y \hookrightarrow x) \to x) \in f_t$, then $(x \hookrightarrow y) \hookrightarrow y \in f_t$. And we have f is a fuzzy sub positive implicative filter.

(3) $\Rightarrow$ (1). Similar to (2) $\Rightarrow$ (1).

Corollary 2 Let f be a fuzzy filter of a residuated lattices A. Then the followings are equivalent

(1) f is a fuzzy sub positive implicative filter,

(2) $f((y \hookrightarrow x) \to x) \ge f((x \to y) \hookrightarrow ((y \to x) \hookrightarrow x))$ for any $x, y \in A$,

(3) $f((y \to x) \hookrightarrow x) \ge f((x \hookrightarrow y) \to ((y \hookrightarrow x) \to x))$ for any $x, y \in A$.

Theorem 8 Let f be a fuzzy filter of a residuated lattices A. Then the followings are equivalent

(1) f is a fuzzy sub positive implicative filter,

(2) $f((x \to y) \hookrightarrow x) = f(x)$ for any $x, y \in A$,

(3) $f((x \hookrightarrow y) \to x) = f(x)$ for any $x, y \in A$.

Proof. (1) $\Rightarrow$ (2). Let f be a fuzzy sub positive implicative filter of A and $f((x \to y) \hookrightarrow x) = t$. Then $(x \to y) \hookrightarrow x \in f_t$. And $1 \in f_t$, $(x \to y) \hookrightarrow (1 \to x) = (x \to y) \hookrightarrow x \in f_t$, we get $x \in f_t$, i.e., $f(x) \ge t = f((x \to y) \hookrightarrow x)$. The inverse inequation is obvious since f is isotone and $x \le (x \to y) \hookrightarrow x$.

(1) $\Rightarrow$ (3). Similar to (1) $\Rightarrow$ (2).

(2) $\Rightarrow$ (1). Let $f((y \to z) \hookrightarrow (x \to y)) \wedge f(x) = t$ for all $x, y, z \in A$, then $(y \to z) \hookrightarrow (x \to y), x \in f_t$. Since $(y \to z) \hookrightarrow (x \to y) = x \to ((y \to z) \hookrightarrow y), x \in f_t$ and f_t is a filter, so $(y \to z) \hookrightarrow y \in f_t$, then $f((y \to z) \hookrightarrow y) = f(y) \ge t = f((y \to z) \hookrightarrow (x \to y)) \wedge f(x)$, and we have f is a fuzzy sub positive implicative filter.

(3) $\Rightarrow$ (1). Similar to (2) $\Rightarrow$ (1).

Corollary 3 Let f be a fuzzy filter of a residuated lattices A. Then the followings are equivalent

(1) f is a fuzzy sub positive implicative filter,

(2) $f(x^- \hookrightarrow x) = f(x)$ for any $x, y \in A$,

(3) $f(x^\sim \to x) = f(x)$ for any $x, y \in A$.

Theorem 9 Let f, g be two fuzzy filters of A which satisfy $f \le g, f(1) =$

$g(1)$. If f is a fuzzy sub positive implicative filter of A , so is g.

Proof. Let $f((x \to y) \hookrightarrow x) = t$ for all $x, y \in A$, then we let $z = (x \to y) \hookrightarrow x, z \to z = 1 \in f_t$. Since $z \to ((x \to y) \hookrightarrow x) = (x \to y) \hookrightarrow (z \to x) = 1 \in f_t$, so we have $(x \to y) \hookrightarrow (z \to x) \leq ((z \to x) \to y) \hookrightarrow (z \to x) \in f_t$. Since f_t is a sub positive implicative filter of A, then we get $g(1) = f(1) \leq f(z \to x) \leq g(z \to x)$. Thus $z \to x \in g_t$ and $x \in g_t$ since $z \in g_t$. Then we have g is a fuzzy sub positive implicative filter.

Corollary 4 Every fuzzy filter f of a residuated lattices A is a fuzzy sub positive implicative filter if and only if χ_A is a fuzzy sub positive implicative filter.

Corollary 5 Every fuzzy sub positive implicative filter f of a non-commutative residuated lattices A is equivalent to a fuzzy Boolean filter.

Corollary 6 Every fuzzy sub positive implicative filter f of a non-commutative residuated lattices A is a fuzzy positive implicative filter.

Acknowledgment

This work is partially supported by China Postdoctoral Science Foundation funded project (Grant No.2013M540716); the National Natural Science Foundation of China (Grant No. 60875034, 61175055); the project TIN-2009-0828; Sichuan Key Technology Research and Development Program of China (Grant No. 2011FZ0051); Wireless Administration of Ministry of Industry and Information Technology of China ([2011]146); the Natural Science foundation of Shaanxi Province (Grant No. 2012JQ1023) and doctor initial fund of Xi'an Shiyou University of China (Grant No. 2011BS017)

References

1. K. Blount, C. Tsinakis. The structure of non-commutative residuated lattices. International Journal of Algebra and Computation, 13(4)(2003) 437-461.
2. P. Hájek, Metamathematics of fuzzy logic, Kluwer, Dordrecht (1998)
3. E. Turunen, Boolean deductive systems of BL-algebras, Arch. Math. Logic 40 (2001) 467-473.
4. X.H. Zhang, Fuzzy logic and its algebric analysis, Science Press, Beijing (2008)
5. W. Wang, X.L. Xin, On fuzzy filters of pseudo BL-algebras. Fuzzy Sets and Systems 162 (2011) 27-38.
6. P. Jipsen, C. Tsinakis. A survey of non-commutative residuated lattices // Ordered Algebraic Structures (J.Martinez, ed.), Kluwer Academic Publishers, Dordrecht, 2002: 19-56.
7. S. Ghorbani, Sub positive implicative filters of non-commutative residuated lattice, World Applied Sciences Journal 12 (2011) 586-590.
8. L. Z. Liu, K. T. Li, Fuzzy Boolean and positive implicative filters of BL-algebras. Fuzzy Sets and Systems 152 (2005) 333-348.

AN ADAPTIVE SPECTRUM ALLOCATION SCHEME BASED ON MATRIX GAME IN MACRO/FEMTOCELL HIERARCHICAL NETWORKS[*]

PENG XU[†,1], MEIRONG CHEN[2], YANG XU[1], ZHENMING SONG[1], DANCHEN WANG[3]

[1]*School of Mathematics, Southwest Jiaotong University, Chengdu, 610031, China*

[2]*Electronic Information and Electric Engineering Department,*
Chengdu Textile College, Chengdu 611731, China

[3]*Intelligent Control Development Center, Southwest Jiaotong University,*
Chengdu, 610031, China

Femtocells has been regarded as one of the most promising approaches to improve indoor coverage and network capacity. The method of decentralized spectrum allocation between users has become more efficient. An adaptive spectrum allocation scheme based on matrix game is proposed, in which femto and macrocell base stations are players and the same spectrum is the resource players will choose to assign users, to minimize the affected interference among each other. The equilibrium is the output of the game, which is also the optimal spectrum allocation manner. The sub-optimal solution is also given to avoid that the equilibrium may not exist. And the comparison results show that the proposed scheme might be a solution for efficiently allocating the spectrum in hierarchical cell networks, as the improvement in terms of throughput, outage probability had been achieved.

1. Introduction

Femtocell systems, known as access point base stations or small cellular home base stations, provide service providers with extension of indoor service coverage and also with expansion of link capacity by drastically reducing the infrastructure costs. The placement of femtocells has a critical effect on the performance of a pre-existing macrocell network, and there are many complicated issues to be overcome for successful deployment of femtocells. When working in macro/femtocells, the main challenges foucused on interference mitigation and management, integration with the macrocell network, etc. Decentralized spectrum allocation between macro and femto users may adopt two manners. One is that all macro and femtocell users are orthogonal through bandwidth splitting; the other is

[*] This work is supported by National Science Foundation of China (Grant No.61175055, 61305074), Sichuan Key Technology Research and Development Program (Grant No.2011FZ0051), Radio Administration Bureau of MIIT of China(Grant No.[2011]146), the Fundamental Research Funds for the Central Universities(Grant No. A0920502051305-25),

[†] Email: pengxup@home.swjtu.edu.cn

that macro and femtocell assign their users with shared bandwidth (i.e. frequency reuse) [1].One conventional approach to improve spectrum efficiency in static manner is to reuse the frequency band in multiple geographical areas or cells[2][3]. However preplanned frequency assignments cannot real-timely satisfy the variety of femtocells. So the methods of dynamic or adaptive spectrum allocation are needed [4][5][6].

In this paper an adaptive frequency allocation scheme based on a non-cooperative game is proposed, through which femto and macro BSs will choose the optimal frequency in shared frequency to assign associated users, where the optimal is defined as minimal interference introduced to users.

2. System model

In system deployment each base station has some options of frequency allocation, and BSs have the opportunity and some methods to deploy the femtocells in dedicated spectrum. There are three methods to allocate spectrum, including orthogonal frequency, frequency reuse and fraction frequency reuse. Assume the macro base station(m-BS) and all femto base stations(f-BSs) have the same spectrum resource, to assign users with adequate frequency to minimize cross-tier interference. The process of spectrum allocation between m-BS and f-BSs accords with a non-cooperative game.

Then the frequency allocation can be defined as a non-cooperative game [7]:

$$G :< N, S, U > \qquad (1)$$

where $N=\{M,F\}$ denotes the set of players, $M=\{$ $mBS\}$ and $F=\{fBS_1,fBS_2,...,fBS_n\}$ denote the macro base station and some femto base stations in one macrocell, respectively. $S=\{f_1,f_2,...,f_m\}$ denotes the frequency that mBS and fBS will allocate, as the strategy set. $U=\{U_M, U_F\}$ represents the relevant utility set for the set M and F, where $u_{ij}^m(k)$ and $u_{ij}^f(k)$ denote the utility of m-BS and f-BS when m-BS assigned ith frequency and the kth f-BS assigned jth frequency, respectively. Proposed Scheme

3. The proposed scheme

Assume that m-BS and all other existed femtocells have adaptively assigned frequencies, and the suitable power control is adapted. Only spectrum allocation of the new femtocell is considered in this part. All new users are classified into femto and macro users, firstly all carrier frequencies of the usable spectrum can be gotten, which is the same for two kinds of users here. Then the m-BS and f-BS begin to allocate the frequencies based on co-channel interference, which are also subject to the Signal to Interference plus Noise Ratio (SINR) of the sub-channel.

The utility set $\tilde{U} = \{\tilde{U}_M, \tilde{U}_F\}$ can be written as:

$$\tilde{U}_M (mBS_i, fBS_j) = \{\tilde{u}_{ij}^m \mid i, j \in 1, 2, \cdots, m\} \qquad (2)$$

$$SINR_{i,m} = \frac{P_{i,m}}{\displaystyle\sum_{m' \in M'-M} P_{i,m'} + \sum_{f \in F} P_{i,f} + N} \qquad (3)$$

$$\tilde{u}_{ij}^m : \sum_{x \in X^m} P'_{i,x} + \sum_{y \in Y^f} P'_{i,y} \qquad (4)$$

$$\tilde{U}_F (mBS_i, fBS_j) = \{\tilde{u}_{ij}^f \mid i, j \in 1, 2, \cdots, m\} \qquad (5)$$

$$SINR_{j,f} = \frac{P_{j,f}}{\displaystyle\sum_{m \in M'} P_{j,m} + \sum_{f' \in F'} P_{j,f'} + N} \qquad (6)$$

$$\tilde{u}_{ij}^f : \sum_{x \in X^m} P'_{j,x} + \sum_{y \in Y^f} P'_{j,y} \qquad (7)$$

where $SINR_{i/j,m/f}$ denotes the SINR of the macro/femto users when communicating with m-BS/f-BS on sub-channel i/j. $P_{i/j,m/f}$ represents the received power of the macro/femto users on sub-channel i/j. N denotes the Noise power. The set of m-BSs is denoted by M', and $M'-M$ denotes the set except the serving m-BS. The set of f-BSs except the serving f-BS is denoted by F'. The existed user sets for macro and femtocell are represented as $x \in X_m$ and $y \in Y_m$, respectively. When the ith sub-channel is allocated to a new macro user m, the interference introduced is mainly for existed macro users and femto users as described in Eq.(4), which is also as the game utility of m-BS. Similar for f-BS, Eq.(7) is also given.

The matrix game is described as a pairwise matrix game[8], where the utility matrix is:

$$(\tilde{u}_{ij}^m, \tilde{u}_{ij}^f)_{m \times m} = \begin{bmatrix} (\tilde{u}_{11}^m, \tilde{u}_{11}^f) & (\tilde{u}_{12}^m, \tilde{u}_{12}^f) & \cdots & (\tilde{u}_{1m}^m, \tilde{u}_{1m}^f) \\ (\tilde{u}_{21}^m, \tilde{u}_{21}^f) & (\tilde{u}_{22}^m, \tilde{u}_{22}^f) & \cdots & (\tilde{u}_{2m}^m, \tilde{u}_{2m}^f) \\ \vdots & \vdots & \ddots & \vdots \\ (\tilde{u}_{m1}^m, \tilde{u}_{m1}^f) & (\tilde{u}_{m2}^m, \tilde{u}_{m2}^f) & \cdots & (\tilde{u}_{mm}^m, \tilde{u}_{mm}^f) \end{bmatrix} \qquad (8)$$

To find out the pure strategy Nash equilibrium, it is needed for m-BS to find the minimum element in each row in $\tilde{U}_F$, and for f-BS in each column in $\tilde{U}_M$.

$$u^f_{ij^*} = \min\{u^f_{ij} \mid j = 1, 2, ..., m\}$$

$$\text{Subject to}: \ SINR_{i,y} > SINR_{th,f}, SINR_{i,x} > SINR_{th,m}$$

(9)

$$u^m_{i^*j} = \min\{u^m_{ij} \mid i = 1, 2, ..., m\}$$

$$\text{Subject to}: \ SINR_{i,x} > SINR_{th,m}, SINR_{i,y} > SINR_{th,f}$$

(10)

If the component (i^*, j^*) does exist, that is the output of Nash equilibrium. Otherwise it means the optimal solution does not exist, the other solution is given as:

$$(i', j') : \min\{ \sum_{i, j \in \{1,2,...,m\}} (\tilde{u}^m_{ij} + \tilde{u}^f_{ij}) \}$$

$$\text{Subject to}: \ SINR_{i,x} > SINR_{th,m}, SINR_{j,y} > SINR_{th,f}$$

(11)

where $SINR_{th,m}$ and $SINR_{th,f}$ denote the each interference constraint for macro and femto users, which are usually decided by network operators and mobile terminals.

4. Simulations and numerical results

Table 1 Simulation parameters

Parameters	Values
Inter macrocell distance	800m
Radius of a femtocell	30m
Number of cells	One tier(7 macrocells)
Macro BS transmit power	20W(43dBm)
Femto Bs transmit power	20mW(13dBm)
Number of used sub-carrier	300
Channel model (Path loss, PL)	$PL_{outdoor}=28+35\log_{10}(d)$ $PL_{indoor}=38.5+20\log_{10}(d)+L_{walls}$ L_{walls}: 7dB, $d \in (0,10]$; 10dB, $d \in (10,20]$; 15dB, $d \in (20,30]$
Log-Normal fading	8dB(outdoor), 4dB(indoor)

The proposed scheme is evaluated in terms of throughput and outage probability, compared to the schemes based on conventional frequency reuse with reuse factor (RF) 3, fractional frequency reuse (FFR) with RF=3, and conventional manner only with SINR, respectively.

The overall network is composed of one tier macrocells, and femtocells are randomly deployed over the macrocells. The number of femto users is varied in one macrocell coverage. The macro and femto users are randomly distributed in the overall network at the ratio 4:1. The simulation parameters are listed in Table 1.

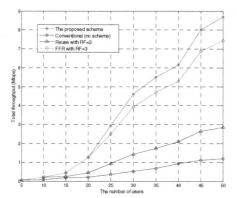

Fig. 1 Throughput versus users

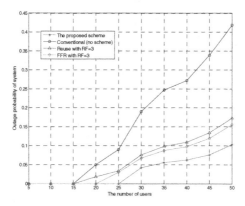

Fig. 2 Outage probabilities versus users

Fig.1 shows the comparison results in terms of total throughput, the merits of the schemes are in the descent order as the proposed, FFR, reuse with RF=3, conventional. That is mainly because the proposed scheme firstly allocates the orthogonal spectrum when spectrum resource is enough, and the throughput at this moment is not obviously different compared with FFR. Along with the number of users increased, the improvement of the proposed scheme is more obvious, up to 16.8%, when spectrum resource is sparse.

The trends of outage probability for four schemes along with the increase of users are shown in Fig. 2. The other three schemes have lower outage probabilities than that of conventional manner. The main reason is that the co-channel interference is reduced in other three schemes. It can also be concluded from Fig.2 that the proposed scheme has the best performance.

5. Conclusions and discussions

The proposed scheme performs best in terms of throughput, outage probability can be obtained. Although the analysis is only as to one femtocell, it is not limited and can be expanded to more femtocells. However the tradeoff between performance improvement and computation complexity still needs to be evaluated in detail, which will be the next research.

References

1. Jie Zhang, Guillaume de la Roche. Femtocells:Technologies and Deployment. UK:Wiley, March 2010.
2. Guan-Ming Su, Yu-Chi Lai, Andres Kwasinski, et al. 3D video communications: Challenges and opportunities. Wiley International Journal of Communication Systems, Oct. 2011, 24(10):1261-1281
3. Abdelnasser A., Hossain E., Dong In Kim. Clustering and Resource Allocation for Dense Femtocells in a Two-Tier Cellular OFDMA Network. IEEE Transactions on Wireless Communications, March 2014, 13(3):1628-1641.
4. Wang Chi Cheung, Quek T.Q.S., Kountouris M. Throughput Optimization, Spectrum Allocation, and Access Control in Two-Tier Femtocell Networks. IEEE Journal on Selected Areas in Communications, April 2012, 30(3):561-574.
5. Peng Xu, Xuming Fang, Meirong Chen, et al. A Stackelberg Game-based Spectrum Allocation Scheme in Macro/Femtocell Hierarchical Networks. Computer Communications, 2013, 36(14):1552-1558
6. Xiaohu Ge, Tao Han, Yan Zhang, et al. Spectrum and Energy Efficiency Evaluation of Two-Tier Femtocell Networks With Partially Open Channels. IEEE Transactions on Vehicular Technology, March 2014, 63(3):1306-1319.
7. John Nash. Non-Cooperative Games. Annals of Mathematics. September, 1951, 54(2):286-295
8. Deng-Feng Li. An Effective Methodology for Solving Matrix Games With Fuzzy Payoffs. *IEEE Transactions on Cybernetics*, April 2013, 43(2):610-621.

THE ALGEBRA STRUCTURE OF LINGUISTIC
TRUTH-VALUED INTUITIONISTIC FUZZY LATTICE

Xin Liu and Ming'e Yin

School of Mathematics, Liaoning Normal University, Dalian 116029, China

Li Zou*

*School of Computer and Information Technology,Liaoning Normal University, Dalian
116029, China*
*State Key Laboratory for Novel Software Technology,Nanjing University,Nanjing
210093,China*
E-mail: zoulicn@163.com

Linguistic truth-valued intuitionistic fuzzy lattice $\mathcal{LI}_{2n} = (LI_{2n}, \cup, \cap, \rightarrow, ((h_n, t), (h_n, f))), ((h_1, t), (h_1, f)))$ based on linguistic truth-valued lattice implication algebra has some special properties. We proof that linguistic truth-valued intuitionistic fuzzy lattice is a triangle algebra. We obtain some triangle algebra structure of $\mathcal{LI}_{2n}$.

Keywords: Lattice implication algebra; Linguistic truth-valued intuitionisitic fuzzy lattice; Triangle algebra.

1. Introduction

In recent years, some alternative methods have been presented for dealing with linguistic information. In,[7,8,12] linguistic information was expressed by means of 2-tuples which are composed by a linguistic term and a numeric value assessed in $[0.5, 0.5)$ which can represent any counting of information which is obtained in the aggregation process. In[11,13] a new model for parametric representation of linguistic truth-values have been proposed. To formalize and infer descriptive words, substantive words and declarative sentence based on type-2 fuzzy sets have been introduced in.[14] Based on the ordering structure of linguistic hedges, hedge algebra have been proposed to deal with Computing Words.[9,10] To manage multi-granular linguistic scales in decision making problems, several computational linguistic approaches have been presented in.[5]

Intuitionistic fuzzy sets (A-IFSs) introduced by Atanassov is a powerful tool to deal with uncertainty.[1,2] A-IFSs concentrate on expressing advantages and disadvantages, pros and cons.[4,17] In this paper, we discuss the algebra structure properties of linguistic truth-valued intuitionistic fuzzy lattice.

2. Linguistic Truth-Valued Intuitionistic Fuzzy Lattice $\mathcal{LI}_{2n}$

Definition 2.1.[15] Let $(L, \vee, \wedge, O, I)$ be a bounded lattice with an order-reversing involution $''$, I and O the greatest and the smallest element of L, respectively, and

$$\rightarrow : L \times L \longrightarrow L$$

be a mapping. $(L, \vee, \wedge, ', \rightarrow, O, I)$ is called a lattice implication algebra (LIA) if the following conditions hold for any $x, y, z \in L$:

(I_1) $x \rightarrow (y \rightarrow z) = y \rightarrow (x \rightarrow z)$;
(I_2) $x \rightarrow x = I$;
(I_3) $x \rightarrow y = y' \rightarrow x'$;
(I_4) $x \rightarrow y = y \rightarrow x = I$ implies $x = y$;
(I_5) $(x \rightarrow y) \rightarrow y = (y \rightarrow x) \rightarrow x$;
(I_6) $(x \vee y) \rightarrow z = (x \rightarrow z) \wedge (y \rightarrow z)$;
(I_7) $(x \wedge y) \rightarrow z = (x \rightarrow z) \vee (y \rightarrow z)$.

Definition 2.2.[15] Let $AD_n = \{h_1, h_2, \cdots, h_n\}$ be a set of n hedge operators and $h_1 < h_2 < \cdots < h_n$, $MT = \{f, t\}$ be "false (f)" and "true (t)", denote $f < t$ and $L_{V(n \times 2)} = AD_n \times MT$ which is called linguistic truth-valued set. Then $\mathcal{L}_{V(n \times 2)} = (L_{V(n \times 2)}, \vee, \wedge, ', \rightarrow, (h_n, f), (h_n, t))$ is called linguistic truth -valued lattice implication algebra from AD_n and MT (Figure.1).

Based on $2n$ linguistic truth-valued lattice implication algebra $\mathcal{L}_{V(n \times 2)}$, we have constructd linguistic truth-valued intuitionistic fuzzy lattice. Formally, denote

$$\mathcal{LI}_{2n} = (LI_{2n}, \cup, \cap)$$

as a linguistic truth-valued intuitionistic fuzzy lattice where $((h_n, t), (h_n, f))$ and $((h_1, t), (h_1, f))$ are the greatest element and the least element of $\mathcal{LI}_{2n}$, respectively(Figure.2).

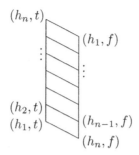

(h_n, t)

(h_1, f)

(h_2, t)
(h_1, t)

(h_{n-1}, f)
(h_n, f)

Fig. 1.   Hasse Diagrams of $\mathcal{L}_{V(n \times 2)}$

Definition 2.3. In the linguistic truth-valued intuitionistic fuzzy lattice $\mathcal{LI}_{2n} = (LI_{2n}, \cup, \cap)$, for any $((h_i, t), (h_j, f)), ((h_k, t), (h_l, f)) \in LI_{2n}$, $((h_i, t), (h_j, f)) \leq ((h_k, t), (h_l, f))$ if and only if $i \leq k$ and $j \leq l$, also

$$((h_i, t), (h_j, f)) \cup ((h_k, t), (h_l, f)) = ((h_{max(i,k)}, t), (h_{max(j,l)}, f)), \quad (1)$$
$$((h_i, t), (h_j, f)) \cap ((h_k, t), (h_l, f)) = ((h_{min(i,k)}, t), (h_{min(j,l)}, f)). \quad (2)$$

3. The Triangle Algebra Structure

From the properties of interval-valued residual lattice,[3] Gasse has proposed Triangle algebra[6] through a constant u and two uniry operators μ and ν.

Definition 3.1.[6] $\mathcal{A} = (A, \cup, \cap, *, \rightarrow, \nu, \mu, 0, u, 1)$ is called a Triangle Algebra, if $(A, \cup, \cap, *, \rightarrow 0, 1)$ is a residual lattice and the following properties are satisfied for any $x, y \in A$,

- T.1 $\nu x \leq x$ T.1' $x \leq \mu x$;
- T.2 $\nu x \leq \nu \nu x$ T.2' $\mu \mu x \leq \mu x$;
- T.3 $\nu(x \cup y) = \nu x \cup \nu y$ T.3' $\mu(x \cup y) = \mu x \cup \mu y$;
- T.4 $\nu(x \cap y) = \nu x \cap \nu y$ T.4' $\mu(x \cap y) = \mu x \cap \mu y$;
- T.5 $\nu 1 = 1$ T.5' $\mu 0 = 0$;
- T.6 $\nu u = 0$ T.6' $\mu u = 1$;
- T.7 $\nu \mu x = \mu x$ T.7' $\mu \nu x = \nu x$;
- T.8 $\nu(x \rightarrow y) \leq \nu x \rightarrow \nu y$);
- T.9 $((\nu x \rightarrow \nu y) \cap (\nu y \rightarrow \nu x)) * ((\mu x \rightarrow \mu y) \cap (\mu y \rightarrow \mu x)) \leq (x \rightarrow y) \cap (y \rightarrow x)$;
- T.10 $(\nu x \rightarrow \nu y) \leq \nu(\nu x \rightarrow \nu y)$.

According to the definition 3.1, we define the unary operators μ and ν in $\mathcal{LI}_{2n}$.

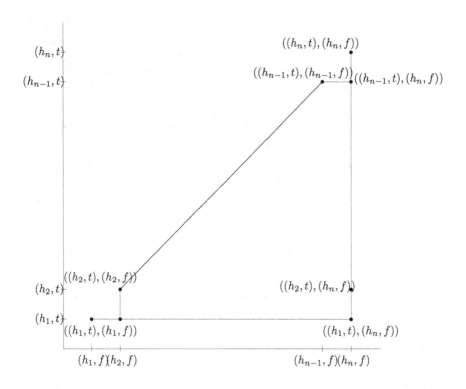

$((h_n, t), (h_n, f))$

$((h_{n-1}, t), (h_{n-1}, f))$ $((h_{n-1}, t), (h_n, f))$

(h_n, t)

(h_{n-1}, t)

$((h_2, t), (h_2, f))$

(h_2, t) $((h_2, t), (h_n, f))$

(h_1, t)

$((h_1, t), (h_1, f))$ $((h_1, t), (h_n, f))$

$(h_1, f)(h_2, f)$ $(h_{n-1}, f)(h_n, f)$

Fig. 2.   Structure Diagrams of $\mathcal{LI}_{2n}$

Definition 3.2. For any $((h_i, t), (h_j, f)) \in LI_{2n}$, we define as follows.

$$\nu((h_i, t), (h_j, f)) = ((h_i, t), (h_i, f)), \quad \mu((h_i, t), (h_j, f)) = ((h_j, t), (h_j, f)).$$

Theorem 3.1.
   $\mathcal{LI}_{2n} = (LI_{2n}, \cup, \cap, *, \rightarrow, \nu, \mu, ((h_1, t), (h_1, f)), ((h_1, t), (h_n, f)),$
$((h_n, t), (h_n, f)))$ is a triangle algebra.

Proposition 3.1. For any $((h_i, t), (h_j, f)), ((h_k, t), (h_l, f)) \in LI_{2n}$,

(1) $\mu((h_i, t), (h_j, f)) = \neg(\nu(\neg((h_i, t), (h_j, f))))$;
(2) $\nu((h_i, t), (h_j, f)) = \neg(\mu(\neg((h_i, t), (h_j, f))))$;
(3) $\mu((h_i, t), (h_j, f)) * (\neg(\mu(\neg((h_k, t), (h_l, f))))) \leq \mu(((h_i, t), (h_j, f)) * ((h_k, t), (h_l, f)))$;
(4) $\mu(\mu((h_i, t), (h_j, f)) * (\neg(\mu((h_k, t), (h_l, f))))) \leq \mu((h_i, t), (h_j, f)) * (\neg(\mu((h_k, t), (h_l, f))))$;

(5) $((\nu((h_i,t),(h_j,f)) \rightarrow \nu((h_k,t),(h_l,f))) \cap (\nu((h_k,t),(h_l,f)) \rightarrow \nu((h_i,t),(h_j,f))))* ((\nu(\neg((h_i,t), (h_j,f))) \rightarrow \nu(\neg((h_k,t),(h_l,f)))) \cap (\nu(\neg((h_k,t),(h_l,f))) \rightarrow \nu(\neg((h_i,t), (h_j,f)))))) \leq (((h_i,t), (h_j,f)) \rightarrow ((h_k,t),(h_l,f))) \cap (((h_k,t),(h_l,f)) \rightarrow ((h_i,t),(h_j,f)));$

(6) $((\mu((h_i,t),(h_j,f)) \rightarrow \mu((h_k,t),(h_l,f))) \cap (\mu((h_k,t),(h_l,f)) \rightarrow \mu((h_i,t),(h_j,f))))* ((\mu(\neg((h_i, t),(h_j,f))) \rightarrow \mu(\neg((h_k,t),(h_l,f)))) \cap (\mu(\neg((h_k,t),(h_l,f))) \rightarrow \mu (\neg((h_i,t), (h_j,f)))))) \leq (((h_i,t),(h_j,f)) \rightarrow ((h_k,t),(h_l,f))) \cap (((h_k,t), (h_l,f)) \rightarrow ((h_i,t),(h_j,f)));$

4. Conclusion

We have got some triangle structure properties of linguistic truth-valued intuitionistic fuzzy lattice. Some more characteristics will be discussed in the future. We can use this approach to deal with linguistic-valued information in some areas, such as evaluation, risk analysis, decision making and so on.

Acknowledgment

This work is partly supported by National Natural Science Foundation of China (61105059,61175055,61372187 and 61173100), Sichuan Key Technology Research and Development Program (2011FZ0051), Radio Administration Bureau of MIIT of China(Grant No.[2011]146), China Institution of Communications(Grant No.[2011]051).

References

1. K. Atanassov, Elements of intuitionistic fuzzy logic. Part I, Fuzzy Set and Systems, Vol.95, 39-52(1998).
2. K.T. Atanassov, Answer to D. Dubois, S. Gottwald, P. Hajek, J. Kacprzyk and H. Prade's paper "Terminological difficulties in fuzzy set theorythe case of 'Intuitionistic Fuzzy Sets' ", Fuzzy Sets and Systems, Vol.156, 496-499(2005).
3. C. Cornelis, G. Deschrijver, E.E. Kerre, Advances and challenges in interval-valued fuzzy logic, *Fuzzy Sets and Systems*. 2006, 157(5):622–627.
4. G. Deschrijver, E.E. Kerre,On the position of intuitionistic fuzzy set theory in the framework of theories modelling imprecision,Information Sciences, Vol.177,1860-1866 (2007)
5. M.Espinilla, J. Liu, L. Martinez, An extended hierarchical linguistic model for decision-making problems, Computatioinal Intelligence, Vol. 27(3),489-512,2011.
6. B. Van Gasse, C. Cornelis, G. Deschrijver and E.E. Kerre, Triangle algebras: A formal logic approach to interval-valued, *Fuzzy Sets and Systems*. 2008, 159: 1042-1060

7. F. Herrera, L. Martineez, A 2-tuple fuzzy linguistic representation model for computing with words, *IEEE Transactions on Fuzzy Systems.* **8** (2000) 746-752.

8. F. Herrera, S. Alonso, F. Chiclana, E. Herrera-Viedma, Computing With Words in Decision Making: Foundations, Trends and Prospects, Fuzzy Optimization and Decision Making. Vol.8(4),337-364 (2009) .

9. N.C. Ho, A topological completion of refined hedge algebras and a model of fuzziness of linguistic terms and hedges, Fuzzy Sets and Systems, Vol.158, 436-451(2007).

10. N.C. Ho and N. V. Long, Fuzziness measure on complete hedge algebras and quantifying semantics of terms in linear hedge algebras, Fuzzy Sets and Systems, Vol.158, 452-471(2007).

11. V.N. Huynh, T.B. Ho and Y. Nakamori, A parametric representation of linguistic hedges in Zadeh's fuzzy logic, International Journal of Approximate Reasoning, Vol.30, 203-223(2002).

12. L. Martinez, D. Ruan, F. Herrera, Computing with Words in Decision support Systems: An overview on Models and Applications, International Journal of Computational Intelligence Systems, Vol.3(4), 382-395(2010).

13. C.H. Nguyen and V.N. Huynh, An algebraic approach to linguistic hedges in Zadeh's fuzzy logic, Fuzzy Set and Systems, Vol.129, 229-254(2002).

14. I. B. Turksen, Meta-linguistic axioms as a foundation for computing with words, Information Sciences, Vol.177, 332-359, 2007.

15. Y. Xu, D. Ruan, K. Y. Qin and J. Liu, *Lattice-valued Logic*, Springer Published, 2004.

16. Y. Xu, D. Ruan, E.E. Kerre and J. Liu, α-resolution principle based on lattice-valued propositional logic LP(X), Information Sciences, Vol.130, 195-223(2000).

17. Z.S. Xu, J. Chen and J. J. Wu, Clustering algoritheorem for intuitionistic fuzzy sets, Information Sciences, Vol.178, 3775-3790(2008).

18. L. Zou, P. Shi, Z. Pei and Y. Xu, On an Algebra of Linguistic Truth-Valued Intuitionistic Lattice-Valued Logic, Journal of Intelligent and Fuzzy Systems, Vol.24, 447-456(2013).

F²-TRANSFORM-BASED SOLUTION OF THE CAUCHY PROBLEM

Irina Perfilieva, Radek Valášek, Viktor Pavliska

*Centre of Excellence IT4Innovations, division of the University of Ostrava
Institute for Research and Applications of Fuzzy Modeling
30. dubna 22, 702 00 Ostrava, Czech Republic*

E-mail:Irina.Perfilieva@osu.cz

We investigate the Cauchy problem for an ordinary differential equation (ODE). We propose two new schemes that compute an approximate solution. Both of them are based on the technique of the second degree F-transform. The quality of new schemes is compared with the exact solution and the Euler method.

Keywords: Cauchy problem, ODE, F-transform

1. Introduction

In this paper, we focus on the Cauchy (initial value) problem for an ordinary differential equation (ODE). We propose to apply the technique of F-(fuzzy) transforms and obtain an approximate solution. Our motivation is based on using average values in the form of F-transform components for the approximation of the second order derivatives instead of various numeric schemes that are dependent on the choice of nodes and computation of function values.

In this paper, we continue the study of fuzzy-based contributions to solutions of classical problems. In this connection, it is well known that fuzzy technique successfully copes with approximation and interpolation problems, control of dynamic systems and solving differential equations. For example, in the lastly mentioned direction, many new techniques (the Hukuhara derivative, differential inclusion) were elaborated for solving fuzzy differential equations, see e.g.[1-5]

Apart from this stream, the technique of F-transforms[6,7] has been proposed for solving ordinary differential equations with the purpose to show its potential in comparison with numerous classical techniques. A numerical method which generalizes the Euler method has been proposed in[8] for an ordinary Cauchy problem. In this contribution, we apply a new technique that uses the second degree F-transform. It is the next step in this direction, and it shows that even a better quality can be achieved in comparison with ordinary numeric schemes.

The following characterizes the structure of the proposed contribution. Necessary details of the F^m-transform are recalled in Section 2. The two new schemes and numeric tests are given in Sections 3. A graphical illustration is shown at the end.

2. F^m-transform

Let us briefly recall necessary details of the F^m-transform as they appeared in.[7]

Let $a = x_1 < \cdots < x_n = b$, $n \geq 3$, be fixed nodes within $[a, b]$ such that $x_k = x_1 + (k-1)h$, $k = 1, \ldots, n$ where $h = \frac{b-a}{n-1}$ be a distance between nodes. Fuzzy sets (basic functions) $A_1, \ldots, A_n : [a, b] \longrightarrow [0, 1]$ establish an *h-uniform fuzzy partition* of $[a, b]$ if they fulfill the following conditions:

(1) for every $k = 1, \ldots, n$, $A_k(x) = 0$ if $x \in [a, b] \setminus [x_{k-1}, x_{k+1}]$ where $x_0 = x_1$, $x_{n+1} = x_n$;
(2) for every $k = 1, \ldots, n$, A_k is continuous on $[x_{k-1}, x_{k+1}]$ where $x_0 = x_1$, $x_{n+1} = x_n$;
(3) for every $x \in [a, b]$, $\sum_{k=1}^n A_k(x) = 1$;
(4) for every $k = 1, \ldots, n$, $\sum_{x \in [a,b]} A_k(x) > 0$;
(5) for every $k = 2, \ldots, n-1$, A_k is symmetrical with respect to the line $x = x_k$.

Let $m = 0, 1, 2, \ldots$ be a fixed degree, $f : [a, b] \longrightarrow \mathbb{R}$ be a square integrable function and $A_1, \ldots, A_n$, $n \geq 3$, be basic functions that establish a fuzzy partition of $[a, b]$. Let moreover, for each $k = 1, \ldots, n$, $P_k^0, P_k^1, P_k^2, \ldots, P_k^m$ be an orthogonal[a] system of polynomials restricted to the interval $[x_{k-1}, x_{k+1}]$. Then the vector

$$F^m[f] = (F_1^m, \ldots, F_n^m),$$

of m-degree polynomials is the F^m-transform of f with respect to $A_1, \ldots, A_n$, where

$$F_k^m = c_{k,0} P_k^0 + c_{k,1} P_k^1 + \cdots + c_{k,m} P_k^m,$$

---

[a]Polynomials P_k^i, P_k^j are orthogonal with respect to the weight given by A_k, i.e. $\int_a^b P_k^i(x) P_k^j(x) A_k(x) dx = 0$.

and

$$c_{k,i} = \frac{\langle f, P_k^i \rangle_k}{\langle P_k^i, P_k^i \rangle_k} = \frac{\int_a^b f(x) P_k^i(x) A_k(x) dx}{\int_a^b P_k^i(x) P_k^i(x) A_k(x) dx}, \quad i = 0, \ldots, m.$$

F_k^m is called the kth F^m-transform component of f.

By using the inversion formula (1), we can approximately reconstruct function f from the vector of its F^m-transform components.

$$f_{F,n}(x) = \sum_{k=1}^n F_k^m A_k(x), x \in [a, b]. \tag{1}$$

The following estimation shows the quality of approximation of $f|_{[x_{k-1}, x_{k+1}]}$ by its kth F^m-transform component.

$$f(x) = F_k^m(x) + O(h^{m+1}), \quad x \in [x_{k-1}, x_{k+1}]. \tag{2}$$

3. New F^2-transform-based Numeric Schemes for the Cauchy Problem

The Cauchy problem consists in solving the following differential equation on the interval $[x_1, x_n]$:

$$y'(x) = f(x, y) \tag{3}$$

with the initial condition $y(x_1) = y_1$. The solution is any function y defined on the interval $[x_1, x_n]$ and such that it fulfills the initial condition at point x_1 and its derivative fulfills (3).

3.1. Numeric scheme I

We assume that all necessary requirements for constructing the F^2-transform of the solution y of (3) are fulfilled, so that on each interval $[x_{k-1}, x_{k+1}]$, the restriction $y|_{[x_{k-1}, x_{k+1}]}$ can be approximated by the F^2 component Y_k, $k = 2, \ldots, n$, where

$$Y_k(x) = c_{k,0} + c_{k,1}(x - x_k) + c_{k,2}((x - x_k)^2 - I_2/h), x \in [x_{k-1}, x_{k+1}],$$

$$\tag{4}$$

$$I_2 = \int_{x_{k-1}}^{x_{k+1}} (x - x_k)^2 A_k(x) dx.$$

Let us choose a h-uniform partition of $[x_1, x_n]$ by triangular shaped basic functions. In this case, the expression for Y_k can be simplified to

$$Y_k(x) = c_{k,0} + c_{k,1}(x - x_k) + c_{k,2}((x - x_k)^2 - h^2/6), x \in [x_{k-1}, x_{k+1}]. \tag{5}$$

We use the following approximation[6,7] for coefficients $c_{k,i}$, $i = 0, 1, 2$:

$$c_{k,i} = y^{(i)}(x_k) + O(h^2),$$

that implies

$$c_{k,0} = y(x_k) + O(h^2),$$
$$c_{k,1} = f(x_k, y_k) + O(h^2),$$
$$c_{k,2} = \frac{f(x_{k+1}, y_{k+1}) - f(x_k, y_k)}{2h} + O(h^2).$$

Substituting into (5) and making simplification, we get

$$Y_k(x_{k+1}) = y(x_k) + h(7f(x_k, y_k) + 5f(x_{k+1}, y_{k+1}))/12 + O(h^2). \qquad (6)$$

The below given numeric scheme is based on (6) and can be used for the computation of approximate values $y_2, \ldots, y_n$ of y at h-equidistant nodes $x_2, \ldots, x_n$.

$$f_1 = y_k + hf(x_k, y_k),$$
$$f_2 = y_k + h(7f(x_k, y_k) + 5f(x_{k+1}, f_1))/12,$$
$$y_{k+1} = y_k + h(7f(x_k, y_k) + 5f(x_{k+1}, f_2))/12.$$

3.2. Numeric scheme II

The numeric scheme I uses functional values of the right-hand side f of (3). The latter can be noisy and/or contains a measurement error. In this case, we propose to approximate the coefficient $c_{k,2}$ in (4) by the linear coefficient of the F^1-transform applied to function f, i.e. by:

$$c_{k,2}^a = \frac{\int_{x_{k-1}}^{x_{k+1}} (x - x_k)f(x, y_k)A_k(x)dx}{\int_{x_{k-1}}^{x_{k+1}} (x - x_k)^2 A_k(x)dx}. \qquad (7)$$

The best results are demonstrated by the following combination of (6) with (5) where the coefficient $c_{k,2}$ is approximated by (7):

$$f_1 = y_k + hf(x_k, y_k),$$
$$f_2 = y_k + h(7f(x_k, y_k) + 5f(x_{k+1}, f_1))/12,$$
$$f_3 = y_k + h(f(x_k, y_k) + 5f(x_{k+1}, f_1))/6,$$
$$y_{k+1} = y_k + h(14f(x_k, y_k) + 5f(x_{k+1}, f_2) + 5f(x_{k+1}, f_3))/24 + 5h^2 c_{k,2}^a/48.$$

3.3. Numeric tests

For the numeric test we choose three examples of the Cauchy problem: with smooth and oscillating right-hand functions.

3.4. *Cauchy problem with smooth right-hand function*

$$y'(x) = x^2 - y, \; y(0) = 1, \; x \in [0,2]. \tag{8}$$

We performed computations by the Runge-Kutta method (second order), the generalized Mid-point method (A. Khastan) and the two Schemes proposed above. The numeric results are in Figure 1.

	Solution	Runge-Kutta	MidPoint	Scheme1	Scheme2
0	1	1	1	1	1
0.1	0.905162582	0.9055	0.90016665	0.904392361	0.904296875
0.2	0.821269247	0.8219275	0.82229997	0.8197224	0.819740743
0.3	0.749181779	0.750144388	0.744039956	0.746860163	0.747182323
0.4	0.689679954	0.690930671	0.691825279	0.686592164	0.687390584
0.5	0.64346934	0.644992257	0.6380082	0.63962941	0.641060603
0.6	0.611188364	0.612967993	0.614556939	0.606614642	0.608820665
0.7	0.593414696	0.595436033	0.587430112	0.588128896	0.591238679
0.8	0.590671036	0.59291961	0.595404216	0.584697424	0.588827983
0.9	0.60343034	0.605892247	0.596682569	0.596795049	0.602052586
1	0.632120559	0.634782484	0.638401002	0.624851011	0.631331908
1.1	0.677128916	0.679978148	0.669335669	0.669253336	0.677045066
1.2	0.738805788	0.741830224	0.746867169	0.730352798	0.739534745
1.3	0.817468207	0.820656352	0.808295535	0.808466497	0.819110704
1.4	0.913403036	0.916743999	0.923541362	0.903881085	0.91605293
1.5	1.02686984	1.030353319	1.015920563	1.016855696	1.030614511
1.6	1.158103482	1.161719754	1.170690549	1.147624585	1.16302421
1.7	1.307316476	1.311056377	1.294115753	1.296399516	1.313488811
1.8	1.474701112	1.478556021	1.490200699	1.463371924	1.482195224
1.9	1.660431381	1.664393199	1.644408913	1.648714862	1.669312402
2	1.864664717	1.868725845	1.883652216	1.852584772	1.874993059

Fig. 1.

3.5. *Cauchy problem with oscillating right-hand function*

$$y'(x) = 1 + 2y\cos(x^2) - \sin(2x^2), \; y(\pi/2) = 2.1951, \; x \in [\pi/2, 3\pi/2]. \tag{9}$$

The numeric results are in Figure 2.

	Solution	Runge-Kutta	MidPoint	Scheme1	Scheme2
1.570796327	2.195062279	2.195062279	2.195062279	2.195062279	2.195062279
1.727875959	1.883280862	1.878335651	1.96351798	1.902565589	1.88219859
1.884955592	1.485003174	1.494428307	1.404840765	1.513808394	1.478742231
2.042035225	1.185604816	1.219630136	1.287480893	1.209400544	1.178625338
2.199114858	1.206758071	1.247748001	1.077243981	1.206505663	1.209379917
2.35619449	1.688183412	1.700697135	1.751476611	1.636137303	1.693136587
2.513274123	2.546629444	2.508013705	2.435428902	2.418127106	2.521294279
2.670353756	3.420050602	3.333476938	3.498618794	3.227290032	3.332582936
2.827433388	3.817593778	3.692376863	3.870171821	3.636462317	3.692201075
2.984513021	3.479187288	3.348299254	3.553460425	3.399299939	3.387995222
3.141592654	2.711291437	2.668238325	2.577387752	2.721950009	2.655896986
3.298672286	2.305201465	2.333276993	2.348027843	2.308186449	2.271520792
3.455751919	2.871344753	2.807462402	2.694190619	2.745914042	2.820701375
3.612831552	4.080084569	3.863786259	4.106894498	3.781441222	3.925068901
3.769911184	4.76709525	4.445837268	4.885516504	4.441726372	4.531281514
3.926990817	4.209785416	3.923630919	4.236331535	4.082267868	4.059442254
4.08407045	3.258242869	3.194712237	3.051758327	3.26824394	3.180950002
4.241150082	3.481872755	3.343080797	3.45071027	3.347751725	3.396576659
4.398229715	4.873145826	4.453645629	4.749790175	4.451438952	4.621417087
4.555309348	5.50119247	4.917844047	5.862702368	5.075598557	5.176724305
4.71238898	4.498590869	4.12305259	4.142271346	4.404208677	4.34042245

Fig. 2.

3.6. Cauchy problem with oscillating right-hand function on a long interval

$$y'(x) = 2x - 8x\cos(x^2),\ y(0) = 0,\ x \in [0,5]. \tag{10}$$

The numeric results are in Figure 3.

	Solution	Runge-Kutta	MidPoint	Scheme1	Scheme2
0	0	0	0	0	0
0.1	-0.029999333	-0.029998	1.54564E-18	-0.024998333	-0.031248244
0.2	-0.119957337	-0.119932009	-0.119976003	-0.109942674	-0.122438746
0.3	-0.269514197	-0.269382345	-0.239632117	-0.25446329	-0.273169291
0.4	-0.477272826	-0.476853038	-0.477666369	-0.457193644	-0.481966106
0.5	-0.739615837	-0.738591888	-0.71060079	-0.714628141	-0.745093063
0.6	-1.049096933	-1.04698961	-1.051149335	-1.019553737	-1.054938864
0.7	-1.392503553	-1.388658048	-1.366281239	-1.359149181	-1.398081869
0.8	-1.748781765	-1.742381891	-1.75510336	-1.712936784	-1.753227285
0.9	-2.087148697	-2.077271969	-2.066947809	-2.050902064	-2.089346052
1	-2.365883939	-2.351612328	-2.38009146	-2.332258841	-2.364510358
1.1	-2.532464006	-2.513061787	-2.521838508	-2.50550703	-2.526091091
1.2	-2.525833393	-2.500993703	-2.550705295	-2.510559807	-2.51310753
1.3	-2.281614604	-2.251757867	-2.281592126	-2.26373107	-2.261521308
1.4	-1.740846083	-1.707425663	-1.774494952	-1.766174495	-1.713043875
1.5	-0.862292788	-0.828028501	-0.866901036	-0.915845864	-0.827472642
1.6	0.362578254	0.39365249	0.331067604	0.277856354	0.40238847
1.7	1.894212853	1.917020979	1.900932641	1.778922367	1.93551494
1.8	3.632994375	3.642129221	3.623455417	3.492709792	3.670993066
1.9	5.415863009	5.406785012	5.454740535	5.262095142	5.445065695
2	7.027209981	6.997839129	7.056734687	6.877353313	7.042500644
2.1	8.228511087	8.180907404	8.306734633	8.104215175	8.226606645
2.2	8.807475029	8.749067625	8.866986719	8.731066484	8.788476321
2.3	8.641077921	8.58473231	8.72886709	8.63012267	8.609622279
2.4	7.758567532	7.720807374	7.797776293	7.819404504	7.723963937
2.5	6.382716866	6.379775174	6.41661195	6.50468341	6.357513973
2.6	4.924194054	4.966325974	4.881986239	5.076992604	4.920996788
2.7	3.909466353	3.995006318	3.852461653	4.046226297	3.936493262
2.8	3.840390966	3.952027525	3.72597927	3.907970678	3.897104129
2.9	5.012546486	5.118625508	4.933070948	4.968250191	5.087339589
3	7.351526059	7.414240724	7.286065137	7.182014672	7.423438596
3.1	10.34665912	10.33638731	10.38530043	10.08158893	10.39198216
3.2	13.15151148	13.06288228	13.2426091	12.86326483	13.15395074
3.3	14.86772884	14.7296863	15.04106679	14.65150308	14.8281856
3.4	14.93958378	14.81127989	15.07409292	14.87586418	14.88002252
3.5	13.49447742	13.44325496	13.57967897	13.60667483	13.4514072
3.6	11.42582898	11.49286248	11.3576333	11.65450803	11.43342491
3.7	10.08329692	10.25301829	9.936535461	10.29801344	10.15289089
3.8	10.62201828	10.81635021	10.41757899	10.6774664	10.72994026
3.9	13.29945142	13.41020226	13.21130587	13.11677739	13.39429888
4	17.15161327	17.10300667	17.20126258	16.78096414	17.18244231
4.1	20.37851746	20.18618109	20.61170413	19.99436121	20.33038458
4.2	21.38183656	21.16332979	21.61539549	21.19229154	21.29423117
4.3	19.89743435	19.80954778	20.0240274	20.00621636	19.84573229
4.4	17.40574094	17.5338877	17.2715389	17.7164958	17.44929143
4.5	16.30789955	16.58308595	16.04355698	16.5589448	16.4383749
4.6	18.20517588	18.42814388	17.963514	18.14477537	18.34037335
4.7	22.48476206	22.4691771	22.52888423	22.07904008	22.52670695
4.8	26.50740462	26.24724795	26.78834072	26.00770651	26.42874127
4.9	27.61516546	27.32539831	27.96267776	27.38524803	27.49814253
5	25.529407	25.48389436	25.58355186	25.73096196	25.50544694

Fig. 3.

Conclusion

In this contribution, we continued study of fuzzy methods that can be applied to numeric solutions of ODE and specially, of the Cauchy problem. We proposed two new schemes that are based on the technique of the second degree F-transform. We showed that approximate solutions that are based on the two new Schemes have better quality than that of Runge-Kutta method in the case where right-hand functions are oscillating.

Acknowledgment

The authors acknowledge that they prepared this paper in connection with the project IT4Innovations Centre of Excellence, reg. no. CZ.1.05/1.1.00/02.0070.

References

1. O. Kaleva, *Fuzzy Sets and Systems* **35**, 309 (1990).
2. P. Diamond and V. Opoitsev, *Int. J. Systems Science* **32**, 1063 (2001).
3. V. Lakshmikantham and J. J. Nieto, *Dynamics Contin. Discrete Impuls. Systems Ser. A Math. Anal.* **10**, 991 (2003).
4. J. J. Nieto, *Fuzzy Sets and Systems* **102**, 259 (2003).
5. B. Bede and L. Stefanini, Solution of fuzzy differential equations with generalized differentiability using LU-parametric representation, in *Proc. Conf. EUSFLAT-LFA11*, (Aix-les-Bains, France, 2011).
6. I. Perfilieva, *Fuzzy Sets and Systems* **157**, 993 (2006).
7. I. Perfilieva, M. Dan?kova and B. Bede, *Fuzzy Sets and Systems* **180**, p. 319 (2011).
8. I. Perfilieva, Fuzzy transform: Application to reef growth problem, in *Fuzzy Logic in Geology*, eds. R. B. Demicco and G. J. Klir (Academic Press, Amsterdam, 2003) pp. 275300.

INTERVAL MIGRATIVE FUNCTIONS

F. T. SANTANA

School of Sciences and Technology, UFRN,
Natal, RN, CEP-59072970, Brazil
E-mail: ab_fabianatsantana@gmail.com

F. L. SANTANA

Mathematics Department, UFRN,
Natal, RN, CEP-59072970, Brazil
E-mail: an_fagner@ccet.ufrn.br
www.ccet.ufrn.br

R. H. N. SANTIAGO & B. BEDREGAL

Department of Informatics and Applied Mathematics, UFRN,
Natal, RN, CEP-59072970, Brazil
E-mail: an_regivan@dimap.ufrn.br

This paper introduces the notion of interval migrative functions. Also, we show a necessary and sufficient condition to a interval function to be migrative and that the interval canonical representation of a migrative function f (in the usual sense) is an interval migrative function and preserves some properties of f.

Keywords: Fuzzy Logic; Interval Mathematics; Migrativity; Aggregation; t-Norm.

Introduction

The migrative functions were introduced in[1] as a binary function on $[0, 1]$ satisfying some conditions. This functions has importance in applications such as decision making (see[2,3]) where two partial information need to be considered and the changes in any of these information reflects in the same way on the decision. The possible uncertainty in the information must be treated somehow. The interval fuzzy logic (or Intuitionistic fuzzy logic, see[4–6]), introduced independently in[7–10] , deal with uncertainty in fuzzy systems by using intervals as membership degrees of fuzzy sets. Interval connectives have been studied(see[11]). To treat uncertainty using intervals, the Moore arithmetic (see[12]) is frequently used. In this work, we introduce the concept of interval migrativity and show some results and a way to obtain an interval migrative function from a migrative function in the usual sense.

1. Interval Migrative Function

In this section, we introduce the notion of interval migrative function, and interval migrative function with respect to an interval t-norm and present some results about that. The set of all intervals will be denoted by $\mathbb{IR}$ and the set of all intervals whose the endpoints lies in the unit interval $[0,1]$ by $\mathbb{I}[0,1]$. If $X \in \mathbb{IR}$, we use the notation $X = [x_i, x_s]$. We use the interval operations introduced by Moore[12], the inclusion order $\subseteq$ and the Kulisch-Miranker order (or product order, see[13]) $\leq_{KM}$ defined by $[x_i, x_s] \leq_{KM} [y_i, y_s] \Leftrightarrow x_i \leq y_i$ and $x_s \leq y_s$.

Definition 1.1. A binary monotonic (in both arguments) function $A : [0,1]^2 \to [0,1]$ is an aggregation function if $A(0,0) = 0$ e $A(1,1) = 1$.

Definition 1.2. A function $G : [0,1]^2 \to [0,1]$ is called migrative if and only if $G(\alpha x, y) = G(x, \alpha y)$ for all $x, y \in [0,1]$ and every $\alpha \geq 0$ such that $\alpha x, \alpha y \in [0,1]$.

Below, we introduce the concept of interval migrative functions.

Definition 1.3. An interval function $G : \mathbb{I}[0,1]^2 \to \mathbb{I}[0,1]$ is migrative if satisfies $G(AX, Y) = G(X, AY)$ for all $X, Y \in \mathbb{I}[0,1]$ and $A \in \mathbb{I}[0,1]$ with $0 \leq a_i \leq a_s \leq 1$. [a]

Example 1.1. Let $T_p : [0,1]^2 \to [0,1]$ be the product T-norm, ie, $T_p(x,y) = xy$. The interval function $IT(X,Y) = [T_p(x_i, y_i), T_p(x_s, y_s)]$ is migrative. Take $X, Y, A \in \mathbb{I}[0,1]$. By the interval arithmetic properties, we have $IT(AX, Y) = IT([a_i, a_s][x_i, x_s], [y_i, y_s]) = IT([a_i x_i, a_s x_s], [y_i, y_s]) = [T_p(a_i x_i, y_i), T_p(a_s x_s, y_s)] = [(a_i x_i)y_i, (a_s x_s)y_s] = [x_i(a_i y_i), x_s(a_s y_s)] = [T_p(x_i, a_i y_i), T_p(x_s, a_s y_s)] = IT([x_i, x_s], [a_i y_i, a_s y_s]) = IT([x_i, x_s], [a_i, a_s][y_i, y_s]) = IT(X, AY)$.

Proposition 1.1. *If $G : \mathbb{I}[0,1]^2 \to \mathbb{I}[0,1]$ is an interval migrative function, then G is symmetric.*

---

[a]Here, AX (or AY) is the Moore product (see[12]) of the intervals A and X.

Proof. Let $G : \mathbb{I}[0,1]^2 \to \mathbb{I}[0,1]$ be an interval migrative function. So, for $X, Y \in \mathbb{I}[0,1]^2$ and $A = [a_i, a_s]$, with $0 \leq a_i \leq a_s \leq 1$, we have $G(AX, Y) = G(X, AY)$. Thus, $G(X, Y) = G([1,1]X, Y) = G([1,1], YX) = G(Y[1,1], X) = G(Y, X)$. So, G is symmetric. $\qquad\square$

One of the most important properties of migrative functions $G : [0,1]^2 \to [0,1]$ is the fact that those functions are characterized by the existence of a function $g : [0,1] \to [0,1]$ such that $G(x,y) = g(xy)$ (see[2]). In the next theorem, we proof that this characterization also occurs in the interval case.

Theorem 1.1. *An interval function* $G : \mathbb{I}[0,1]^2 \to \mathbb{I}[0,1]$ *is migrative if, and only if, exists an interval function* $g : \mathbb{I}[0,1] \to \mathbb{I}[0,1]$, *such that* $G(X,Y) = g(XY)$ *for all* $X, Y \in \mathbb{I}[0,1]$.

Proof. ($\Leftarrow$) Given an interval function $G : \mathbb{I}[0,1]^2 \to \mathbb{I}[0,1]$, suppose that exists an interval function $g : \mathbb{I}[0,1] \to \mathbb{I}[0,1]$, such that $G(X,Y) = g(XY)$ for all $X, Y \in \mathbb{I}[0,1]$. Consider $A \in \mathbb{I}[0,1]$. Since the interval multiplication is associative and commutative (see[12]), we have $(AX)Y = X(AY)$. So, $G(AX, Y) = g((AX)Y) = g(X(AY)) = G(X, AY)$, ie, G is migrative.
($\Rightarrow$) Suppose that the interval function $G : \mathbb{I}[0,1]^2 \to \mathbb{I}[0,1]$ is migrative. Define $g : \mathbb{I}[0,1] \to \mathbb{I}[0,1]$ by $g(X) = G([1,1], X)$. Thus, we have $G(X,Y) = G([1,1]X, Y) = G([1,1], XY) = g(XY)$. $\qquad\square$

Definition 1.4. An interval function $G : \mathbb{I}[0,1]^2 \to \mathbb{I}[0,1]$ is an interval aggregation function if it is monotonic(in both arguments) and $G([0,0],[0,0]) = [0,0]$ and $G([1,1],[1,1]) = [1,1]$.

The following lemmas will be used to proof under what conditions an interval migrative function is also an aggregation function.

Lemma 1.2. *Let* $G : \mathbb{I}[0,1]^2 \to \mathbb{I}[0,1]$ *be an interval migrative function. So, G is monotonic(in both arguments) if, and only if,* $g : \mathbb{I}[0,1] \to \mathbb{I}[0,1]$, *where* $G(X,Y) = g(XY)$, *is monotonic.*

Proof. ($\Rightarrow$) Take $X, Y \in \mathbb{I}[0,1]$. Suppose that $X \leq_{KM} Y$. Since G is migrative and monotonic, we have $G([1,1], X) \leq_{KM} G([1,1], Y)$ and $G(X,Y) = g(XY)$. So, $g([1,1]X) \leq_{KM} g([1,1]Y)$, ie, $g(X) \leq_{KM} g(Y)$.
($\Leftarrow$) Take $X_1, X_2, Y_1, Y_2 \in \mathbb{I}[0,1]$ with $X_1 \leq_{KM} Y_1$ e $X_2 \leq_{KM} Y_2$. From the properties of interval multiplication and $\leq_{KM}$, we have $X_1 X_2 \leq_{KM}$

$Y_1 Y_2$. Since g is monotonic, $g(X_1 X_2) \leq_{KM} g(Y_1 Y_2)$, so $G(X_1, X_2) \leq_{KM} G(Y_1, Y_2)$, for all $X, Y \in \mathbb{I}[0,1]$. □

Lemma 1.3. *Let* $G : \mathbb{I}[0,1]^2 \to \mathbb{I}[0,1]$ *be an interval migrative function. So,* $G([1,1],[1,1]) = [1,1]$ *if, and only if,* $g([1,1]) = [1,1]$*, where* $G(X,Y) = g(XY)$*.*

Proof. It is straightforward. □

Lemma 1.4. *Let* $G : \mathbb{I}[0,1]^2 \to \mathbb{I}[0,1]$ *be an interval migrative function. So,* $G([0,0],[0,0]) = [0,0]$ *if, and only if,* $g([0,0]) = [0,0]$*, where* $G(X,Y) = g(X,Y)$*.*

Proof. It is straightforward. □

Theorem 1.5. *An interval migrative function* $G : \mathbb{I}[0,1]^2 \to \mathbb{I}[0,1]$ *is an interval aggregation function if, and only if, exists a monotonic function* $g : \mathbb{I}[0,1] \to \mathbb{I}[0,1]$ *such that* $G(X,Y) = g(XY)$*,* $g([0,0]) = [0,0]$ *and* $g([1,1]) = [1,1]$*.*

Proof. ($\Rightarrow$) Suppose that the function $G : \mathbb{I}[0,1]^2 \to \mathbb{I}[0,1]$ is an interval aggregation function. So, $G([0,0],[0,0]) = [0,0]$, $G([1,1],[1,1]) = [1,1]$ and G is monotonic in both arguments. Since G is migrative, by the lemma 1.2, exists $g : \mathbb{I}[0,1] \to \mathbb{I}[0,1]$ monotonic such that $G(X,Y) = g(XY)$. Thus, by the lemmas 1.3 and 1.4, we have $g([1,1]) = g([1,1].[1,1]) = G([1,1],[1,1]) = [1,1]$ and $g([0,0]) = g([0,0].[0,0]) = G([0,0],[0,0]) = [0,0]$.
($\Leftarrow$) It is straightforward. □

2. Canonical Interval Representation and Migrativity

In this section, we show how to obtain an interval migrative function from a real migrative function using the canonical interval representation. The canonical interval representation of a non-asymptotic function $f : \mathbb{R} \to \mathbb{R}$ (see[14]), denoted by $\widehat{f}$, is defined by $\widehat{f}([a,b]) = [\min\{f([a,b])\}, \max\{f([a,b])\}]$. In[14], the authors proved that this function is the best interval representation of a real function.

An important fact about interval arithmetic, which will be used, is that for $A, B \in \mathbb{R}$ and $O = \{+, \times, -, \div\}$(the set of interval operations), if $*'$ is the real operation relative to the interval operation $* \in O$, we have $A * B = \{a *' b | a \in A \text{ and } b \in B\}$. The proof of this fact can be found in[12].

The following theorem shows that the interval canonical representation of a real migrative function is an interval migrative function.

Theorem 2.1. *If $G : [0,1]^2 \to [0,1]$ is migrative, then $\widehat{G} : \mathbb{I}[0,1]^2 \to [0,1]$ is an interval migrative function.*

Proof. Let $G : [0,1]^2 \to [0,1]$ be a migrative function. For $X, Y, A \in \mathbb{I}[0,1]$, we have:

$$\begin{aligned}
\widehat{G}(AX, Y) &= \widehat{G}([a_i x_i, a_s x_s], [y_i, y_s]) \\
&= [min\{G([a_i x_i, a_s x_s], [y_i, y_s])\}, max\{G([a_i x_i, a_s x_s], [y_i, y_s])\}]
\end{aligned}$$

and

$$\begin{aligned}
\widehat{G}(X, AY) &= \widehat{G}([x_i, x_s], [a_i y_i, a_s y_s]) \\
&= [min\{G([x_i, x_s], [a_i y_i, a_s y_s])\}, max\{G([x_i, x_s], [a_i y_i, a_s y_s])\}]
\end{aligned}$$

We must proof that

$$c = min\{G([a_i x_i, a_s x_s], [y_i, y_s])\} = min\{G([x_i, x_s], [a_i y_i, a_s y_s])\} = d$$

and

$$e = max\{G([a_i x_i, a_s x_s], [y_i, y_s])\} = max\{G([x_i, x_s], [a_i y_i, a_s y_s])\} = f.$$

As seen above, there are $a, a' \in A$, $x, x' \in X$ and $y, y' \in Y$ such that $c = G(ax, y) = G(x, ay)$ and $d = G(x', a'y') = G(a'x', y')$. Suppose that $c < d$. So, $c = G(x, ay) = G(ax, y) < G(x', a'y') = d$, which contradicts $c = min\{G([a_i x_i, a_s x_s], [y_i, y_s])\}$. So, $c \geq d$. Analogously, we can proof that $c \leq d$, and so, $c = d$. Similarly, we proof that $e = f$.

Thus, $\widehat{G}(AX, Y) = \widehat{G}(X, AY)$, which implies that $\widehat{G}$ is an interval migrative function. $\square$

In the next theorem we investigate the relations between G and $\widehat{G}$ and g and $\widehat{g}$.

Theorem 2.2. *If $G : [0,1]^2 \to [0,1]$ is migrative and $G(x, y) = g(xy)$ for some $g : [0,1] \to [0,1]$, then $\widehat{G}(X, Y) = \widehat{g}(XY)$.*

Proof. We have

$$\begin{aligned}
\widehat{G}(X, Y) &= [min\{G(X, Y)\}, max\{G(X, Y)\}] \\
&= [min\{g(XY)\}, max\{g(XY)\}] \\
&= \widehat{g}(XY).
\end{aligned}$$
$\square$

3. Final Remarks

In this paper we introduced the concept of interval migrativity and investigate some results of such functions. Also, we showed how to obtain an interval migrative function from a migrative function using the canonical interval representation. In future works, we can investigate more results about interval migrative function and ways to obtain these kind of interval function from real functions. Also, we can introduce a notion of interval migrative function with respect to a interval t-norm, in a similar way to[15] .

References

1. F. Durante, P. Sarkoci, A Note on the Convex Combinations of Triangular Norms, *Fuzzy Sets and Systems* **159**, 7780 (2008).
2. H. Bustince, J. Montero, R. Mesiar, Migrativity of Aggregation Functions, *Fuzzy Sets System.* 160 (2009) 766777.
3. J.Montero, D.Gmez, S.Muoz, Fuzzy Information Representation for Decision Aiding, *in:Proc. of the IPMU Conference*, Mlaga, Spain, 2227, (2008).
4. K. T. Atanassov, Intuitionistic Fuzzy Sets, *Fuzzy Sets and Systems* **20**, $87-96$ (1986).
5. J. Goguen, L-Fuzzy Sets, *Journal of Mathematical Analysis and Applications* **18**, $145-174$ (1967).
6. G. Deschriijver, E.E. Kerre, On the Relationship Between Some Extensions of Fuzzy Set Theory, *Fuzzy Sets and Systems* **133**, $227-235$ (2003).
7. L. A. Zadeh, The Concept of Linguistic Variable and Its Application to Aprproximate Reasoning-I, *Information sciences* **8**, $199-249$.
8. I. Grattan-Guiness, Fuzzy Membership Mappe Onto Interval and Many-Valued Fuzzy Sets, *Zeitschrift fur Mathematische Logik und Grundladen der Mathematik* **22** , $149-160$ (1975).
9. K. Jahn, Interval-Wertige Mengen, *Mathematische Nachrichten,* **68**, $115-132$ (1975).
10. R. Sambuc, Fonction ϕ-Floues: Application l'Aide au Diagnostic en pathologie Thyroidienne, PhD Thesis, University of Marseille, (Marseille, France 1975).
11. B. C Bedregal, A. Takahashi, The Best Interval Representations of T-Norms and Automorphisms, *Fuzzy Sets and Systems* **157**, $3220-3230$, (2006).
12. R. E. Moore, *Automatic Error Analysis in Digital Computation.* Technical Report LMSD84821, Lockheed Missiles and Space Division Co. (1959).
13. U. Kulisch, W. Miranker, *Computer Arithmetic in Theory and Practice*, (New York Academic Press, New York, 1981).
14. R. H. N. Santiago, B. C. Bedregal, B. M. Acioly. Formal Aspects of Correctness and Optimality of Interval Computations, *Formal Aspects of Computing* **18**, $231-243$ (2006).
15. J. Fodor, I. J. Rudas, An Extension of the Migrative Property for Triangular Norms, *Fuzzy Sets and Systems* **168**, $370-80$, (2011).

SEARCHING FOR A CONSENSUS SIMILARITY FUNCTION FOR GENERALIZED TRAPEZOIDAL FUZZY NUMBERS

E. VICENTE, A. MATEOS* and A. JIMÉNEZ-MARTÍN

Decision Analysis and Statistics Group, Universidad Politécnica de Madrid, Campus de Montegancedo s/n, Boadilla del Monte, 28660-Madrid, Spain
* E-mail: amateos@fi.upm.es

There is controversy regarding the use of the similarity functions proposed in the literature to compare generalized trapezoidal fuzzy numbers since conflicting similarity values are sometimes output for the same pair of fuzzy numbers. In this paper we propose a similarity function aimed at establishing a consensus. It accounts for the different approaches of all the similarity functions. It also has better properties and can easily incorporate new parameters for future improvements. The analysis is carried out on the basis of a large and representative set of pairs of trapezoidal fuzzy numbers.

Keywords: Similarity function; Generalized trapezoidal fuzzy number; Consensus.

1. Introduction

A great variety of similarity functions have been proposed in the literature to compare fuzzy numbers. The usual parameters are distance, shape and size, which are then aggregated in different ways leading to different functions.

However, there is controversy regarding the use of similarity functions since different similarity functions sometimes output conflicting similarity values for the same pair of trapezoidal fuzzy numbers. Moreover, their performance is often analyzed based on biased sets of fuzzy numbers, clearly highlighting the benefits but disguising the associated drawbacks.

In this paper we propose a similarity function for generalized trapezoidal fuzzy numbers aimed at establishing a consensus between the similarity functions reported in the literature, whose performance is analyzed on the basis of a large and representative set of pairs of trapezoidal fuzzy numbers.

In Section 2 we review the most representative similarity functions in the literature and the set of pairs of fuzzy numbers commonly used for analyzing their performance. In Section 3 we develop a method for deriving a representative set of pairs of fuzzy numbers. We also propose a stable consensus similarity function. Finally, we conclude with the advantages of the proposed consensus function in Section 4.

2. Similarity Functions for Generalized Trapezoidal Fuzzy Numbers

The similarity measures of fuzzy numbers are usually based on a comparison of various associated parameters, such as distance, shape or size. One of the first measures of similarity was proposed by Chen[1] in 1996. It used the geometric distance between the considered fuzzy numbers. However, this function is not applicable for generalized fuzzy numbers.

Chen[2] himself extended his similarity measure in 2003 to generalized trapezoidal fuzzy numbers, incorporating the distance between the centers of gravity of the compared numbers to the similarity function. Another measure proposed by Chen[3] in 2009 accounted for the perimeter and height of the considered generalized trapezoidal fuzzy numbers.

Gomathi and Sivaraman[4] proposed using the geometric mean rather than the average distance between vertices. Wen et al.[5] added the area of the considered fuzzy numbers to the similarity function.

In 2009 Sridevi and Nadarajan[6] replaced Chen's[3] geometrical distance by the fuzzy distance $1 - \sum_{i=1}^{4} \frac{\mu_d(x_i)}{4}$, with $\mu_d(x_i) = 1 - (x_i/d)$ if $0 \le x_i \le d$ (0 otherwise), $d \in (0,1]$ and $x_i = | a_i - b_i |$. If $d = 1$ we have Chen's similarity function. In the same year, Wei and Chen[7] proposed a measure adding the perimeter and height of generalized trapezoidal fuzzy numbers to the geometric distance.

Xu et al.[8] proposed the geometrical distance and the distance between the centers of gravity of the compared numbers in 2010. However, this function had a serious drawback since $S(\tilde{a}, \tilde{b}) \ne 1 - |a - b| ; \forall a, b \in \mathbb{R}$.

The most recent proposals are by Zhu and Xu[9] in 2012 and Vicente et al.[10] in 2013. However, Zhu and Xu's function is not well defined since the similarity between $\tilde{a} = (0.01, 0.01, 0.01, 0.01; 0.5)$ and $\tilde{b} = (1, 1, 1, 1; 1)$ is $S(\tilde{a}, \tilde{b}) = \sqrt{-0.0021}$, whereas the function by Vicente et al. is too demanding because it imposes a penalty of $(1 - \alpha - \beta)$ when the compared numbers do not share area.

Arbitrary sets of fuzzy numbers are usually used to compare the proposed similarity functions, in such a way that the benefits of the proposed function are clearly shown but the associated drawbacks remain hidden. Chen originally proposed a set with only 15 pairs of fuzzy numbers, which was enlarged afterwards by other authors, such as Sridevi and Nadarajan[6] (26 pairs), Xu et al.[8] (30 pairs) or Vicente-Cestero et al.[11] (35 pairs), but other authors, such as Gomathi and Sivaraman[4], continue to use small sets of pairs (5 pairs). Besides, some sets are clearly deficient. For example, Xu et al. and Gomathi and Sivaraman use fuzzy numbers with zero height, which does not make sense.

Figure 1 shows the performances of the above similarity functions on the basis of the set of pairs proposed by Chen and Chen[2] (15 pairs). The similarity output by the different functions varies enormously for some pairs, especially, 3, 4, 8, 10, 11 and 15.

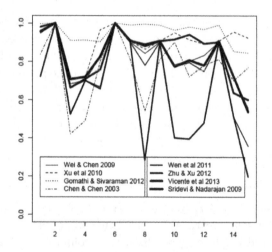

Fig. 1. Similarity values on the set of Chen and Chen

Different criteria could be used to search for a consensus among the considered similarity functions. We have considered the Pearson correlation coefficient, i.e., the consensus function should maximize the Pearson correlation coefficient regarding the other similarity functions. The functions by Gomathi and Sivaraman and by Zhu and Xu will not be considered henceforth since they generate atypical data associated with incorrectly processed pairs. An analytical expression of a similarity function that satisfies these criteria is derived in Section 3.

3. Deriving a Consensus Similarity Function

The most used parameters in similarity functions are the arithmetic and geometric distances, distances between the centers of gravity, differences between the heights, perimeters and areas. We consider the following families of similarity functions:

$$S_1(\widetilde{a}, \widetilde{b}) = 1 - (w_1 d_1 + w_2 d_2 + w_3 d_3),$$

$$S_2(\widetilde{a}, \widetilde{b}) = 1 - (w_1 d_1 + w_2 d_2 + w_3 d_3) \left(\frac{d_4}{d_5}\right)^{v_1} \left(\frac{d_6}{d_7}\right)^{v_2} \left(\frac{d_8}{d_9}\right)^{v_3} \left(\frac{d_{10}}{d_{11}}\right)^{v_4} \left(\frac{d_{12}}{d_{13}}\right)^{v_5},$$

$$S_3(\widetilde{a}, \widetilde{b}) = 1 - (w_1 d_1 + w_2 d_2 + w_3 d_3) \prod_{i=1}^{n} \left(\frac{v_{1i} d_4 + v_{2i} d_6 + v_{3i} d_8 + v_{4i} d_{10} + v_{5i} d_{12}}{v_{1i} d_5 + v_{2i} d_7 + v_{3i} d_9 + v_{4i} d_{11} + v_{5i} d_{13}}\right),$$

$$S_4(\widetilde{a}, \widetilde{b}) = [1 - (w_1 d_1 + w_2 d_2 + w_3 d_3)] \prod_{i=1}^{n} \left(\frac{v_{1i} d_4 + v_{2i} d_6 + v_{3i} d_8 + v_{4i} d_{10} + v_{5i} d_{12}}{v_{1i} d_5 + v_{2i} d_7 + v_{3i} d_9 + v_{4i} d_{11} + v_{5i} d_{13}}\right),$$

with $\widetilde{a} = (a_1, a_2, a_3, a_4; w_1)$ and $\widetilde{b} = (b_1, b_2, b_3, b_4; w_2)$, $d_1 = (\sum |a_i - b_i|)/4$, the Euclidean distance; $d_2 = d\left((X_{\widetilde{a}}, Y_{\widetilde{a}}), (X_{\widetilde{b}}, Y_{\widetilde{b}})\right)$, the distance between their centers of gravity; $d_3 = (\prod_{i=1}^{4} | a_i - b_i |)^{1/4}$, the geometric mean; $d_4 = min\{P_{\widetilde{a}}, P_{\widetilde{b}}\}$ ($d_5 = max\{P_{\widetilde{a}}, P_{\widetilde{b}}\}$), the minimum (maximum) of their perimeters; $d_6 = min\{A(\widetilde{a}), A(\widetilde{b})\}$ ($d_7 = max\{A(\widetilde{a}), A(\widetilde{b})\}$), the minimum (maximum) of their areas; $d_8 = min\{w_{\widetilde{a}}, w_{\widetilde{b}}\}$, $d_9 = max\{w_{\widetilde{a}}, w_{\widetilde{b}}\}$, $d_{10} = min\{Q_{\widetilde{a}}, Q_{\widetilde{b}}\}$, $d_{11} = max\{Q_{\widetilde{a}}, Q_{\widetilde{b}}\}$, with $Q_{\widetilde{a}} = \sqrt{(a_2 - a_1)^2 + (a_3 - a_2)^2 + (a_4 - a_3)^2 + w_{\widetilde{a}}^2}$; and $d_{12} = \int_0^1 \mu_{\widetilde{a} \cap \widetilde{b}}(x) dx$ ($d_{13} = \int_0^1 \mu_{\widetilde{a} \cup \widetilde{b}}(x) dx$), the intersection area (union), $w_1, w_2, w_3, v_j, v_{ji} \in [0, 1]$, with $w_1 + w_2 + w_3 = 1$, $\sum v_j = 1$ and $\sum v_{ji} = 1$.

Note that the second family generalizes to the first family when we consider $v_i = 0 \ \forall i$. The third family generalizes to the second family when we consider $n = 5$ and $(v_i = 1, v_{ji} = 0 \ \forall i \neq j) \ \forall i = 1, ..., 5$.

We have found using Monte Carlo simulation that the functions that best fit the consensus are from the fourth family ($S_4(\widetilde{a}, \widetilde{b})$) with $n = 1$. Therefore, we focus on this family with $n = 1$ to identify the consensus function.

Then, the problem is to compute the values $w_i, v_j \in [0, 1]$ that maximizes the minimum Pearson correlation coefficient R_i between the function S_4 and each considered similarity function on the basis of 48 pairs of fuzzy numbers taken from Xu et al., Gomathi and Sivaraman, Sridevi and Nadarajan and Wei and Chen:

$$max \ z = \min_i \{R_i\}$$
$$s.t. \quad w_1 + w_2 + w_3 = 1, \qquad 0 \leq w_i \leq 1, \forall i$$
$$v_1 + v_2 + v_3 + v_4 + v_5 = 1, \ 0 \leq v_j \leq 1, \forall j$$

However, the above optimization problem is complex and it is necessary to use metaheuristics to solve it. The optimum solution using *simulated annealing*[12] is w_1^*=0.234, w_2^*=0.744, w_3^*=0.022, v_1^*=0.109, v_2^*=0.123, v_3^*=0.15, v_4^*=0.604 and v_5^*=0.013. Note that the most relevant parameters in the optimal solution are w_2^*, associated with the distance between the centers of gravity; and v_4^*, associated with elements $Q_{\tilde{a}}$ and $Q_{\tilde{b}}$ proposed by Gomathi and Sivaraman to reduce computational time for the perimeter assessment.

The correlation coefficients of the consensus function regarding the similarity functions by Wei and Chen, Chen, Xu et al, Wen et al, Vicente et al and Sridevi and Nadarajan are 0.96, 0.92, 0.90, 0.91, 0.96 and 0.95, respectively. Figure 2 shows how the fit of the consensus function compared with the considered similarity functions.

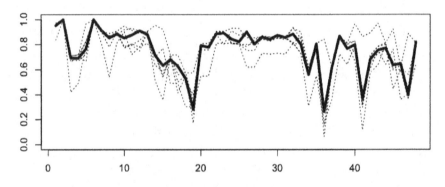

Fig. 2. Comparing the values output by the consensus function

4. Conclusion

We have proposed a consensus function on the basis of different similarity functions reported in the literature for generalized trapezoidal fuzzy numbers. The proposed function has better properties than some similarity functions reported in the literature, such as those proposed by Xu et al, which does not properly measure the similarity between two real numbers, or by Zhu and Xu, which is not fully defined.

The proposed function aggregates the approaches of different similarity functions whose outputs vary enormously, making a consensus necessary. Besides, it can easily incorporate new perspectives (parameters) for future improvements. The appropriateness of parameters can be evaluated, and parameters with low weights can be discarded, leading to a refined function with fewer parameters.

Acknowledgments

This paper was supported by the Madrid Regional Government project S-05505/TIC/0230 and the Spanish Ministry of Science and innovation project MTM2011-28983-C03-03.

References

1. S. M. Chen, New methods for subjective mental workload assessment and fuzzy risk analysis, *Cybernetics and Systems*, *27*, 449-472 (1996).
2. S. J. Chen, S. M. Chen, Fuzzy risk analysis based on similarity measures of generalized fuzzy numbers, *IEEE Transactions on Fuzzy Systems*, *11*, 45-56, (2003).
3. S. M. Chen, J.-H. Chen, Fuzzy risk analysis based on similarity measures between interval-valued fuzzy numbers and interval-valued fuzzy number arithmetic operators, *Expert Systems with Applications*, *36*, 6309-6317, (2009).
4. V. L. Gomathi Nayagam, G. Sivaraman, A novel similarity measure between generalized fuzzy numbers, *International Journal of Computer Theory and Engineering*, *4*, 448-450, (2012).
5. J. Wen, X. Fan, D. Duanmu, D. Yong, A modified similarity measure of generalized fuzzy numbers, *Procedia Engineering*, *15*, 2773-2777, (2011).
6. B. Sridevi, R. Nadarajan, Fuzzy similarity measure for generalized fuzzy numbers, *International Journal of Open Problems in Computer Science and Mathematics*, *2*, 111-116, (2009).
7. S. H. Wei, S. M. Chen, A new approach for fuzzy risk analysis based on similarity measures of generalized fuzzy numbers, *Expert Systems with Applications*, *36*, 589-598, (2009).
8. Z. Xu, S. Shang, W. Qian, W. Shu, A method for fuzzy risk analysis based on the new similarity of trapezoidal fuzzy numbers, *Expert Systems with Applications*, *37*, 1920-1927, (2010).
9. L. Zhu, R. Xu, *Fuzzy risk analysis based on similarity measure of generalizard fuzzy numbers*, Fuzzy Enginering and Operations Research. Berlin/Heidelberg: Springer, 569-587, (2012).
10. E. Vicente, A. Mateos, A. Jiménez, A new similarity function for generalized trapezoidal fuzzy numbers, *Lecture Notes in Artificial Intelligence*, *7894*, 400-411, (2013).
11. E. Vicente-Cestero, A. Mateos, A. Jiménez-Martín, Similarity functions for generalized trapezoidal fuzzy numbers: An improved comparative analysis, *Journal of Intelligence and Fuzzy Systems*, under revision, (2014).
12. S. Kirkpatrick, C. D. Gelatt, C. D. Vecchi, Optimization by simulated annealing, *Science*, *220*, 671-680, (1983).

OUTLINE OF 2^n-VALUED PROPOSITIONAL CALCULUS WITH A BIG DATA SETTING[*]

LONG HONG

College of Computer, Nanjing University of Posts and Telecommunications
Nanjing, 210003, P. R. China
Department of Computer Science and Electrical Engineering, University of Missouri-
Kansas City
Kansas City, 64112, U. S. A. and
State Key Laboratory of Software Development Environment
Beijing, 100090, P. R. China

NINGNING ZHOU

College of Computer, Nanjing University of Posts and Telecommunications
Nanjing, 210003, P.R.China and
State Key Laboratory of Software Development Environment
Beijing, 100090, P.R.China

This paper aims at establishing an outline of 2^n-valued propositional calculus (2^nP) to set logical foundation for big data science. After introducing the characteristics of big data and the significance of researching on big data, we briefly analyze features of famous L_n system. This paper specifies 2^nP from logical semantic and syntax. We firstly define connectives including negation $\neg$ and disjunction $\vee$, and define conjunction $\wedge$ and implications $\rightarrow$ based on them; we prove the $\{\neg, \rightarrow\}$ is adequate set of connective. Then we structure the axiom set including all axioms of classical logic, and prove modus ponens and the consistent of 2^nP, yet give the soundness theorem and the adequate theorem of 2^nP.

Keywords: 2^n-valued logic; big data; propositional calculus.

1. Introduction

Recently, 'big data' has become a hot word in science and technology. Since tremendous value was contained in big data, funding agencies of many countries have created some support programmes for researching on it, which shows that these two small words make a big science [1].

[*] This work was supported by the National Natural Science Foundation of China under Grant No.61170322 and by the Open Fund of the State Key Laboratory of Software Development Environment under Grant No.SKLSDE-2011KF-04..

Big data are big in four ways: the volume of the data that systems must sample, or process, or disseminate; the number and complexity of the data types; the rate at which the data streams in or out; and the potential value. According to statistics of IDC, the amount of creating and reproducing data in 2011 reached 2^{70} bytes, 75% of which came from individual pictures, files of video and voice, and so on [2].

Confronting these data called data mountain [3] and data deluge [4], people look forward to big data science to decrease non-sense ones [5]. However, for making big data become a category of science, it is necessary to study universality problems as the foundation of big data science. Classification, a qualitative analysis, is a key-link in the scientific research chain, and the essence of truth value in logic is qualitative effect. Therefore, establishing the logic fitting well with big data possesses the role of cornerstone for big data science.

The 2^m bytes is a value expression for the amount of big data, and we intuitively feel that there is certain interconnection between it and 2^n-valued logic studied in this paper. For instance, in categorizing big data, we may firstly divide it into 2^1 types that are primitive data and derivative data and then continue with the same analysis according to different cases. We shall explore the relations in other papers.

2^n-valued logic belongs to multi-value logic. In 1920, J Łukasiewicz [6] presented three valued logic, and called it a first system of non-Aristotelian logic; E L Post [7] put forward a m-valued truth-system of his own in1921. As both of that broke through the shackles of two valued logic, Łukasiewicz and Post set a cornerstone for naturally describing 'neither true nor false'. In 1930, Łukasiewicz and A Tarski [8] extended three value system, L_3, to n-valued system L_n whose truth set is $S_{Ln}=\{0, 1/n\text{-}1, 2/n\text{-}1, \ldots, n\text{-}2/n\text{-}1, 1\}$, and its main connectives are negation $\neg$, and implication $\rightarrow$. Let x, x_1, $x_2 \in S_{Ln}$, then the truth function of these connectives are as follows:

$\neg x = 1-x$;

$x_1 \rightarrow x_2 = \min(1, 1-x_1+x_2)$.

Łukasiewicz also formulated an axiom system for L_n, which consists of the following five sentences using Polish notation:

$$\text{'}CpCqp\text{'}, \text{'}CCpqCCqrCpr\text{'}, \text{'}CCCpqqCCqpp\text{'},$$
$$\text{'}CCCpqCqpCqp\text{'}, \text{'}CCNpNqCqp\text{'}.$$

The system L_n has rich connotation. For a long time past, many scholars have dedicated tremendous amount of effort to study L_n and achieved great results. However, the systems L_n are incomplete and are merely sub-systems of classic logic system.

This paper aims at establishing an outlook of 2^n–valued propositional calculus that incarnates self-features and continues to have axiom model in classic logic. It is necessary to explain drawing inspiration to us, which are from two aspects:

(1) Describing the connectives of Principia Mathematic System, Post firstly leaded negation and disjunction into his study and then used them to define other connectives [7], which is natural structuring procedure from simple to manifold, and has a methodological significance.

(2) When expounded logical consequence and relevant, Belnap [9] believed that for A to be relevant to B in the required sense, a necessary condition is that A and B have some propositional variable in common, and gave a truth table meeting this condition, in which the operation of disjunction connective was difference from selecting maximum in general OR operation.

2. Structure of 2^n-Value Propositional Calculus

2.1. Semantics of 2^n Valued Logic

Denote $x_{n-1}x_{n-1}...x_0$ as truth of 2^n valued logic and S_2^n as the set of truth, where $n \in N$, $x_i \in \{0, 1\}$, $0 \le i \le n-1$.

Definition 1. Let $x, y \in S_2^n$.

(1) The symbol $\neg$ is called negation connective if

$$\neg x_i = \begin{cases} 1 & x_i = 0 \\ 0 & x_i = 1 \end{cases};$$

(2) The symbol $\vee$ is called disjunction connective if

$$x_i \vee y_i = \begin{cases} 0 & x_i = y_i = 0 \\ 1 & others \end{cases}.$$

Definition 2. Let $x, y \in S_2^n$.

(1) The symbol $\wedge$ is called conjunction if $x \wedge y = \neg(\neg x \vee \neg y)$;

(2) The symbol $\rightarrow$ is called implication if $x \rightarrow y = \neg x \vee y$.

According to Def.1 and Def.2, the 2^n ($n=2$) valued truth table is show in Table 1

Table 1. The truth table of 2^2 value logic. The operations of $\neg,\vee$ and are all bit calculation.

q	¬p	p∨q				p→q				p∧q			
p		11	10	01	00	11	10	01	00	11	10	01	00
11	00	11	11	11	11	11	10	01	00	11	10	01	00
10	01	11	10	11	10	11	11	01	01	10	10	00	00
01	10	11	11	01	01	11	10	11	10	01	00	01	00
00	11	11	10	01	00	11	11	11	11	00	00	00	00

Lemma 1. $\neg\neg x = x$.

Proof. Let $x_i = 1$. By Def.1(a), $\neg x_i = 0$ and $\neg\neg x_i = 1 = x_i$; let $x_i = 0$, then $\neg x_i = 1$ and $\neg\neg x_i = 0 = x_i$. Hence,

$$\neg\neg x_i = x_i. \tag{1}$$

Now, let $x = x_{n-1}\, x_{n-1} \ldots x_0$. By Def.1($a$) and (1),

$$\neg x = \neg x_{n-1}\neg x_{n-1} \ldots \neg x_0 \tag{2}$$

By (2), Def.1(a) and (1), $\neg\neg x = \neg\neg x_{n-1}\neg\neg x_{n-1} \ldots \neg\neg x_0 = x_{n-1}\, x_{n-1} \ldots x_0 = x$.

Lemma 2. $x \vee y = \neg x \rightarrow y$.

Proof. By Def. 2(b) and Lem. 1,

$\neg x \rightarrow y = \neg\neg x \vee y$

$\qquad = x \vee y$.

Lemma 3. $x \wedge y = \neg(x \rightarrow \neg y)$.

Proof. By Def. 2,

$\neg(x \rightarrow \neg y) = \neg(\neg x \vee \neg y)$

$\qquad = x \wedge y$.

Theorem 4. The truth set $\{\neg, \rightarrow\}$ is an adequate set of connective.

By Lem. 2 and Lem. 3, Th. 4 follows.

2.2. Syntax of 2^n-Valued Propositional ($2^n P$)

By Th.4, we can use negation connective $\neg$ and implication connective $\rightarrow$ to describe syntax succinctly.

2.2.1. Formal Language

(1) Alphabet of symbols

a. Propositional symbols: p, q, r, p_i, q_i, r_i, where $i \in N$;

b. Connectives: $\neg, \rightarrow$;

c. Others:), (,

(2) Set of well-formed formula (*wff*)

a. proposition symbols are *wff*s;

b. If A is *wff*, then $\neg A$ is *wff*;

c. If A and A are *wff*, then $A \rightarrow B$ is *wff*.

d. The set of all *wff*s is generated by a, b, and c.

2.2.2. Axioms and Rule of Deduction

(1) Axioms

Ax1: $A \rightarrow (B \rightarrow A)$

Ax2: $(\neg A \rightarrow B) \rightarrow ((\neg A \rightarrow \neg B) \rightarrow A)$

Ax3: $(A \rightarrow (B \rightarrow C)) \rightarrow ((A \rightarrow B) \rightarrow (A \rightarrow C))$

Ax4: $((A \rightarrow \neg A) \rightarrow A) \rightarrow A$

(2) Rule of deduction

MP: $A, A \rightarrow B \vdash B$

Here, the listed four axioms are schemes to specify all of infinite axioms. In modus ponens, B is the direct consequence from A and $A \rightarrow B$, namely B is yielded by A and $A \rightarrow B$.

2.3. System Characteristics

Definition 3. Denote Γ as a formulas set of $2^n P$. The mapping

$$V: \Gamma \rightarrow S_{2n}$$

is called a valuation of $2^n P$. When $A \in \Gamma$, there exists a

$$V(A) \in S_{2n} = \{2^n-1, 2^n-2, \ldots, 1, 0\} = \{\underbrace{11\ldots1}_{n \text{ bits}}, \underbrace{1\ldots10}_{n \text{ bits}}, \ldots, \underbrace{0\ldots01}_{n \text{ bits}}, \underbrace{0\ldots00}_{n \text{ bits}}\}.$$

Definition 4. Let $A \in \Gamma$. If for every valuation V, $V(A)=2^n-1$, then A is a tautology and write $\vDash A$; if A is last member of some deduction from Γ, then A is yielded by Γ, denoted as $\Gamma \vdash A$.

Lemma 5. $V(A \rightarrow B) = 2^n-1$ if $V(A) = V(B)$.

Proof. Let $V(A) = V(B) = x_{n-1} x_{n-1} \ldots x_0$, then

$$V(A \rightarrow B) = V(\neg A \vee B)$$
$$= V(\neg A) \vee V(B)$$
$$= (\neg x_{n-1} \neg x_{n-1} \ldots \neg x_0) \vee (x_{n-1} x_{n-1} \ldots x_0)$$
$$= \underbrace{11\ldots1}_{n \text{ bits}} = 2^n-1.$$

Theorem 6. Let $A, A \rightarrow B \in \Gamma$. B is a tautology if both A and $A \rightarrow B$ are tautologies.

Proof. Assume A and $A \rightarrow B$ are tautologies. Suppose B is not a tautology. By Lem. 5, only when $V(A)=V(B)$, $A \rightarrow B$ has be a tautology, so A is not a tautology, which contradicts the given condition. Hence, B is a tautology.

Theorem 7. $\Gamma \vdash A \Rightarrow \vDash A$.

The proof is completed by induction on the number of *wffs* in sequence of *wffs* that infer A, and omit it here.

From semantics, an axiom system is consistent if and only if all proved *wffs* in this system are tautology.

Theorem 8. $2^n P$ is consistent.

Proof. Suppose that $2^n P$ is not consistent, namely there is a $A \in \Gamma$ such that $\Gamma \vdash A$ and $\Gamma \vdash \neg A$. By Th.7, both A and $\neg A$ are tautology, which is contradiction. So, $2^n P$ is consistent.

In general, the extension of a logic system is a reform system formed by enlarging the set of axioms so that all theorems of old system remain in new one. **Definition 5.** Let $A \in \Gamma$. An extension of 2^np is consistent if there is not both A and $\neg A$ that are theorems in the extension.

Theorem 9. $\vDash A \Rightarrow \Gamma \vdash A$.

The proof is mitted here.

3. Concluding Remarks

This paper has merely structured 2^n valued logic initially, and there are many studies to perfect the system. Even though 2^nP is the extension of Boolean Logic, it conforms to big data era. Therefore, maybe 2^nP plays a cornerstone for big data science. Since digital logic and binary number system had been used in digital computer, we believe that 2^nP will broaden logical foundation of computer science and artificial intelligence.

Acknowledgments

The authors would like to thank Xi-An Xiao for his valuable suggestions, and thank reviewer for pointing out a mistake in this paper.

References

1. Elena Aronova, Karen S. Baker and Naomi Oreskes, *Historical Studies in the Natural Science*, **40**,183(2010).
2. Li Guojie and Cheng Xueqi, *Bulletin of Chinese Academy of Sciences*, **6**, 647(2012).
3. Nancy R. Gough and Michael B. Yaffe, *Science Signaling*, **4**, 2(2011)
4. Gordon Bell, Tony Hey and Alex Szalay, *Science*, **323**,1297(2009).
5. Chris A. Mattmann, *Nature,* **493**, 473(2013).
6. J Łukasiewicz, *The Polish Review*, **13**, 43 (1968).
7. E L Post, *American Journal of Mathematics*, **43**, 163 (1921).
8. A Tarski, *Oxford at The Clarendon Press*, 38 (1956).
9. Nuel D. Belnap, JR, *The Journal of Symbolic Logic*, **25**, 144 (1960).

GRAFICAL ILLUSTRATIONS OF REAL-VALUED BOOLEAN CONSISTENT LOGICAL RELATIONS

DRAGAN RADOJEVIC[*]

*Mihajlo Pupin Institute, University of Belgrade, Volgina 15
Belgrade, 11000, Serbia*

This paper presents the graphical illustration of the Boolean consistent real-valued relations on the example of two two-dimensional objects. Consistent real-valued relations are based on the real-valued realization of the Boolean algebra.

1. Introduction

The real-valued Boolean algebra [1, 2, 3] is a framework for the realization of the real-valued relations, such as classical (two-valued) Boolean algebra is for the classical two-valued relations. In this paper, the real-valued logical relations are illustrated by the two cases of two two-dimensional objects $A = (a_1, a_2)$, $B = (b_1, b_2)$, which are given in the following Figure 1.

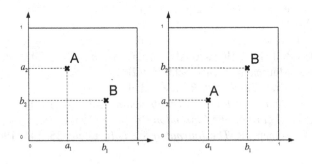

Figure 1: Analyzed cases I and II

---

[*] This work is supported by the Ministry of Education and Science of the Republic of Serbia.

2. Real-valued relations

The logical Boolean consistent real-valued relations are realized on the basis of the preferential structures which rely on the order relation $(A \leq B)$, [4, 5].

$$(A = B) = (A \leq B) \wedge (A \geq B),$$
$$(A < B) = (A \leq B) \wedge \overline{(A \geq B)},$$
$$(A > B) = \overline{(A \leq B)} \wedge (A \geq B),$$
$$(A \diamond B) = \overline{(A \leq B)} \wedge \overline{(A \geq B)},$$
$$(A \Leftrightarrow B) = (A = B) \vee (A \diamond B),$$
$$(A \veebar B) = \overline{(A \Leftrightarrow B)}.$$

The basic is a relation of order [4, 5], which is defined in scalar case as follows:

$$a \leq b =_{def} 1 - a + min(a,b).$$

2.1 Order relations $A \leq B$

$$(A \leq B) = (a_1 \leq b_1) \wedge (a_2 \leq b_2),$$
$$= (1 - a_1 + min(a_1,b_1))(1 - a_2 + min(a_2,b_2)).$$

case I $(a_1 < b_1, \ b_2 < a_2)$

$$(A \leq B) = (1 - a_1 + a_1)(1 - a_2 + b_2),$$
$$= 1 - a_2 + b_2.$$

case II $(a_1 < b_1, a_2 < b_2)$

$$(A \leq B) = (1 - a_1 + min(a_1,b_1))(1 - a_2 + min(a_2,b_2)),$$
$$= 1.$$

(2.1)

2.2 Order relations $A \geq B$

case I $(a_1 < b_1, \ b_2 < a_2)$

$$(B \leq A) = (1 - b_1) + a_1.$$

case II $(a_1 < b_1, \ a_2 < b_2)$

$$(B \leq A) = (1 - b_1)(1 - b_2) + (1 - b_1)a_2 + a_1(1 - b_2) + a_1 a_2.$$

(2.2)

2.3 Equivalence relations $A = B$

$$(A = B) = (A \leq B)(B \leq A),$$
$$= \left(\left(1 - a_1 + min\left(a_1, b_1\right)\right)\left(1 - a_2 + min\left(a_2, b_2\right)\right) \right)$$
$$\left(\left(1 - b_1 + min\left(a_1, b_1\right)\right)\left(1 - b_2 + min\left(a_2, b_2\right)\right) \right)$$

case I $\quad \left(a_1 < b_1, \quad b_2 < a_2\right)$

$$(A = B) = \left(1 - a_2 + b_2\right)\left(1 - b_1 + a_1\right), \tag{2.3}$$
$$= a_1 b_2 + a_1\left(1 - a_2\right) + \left(1 - b_1\right)b_2 + \left(1 - b_1\right)\left(1 - a_2\right).$$

case II $\quad \left(a_1 < b_1, \quad a_2 < b_2\right)$

$$(A = B) = \left(1 - b_1 + a_1\right)\left(1 - b_2 + a_2\right),$$
$$= a_1 a_2 + a_1\left(1 - b_2\right) + \left(1 - b_1\right)a_2 + \left(1 - b_1\right)\left(1 - b_2\right).$$

2.4 Uncertainty relations $A <> B$

$$(A <> B) = \overline{(A \leq B)(B \leq A)}$$
$$= \left(\left(a_1 > b_1\right) \vee \left(a_2 > b_2\right)\right) \wedge \left(\left(b_1 > a_1\right) \vee \left(b_2 > a_2\right)\right).$$

case I $\quad \left(a_1 < b_1, \quad b_2 < a_2\right)$

$$(A <> B) = \left(a_2 - b_2\right)\left(b_1 - a_1\right).. \tag{2.4}$$

case II $\quad \left(a_1 < b_1, \quad a_2 < b_2\right)$

$$(A <> B) = 0.$$

2.5 Similarity relations $A \Leftrightarrow B$

$$(A \Leftrightarrow B) = (A = B) \vee (A <> B)$$
$$= (A \leq B)(A \geq B) + \left(\overline{A \leq B}\right)\left(\overline{A \geq B}\right)$$

case I $\quad \left(a_1 < b_1, \quad b_2 < a_2\right)$

$$(A \Leftrightarrow B) = \left(1 - a_2 + b_2\right)\left(1 - b_1 + a_1\right) + \left(a_2 - b_2\right)\left(b_1 - a_1\right),$$
$$= a_1 b_2 + a_1\left(1 - a_2\right) + \left(1 - b_1\right)b_2 + \tag{2.5}$$
$$\left(1 - b_1\right)\left(1 - a_2\right) + \left(a_2 - b_2\right)\left(b_1 - a_1\right).$$

case II $\quad \left(a_1 < b_1, \quad a_2 < b_2\right)$

$$(A \Leftrightarrow B) = \left(1 - b_1 + a_1\right)\left(1 - b_2 + a_2\right),$$
$$= a_1 a_2 + a_1\left(1 - b_2\right) + \left(1 - b_1\right)a_2 + \left(1 - b_1\right)\left(1 - b_2\right).$$

2.6 Diversity relations $A \veebar B$

$$\left(A \veebar B\right) = \overline{\left(A \Leftrightarrow B\right)}.$$

$$\left(A \veebar B\right) = \overline{\left(A = B\right)} \wedge \overline{\left(A \Leftrightarrow B\right)}$$

case I $\quad \left(a_1 < b_1, \quad b_2 < a_2\right)$

$$\left(A \veebar B\right) = 1 - \left(1 - a_2 + b_2\right)\left(1 - b_1 + a_1\right) - \left(a_2 - b_2\right)\left(b_1 - a_1\right). \qquad (2.6)$$

case II $\quad \left(a_1 < b_1, \quad a_2 < b_2\right)$

$$\left(A \veebar B\right) = 1 - \left(1 - b_1 + a_1\right)\left(1 - b_2 + a_2\right),$$

$$= 1 - \left(1 - b_1\right)a_2 - \left(1 - b_1\right)\left(1 - b_2\right) - a_1 a_2 - a_1 \left(1 - b_2\right).$$

2.7 Relations of "less than" $A < B$

$$\left(A < B\right) = \left(\overline{B \leq A}\right)\left(A \leq B\right).$$

case I $\quad \left(a_1 < b_1, \quad b_2 < a_2\right)$

$$\left(A < B\right) = \left(b_1 - a_1\right)\left(1 - a_2 + b_2\right) \qquad (2.7)$$

$$= \left(b_1 - a_1\right)\left(1 - a_2\right) + \left(b_1 - a_1\right)b_2.$$

case II $\quad \left(a_1 < b_1, a_2 < b_2\right)$

$$\left(A < B\right) = \left(b_1 - a_1\right) + \left(b_2 - a_2\right) - \left(b_1 - a_1\right)\left(b_2 - a_2\right).$$

2.8 Relations of "greater than" $A > B$

$$\left(A > B\right) = \left(A \geq B\right)\left(\overline{A \leq B}\right).$$

case I $\quad \left(a_1 < b_1, \quad b_2 < a_2\right)$

$$\left(A > B\right) = \left(1 - b_1\right)\left(a_2 - b_2\right) + \left(a_2 - b_2\right)a_1. \qquad (2.8)$$

case II $\quad \left(a_1 < b_1, a_2 < b_2\right)$

$$\left(A > B\right) = 0.$$

All other Boolean consistent binary real-valued relations based on two order relations $A \leq B$ and $A \geq B$, can be represented by corresponding Hasse diagram, Figures 2 and 3 as in classical (two-valued) relations [5, 7].

268

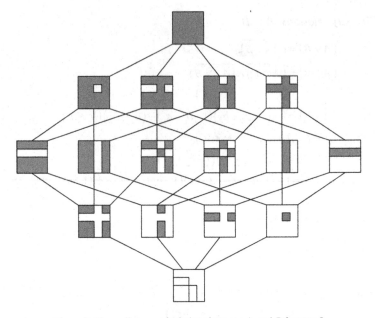

Figure 2: Hasse diagram of relations between *A* and *B* for case I

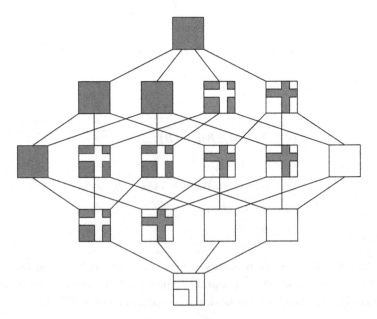

Figure 3: Hasse diagram of relations between *A* and *B* for case II

3. Conclusion

The real-valued logical relations based on the real-valued realization of the Boolean algebra, known also as the interpolative Boolean algebra, are consistent generalizations of the classical two-valued logical relations. The above described graphical illustrations of the relations between objects described with two attributes each, which values from the real interval [0, 1] are, on one hand, simple enough and, on the other hand, informative enough to illustrate relevant phenomenon of the consistent generalization. The described logical relations are of great practical importance for the real implementation. In the existing real applications dominate geometrical approaches for treating similarities, diversities, un-distinguishability, and similar. In all cases the stated geometrical approaches can be treated consistently according to the appropriate logical approaches: closeness by the similarity relation, distance by the diversity relation, etc.

References

1. Radojević, D. (2000). New [0,1]-valued logic: A natural generalization of Boolean logic. Yugoslav Journal of Operational Research, 10 (2), 185-216.

2. Radojević, D. (2008). Interpolative Realization of Boolean Algebra as a Consistent Frame for Gradation and/or Fuzziness. In Nikravesh, M. *et al.* (eds.) Forging New Frontiers: Fuzzy Pioneers II, 218, 295-317.

3. Radojević D., Real-Valued Realizations of Boolean Algebra are a Natural Frame for Consistent Fuzzy Logic, In R. Sesing, E. Trillas, C. Moraga and S. Termini, editors, On Fuzziness: A Homage to Lotfi A. Zadeh, Studies in Fuzziness and Soft Computing 299, pages 559-565, Springer-Verlag, 2013.

4. Arrow, K. J., (1951b, 2nd ed. 1963). *Social Choice and Individual Values*. Wiley, New York. ISBN 0-300-01364-7.

5. Radojević, D. (2005). Interpolative relations and interpolative preference structures. Yugoslav Journal of Operational Research, 15(2), 171-189.

6. Baczynski M., Jayaram B., Fuzzy Implications, Series: Studies in fuzziness and Soft Computing, Springer, 2008.

7. Radojević, D. (2010) Generalized (Real-Valued) order and Equivalence Relations, SYM-OP-IS 2010, 451-454.

α-RESOLUTION METHOD FOR LATTICE-VALUED HORN GENERALIZED CLAUSES IN LATTICE-VALUED PROPOSITIONAL LOGIC SYSTEM

Weitao Xu*, Wenqiang Zhang and Dexian Zhang

*College of Information Science and Engineering,Henan University of Technology,
Zhengzhou, 450001, China,
* E-mail: hnxmxwt@163.com*

Yang Xu†, Xiaodong Pan

*School of Mathematics, Southwest Jiaotong University,
Chengdu, 610031, China
† E-mail: xuyang@home.swjtu.edu.cn*

This paper presents an α-resolution method for lattice-valued horn generalized clauses in lattice-valued propositional logic system $\mathcal{L}P(X)$ based on lattice implication algebra. In this approach, We give lattice-valued horn generalized clause and the correlative concepts in $\mathcal{L}P(X)$. The α-resolution of two lattice-valued horn generalized clauses is also represented in $\mathcal{L}P(X)$. It reflects the resolution rules in a resolution process, which aims at deleting α-resolution literals and obtaining a resolvent. This method can provide an efficient tool for automated reasoning in lattice-valued propositional logic system and lattice-valued first-order logic system.

Keywords: automated reasoning; lattice-valued logic; α-resolution; lattice-valued horn g-clause; lattice implication algebra.

1. Introduction

Automated reasoning is one of the most important branches in Artificial Intelligence. Since the resolution principle is presented by Robinson in 1965,[4] resolution-based automated reasoning become a research focus by many scholars.

Based on Robinson's resolution principle, many resolution methods are studied in classical logic system. Specially, there are three typical resolution methods such as semantic resolution, linear resolution and lock resolution. Liu deeply studied these resolution methods and extended them to the set of the generalized clauses.[6] Lu also presented the resolution principle for the set of horn clauses.[5] However, these classical resolution principle based on classical logic is easy to deal with certain problem. In fact, there exists much uncertain information or knowledge in a real world. Hence, the non-classical logic were focused by many scholars. At the same time, the resolution based on non-classical logic also paid many attention.

Lattice-valued logic is an important non-classical logic, which plays an important role in dealing with comparability and incomparability. In order to establish the theories and methods to simultaneously deal with fuzziness and incomparability of processed object itself and uncertainty in the course of information processing, Xu presented lattice implication algebra by combining lattice with implication algebra.[7] Subsequently, Xu et al. established lattice-valued propositional logic system $\mathcal{L}P(X)$ and lattice-valued first-order logic system $\mathcal{L}F(X)$ based on lattice implication algebra.[8,9,11] These logic systems, which have not only stick syntax proof but also sound semantic interpretation, provide a scientific and reasonable logical foundation for intelligent information processing and theorem automated proving. In the frame of lattice-valued propositional logic system $\mathcal{L}P(X)$, Xu et al. established α-resolution principle for the generalized clauses.[10,11] The α-resolution principle provides a crucial foundation to construct resolution method for automated reasoning.

In this paper, α-resolution method for lattice-valued horn generalized clauses is established in lattice-valued propositional logic system $\mathcal{L}P(X)$ based on lattice implication algebra. The paper is organized as follows. In section 2, we recall some basic conception. In section 3, α-resolution method is established for lattice-valued horn g-clauses in $\mathcal{L}P(X)$. In section 4, the conclusions and future works are given.

2. α-resolution method for lattice-valued horn generalized clauses

We refer the readers to[7-11] for more details of the concepts and properties about lattice implication algebra, lattice-valued propositional logic system and α-resolution principle based on $\mathcal{L}P(X)$.

In the following, generalized literal and generalized clause are denoted as g-literal and g-clause respectively.

Definition 2.1. Let $\mathcal{L}P(X)$ be lattice-valued propositional logic system, p is called a positive literal, then p' is called a negative literal.

Definition 2.2. Let $\mathcal{L}P(X)$ be lattice-valued propositional logic system, g is called a positive g-literal, then g' is called a negative g-literal.

Example 2.1. In $\mathcal{LP}(X)$, p and q are positive literals, then

(1) $p \to q$, $p' \to q$, $p' \to q'$, $p \to q'$ are also positive g-literals.

(2) $(p \to q)'$, $(p' \to q)'$, $(p' \to q)'$, $(p \to q')'$ are called negative g-literals.

Remark 2.1. A positive literal is still called a positive g-literal, a negative literal is still called a negative g-literal.

Definition 2.3. In $\mathcal{LP}(X)$, let r be a positive g-literal, and $h_1, h_2, \cdots, h_m$ are the negative g-literals, the clauses with at most one positive g-literal of the following form

$$h_1 \vee h_2 \vee \cdots \vee h_m \vee r, \quad or \quad h_1 \vee h_2 \vee \cdots \vee h_m, \quad or \quad r$$

are called lattice-valued horn generalized clauses, shortly for lattice-valued horn g-clause.

Definition 2.4. In $\mathcal{LP}(X)$, if a lattice-valued horn g-clause contains only one positive g-literal, then it is called unit lattice-valued horn g-clause.

Definition 2.5. In lattice-valued horn g-clause, if the rightmost g-literal is a positive g-literal, then it is called a normal lattice-valued horn g-clause.

Definition 2.6. In $\mathcal{LP}(X)$, let S be a set of the g-clauses. S is called a set of lattice-valued horn g-clauses if every g-clause in S is lattice-valued horn g-clause.

Definition 2.7. In $\mathcal{LP}(X)$, let H_1 and H_2 be lattice-valued horn g-clauses. The resolvent of H_1 and H_2 are as follows.

(1) $H_1 = h_1 \vee h_2 \vee \cdots \vee h_m \vee r_1$, $H_2 = g_1 \vee g_2 \vee \cdots \vee g_n \vee r_2$.

    (a) If $r_1 \wedge r_2 \leq \alpha$, then the resolution of H_1 and H_2 is represented as

$$\frac{h_1 \vee \cdots \vee h_m \vee \boxed{r_1} \qquad g_1 \vee \cdots \vee g_n \vee \boxed{r_2}}{\alpha \vee h_1 \vee \cdots \vee h_m \vee g_1 \vee \cdots \vee g_n},$$

and the resolvent of H_1 and H_2 is

$$R_\alpha(H_1, H_2) = \alpha \vee h_1 \vee \cdots \vee h_m \vee g_1 \vee \cdots \vee g_n.$$

    (b) If $r_1 \wedge g_i \leq \alpha$, then the resolution of H_1 and H_2 is represented as

$$\frac{h_1 \vee \cdots \vee h_m \vee \boxed{r_1} \qquad g_1 \vee \cdots \vee \boxed{g_i} \vee \cdots \vee g_n \vee r_2}{\alpha \vee h_1 \vee \cdots \vee h_m \vee g_1 \vee \cdots \vee g_{i-1} \vee g_{i+1} \vee \cdots \vee g_n \vee r_2},$$

and the resolvent of H_1 and H_2 is

$$R_\alpha(H_1, H_2) = \alpha \vee h_1 \vee \cdots \vee h_m \vee g_1 \vee \cdots \vee g_{i-1} \vee g_{i+1} \vee \cdots \vee g_n \vee r_2.$$

(c) If $h_i \wedge r_2 \leq \alpha$, then the resolution of H_1 and H_2 is represented as

$$\frac{h_1 \vee \cdots \vee \boxed{h_i} \vee \cdots \vee h_m \vee r_1 \qquad g_1 \vee \cdots \vee g_n \vee \boxed{r_2}}{\alpha \vee h_1 \vee \cdots \vee h_{i-1} \vee h_{i+1} \vee \cdots \vee h_m \vee g_1 \vee \cdots \vee g_n \vee r_1},$$

and the resolvent of H_1 and H_2 is

$$R_\alpha(H_1, H_2) = \alpha \vee h_1 \vee \cdots \vee h_{i-1} \vee h_{i+1} \vee \cdots \vee h_m \vee g_1 \vee \cdots \vee g_n \vee r_1.$$

(2) $H_1 = h_1 \vee h_2 \vee \cdots \vee h_m \vee r$, $H_2 = g_1 \vee g_2 \vee \cdots \vee g_n$.

(a) If $r \wedge g_i \leq \alpha$, then the resolution of H_1 and H_2 is represented as

$$\frac{h_1 \vee \cdots \vee h_m \vee \boxed{r} \qquad g_1 \vee \cdots \vee \boxed{g_i} \vee \cdots \vee g_n}{\alpha \vee h_1 \vee \cdots \vee h_m \vee g_1 \vee \cdots \vee g_{i-1} \vee g_{i+1} \vee \cdots \vee g_n},$$

and the resolvent of H_1 and H_2 is

$$R_\alpha(H_1, H_2) = \alpha \vee h_1 \vee \cdots \vee h_m \vee g_1 \vee \cdots \vee g_{i-1} \vee g_{i+1} \vee \cdots \vee g_n.$$

(b) If $h_i \wedge g_j \leq \alpha$, then the resolution of H_1 and H_2 is represented as

$$\frac{h_1 \vee \cdots \vee \boxed{h_i} \vee \cdots \vee h_m \vee r \qquad g_1 \vee \cdots \vee \boxed{g_j} \vee \cdots \vee g_n}{\begin{array}{c} \alpha \vee h_1 \vee \cdots \vee h_{i-1} \vee h_{i+1} \vee \cdots \vee g_1 \\ \vee \cdots \vee g_{j-1} \vee g_{j+1} \vee \cdots \vee g_n \vee r \end{array}},$$

and the resolvent of H_1 and H_2 is

$$R_\alpha(H_1, H_2) = \alpha \vee h_1 \vee \cdots \vee h_{i-1} \vee h_{i+1} \vee \cdots \vee g_1$$
$$\vee \cdots \vee g_{j-1} \vee g_{j+1} \vee \cdots \vee g_n \vee r$$

(3) $H_1 = h_1 \vee h_2 \vee \cdots \vee h_m \vee r_1$, $H_2 = r_2$.

(a) If $r_1 \wedge r_2 \leq \alpha$, then the resolution of H_1 and H_2 is represented as

$$\frac{h_1 \vee \cdots \vee h_m \vee \boxed{r_1} \qquad \boxed{r_2}}{\alpha \vee h_1 \vee \cdots \vee h_m},$$

and the resolvent of H_1 and H_2 is

$$R_\alpha(H_1, H_2) = \alpha \vee h_1 \vee h_2 \vee \cdots \vee h_m.$$

(b) If $h_m \wedge r_2 \leq \alpha$, then the resolution of H_1 and H_2 is represented as

274

$$\frac{h_1 \vee h_2 \vee \cdots \vee h_{m-1} \vee \boxed{h_m} \vee r_1 \qquad \boxed{r_2}}{\alpha \vee h_1 \vee \cdots \vee h_{m-1} \vee r_1},$$

and the resolvent of H_1 and H_2 is

$$R_\alpha(H_1, H_2) = \alpha \vee h_1 \vee \cdots \vee h_{m-1} \vee r_1.$$

(4) $H_1 = h_1 \vee h_2 \vee \cdots \vee h_m$, $H_2 = r$.

If $h_m \wedge r \leq \alpha$, then the resolution of H_1 and H_2 is represented as

$$\frac{h_1 \vee \cdots \vee \boxed{h_m} \qquad \boxed{r}}{\alpha \vee h_1 \vee \cdots \vee h_{m-1}},$$

and the resolvent of H_1 and H_2 is

$$R_\alpha(H_1, H_2) = \alpha \vee h_1 \vee \cdots \vee h_{m-1}.$$

Where, $h_i(i = 1, 2, \cdots, m)$ and $g_i(i = 1, 2, \cdots, n)$ are the negative g-literals, r, r_1 and r_2 are the positive g-literals.

Definition 2.8. In $\mathcal{L}P(X)$, let $S = \{H_1, \cdots, H_i, \cdots, H_n\}$ be a set of lattice-valued horn g-clauses, $\alpha \in L$. $\omega = \{D_1, D_2, \cdots, D_i, \cdots, D_k\}$ is an α-resolution deduction from S to lattice-valued horn g-clause D_k if it satisfies the following condition

(1) $D_i \in S, i = 1, 2, \cdots, k$; or

(2) there exist m and j, such that $D_i = R_\alpha(D_m, D_j)(m < i, j < i)$.

Theorem 2.1. *Suppose S is a set of lattice-valued horn g-clauses in $\mathcal{L}P(X)$, $\alpha \in L$, and $\omega = \{D_1, \cdots, D_i, \cdots, D_k\}$ is an $\alpha-$ resolution deduction from S to lattice-valued horn g-clause D_k. If D_k is $\alpha - \diamond$, then $S \leq \alpha$, i.e., if $D_k = \alpha$, then $S \leq \alpha$.*

Theorem 2.2. *Let S is a set of lattice-valued horn g-clauses in lattice-valued propositional logic system $\mathcal{L}P(X)$, $\alpha \in L$. If $S \leq \alpha$, then there exists an α-resolution deduction from the set S to $\alpha - \diamond$.*

3. Acknowledgments

This paper is supported by the National Natural Science Foundation of China(No.61175055, U1304609, 61100046, 61300123), the National High Technology Research and Development Program of China(863 Program, No.2012AA101608), the High-level Talent Foundation of Henan University of Technology(No.2012BS012), Key Technology Research Program of the Education Department Henan Province(No.13B520945).

4. Conclusions and future work

Lattice-valued horn g-clause is an important type of g-clauses in lattice-valued propositional logic system $\mathcal{L}P(X)$. In this paper, α-resolution method for lattice-valued horn g-clauses is established in $\mathcal{L}P(X)$. The completeness theorem is also given. In future work, an automated reasoning algorithm can be constructed in $\mathcal{L}P(X)$, and α-resolution method can be studied in lattice-valued first-order logic system $\mathcal{L}F(X)$.

References

1. C.L. Chang, R.C.T. Lee, *Symbolic Logic and Mechanical Theorem Proving*, Academic Press, New York 1973.
2. D.W. Loveland, *Automated Theorem Proving: A logical Basis*, North-Holland, Amsterdam 1978.
3. Jun Liu, Da Ruan, Yang Xu, Zhengming Song, *A resolution-like strategy based on lattice-valued logic*, IEEE Transactions on Fuzzy Systems 11(4) (2003) 560-567.
4. J.A. Robinson, *A machine-oriented logic based on the resolution principle*, J. ACM 12(1) (1965) 23-41.
5. R.Q. Lu, *Resolution principle*, Science China 7 (1981) 896-903 (in Chinese).
6. X.H. Liu, *Resolution-based Automated Reasoning*, Academic Press of China, Beijing, China, 1994 (in Chinese).
7. Y. Xu, *Lattice implication algebra*, J. Southwest Jiaotong University 28(1) (1993) 20-27 (in Chinese).
8. Y. Xu, K. Qin, *Lattice-valued propositionallogic(I)*, J. Southwest Jiaotong University 2 (1993) 123-128 (English version).
9. Y. Xu, K. Qin, *Lattice-valued propositional logic(II)*, J. Southwest Jiaotong University 1 (1994) 22-27 (English version).
10. Y. Xu, D. Ruan, E.E. Kerre, J. Liu, *α-Resolution principle based on lattice-valued propositional logic LP(X)*, Information Science 130(1-4) (2000) 195-223.
11. Y. Xu, D. Ruan, K. Qin and J. Liu, *Lattice-Valued Logic: An alternative approach to treat fuzziness and incomparability*, Berlin: Springer-Verlag 2003.
12. Y. Xu, J. Liu, D. Ruan, X.B. Li, *Determination of α-Resolution in Lattice-Valued First-order Logic LF(X)*, Information Sciences 181(10) (2011) 1836-1862.

FUZZIFICATION OF BOOLEAN NETWORKS

VLADIMIR DOBRIĆ

Faculty of Organizational Sciences, University of Belgrade, Jove Ilića 154
Belgrade,11000, Serbia

Boolean networks are models of complex dynamical systems. Modelling complex systems with Boolean networks is adequate in situations in which binary view is valid. If the situation is not "black and white", Boolean networks are inadequate/ oversimplified models. For modelling real world complex systems, Boolean networks lack descriptive power - fuzzification of the model is required. Boolean networks are fuzzified using the interpolative Boolean algebra. Fuzzy model keeps the Boolean frame.

1. Introduction

Boolean networks are mostly used in biology [1, 2]. Applications in other domains are rare [3, 4, 5]. Boolean network is a directed graph, with an assignment of binary state and Boolean function to each node. The state of the node is the value of its Boolean function whose arguments are the states of node's predecessors from the previous time step. Boolean network evolves in discrete time steps from an initial assignment of states for each node. Boolean network dynamics can be ordered, complex or chaotic.

Boolean networks facilitate qualitative analysis of dynamics of complex systems. Modelling complex systems with Boolean networks is adequate only for problems in which binary view is valid. Since most problems are not "black and white", applicability of model is highly restricted. Modelling real world complex systems with classical Boolean networks is oversimplification of reality. More descriptive power is required. Incorporation of fuzzy view into Boolean networks is needed when modelling real world complex systems. Boolean consistent fuzzification of model is achieved using the interpolative Boolean algebra.

2. Boolean networks

Boolean network is a directed graph whose nodes represent system components and edges represent causal relationships between components:

$$BN = (N, E) \tag{1}$$

Here N is a set of nodes and E is a set of directed edges.

Node's predecessors are nodes from which its incoming edges come from. Node's successors are nodes to which its outgoing edges point to. Dynamics is introduced on Boolean network by assigning to each node a time-dependent binary variable and a Boolean function. The state of a node is the value of its Boolean function whose arguments are the states of node's predecessors from the previous time step. If the node N_i has K_i predecessors, the update rule is given as:

$$N_i(t) = f_i\left(N_{i_1}(t-1), N_{i_2}(t-1), ..., N_{i_{K_i}}(t-1)\right) \qquad (2)$$

Here $N_i(t) \in \{0,1\}$ is the state of the node N_i at time t, $N_{i_1}(t-1), N_{i_2}(t-1), ..., N_{i_{K_i}}(t-1)$ are the states of its predecessors at time t-1, and f_i is a Boolean function associated to it.

Dynamics of Boolean network is defined by equations which update the states of the nodes in the network:

$$\begin{bmatrix} N_1(t) \\ \vdots \\ N_M(t) \end{bmatrix} = \begin{bmatrix} f_1\left(N_{1_1}(t-1), N_{1_2}(t-1), ..., N_{1_{K_1}}(t-1)\right) \\ \vdots \\ f_M\left(N_{M_1}(t-1), N_{M_2}(t-1), ..., N_{M_{K_M}}(t-1)\right) \end{bmatrix} \qquad (3)$$

Here $N(t) = [N_i(t) \,|\, i=1,...,M]^T$ is the state of a Boolean network at time t, M is the number of nodes in the network.

Boolean network evolves in discrete time steps from an initial assignment of states for each node. For simplicity, synchronous and deterministic state update is assumed in this paper. Since the state space is finite (2^M), Boolean network dynamics eventually reaches point or cycle attractors. Each attractor has a basin of attraction which is a set of states that eventually converge to that attractor. Dynamical behavior of Boolean network can be fundamentally different depending on which basin of attraction the initial state is located (ordered, critical or chaotic regime).

3. Fuzzification of Boolean networks

Fuzzification of Boolean networks is streightforward using the interpolative Boolean algebra [6, 7, 8, 9, 10]. States of nodes become fuzzy ([0, 1] valued), while Boolean functions are mapped into generalized Boolean polynomials which become the update rules in the fuzzy model. Any Boolean function can be mapped into uniquely corresponding generalized Boolean polynomial according to the following rules:

$$\left[N_i \wedge N_j\right]^{\otimes} =_{def} \begin{cases} N_i \otimes N_j, & i \neq j \\ N_i, & i = j \end{cases}$$

$$\left[N_i \vee N_j\right]^{\otimes} =_{def} N_i + N_j - \left(N_i \wedge N_j\right)^{\otimes} = N_i + N_j - N_i \otimes N_j$$

$$\left[\neg N_i\right]^{\otimes} =_{def} 1 - N_i$$

$$\left[f_i\left(N_1,...,N_M\right) \wedge f_j\left(N_1,...,N_M\right)\right]^{\otimes} =_{def} f_i^{\otimes}\left(N_1,...,N_M\right) \otimes f_j^{\otimes}\left(N_1,...,N_n\right)$$

$$\left[f_i\left(N_1,...,N_M\right) \vee f_j\left(N_1,...,N_M\right)\right]^{\otimes} =_{def} f_i^{\otimes}\left(N_1,...,N_M\right) + f_j^{\otimes}\left(N_1,...,N_M\right) - \\ f_i^{\otimes}\left(N_1,...,N_M\right) \otimes f_j^{\otimes}\left(N_1,...,N_n\right) \quad (4)$$

$$\left[\neg f_i\left(N_1,...,N_M\right)\right]^{\otimes} =_{def} 1 - f_i^{\otimes}\left(N_1,...,N_M\right)$$

$$N_i, N_j \in N; f_i\left(N_1,...,N_M\right), f_j\left(N_1,...,N_M\right) \in BA(N).$$

A generalized product $\otimes : [0, 1] \times [0, 1] \rightarrow [0, 1]$ is a binary operation with the following properties:

1. Commutativity:

$$N_i \otimes N_j = N_j \otimes N_i \quad (5)$$

2. Associativity:

$$\left(N_i \otimes N_j\right) \otimes N_k = N_i \otimes \left(N_j \otimes N_k\right) \quad (6)$$

3. Monotonicity:

$$N_i \leq N_j \quad \Rightarrow \quad N_i \otimes N_k \leq N_j \otimes N_k \quad (7)$$

4. Boundary:

$$N_i \otimes 1 = N_i \quad (8)$$

5. Non-negativity:

$$\bigotimes_{N_i \in S} N_i \bigotimes_{A_j \in N \setminus S} \left(1 - N_j\right) \geq 0 \quad (9)$$

The state of a node N_i is the value of its generalized Boolean polynomial whose arguments are the states of node's predecessors in the previous time step:

$$N_i(t) = \left[f_i\left(N_{i_1}(t-1), N_{i_2}(t-1), ..., N_{i_{K_i}}(t-1) \right) \right]^\otimes =$$
$$= f_i^\otimes\left(N_{i_1}(t-1), N_{i_2}(t-1), ..., N_{i_{K_i}}(t-1) \right) \tag{10}$$

Here $N_i(t) \in [0,1]$ is the state of the node N_i at time t, $N_{i_1}(t-1), N_{i_2}(t-1), ..., N_{i_{K_i}}(t-1)$ are the states of node N_i predecessors at time t-1, K_i is the number of predecessors of the node N_i, and $f_i^\otimes\left(N_{i_1}(t-1), N_{i_2}(t-1), ..., N_{i_{K_i}}(t-1) \right)$ is the generalized Boolean polynomial that corresponds to Boolean function $f_i\left(N_{i_1}(t-1), N_{i_2}(t-1), ..., N_{i_{K_i}}(t-1) \right)$ associated to node N_i.☐☐

Dynamics of fuzzy model is defined by the following equations:

$$\begin{bmatrix} N_1(t) \\ \vdots \\ N_M(t) \end{bmatrix} = \begin{bmatrix} \left[f_1\left(N_{1_1}(t-1), N_{1_2}(t-1), ..., N_{1_{k_1}}(t-1) \right) \right]^\otimes \\ \vdots \\ \left[f_M\left(N_{M_1}(t-1), N_{M_2}(t-1), ..., N_{M_{K_M}}(t-1) \right) \right]^\otimes \end{bmatrix} =$$
$$= \begin{bmatrix} f_1^\otimes\left(N_{1_1}(t-1), N_{1_2}(t-1), ..., N_{1_{k_1}}(t-1) \right) \\ \vdots \\ f_M^\otimes\left(N_{M_1}(t-1), N_{M_2}(t-1), ..., N_{M_{K_M}}(t-1) \right) \end{bmatrix} \tag{11}$$

Here $N(t) = \left(N_i(t) \mid i = 1,...,M \right)^T$ is the state of Boolean network at time t, M is the number of nodes in the network.

4. Illustrative example

Consider the following equations (taken from [11]) which define the dynamics of classical Boolean network:

$$\begin{aligned} A(t+1) &= B(t) \vee C(t) \\ B(t+1) &= A(t) \Leftrightarrow C(t) \\ C(t+1) &= A(t) \wedge D(t) \\ D(t+1) &= \left(A(t) \rightarrow B(t) \right) \underline{\vee} C(t) \end{aligned} \tag{12}$$

Dynamics of fuzzy model is defined by the following equations:

$$A(t+1) = \left[B(t) \vee C(t)\right]^{\otimes} = B(t) + C(t) - B(t) \otimes C(t)$$

$$B(t+1) = \left[A(t) \Leftrightarrow C(t)\right]^{\otimes} = 1 - A(t) - B(t) + 2A(t) \otimes B(t)$$

$$C(t+1) = \left[A(t) \wedge D(t)\right]^{\otimes} = A(t) \otimes D(t) \tag{13}$$

$$D(t+1) = \left[\left(A(t) \rightarrow B(t)\right) \veebar C(t)\right]^{\otimes} =$$

$$= 1 - A(t) - C(t) + A(t) \otimes B(t) + 2A(t) \otimes C(t) - 2A(t) \otimes B(t) \otimes C(t)$$

For any crisp initial conditions and any generalized product (or T-norm), fuzzy model shows the same dynamics like the classical model. Ordered behavior can be observed/ cycle attractor (1, 1, 1, 1) – (1, 1, 1, 0) – (1, 1, 0, 0) – (1, 0, 0, 1) – (0, 0, 1, 0) – (1, 0, 0, 0) – (0, 0, 0, 0) – (0, 1, 0, 1) – (1, 1, 0, 1) – (1, 0, 1, 1) - (1, 1, 1, 1) is reached. For any fuzzy initial conditions and generalized product $(\otimes = *)$, model shows ordered behavior (Figure 1.) - point attractor (0.6478, 0.4563, 0.3522, 0.5437) is reached. For generalized product $(\otimes = min)$, chaotic behavior can be observed.

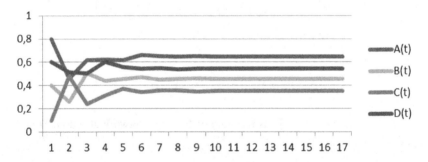

Figure 1. Ordered dynamics of fuzzy model for $(\otimes = *)$

5. Conclusion

Boolean networks are used for modelling complex dynamical systems. It is reasonable to apply Boolean networks only to problems in which binary view is valid. For most real world problems, since they are not "black and white", Boolean networks are inadequate/ oversimplified models of reality. Real world problems require more descriptive power - fuzzy view needs to be incorporated into Boolean networks. Boolean consistent fuzzification of Boolean networks is achieved using the interpolative Boolean algebra.

References

1. Kauffman, S. A., *Origins of Order: Self-Organization and Selection in Evolution*, Oxford University Press, (1993).
2. Rui-Sheng Wang, Assieh Saadatpour, Reka Albert, *Boolean modeling in systems biology: an overview of methodology and applications*, Physical biology **9**, (2012).
3. Andrea Roli, Mattia Manfroni, Carlo Pinciroli, Mauro Birattari. *On the Design of Boolean Network Robots, Applications of Evolutionary Computation*, Springer Berlin Heidelberg, (2011).
4. Geoff Easton, Roger J. Brooks, Kristina Georgieva, Ian Wilkinson, *Understanding the dynamics of industrial networks using Kauffman Boolean networks*, Advances in Complex Systems, Vol. 11, No. 1, (2008).
5. Jia-Wen Gu, Wai-Ki Ching, Tak-Kuen Siu, Harry Zheng, *On Modeling Credit Defaults: A Probabilistic Boolean Network Approach*, Risk and Decision Analysis, Volume 4, Number 2, (2013).
6. Dragan Radojevic, *New [0,1]-valued logic: A natural generalization of Boolean logic*, Yugoslav Journal of Operational Research - YUJOR, Belgrade, Vol. 10, No 2, (2000).
7. Dragan Radojevic, *Fuzzy Set Theory in Boolean Frame*, Int. J. of Computers, Communications & Control, Vol. III, (2008).
8. Dragan Radojevic, *Real-Valued Realizations of Boolean Algebras Are a Natural Frame for Consistent Fuzzy Logic*, On fuzzines, Studies in Fuzziness and Soft Computing, Volume 299, (2013).
9. Dragan Radojevic, *Logical Aggregation Based on Interpolative Boolean Algebra*, Mathware & Soft Computing 15, (2008).
10. Dragan Radojević, *Interpolative relations and interpolative preference structures*, Yugoslav Journal of Operational Research – YUJOR , Belgrade, Vol. 15, No 2, (2005).
11. Daizhan Cheng, Hongsheng Qi, Zhiqiang Li, Jiang B. Liu, *Stability and stabilization of Boolean networks*, International Journal of Robust and Nonlinear Control, Volume 21, Issue 2, (2011).

A METHOD OF DATA CLUSTERING BASED ON DYNAMIC LEARNING[*]

XIAOHONG LIU

College of Management, Southwest University for Nationalities, Chengdu, 610041, P.R.China

Data clustering is widely used in management decision and other fields. The traditional methods of data clustering based on offline calculating are faced with the challenge of speed and cost in the process of emergency decision making of social problem. Therefore, it's necessary to research a new method of data clustering as online using intelligent technologies. On discussing on the problem of data clustering, analyzing the basic assumption and selection criteria, a dynamic program of data clustering based online is put forward in this paper. The theory of dynamic learning is used in establishing an algorithm of data clustering.

1. Introduction

Technology of data clustering was first proposed by Ivakhnenko in 1967. With it's widely developed and applied in many fields, this technology has become one of important contents in the field of artificial intelligence. Through the data clustering, we can improve the actual meanings of data. Therefore, the value of application data clustering is self-evident. The technology and methods of data clustering have been applied in many fields, such as engineering, economics and management etc. Especially, with the internet rapidly developed and its widely applied, we have been facing with massive data, how to fast the data clustering and enhance its commercial value has become a new topic. There are lots of literatures related to data clustering based on offline calculating, and one main purpose of these literatures is to improve the clustering precise as possible. However, for many emergency cases, such as unexpected mass events and natural disasters, the speed of making decision based on satisfaction is more important than the quality of decision based on science. The online data clustering plays a very important role, especially in the process of emergency

[*] This work is partially supported by State Bureau of Foreign Expert's Affairs project of China (grant No. 2013-12) and supported by grant 12XNZ007 of State Ethnic Affairs Commission of China, and supported by grant 2014XWD-S1202 of Southwest University for Nationalities.

decision-making. In the process of this decision-making, the decision makers need to make decision as soon as possible when they get the data; therefore, the online data clustering is very useful for them. However, in many emergency cases, due to lack of scientific basis, the decision problem is made mainly depending of human being's experience or feeling. The main goal of this paper is to improve the validity of online data clustering. Firstly, we discuss on the problem of data clustering; secondly, analyze the basic assumption and selection criteria; thirdly, a dynamic program of data clustering based online is put forward; lastly, the theory of dynamic learning is used in establishing an algorithm of data clustering.

2. Discussing on the problem of data clustering

In order to understand the problem of data clustering, we explain the concept of data clustering. The data clustering is a dividing a group of data in accordance with condition of one or more attributes. Accordingly, a group of data is divided into two parts, i.e. that data met the dividing condition is called as the same data clustering, or the new data clustering. Through the data clustering, we could find that the specific relationship between data, therefore, the value of application is effectively improved.

In the field of management decision-making, we are faced with uncertainty of many attributes. We can use the data to express each attribute, but do not know the regularity of data in advance. In order to improve the validity of management decision-making, we are used to classify the attribute with the same or similar, in fact, which is one of problems of data clustering. Therefore, the data clustering is widely used in the process of management decision-making, such as in human resource management, the relative evaluation of human resources is a widely used in different type of organizations, according to its theory, the result is to get the index scores through comparison of various human resources, and to determine the corresponding evaluation grade, the result is used in other functions of human resource management. However, a key problem of this evaluation is that its reliability and validity is not satisfied in practice. We are faced with the difficulty of how to improve the data clustering using this tool.

Generally speaking, the difficulty of data clustering includes two aspects: one is to determine the division basis, i.e. according to divided rule to classify the data; the other is the response speed of data classification, especially in emergency conditions, need to fast get the data clustering.

In the process of different decision-making, we may define the condition according to the need of decision. We focuses on putting forward a fast data clustering based on the dynamic learning model, especially for management decision problem with massive data, we do not know data's regular in advance. The data clustering is a relatively effective method for data classified, and is to provide theoretical basis for management decision-making.

3. The basic assumptions and selection criteria

3.1. *The basic assumptions*

Classifying data: (1) according to the result of comparison data, the data is divided into the same data clustering and new data clustering. The same data clustering is a set of composed with the same condition, i.e. the absolute value of difference of each data comparison with the average is less than the given value, or that is the new data clustering. (2) According to the availability of data, the data is divided into valid data and invalid data. The valid data is that its power weight is not zero, or that is invalid data.

Cost of data: (1) the directly cost of data includes data acquisition, payment to the experimental cost and organization expert sensory evaluation of costs; (2) the indirectly cost data is data acquisition opportunity cost, mainly refers to obtain some data and give up to get the other effective data proceeds.

Returns of data: (1) the valid data can positively support the decision therefore, it is necessary to effectively increase valid data through data clustering; (2) the invalid data is not only waste cost, but decrease the quality of decision also, therefore, it is necessary to filter out the invalid data.

3.2. *selection criteria*

Data weight: suppose n data, w_i denotes the weight of the ith data, $i = 1,2,..., n$, the weights are equal in the front of three data, i.e. $w_1 = w_2 = w_3 = \frac{1}{3}$. From the fourth data, dynamic adjustment of the weight according to the data and the differences of average, adjustment principle is the data weight is proportional function absolute value and the average, which is closer to the average of its weight is greater, and vice versa smaller.

Data weighted average: suppose n data, X_i and $\overline{X}_i$ denotes the data value of ith and the data weighted average from one to i respectively, and $\overline{X}_i = \sum_{t=1}^{i} w_t X_t$, $t = 1,2,..., i$.

Judgment criteria of clustering: set the same clustering judgment condition is $\varepsilon > 0$, for the ith data, (1) if $|X_i - \overline{X}_i| \le \varepsilon$, then called it as the same data clustering, and if $w_i > 0,$ then called it as a valid data, or invalid data. (2) If $\left| X_i - \overline{X}_i \right| > \varepsilon,$ then called as a new data clustering.

Judgment criteria of new clustering: set condition of a new clustering as $\delta > 0$, and $\delta = m\varepsilon$, $m = 2,3,..r$, $r = \min\left\{ n, \left[\dfrac{n}{\varepsilon} \right] \right\}$, for the ith data, if (1)

$\overline{X}_i + (m-1)\varepsilon < X_i < \overline{X}_i + m\varepsilon$, or (2) $\overline{X}_i - m\varepsilon < X_i < \overline{X}_i - m\varepsilon + \varepsilon$, then called it as the mth new clustering.

4. Dynamic programs of data clustering based online

In order to quickly get the result of data clustering, an online dynamic process is shown in Figure 1.

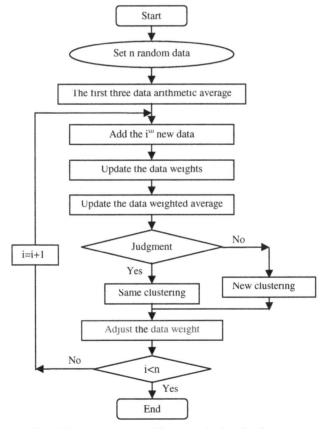

Figure 1 Dynamic program of data clustering based online

The main goal of Figure 1 is to divide n random data (i.e. do not know the basic rules of data) into clustering by online. The basic idea is by comparing the new data and the weighted average, dynamically adjusting the weight and its weighted average, to get an efficient clustering for the new data.

This method of online data clustering is consisted of four steps:

The 1st step, the weight of in the front of three samples (with equal probability events), get the arithmetic average.

The 2nd step, according to the rule, we can calculate the new data and the weighted average respectively.

The 3rd step, according to the judgment criteria of clustering, we can determine the new data belongs to which data clustering.

The 4th step, dynamically adjust the weight, cycle from the 2nd step to the 4th, until the exit criteria are met.

5. A dynamic learning algorithm of data clustering

In order to improve its speed and efficiency, we use a dynamic learning model to build the method of data clustering which is shown in figure 2.

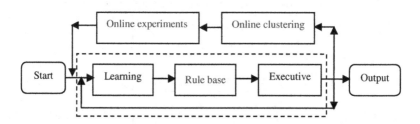

Figure 2 A dynamic learning model

Learning stage: suppose that there are n data, through self-learning stage, calculating the weight of each data and the weighted average, by comparing the difference between the new data and the weighted average to judge the effectiveness of data. The learning stage is divided into two steps.

(1) Get the first three data, set their weight is w_1, w_2 and w_3 respectively.

(2) From the ith data ($i \geq 4$), according to formula (1) to calculate weighted average when adding the new data

$$\overline{X}_i = \alpha \overline{X}_{i-1} + (1 - \alpha) X_i, \quad 0 \leq \alpha \leq 1. \tag{1}$$

If $|X_i - \overline{X}_t| \leq \varepsilon$, then we adjust w_t in the same clustering. According to *data weight*, i.e. the data weight is proportional function absolute value and the average, the weight is calculated according to formula (2) and (3):

$$\lambda_t = 1 - \frac{|X_t - \overline{X}_t|}{\sum_{t=1}^{i} |X_t - \overline{X}_t|}, \quad t = 1, 2, \ldots, i \quad (2)$$

The formula of the weight of data after normalized is shown as (3):

$$w_t = \frac{\lambda_t}{\sum_{t=1}^{i} \lambda_t} \quad (3)$$

If $|X_i - \overline{X}_i| > \varepsilon$, then we set $w_i = 0$, $\sum_{t=1}^{i} w_t = 1$.

6. Conclusions

Online data clustering is an important data processing method. There are many factors influencing the effectiveness of data clustering, and the most bases of data clustering are the average value and its error. Through comparing the new data with the weighted average of the data to calculate different to determine the clustering, dynamic program and its online algorithm based on dynamic learning are presented in this paper. This work has theoretical and practical significance for the data clustering, which built the foundation for the development of intelligent sensory evaluation. It must be pointed out is that only from the weighted average and error to determine the clustering is not enough. Because the actual problem is more complex and diverse, the data clustering should meet the needs of practical problems, the further study of data clustering is to do simulation and improve its application.

References

1. Ivakhnenko A G,Heristic self-organizing in problems of engineering cybernetics, *Automatica*.2,6 (1967).
2. Dimitriadou E, Dolniar S, Weingessal A, An examination of indexes for determining the number of clusters in binary data sets, *Psychometrika*. 1,67(2002).
3. Sun H J, Wang S R, Jiang Q S, FCM- based model selection algorithms for determining the number of clusters, *Pattern Recognition*.10,37(2004).
4. Min Song-qiang, He Chang-zhang, Reviews of evolutional group method of data handling, Application *Research of Computer*.2, 27(2010).

CONJUGATE FUZZY S-IMPLICATIONS OBTAINED BY OWA-OPERATORS

I. BENITEZ, R. REISER and A. YAMIN

CDTEC,UFPEL,Pelotas/RS-Brazil

{benitez,reiser,adenauer}@inf.ufpel.edu.br,

B. BEDREGAL

DIMAP,UFRN,Natal/RN-Brazil

bedregal@dimap.ufrn.br

The aggregating fuzzy (S,N)-subimplications is obtained by the OWA-operator performed over the families of triangular sub(co)norms along with fuzzy negations. (S,N)-subimplications are characterized by the generalized associativity and distributive properties together with extensions of the exchange and neutrality principles. As the main results, these families of subimplications extend related S-implications by preserving their corresponding properties. We also discuss the action of automorphisms on such fuzzy implication classes.

Keywords: OWA-operators; fuzzy t-sub(co)norm; fuzzy (sub)implication.

1. Introduction

This paper deals with the current status of the theory of aggregation operators to obtain classes of fuzzy implications by considering extensions of associativity, exchange principle and distributivity properties. Differently of previous[1] related to the arithmetic media, here we focus on the ordered weighted average (OWA) operator, which is applied into a family of fuzzy connectives to generate new fuzzy connectives, preserving the same properties verified by the corresponding family. As the main contribution, this paper introduces the related class of aggregating fuzzy S-subimplications, describing the conjugate functions related to the member of such class.

2. Preliminaries

Consider concepts of fuzzy connectives[2,3] in the unit interval $U = [0, 1]$.

Definition 2.1. [4, Def. 0] A mapping $\rho: U \to U$ is an **order automorphism** if it is continuous, strictly increasing and verifies the boundary conditions $\rho(0)=0$ and $\rho(1)=1$, i.e., if it is an increasing bijection on U.

Order automorphisms are closed under composition and inverse operators. When $\rho(\vec{x}) = (\rho(x_1), \ldots, \rho(x_n)) \in U^n$, the action of an order automorphism ρ on a function $f \colon U^n \to U$, refereed as f^ρ and named **the ρ-conjugate of f**, is defined as $f^\rho(\vec{x}) = \rho^{-1}(f(\rho(\vec{x})))$, $\vec{x} = (x_1, \ldots, x_n) \in U^n$. The family of all automorphisms is referred as $Aut(U)$.

Proposition 2.1. *[5, Prop. 2.1] Let $\rho \in Aut(U)$, $\rho(xy) = \rho(x)\rho(y)$ iff there exists a real number $r > 0$ such that $\rho(x) = x^r$, for all $x, y \in U$.*

A **fuzzy negation** (FN) $N \colon U \to U$ satisfies:
N1 : $N(0) = 1$ and $N(1) = 0$; **N2** : If $x \geq y$ then $N(x) \leq N(y)$, $\forall\, x, y \in U$.
Fuzzy negations satisfying the involutive property are called **strong FNs**:
N3 : $N(N(x)) = x$, $\forall\, x \in U$.

The standard negation $N_S(x) = 1 - x$ is a strong fuzzy negation.

A **fuzzy subimplicator** $I \colon U^2 \to U$ satisfies the conditions:
I0 : $I(1,1) = I(0,1) = I(0,0) = 1$;
A fuzzy subimplicator $I \colon U^2 \to U$ also satisfying the boundary condition:
I1 : $I(1,0) = 0$;
is called **fuzzy implicator**. And, a fuzzy (sub)implicator I verifying:
I2 : If $x \leq z$ then $I(x,y) \geq I(z,y)$ (left antitonicity);
I3 : If $y \leq z$ then $I(x,y) \leq I(x,z)$ (right isotonicity);
I4 : $I(0,y) = 1$ (left boundary property);

is called a **fuzzy (sub)implication** [6, Def. 6].[7]

3. Aggregation functions

In [8, Def. 2], an *n*-ary *aggregation* function $A \colon U^n \to U$ demands, for all $\vec{x} = (x_1, x_2, \ldots, x_n)$, $\vec{y} = (y_1, y_2, \ldots, y_n) \in U^n$, the following conditions:

A1: Boundary Conditions $A(0,0,\ldots,0) = 0$ and $A(1,1,\ldots,1) = 1$;
A2: Monotonicity If $\vec{x} \leq \vec{y}$ then $A(\vec{x}) \leq A(\vec{y})$ where $\vec{x} \leq \vec{y}$ iff $x_i \leq y_i$, for all $0 \leq i \leq n$.

Some extra usual properties for aggregation functions are the following:

A3: Symmetry $A(\vec{x_\sigma}) = A(x_{\sigma_1}, \ldots, x_{\sigma_n}) = A(\vec{x})$, for all σ-permutation;
A4: Compensation $\min_{i=1}^n(x_i) \leq A(\vec{x}) \leq \max_{i=1}^n(x_i)$;
A5: Idempotency $A(x, x, \ldots, x) = x$, for all $x \in U$;
A6: Distributivity: $A(F(x, y_1), \ldots, F(x, y_n)) = F(x, A(y_1, \ldots, y_n))$, for all $x, y_1, \ldots, y_n \in U$ and $F \colon U^k \to U$.

The previous properties usually demanded from an aggregation function A can also be naturally extended to its conjugate function A^ρ.

Proposition 3.1. *Let $A \colon U^n \to U$ be a function and ρ be an order automorphism. For $i = \{1, \ldots, 5\}$, A^ρ satisfies **Ai** iff A satisfies **Ai**.*

Proposition 3.2. *Let* $\sigma\colon \mathbb{N}_n \to \mathbb{N}_n$, *with* $\mathbb{N}_n = \{1,\ldots,n\}$, *be a permutation ordering the elements:* $x_{\sigma(1)} \leq \ldots \leq x_{\sigma(n)}$. *Let* $w_1,\ldots,w_n$ *be non negative weights* $(w_i \leq 0)$ *such that* $\sum_{i=1}^{n} w_i = 1$. *The operator* $\mathcal{A}\colon U^n \to U$ *and its conjugate operator* $(\mathcal{A})^\rho\colon U^n \to U$, *respectively given as:*

$$\mathcal{A}(\vec{x}) = \sum_{i=1}^{n} w_i x_{\sigma(i)} \quad and \quad (\mathcal{A})^\rho(\vec{x}) = \rho^{-1} \sum_{i=1}^{n} w_i \rho(x_{\sigma(i)}), \qquad (1)$$

verify property **A**k, *for* $k \in \{3,4,5\}$.
Proof. Straightforward. □

A **triangular sub(co)norm** (t-sub(co)norm)[9] is a binary aggregation function $(S)T\colon U^2 \to U$ such that, for all $x,y \in U$, the following holds:

T0: $T(x,y) \leq \min(x,y)$;   **S0**: $S(x,y) \geq \max(x,y)$;

and also verifying the properties:

T1: $T(x,y) = T(y,x)$;   **S1**: $S(x,y) = S(y,x)$;
T2: $T(x,T(y,z))=T(T(x,y),z)$; **S2**: $S(x,S(y,z))=S(S(x,y),z)$;
T3: $T(x,z) \leq T(y,z)$, if $x \leq y$; **S3**: $S(x,z) \leq S(y,z)$, if $x \leq y$.

A **t-(co)norm** is a t-sub(co)norm satisfying the condition:

T4: $T(x,1) = x$;   **S4**: $S(x,0) = x$;

Proposition 3.3. *For* $i \geq 1, T_{P_i}(S_{P_i})\colon U^2 \to U$ *is a t-sub(co)norm given by*

$$T_{Pi}(x,y) = \frac{1}{i}xy, \quad \left(S_{Pi}(x,y) = 1 - \frac{1}{i}(1 - x - y + xy)\right) \forall x,y \in U. \quad (2)$$

Proof. Straightforward. □

The families of all t-sub(co)norms T_{Pi} (S_{Pi}) is referred as $\mathcal{T}_P$ $(\mathcal{S}_P)$. When $i = 1$, Eq.(2a) and Eq.(2b) are the product t-norm $T_P(x,y) = xy$ and the t-conorm named as algebraic sum $S_P(x,y) = x + y - xy$.

4. Fuzzy (S,N)-(sub)implication class

The main results considered in this section are reported from[1,4] and.[10] A function $I_{S,N}\colon U^2 \to U$ is called an (strong) **(S,N)-(sub)implication** if there exists a t-(sub)conorm S and a (strong) fuzzy negation N such that

$$I_{S,N}(x,y) = S(N(x),y), \forall x,y \in U. \qquad (3)$$

If N is a strong FN, then $I_{S,N}$ is called an **S-(sub)implication**. The family of all (S,N)-subimplicators is referred as $\mathcal{I}_{(S,N)}$.

Proposition 4.1. *[1, Prop. 4.10] The next statements are equivalent:*
1. $I \in \mathcal{I}_{(S,N)}$ *underlies a continuous FN* N *and a t-subconorm* S *at point* 0;

2. I is continuous at point $x = 1$ in the first component satisfying **I3** and the two additional conditions:

I5 : **Exchange Principle:** $I(x, I(y, z)) = I(y, I(x, z))$, $\forall x, y, z \in U$;
I6 : **Contrapositive Symmetry:** $I(x, y) = I(N(y), N(x))$, $\forall x, y \in U$.

Proposition 4.2. The binary function $I_{S_i} : U^2 \to U$, defined as

$$I_{S_i}(x, y) = 1 - \frac{1}{i}(x - xy), \ \forall i \geq 1, \forall x, y \in U, \tag{4}$$

is a strong fuzzy S-subimplication.

Proof. Taking $S_i(x, y) = 1 - \frac{1}{i}(1 - x - y + xy)$, for $i \leq 1$. S_i is clearly a t-subconorm, and we have that $S_i(N_S(x), y) = 1 - \frac{1}{i}(1 - (1-x) - y + (1-x)y) = 1 - \frac{1}{i}(x - xy)$. So, $I_{S_i}(x, y) = S_i(N_S(x), y)$ is an (S_i, N_S)-implication. $\square$

Proposition 4.3. [1, Prop. 4.10] An (S,N)-subimplication in $\mathcal{I}$ verifies Property $\mathbf{I_k}$, for $\mathbf{k} \in \{0, 2 \ldots, 6\}$.

Theorem 4.1. The operator $I_{S_i} : U^2 \to U$ is an (S_i, N_S)-implication underlying the continuous negation N_S and t-subconorm S_{P_i} at point 0.

Proof. Straightforward from Props. 4.1, 4.2 and 4.3. $\square$

5. Aggregating fuzzy connectives from the OWA-operator

Consider $A \colon U^n \to U$ as an n-ary aggregation function and $\mathcal{F} = \{F_i \colon U^k \to U\}$, with $i \in \{1, 2, \ldots, n\}$ as a family of functions.

Definition 5.1. [1, Prop. 5.1] An k-ary function $\mathcal{F}_A \colon U^k \to U$ is called as $(A, \mathcal{F})$-**operator on** U and given by:

$$\mathcal{F}_A(x_1, \ldots, x_k) = A(F_1(x_1, \ldots, x_k), \ldots, F_n(x_1, \ldots, x_k)). \tag{5}$$

Proposition 5.1. [1, Prop. 6.1] Let $A \colon U^n \to U$ be an aggregation and $(\mathcal{S})\mathcal{T} = \{(S_i)T_i \colon U^2 \to U\}$, with $i \in \{1, 2, \ldots, n\}$ be a family of t-sub(co)norms. Then the function $(S_A \colon U^2 \to U)$ $\mathcal{T}_A \colon U^2 \to U$, called $((A, \mathcal{S})$-operator) $(A, \mathcal{T})$-operator, is a t-sub(co)norm whenever the A satisfies property $\mathbf{A6}$ and for all i, j such that $0 \leq i, j \leq n$ and $x, y, z \in U$, each t-sub(co)norm T_i (S_i) satisfies the **generalized associativity**:

$$T_i(x, T_j(y, z)) = T_i(T_j(x, y), z); \quad S_i(x, S_j(y, z)) = S_i(S_j(x, y), z). \tag{6}$$

Proposition 5.2. For all $i, j \geq 1$, each pair $T_{P_i}, T_{P_j} \in \mathcal{T}_P$ and $S_{P_i}, S_{P_j} \in \mathcal{S}_P$ verifies Eqs. (6)a and (6)b, respectively.

Proof. For all x, y, $z \in U$, $T_{Pi}(x, T_{Pj}(y,z)) = T_{Pi}(x, \frac{1}{j}yz) = \frac{1}{ij}(xyz) = \frac{1}{i}(T_{Pj}(x,y) \cdot z) = T_{Pi}(T_{Pj}(x,y), z)$ Then, $\mathcal{T}_P$ satisfies the Eq.(6)a. The proof for $\mathcal{S}_P$ and related to Eq.(6) can be analogously obtained. $\qquad\square$

Proposition 5.3. *Based on the OWA-operator, Property* **A6** *is verified by both operators* $(\mathcal{S}_P)_\mathcal{A}, (\mathcal{T}_P)_\mathcal{A} \colon U^2 \to U$, *respectively given as follows*

$$(\mathcal{T}_P)_\mathcal{A}(x, \vec{y}) = \sum_{i=0}^{n} w_i T_{P\sigma(i)}(x,y) \quad (\mathcal{S}_P)_\mathcal{A}(x, \vec{y}) = \sum_{i=0}^{n} w_i S_{P\sigma(i)}(x,y). \qquad (7)$$

Proof. For all $x \in U$, $\vec{y} \in U^n$ and $T_i \in \mathcal{T}$, $(\mathcal{T}_P)_\mathcal{A}(x, \vec{y}) = \mathcal{A}(\frac{1}{i}x(y_1, \ldots, y_n)) = \frac{1}{i}x(w_1 y_{\sigma(1)}, \ldots, w_n y_{\sigma(n)}))$. Therefore, $(\mathcal{T}_P)_\mathcal{A}(x, \vec{y}) = \frac{1}{i}x\,\mathcal{A}(\vec{y}) = T_{Pi}(x, \mathcal{A}(\vec{y}))$. Therefore $(\mathcal{T}_P)_\mathcal{A}$ satisfies **A6**. $\qquad\square$

Corollary 5.1. *The operator* $((\mathcal{S}_P)_\mathcal{A})$ $(\mathcal{T}_P)_\mathcal{A}$ *is a t-sub(co)norm.*

Proof. Straightforward from Props. 5.1, 5.2 and 5.3. $\qquad\square$

The following proposition, states the conditions under which a fuzzy subimplication I_M verifies the generalized exchange principle.

Proposition 5.4. *[1, Prop. 7.1] Let $A \colon U^n \to U$ be an n-ary aggregation function and $\mathcal{I} = \{I_i \colon U^k \to U\}$, for $i \in \mathcal{K} = \{1, 2, \ldots, n\}$ be a family of fuzzy subimplication functions. $\mathcal{I}_A$ verifies* **I5** *if the aggregation A verifies* **A6** *and the* **Generalized Exchange Principle** *is held:*

I10: $I_i(x, I_j(y, z)) = I_i(y, I_j(x, z))$, $\forall x, y, z \in U$, $I_i, I_j \in \mathcal{I}$, $i, j \in \mathcal{K}$.

Proposition 5.5. *[1, Theom. 5.2] Let $A \colon U^n \to U$ be an n-ary idempotent aggregation and the family $\mathcal{I}_{(S_P, N_S)}$ of S-subimplications. For $k \in \{0, 2, 3, 4, 6\}$, $(\mathcal{I}_{(S_P, N_S)})_A$ verifies* **Ik** *if each $I_i \in \mathcal{I}_{(S_P, N_S)}$ verifies* **Ik**.

Now, the main properties of aggregating fuzzy (S,N)-subimplications obtained by considering the OWA-operator are described.

Proposition 5.6. *The operator $(\mathcal{I}_{(S_P, N_S)})_\mathcal{A}$ verifies* **I5**.

Proof. According to Prop. 5.4, we have the following. (i) For all $x, y_1, \ldots, y_n \in U$, $\mathcal{A}(I_{S_i}(x, y_1), \ldots, I_{S_i}(x, y_n)) = w_1(1 - \frac{1}{i}(x - xy_{\sigma(1)})), \ldots, w_n(1 - \frac{1}{i}(x - xy_{\sigma(n)})) = \sum_{i=0}^{n} w_i - \frac{1}{i}(x - x\sum_{i=0}^{n} w_i y_{\sigma(i)}) = 1 - \frac{1}{i}(x - x \cdot \mathcal{A}(\vec{y})) = I_{S_i}(x, \mathcal{A}(\vec{y}))$. Therefore, $\mathcal{A}$ verifies **A6**. (ii) And, for $I_{Pi_1}, I_{Pi_2} \in \mathcal{I}$, $I_{Pi_1}(x, I_{Pi_2}(y, z)) = I_{Pi_1}(x, 1 - \frac{1}{i_2}(y - yz)) = 1 - \frac{1}{i_1}(x - x(1 - \frac{1}{i_2}(y - yz))) = 1 - \frac{xy}{i_1 i_2} = 1 - \frac{1}{i_1}(y - y(1 - \frac{1}{i_2}(x - xz))) = I_{Pi_1}(y, I_{Pi_2}(x, z))$. So, $\mathcal{I}_A$ verifies **I10**. Concluding, $\mathcal{I}_A$ verifies **I5**. $\qquad\square$

Corollary 5.2. *The operator* $(\mathcal{I}_{(S_P,N_S)})_{\mathcal{A}}$ *is a S-subimplication given by*

$$\mathcal{I}_{\mathcal{A}}(x,y) = (\mathcal{S}_P)_{\mathcal{A}}(N_S(x),y) \tag{8}$$

Proof. Straightforward from Props. 5.1, 5.5 and 5.6. □

Proposition 5.7. *The action of an automorphism* ρ *on a S-subimplication* $(\mathcal{I}_{(S_P,N_S)})_{\mathcal{A}}$ *is also a S-subimplication given by*

$$(\mathcal{I}_{(S_P,N_S)_{\mathcal{A}}})^{\rho}(x,y) = (\mathcal{S}_P)_{\mathcal{A}^{\rho}}^{\rho}(N_S(x),y) \tag{9}$$

Proof. The following holds, since a sigma permutation σ preserved by an automorphism ρ: $(\mathcal{I}_{(S_P,N_S)_{\mathcal{A}}})^{\rho}(x,y) = \rho^{-1}\left(\mathcal{I}_{(S_P,N_S)_{\mathcal{A}}}(\rho(x),\rho(y))\right) = \sum_{i=0}^{n} w_i(I_{S_{P_{\sigma(i)}},N_S}(\rho(x),\rho(y)) = \sum_{i=0}^{n} w_i(1 - \frac{1}{\sigma(i)}(\rho(x) - \rho(x)\rho(y))) = \rho^{-1}\sum_{i=0}^{n} w_i\rho\left(S_{P_{\sigma(i)}}^{\rho}(x,y)\right) = \mathcal{I}_{(S_P^{\rho},\mathcal{A}^{\rho})}(x,y).$ □

6. Conclusion and Final Remarks

Conjugate fuzzy (S,N)-subimplications with respect to the OWA-operator were considered. Since such classes of subimplication are represented by t-sub(co)norms which are characterized by generalized associativity, the corresponding (S,N)-subimplications are characterized by distributive n-ary aggregation together with related generalizations, as the exchange and neutrality principles. Our perspectives considers the interrelations in classes of representable subimplications.

References

1. R. Reiser, B. Bedregal and M. Baczyński, *Inf. Science* **253**, 126 (2013).
2. B. Bedregal, G. Dimuro, R. Santiago and R. Reiser, *Inf. Science* **180**, 1373 (2010).
3. Y. Shi, B. V. Gasse, D. Ruan and E. E. Kerre, *Fuzzy Sets and Systems* **159**, 2988 (2008).
4. H. Bustince, P. Burillo and F. Soria, *Fuzzy Sets Systems* **134**, 209 (2003).
5. B. Bedregal, G. Dimuro, H. Bustince and E. Barrenechea, *Inf. Science* **249**, 148 (2013).
6. E. K. G. Cornelis, G. Deschrijver, *Intl. J. of Approx. Reasoning* , 55 (2004).
7. L. Kitainik, *Fuzzy Decision Procedures with Binary Relations* (Kluwer Academic Publisher, Dordrecht, 1993).
8. H. Bustince, T. Calvo, B. D. Baets, J. C. Fodor, R. Mesiar, J. Montero, D. Paternain and A. Pradera, *Information Science* **180**, 1977 (2010).
9. E. P. Klement, R. Mesiar and E. Pap, *Triangular Norms* (Kluwer Academic Publisher, Dordrecht, 2000).
10. M. Baczyński and B. Jayaram, *Fuzzy Sets and Systems* **159**, 1836 (2008).

QUASI-HOMOGENEOUS OVERLAP FUNCTIONS

L. M. COSTA

Department of Informatics and Applied Mathematics, Federal University of Rio Grande do Norte ,
Natal, Rio Grande do Norte 59078/970, Brazil
E-mail: lucelialimastm@gmail.com

B.R.C. BEDREGAL

Department of Informatics and Applied Mathematics, Federal University of Rio Grande do Norte ,
Natal, Rio Grande do Norte 59078/970, Brazil
E-mail: brcbedregal@gmail.com

In this paper, we studied the classes of quasi-homogeneous overlap functions. In which we demonstrate that all the class of quasi-homogeneous overlap functions properly contains the class of quasi-homogeneous t-norms, that is, all quasi-homogeneous t-norm is a quasi-homogeneous overlap function, but not all overlap function quasi-homogeneous is a quasi-homogeneous t-norm.

Keywords: Overlap functions; quasi-homogeneous; t-norms

1. Introduction

Homogeneity of order k of real functions reflects their regularity with respect to the inputs with same ratio in the form:

$$F(\lambda x_1, \cdots, \lambda x_n) = \lambda^k F(x_1, \cdots, x_n).$$

On the other hand, a generalized homogeneity should reflect the multiplicative constant λ as well as the original value $F(x1, \cdots, xn)$, and thus it should be expressed as:

$$F(\lambda x_1, \cdots, \lambda x_n) = G(\lambda, F(x_1, \cdots, x_n)),$$

where G is a binary function.

Ebanks[1] introduced the concept of quasi-homogeneity considering $G(a, b) = \varphi^{-1}(f(a)\varphi(b))$, with φ be a strictly monotone and continuous function and

f an arbitrary function. Hence a function F is called quasi-homogeneous if

$$F(\lambda x_1, \cdots, \lambda x_n) = \varphi^{-1}(f(\lambda)\varphi(F(x_1, \cdots, x_n))).$$

Overlap functions were defined by Bustince[4] where he proposed the construction of a method and analyzed the conditions ensuring that t-norms are overlap functions. It's essentially characterized by symmetry and the properties of monotonicity . Mesiar[6] discussed the class of quasi-homogeneous copulas through its representation and characterization. As a consequence, constructed a new method for copulas when only their diagonal section is known, is obtained.

Based on paper Mesiar,[6] discussed the class of quasi- homogeneous overlap functions through their representation and characterization. In the next section, we show some notions and results on overlap functions, ho- mogeneity of t-norms and quasi- homogeneity of t-norms . In section 3, we represent and characterize the quasi- homogeneous overlap functions through theorems and corollaries . Finally, some concluding remarks are included.

2. Preliminaries

Some concepts and results on overlap functions, can be found in.[5] Recall that a binary function $\mathcal{B} : [0,1]^2 \to [0,1]$ is said to be a overlap function if it satisfies the following properties:

1) $\mathcal{B}$ is symmetric;
2) $\mathcal{B}(x,y) = 0$ if and only if $xy = 0$;
3) $\mathcal{B}(x,y) = 1$ if and only if $xy = 1$;
4) $\mathcal{B}$ is non-decreasing;
5) $\mathcal{B}$ is continuous.

Corollary 2.1.[3] $\mathcal{B} : [0,1]^2 \to [0,1]$ *is an associative overlap function if and only if $\mathcal{B}$ is a continuous and positive t-norm.*

Definition 2.1. A function $F : [0,1]^2 \to [0,1]$ is said to be homogeneous of order $k > 0$ if it satisfies

$$F(\alpha x, \alpha y) = \alpha^k F(x,y), \forall x, y, \alpha \in [0,1].$$

The homogeneity condition has been characterized for T-norms as well as for overlap functions and the results are as follows:

Theorem 2.1.[2] *A t-norm T is homogeneous of order k if and only if either $k = 1$ and T is the minimum t-norm, or $k = 2$ and T is the product t-norm.*

Proposition 2.1. *Let $F_i : [0,1]^2 \to [0,1]$ be a finite family of homogeneous functions of order k_i and $F : [0,1]^2 \to [0,1]$ their convex sum for the respective weights $w_i, i = 1, \cdots, n$ and $\sum_{i=1}^{n} w_i = 1$. Then, F is homogeneous of order k if and only if for each i with $w_i > 0$, it holds that $k_i = k$.*

Proof. $\Rightarrow$) See[3]

$\Leftarrow$) Consider $k_i = k$ for all $i \in I$ and $w_i > 0$. Then

$$F(\alpha x, \alpha y) = \sum_{i \in I} w_i F_i(\alpha x, \alpha y) = \sum_{i \in I} w_i \alpha^{k_i} F_i(x,y) = \sum_{i \in I} w_i \alpha^{k} F_i(x,y)$$

$$= \alpha^k \sum_{i \in I} w_i F_i(x,y).$$

Therefore,

$$\alpha^k \sum_{i \in I} w_i F_i(x,y) = \alpha^k F(x,y).$$

$\square$

Proposition 2.2.[3] *A function $F : [0,1]^2 \to [0,1]$ is homogeneous of order k and has 1 as neutral element if and only if*

$$F(x,y) = \begin{cases} 0 & se\ x = y = 0 \\ \frac{y}{x} x^k & se\ x \neq 0 \land y \leq x \\ \frac{x}{y} y^k & se\ y \neq 0 \land y > x, \end{cases} \tag{1}$$

Note that in equation (1) if $k = 1$, then F is the minimum t-norm, and if $k = 2$, F is the product t-norm.

Theorem 2.2. [3] *For any $k \geq 1$, the function $F : [0,1]^2 \to [0,1]$, defined in (1), is an overlap function.*

The following result is immediate.

Corollary 2.2. *The unique overlap function that is homogeneous of order $k \geq 1$ and has 1 as neutral element is the function $F : [0,1]^2 \to [0,1]$ defined in (1).*

The following proposition states that the smaller the homogeneous overlap function is, the greater its homogeneity order. However, to guarantee the converse is required 1 as the neutral element.

Proposition 2.3.[3] *Let $\mathcal{O}_1, \mathcal{O}_2 : [0,1]^2 \to [0,1]$ be homogeneous overlap functions of order k_1 e k_2, respectively. then, it holds that:*

i) If $\mathcal{O}_1 \leq_\mathcal{O} \mathcal{O}_2$ then $k_1 \geq k_2$;
ii) Whenever $\mathcal{O}_1$ and $\mathcal{O}_2$ have 1 as neutral element, if $k_1 \geq k_2$ then $\mathcal{O}_1 \leq_\mathcal{O} \mathcal{O}_2$.

3. Quasi-homogeneous

Many studies have been made on generalizations of the homogeneity condition, specially in the framework of t-norms. One of these generalizations of homogeneity was introduced by Ebanks [1], where he extended homogeneous t-norms for quasi-homogeneous t-norms, that is, for t-norms T satisfying

$$\varphi(T(\lambda x, \lambda y)) = f(\lambda)\varphi(T(x,y)), \forall x, y, \lambda \in I,$$

where $\varphi : I \to \mathbb{R}$ is continuous and strictly monotonic and $f : I \to I$ is arbitrary.

Definition 3.1.[6] A function $F : [0,1]^2 \to [0,1]$ is said to be quasi- homogeneous if there exists a continuous, strictly monotonic function $\varphi : [0,1] \to \mathbb{R}$ and a function $f : [0,1] \to [0,1]$ such that

$$F(\lambda x, \lambda y) = \varphi^{-1}(f(\lambda)\varphi(F(x,y))), \forall x, y, \lambda \in [0,1].$$

In this case it will be said that F is (φ, f)-quasi-homogeneous. Quasi- homogeneous t-norms have been characterized allowing for new solutions.

Theorem 3.1.[2] *A t-norm T is quasi-homogeneous if and only if is a member of the family T_α with $0 \leq \alpha \leq +\infty$, where*

$$T_\alpha(x,y) = (x^{-\alpha} + y^{-\alpha} - 1)^{-1/\alpha} \text{ to } 0 < \alpha < \infty.$$

$T_0 = T_p$ *is the product t-norm and $T_{+\infty} = T_M$ is the minimum t- norm.*

Here, $f_\alpha(\lambda) = \lambda^c$ with $c > 0$ arbitrary, and for all $\alpha \in [0, +\infty]$, and φ_α are given

$$\varphi_\alpha(x) = k(1 + x^\alpha)^{-c/\alpha} \text{ to } 0 < \alpha < +\infty.$$

and

$$\varphi_0(x) = kx^{c/2} \text{ and } \varphi_{+\infty}(x) = kx^c, \text{ with } k \neq 0.$$

4. Quasi-homogeneous overlap functions

In this section, we will represent and characterize the quasi-homogeneous overlap functions that satisfy the definition 3.1.

Proposition 4.1. *Let F be a homogeneous function as defined in (1). Let $\varphi(x) = x^r$ be with $r > 0$; and $f(x) = \varphi(x)^k$, then F is an overlap function (φ, f)-quasi-homogeneous.*

Proof. By Theorem 2.2 have that F is a overlap function. The following we will show that F is a overlap function (φ, f)-quasi-homogeneous.
Case 1: If $\lambda x = \lambda y = 0 \Rightarrow x = y = 0$ or $\lambda = 0$ then
$F(\lambda x, \lambda y) = 0$.
If $x = y = 0$, then

$$\varphi^{-1}(f(\lambda)\varphi(F(x,y))) = \varphi^{-1}(0) = 0 = F(\lambda x, \lambda y).$$

If $\lambda = 0$ then

$$\varphi^{-1}(f(\lambda)\varphi(F(x,y))) = \varphi^{-1}(f(0)\varphi(F(x,y)))$$
$$= \varphi^{-1}(0) = 0 = F(\lambda x, \lambda y).$$

So, in this case

$$F(\lambda x, \lambda y) = \varphi^{-1}(f(\lambda)\varphi(F(x,y))).$$

Case 2: If $\lambda x \neq 0$ and $\lambda y \leq \lambda x \Rightarrow x \neq 0, \lambda \neq 0$ e $y \leq x$, then

$$F(\lambda x, \lambda y) = \frac{y}{x}(\lambda x)^k.$$

Therefore,

$$\varphi^{-1}(f(\lambda)\varphi(F(x,y))) = \varphi^{-1}\left(\varphi(\lambda)^k\varphi\left(\frac{y}{x}x^k\right)\right)$$
$$= \sqrt[r]{\left(\lambda^k\frac{y}{x}x^k\right)^r} = \frac{y}{x}(\lambda x)^k = F(\lambda x, \lambda y).$$

So, in this case

$$F(\lambda x, \lambda y) = \varphi^{-1}(f(\lambda)\varphi(F(x,y))).$$

The case 3 is similar.
Thus, F is an overlap function (φ, f)-quasi-homogeneous.

□

Theorem 4.1. *All quasi-homogeneous t-norm is a quasi-homogeneous overlap function.*

Proof. Let T be a quasi-homogeneous t-norm, then by the theorem 3.1, T is a member of the family T_α with $0 < \alpha < 1$. By Corollary 2.1, to prove that T is a quasi-homogeneous overlap function, we need to show that T is continuous and positive. It is easy to see that T is continuous. So, it remains to show that T is positive. Supose that $T_\alpha(x; y) = 0$ for some $x, y \in (0, 1)$. Without loss of generality we can assume that $x \leq y$. Since T_α is increasing, then $T_\alpha(x; x) = 0$. On the other hand,

$$
\begin{aligned}
T_\alpha(x, x) &= (x^{-\alpha} + x^{-\alpha} - 1)^{\frac{-1}{\alpha}} \\
&= \frac{1}{(2x^{-\alpha} - 1)^{\frac{1}{\alpha}}} \\
&= \frac{1}{x(2 - x^\alpha)^{\frac{1}{\alpha}}}.
\end{aligned}
$$

So, because $x \neq 0$, then $T_\alpha(x, x) \neq 0$ which is a contradiction. Therefore, $T_\alpha(x, y) \neq 0$ for each $x, y \in (0; 1)$, that is, T_α is positive.

5. Conclusion

In this paper we conclude that all the class of quasi-homogeneous overlap functions properly contains the class of quasi-homogeneous t-norms, that is, all quasi-homogeneous t-norm is a quasi-homogeneous overlap function, but not all overlap function quasi-homogeneous is a quasi-homogeneous t-norm.

References

1. Ebanks B. R. Ebanks. Quasi-homogeneous associative functions.*Internal. J. Math. Sci.* (21), 351-358, (1998).
2. Alsina C. Alsina, M. J. Frank & B. Schweizer. Associative functions. Triangular norms and copulas. *World Scientific Publishing Co.*, Singapore (2006).
3. Bedregal B. C. Bedregal, G. P. Dimuro, H. Bustince & E. Barrenechea. New results on overlap and grouping functions. *Information Sciences*, (2013).
4. Bustince2 H. Bustince, J. Fernández, R. Mesiar & R. Orduna. Overlap functions. *Nonlinear Analisis* (72) (3-4)1488-1499, (2010).
5. Bustince3 H. Bustince, M. Pagola, R. Mesiar, F. Herrera & E. Hüllermeier. Grouping, Overlap, and generalized Bi-entropic functions for fuzzy modeling of pairwise comparisons. *IEEE Transactions on Fuzzy Systems* 20 (3), 906-929, (2012).
6. Mesiar R. Mesiar & J. Torrens. On quasi-homogeneous copulas. *Kybernetika*, (44), number 6, page 745-756, (2008).

INVERSE LIMITS IN FUZZY DYNAMICAL SYSTEMS INDUCED BY INTERVAL MAPS

J. P. Boroński and J. Kupka

Institute for Research and Applications of Fuzzy Modeling -
Centre of Excellence IT4Innovations -
University of Ostrava,
30. dubna 22, 701 03 Ostrava, Czech Republic
E-mails: Jan.Boronski@osu.cz, Jiri.Kupka@osu.cz
www: irafm.osu.cz

Within this contribution we establish a theoretical background necessary for studying inverse limits of fuzzy dynamical systems induced by crisp (non-fuzzy) ones. First, we elaborate topological properties of the space of fuzzy sets, such as connectedness and compactness. Second, we focus our attention on dynamical conditions sufficient for the existence of indecomposable continua in the inverse limit space.

Keywords: Fuzzy dynamical system; Zadeh's extension, inverse limit spaces.

1. Introduction

This short paper contributes to theory of inverse limit spaces and fuzzy dynamical systems. There has been a lot of attention (Ref. 1,2) to the problem of relating the dynamical behavior of a map and the topological structure of respective inverse limit space. For instance, Barge and Martin[1] showed that for an interval map $\varphi : I \to I$ which is chaotic (reps. turbulent) its inverse limit space X_φ must contain an indecomposable subcontinuum, and they also showed (Ref. 2) that this inverse limit can be realized as an attractor of some planar homeomorphism $\varphi : \mathbb{R}^2 \to \mathbb{R}^2$.

This work follows recent work devoted to our study of fuzzy dynamical systems that are induced by ordinary (non-fuzzy) ones (Ref. 3–5). We have started to study inverse limit spaces of such fuzzy dynamical systems. Within this work we are able to mention only a few initial results and only ideas of their proofs - we elaborate some topological properties of various spaces of fuzzy sets (Section 3) and we show that inverse limit spaces of fuzzy dynamical systems induced by a huge class of (turbulent) interval maps possess an indecomposable subcontinuum (Section 4). Before showing these results we have to introduce some basic notions.

2. Definitions

2.1. *Fuzzy mathematics, notation*

Throughout this paper $\mathbb{R}$ denotes the set of real numbers and I denotes the closed unit interval $[0, 1]$. Now we recall some basic notions from fuzzy mathematics. A *fuzzy set* A on a given metric space (X, d_X) (resp. universum, universal space) is a map $A : X \to I$. Further, for any $\alpha \in (0, 1]$, an α-*cut* $[A]_\alpha$ of A is defined by $[A]_\alpha := \{x \in X \,|\, A(x) \geq \alpha\}$. It should be mentioned that if a fuzzy set A is upper semi-continuous then every α-cut is a closed subset of X. A *support* $supp(A)$ of a given fuzzy set A is defined as $supp(A) = \overline{\{x \in X \,|\, A(x) > 0\}}$ where $\overline{\{\ldots\}}$ denotes a topological closure.

An *empty* fuzzy set is the function $\emptyset_X : X \to I$ which is identically equal to 0 on X. The space of non-empty fuzzy sets on X is denoted by $\mathbb{F}(X)$. A fuzzy set A is *normal* if $A(x) = 1$ for some $x \in X$. The space of normal upper semi-continuous fuzzy sets on X with compact supports is denoted by $\mathbb{F}^1(X)$. Since X is equipped with some topological structure, by $\mathbb{F}_k(X)$ we denote fuzzy sets from $\mathbb{F}(X)$ for which α-cuts consist of at most k connected components. Then we can intuitively combine our notation, e.g. $\mathbb{F}^1_2(X)$ contains normal upper semi-continuous fuzzy sets for which every α-cut has at most two connected components etc. Especially, $\mathbb{F}^1_1(X)$ denotes a system of fuzzy sets on the interval X which are usually called *fuzzy numbers*.

2.2. *Metrics*

Before we define metrics on the space $\mathbb{F}(X)$ of fuzzy sets, we need to introduce some notions on the space $\mathbb{K}(X)$ of nonempty closed subsets of X. The space $\mathbb{K}(X)$ is equipped with the metric topology induced by well-known Hausdorff metric D_X on the space X defined as follows. The *Hausdorff metric* D_X between $A, B \in \mathbb{K}(X)$ is defined, as usual, by

$$D_X(A, B) = \inf\{\varepsilon > 0 \,|\, A \subseteq U_\varepsilon(B) \text{ and } B \subseteq U_\varepsilon(A)\},$$

where $U_\varepsilon(A) = \{x \in X \,|\, D(x, A) < \varepsilon\}$ and $D(x, A) = \inf_{a \in A} d_X(x, a)$. It is well known that $(\mathbb{K}(X), D_X)$ is compact, complete and separable whenever X is compact, complete and separable. We are ready to define metrics on the space of fuzzy sets $\mathbb{F}(X)$.

We use the following notation - for any $A \in \mathbb{F}(X)$,

$$end(A) = \{(x, a) \in X \times I \mid A(x) \geq a\} \tag{1}$$

is the so-called *endograph* of A and

$$send(A) = end(A) \cap (supp(A) \times I) \tag{2}$$

denotes the *sendograph* (abr. *supported endograph*) of the fuzzy set A.

The most frequently used metric is probably the *supremum* metric d_∞ defined as $d_\infty(A, B) = \sup_{\alpha \in (0,1]} D_X([A]_\alpha, [B]_\alpha)$ for $A, B \in \mathbb{F}^1(X)$. Further, the *sendograph* metric $d_S(A, B) = D_{X \times I}(send(A), send(B))$ is defined only for nonempty fuzzy sets $A, B \in \mathbb{F}(X)$. And finally, the *endograph* metric d_E is defined correctly for any two $A, B \in \mathbb{F}(X)$ by $d_E(A, B) = D_{X \times I}(end(A), end(B))$. For basic properties and constructions of metric spaces of fuzzy sets we refer e.g. to Ref. 4 and references therein. Below we use the following relationship among metrics defined above - for $A, B \in \mathbb{F}(X)$,

$$d_E(A, B) \leq d_S(A, B) \leq d_\infty(A, B). \tag{3}$$

2.3. Dynamical systems

A discrete dynamical system is a pair (X, f) where X is a metric space and $f : X \to X$ is continuous. A *continuum* is a compact and connected metric space containing at least two points. A continuum is *decomposable* if it is the union of two proper subcontinua. A continuum is *indecomposable* if it is not decomposable. We call a map $f : X \to X$ is *turbulent* if there are continua Y, U and V such that $f(U) = f(V) = Y$ and $int(U) \cap int(V) = \emptyset$. It is also known that turbulence of $f : X \to X$ implies turbulence of the extension $\hat{f}$ (Ref. 7). Finally, for the definition of a *topoogical entropy* of f we refer to Ref. 6.

2.4. Zadeh's extension

It is currently well known that any map $f : X \to Y$ can be naturally extended to a map $\hat{f} : \mathbb{F}(X) \to \mathbb{F}(Y)$. This map is called a *fuzzification* (or *Zadeh's extension*) of the map $f : X \to Y$ and is defined by the expression

$$(\hat{f}(A))(x) = \sup_{y \in f^{-1}(x)} \{A(y)\} \tag{4}$$

for arbitrary $A \in \mathbb{F}(X)$ and $x \in X$. Fuzzy extensions of f were already studied in several papers (e.g. Ref. 4 and references therein). For instance, it is known that $\hat{f}$ is continuous, if the particular spaces of fuzzy sets are equipped with metric topologies induced by the metrics above, provided $f : X \to Y$ is continuous as well.

2.5. *Inverse limit spaces*

Suppose a map $f : X \to X$ is given on a metric space X. The *inverse limit space* $X_\leftarrow = \varprojlim\{f, X\}$ is the space given by

$$X_\leftarrow = \{(x_1, x_2, x_3, \ldots) \in X^{\mathbb{N}} : f(x_{i+1}) = x_i\}.$$

The topology of $X_\leftarrow$ is induced from the product topology of $X^{\mathbb{N}}$, with the basic open sets in $X_\leftarrow$ given by

$$U_\leftarrow = (f^{i-1}(U), f^{i-2}(U), \ldots, U, f^{-1}(U), f^{-2}(U), \ldots),$$

where U is an open subset of the i-th factor space X. The map f is called a *bonding map*. To emphasize the interplay between topology and dynamics of inverse limit spaces we can state the following results.

Theorem 2.1. *(Ref. 2) If G is a graph and $f : G \to G$ is a map then $G_f = \varprojlim\{f, G\}$ can be embedded in a sphere $\mathbb{S}^n$ of dimension at most $n = 4$, so that G_f is a global attractor of a homeomorphism $h : \mathbb{S}^n \to \mathbb{S}^n$ and*

$$h|G_f = \sigma_f.$$

Indecomposable continua allows us to "classify" interval dynamical systems. For instance, Barge & Martin in Ref. 1 also showed that if $f : [0, 1] \to [0, 1]$ is chaotic then $\varprojlim\{f, [0, 1]\}$ contains an indecomposable subcontinuum. They also proved that if $f : [0, 1] \to [0, 1]$ is piecewise linear and topological entropy is zero then $\varprojlim\{f, [0, 1]\}$ does not contain an indecomposable subcontinuum.

3. Connectedness, compactness etc.

It is known that $(\mathbb{K}(X), D_X)$ is compact and connected whenever the space X is compact and connected. In this section we summarize the same properties for various spaces of fuzzy sets.

3.1. *Compactness*

In this subsection we assume that X is a compact metric space. Then it is known (e.g. in Ref. 4 and references therein) that $(\mathbb{F}(X), d_E)$ (resp

$(\mathbb{F}_k^1(X), d_E)$ for $k \in \mathbb{N}$) is compact, but $(\mathbb{F}(X), d_\infty)$, $(\mathbb{F}(X), d_S)$ (resp $(\mathbb{F}_k^1(X), d_\infty)$, $(\mathbb{F}_k^1(X), d_S)$ for $k \in \mathbb{N}$) are not compact.

3.2. Connectedness

In this section we study connectedness of spaces of fuzzy set over a connected compact subset $X = J \subseteq \mathbb{R}$. Below we use the fact that every path-connected topological space is connected.

Lemma 3.1. *The space* $(\mathbb{F}_1^1(X), d_\infty)$ *is path connected, and hence connected.*

Proof. It is sufficient to show that the space $(\mathbb{F}_1^1(X), d_\infty)$ is path connected. Let $A, B \in \mathbb{F}_1^1(I)$ be such that $A \neq B$. We will find a path γ between A and B, i.e. a continuous map $\gamma : I \to \mathbb{F}_1^1(I)$ such that $\gamma(0) = A$ and $\gamma(1) = B$. Within this proof we use the fact that fuzzy sets can be "reconstructed" with the help of their α-cuts and the path γ is then constructed with the help of convex combinations of α-cuts of A and B. $\quad\square$

Due to space reasons we cannot provide proofs of the following statements. They will be provided in the extended version of this contribution. It can be proven that we can expect connectedness in many subspaces of fuzzy sets.

Lemma 3.2. *For any* $k \in \mathbb{N}$, *the space* $(\mathbb{F}_k^1(X), d_\infty)$ *is path connected, and hence connected.*

Lemma 3.3. *The space* $(\mathbb{F}^1(X), d_\infty)$ *is connected.*

According to (3), we can obtain the following consequences.

Corollary 3.1. *For any* $k \in \mathbb{N}$ *and* $d \in \{d_E, d_S\}$, *the space* $(\mathbb{F}_k^1(X), d)$ *is path connected, and hence connected.*

Corollary 3.2. *For* $d \in \{d_E, d_S\}$, *the space* $(\mathbb{F}(X), d)$ *is path connected, and hence connected.*

4. Inverse limit spaces of fuzzy dynamical systems

Here we present the main result of this contribution describing a part of the inverse limit space of some induced fuzzy dynamical systems.

Theorem 4.1. *Suppose that* $f : X \to X$ *is a turbulent map on a continuum. Then* $\hat{X}_{\hat{f}} = \varprojlim\{\hat{f}, \mathbb{F}^1(X)\}$ *contains an indecomposable subcontinuum.*

Proof. The idea of the proof is the following. It is well known that a continuum K is indecomposable if and only if for every subcontinuum $C \subseteq K$ we have $int(C) = \emptyset$. As f is turbulent so is $\hat{f}$. Without loss of generality we may assume that there are subcontinua U and V such that $\hat{f}(U) = \hat{f}(V) = \mathbb{F}^1(X)$ and $int(U) \cap int(V) = \emptyset$. By contradiction, suppose there is a subcontinuum $C \subseteq \hat{X}_{\hat{f}}$ such that $int(C) \neq \emptyset$. Let C_n be its projection onto the n-th factor space. Then $C_{n+1} \cap int(U) = \emptyset$ or $C_{n+1} \cap int(V) = \emptyset$. However, for any open set $W \subseteq \hat{X}_{\hat{f}}$ we must have that $W_i \cap U \neq \emptyset$ and $W_i \cap V \neq \emptyset$ so we obtain a contradiction. $\square$

5. Conclusions

Within this work we elaborate a part theoretical background necessary for studying inverse limit spaces of fuzzy dynamical systems. We also proved that, for majority of interval maps (e.g. Ref. 8), inverse limit spaces of their fuzzy extensions contain an indecomposable subcontinuum. Due to space reasons we could not provide full proofs and other results related to this topic.

Acknowledgments

This work was supported by the European Regional Development Fund in the IT4Innovations Centre of Excellence project (CZ.1.05/1.1.00/02.0070).

References

1. M. Barge, J. Martin, *Chaos, periodicity, and snakelike continua*, Trans. Amer. Math. Soc. **289** (1985), No. 1, 355–365.
2. M. Barge, J. Martin, *The construction of global attractors*, Proc. Amer. Math. Soc. **110** (1990), No. 2, 523–525.
3. J. S. Cánovas and J. Kupka, *On the topological entropy on the space of fuzzy numbers*, Fuzzy Sets and Systems, Available online 30 May 2013, http://dx.doi.org/10.1016/j.fss.2013.05.013.
4. J. Kupka, *On Fuzzifications of Discrete Dynamical Systems*, Information Sciences **181** (2011), 13, pp. 2858–2872.
5. J. Kupka, *On Devaney chaotic induced dynamical systems*, Fuzzy Sets and Systems **177** (2011), Iss 1, pp. 34–44.
6. R. Bowen, *Entropy for group endomorphism and homogeneous spaces,* Trans. Amer. Math. Soc. **153** (1971), 401–414.
7. H. Román-Flores, Y. Chalco-Cano, G.N. Silva, J. Kupka, *Chaos, Solitons & Fractals* **44** (2011), No. 11, 990–994.
8. L. S. Block and W. A. Coppel, *Dynamics in one dimension*, Lecture Notes in Mathematics, **1513** Springer-Verlag, Berlin, 1992.

EXTENSION OF N-DIMENSIONAL LATTICE-VALUED NEGATIONS

E. S. Palmeira

Departamento de Ciências Exatas e Tecnológicas
Universidade Estadual de Santa Cruz - UESC,
Ilhéus, 45662-900, Brazil
* E-mail: espalmeira@uesc.br

B. C. Bedregal

Departamento de Informática e Matemática Aplicada
Universidade Federal do Rio Grande do Norte
Natal, 59078-970, Brazil
E-mail: bedregal@ufrn.dimap.br

In this paper we apply a method to extend n-dimensional lattice-valued fuzzy negations by preserving the largest possible number of properties of these negations which are invariants under homomorphisms. Further, we also prove some related results and properties.

Keywords: Lattice; n-dimensional negation; extension; e-operator.

1. Introdution

Let L and K be nonempty sets and suppose that $M \subseteq L$. Given a function $f : M \longrightarrow K$, if we want to extend the domain of f to cover the whole L, what is the best choice to define $f(x)$ for the elements $x \in L \backslash M$ in order to preserve the largest possible number of properties of f? This a very complex problem and a answer for this question is not so simple.

Palmeira et al.[8] provided a method to extend t-norms, t-conorms and fuzzy negations using a special mapping (namely e-operator). Also in this work, we apply this extension method for n-dimensional t-norms. As a natural consequence of our researches we discuss here about the extension of n-dimensional fuzzy negations.

We begin in Section 2 recalling some definitions and results related to lattices, lattice homomorphisms, retractions, sublattices and fuzzy negations. Also in this section, we present the notion of (r, s)-sublattices and describe the extension method via e-operators. Sections 3 is devoted to discuss about n-dimensional negations on $L_n(L)$ and it extension.

2. Preliminaries

Let L be a nonempty set. If $\wedge_L$ and $\vee_L$ are two binary operations on L, then $\langle L, \wedge_L, \vee_L \rangle$ is a *lattice* provided that for each $x, y, z \in L$, the following properties hold:

(1) $x \wedge_L y = y \wedge_L x$ and $x \vee_L y = y \vee_L x$;
(2) $(x \wedge_L y) \wedge_L z = x \wedge_L (y \wedge_L z)$ and $(x \vee_L y) \vee_L z = x \vee_L (y \wedge_L z)$;
(3) $x \wedge_L (x \vee_L y) = x$ and $x \vee_L (x \wedge_L y) = x$.

If in $\langle L, \wedge_L, \vee_L \rangle$ there are elements 0 and 1 such that, for all $x \in L$, $x \wedge_L 1 = x$ and $x \vee_L 0 = x$, then $\langle L, \wedge_L, \vee_L, 0, 1 \rangle$ is called a *bounded lattice*.

Definition 2.1. A homomorphism r of a lattice L onto a lattice M is said to be a retraction if there exists a homomorphism s of M into L which satisfies $r \circ s = id_M$. A lattice M is called a retract of a lattice L if there is a retraction r, of L onto M, and s is then called a pseudo-inverse of r.

Definition 2.2. Let L and M be arbitrary bounded lattices. We say that M is a (r, s)-sublattice of L if M is a retract of L (i.e. M is a sublattice of L up to isomorphisms). In other words, M is a (r, s)-sublattice of L if there is a retraction r of L onto M with pseudo-inverse $s : M \to L$.

Definition 2.3. Every retraction $r : L \longrightarrow M$ (with pseudo-inverse s) which satisfies $s \circ r \leqslant id_L$[a] ($id_L \leqslant s \circ r$) is called a lower (an upper) retraction. In this case, M is a lower (an upper) retract of L.

Definition 2.4. Let M be a (r_1, s)-sublattice of L. If r_1 is a lower retraction and there is an upper retraction $r_2 : L \longrightarrow M$ such that its pseudo-inverse is also s, then M is called a full (r_1, r_2, s)-sublattice of L. Notation: $M \trianglelefteq L$ with respect to (r_1, r_2, s).

Definition 2.5.[1] A function $N : L \longrightarrow L$ is called a fuzzy negation if it satisfies:

(1) $N(0_L) = 1_L$ and $N(1_L) = 0_L$;
(2) If $x \leqslant_L y$ then $N(y) \leqslant_L N(x)$, for all $x, y \in L$.

---

[a] If f and g are functions on a lattice L it is said that $f \leqslant g$ if and only if $f(x) \leqslant_L g(x)$ for all $x \in L$.

Involutive property:

$$N(N(x)) = x, \forall x \in L \tag{1}$$

Equivalence Point:

$$N(x) = x \tag{2}$$

2.1. Extension Method via e-operators

To solve the problem of extending fuzzy logic connectives we have developed in[6-8] a special operators which plays a fundamental hole in our extension method. In which follows we define this operator and present some relevant properties of it.

Definition 2.6. Let $M \trianglelefteq L$ with respect to (r_1, r_2, s). A mapping $\odot :$ $M \times M \longrightarrow L$ is called an *e-operator on M* if it is isotonic and satisfies, for each $a, b \in M$ and for each $x \in L$, the following conditions:

$$r_1(a \odot b) = a \wedge_M b \quad and \quad r_2(a \odot b) = a \vee_M b \tag{3}$$

$$r_1(x) \odot r_2(x) = x \tag{4}$$

In other words, if $M \trianglelefteq L$ with respect to (r_1, r_2, s) (by Definition 2.4, there are two retractions $r_1, r_2 : L \longrightarrow M$ with the same pseudo-inverse $s : M \longrightarrow L$ such that $s \circ r_1 \leqslant id_L \leqslant s \circ r_2$) the e-operator $\odot$ describes an isotonic way to relate retractions r_1 and r_2 with the meet and join operators of M, respectively, by (3).

Lemma 2.1. *Consider $M \trianglelefteq L$ with respect to (r_1, r_2, s) and let $\odot$ be an e-operator on M. Then, for all $a, b \in M$ and $x, y \in L$, the following properties hold:*

(1) $a \leqslant_M b$ if and only if $r_1(a \odot b) = a$ and $r_2(a \odot b) = b$;
(2) For every $a \in M$ we have $s(a) = a \odot a$;
(3)

$$r_1(x) \leqslant_M r_1(y) \ and \ r_2(x) \leqslant_M r_2(y) \ iff \ x \leqslant_L y; \tag{5}$$

(4) $r_1(x) = r_1(y)$ and $r_2(x) = r_2(y)$ if and only if $x = y$;
(5) $\odot$ is commutative.

Theorem 2.1. *Let $M \unlhd L$ with respect to (r_1, r_2, s) and $\odot$ an e-operator on M. If N is a fuzzy negation on M, then $N_\odot^E(x) = N(r_1(x)) \odot N(r_2(x))$ is a fuzzy negation on L. Moreover,*

(1) If N is involutive (i.e., it satisfies (1)) then $N_\odot^E$ is also involutive.

(2) If a is an equilibrium point of fuzzy negation N then $s(a)$ is an equilibrium point of $N_\odot^E$.

3. On n-dimensional Negations

The n-dimensional fuzzy set theory has been studied as a way to generalize the fuzzy set theory valued to the simplex $L_n([0,1]) = \{x = (x_1, x_2, \ldots, x_n) \in [0,1]^n \mid x_1 \leqslant x_2 \leqslant \cdots \leqslant x_n\}$ for a fixed $n \in \mathbb{N} - \{0\}$ (see[9]). We think about the fuzzy operators (t-norms, t-conorms and fuzzy negations) on $L_n([0,1])$. For $n = 2$, a good formalization about interval-valued fuzzy logic is given by Deschrijver and partners in.[3–5] Recent studies for arbitrary n have been done by Bedregal et al. in[2] where a formalization of n-dimensional aggregation functions, particulary t-norms, fuzzy negations and automorphisms on $L_n([0,1])$ is carried out.

Based on this framework, an interesting issue is the generalization of lattice-valued aggregation functions to higher dimension using a bounded lattice L instead of $[0,1]$ on the definition of $L_n([0,1])$.

One can naturally define a lattice version of the set $L_n([0,1])$, namely

$$L_n(L) = \{\mathbf{x} = (x_1, x_2, \ldots, x_n) \in L^n \mid x_1 \leqslant_L x_2 \leqslant_L \cdots \leqslant_L x_n\} \quad (6)$$

where L is a bounded lattice.

For each $\mathbf{x}, \mathbf{y} \in L_n(L)$ we define by

$$\mathbf{x} \wedge \mathbf{y} = (x_1 \wedge_L y_1, x_2 \wedge_L y_2, \ldots, x_n \wedge_L y_n)$$

and

$$\mathbf{x} \vee \mathbf{y} = (x_1 \vee_L y_1, x_2 \vee_L y_2, \ldots, x_n \vee_L y_n)$$

the meet and join operations on $L_n(L)$, respectively.

Denote $/x/ = (x, x, \ldots, x)$ for each $x \in L$. Thus, $/0_L/$ and $/1_L/$ are a bottom and a top element of $L_n(L)$. As an easy exercise one can prove that $\langle L_n(L), \wedge, \vee, /0_L/, /1_L/ \rangle$ is a bounded lattice.

A partial order on $L_n(L)$ is given by

$$\mathbf{x} \leqslant \mathbf{y} \iff x_i \leqslant_L y_i \text{ for each } i = 1, 2, \ldots, n$$

Definition 3.1. Let $N_1, N_2, \ldots, N_n : L \to L$ be fuzzy negations such that $N_1 \leqslant N_2 \leqslant \cdots \leqslant N_n$. Then

$$\widetilde{N_1 \cdots N_n}(\mathbf{x}) = (N_1(x_1), \ldots, N_n(x_n)) \qquad (7)$$

is an n-dimensional fuzzy negation. In case that $N_1 = N_2 = \cdots = N_n$ we denote $\widetilde{N_1 \cdots N_n}$ by $\mathcal{N}_N$.

In this work we lead only with n-dimensional fuzzy negation $\mathcal{N}_N$, but every result presented here remains valid for $\widetilde{N_1 \cdots N_n}$.

Proposition 3.1. *Let $M \trianglelefteq L$ with respect to (r_1, r_2, s), $\odot$ be an e-operator on M and N be a fuzzy negation on M. Then $\mathcal{N}_{N_\odot^E} : L_n(L) \longrightarrow L_n(L)$ given by*

$$\mathcal{N}_{N_\odot^E}(\mathbf{x}) = (N_\odot^E(x_1), N_\odot^E(x_2), \ldots, N_\odot^E(x_n))$$

is a n-dimensional fuzzy negation on $L_n(L)$.

Proof. Straightforward from Theorem 2.1 and Definition 3.1. $\qquad \square$

Proposition 3.2. *Let M be a (r, s)-sublattice of L. If $M \trianglelefteq L$ with respect to (r_1, r_2, s) then $L_n(M) \trianglelefteq L_n(L)$ with respect to $(\mathfrak{r}_1, \mathfrak{r}_2, \mathfrak{s})$ where $\mathfrak{r}_1$, $\mathfrak{r}_2$ and $\mathfrak{s}$ are suitable homomorphisms defined from r_1, r_2 and s respectively.*

Proposition 3.3. *Let $M \trianglelefteq L$ with respect to (r_1, r_2, s) and let $\odot$ be an e-operator on M. The function $\odot^n : L_n(M) \times L_n(M) \longrightarrow L_n(L)$ given by*

$$\mathbf{a} \odot^n \mathbf{b} = (a_1 \odot b_1, a_2 \odot b_2, \ldots, a_n \odot b_n) \qquad (8)$$

for all $\mathbf{a}, \mathbf{b} \in L_n(M)$ is an e-operator on $L_n(M)$.

Proof. Straightforward from Proposition 3.2 and from the fact that $\odot$ is an e-operator on M. $\qquad \square$

Proposition 3.4. *Let $M \trianglelefteq L$ with respect to (r_1, r_2, s) and $\odot$ be an e-operator on M. If $\mathcal{N}$ is a fuzzy negation on $L_n(M)$ then the function $\mathcal{N}_\odot^E : L_n(L) \longrightarrow L_n(L)$ given by*

$$\mathcal{N}_\odot^E(\mathbf{x}) = \mathcal{N}(\mathfrak{r}_1(\mathbf{x})) \odot^n \mathcal{N}(\mathfrak{r}_2(\mathbf{x}))$$

for all $\mathbf{x} \in L_n(L)$, is a fuzzy negation on $L_n(L)$.

Proof. Notice that $\mathcal{N}_\odot^E(/0_L/) = \mathcal{N}(\mathfrak{r}_1(/0_L/)) \odot^n \mathcal{N}(\mathfrak{r}_2(/0_L/)) = \mathcal{N}(/0_L/) \odot^n \mathcal{N}(/0_L/) = /1_L/ \odot^n /1_L/ = /1_L/$. Analogously it can be proved that $\mathcal{N}_\odot^E(/1_L/) = /0_L/$.

Now, if $\mathbf{x} \leqslant \mathbf{y}$ then $x_i \leqslant y_i$ for every $i \in \{1, 2, \ldots, n\}$ and hence $r_1(x_i) \leqslant_L r_1(y_i)$, $r_2(x_i) \leqslant_L r_2(y_i)$, $N(r_1(y_i)) \leqslant_L N(r_1(x_i))$ and $N(r_2(y_i)) \leqslant_L N(r_2(x_i))$ for each $i \in \{1, 2, \ldots, n\}$. Therefore, $\mathcal{N}_\odot^E(\mathbf{y}) = \mathcal{N}(\mathfrak{r}_1(\mathbf{y})) \odot^n \mathcal{N}(\mathfrak{r}_2(\mathbf{y})) \leqslant \mathcal{N}(\mathfrak{r}_1(\mathbf{x})) \odot^n \mathcal{N}(\mathfrak{r}_2(\mathbf{x})) = \mathcal{N}_\odot^E(\mathbf{x})$. $\square$

4. Final Remarks

The method of extending fuzzy connectives via e-operators presented in[8] proved to be efficient to solve the challenge of defining extensions that are able to preserve the largest possible number of properties of fuzzy connectives. This good results remain valid for n-dimensional fuzzy negations, as we could see in this paper.

For further works, we would like still applying this extension method for other fuzzy operators in order to test its efficiency in preserving the main properties of these operators.

References

1. B. C. Bedregal. On Interval Fuzzy Negations. *Fuzzy Sets and Systems*, 161:2290-2313, 2010.
2. B. C. Bedregal, G. Beliakov, H. Bustince, T. Calvo, R. Mesiar and D. Paternain. A Class of Fuzzy Multisets with a Fixed Number of Memberships. *Information Science*, 189:1-17, 2012.
3. G. Deschrijver. The Archimedean property for t-norms in interval-valued fuzzy set theory. *Fuzzy Sets and Systems*, 157(17): 2311-2327, 2006.
4. G. Deschrijver. A representation of t-norms in interval-valued L-fuzzy set theory. *Fuzzy Sets and Systems*, 159(13): 1597-1618, 2008.
5. G. Deschrijver. Triangular norms which are meet-morphisms in interval-valued fuzzy set theory. *Fuzzy Sets and Systems*, 181(1): 88-101, 2011.
6. E. S. Palmeira and B. C. Bedregal. Extension of Fuzzy Logic Operators Defined on Bounded Lattices via Retractions. *Computer & Mathematics with Applications*, 63: 1026–1038, 2012.
7. E. S. Palmeira, B. C. Bedregal, J. Fernandez and A. Jurio. On the Extension of Lattice-valued Implications via Retractions. *Fuzzy Sets and Systems*, 2013 (in press).
8. E. S. Palmeira, B. C. Bedregal, R. Mesiar and J. Fernandez. A New Way to Extend T-norms, T-conorms and Negations. *Fuzzy Sets and Systems*, 2013 (in press).
9. Y. Shang, X. Yuan and E. S. Lee. The n-Dimensional Fuzzy Sets and Zadeh Fuzzy Sets Based on the Finite Valued Fuzzy Sets. *Computers & Mathematics with Applications*, 60: 442–463, 2010.

FUZZY HOMOMORPHISM IN FUZZY LATTICES PRESERVING IDEALS

I. MEZZOMO

Department of Mathematical Sciences, Technology and Humanities – DCETH
Rural Federal University of SemiArid – UFERSA
Angicos – Rio Grande do Norte, Brazil, 59.515-000
E-mail: imezzomo@ufersa.edu.br

B. BEDREGAL and R. H. N. SANTIAGO

Group for Logic, Language, Information, Theory and Applications - LOLITA
Department of Informatics and Applied Mathematics – DIMAp
Federal University of Rio Grande do Norte – UFRN
Natal – Rio Grande do Norte, Brazil, 59.072-970
E-mail: {bedregal, regivan}@dimap.ufrn.br

In this paper we consider the notion of Fuzzy Lattices which was introduced by Chon in 2009. We define the fuzzy homomorphism between fuzzy lattices and proved some results of fuzzy homomorphism on bounded fuzzy lattices. Also, we prove some results involving fuzzy homomorphism and ideals.

Keywords: Fuzzy Lattices; Fuzzy Homomorphism; Ideals.

1. Introduction

The concept of fuzzy sets as well as fuzzy relations was first introduced by Zadeh.[9] In 1971, Zadeh[10] defined fuzzy orderings, which are transitive fuzzy relations. In particular, a fuzzy partial ordering is a fuzzy ordering which is also reflexive and antisymmetric.

In 2009, Chon in,[2] considering Zadeh's fuzzy orders,[10] proposed a new notion for fuzzy lattices and studied the level sets of such structures, he also provided some results for distributive and modular fuzzy lattices.

As a continuation of these studies, in this work, using the definition of ideals of fuzzy lattices and fuzzy homomorphism defined in[5] and,[6] respectively, we prove some results involving fuzzy homomorphism and ideals.

The following references can be used as bibliographical source:[1,3,4]

2. Fuzzy Lattices

Let X and Y be non-empty sets and $x \in X$ and $y \in Y$. A fuzzy relation A is a mapping from the Cartesian product $X \times Y$ to the interval $[0,1]$; $A : X \times Y \to [0,1]$. If $X = Y$, then we say that A is a binary fuzzy relation on X.

Let X be a nonempty set. A fuzzy relation A on X is *fuzzy reflexive*, if $A(x,x) = 1$, for all $x \in X$. A is *fuzzy symmetric*, if $A(x,y) = A(y,x)$, for all $x, y \in X$. A is *fuzzy transitive*, if $A(x,z) \geq \sup_{y \in X} \min\{A(x,y), A(y,z)\}$ for all $x, y, z \in X$. A is *fuzzy antisymmetric*, if $A(x,y) > 0$ and $A(y,x) > 0$ implies $x = y$. The fuzzy reflexivity, symmetry, antisymmetry and transitivity notion were first defined by Zadeh in.[10]

A fuzzy relation A is a *fuzzy partial order relation* if A is fuzzy reflexive, fuzzy antisymmetric and fuzzy transitive. A fuzzy partial order relation A is a *fuzzy total order relation* if $A(x,y) > 0$ or $A(y,x) > 0$ for all $x, y \in X$. If A is a fuzzy partial order relation on a set X, then (X, A) is called a *fuzzy partially ordered set* or *fuzzy poset*. If A is a fuzzy total order relation in a set X, then (X, A) is called *fuzzy totally ordered set* or a *fuzzy chain*. For more details see.[2,10]

According to Chon,[2] Definition 3.1, given a fuzzy poset (X, A) and a subset $Y \subseteq X$, $u \in X$ is said to be an upper bound for Y whenever $A(y,u) > 0$, for all $y \in Y$. It is also called the least upper bound (or Supremum) of Y iff $A(u, u_0) > 0$ for every upper bound u_0 of Y. Dually, $v \in X$ is said to be a lower bound for Y whenever $A(v,y) > 0$, for all $y \in Y$. A lower bound v_0 for Y is the greatest lower bound (or Infimum) of Y iff $A(v, v_0) > 0$ for every lower bound v for Y.

We denote a supremum of the set $\{x,y\}$ by $x \vee y$ and a infimum of the set $\{x,y\}$ by $x \wedge y$.

Definition 2.1. [2, Definition 3.2] A fuzzy poset (X, A) is a fuzzy lattice iff $x \vee y$ and $x \wedge y$ exist for all $x, y \in X$.

In Mezzomo *et. al*,[8] Definition 3.4, we have that a fuzzy lattice $\mathcal{L} = (X, A)$ is bounded if there exists $\perp$ and $\top$ in X such that for any $x \in X$ we have that $A(\perp, x) > 0$ and $A(x, \top) > 0$.

For more details see.[2,6–8]

3. Fuzzy Homomorphism

Definition 3.1. [6, Definition 5.1] Let $\mathcal{L} = (X, A)$ and $\mathcal{M} = (Y, B)$ be bounded fuzzy lattices. A mapping $h : X \to Y$ is a *fuzzy homomorphism* from $\mathcal{L}$ into $\mathcal{M}$ if, for all $x, y \in X$:

(i) $h(x \wedge_{\mathcal{L}} y) = h(x) \wedge_{\mathcal{M}} h(y)$;
(ii) $h(x \vee_{\mathcal{L}} y) = h(x) \vee_{\mathcal{M}} h(y)$;
(iii) $h(\perp_{\mathcal{L}}) = \perp_{\mathcal{M}}$;
(iv) $h(\top_{\mathcal{L}}) = \top_{\mathcal{M}}$.

Like in crisp algebra, fuzzy homomorphisms can be classified as:

(i) monomorphism — injective fuzzy homomorphism;
(ii) epimorphism — surjective fuzzy homomorphism;
(iii) isomorphism — bijective fuzzy homomorphism.

Proposition 3.1. *[6, Proposition 5.1] Let $\mathcal{L} = (X, A)$ and $\mathcal{M} = (Y, B)$ be bounded fuzzy lattices and let a mapping $h : X \to Y$ be a fuzzy homomorphism. For all $x, y \in X$, if $A(x, y) > 0$, then $B(h(x), h(y)) > 0$.*

Definition 3.2. [6, Definition 5.2] Let $\mathcal{L} = (X, A)$ and $\mathcal{M} = (Y, B)$ be bounded fuzzy lattices. A mapping $h : X \to Y$ is a *fuzzy order-homomorphism* from $\mathcal{L}$ into $\mathcal{M}$ if, for all $x, y \in X$, satisfies the following conditions:

(i) If $A(x, y) > 0$ then $B(h(x), h(y)) > 0$;
(ii) $h(\perp_{\mathcal{L}}) = \perp_{\mathcal{M}}$;
(iii) $h(\top_{\mathcal{L}}) = \top_{\mathcal{M}}$.

Lemma 3.1. *Let $\mathcal{L} = (X, A)$ and $\mathcal{M} = (Y, B)$ be bounded fuzzy lattices. If $h : X \to Y$ is a fuzzy monomorphism, then $A(x, y) > 0 \Leftrightarrow B(h(x), h(y)) > 0$.*

Proof. ($\Rightarrow$) By *Mezzomo et.al*,[6] Proposition 5.1, each fuzzy homomorphism is a fuzzy order homomorphism. So, $A(x, y) > 0 \Rightarrow B(h(x), h(y)) > 0$.

($\Leftarrow$)

$$B(h(x), h(y)) > 0 \Rightarrow h(x) \vee_{\mathcal{M}} h(y) = h(y) \text{ (By [2, Proposition 3.3])}$$
$$\Rightarrow h(x \vee_{\mathcal{L}} y) = h(y)$$
$$\Rightarrow x \vee_{\mathcal{L}} y = y \qquad \text{(Because } h \text{ is injective)}$$
$$\Rightarrow A(x, y) > 0 \qquad \text{(By [2, Proposition 3.3])} \quad \square$$

Definition 3.3. Let X and Y be sets and $h : X \to Y$ be a map. So, for all $Z \subseteq X$, the set defined by $h(Z) = \{h(x) : x \in Z\}$ is called *image* of Z from Y induced by h. On the other hand, for each $W \subseteq Y$, the set $\overleftarrow{h}(W) = \{x \in X : h(x) \in W\}$ is called *inverse image* of W from X induced by h.

Definition 3.4. [5, Definition 4.1] Let $\mathcal{L} = (X, A)$ be a fuzzy lattice and $I \subseteq X$. I is an *ideal* in $\mathcal{L}$, if satisfies the following conditions:

(i) If $x \in X$, $y \in I$ and $A(x, y) > 0$, then $x \in I$;
(ii) If $x, y \in I$, then $x \vee_{\mathcal{L}} y \in I$.

Definition 3.5. Let $\mathcal{L} = (X, A)$ be a fuzzy lattice and $y \in X$. The set $\downarrow y = \{x \in X : A(x, y) > 0\}$ is called *principal ideal* of $\mathcal{L}$ generated by y.

Notice that some fuzzy homomorphisms do not preserve ideals, i.e. if h is a fuzzy homomorphism and I is an ideal of $\mathcal{L}$, then $h(I)$ is not necessarily an ideal of $\mathcal{M}$. The example below illustrates this case.

Example 3.1. Let $\mathcal{L} = (X, A)$ and $\mathcal{M} = (Y, B)$ be the fuzzy lattices as defined in Figure 1 and let $h : \mathcal{L} \to \mathcal{M}$ be the fuzzy homomorphism defined by $h(x) = x'$, $h(y) = y'$, $h(z) = z'$ and $h(w) = w'$. The set $I = \{y, z, w\}$ is an ideal of $\mathcal{L}$, but their image $h(I) = \{y', z', w'\}$ is not an ideal of $\mathcal{M}$ because $y' \in h(I)$ and $B(v', y') > 0$, but $v' \notin h(I)$. Therefore, I is an ideal of $\mathcal{L}$ and $h(I)$ is not an ideal of $\mathcal{M}$. ∎

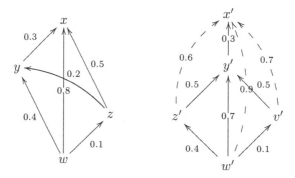

Fig. 1. Representations of the fuzzy lattices $\mathcal{L}$ and $\mathcal{M}$, respectively.

The next proposition show us that the converse situation occurs.

Proposition 3.2. *Let $\mathcal{L} = (X, A)$ and $\mathcal{M} = (Y, B)$ be bounded fuzzy lattices, $I \subseteq X$ and $h : X \to Y$ a fuzzy homomorphism. Then, if $h(I)$ is an ideal of $\mathcal{M}$, then I is an ideal of $\mathcal{L}$.*

Proof. (i) Given $x \in X$ and $y \in I$ such that $A(x,y) > 0$, since h is a fuzzy homomorphism, by Proposition 3.1, $B(h(x), h(y)) > 0$. By Definition 3.3, if $y \in I$, then $h(y) \in h(I)$. By hypothesis, $h(I)$ is an ideal of $\mathcal{M}$, so by Definition 3.4 (i), $h(x) \in h(I)$. Hence, by Definition 3.3, we have that $x \in I$.

(ii) Given $x, y \in I$, according to Definition 3.3, $h(x), h(y) \in h(I)$. By hypothesis, $h(I)$ is an ideal of $\mathcal{M}$ so, by Definition 3.4 (ii), $h(x) \vee_{\mathcal{M}} h(y) \in h(I)$. Hence, because h is a fuzzy homomorphism, by Definition 3.1, $h(x \vee_{\mathcal{L}} y) = h(x) \vee_{\mathcal{M}} h(y) \in h(I)$. Therefore, by Definition 3.3, $x \vee_{\mathcal{L}} y \in I$. $\square$

Proposition 3.3. *Let $\mathcal{L} = (X, A)$ and $\mathcal{M} = (Y, B)$ be bounded fuzzy lattices, $I \subseteq X$ and $h : X \to Y$ a fuzzy isomorphism. Then, $h(I)$ is an ideal of $\mathcal{M}$ iff I is an ideal of $\mathcal{L}$.*

Proof. ($\Rightarrow$) Straightforward from Proposition 3.2.
($\Leftarrow$) Let I be an ideal of $\mathcal{L}$.

(i) Given $x', y' \in Y$ such that $y' \in h(I)$ and $B(x', y') > 0$. Because $y' \in h(I)$, then there exist $y \in I$ such that $h(y) = y'$ and because h is surjective there exist $x \in X$ such that $h(x) = x'$. Since h is an injective fuzzy order-homomorphism, by Lemma 3.1, $A(x, y) > 0$. By hypothesis, I is an ideal of $\mathcal{L}$. So by Definition 3.4 (i), $x \in I$ and therefore, $x' = h(x) \in h(I)$.

(ii) Let $x' \in h(I)$ and $y' \in h(I)$. So, there exists at least one $x, y \in X$ such that $h(x) = x'$ and $h(y) = y'$. By Definition 3.3, $x, y \in \overleftarrow{h}(h(I))$ and because h is bijective, $x, y \in I$. By hypothesis, I is an ideal of $\mathcal{L}$, so by Definition 3.4 (ii), $x \vee_{\mathcal{L}} y \in I$. Hence, by Definition 3.3, $h(x \vee_{\mathcal{L}} y) \in h(I)$. Therefore, by Definition 3.1, $x' \vee_{\mathcal{M}} y' = h(x) \vee_{\mathcal{M}} h(y) = h(x \vee_{\mathcal{L}} y) \in h(I)$. $\square$

Theorem 3.1. *Let $\mathcal{L} = (X, A)$ and $\mathcal{M} = (Y, B)$ be bounded fuzzy lattices and let $h : X \to Y$ be a fuzzy homomorphism. If the inverse image induced by h is always finite, then the inverse image of all principal ideals of $\mathcal{M}$ are principal ideals of $\mathcal{L}$.*

Proof. Suppose that h is a fuzzy homomorphism and $\downarrow y'$ is a principal ideal generated by $y' \in Y$.

(i) Given $x, y \in X$ such that $y \in \overleftarrow{h}(\downarrow y')$ and $A(x, y) > 0$, by Definition 3.3, $h(y) \in \downarrow y'$. Because h is a fuzzy homomorphism, $B(h(x), h(y)) > 0$. Since $\downarrow y'$ is an ideal, then $h(x) \in \downarrow y'$. Therefore, by Definition 3.3, $x \in \overleftarrow{h}(\downarrow y')$.

(ii) Given $x, y \in X$ such that $x, y \in \overleftarrow{h}(\downarrow y')$. By Definition 3.3, we have that $h(x) \in \downarrow y'$ and $h(y) \in \downarrow y'$. By hypothesis, $\downarrow y'$ is an ideal of $\mathcal{M}$.

So, by Definition 3.4 (ii), $h(x) \vee_{\mathcal{M}} h(y) \in\downarrow y'$. Hence, because h is a fuzzy homomorphism, $h(x \vee_{\mathcal{L}} y) \in\downarrow y'$. Therefore, by Definition 3.3, $x \vee_{\mathcal{L}} y \in \overleftarrow{h}(\downarrow y')$.

(iii) Because $\overleftarrow{h}$ always return a finite set, then $\overleftarrow{h}(y')$ is finite, and so, $\bigvee \overleftarrow{h}(y')$ there exists. Also, for all $y \in \overleftarrow{h}(y')$, trivially $h(y) = y'$, and so $h(\bigvee \overleftarrow{h}(y')) = \bigvee_{y \in \overleftarrow{h}(y')} h(y) = y'$. Therefore, $\overleftarrow{h}(\downarrow y') =\downarrow \bigvee \overleftarrow{h}(y')$. $\qquad\square$

4. Conclusion

In this paper, we study the notion of fuzzy lattices defined by Chon[2] using the fuzzy order relation notion defined by Zadeh[10] and consider the notion of fuzzy lattices homomorphisms and prove that if h is a homomorphism and the image of a set $h(I)$ is an ideal, then I is an ideal. Also, we prove that if the inverse image induced by h is finite, then the inverse image of all principal ideals of $\mathcal{M}$ are principal ideals of $\mathcal{L}$. In terms of future works one promising idea is the investigation of the behaviour from fuzzy homomorphism on prime and maximal ideals. Also, the study of the fuzzy homomorphism involving kinds of fuzzy ideals on fuzzy lattices.

References

1. G. Birkhoff, *Lattice Theory*, Volume 25 of AMS Colloquium Publications, American Mathematical Society 1967.
2. I. Chon, *Fuzzy partial order relations and fuzzy lattices*, Korean Journal Mathematics 17 (4) (2009) 361-374.
3. B.A. Davey, H.A. Priestley, *Introduction to Lattices and Order*, Cambridge University Press, Cambridge, 2002.
4. G. Grätzer, *General Lattice Theory*, Birkhuser Verlag, Basel-Boston-Berlin, 2000.
5. I. Mezzomo, B.C. Bedregal, R.H.N. Santiago, *Kinds of ideals of fuzzy lattice*, Second Brazilian Congress on Fuzzy Systems - 2012, 657-671.
6. I. Mezzomo, B.C. Bedregal, R.H.N. Santiago, *Types of fuzzy ideals in fuzzy lattices*, Preprint submitted to The Journal of Intelligent and Fuzzy Systems.
7. I. Mezzomo, B.C. Bedregal, R.H.N. Santiago, *α-ideals of fuzzy lattices*, IFSA World Congress and NAFIPS Annual Meeting (IFSA/NAFIPS), 2013 Joint - 157-162. DOI: 10.1109/IFSA-NAFIPS.2013.6608392.
8. I. Mezzomo, B.C. Bedregal, R.H.N. Santiago, *Operations on bounded fuzzy lattices*, IFSA World Congress and NAFIPS Annual Meeting (IFSA/NAFIPS) - 2013 Joint, 151-156. DOI: 10.1109/IFSA-NAFIPS.2013.6608391.
9. L.A. Zadeh, *Fuzzy sets*, Information and Control 8 (1965) 338-353.
10. L.A. Zadeh, *Similarity relations and fuzzy orderings*, Information Sciences 3 (1971) 177-200.

ON MONOTONIC INCLUSION INTERVAL UNINORMS

F. L. SANTANA

Mathematics Department, UFRN,
Natal, RN, CEP-59072970, Brazil
* E-mail: ab_fagner@ccet.ufrn.br
www.ccet.ufrn.br

R. H. N. SANTIAGO

Department of Informatics and Applied Mathematics, UFRN,
Natal, RN, CEP-59072970, Brazil
E-mail: an_regivan@dimap.ufrn.br

F. T. SANTANA

School of Sciences and Technology, UFRN,
Natal, RN, CEP-59072970, Brazil
E-mail: an_fabianatsantana@gmail.com

In this paper, some results about interval uninorms with the additional property of monotonicity inclusion are introduced; e.g construction of interval uninorms from usual uninorms and constructions of interval t-norms and t-conorms from interval uninorms. It is also shown that the neutral element of this type of interval uninorm must be a degenerate interval.

Keywords: Uninorms; Neutral Element; Interval Fuzzy.

Introduction

A uninorm operator (concept introduced in[1]) is an aggregation function $U : [0, 1] \times [0, 1] \longrightarrow [0, 1]$, that is commutative, associative, monotonic and has a neutral element. The difference between uninorms and t-norms/t-conorms is that the neutral element can be any number $e \in [0, 1]$. Of course, if $e = 1$, then U is a t-norm and if $e = 0$, then U is a t-conorm. The uninorms has applications in several areas (see[2]). For example, in multicriteria decision making, an uninorm can be used to aggregate the evaluation of alternatives, where the neutral element represents a level of satisfaction (see[3]). Some aggregation functions on $[0, 1]$ have been used in fuzzy logic as logical connectives (t-norms are conjunctions and t-conorms are disjunctions). Thinking about applications of fuzzy logic, we can realize that determination of membership degrees could have some kind of uncertainty, since different specialists can assign differents degrees. The interval fuzzy logic (or equivalently intuitionistic fuzzy logic, see[4-6]), introduced independently in[7-10] deal with this uncertainty by using intervals (pairs of real numbers) as membership degrees. Interval Uninorms were introduced in[11] , but in that paper, only the monotonicity by product order (or Kulish-Miranker order, see[12]) is required. In this paper, we show some natural ways to obtain an interval uninorm from usual ones, and we note that this interval uninorms also are monotonic with respect to $\subseteq$. So, we only consider uninorms that are $\subseteq$-monotonic and follow the ideas of[13,14] . We show that in this kind of uninorm, the neutral element is a degenerate interval. We also show a way to obtain interval $\subseteq$-monotonic t-norms and t-conorms from interval uninorms.

1. Interval Uninorms

The set of all intervals will be denoted by $\mathbb{IR}$ and the set of all intervals whose the ends lies on the unit interval $[0,1]$ by $\mathbb{I}[0,1]$. If $X \in \mathbb{IR}$, we use the notation $X = [\underline{x}, \overline{x}]$. We use the interval operations introduced in[15] , the inclusion order $\subseteq$ and the Kulisch-Miranker order (or product order) $\leq_{km}$ defined by $[\underline{x}, \overline{x}] \leq_{km} [\underline{y}, \overline{y}] \Leftrightarrow \underline{x} \leq \underline{y}$ and $\overline{x} \leq \overline{y}$.

Definition 1.1. A function $U : \mathbb{I}[0,1] \times \mathbb{I}[0,1] \longrightarrow \mathbb{I}[0,1]$ is a $\subseteq$-monotonic interval uninorm (i-uninorm for short) if satisfies:

(1) $U(X,Y) = U(Y,X)$; (Commutativity)
(2) $U(X,U(Y,Z)) = U(U(X,Y),Z)$; (Associativity)
(3) $U(X,Y) \leq_{km} U(Z,W)$ if $X \leq_{km} Z$ and $Y \leq_{km} W$; ($\leq_{km}$-Monotonicity)
(4) $U(X,Y) \subseteq U(Z,W)$ if $X \subseteq Z$ and $Y \subseteq W$; ($\subseteq$-Monotonicity)
(5) There exists an element $E \in [0,1]$ such that $U(E,X) = X$, for all $X \in \mathbb{I}[0,1]$. (Neutral Element)

Theorem 1.1. *If U_1 and U_2 are two uninorms such that $U_1(x,y) \leq U_2(x,y)$, for all $x,y \in [0,1]$ and it's neutral elements are equals[a] have*

---

[a]This requirement allows that the neutral element be well defined. Since $U_1(x,y) \leq U_2(x,y)$, if e_1 and e_2 are the neutral elements of U_1 and U_2, we must have $U_1(e_1,e_2) = e_2$ and $U_2(e_1,e_2) = e_1$, so $e_2 \leq e_1$ and as will be seen, we must have $e_1 \leq e_2$.

seen then the function $U : \mathbb{I}[0,1] \times \mathbb{I}[0,1] \longrightarrow \mathbb{I}[0,1]$ *defined by* $U(X,Y) = [U_1(\underline{x},\underline{y}), U_2(\overline{x},\overline{y})]$ *is a i-uninorm.*

Proof. The first two conditions of the i-uninorm definition are immediate. For the third condition, suppose that $X \leq_{km} Z$ and $Y \leq_{km} W$, ie, $\underline{x} \leq \underline{z}$, $\overline{x} \leq \overline{z}$, $\underline{y} \leq \underline{w}$ and $\overline{y} \leq \overline{w}$. By the monotonicity of the usual uninorms, we have $U_1(\underline{x},\underline{y}) \leq U_1(\underline{z},\underline{w})$ and $U_2(\overline{x},\overline{y}) \leq U_2(\overline{z},\overline{w})$, so $[U_1(\underline{x},\underline{y}), U_2(\overline{x},\overline{y})] \leq_{km} [U_1(\underline{z},\underline{w}), U_2(\overline{z},\overline{w})]$ which means that $U(X,Z) \leq_{km} U(Y,W)$. The $\subseteq$-monotonicity (condition 4) is proved analogously. For the last condition, take $E = [e,e]$ such that e is the commom neutral element of U_1 and U_2. Thus, for every $X \in \mathbb{I}[0,1]$, we have $U(E,X) = [U_1(e,\underline{x}), U_2(e,\overline{x})] = [\underline{x},\overline{x}] = X$. $\qquad\square$

In this last theorem, we consider that the neutral elements of U_1 and U_2 are the same. With this assumption the i-uninorms have degenerate intervals as neutral elements. In the next results we prove that every i-uninorm have this property.

Lemma 1.2. *Let* $U : \mathbb{I}[0,1] \times \mathbb{I}[0,1] \longrightarrow \mathbb{I}[0,1]$ *be a i-uninorm with neutral element* E.

(1) If $E \leq_{km} X$, *then* $Y \leq_{km} U(X,Y)$, *for all* $Y \in \mathbb{I}[0,1]$;
(2) If $X \leq_{km} E$, *then* $U(X,Y) \leq_{km} Y$, *for all* $Y \in \mathbb{I}[0,1]$;
(3) If $E \subseteq X$, *then* $Y \subseteq U(X,Y)$, *for all* $Y \in \mathbb{I}[0,1]$;
(4) If $X \subseteq E$, *then* $U(X,Y) \subseteq Y$, *for all* $Y \in \mathbb{I}[0,1]$.

Proof.

(1) Since $E \leq_{km} X$, we have $Y = U(E,Y) \leq_{km} U(X,Y)$, so $Y \leq_{km} U(X,Y)$;
(2) Since $X \leq_{km} E$, we have $U(X,Y) \leq_{km} U(E,Y) = Y$, so $Y \leq_{km} U(X,Y)$;
(3) Since $E \subseteq X$, we have $Y = U(E,Y) \subseteq U(X,Y)$, so $Y \subseteq U(X,Y)$;
(4) Since $X \subseteq E$, we have $U(X,Y) \subseteq U(E,Y) = Y$, so $U(X,Y) \subseteq Y$. $\quad\square$

Lemma 1.3. *Let* $U : \mathbb{I}[0,1] \times \mathbb{I}[0,1] \longrightarrow \mathbb{I}[0,1]$ *be a i-uninorm with neutral element* $E = [\underline{e}, \overline{e}]$.

(1) $U([\underline{e},\underline{e}], [x,x]) = [x,x]$, *for all* $x \in [0,1]$;
(2) $U([\overline{e},\overline{e}], [x,x]) = [x,x]$, *for all* $x \in [0,1]$.

Proof.

(1) Since $[\bar{e},\bar{e}] \subseteq [\underline{e},\bar{e}]$, the above lemma garantees that $U([\bar{e},\bar{e}],[x,x]) \subseteq U(E,[x,x]) = [x,x]$. Thus, $U([\bar{e},\bar{e}],[x,x])$ is an interval and also a subset of $[x,x]$, so $U([\bar{e},\bar{e}],[x,x]) = [x,x]$;

(2) Since $[\underline{e},\underline{e}] \subseteq [\underline{e},\bar{e}]$, we have $U([\underline{e},\underline{e}],[x,x]) \subseteq U(E,[x,x]) = [x,x]$. Thus, $U([\underline{e},\underline{e}],[x,x]) = [x,x]$. $\square$

Theorem 1.4. *If $U : \mathbb{I}[0,1] \times \mathbb{I}[0,1] \longrightarrow \mathbb{I}[0,1]$ is a i-uninorm, then its neutral element must to be a degenerated interval.*

Proof. Suppose that $E = [\underline{e},\bar{e}]$. Follows from the lemma 1.3 $U([\underline{e},\underline{e}],[\bar{e},\bar{e}] = [\underline{e},\underline{e}]$ and $U([\underline{e},\underline{e}],[\bar{e},\bar{e}]) = [\bar{e},\bar{e}]$. Thus, we have $[\underline{e},\underline{e}] = [\bar{e},\bar{e}]$, i.e., $\underline{e} = \bar{e}$. $\square$

2. i-t-Norms and i-t-Conorms from i-Uninorms

We consider the definitions of interval t-norms (i-t-norms) in[14] and interval t-conorms (i-t-conorms) in.[16] In this definitions, the $\subseteq$-monotonicity is also required. With respect to interval operations, for intervals $X, Y, Z, [e, e]$ ($e > 0$) and $[1, 1]$ the following results are valids:

(1) $E \cdot X = [e\underline{x}, e\bar{x}]$;
(2) $\dfrac{X}{[e,e]} = [\dfrac{\underline{x}}{e}, \dfrac{\bar{x}}{e}]$;
(3) $[1,1] \cdot X = X$;
(4) $0 \notin [1,1] - [e,e]$.

The next results status that i-t-norms and i-t-conorms can be obtained from i-uninorms[b].

Theorem 2.1. *Let $U : \mathbb{I}[0,1] \times \mathbb{I}[0,1] \longrightarrow \mathbb{I}[0,1]$ be a i-uninorm with neutral element $E = [e, e]$, where $e \neq 0$. The function $T : \mathbb{I}[0,1] \times \mathbb{I}[0,1] \longrightarrow \mathbb{I}[0,1]$ defined by:*

$$T(X,Y) = \frac{U(E \cdot X, E \cdot Y)}{E}$$

is a i-T-norm.

Proof. The commutativity and the associativity of T are straightforward. Also, is easy to see that $[1,1]$ is, in fact, the neutral element of T. We must check the two monotonicities.

---

[b]This is a generalization of the ideas exposed in.[17]

For $\leq_{km}$-Monotonicity, suppose that $X \leq_{km} Y$ and $Z \leq_{km} W$, ie, $\underline{x} \leq \underline{y}$, $\overline{x} \leq \overline{y}$, $\underline{z} \leq \underline{w}$ and $\overline{z} \leq \overline{w}$. Thus, we have $e\underline{x} \leq e\underline{y}$, $e\overline{x} \leq e\overline{y}$, $e\underline{z} \leq e\underline{w}$ and $e\overline{z} \leq e\overline{w}$, which implies $E \cdot X \leq_{km} E \cdot Y$ and $E \cdot Z \leq_{km} E \cdot W$, so $U(E{\cdot}X, E{\cdot}Z) \leq_{km} U(E{\cdot}Y, E{\cdot}W) \Rightarrow \dfrac{U(E \cdot X, E \cdot Z)}{E} \leq_{km} \dfrac{U(E \cdot Y, E \cdot W)}{E}$, i.e., $T(X,Z) \leq_{km} T(Y,W)$.

Finally, for $\subseteq$-Monotonicity, suppose that $X \subseteq Y$ and $Z \subseteq W$, ie, $\underline{x} \geq \underline{y}$, $\overline{x} \leq \overline{y}$, $\underline{z} \geq \underline{w}$ and $\overline{z} \leq \overline{w}$. Thus, we have $e\underline{x} \geq e\underline{y}$, $e\overline{x} \leq e\overline{y}$, $e\underline{z} \geq e\underline{w}$ and $e\overline{z} \leq e\overline{w}$, which implies $E \cdot X \subseteq E \cdot Y$ and $E \cdot Z \subseteq E \cdot W$, so $U(E \cdot X, E \cdot Z) \subseteq U(E \cdot Y, E \cdot W) \Rightarrow \dfrac{U(E \cdot X, E \cdot Z)}{E} \subseteq \dfrac{U(E \cdot Y, E \cdot W)}{E}$, ie, $T(X,Z) \subseteq T(Y,W)$. $\qquad\square$

Theorem 2.2. *Let $U : \mathbb{I}[0,1] \times \mathbb{I}[0,1] \longrightarrow \mathbb{I}[0,1]$ be a i-uniform with neutral element $E = [e,e]$, where $e \neq 1$. The function $S : \mathbb{I}[0,1] \times \mathbb{I}[0,1] \longrightarrow \mathbb{I}[0,1]$ defined by:*

$$S(X,Y) = \frac{U(E + [1-e, 1-e].X, E + [1-e, 1-e].Y) - E}{[1-e, 1-e]}$$

is a i-T-conorm.

Proof. Again, the commutativity and the associativity of S and the fact that $[0,0]$ is the neutral element of S are straightforward.

Suppose that $X \leq_{km} Y$ and $Z \leq_{km} W$. It follows immediately from the properties of interval arithmetic that $E + [1 - e, 1 - e] \cdot X \leq_{km} E + [1-e, 1-e] \cdot Y$, so $\dfrac{U(E + [1-e, 1-e] \cdot X, E + [1-e, 1-e] \cdot Z) - E}{[1-e, 1-e]} \leq_{km}$ $\dfrac{U(E + [1-e, 1-e] \cdot Y, E + [1-e, 1-e] \cdot W) - E}{[1-e, 1-e]}$, ie, $S(X,Z) \leq_{km} S(Y,W)$.

The proof of $\subseteq$-Monotonicity is analogous to the proof of $\leq_{km}$-Monotonicity. $\qquad\square$

3. Final Remarks

In this paper we introduced some results about interval uninorms that are $\subseteq$-monotonic. Also, we show how to obtain interval t-norms and interval t-conorms from such interval uninorms and from given two uninorms (satisfying some conditions) we can obtain an interval uninorm. In future works, we will study some other conections between interval uninorms and others interval fuzzy connectives and use the Canonical Interval Representation[18] to construct an interval uninorm from an usual uninorm.

References

1. R. R. Yager, A. Rybalov, Uninorm Aggregation Operators, *Fuzzy sets and Systems* **80**, 111 − 120 (1996).
2. R. R. Yager, Uninorms in Fuzzy Systems Modeling, *Fuzzy Sets and Systems*, **122**, 167 − 175 (2001).
3. K. C. Maes, B. Baets, A Counter View on Uninorm Properties, *Kybernetika* **42**, 303 − 318 (2006).
4. K. T. Atanassov, Intuitionistic Fuzzy Sets, *Fuzzy Sets and Systems* **20**, 87−96 (1986).
5. J. Goguen, L-Fuzzy Sets, *Journal of Mathematical Analysis and Applications* **18**, 145 − 174 (1967).
6. G. Deschriijver, E.E. Kerre, On the Relationship Between Some Extensions of Fuzzy Set Theory, *Fuzzy Sets and Systems* **133**, 227 − 235 (2003).
7. L. A. Zadeh, The Concept of Linguistic Variable and Its Application to Aprproximate Reasoning-I, *Information sciences* **8**, 199 − 249.
8. I. Grattan-Guiness, Fuzzy Membership Mappe Onto Interval and Many-Valued Fuzzy Sets, *Zeitschrift fr Mathematische Logik und Grundladen der Mathematik* **22** , 149 − 160 (1975).
9. K. Jahn, Interval-Wertige Mengen, *Mathematische Nachrichten*, **68**, 115−132 (1975).
10. R. Sambuc, Fonction ϕ-Floues: Application l'Aide au Diagnostic en pathologie Thyroidienne, PhD Thesis, University of Marseille, (Marseille, France 1975).
11. G. Deschrijver, E. E. Kerre, Uninorms in L^*-Fuzzy Set Theory, *Fuzzy Sets and Systems*, **148**, 243 − 262 (2004).
12. U. Kulisch, W. Miranker, *Computer Arithmetic in Theory and Practice*, (New York Academic Press, New York 1981).
13. B. C. Bedregal, On Interval Fuzzy Negation, *Fuzzy Sets and Systems* **161**, 2290 − 2313 (2010).
14. B. C Bedregal, A. Takahashi, The Best Interval Representations of T-Norms and Automorphisms, *Fuzzy Sets and Systems* **157**, 3220 − 3230, (2006).
15. R. E. Moore, *Automatic Error Analysis in Digital Computation*. Technical Report LMSD84821, Lockheed Missiles and Space Division Co. (1959).
16. B. C Bedregal, A. Takahashi, Interval Valued Versions of T-Conorms, Fuzzy Negations and Fuzzy Implications, *Proceedings of IEEE International Conference on Fuzzy Systems*, 1981 − 1987, (2006).
17. M. Baczynski, B. Jayaram, *Fuzzy Implications*, (Springer-Verlag, Berlin Heiderberg, 2008).
18. R. N. Santiago, B. C. Bedregal, B. M. Acioly. Formal Aspects of Correctness and Optimality of Interval Computations, *Formal Aspects of Computing* **18**, 231 − 243 (2006).

DISTANCE MEASURES WITH PROBABILITIES, OWA OPERATORS AND WEIGHTED AVERAGES[*]

JOSÉ M. MERIGÓ[1], LIGANG ZHOU[2], DEJIAN YU[3]

[1]*Manchester Business School, University of Manchester,*
Booth Street West, Manchester, M156PB, UK
[2]*School of Mathematical Sciences, Anhui University,*
230601 Hefei, Anhui, China
[3]*School of Information, Zhejiang University of Finance and Economics,*
310018 Hangzhou, China

New aggregation operators are introduced by using distance measures with the ordered weighted average, the probability and the weighted average. This approach is developed by using the Minkowski distance which uses generalized means in the aggregation process. In order to do this, it is introduced the generalized probabilistic ordered weighted averaging weighted averaging distance (GPOWAWAD) operator. It provides a parameterized family of aggregation operators between the minimum distance and the maximum one considering subjective and objective information in the analysis. Some of its main properties and particular cases are also studied.

1. Introduction

Aggregation operators (or functions) are very useful techniques for collecting the information providing summarized results [1-2]. Some very popular techniques in this framework are the probability and the weighted average. They give importance to the variables according to some available subjective or objective information. Another popular aggregation operator is the ordered weighted average (OWA) [3-4]. It provides a parameterized family of aggregation operators between the minimum and the maximum. A key issue in the OWA operator is how to integrate it with some other key concepts such as

---

[*] This work is supported by the European Commission through the project PIEF-GA-2011-300062.
Email address: jose.merigolindahl@mbs.ac.uk

the probability and the weighted average. Yager, Engemann and Filev [5-6] developed the immediate probability and Merigó [7] the probabilistic OWA (POWA) operator. Torra [8] introduced the weighted OWA (WOWA) operator, Yager [9] the importance OWA, Xu and Da [10] the hybrid average and Merigó [11] the OWA weighted average (OWAWA). Recently, Merigó et al. [12] have suggested a more general approach that integrates all three concepts in the same formulation and considering the degree of importance that each concept has in the formulation. This aggregation operator is known as the probabilistic OWA weighted average (POWAWA).

Some other techniques useful for representing the information are the generalized aggregation operators. As the name indicates, these aggregation operators use generalized and quasi-arithmetic means in the analysis. Thus, they contain a wide range of aggregation operators that include the arithmetic mean, the geometric mean and the quadratic mean.

Distance measures are used for measuring the differences between two elements, sets or fuzzy sets [13]. Usually, when dealing with sets of elements, it is necessary to normalize the distances into an average result such as the normalized Hamming distance and the normalized Minkowski distance. Recently, it has also been suggested the use of the OWA operator with distance measures [14-15]. In this context, it is possible to develop a wide range of new distance measures by using the available aggregation operators that have been recently introduced in the literature.

The aim of this paper is to introduce the generalized probabilistic OWA weighted averaging distance (GPOWAWAD) operator. It provides distance measures in a unified framework between the probability, the weighted average and the OWA operator. Moreover it uses the Minkowski distance that includes the Hamming and the Euclidean distance as particular cases. Therefore, this distance aggregation operator can represent a wide range of aggregation operators as particular cases and can deal with a wide range of complex granularities in the information. A further generalization by using quasi-arithmetic means is also introduced: the quasi-arithmetic POWAWAD (Quasi-POWAWAD) operator.

This paper is organized as follows. Section 2 introduces the GPOWAWAD operator. Section 3 analyzes a wide range of particular cases and Section 4 presents the Quasi-POWAWAD operator. Section 5 summarizes the main findings and conclusions of the paper.

2. The GPOWAWAD operator

The GPOWAWAD operator is a distance aggregation operator that integrates the probability, the weighted average and the OWA operator in the same formulation considering the degree of importance that each sub aggregation has in the problem. Moreover, it uses generalized means providing a general framework that includes a wide range of particular cases including quadratic and harmonic aggregations. By using generalized means, this approach is implicitly using a generalization of the Minkowsi distance [16]. Its main advantage is that it can aggregate distance measures considering subjective and objective information and the attitudinal character of the decision maker. It can be defined as follows for two sets $X = \{x_1, x_2, ..., x_n\}$ and $Y = \{y_1, y_2, ..., y_n\}$.

Definition 1. A GPOWAWAD operator is a mapping $GPOWAWAD: R^n \times R^n \rightarrow R$ of dimension n, if it has an associated weighting vector W, with $\sum_{j=1}^{n} w_j = 1$ and $w_j \in [0, 1]$, a probabilistic vector P, with $\sum_{i=1}^{n} p_i = 1$ and $p_i \in [0, 1]$, and a weighting vector V that affects the weighted average, with $\sum_{i=1}^{n} v_i = 1$ and $v_i \in [0, 1]$, such that:

$GPOWAWAD\ (\langle x_1, y_1 \rangle, \langle x_2, y_2 \rangle, ..., \langle x_n, y_n \rangle) =$

$$= C_1 \left(\sum_{j=1}^{n} w_j b_j^\lambda \right)^{1/\lambda} + C_2 \left(\sum_{i=1}^{n} v_i |x_i - y_i|^\delta \right)^{1/\delta} + C_3 \left(\sum_{i=1}^{n} p_i |x_i - y_i|^\chi \right)^{1/\chi}, \quad (1)$$

where b_j is the jth largest of the arguments $|x_i - y_i|$, C_1, C_2 and $C_3 \in [0, 1]$ with $C_1 + C_2 + C_3 = 1$ and λ, δ and χ are parameters such that λ, δ and $\chi \in \{-\infty, \infty\} - \{0\}$.

Note that in fuzzy set theory it is very practical to simplify the mapping to $[0, 1]$. That is, $[0, 1]^n \times [0, 1]^n \rightarrow [0, 1]$. Note also that it is possible to distinguish between descending GPOWAWAD and ascending GPOWAWAD operators. The weights of these operators are related by $w_j = w^*_{n-j+1}$.

Observe that if some of the weighting vectors are not normalized, i.e., $W = \sum_{j=1}^{n} w_j \neq 1$, $V = \sum_{i=1}^{n} v_i \neq 1$ and $P = \sum_{i=1}^{n} p_i \neq 1$, then, we can express the GPOWAWAD operator as:

$GPOWAWAD\ (\langle x_1, y_1 \rangle, \langle x_2, y_2 \rangle, ..., \langle x_n, y_n \rangle) =$

$$= \frac{C_1}{W} \left(\sum_{j=1}^{n} w_j b_j^\lambda \right)^{1/\lambda} + \frac{C_2}{V} \left(\sum_{i=1}^{n} v_i |x_i - y_i|^\delta \right)^{1/\delta} + \frac{C_3}{P} \left(\sum_{i=1}^{n} p_i |x_i - y_i|^\chi \right)^{1/\chi}. \quad (2)$$

The GPOWAWAD operator accomplishes reflexivity when $f(\langle x_1, y_1 \rangle, \langle x_2, y_2 \rangle, \ldots, \langle x_n, y_n \rangle) = 0$ if and only if $x_i = y_i$ for all $i \in [1, n]$. And the commutativity when $f(\langle x_1, y_1 \rangle, \langle x_2, y_2 \rangle, \ldots, \langle x_n, y_n \rangle) = f(\langle y_1, x_1 \rangle, \langle y_2, x_2 \rangle, \ldots, \langle y_n, x_n \rangle)$. The GPOWAWAD operator is also monotonic, bounded and idempotent.

When analysing the weights, sometimes it becomes useful to characterize them. A very common technique for doing so is the entropy of dispersion which can be defined as follows:

$$H(\hat{V}) = -\left(C_1 \sum_{j=1}^{n} w_j \ln(w_j) + C_2 \sum_{i=1}^{n} v_i \ln(v_i) + C_3 \sum_{i=1}^{n} p_i \ln(p_i) \right). \tag{3}$$

As we can see, if $C_1 = 1$, we get the Yager entropy [3] and if $C_2 = 1$ or $C_3 = 1$, the Shannon entropy [17]. If $C_1 = 0$, we get the entropy of the PWA operator [18], if $C_2 = 0$, the entropy of the POWA operator [7] and if $C_3 = 0$, the entropy of the OWA weighted average [11].

3. Families of GPOWAWAD operators

By analyzing different values in the parameters of the GPOWAWAD operator we may obtain a wide range of particular cases. For example:

- If $C_1 = 1$, we get the Minkowski OWA distance (MOWAD).
- If $C_2 = 1$, we get the weighted Minkowski distance.
- If $C_3 = 1$, we get the probabilistic Minkowski distance.
- If $C_1 = 0$, we form the generalized probabilistic weighted averaging distance (GPWAD).
- If $C_2 = 0$, we form the generalized probabilistic OWAD (GPOWAD).
- If $C_3 = 0$, we form the generalized OWAWA distance (GOWAWAD).
- The GPOWAWA operator (if one of the sets is empty).
- If $\lambda = \delta = \chi = 1$, the POWAWAD.
- If $\lambda = \delta = \chi = 2$, the Euclidean POWAWAD.
- If $\lambda = \delta = \chi = -1$, the harmonic POWAWAD.
- If $\lambda = \delta = \chi \to 0$, the geometric POWAWAD.
- The arithmetic GPWAD (if $w_j = 1/n$, for all j).
- The arithmetic GPOWAD (if $v_i = 1/n$, for all i).
- The arithmetic GOWAWAD (if $p_i = 1/n$, for all i).
- The normalized Minkowski distance (if $v_i = 1/n$, $p_i = 1/n$, for all i, and $w_j = 1/n$, for all j).
- The maximum GPWAD ($w_1 = 1$ and $w_j = 0$, for all $j \neq 1$).
- The minimum GPWAD ($w_n = 1$ and $w_j = 0$, for all $j \neq n$).

Other families of GPOWAWAD operators could be used following the OWA literature and its extensions [4,12,14].

4. The Quasi-POWAWAD operator

The GPOWAWAD operator can be further generalized by using quasi-arithmetic means [19-20]. Thus, we obtain the quasi-arithmetic POWAWAD (Quasi-POWAWAD) operator. Its main strength is that it provides a more general approach that includes more particular cases than the GPOWAWAD operator since it includes it as a particular case. It is defined as follows for two sets $X = \{x_1, x_2, ..., x_n\}$ and $Y = \{y_1, y_2, ..., y_n\}$.

Definition 2. A Quasi-POWAWAD operator is a mapping $Quasi\text{-}POWAWAD$: $R^n \times R^n \rightarrow R$ of dimension n, that has an associated weighting vector W, with $\sum_{j=1}^{n} w_j = 1$ and $w_j \in [0, 1]$, a probabilistic vector P, with $\sum_{i=1}^{n} p_i = 1$ and $p_i \in [0, 1]$, and a weighting vector V that affects the weighted average, with $\sum_{i=1}^{n} v_i = 1$ and $v_i \in [0, 1]$, such that:

$$Quasi\text{-}POWAWAD \, (\langle x_1, y_1 \rangle, \langle x_2, y_2 \rangle, ..., \langle x_n, y_n \rangle) =$$

$$= C_1 f^{-1}\left(\sum_{j=1}^{n} w_j f(b_j) \right) + C_2 g^{-1}\left(\sum_{i=1}^{n} v_i g(|x_i - y_i|) \right) + C_3 h^{-1}\left(\sum_{i=1}^{n} p_i h(|x_i - y_i|) \right), \quad (4)$$

where b_j is the jth largest of the arguments $|x_i - y_i|$, C_1, C_2 and $C_3 \in [0, 1]$ with $C_1 + C_2 + C_3 = 1$ and f, g and h are strictly continuous monotonic functions.

Note that if $f = b^\lambda$, $g = |x_i - y_i|^\delta$ and $h = |x_i - y_i|^\gamma$, the Quasi-POWAWAD becomes that GPOWAWAD operator.

5. Conclusions

This paper has introduced the GPOWAWAD operator. It is an aggregation operator that permits to study distance measures in a more complete and flexible way because it can deal with different sources of information in the analysis including the probability, the weighted average and the OWA operator. The use of generalized has shown the possibility of including the Hamming and the Euclidean distance in the same formulation. Some other particular cases have also been considered. The paper has ended with the Quasi-POWAWAD operator, a further generalization of the GPOWAWAD by using quasi-arithmetic means. In future research, further extensions will be considered including the use of Choquet integrals and norms.

References

1. G. Beliakov, A. Pradera and T. Calvo, *Aggregation functions: A guide for practitioners* (Springer-Verlag, Berlin-Heidelberg, 2007).
2. M. Grabisch, J.L. Marichal and R. Mesiar, E. Pap, Aggregation functions: Means, *Inform. Sci.* **181**, 1 (2011).
3. R.R. Yager, On ordered weighted averaging aggregation operators in multi-criteria decision making, *IEEE Trans. Syst. Man Cybern. B* **18**, 183 (1988).
4. R.R. Yager, J. Kacprzyk and G. Beliakov. *Recent developments on the ordered weighted averaging operators: Theory and practice.* (Springer-Verlag, Berlin-Heidelberg, 2011).
5. R.R. Yager, K.J. Engemann and D.P. Filev, On the concept of immediate probabilities, *Int. J. Intelligent Syst.* **10**, 373 (1995).
6. K.J. Engemann, D.P. Filev and R.R. Yager, Modelling decision making using immediate probabilities, *Int. J. General Syst.* **24**, 281 (1996).
7. J.M. Merigó, Probabilities with OWA operators, *Expert Syst. Applic.* **39**, 11456 (2012).
8. V. Torra, The weighted OWA operator, *Int. J. Intelligent Syst.* **12**, 153 (1997).
9. R.R. Yager, Including importances in OWA aggregation using fuzzy systems modelling, *IEEE Trans. Fuzzy Syst.* **6**, 286 (1998).
10. Z.S. Xu and Q.L. Da, An overview of operators for aggregating information. *Int. J. Intelligent Syst.* **18**, 953 (2003).
11. J.M. Merigó, A unified model between the weighted average and the induced OWA operator, *Expert Syst. Applic.* **38**, 11560 (2011).
12. J.M. Merigó, C. Lobato-Carral and A. Carrilero-Castillo, Decision making in the European Union under risk and uncertainty, *Eur. J. Int. Management*, **6**, 590 (2012).
13. A. Kaufmann, *Introduction to the theory of fuzzy subsets* (Academic Press, New York, 1975).
14. J.M. Merigó and A.M. Gil-Lafuente, New decision-making techniques and their application in the selection of financial products, *Inform. Sci.* **180**, 2085 (2010).
15. Z.S. Xu and J. Chen, Ordered weighted distance measure, *J. Syst. Sci. Syst. Eng.* **17**, 432 (2008).
16. J.M. Merigó and M. Casanovas, A new Minkowski distance based on induced aggregation operators, *Int. J. Computational Intelligence Syst.* **4**, 123 (2011).
17. C.E. Shannon, A mathematical theory of communication, *Bell Systems Technical J.* **27**, 379 (1948).
18. J.M. Merigó. The probabilistic weighted average and its application in multi-person decision making, *Int. J. Intelligent Syst.* **27**, 457 (2012).
19. J.M. Merigó and M. Casanovas, The uncertain induced quasi-arithmetic OWA operator, *Int. J Intelligent Syst.* **26**, 1 (2011).
20. J.M. Merigó and R.R. Yager, Generalized moving averages, distance measures and OWA operators, *Int. J Uncert. Fuzz. Knowledge-Based Syst.* **21**, 533 (2013).

A RULE BASE AND ITS INFERENCE METHOD USING EVIDENTIAL REASONING[*]

LIUQIAN JIN AND YANG XU

Intelligent Control Development Center , Southwest Jiaotong University, Chengdu, China, 610031

XIN FANG

School of Transportation and Logistics , Southwest Jiaotong University, Chengdu, China, 610031

In this paper, a rule base representation with certainty factors is proposed firstly along with its inference method. Such a rule base is designed with certainty factors embedded in the consequence terms, rule terms as well as in the antecedent terms, which is shown to be capable of capturing uncertainty. As the evidential reasoning approach is applied to the rule combination, the overall representation and inference framework can be applied in rule based system for human decision making due to the fact. A numerical example is examined to show the implementation process of the proposed method, as comparing with a classical approache we can see its high perfprmance.

1. Introduction

Among many alternative means for knowledge representation, rules seem to be one of the most common forms for expressing various types of knowledge for a number of reasons [9, 4, 5]. Most phenomena in our world are uncertain, the knowledge of phenomena are uncertainty with randomness, vagueness, incompleteness, ignorance and so on. Uncertainty is an important characteristic of knowledge, so how to represent and infer the uncertainty is an important point of knowledge representation and reasoning [2].

Uncertainty information is also processed in knowledge systems. In fact, uncertainty can be modeled by probabilities, or by fuzzy sets, or by possibilities, or by any other single methods. So how to build the uncertainty reasoning methods is a hot spots [3].

[*] This work is supported by National Science Foundation of China (Grant No. 61175055), Sichuan Key Technology Research and Development Program (Grant No. 2011FZ0051), Radio Administration Bureau of MIIT of China (Grant No. [2011] 146), China Institution of Communications (Grant No. [2011] 051).

In this paper, different from the existing representations, there are multiple consequent attributes in a rule, the antecedent attribute values and consequent attribute values are with certainty factors. This representation is more in tune with human knowledge and reduces the loss of information.

The rest of this paper is organized as follows. Certainty rule base and its inference framework are proposed in Section 2, including the structure and representation of certainty rule base and inference method. The proposed rule representation and inference methodology are demonstrated in Section 3 using a numerical example and compare with the Dempster-Shafer Theory. Conclusion are drawn in Section 4.

2. Certainty rule base inference method using the evidential reasoning approach

The structure and representation of Certainty Rule Base (CeRB) and its inference method are given in this section. The starting point of constructing a rule base is to collect If-then rules from domain experts or through data mining based on domain knowledge. A knowledge base and an inference engine are then designed to infer useful consequents with certainty factors from rules and observation facts that are provided by users.

First of all, we should represent the knowledge and fact with uncertainty.

Definition 1 A rule base model can be formally represented as follows:

$$R= \langle (X, A), (Y, C), CF, W, F \rangle$$

where $X=\{X_i|\ i=1, \cdots, M\}$ is the set of antecedent attributes; $A_i=\{A_{i,Ii}|\ Ii=1, \cdots, L_{Ai}\}$ is the set of attribute values for X_i, let $A=\{A_i|\ i=1, \cdots, M\}$ as the set of antecedent attribute value sets; $Y=\{Y_j|\ j=1, \cdots, N\}$ is the set of consequent attributes; $C_j=\{C_{j,Jj}|\ Jj=1, \cdots, L_{Cj}\}$ is the set of attribute values for Y_j, let $C=\{C_j|\ j=1, \cdots, N\}$ as the set of consequent attribute value sets; $W=\{w_i|\ 0 \leq w_i \leq 1,\ i=1, \cdots, M,$ $\sum_{i=1}^{M} w_i = 1\ \}$ is the set of antecedent attribute weights, w_i is the weight of A_i; CF is certainty factor; F is a logical function.

The kth rule in a rule base in forms of a certainty rule can be written as R^k:

$$\text{If } \left(X_1 = A_1^k, CF^k \left(X_1 = A_1^k \right) \right) \wedge \cdots \wedge \left(X_M = A_M^k, CF^k \left(X_M = A_M^k \right) \right)$$

$$\text{then } \left(Y_1 = C_1^k, CF^k \left(Y_1 = C_1^k \right) \right) \wedge \cdots \wedge \left(Y_N = C_N^k, CF^k \left(Y_N = C_N^k \right) \right)$$

with rule certainty factor $CF^k(R^k)$,

and antecedent attribute weights $w_1, w_2, \cdots, w_M$

where $A_i^k \in A_i$ or $A_i^k = \varnothing$, $0 \leq CF^k \left(X_i = A_i^k \right) \leq 1$; $C_j^k \in C_j$ or $C_j^k = \varnothing$,

$0 \leq CF^k \left(Y_j = C_j^k \right) \leq 1$; $0 \leq CF^k \left(R^k \right) \leq 1$; $0 \leq w_i \leq 1$, $\sum_{i=1}^{M} w_i = 1$.

Remark:

$$\alpha_i^k = CF^k\left(X_i = A_i^k\right), \qquad i=1,2,\cdots,M \ ;$$

$$\beta_j^k = CF^k\left(Y_j = C_j^k\right), \qquad j=1,2,\cdots,N \ ; \ \gamma^k = CF^k\left(R^k\right) \ ;$$

then the kth rule R^k can be written as:

$$\text{If } \left(A_1^k,\alpha_1^k\right)\wedge\left(A_2^k,\alpha_2^k\right)\wedge\cdots\wedge\left(A_M^k,\alpha_M^k\right)$$

$$\text{then } \left(C_1^k,\beta_1^k\right)\wedge\left(C_2^k,\beta_2^k\right)\wedge\cdots\wedge\left(C_N^k,\beta_N^k\right)$$

with rule certainty factor γ^k, and antecedent attribute weights $w_1, w_2, \cdots, w_M$ where $\alpha_i^k, (i=1,2,\cdots,M)$ is the certainty factor of A_i^k, some antecedent attributes may be not needed in this rule, in this case, $A_i^k = \varnothing$ ($\varnothing$ means default, empty set), if $A_i^k = \varnothing$ then $\alpha_i^k = 0$ and this antecedent attribute can be left out; so as the consequent.

With the representation of certainty rule, the certainty rule base inference method should be given.

There is an input vector remarked as

$$Input()=\{(a_1, \alpha_1), (a_2, \alpha_2), \cdots, (a_M, \alpha_M)\},$$

where $a_i, (i=1,2, \cdots, M)$ is one-to-one correspondence with the ith antecedent attribute X_i, $a_i = \varnothing$ is allowed but not all of them; α_i, $(i=1,2, \cdots, M)$ is the certainty factor of a_i, if $a_i = \varnothing$ then $\alpha_i = 0$, the higher the number value of α_i, the greater the degree of certainty.

Suppose that the input fact and the kth rule R^k match successfully, it means that for all i with which $A_i^k \neq \varnothing$, a_i is equal to A_i^k. But the certainty factor of each input value and antecedent attribute value may be different, so based on the similarity measure there is a matching degree should be given as certainty factors.

So the certainty factor of A_i^k with the input fact for inference can be given as an individual matching degree as follows[7]:

$$\tilde{\alpha}_i^k = \begin{cases} \min\{1-\alpha_i^k+\alpha_i, 1-\alpha_i+\alpha_i^k\}, & A_i^k \neq \varnothing \\ 1, & A_i^k = \varnothing \end{cases} \quad (i=1,2,\cdots,M).$$

The weight set of the antecedent attribute of the kth rule R^k is given as $W^k = \{w_1^k, w_2^k, \cdots, w_M^k\}$, with

$$w_i^k = \begin{cases} w_i & A_i^k \neq \varnothing \\ 0 & A_i^k = \varnothing \end{cases} \quad (i=1,2,\cdots,M),$$

after normalization, the weight set is obtained as

$$\tilde{W}^k = \{\tilde{w}_1^k, \tilde{w}_2^k, \cdots, \tilde{w}_M^k\}, \quad \tilde{w}_i^k = \frac{w_i^k}{\sum_{l=1}^{M} w_l^k} (i=1,2,\cdots,M).$$

the aggregation function of antecedent

$$\tilde{\alpha}^k = \prod_{i=1}^{M} \left(\tilde{\alpha}_i^k \right)^{\bar{w}_i^k}$$

where

$$\bar{w}_i^k = \frac{\tilde{w}_i^k}{\max\limits_{l=1,\cdots,M} \left\{ \tilde{w}_l^k \right\}},$$

$\bar{w}_i^k$ is weighted geometric averaging operator [1].

The weight w_R^k of the kth rule and the weight w_A^k of the antecedent can be given as follows:

$$w_R^k = \frac{\gamma^k}{\tilde{\alpha}^k + \gamma^k}, \quad w_A^k = \frac{\tilde{\alpha}^k}{\tilde{\alpha}^k + \gamma^k}.$$

Then the basic probability mass $m_R(\wedge C^k)$ assigned to $\wedge C^k$ (the consequent of the kth rule) and the unassigned mass $m_R(\Xi^k)$ caused by the uncertainty of rule R^k and the basic probability mass $m_A(\wedge C^k)$ assigned to $\wedge C^k$ and the unassigned mass $m_A(\Xi^k)$ caused by the attribute $\wedge A^k$ are given as follows:

$$m_R\left(\wedge C^k\right) = w_R^k \gamma^k ; \quad m_R\left(\varnothing\right) = 0 ; \quad m_R\left(\Xi^k\right) = 1 - w_R^k \gamma^k ; \quad \bar{m}_R\left(\Xi^k\right) = 1 - w_R^k ;$$

$$m_A\left(\wedge C^k\right) = w_A^k \tilde{\alpha}^k ; \quad m_A\left(\varnothing\right) = 0 ; \quad m_A\left(\Xi^k\right) = 1 - w_A^k \tilde{\alpha}^k ; \quad \bar{m}_A\left(\Xi^k\right) = 1 - w_A^k .$$

Based on Dempster-Shafer theory and evidential reasoning approach, the probability masses of the evidence combinations are given as follows:

$$N^k = 1 - \sum_{E \cap F = \varnothing} m_R\left(E\right) m_A\left(F\right) = 1 ;$$

$$m\left(\wedge C^k\right) = \left[m_R\left(\wedge C^k\right) m_A\left(\wedge C^k\right) + m_R\left(\wedge C^k\right) m_A\left(\Xi^k\right) + m_R\left(\Xi^k\right) m_A\left(\wedge C^k\right) \right] \Big/ N^k$$
$$= w_R^k \gamma^k + w_A^k \tilde{\alpha}^k - w_A^k w_R^k \tilde{\alpha}^k \gamma^k$$

$$\bar{m}\left(\Xi^k\right) = \left[\bar{m}_R\left(\Xi^k\right) \bar{m}_A\left(\Xi^k\right) \right] \Big/ N^k = \left(1 - w_R^k\right)\left(1 - w_A^k\right) .$$

The certainty factor of the consequent $\wedge C^k$ is given as following:

$$\tilde{\beta}^k = \frac{m\left(\wedge C^k\right)}{1 - \bar{m}\left(\Xi^k\right)} = \frac{w_R^k \gamma^k + w_A^k \tilde{\alpha}^k - w_A^k w_R^k \tilde{\alpha}^k \gamma^k}{1 - \left(1 - w_R^k\right)\left(1 - w_A^k\right)} .$$

Based on similarity measure, for each certainty factor of the consequent attribute value is given as follows:

$$\tilde{\beta}_j^k = \left(1 - \beta_j^k + \tilde{\beta}^k\right) \beta_j^k .$$

3. Numerical example

A numerical example is discussed in this section to show the exercise method and demonstrate the algorithm's efficacy.

Suppose R is a certainty rule base with antecedent attribute set X, antecedent attribute value set A, consequent attribute set Y, consequent attribute value set C, certainty factor set CF, antecedent attribute weight set W, and logical function F. R is given as follows:

$$R= \langle(X, A), (Y, C), CF, W, F\rangle$$

where $X=\{x_1, x_2, x_3, x_4\}$, $A=\{A_1, A_2, A_3, A_4\}$, $A_1=\{a_{11}, a_{12}, a_{13}\}$, $A_2=\{a_{21}, a_{22}, a_{23}\}$, $A_3=\{a_{31}, a_{32}\}$, $A_4=\{a_{41}, a_{42}\}$, $Y=\{x_4, x_5\}$, $C=\{C_1, C_2\}$, $C_1=\{a_{41}, a_{42}\}$, $C_2=\{a_{51}, a_{52}\}$, $W=\{0.4, 0.15, 0.2, 0.25\}$, $w_A=0.5$, $w_R=0.5$.

The rule base R with certainty factors is given in Table 1.

Table 1. Certainty Rule Base

Rule	Antecedent	Consequent	CF of Rule
R^1	$(a_{11},0.7)\wedge(a_{21},0.6)$	$(a_{41},0.7)$	0.9
R^2	$(a_{13},0.8)\wedge(a_{32},0.7)$	$(a_{42},0.6)$	0.9
R^3	$(a_{22},0.6)\wedge(a_{31},0.8)$	$(a_{42},0.6)$	0.8
R^4	$(a_{23},0.7)\wedge(a_{32},0.6)$	$(a_{41},0.7)$	0.8
R^5	$(a_{32},0.8)\wedge(a_{41},0.7)$	$(a_{51},0.7)$	0.7
R^6	$(a_{32},0.6)\wedge(a_{42},0.6)$	$(a_{52},0.5)$	0.6
R^7	$(a_{11},0.6)\wedge(a_{21},0.7)\wedge(a_{31},0.8)$	$(a_{42},0.7)\wedge(a_{51},0.6)$	0.7
R^8	$(a_{11},0.7)\wedge(a_{23},0.6)\wedge(a_{42},0.8)$	$(a_{52},0.8)$	0.9
R^9	$(a_{12},0.7)\wedge(a_{22},0.7)\wedge(a_{31},0.6)$	$(a_{41},0.6)\wedge(a_{51},0.7)$	0.9
R^{10}	$(a_{12},0.6)\wedge(a_{23},0.7)\wedge(a_{32},0.5)$	$(a_{41},0.7)\wedge(a_{52},0.6)$	1

with the weights of the antecedent attribute: $W =\{0.4,0.15,0.2,0.25\}$.

The actual input vector is $Input()$as follows:

$$Input()=\{(a_{11}, 0.6), (a_{21}, 0.8), (a_{31}, 0.6)\}.$$

Based on the certainty rule base and input vector , the R^1 and R^7 match, the certainty factors of the consequent attribute values and intermediate datas are given in Table 2.

Table 2. The certainty factors of the consequent attribute values and intermediate datas

Rule	$\tilde{\alpha}_1^k$	$\tilde{\alpha}_2^k$	$\tilde{\alpha}_3^k$	$\tilde{\alpha}_4^k$	w_1^k	w_2^k	w_3^k	w_4^k
R^1	0.9	1	0	0	0.4	0.15	0	0
R^7	1	1	0.8	0	0.4	0.15	0.2	0

Rule	$\tilde{w}_1^k$	$\tilde{w}_2^k$	$\tilde{w}_3^k$	$\tilde{w}_4^k$	$\overline{w}_1^k$	$\overline{w}_2^k$	$\overline{w}_3^k$	$\overline{w}_4^k$
R^1	0.73	0.27	0	0	1	0.370	0	0
R^7	0.53	0.2	0.27	0	1	0.377	0.5	0

Rule	$\bar{\alpha}^k$	γ^k	w_A^k	w_R^k	$\tilde{\beta}^k$	$\tilde{\beta}_1^k$	$\tilde{\beta}_2^k$
R^1	0.9	0.9	0.500	0.500	0.930	0.904	0
R^7	0.899	0.7	0.562	0.438	0.871	0.820	0.763

For R^1, the consequent is $(a_{41}, 0.904)$; for R^7, the consequent is $(a_{42}, 0.820)$ $\wedge$ $(a_{51}, 0.763)$, then we can the result as (a_{41}, a_{51}).

With the MYCIN inference model, the certainty factors of antecedents and rules as well as the weights of antecedent attributes are ignored, so the result lost some information. The consequents $(a_{41}, 0.42)$ and $(a_{42}, 0.42) \wedge (a_{51}, 0.36)$, in this case, we can'n make a decision which between a_{41} and a_{42} is better.

With the belief rule-base inference methodology using the evudential reasoning approach (RIMER), the certainty factors of antecedents and multi-consequent attributes are ignored. The consequents $(a_{41}, 0.7)$ and $(a_{42}, 0.7) \wedge (a_{51}, 0.6)$, in this case, we also can'n make a decision which between a_{41} and a_{42} is better.

By the numeration and comparison, certainty rule base its inference method shows its implementablility, advantage and application value, as there are still some problems should be researched, we will continuously improve this method.

4. Conclusion

In this paper, a new rule base representation, called certainty rule base, was proposed as a great extension of traditional fuzzy rule based systems and belief rule base introduced in [4] in term of modified performance. Finally, there is a sample numerical example, which was shown there is not a problem for practical application and its advantages.

References

1. Aczél J, Saaty T L. Procedures for synthesizing ratio judgements. Journal of mathematical psychology, 1983, 27(2): 93-102.
2. Fengbao Yang, Xiaoxia Wang. Combination method of conflictive evidences in D-S evidence theory. Beijing: National defense industry press, 2010.2.
3. Hans-Jürgen Zimmermann. Fuzzy sets and operations research for decision support. Beijing normal university press, 2009.4.
4. Jianbo Yang, Jun Liu, Jin Wang. Belief rule-base inference methodology using the evidential reasoning approach--RIMER. IEEE transactions on systems, man, and cybernetics--part A: systems and humans, 2006, 36(2): 266-285.
5. Jianbo Yang, Dongling Xu. Evidential reasoning rule for evidence combination. Artificial Intelligence, 2013, 205: 1-29.
6. Jun Liu, Lius Martinez, Alberto Calzada, et al. A novel belief rule base representation, generation and its inference methodology. Knowledge-Based Systems, 2013, 53: 129-141.
7. Liuqian Jin, Yang Xu. A rule-based inference method using Dempster-Shafer theory. The 2013 International Conference on Intelligent System and Knowledge Engineering (ISKE 2013). Shenzhen, November 20-23, 2013
8. Liuqian Jin, Yang Xu. A novel rule base representation and its inference methodology using the evidential reasoning approach. (Completed)
9. Ron Sun. Robust reasoning: Integrating rule-based and similarity-based reasoning. Artificial Intelligence, 1995, 75(2): 241-295.
10. Zhibin Wu, Jiuping Xu. A consistency and consensus based decision support model for group decision making with multiplicative preference relations. Decision Support Systems, 2012, 52: 757-767.

BIPOLARITY IN SOCIAL SCIENCES AND MATHEMATICS*

CAMILO A. FRANCO

Department of Food and Resource Economics, University of Copenhagen,
Frederiksberg, DK-1958, Denmark

J. TINGUARO RODRÍGUEZ, JAVIER MONTERO

Faculty of Mathematics, Complutense University, Madrid, 28040, Spain

The polarity of concepts and the dialectic process by which its meaning emerges has been subject of interest since the ancient Greeks. Recently, the term Bipolarity has been used in social and mathematical sciences, referring to the measurement of the meaning of concepts. It is claimed that the measuring process has to consider at least an associated pair of meaningful opposites, such that some type of structure is used to analyze the aspect of reality that is being modeled. From this point of view, we take a quick overview on the genealogy of Bipolarity, discussing some ideas about the nature of negative knowledge, and how it has been examined recently, and not so recently, by the mathematical community.

1. Introduction

In 1958, Ch. Osgood *et al* [10] proposed a semantic theory based on the semantic differential scale (SD). This theory became a corner-stone in economic and decision models dealing with subjective measurements of attitudes and perceptions. The SD scale of Osgood is commonly known as the *bipolar univariate model*, while a modified SD scale, initially proposed by K. Kaplan, can be referred to as the *unipolar bivariate model* (see e.g. [7]). In decision theory, some well-known examples using the bipolar univariate model are Prospect Theory [12] and its generalization by means of the Choquet integral w.r.t. bi-capacities [8], while for unipolar bivariate modeling, some examples consist in the Four-Valued Model for Partial Comparability Theory [11] and the Preference-Aversion Model [5].

The SD scale of Osgood, or bipolar univariate model, is a one-dimensional structure whose end-points are opposite references. These references are taken to be *reciprocal*, such that the known value of one of them entails (by some

---

* Financial support from the Center for research in the Foundations of Electronic Markets (CFEM), funded by the Danish Council for Strategic Research, and from the Government of Spain, Grant TIN2012-32482, is gratefully acknowledged.

mathematical operation such as Negation) the value of the other. The SD scale became a very popular tool for measuring attitudes in an easy way, where the individual is asked to value a concept on the SD scale, such that the value can be negative, neutral or positive. In this way, the concept cannot be positive and negative at the same time. According to some critics (see [9] for a detailed exposition of these matters until 1972, and for a more recent one from 1997, see [2]), the SD scale does not allow measuring ambivalence, an attitude essentially different from the SD's neutral-indifference state.

Therefore, the nature of ambivalence (apart from a neutral-indifferent attitude) requires to separately measuring the positive and negative components inherent to every attitudinal response (implicitly aggregated under the SD scale). In 1972, Kaplan [9] proposed a modification to the SD technique, where individuals are presented both with a positive and a negative unipolar scale. Such modification was a response to the restrictive *reciprocal bipolar structure* of the bipolar univariate model, which did not allow examining in an analytical way how the emergence of ambivalence occurred and how it could be resolved.

2. Reflecting on the Bipolarity of Concepts and Intuitionistic Ideas

In a general sense, bipolarity refers to the polarity of the meaning of concepts and the nature of positive and negative knowledge. Hence, it is deeply related with that which we consider to be valid or even relevant knowledge. Take for example the *intuitionistic* philosophical-mathematical position (referring to a position defended in the last 19th and early 20th century by H. Poicaré and L.E.J. Brouwer), where the truth/provability of a proposition P can only be associated to the explicit mathematical construction of P. In consequence, the proof of the impossibility of P cannot be taken as the proof of its negative affirmation not-P [1] (this leads e.g., to the questioning of the principle of the excluded middle, where it holds either P or not-P, and the validity of some mathematical demonstrations that make use of it, such as the existence of non-denumerable sets).

At the current state of things, *bipolarity* has been examined in mathematics following a typology where bipolarity types I, II and III exist [4]. The first two respectively refer to the above mentioned univariate and bivariate models, while the third one stands as a proposal on its own (it still remains to be further explored). At first instance, type-III bipolarity seems to refer to a bivariate model with more than one pair of opposite references, possibly describing the different sources of information or the multiple dimensions building up the meaning of concepts. As it seems, this third type is the most general setting for modeling complex (real-life) bipolar knowledge, due to the fact that the meaning of concepts refers to the use that they are given in reality (by our brain), and such use can be represented through (multiple) positive and aversive stimuli. Then, as it has been argued before, at least both indifference and ambivalence neutral states have to be accounted for in the model's valuation structure so it can be a good representation of reality.

One of the consequences of taking a third-type bipolar approach, is that negative information/knowledge exists independently from the positive one (i.e., from the intuitionistic point of view, the construction of a proof on the impossibility of proposition P does not imply having a proof for the affirmation of not-P). Hence, what seems more appealing in order to understand concepts and reality is to explore the neutral states that arise in between such opposites, and not refer to the opposite binary pole by assuming that negative information/knowledge exists only as the complement of the positive, or in other words, as the associated (by some mathematical operation) negative counterpart of the positive.

Following this line of thought, bipolarity can be understood in a general way by paired structures where a reference concept is represented as P, and its meaning can be decomposed into the pairs Q and V, but also into pairs A and Z, or even so, each pair Q and V could be decomposed into their respective pairs of (Q^+, Q^-) and (V^+, V^-). Take for example, P="size", Q="tall", V="short", and A="big", Z="small". Under the univariate model (bipolarity type I), the verification of P can be Q or V, but never Q and V. Indeed, this is black or white binary modeling of reality. In real-life problems, complexity is an undeniable quality that refers to something being both positive and negative at the same time. Then P can be both Q and V, requiring an explicit measurement of both Q and V, and the same happens for A and Z, and for any other pair of *meaningful opposites* (a term firstly introduced in [10]), where such complexity builds on as much as it is needed.

3. Some Results on Bipolar Preference Modeling

Here we present some results regarding the representation of knowledge and its relation to bipolarity in preference modeling. The first result refers to the distinction of need and preference. It is well known that classical economic theory assumes that the individual decides according to a subjective measure of utility, built on the perception of desire [3]. Nonetheless, it can be argued that the individual decides according to his needs and desires, a position that requires the previous demonstration that an effective distinction between preference and need is possible.

It has been shown that only under a (bipolar type-III) frame that aggregates separately positive and negative preferences, in the form of perceptions of desire and rejection, it is possible to distinguish between preferences and needs [5].

On the other hand, it has been shown that the use of a reciprocal structure in preference modeling reduces the representation of knowledge, resulting in the consequent loss of information [6]. In this way, if the inverse preference is taken as the negative counterpart of preference, the individual's decision possibilities reduce to that of desiring (more or less) some alternative, without possibly revealing rejection. The consequence of this type of modeling, commonly associated to mainstream economic theory, is a poor representation of reality, in the sense that it does not acknowledge the potential complexity of human behavior and attitudes.

References

1. L.E.J. Brouwer. Intuitionism and formalism. Bulletin (New Series) of the American Mathematical Society 37 (1999), 55-64. Reprinted from Bull. Amer. Math. Soc. 20 (1913), 81-96.
2. J. Cacioppo, W. Gardner, G. Bernston. Beyond bipolar conceptualizations and measures: the case of attitudes and evaluative space. Personality and Social Psychology Review 1 (1997), 3-26.
3. G. Debreu. Theory of value. An axiomatic analysis of economic equilibrium. Yale University Press, New Haven (1959)
4. D. Dubois, H. Prade. An introduction to bipolar representations of information and preference. International Journal of Intelligent Systems 23 (2008), 866-877.
5. C. Franco, J. Montero, J.T. Rodríguez. A fuzzy and bipolar approach to preference modeling with application to need and desire. Fuzzy Sets and Systems 214 (2013), 20-34.
6. C. Franco, J.T. Rodríguez, J. Montero. An ordinal approach to computing with words and the preference-aversion model. Information Sciences 258 (2014), 239-248.
7. M. Grabisch, S. Greco, M. Pirlot. Bipolar and bivariate models in multi-criteria decision analysis: descriptive and constructive approaches. International Journal of Intelligent Systems 23 (2008), 930-969.
8. M. Grabisch, Ch. Labreuche. A decade of application of the Choquet and Sugeno integrals in multi-criteria decision aid. Annals of Operations Research 175 (2010), 247-290.
9. K. Kaplan. On the ambivalence-indifference problem in attitude theory and measurement: a suggested modification of the semantic differential technique. Psychological Bulletin 77 (1972), 361-372.
10. Ch. Osgood, G. Suci, P. Tannenbaum. The Measurement of Meaning. University of Illinois Press, Urbana (1958).
11. A. Tsoukiàs, Ph. Vincke. A new axiomatic foundation of the partial comparability theory. Theory and Decision 39 (1995), 79-114.
12. A. Tversky, D. Kahneman. Advances in prospect theory: cumulative representation of uncertainty. Journal of Risk and Uncertainty 5 (1992), 297-323.

α-SEMI-LOCK SEMANTIC RESOLUTION METHOD BASED ON LATTICE-VALUED PROPOSITIONAL LOGIC LP(X)

XIAOMEI ZHONG[1], YANG XU[1], XINGXING HE[1]

[1]*School of Mathematics, Southwest Jiaotong University*
Chengdu, Sichuan 610031, P.R. China
zhongxm2013@home.swjtu.edu.cn, xuyang@home.swjtu.edu.cn,
x.he@home.swjtu.edu.cn

On the basis of multiary α-resolution principle, a multiary α-resolution automated reasoning method--α-semi-lock semantic resolution method is studied in lattice-valued propositional logic system LP(X) based on lattice implication algebra. Concretely, α-semi-lock semantic resolution method is established in LP(X), as well as its soundness and condition completeness.

1. Introduction

Since lattice-valued logic based on lattice implication algebra (LIA) is a kind of important multi-valued logic, which can describe both comparability and incomparability simultaneously, it is very necessary to further study resolution-based automated reasoning in lattice-valued propositional logic LP(X) based on LIA. In view of this idea, in 2000, Xu et al., established α-resolution principle [8] in LP(X), as well as its soundness and weak completeness. Since then, some researchers have investigated a variety of α-resolution automated reasoning methods in LP(X) and achieved some important results [2, 5-7]. Last year, Xu et al., further improved α-resolution principle and extended it into a more general form--multiary α-resolution principle [11], which enhances the ability of α-resolution automated reasoning to some extent.

During the process of using α-resolution automated reasoning to solve practical problems, principle can only play the role of guiding, which allows the establishment of specific α-resolution methods based on multiary α-resolution principle become very important. As lock resolution method [4] and semantic resolution method [3] are two types of classical resolution-based automated reasoning methods in classical 2-valued logic, so it is necessary for us to establish the corresponding α-lock semantic resolution method in LP(X) by combing the characteristics of lock resolution method and semantic resolution method.

This paper is organized as follows: in Section 2, some preliminary relevant concepts and conclusions about lattice-valued propositional logic LP(X) and multiary α-resolution principle are reviewed. In Section 3, α-semi-lock semantic resolution method based on LP(X) is established, as well as its soundness and condition completeness.

2. Preliminaries

In this section, we will review some elementary concepts and conclusions of lattice-valued propositional logic LP(X) based on LIA and multiary α-resolution principle. We refer the readers to [9, 11] for more details.

Definition 2.1 [9] Let $(L, \vee, \wedge, O, I)$ be a bounded lattice with an order-reversing involution $'$, I and O the greatest and the smallest element of L respectively, and $\rightarrow: L \times L \rightarrow L$ be a mapping. $(L, \vee, \wedge, ', \rightarrow, O, I)$ is called an LIA if the following conditions hold for any $x, y, z \in L$:

(I_1) $x \rightarrow (y \rightarrow z) = y \rightarrow (x \rightarrow z)$;　(I_2) $x \rightarrow x = I$;　(I_3) $x \rightarrow y = y' \rightarrow x'$;

(I_4) $x \rightarrow y = y \rightarrow x = I$ implies $x = y$;　(I_5) $(x \rightarrow y) \rightarrow y = (y \rightarrow x) \rightarrow x$;

(l_1) $(x \vee y) \rightarrow z = (x \rightarrow z) \wedge (y \rightarrow z)$;　(l_2) $(x \wedge y) \rightarrow z = (x \rightarrow z) \vee (y \rightarrow z)$.

Example 2.1 [9] **(Łukasiewicz implication algebra on finite chain)** Let $L_n = \{a_i \mid i = 1, 2, \ldots, n\}$, $a_1 < a_2 < \ldots < a_n$. For any $1 \leq j, k \leq n$, define

$a_j \vee a_k = a_{max\{j, k\}}$, $a_j \wedge a_k = a_{min\{j, k\}}$, $(a_j)' = a_{n-j+1}$, $a_j \rightarrow a_k = a_{min\{n-j+k, n\}}$.

Then $(L_n, \vee, \wedge, ', \rightarrow, a_1, a_n)$ is an LIA.

Example 2.2 [10] Let $\mathcal{L}_n = (L_n, \vee_1, \wedge_1, '^1, \rightarrow_1, a_1, a_n)$ be the Łukasiewicz implication algebra in Example 2.1. $L_2 = \P b_1{}^c b_2 \Diamond$, $b_1 < b_2$, $\mathcal{L}_2 = (L_2, \vee_2, \wedge_2, '^2, \rightarrow_2, b_1, b_2)$ is also a Łukasiewicz implication algebra. For any $(a_i, b_j), (a_k, b_m) \in L_n \times L_2$, define

$(a_i, b_j) \vee (a_k, b_m) = (a_i \vee_1 a_k, b_j \vee_2 b_m)$, $(a_i, b_j) \wedge (a_k, b_m) = (a_i \wedge_1 a_k, b_j \wedge_2 b_m)$,

$(a_i, b_j)' = (a_i'^1, b_j'^2)$,　$(a_i, b_j) \rightarrow (a_k, b_m) = (a_i \rightarrow_1 a_k, b_j \rightarrow_2 b_m)$.

Then $(L_n \times L_2, \vee, \wedge, ', \rightarrow, (a_1, b_1), (a_n, b_2))$ is an LIA, denoted as $\mathcal{L}_n \times \mathcal{L}_2$.

Definition 2.2 [9] Let X be the set of propositional variables, $(L, \vee, \wedge, ', \rightarrow, O, I)$ be an LIA, $T = L \cup \{', \rightarrow\}$ be a type with $ar(') = 1$, $ar(\rightarrow) = 2$ and $ar(a) = 0$ for any $a \in L$. The proposition algebra of the lattice-valued proposition calculus on the set X of propositional variables is the free T algebra on X and denoted by LP(X).

Definition 2.3 [9] A mapping v: LP(X) $\rightarrow L$ is called a valuation of LP(X), if it is a T-homomorphism.

Definition 2.4 [8] Let F be a logical formula in LP(X), $\alpha \in L$. If $v(F) \leq \alpha$ holds for any valuation v of LP(X), we say F is a α-false formula.

In LP(X), all constants, literals and IESFs are called generalized literals. The disjunction of a finite number of generalized literals is a generalized clause. Here, the definition of literal is the same as that in classical 2-valued logic.

Definition 2.5 [11] Let $C_i = p_{i1} \vee \cdots \vee p_{im_i}$ $(i = 1, 2,\ldots, m)$ be generalized clauses of LP(X), $H_i = \left\{ p_{i1}, \cdots, p_{im_i} \right\}$ the set of all generalized literals occurring in C_i, and $\alpha \in L$, and m represents the number of generalized clauses involved in m-ary α-resolution, m_i represents the number of generalized literals in the ith generalized clause. If there exist generalized literals $x_i \in H_i$ $(i = 1, 2,\ldots, m)$ such that $x_1 \wedge x_2 \wedge \ldots \wedge x_m \leq \alpha$, then

$$C_1(x_1 = \alpha) \vee C_2(x_2 = \alpha) \vee \ldots \vee C_m(x_m = \alpha)$$

is called an m-ary α-resolvent of C_1, $C_2,\ldots,$ and C_m, denoted by $R_{p(m-\alpha)}(C_1(x_1),$ $C_2(x_2),\ldots, C_m(x_m))$ where "p" in "$R_{p(m-\alpha)}$" represents "propositional logic", "m" means "m-ary", here $x_1, x_2, \ldots, x_m$ are called an m-ary α-resolution group.

Definition 2.6 [6] Let C be a generalized clause in LP(X). C is called a locked generalized clause if each disjunct occurring in C is assigned a positive integer in its lower left corner (the same disjunct appearing in different locations can be labeled different positive integer). The positive integer is called a lock of the disjunct.

3. α-Semi-lock semantic resolution for LP(X)

Definition 3.1 Let v_0 be a valuation in LP(X), $\alpha \in L$. N, $E_1,\ldots, E_q$ are sets composed of some locked generalized clauses in LP(X). The sequence $(N, E_1,\ldots, E_q)$ is called an α-semi-lock semantic clash (α-SLS clash for short) (w.r.t. v_0), if N, $E_1,\ldots, E_q$ satisfy the following conditions:

(1) For any generalized clause $C \in E_i$, $v_0(C) \leq \alpha$, where $i = 1, 2,\ldots, q$.

(2) Let $R_0 = \underset{C \in N}{\vee} C$. For any $i = 1, 2,\ldots, q$, there exists a multiary α-resolvent R_i of N_i and E_i, where $N_1 = N$, $N_2 = \{R_1\} \cup N_2^*$, $N_2^* \subseteq N$ and for any $i = 3,\ldots, q$, $N_i = \{R_{i-1}\} \cup N_i^*$, $N_i^* \subseteq N \cup \{R_1,\ldots, R_{i-2}\}$.

(3) For any generalized clause $C \in E_i$, the α-resolution literal g of C is the disjunct which has the smallest lock among disjuncts occurring in C, $i = 1, 2,\ldots, q$.

(4) $v_0(R_q) \leq \alpha$.

R_q is called the α-SLS resolvent of this clash. $E_1,\ldots, E_q$ are called electrons and N is called the core of this clash.

Remark 3.1 (1) For any generalized clause C occurring in Definition 3.1, if the same disjunct occurs in different locations of C, then retain the one with the smallest lock and delete others. For example, let $C = {}_3g \vee {}_1g \vee {}_6h \vee {}_4h \vee {}_8h$ be a locked generalized clause, if g and h are different disjuncts, then we rewrite C as $C = {}_1g \vee {}_4h$.

(2) For any disjunct g occurring in E_i ($i = 1, 2,\ldots, q$), $v_0(g) \le \alpha$. In fact, let generalized clause $C \in E_i$ and $C = C^* \vee g$, if $v_0(g) \not\le \alpha$, then $v_0(C) \not\le \alpha$, which contradicts to $v_0(C) \le \alpha$.

Example 3.1 Let $C_1 = {}_1(x \to y)$, $C_2 = {}_2(x \to z)' \vee {}_6(s \to t)$, $C_3 = {}_3y' \vee {}_4(y \to z)$, $C_4 = {}_5(s \to t)' \vee {}_7(r \to (a_2, b_1))$ be four locked generalized clauses in lattice-valued propositional logic $(\mathcal{L}_9 \times \mathcal{L}_2)P(X)$ based on $\mathcal{L}_9 \times \mathcal{L}_2$ and $S = C_1 \wedge C_2 \wedge C_3 \wedge C_4$, where $\mathcal{L}_9 \times \mathcal{L}_2$ is the same LIA with eighteen elements as that in Example 2.2, x, y, z, r, s, t are propositional variables, $(a_2, b_1) \in L_9 \times L_2$. Suppose $\alpha = (a_6, b_2) \in L_9 \times L_2$, v_0 is the valuation of $(\mathcal{L}_9 \times \mathcal{L}_2)P(X)$ such that $v_0(x) = I$, $v_0(y) = v_0(z) = (a_2, b_2)$, $v_0(s) = (a_8, b_2)$, $v_0(t) = (a_6, b_1)$, $v_0(r) = (a_7, b_1)$, then we can obtain an α-SLS clash $(N, E_1,\ldots, E_q)$ by Definition 3.1.

In fact, since $v_0(C_1) = (a_2, b_2) < \alpha$, $v_0(C_2) = (a_8, b_1) \parallel \alpha$ (here $\parallel$ means incomparable), $v_0(C_3) = I > \alpha$, $v_0(C_4) = (a_4, b_2) < \alpha$, so we can obtain an α-SLS clash (w.r.t. v_0) (N, E_1, E_2, E_3): $N = \{C_2, C_3\}$, $E_1 = \{C_1\}$, $E_2 = \{C_1\}$, $E_3 = \{C_4\}$ and the α-SLS resolvent R_3 of this clash is ${}_7(r \to (a_2, b_1)) \vee \alpha$, where $R_1 = {}_4(y \to z) \vee {}_6(s \to t) \vee \alpha$, $N_2 = \{C_2, R_1\}$, $R_2 = {}_6(s \to t) \vee \alpha$, $N_3 = \{R_2\}$.

Theorem 3.1 Suppose v_0 is a valuation of LP(X), $\alpha \in L$ and $N, E_1,\ldots, E_q$ are sets composed of some locked generalized clauses in LP(X). If $(N, E_1,\ldots, E_q)$ is an α-SLS clash (w.r.t. v_0), then $\bigwedge_{C \in N \cup E_i \cup \ldots \cup E_q} C \le R_q$, where R_q is the α-SLS resolvent of $(N, E_1,\ldots, E_q)$.

Proof. According to the soundness of multiary α-resolution principle in LP(X) [11], we can obtain the result easily.

Definition 3.2 Suppose $S = C_1 \wedge C_2 \wedge \ldots \wedge C_m$, where $C_1, C_2,\ldots, C_m$ are locked generalized clauses in LP(X), v_0 is a valuation of LP(X) and $\alpha \in L$. $\{D_1, D_2,\ldots, D_t\}$ is called an α-semi-lock semantic resolution deduction (w.r.t. v_0) (α-SLS resolution deduction for short) from S to generalized clause D_t, if it satisfies the following conditions:

(1) $D_i \in \{C_1, C_2,\ldots, C_m\}$ or

(2) D_i is an α-SLS resolvent (w.r.t v_0), where the core and electrons of the clash taking D_i as its α-SLS resolvent are subsets of $\{D_j \mid j < i\} \cup \{C_1, C_2,\ldots, C_m\}$.

The symbol $\alpha\text{-}\odot$ in the following represents an α-false generalized clause in LP(X).

Theorem 3.2 (Soundness) Suppose $S = C_1 \wedge C_2 \wedge \ldots \wedge C_m$, where $C_1, C_2,\ldots, C_m$ are locked generalized clauses in LP(X), $\alpha \in L$. v_0 is a valuation of LP(X) and $\{D_1, D_2,..., D_t\}$ is an α-SLS resolution deduction from S to generalized clause D_t. If D_t is α-⊙, then $S \le \alpha$, i.e., if $D_t \le \alpha$, then $S \le \alpha$.

Proof. According to Theorem 3.1, $S \le D_1 \wedge D_2 \wedge...\wedge D_t \le D_t$, so we can obtain the result easily.

Theorem 3.3 (Condition completeness) Let $S = C_1 \wedge C_2 \wedge...\wedge C_m$, where $C_1, C_2,..., C_m$ are locked generalized clauses in LP(X). v_0 is a valuation of LP(X) and $\alpha \in L$. If the following conditions hold:

(1) $S \le \alpha$,

(2) $S^0 \ne \phi$, where $S^0 = \{C_i | v_0(C_i) \le \alpha, i \in \{1, 2,..., m\}\}$,

(3) there exists at least a locked generalized clause $C_j \in \{C_1, C_2,..., C_m\}$, such that for any disjunct g of C_j, $v_0(g) \not\le \alpha$,

then there exists an α-SLS resolution deduction (w.r.t. v_0) from S to α-⊙.

Proof. According to the condition completeness of α-QLS resolution in LP(X) [5], we can obtain the result easily.

Example 3.2 Let $C_1 = (x \rightarrow y)$, $C_2 = (x \rightarrow z)' \vee (s \rightarrow t)$, $C_3 = y' \vee (y \rightarrow z) \vee (s \rightarrow (a_4, b_1))$, $C_4 = (s \rightarrow t)' \vee (r \rightarrow (a_2, b_1))'$, $C_5 = r \rightarrow (a_5, b_1)$ be five generalized clauses in $(\mathcal{L}_9 \times \mathcal{L}_2)$P(X) and $S = C_1 \wedge C_2 \wedge C_3 \wedge C_4 \wedge C_5$, where $(a_4, b_1), (a_2, b_1), (a_5, b_1) \in L_9 \times L_2$ and x, y, z, r, s, t are propositional variables. If $\alpha = (a_6, b_1) \in L_9 \times L_2$, then $S \le \alpha$ and there exists an α-SLS resolution deduction from S to α-⊙.

In fact, we only need to find an α-SLS resolution deduction from S to α-⊙. Let C_1, C_2, C_3, C_4, C_5 have the following locks:

$C_1 = {}_1(x \rightarrow y)$, $C_2 = {}_2(x \rightarrow z)' \vee {}_3(s \rightarrow t)$, $C_3 = {}_4y' \vee {}_5(y \rightarrow z) \vee {}_6(s \rightarrow (a_4, b_1))$,
$C_4 = {}_7(s \rightarrow t)' \vee {}_8(r \rightarrow (a_2, b_1))'$, $\qquad\qquad C_5 = {}_9(r \rightarrow (a_5, b_1))$.

Suppose v_0 is the valuation in $(\mathcal{L}_9 \times \mathcal{L}_2)$P(X) such that $v_0(x) = I$, $v_0(y) = (a_5, b_1)$, $v_0(z) = (a_2, b_2)$, $v_0(s) = (a_6, b_2)$, $v_0(t) = (a_3, b_1)$, $v_0(r) = (a_6, b_1)$. Hence we have $v_0(C_1) < \alpha$, $v_0(C_2) > \alpha$, $v_0(C_3) > \alpha$, $v_0(C_4) \| \alpha$, $v_0(C_5) > \alpha$. Since the conditions (2) and (3) of Theorem 3.2 hold, so we have the following α-SLS resolution deduction:

(1) ${}_1(x \rightarrow y)$

(2) ${}_2(x \rightarrow z)' \vee {}_3(s \rightarrow t)$

(3) ${}_4y' \vee {}_5(y \rightarrow z) \vee {}_6(s \rightarrow (a_4, b_1))$

(4) ${}_7(s \rightarrow t)' \vee {}_8(r \rightarrow (a_2, b_1))'$

(5) ${}_9(r \rightarrow (a_5, b_1))$

(6) ${}_6(s \rightarrow (a_4, b_1))' \vee {}_3(s \rightarrow t) \vee \alpha$ by (1), (2), (3)

(7) ${}_8(r \rightarrow (a_2, b_1))' \vee {}_3(s \rightarrow t) \vee \alpha$ by (1), (4), (6)

(8) ${}_8(r \rightarrow (a_2, b_1))' \vee \alpha$ by (4), (7)

(9) α by (5), (8)

Hence, there exists an α-SLS resolution deduction form S to α-⊙, i.e., $S \le \alpha$.

Acknowledgments

This work is partially supported by the National Natural Science Foundation of P. R. China (Grant No. 61175055, 61100046, 61305074); Fundamental Research business expense special funds for the Central Universities (Grant No. A0920502051305-26).

References

1. J. P. Robinson, *A machine-oriented logic based on the resolution principle. J. ACM.,* **12,** 23-41 (1965).
2. J. Ma, W.J. Li, D. Ruan, Y. Xu, *Filter-based resolution principle for lattice-valued propositional logic LP(X), Information Sciences,* **177,** 1046-1062 (2007).
3. J. R. Slagle, *Automatic theorem proving with renamable and semantic resolution. J. ACM.,* **14(4),** 687-697 (1967).
4. R.S. Boyer, *Locking: a restriction of resolution, Doctoral Dissertation, University of Texas at Austin,* (1971).
5. X.M. Zhong, Y. Xu, J. Liu, S.W. Chen, *α-Quasi-lock semantic resolution method based on lattice-valued logic, International Journal of Computational Intelligence Systems,* doi=10.1080/18756891.2013.859868, (2013). (accepted)
6. X.X. He, Y. Xu, J. Liu, D. Ruan, *α-Lock resolution method for a lattice-valued first-order logic. Engineering Applications of Artificial Intelligence,* **24,** 1274-1280 (2011).
7. W.T. Xu, Y. Xu, *α-Generalized linear resolution method based on lattice-valued propositional logic LP(X), 8th International Conference on Fuzzy Systems and Knowledge Discovery, July 26-28, Shanghai, China,* 1413-1416 (2011).
8. Y. Xu, D. Ruan, E.E. Kerre, J. Liu, *α-Resolution principle based on lattice-valued propositional logic LP(X), Inform. Sciences,* **130,** 195-223 (2000).
9. Y. Xu, D. Ruan, K.Y. Qin and J. Liu, *Lattice-Valued Logic: An Alternative Approach to Treat Fuzziness and Incomparability, Springer-Verlag, Heidelberg* (2003).
10. Y. Xu, S. W. Chen, J. Ma, *Linguistic truth-valued lattice implication algebra and its properties, in Proc. IMACS MuLticonference on Computational Engineering in Systems Applications, Beijing, China,* 1413-1418 (2006).
11. Y. Xu, J. Liu, X.M. Zhong, S.W. Chen, *Multiary α-Resolution principle for a lattice-valued logic, IEEE transactions on fuzzy systems,* **21(5),** 898-912 (2013).

SEMANTICS OF PROPOSITIONAL FUZZY MODAL LOGIC WITH EVALUATED SYNTAX BASED ON MV-ALGEBRAS

Xiaodong Pan* and Hairui Jia and Yang Xu

Intelligent Control Development Center, School of Mathematics, Southwest Jiaotong University, Chengdu, Sichuan, 610031, P.R. China
* E-mail: xdpan1@163.com

Weitao Xu

College of Information Science and Engineering, Henan University of Technology Zhengzhou, Henan, 450001, P.R. China
E-mail: hnxmxwt@163.com

This article deals with propositional fuzzy modal logic with evaluated syntax based on MV-algebras. We focus on its semantic theory from the viewpoint of Pavelka's graded semantics of propositional fuzzy logic, investigate the L-tautologies based on different Kripke frames. We also define the notion of L-semantic consequence operation, its some basic properties are presented.

Keywords: Propositional fuzzy modal logic; L-tautology; Consequence operation; MV-algebra; Evaluated syntax.

1. Introduction

Fuzzy logics with evaluated syntax have been introduced by Pavelka [13] in 1979. Pavelka broke through the traditional method of fuzzy logics, and established a kind of graded, complete fuzzy propositional logic. In this kind of fuzzy logics, not only the set of truth values has been expanded, but also the formal language has been extended by a set of logical (truth) constants that are names of all truth values, and some formulas which are not always fully true have been introduced into the set of axioms, each formula being in the syntax assigned a value. The inference rules can transmit the truth values among formulas, that is to say, the truth values of formulas as conclusion can be obtained from the truth values of formulas as premise by computation. After that, Novak [9-12] extended Pavelkas fuzzy logic to first-order fuzzy logic, and furthermore, to fuzzy type theory. Since the process of inference involves the transmission of truth values of formulas, and so fuzzy logic with evaluated syntax is suitable to model humans reasoning based on fuzzy information, thus making it possible to build artificially computer-based systems able to simulate humans intelligence by computer.

One of the most important directions extending fuzzy logic is the modal extensions of fuzzy logics, there are already various modal extensions of fuzzy logics, most of which are based on finitely valued logics with traditional syntax, see [5-8], The basic idea was to retain the general notion of possible world semantics, while allowing formulas to have values in a many-valued space, at each possible world. What seems not to have been considered is allowing the accessibility relation between possible worlds itself to be many-valued. But many-valued accessibility is a very natural notion. After all, some worlds alternative to this one are more relevant, others less, as one intuitively thinks of these things. In [1, 2], Bou also developed fuzzy modal logic with many-valued accessibility relation in the traditional way.

In this paper, we establish a kind of graded semantic theory for propositional fuzzy modal logic with evaluated syntax based on MV-algebras, allow the accessibility relation between worlds also to be many-valued, and introduce graded modal connectives into the formal languages. We also propose the notion of satisfiability with certain level for a set of formulas from the viewpoint of approximating reasoning. Furthermore, we define the semantic consequence operation concerning a set of formulas, and the consistency of fuzzy information.

2. Preliminaries

The set of truth values is supposed to form an MV-algebra[2]. An algebraic structure $\mathcal{L} = (L, \oplus, ', 0)$ with similarity type $\langle 2, 1, 0 \rangle$ is an MV-algebra if and only if $(L, \oplus, 0)$ is an abelian monoid with neutral element 0, and if furthermore for all $x, y \in L$ there hold true

(i) $x'' = x$, (ii) $x \oplus 0' = 0'$, (iii) $(x' \oplus y)' \oplus y = (y' \oplus x)' \oplus x$.

Such an MV-algebra is nontrivial if and only if it contains at least two elements. By denoting $x \otimes y = (x' \oplus y')'$ and $1 = 0'$, it follows that $(L, \otimes, ', 1)$ is also an MV-algebra, which is known as the dual MV-algebra of $(L, \oplus, ', 0)$. Notice also that it is possible to derive a lattice structure from that of MV-algebra, since $x \leqslant_L y$ iff $x' \oplus y = 1$ iff $x \otimes y' = 0$ defines a partial order on L, in such a way that $(L, \leqslant_L, \vee, \wedge, 0, 1)$ is a lattice with the meet and join operations respectively given, for all $x, y \in L$, by $x \wedge y = (x' \otimes y)' \otimes y$, $x \vee y = (x' \oplus y)' \oplus y$, and 0 and 1 are the bottom and top elements, respectively. The following is an equivalent definition of MV-algebra, which is also known as a lattice implication algebra which has been introduced by Xu et. al. in [15, 16]. The equivalency between these two definitions has been proved by Wang in [14].

Definition 2.1. A bounded lattice $(L, \vee, \wedge, 0, 1)$ with order reversing involution $'$ and a binary operation $\to$ is called a lattice implication algebra if it satisfies the following axioms: for all $x, y, z \in L$,

(I_1) $x \to (y \to z) = y \to (x \to z)$, (I_2) $x \to x = 1$, (I_3) $x \to y = y' \to x'$,

(I_4) $x \to y = y \to x = 1 \Rightarrow x = y$, (I_5) $(x \to y) \to y = (y \to x) \to x$,

(L_1) $(x \vee y) \to z = (x \to z) \wedge (y \to z)$, (L_2) $(x \wedge y) \to z = (x \to z) \vee (y \to z)$.

In what follows, we will use the equivalent definition in most cases for convenience.

Let $\mathcal{P}_{FM}$ be the propositional fuzzy modal logic system with evaluated syntax based on MV-algebras, the language J of $\mathcal{P}_{FM}$ consists of: (1) the set of propositional variable: $S = \{p_1, p_2, p_3, \cdots\}$; (2) the set of constants: $\overline{L} = \{\overline{a} | a \in L\}$; (3) logical connectives: $\neg, \Rightarrow, \{\Box_\beta\}_{\beta \in L \setminus \{0\}}$, where for any $\beta \in L \setminus \{0\}$, $\Box_\beta$ (it is necessary to the degree β, also read "box beta") is modal connective; (4) auxiliary symbols: $)$, $($.

The set $\mathcal{F}_J$ of well-formed formulas of $\mathcal{P}_{FM}$ is the least set Y satisfying the following conditions: (1) $S \subset Y$; (2) $\overline{L} \subset Y$; (3) if $A, B \in Y$, then $\neg A, A \Rightarrow B \in Y$, and for any $\beta \in L \setminus \{0\}$, $\Box_\beta A \in Y$.

In what follows, unless otherwise stated, L always represents a complete MV-algebra(For more details, please refer to ref.[3]), and the set $\mathbb{N} \setminus \{0\}$ will be denoted by $\mathbb{N}^+$.

For the sake of convenience, we introduce some abbreviations as follows: for any $A, B, C \in \mathcal{F}_J, n \in \mathbb{N}^+, \beta \in L \setminus \{0\}$,

$A \vee B \triangleq (A \Rightarrow B) \Rightarrow B, A \wedge B \triangleq \neg(\neg A \vee \neg B), A\&B \triangleq \neg(A \Rightarrow \neg B), A \triangledown B \triangleq \neg A \Rightarrow B, A \Leftrightarrow B \triangleq (A \Rightarrow B) \wedge (B \Rightarrow A), \diamond_\beta A \triangleq \neg \Box_\beta \neg A, A^0 \triangleq I, A^n \triangleq A^{n-1}\&A, 0A \triangleq O, nA \triangleq (n-1)A \triangledown A$.

3. L-tautology theory

In this section, we investigate L-tautologies in $\mathcal{P}_{FM}$. Semantically, the propositional fuzzy logic based on MV-algebras can be characterised by a structure $S_{\mathcal{P}_F} = \langle L, D, \{f_c; c \in \{\neg, \Rightarrow\}\} \rangle$, where L is an MV-algebra, $D \subset L \setminus \{0\}$ is the set of designated values which are the values that are preserved in valid inferences. For each connective, c, f_c is the truth function it denotes.

An L-valued Kripke frame is a pair $\mathcal{F} = \langle W, R \rangle$ where W is a non-empty set of worlds, R is a binary L-fuzzy accessibility relation on W. An interpretation for $\mathcal{P}_{FM}$ is a structure (or model) $\langle W, R, S_{\mathcal{P}_F}, v \rangle$ (denoted as $\langle W, R, v \rangle$ below when without confusion or errors), where $\langle W, R \rangle$ is an L-valued Kripke frame, $S_{\mathcal{P}_F}$ is the structure as defined above, and for each propositional parameter, p, and world, ω, v assigns the parameter a value, $v_\omega(p)$, in L. This is extended to a map from $\mathcal{F}_J$ to L at a world ω by applying the following truth functions recursively:

$v_\omega(\neg A) = (v_\omega(A))'; v_\omega(A \Rightarrow B) = v_\omega(A) \to v_\omega(B);$

for all $a \in L, v_\omega(\overline{a}) = a;$

for any $\beta \in L \setminus \{0\}, v_\omega(\square_\beta A) = \bigwedge \{v_{\omega'}(A) : \omega' \in W, R(\omega, \omega') \geqslant \beta\};$

for any $\beta \in L \setminus \{0\}, v_\omega(\diamond_\beta A) = \bigvee \{v_{\omega'}(A) : \omega' \in W, R(\omega, \omega') \geqslant \beta\}.$

Definition 3.1. Let $0 < \alpha \in L$, a modal formula A is α-tautology in a structure $\mathcal{M} = \langle W, R, v \rangle$, denoted $\mathcal{M} \models_\alpha A$, provided $\bigwedge_{\omega \in W} v_\omega(A) = \alpha$. A modal formula A is α-tautology in a frame $\mathcal{F} = \langle W, R \rangle$, denoted $\mathcal{F} \models_\alpha A$, provided that A is an α-tautology in any structure based on $\mathcal{F}$. And if **K** is a class of frames then we write $\mathbf{K} \models_\alpha A$ to mean that A is an α-tautology in all frames in this class.

For any kind of α-tautology A mentioned above, if there exists $\omega \in W$ in some structure $\mathcal{M}$ such that $v_\omega(A) = \alpha$, then A is called a reachable α-tautology.

The set of all α-tautologies in a structure $\mathcal{M}$ (a frame $\mathcal{F}$, a class of frames **K**) will be denoted by $\alpha - Tau(\mathcal{M})$ ($\alpha - Tau(\mathcal{F})$, $\alpha - Tau(\mathbf{K})$). The set of all reachable α-tautologies in a structure $\mathcal{M}$ (a frame $\mathcal{F}$, a class of frames **K**) will be denoted by $[\alpha) - Tau(\mathcal{M})$ ($[\alpha) - Tau(\mathcal{F})$, $[\alpha) - Tau(\mathbf{K})$).

In the following, we always assume that $\alpha > 0$ unless otherwise stated.

Example 3.1. For any $\beta \in L \setminus \{0\}$, the following modal formulas are 1-tautology in all frames:
(1) $\square_\beta(A \wedge B) \Leftrightarrow (\square_\beta A \wedge \square_\beta B)$, $\diamond_\beta(A \vee B) \Leftrightarrow (\diamond_\beta A \vee \diamond_\beta B)$;
(2) for all $\overline{a} \in \overline{L}$, $\square_\beta(\overline{a} \Rightarrow A) \Leftrightarrow (\overline{a} \Rightarrow \square_\beta A)$;
(3) $\square_{\beta_i} A \Rightarrow \square_{\beta_j} A$, $\diamond_{\beta_j} A \Rightarrow \diamond_{\beta_i} A$, if $\beta_i \leqslant \beta_j$;
(4) $\neg\neg\square_\beta A \Leftrightarrow \square_\beta \neg\neg A$;
(5) all tautologies in propositional fuzzy logic.

Theorem 3.1. *If L is a completely distributive lattice, then for any $\beta \in L \setminus \{0\}$, $\square_\beta(A \Rightarrow B) \Rightarrow (\square_\beta A \Rightarrow \square_\beta B)$ is 1-tautology in all frames.*

Proof. It suffices to show that in any structure $\mathcal{M} = \langle W, R, v \rangle$ and any world $\omega \in W$, $v_\omega(\square_\beta(A \Rightarrow B)) \leqslant v_\omega(\square_\beta A \Rightarrow \square_\beta B)$, that is, $\bigwedge \{v_{\omega'}(A) \to$

$v_{\omega'}(B) : R(\omega,\omega') \geqslant \beta, \omega' \in W\} \leqslant \bigwedge\{v_{\omega'}(A) : R(\omega,\omega') \geqslant \beta, \omega' \in W\} \to \bigwedge\{v_{\omega'}(B) : R(\omega,\omega') \geqslant \beta, \omega' \in W\}$. Let $X = \{\omega' : R(\omega,\omega') \geqslant \beta, \omega' \in W\}$, and let a_x and b_x be $v_x(A)$ and $v_x(B)$, respectively. We will show that:

$$\bigwedge\{a_x \to b_x : x \in X\} \leqslant \bigwedge\{a_x : x \in X\} \to \bigwedge\{b_x : x \in X\}.$$

Since for any $x_0 \in X$, $\bigwedge\{a_x \to b_x : x \in X\} \leqslant a_{x_0} \to b_{x_0} \leqslant \bigwedge\{a_x : x \in X\} \to b_{x_0}$; note that L is completely distributive, it follows from the arbitrariness of x_0 that $\bigwedge\{a_x \to b_x : x \in X\} \leqslant \bigwedge_{x \in X}\left\{\bigwedge\{a_x : x \in X\} \to b_x\right\} = \bigwedge\{a_x : x \in X\} \to \bigwedge\{b_x : x \in X\}$. This completes the proof. $\square$

Proposition 3.1. *For any $\beta \in L \setminus \{0\}$, if $A \in 1 - Tau(\mathcal{M})(1 - Tau(\mathcal{F}), 1 - Tau(\mathbf{K}))$, than $\square_\beta A \in 1 - Tau(\mathcal{M})(1 - Tau(\mathcal{F}), 1 - Tau(\mathbf{K}))$.*

Proof. Suppose that $\square_\beta A \notin 1 - Tau(\mathcal{M})$. Then there is some world in the structure $\mathcal{M} = \langle W, R, v \rangle$, ω, such that $v_\omega(\square_\beta A) \neq 1$. Thus, for some world $\omega' \in W$ such that $R(\omega, \omega') \geqslant \beta$, $v_{\omega'}(A) \neq 1$. Hence $A \notin 1 - Tau(\mathcal{M})$. The rest are obvious. $\square$

Proposition 3.2. *Let $\mathcal{M} = \langle W, R, v \rangle$ be a structure and $\beta \in L \setminus \{0\}$. If R is β-reflexive and $A \in [\alpha) - Tau(\mathcal{M})$, than $\square_\beta A \in [\alpha) - Tau(\mathcal{M})$.*

Proof. Since $A \in [\alpha) - Tau(\mathcal{M})$, then $\bigwedge_{\omega \in W} v_\omega(A) = \alpha$ and there is some world $\omega_0 \in W$ such that $v_{\omega_0}(A) = \alpha$. Note that R is β-reflexive, that is, $R(\omega, \omega) \geqslant \beta$ for any $\omega \in W$. Thus,

$$\bigwedge_{\omega \in W} v_\omega(\square_\beta A) = \bigwedge_{\omega \in W} \left(\bigwedge\{v_{\omega'}(A) : R(\omega, \omega') \geqslant \beta\} \right)$$
$$= \bigwedge_{\omega \in W, \omega \neq \omega_0} \left(\bigwedge\{v_{\omega'}(A) : R(\omega, \omega') \geqslant \beta\} \right) \wedge \bigwedge\{v_{\omega'}(A) : R(\omega_0, \omega') \geqslant \beta\}$$
$$= \alpha.$$

Hence, $\square_\beta A \in [\alpha) - Tau(\mathcal{M})$. $\square$

Proposition 3.3. *Let $\mathcal{M} = \langle W, R, v \rangle$ be a structure. For any $\beta \in L \setminus \{0\}$, the following conclusions hold:*
(1) if R is β-reflexive, then $\square_\beta A \Rightarrow A \in 1 - Tau(\mathbf{M})$;
(2) if R is symmetric, then $A \Rightarrow \square_\beta \diamond_\beta A \in 1 - Tau(\mathbf{M})$;
(3) if R is max-min transitive, then $\square_\beta \Rightarrow \square_\beta\square_\beta A \in 1 - Tau(\mathbf{M})$.

4. Semantic consequence operation and consistency of information

In 1979, Pavelka defined the semantic and syntactic consequence operations as self-mappings on $L^{\mathcal{F}_J}$, the semantic and syntactic deductions were presented in the form of L-consequence operation. In this way, we define the notion of L-consequence operation in $\mathcal{P}_{FM}$ in this section.

As a naturally extension of the notion of validity in propositional fuzzy logic with evaluated syntax, we understand validity in $\mathcal{P}_{FM}$ as follows:

$\Sigma \vDash_\alpha A$ if and only if for every structure, $\langle W, R, v \rangle$, and for every $\omega \in W$, whenever $v_\omega(B) \in D$ for every $B \in \Sigma$, $v_\omega(A) \in D$. Where $D \subset L \setminus \{0\}$ is the set of designated values which satisfies: for any $\alpha_1 \in D$, if $\alpha_1 \leqslant \alpha_2$, then $\alpha_2 \in D$.

In the following, D always denotes a set of designated values unless otherwise stated.

Definition 4.1. Let $M \subset \mathcal{F}_J$. Define $M_D \subset L^{\mathcal{F}_J}$ as

$$M_D \triangleq \Big\{ X \in L^{\mathcal{F}_J} \,\Big|\, \forall A \in \mathcal{F}_J, \text{ if } A \in M \text{ and } A \text{ is not a constant}, \text{then}$$
$$X(A) \in D; \text{ if } A \in M \text{ and } A = \bar{a} \text{ is a constant}, \text{then } X(A) = a;$$
$$\text{otherwise}, X(A) = 0 \Big\}.$$

Let $X \in M_D$. For any $A \in M$, the value $X(A)$ represents the initial truth value of A with regard to M, and X is called information with regard to M in $\mathcal{P}_{FM}$.

Definition 4.2. Let $\mathcal{M} = \langle W, R, v \rangle$ be a structure and $M \subset \mathcal{F}_J$. We say that $\mathcal{M}$ is a model of M, or $\mathcal{M}$ satisfies M on the level of D if there is a world ω such that $v_\omega(A) \in D$ for any $A \in M$ that is not a constant. We say that M is satisfiable on the level of D if there is a structure $\mathcal{M} = \langle W, R, v \rangle$ such that $\mathcal{M}$ is a model of M on the level of D.

Proposition 4.1. M is satisfiable on the level of D if and only if there exist $X \in M_D$, structure $\mathcal{M} = \langle W, R, v \rangle$ and world ω such that $v_\omega \geqslant X$.

Definition 4.3. Let $X \in M_D$. If $\overline{X} \in L^{\mathcal{F}_J}$ satisfying

$$\overline{X}(A) = \begin{cases} 1, & \text{if there exists } B \in M \text{ such that } X(B) = a > 0 \text{ and} \\ & A = \bar{a} \Rightarrow B; \\ 0, & \text{otherwise.} \end{cases}$$

then we say $\overline{X}$ a substitution of X on the level of D.

If $\overline{X}$ is a substitution of X on the level of D, then we can consider $\overline{X}$ as a classical subset of $\mathcal{F}_J$, and for any $A \in \mathcal{F}_J$, if $A \in M$, then $\overline{X}(\overline{X(A)} \Rightarrow A) = 1$; otherwise, $\overline{X}(\overline{X(A)} \Rightarrow A) = 0$.

Theorem 4.1. *Let $\mathcal{M} = \langle W, R, v \rangle$ be a structure. Then $\mathcal{M}$ is a model of M on the level of D if and only if there is a world ω and $X \in M_D$, and a substitution $\overline{X}$ of X on the level of D such that $v_\omega \geqslant \overline{X}$.*

Remark 4.1. One could see that by Theorem 4.1, the satisfiability of an L-fuzzy set of formulas can be convert into the satisfiability of a classical set of formulas.

In classical logic, we say that A can be derived from M, that is to say, $M \vDash A$ if and only if for any valuation v, if $v(B) = 1$ for any $B \in M$, then we have $v(A) = 1$; we could show this deduction in the form of sets as well, $M \vDash A$ if and only if $A \in \bigcap \{T_v | M \subset T_v, v \text{ is a valuation}\}$, where $T_v = \{p | p \text{ is a well-formed formula } and \ v(p) = 1\}$.

In the following, we generalize the notion of semantic deduction, and define the semantic deduction of M on the level of D in $\mathcal{P}_{FM}$ as follows:

Definition 4.4. Let $\mathcal{M} = \langle W, R, v \rangle$ be a structure and $M \subset \mathcal{F}_J$. Define the mapping: $\mathfrak{C}_{\mathcal{M},D}^M : M_D \to L^{\mathcal{F}_J}$ as follows: for any $X \in M_D$, and for any $A \in \mathcal{F}_J$, $\mathfrak{C}_{\mathcal{M},D}^M(X)(A) = \bigwedge_{\omega \in W} \{v_\omega(A) | v_\omega \geqslant X\}$.

Remark 4.2. In definition 4.4, if $\{\omega \in W | v_\omega \geqslant X\} = \emptyset$, i.e, there exists no $\omega \in W$ such that $v_\omega \geqslant X$, then we let $\mathfrak{C}_{\mathcal{M},D}^M(X) = I_{\mathcal{F}_J}$, here we call X inconsistent information in the structure $\mathcal{M}$. Conversely, if $\{\omega \in W | v_\omega \geqslant X\} \neq \emptyset$, then we call X consistent information in the structure $\mathcal{M}$. If for any $X \in M_D$, X is consistent in the structure $\mathcal{M}$, then M is said to be consistent on the level of D in the structure $\mathcal{M}$.

We just define these notions above in a structure $\mathcal{M}$, similarly, it is easy to extend them into a frame $\mathcal{F} = \langle W, R \rangle$, and a class of frames $\mathbf{K}$. Here we will not explain it again.

5. Conclusion

This paper focused on the graded semantics of propositional fuzzy modal logic with evaluated syntax based on MV-algebras, presented its some basic properties. Further, we need to develop the logical calculus with evaluated syntax corresponding to the established semantics, and establish the corresponding proof theory.

Acknowledgments

The work was partially supported by the National Natural Science Foundation of China (Grant No. 61100046, 61305074, 61175055) and the application fundamental research plan project of Sichuan Province(Grant No. 2011JY0092).

References

1. F. Bou, F. Esteva, *Exploring a syntactic notion of modal many-valued logics*, Mathware & Soft computing 15(2008) 175-181.
2. F. Bou, L. Godo, F. Esteva, R.O. Rodriguez *On the minimum many-valued modal logic over a finite residuated lattice*, Journal of Logic and Computation 5(2011) 739-790.
3. C. C. Chang, *Algebraic analysis of many-valued logics*, Transactions of the American Mathematical Society 88(1958) 476-490.
4. R. L. O. Cignoli, I.M.L. D'Ottaviano, D. Mundici,*Algebraic foundations of many-valued reasoning*, Kluwer (2000).
5. M. C. Fitting, *Many-valued modal logics*, Fundamenta Informaticae 15(1992) 235-254.
6. M. C. Fitting, *Many-valued modal logics II*, Fundamenta Informaticae 17(1992) 55-73.
7. P. Hájek, *On fuzzy modal logics S5($\mathfrak{C}$)*, Fuzzy Sets Syst. 161(2010) 2389-2396.
8. A.M. Mironov, *Fuzzy modal logics*, Journal of Mathematical Sciences 128(2005) 3461-3483.
9. V. Novák, *On fuzzy type theory*, Fuzzy Sets Syst. 149(2005) 235-273.
10. V. Novák, *Which logic is the real fuzzy logic?*, Fuzzy Sets Syst. 157(2006) 635-641.
11. V. Novák, *Fuzzy logic with countable evaluated syntax revisited*, Fuzzy Sets Syst. 158(2007) 929-936.
12. V. Novák, *Reasoning about methematical fuzzy logic and its future*, Fuzzy Sets Syst. 192(2012) 25-44.
13. J. Pavelka, *On fuzzy logic I: Many-valued rules of inference, II: Enriched residuated lattices and semantics of propositional calculi, III: Semantical Conpleteness of some many-valued propositional calculi.* Zeitschr F Math Logik Und Grundlagend Math, 25(1979) 45-52; 119-134; 447-464.
14. G.J. Wang, *MV-algebras, BL-algebras, R_0-algebras, and multiple-valued logic*, Fuzzy Systems and Mathematics 16, 2(2002) 1-15.(in Chinese)
15. Y. Xu, *Lattice implication algebras*, J. Southwest Jiaotong Univ. 28, 1(1993) 20-27.(in Chinese)
16. Y. Xu, D. Ruan, K.Y. Qin, J. Liu, Lattice-Valued Logic-An Alternative Approach to Treat Fuzziness and Incomparability, Springer-Verlag Berlin Heidelberg New York Press (2003).

FORMAL LOGICAL TRANSFORMATION OF HIERARCHICAL HUMAN ACTIVITY FOR REASONING BASED RECOGNITION

SHUWEI CHEN, JUN LIU, HUI WANG, AND JUAN AUGUSTO

School of Computing and Mathematics, University of Ulster, Northern Ireland, UK

This paper proposes a formal framework which represents the composite human activity under consideration by a hierarchical ordering structure and discusses how they can be modelled and transferred into a formal syntactical logical formula, i.e., logical predicate algebra. This has placed a foundation for recognizing the composite activity based on the transformed logical formulas using automated reasoning methodology.

1. Introduction

The understanding of context and human activities is a core component that supports and enables all kinds of context-aware applications, including user behavior modelling for marketing and advertising, health care and home monitoring, video surveillance, and context-based personal assistants, etc. [1, 2]. In the main approaches classified in human activity recognition, compared with the single-layer approaches representing and recognizing low level activity as a particular class of image sequences, hierarchical approaches are concerned with modelling a complex scene, the inherent structure and semantics of complex activities requiring higher-level representation and reasoning methods. The major advantage of hierarchical approaches over single-layered ones is their ability to recognize high-level activities with more complex structures. They are especially suitable for a semantic-level analysis of interactions between humans and/or objects as well as complex group activities. By encapsulating structurally redundant subevents shared by multiple high-level activities, hierarchical approaches model the activities with a lesser amount of training and recognize them more efficiently [3]. In addition, the hierarchical modeling of high-level activities makes recognition systems to incorporate human knowledge (i.e., prior knowledge of the activity) much easier. Human knowledge can be included in the system by listing semantically meaningful sub-activities composing a high-level activity and/or by specifying their relationships.

One of the major challenging problems for these applications is how to bridge the semantic gap between high level human understanding and given low level data. Note that a hierarchical structure can be considered as an ordering structure representing the underlying semantic relationship of considered task, e.g., in human activity recognition, composite activity can be decomposed into simpler activities, e.g., interactions and actions, and further into gestures and poses based on its semantic ordering relation. This challenge can be further elaborated as: how to model appropriately a hierarchical structure reflecting the semantic ordering and establish the corresponding reasoning mechanism directly based on this hierarchical structure to achieve the required task.

This paper proposes a formal framework which represents the composite activity under consideration by a hierarchical ordering structure and discusses how they can be transferred into first-order logical predicate algebra. It places a foundation for recognizing the composite activity based on the transformed logical formulas using automated reasoning methodology.

2. Hierarchical Activity Representation Structure

Hierarchy, in mathematical terms, is a partially ordered set, which is a collection of parts with ordered asymmetric relationships inside a whole, i.e., upper levels are above lower levels, and the relationship upwards is asymmetric with the relationships downwards.

Human activities, according to their complexity, can be conceptually categorized into four different levels: gestures, actions, interactions, and group activities [3]. These composite activities are intuitively composed of a series of simpler activities, atomic actions, gestures and properties of objects, mainly people, according to their semantic meanings. Therefore, in human activity context, the decomposition of composite activity into mid-level interactions and actions, and further into low-level features and gestures will naturally generate a hierarchical representation structure, which is essentially a partially ordered structure in terms of semantic ordering of the activity under consideration. These ordering relations include temporal or spatial ordering, e.g., "meet", "join", among different actions and gestures. This structure is constructed based on the knowledge of the semantic meaning of the considered activity. In order to further handle the activity recognition task, we need to represent the activity in a formal way. One hierarchical structure itself provides individual representation of one composite activity based on its semantic meaning. It is common that a complex activity may be composed of several smaller composite activities, i.e., one hierarchy can be linked with another hierarchy, not only through "meet" or "join", but also negation or one hierarchy may imply another hierarchy. Figure 1 shows the four logical link relations: implication, negation, meet and join, between different hierarchies (composite events). The formal representation framework into predicate formula will be discussed in Section 3.

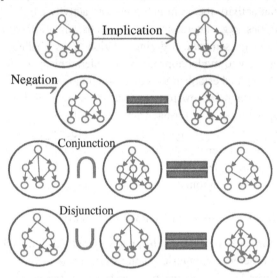

Figure 1. Complex activity connected logically via different hierarchical hierarchies

3. From Hierarchical Activity Structure to Logical Formulae

Based on Figure 1, the generation of the corresponding logical predicates can be achieved according to the following ways.

3.1. *Elements of the Hierarchical Structure*

The elements of the hierarchical structure are as follows.
1) The set of variables: X represents the corresponding people or objects;
2) The set of constants: A to represent the specific people or objects;
3) The set T of temporal relations between actions and gestures;
4) Logical connectives: $\vee$, $\wedge$, $\neg$, and $\rightarrow$, as defined in subsection.
5) The set F of functions for describing the corresponding activities, actions, and gestures of people or objects.

These functions include the following types according to their semantic layers.
1) $G_i(\cdot)$: Highest level group activities whose number of parameters varies for different activities;
2) $H_i(x_j, x_k)$: Interactions between two people or objects x_j and x_k;
3) $F_i(x_j)$: Single-actor actions of person x_j;
4) $Q_i(x_j)$: Gestures of person x_j.

3.2. *Temporal Relations between Actions and Gestures*

Note that temporal relations between these gestures and actions are also necessary for human activity recognition. For example, "arm around" should happen when "arm stretch" finishes for embrace interaction. We adopt the popular temporal relations among time intervals from Allen's interval temporal logic [4, 5]. Allen's interval temporal logic defines six predicates: 'before', 'meets', 'overlaps', 'starts', 'during', and 'finishes', which are denoted as T_1, T_2, T_3, T_4, T_5, T_6 accordingly for the following activity recognition. Each activity or gesture is associated with a time interval describing its start and end points, e.g., start frame and end frame for video based activity recognition. The parameters of each predicate are two time intervals (corresponding to two activities), and the predicate decides whether the corresponding temporal relation between them hold or not. For example, let a and b be two time intervals, (a_{start}, a_{end}) and (b_{start}, b_{end}), then the corresponding predicates are defined as follows.

- before$(a, b) \Longleftrightarrow a_{end} < b_{start}$; starts$(a, b) \Longleftrightarrow a_{start} = b_{start}$ and $a_{end} < b_{end}$;
- meets$(a, b) \Longleftrightarrow a_{end} = b_{start}$; during$(a, b) \Longleftrightarrow a_{start} > b_{start}$ and $a_{end} < b_{end}$;
- overlaps$(a, b) \Longleftrightarrow a_{start} < b_{start} < a_{end}$;
- finishes$(a, b) \Longleftrightarrow a_{end} = b_{end}$ and $a_{start} > b_{start}$.

3.3. *Logical Connectives and Formulas*

The logical connectives reflect the semantic relationship between different actions and gestures described as functions above. They generally consist of four operations as follows: 1) $\vee$: disjunction, describing the 'or' or 'join' relation between actions and gestures; 2) $\wedge$: conjunction, describing the 'and' or 'meet' relation between actions and gestures; 3) $\neg$: negation, describing the negation of certain activity or gesture; 4) $\rightarrow$: implication, describing that certain activity is the logical consequence of some actions and gestures. The following logical algebra can be defined based on [6].

Definition 3.1. The set Y of logical formulas for activity recognition is defined as the least set satisfying: $(1) X \subseteq Y$; $(2) A \subseteq Y$; $(3) T \subseteq Y$; $(4) F \subseteq Y$; (5) If $p, q \in Y$, then $p \vee q \in Y$, $p \wedge q \in Y$, $\neg p \in Y$, $p \rightarrow q \in Y$.

Note that the above definition is a generic one. There may be some formulas that do not have real meanings in activity recognition.

We consider here only interactions "hug" as an example for illustration purpose. The corresponding hierarchical structures of this interaction are constructed as follows based on the underlying semantic ordering relationships of them. For simplicity, the input video level and the image features are not shown here.

358

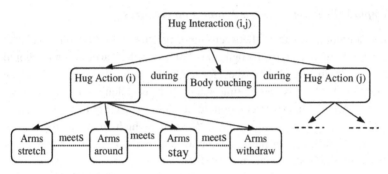

Figure 2. Hierarchical structure of *Hug* interaction

Based on the hierarchical structure shown as in Figure 2, the generation of the corresponding logical formulas can be achieved according to the above procedures. Here we list only the related, not all the formulas: $H_1(x_1, x_2)$-Hug interaction of person x_1 and person x_2; $H_2(x_1, x_2)$-Body touching of person x_1 and person x_2; $F(x)$-Hug action of person x; $Q_1(x)$-Arm stretch gesture of person x; $Q_2(x)$-Arm around gesture of x; $Q_3(x)$-Arm stay gesture of person x; $Q_4(x)$-Arm withdraw gesture of person x; $T_2(Q_i, Q_j)$-Gesture Q_i and Q_j 'meets' (temporal relation); $T_5(H_i, H_j)$-Action H_j happen 'during' activity H_i (temporal relation).

After predicates representation, the logical formulas for "hug" are constructed as follows according to the underlying logical interactions along with appropriate logical connectives. Note that we have not included the quantifiers in these formulas, which means that the free variables appeared are universally quantified. The logical formulas for *hug* interaction:

$$(F(x_1) \wedge H_2(x_1, x_2) \wedge T_5(H_2(x_1, x_2), F(x_1)) \vee (F(x_2) \wedge H_2(x_2, x_1) \wedge$$
$$T_5(H_2(x_2, x_1), F(x_2)) \rightarrow H_1(x_1, x_2), \qquad (3.1)$$
$$Q_1(x_1) \wedge Q_2(x_1) \wedge Q_3(x_1) \wedge Q_4(x_1) \wedge T_2(Q_1(x_1), Q_2(x_1)) \wedge T_2(Q_2(x_1), Q_3(x_1)) \wedge$$
$$T_2(Q_3(x_1), Q_4(x_1)) \rightarrow F(x_1), \qquad (3.2)$$
$$Q_1(x_2) \wedge Q_2(x_2) \wedge Q_3(x_2) \wedge Q_4(x_2) \wedge T_2(Q_1(x_2), Q_2(x_2)) \wedge T_2(Q_2(x_2), Q_3(x_2)) \wedge$$
$$T_2(Q_3(x_2), Q_4(x_2)) \rightarrow F(x_2). \qquad (3.3)$$

The 'or' relation (corresponding to logical connective 'disjunction') in first logical formula (3.1) shows that the event is also defined as 'hug' when a person is hugging another person while he/she has no the corresponding action.

We treat the activity to be recognized as the high-level node, which is represented as the disjunctive normal forms of the mid-level action nodes, and the mid-level action nodes are consequently the disjunctive normal forms of the low-level gesture or feature nodes denoted as literals (atomic formulas or their negations). The temporal relations between gestures and actions contribute also to the disjunctive normal forms at the corresponding layers, by acting as functions which take the gestures and actions as their variables. This process is semantically nature due to the fact that the high-level activity is essentially composed some lower level actions and gestures. In other words, although the hierarchical structure is constructed according to the semantic understanding of the activity, it naturally has a close relationship to logic representation.

4. Conclusions

Formalization is the key and fundamental issue in different applications, once formalized into first-order logic formula, there are formal reasoning methodologies and tools available for reasoning and decision making purpose. This work provided a formalization framework which works in the human activity recognition application context to model activity into hierarchical structure which is then transferred into the first-order logic formula, and the recognition will be conducted in a feasible way using automated reasoning tools [7, 8]. Due to the limited size, details of formalization were skipped.

Acknowledgment

This work has been partially supported by the research project TIN2012-31263, and the EU-FP7 project – SAVASA under grant agreement number 285621.

References

1. O. Lara and M. Labrador. A survey on human activity recognition using wearable sensors. *IEEE Communications Surveys Tutorials*, 15(3): 1192–1209, 2013.

2. P. Turaga, R. Chellappa, V. S. Subrahmanian, and O. Udrea. Machine recognition of human activities: A survey. *IEEE Transactions on Circuits and Systems for Video Technology*, 18(11):1473–1488, 2008.

3. J. K. Aggarwal and M. S. Ryoo, Human activity analysis: a review, *ACM Computing Surveys*, 43(3): Article 16, 2011.

4. J. F. Allen & G. Ferguson, Actions and events in interval temporal logic. *Journal of Logic and Computation*, 4(5), p. 531–579, 1994.

5. M.S. Ryoo & J.K. Aggarwal, Semantic representation and recognition of continued and recursive. *International Journal of Computer Vision*, 32(1), pp. 1–24, 2009.

6. D.W. Barnes and J.M. Mack, *An Algebraic Introduction to Mathematical Logic*. Springer, 1975.

7. S.W. Chen, J. Liu, H. Wang, J.C. Augusto, A hierarchical human activity recognition framework based on automated reasoning, *Proceedings of the 2013 IEEE International Conference on Systems, Man, and Cybernetics* (SMC2013), Manchester, UK, 13-16 October, 2013, IEEE Press, pp. 3495-3499.

8. G. J. Wang and H. J. Zhou, Introduction to Mathematical Logic and Resolution Principle, 2nd ed., Oxford: Alpha Science International Limited, 2009.

PART 4

SOFT COMPUTING AND APPLIED RESEARCH

.

PARTICLE SWARMS APPLIED TO THE QUADRATIC ASSIGNMENT PROBLEM FOR SOLVING THE IN-CORE FUEL MANAGEMENT OPTIMIZATION

ANDERSON ALVARENGA DE MOURA MENESES

Instituto de Engenharia e Geociências, Universidade Federal do Oeste do Pará
Av. Vera Paz, s/n – Salé, Santarém, PA, 68005-110, Brazil

The In-Core Fuel Management Optimization (ICFMO) is a prominent and real-world combinatorial problem in Nuclear Engineering, with a large number of sub-optimal solutions, disconnected feasible regions and approximation hazards. For the sake of previous validation, optimization techniques are applied to benchmark combinatorial problems prior to applications to the ICFMO itself. In the present work, the investigation on the application of Particle Swarm Optimization (PSO) to the Quadratic Assignment Problem (QAP) is reported. The Random Keys (RK), an encoding model used to map particles' positions in a continuous search space into combinatorial solutions, allowed promising results without constructive heuristics and local search. The application of PSO with RK to the QAP forms a basis for further investigation on the RK encoding scheme for the ICFMO.

1. Introduction

The In-Core Fuel Management Optimization (ICFMO) or Loading Pattern (LP) Optimization is a prominent real-world problem in Nuclear Engineering. Its goal is to determine the LP for producing full power within adequate safety margins [1]-[6]. Its high complexity is characterized by a large number of feasible solutions, large number of sub-optimal solutions, disconnected feasible regions, high dimensionality, complex and time-consuming evaluation function (which involves Reactor Physics calculations) as well as approximation hazards. Several metaheuristics such as Simulated Annealing, Genetic Algorithms, Ant Colonies Optimization, and Artificial Bee Colonies have been investigated for application to the ICFMO, as well as the Particle Swarm Optimization (PSO) [2], [3], [7].

Prior to the investigation of metaheuristics directly applied to the ICFMO, the validation of the code is often made with benchmark combinatorial problems such as the Traveling Salesman Problem (TSP), as described in [2] and [3]. However, the formulation of the ICFMO based on an Assignment Problem (AP) is also possible [4] and, to the best of our knowledge, no report of PSO with Random Keys (PSORK) applied to the Quadratic Assignment Problem (QAP) without local search and constructive heuristics and finding the global minimum has been made yet, as presented herein.

Rather than only solving the QAP, for which there exist several competitive algorithms, the present work is part of the investigation and development of new techniques for the ICFMO, using benchmark problems such as the TSP and QAP. The idea of using such benchmark problems is straightforward. The ICFMO depends on real-world characteristics which vary from one power plant to another such as the cycle of operation, specificities of the fuel assemblies, maintenance planning as well as economic objectives, therefore it is not possible to benchmark the ICFMO itself. Thus applying algorithms to complex problems such as the TSP and QAP helps producing insights about the performance of those techniques for the ICFMO.

Particularly, the present work is part of an ongoing investigation, in which the PSORK algorithm is applied to the QAP, in order to go deeper in the performance and behavior of RK model observing how it works in the context of an assignment problem, and not only with the TSP as done before [2], [3]. Thus we are also applying the PSORK algorithm to a complex assignment problem such as the QAP, with competitive results, although not using local search or constructive heuristics. This point is critically important in our investigation since local search or constructive heuristics used in benchmark problems such as the QAP are mostly useless or senseless for the ICFMO.

The remaining of the present paper is structured as follows. The theoretical background is described in section 2. The computational experimental results are reported in section 3. In section 4 we discuss the results and conclusions are drawn in section 5.

2. Theoretical Background

2.1. *Quadratic Assignment Problem (QAP)*

The QAP was stated by Koopmans and Beckman in 1957 [8]. According to its formulation, given two n × n matrices (a_{ij}) and (b_{ij}), respectively flow and distance matrices, the goal is to find a permutation π^* with the minimization given by

$$\min_{\pi \in \Pi(n)} f(\pi) = \sum_{i=1}^{n} \sum_{j=1}^{n} a_{ij} b_{\pi_i \pi_j}, \tag{1}$$

where $\Pi(n)$ is the set of permutations of n elements. According to [9], "QAP instances of size larger than 20 are considered intractable" and "a large number of real-world problems lead to QAP instances of considerable size that cannot be solved exactly". See also [10] for more information on the QAP.

Besides the possibility of stating the ICFMO as an AP [4], the analogy between the QAP and the ICFMO is due to the following fact. In the QAP, two apparently similar permutations π_A and π_B will probably have very different evaluations $f(\pi_A)$ and $f(\pi_B)$, calculated with Eq. (1). In the ICFMO, two apparently similar permutations may also have very different evaluations (or even be unfeasible), although the evaluations are made with Reactor Physics codes.

In the present work the tests were performed with the instance *tai12a*, from the QAPLib (http://www.opt.math.tu-graz.ac.at/qaplib/), in which $n = 12$. The global minimum of this instance is 224416.

2.2. *Particle Swarm Optimization (PSO) with Random Keys (RK)*

The PSO algorithm is a metaheuristic that models a collaborative search, based on the social aspects of intelligence [7], belonging to the paradigm of Swarm Intelligence. The balance between individual cognition and social learning is seen in the PSO's equations, in which a swarm with P particles "flies" in an n-dimensional search space. Each particle i ($i = 1, 2, ..., P$) in the iteration t has a position $x_i^t = (x_{i1}^t, x_{i2}^t, ..., x_{in}^t)$ and a velocity $v_i^t = (v_{i1}^t, v_{i2}^t, ..., v_{in}^t)$, which are updated according to the equations

$$v_{ij}^{t+1} = w^t v_{ij}^t + c_1 r_1^t (pbest_{ij} - x_{ij}^t) + c_2 r_2^t (gbest_j - x_{ij}^t) \tag{2}$$

and

$$x_{ij}^{t+1} = x_{ij}^t + v_{ij}^{t+1} \quad , \tag{3}$$

where j is the dimension ($j = 1, 2,..., n$); c_1 and c_2 are acceleration constants; r_1^t and r_2^t are uniformly distributed random numbers in the interval [0, 1]; $pbest_{ij}$ is the jth coordinate of the best position reached by the particle i until the iteration t; $gbest_j$ is the jth coordinate of the best position reached by the best particle of the swarm until the iteration t.

The inertia weight w^t decreases linearly according to the equation

$$w^t = w - \frac{w - w_{min}}{t_{max}} t \quad , \tag{4}$$

where w is the maximum inertia constant, w_{min} is the minimum inertia constant, t_{max} is the maximum number of iterations and t is the current iteration.

The RK model was proposed by Bean in 1994 [11]. The RK encoding model maps particles' positions of a continuous search space into combinatorial solutions. For example, if the key sequence (position) in a five-dimensional space x_i^t = (0.39; 0.12; 0.54; 0.98; 0.41) had been obtained, the resulting combinatorial solution would be (2, 1, 5, 3, 4) since 0.12 is the lowest number and is the *second* coordinate in x_i^t; 0.39, which is the second lowest number, is the *first* coordinate; 0.41 is the third lowest number and is the *fifth* coordinate and so forth. More information on the application of the PSORK algorithm to the TSP and the ICFMO is found in [3].

Thus the PSORK algorithm consists in particles flying in a continuous search space, having their positions mapped into discrete solutions and evaluated according to the objective function of the problem.

3. Computational Experimental Results

The code was implemented in FORTRAN, in the Microsoft Developer Studio. The experiments were performed in a notebook with an Intel Pentium Dual Core T3400, 2.16 GHz processor (4 GB RAM). The swarms had 100 particles, with w = 0.9, w_{min} = 0.2, $c_1 = c_2$ = 1.8 (similarly to the values used successfully for the TSP and ICFMO [3]), and the initial velocity coordinates were set to $v_{ij}^0 = 30 \times u_{ij}^0$, where u_{ij}^0 is a uniformly distributed random number in the interval [0, 1]. The stopping criterion was t_{max} = 1000 iterations. The results for 10 seeds are exhibited in the Table 1.

Table 1. Results for the PSORK algorithm applied to the QAP instance *tai12a*.

Test	Result
#1	243460
#2	**224416**[1]
#3	236006
#4	232164
#5	**224416**[1]
#6	242968
#7	237560
#8	230704
#9	233848
#10	**224416**[1]
Average	**232996**

[1] Global minimum.

4. Discussion

In three out of ten tests the swarms reached the global minimum for the instance *tai12a*. Notice that the PSORK algorithm does not use constructive heuristics or local search procedure. Besides, in six out of ten tests the results are within a 5% relaxation for this instance (235637).

The average value of 232996 (in 100000 evaluations) cannot be directly compared to the average value 239400 (for five tests, in 72000 evaluations) of the Variable Neighborhood PSO described in [12] since the overall number of evaluations is different, although it gives an idea of the algorithms' performance.

5. Conclusion

In the present work, we report the application of the PSORK algorithm to the QAP, used as a benchmark problem for the ICFMO. The ICFMO is a prominent problem in Nuclear Engineering with high complexity given the large number of feasible and sub-optimal solutions, disconnected feasible regions, high dimensionality, complex and time-consuming evaluation function (which involves Reactor Physics calculations) as well as approximation hazards. Due to its specificities, the ICFMO cannot be benchmarked itself, thus the use of benchmark combinatorial problems such as the QAP is necessary. The investigation on methods that do not use constructive heuristics or local search procedures is particularly important, since heuristics for the QAP cannot be used for the ICFMO. The global minimum found for the QAP instance *tai12a* as well the other results demonstrates that the PSORK algorithm is promising for the QAP. Ongoing research comprises the application of PSORK to other QAP instances as well as further investigation on the improvement of RK model for application to the ICFMO.

Acknowledgments

This research is supported by CNPq (Conselho Nacional de Desenvolvimento Científico e Tecnológico, Brazil – Project no. 472912/2013-5).

References

1. S. Levine, In-Core Fuel Management of Four Reactor Types. In: Handbook of Nuclear Reactor Calculation, vol. II, CRC Press (1987).
2. A.A.M. Meneses, R. Schirru, Particle Swarm Optimization applied to the combinatorial problem in order to solve the Nuclear Reactor Fuel Reloading Problem. In: Proceedings of the Seventh International FLINS Conference on Applied Artificial Intelligence (2006).

3. A.A.M. Meneses, M.D. Machado, R. Schirru, Particle Swarm Optimization applied to the nuclear reload problem of a Pressurized Water Reactor, Progress in Nuclear Energy 51, 319-326 (2009).

4. A.A.M. Meneses, L.M. Gambardella, R. Schirru, A new approach for heuristics-guided search in the In-Core Fuel Management Optimization, Progress in Nuclear Energy 52, 339-351 (2010).

5. A.A.M. Meneses, R. Schirru, L.M. Gambardella, A Class-Based Search for the In-Core Fuel Management Optimization of a Pressurized Water Reactor, Annals of Nuclear Energy 37, 1554-1560 (2010).

6. I.M.S. Oliveira, R. Schirru, Swarm intelligence of artificial bees applied to In-Core Fuel Management Optimization, Annals of Nuclear Energy 38, 1039-1045 (2011).

7. J. Kennedy, R.C. Eberhart, Swarm Intelligence, Morgan Kaufmann Publishers, California, USA (2001).

8. T.C. Koopmans, M.J. Beckmann, Assignment problems and the location of economic activities, Econometrica 25, 53-76 (1957).

9. E.D. Taillard, L.M. Gambardella, Adaptive Memories for the Quadratic Assignment Problem, Technical Report IDSIA 87-97 (1997).

10. R.K. Ahuja, J.B. Orlin, A. Tiwari, A greedy genetic algorithm for the quadratic assignment problem, Computers & Operations Research 27, 917-934 (2000).

11. J.C. Bean, Genetic algorithms and random keys for sequencing and optimization, ORSA Journal of Computing 6, 154-160 (1994).

12. H. Liu, A. Abraham, An Hybrid Fuzzy Variable Neighborhood Particle Swarm Optimization Algorithm for Solving Quadratic Assignment Problems, Journal of Universal Computer Science 13, 1309-1331 (2007).

MQDM: AN ITERATIVE FUZZY METHOD FOR GROUP DECISION MAKING

RAMÓN SOTO C., M. ELENA ROBLES-BALDENEGRO

Department of Accounting, University of Sonora, Blvd. Transversal & Rosales Hermosillo, Sonora, 83000, México

VICTORIA LOPEZ

Faculty of Informatics, Complutense University of Madrid Madrid 28040, Spain

JUAN A. CAMALICH

MoviQuest, S.C., Ángela Peralta No.51, Col. Periodista C.P. Hermosillo, Sonora 83156, México

The current communication technologies have resulted in a modern world characterized by a remarkable increase in social interactions. In this new context and because of the globalization of all human activities make the collective participation in decision-making processes take an increasingly prominent role. In this paper, a new method for group decision making from a set of imprecise opinions called "moviQuest Decision Making" (MQDM), is presented. This method allows to integrate the opinions of heterogeneous groups of agents for iterative collective decision making.

1. Introduction

In this paper we present a new iterative method for group decision making called 'moviQuest Decision Making' (MQDM). Fuzzy trends encoding method [5] is used to capture the underlying fuzzy sentiments in the opinion given by the participants. This encoding method has been used to integrate three types of opinions: 1) scalar values with f xed distribution, 2) ordered linguistic values and 3) non-stationary time series values [5, 6]. In this article we will focus on the use of ordered linguistic values as a primary resource in collective decision making. Extending the use of this method to take decisions on numeric values is straightforward.

2. Fuzzy trends encoding

2.1. *Ordered linguistic values*

Ordered linguistic values are linguistic labels associated with an order determined by a semantic rule. Many questions can be expressed so that the possible answers are expressed by a Likert-type scale, being this a particularly interesting case of ordered linguistic values. In MQDM, ordered linguistic values are encoded using the fuzzy sets 'Disagree', 'Neutral' and 'Agree' (Figure 1).

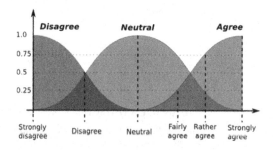

Figure 1. Fuzzy sets for encoding answers to a Likert-scale question.

The membership function for 'Neutral' fuzzy set is def ned by the logistic curve:

$$
\mu_N(x) = \begin{cases} 0 & x \leq v - \lambda \\ 2\left[\frac{v-\lambda-x}{\lambda}\right]^2 & v - \lambda < x \leq v - \frac{\lambda}{2} \\ 1 - 2\left[\frac{v-x}{\lambda}\right]^2 & v - \frac{\lambda}{2} < x \leq v + \frac{\lambda}{2} \\ 2\left[\frac{v+\lambda-x}{\lambda}\right]^2 & v + \frac{\lambda}{2} < x \leq v + \lambda \\ 0 & x > v + \lambda \end{cases} \tag{1}
$$

where v is the modal value of the 'Neutral' fuzzy set and λ is the fuzzy set bandwidth. The fuzzy sets 'Disagree' and 'Agree' are defined accordingly. The number of linguistic values and the corresponding value of membership in the fuzzy sets are def ned during the design of the questionnaire.

2.2. *Fuzzy representation*

The representation of fuzzy values in MQDM method follows the scheme used in the Fuzzy Inductive Reasoning (FIR) technique [1]. Such encoding uses triplets with the following structure:

$$r(x) = (\alpha_{max}, \mu_{max}, side) \qquad (2)$$

where α_{max} is the name of the fuzzy set in which the quantitative value x has the largest membership value, μ_{max} is the membership value of x in the fuzzy set α_{max} and side is an additional qualitative value that describes the side on the membership function curve where the quantitative value x is located (**Left**, **Center** or **Right**). The center for the decreasing logistic curve is taken at $x = \upsilon - \lambda$, while for the growing logistic curve is taken at $x = \upsilon + \lambda$.

Two complementary concepts to this representation are those of 'neighboring fuzzy sets' and 'pointing out to'. These concepts are defi ed as follows [3]:

Definition 1: Two fuzzy sets α and β are said to be 'neighboring fuzzy sets' iff $\alpha \neq \beta$ and $\alpha \cap \beta \neq \phi$, being ϕ the empty set. This relations is represented as $\mathcal{N}(\alpha, \beta)$.

Definition 2: The variable x is said to 'point out to' the fuzzy set α (denoted $x \mapsto \alpha$) iff: 1) $x \in \beta$ and $\mathcal{N}(\alpha, \beta)$, and 2) α is located at the same side of β where x is placed on.

3. Iterative fuzzy aggregation

3.1. *Iterative group decision making*

The method for MQDM decision making is performed as an iterative process sketched in Figure 2.

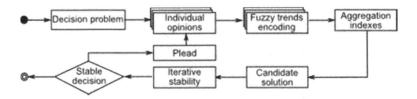

Figure 2. Iterative fuzzy aggregation process.

The core of such a method is the aggregation of the individual fuzzy coded opinions for generating a candidate solution [2]. After the first voting round, participants have the opportunity to argue for or against the possible solutions and re-vote. If collective decision stands, the process concludes. Otherwise, a new round of argument is generated and returned to vote. The process is repeated until a stable decision on the previous iteration. The basis for this aggregation is the computation of the *Fuzzy aggregation indexes*.

3.2. *Fuzzy aggregation indexes*

MQDM uses a set of fuzzy aggregation indexes to accumulate the opinions given by the participants, taking also into account the 'inclination' of the participant for other possible solutions. We def ne the fuzzy aggregation index at iteration i for the fuzzy class α as follows:

$$I_\alpha^{(i)} = \frac{\sum_{j=1}^n w_j^i v_j^i}{w_j^i} \tag{3}$$

being n the number of votes issued. If x_j^i is the opinion given by the agent A_j at iteration i and $X_j^i = (\alpha_j^i, \mu_j^i, s_j^i)$ the corresponding coded value, then V_j^i is computed as:

$$V_j^i = \begin{cases} \mu & X_j^i \in \alpha \\ 1 - \mu & X_j^i \in \beta \text{ and } \mathcal{N}(\alpha, \beta) \text{ and } x \mapsto \alpha \\ 0 & \text{Any other case} \end{cases} \tag{4}$$

W_j^i is the conf dence the system has on the opinion of agent A_j and is defined as:

$$W_j^i = \begin{cases} \kappa_j\left(1 - \bar{E}_j\right)\left(\frac{2}{1+e^{-8\Omega_\gamma^3}} - 1\right)\left(\frac{1-\omega-\mathcal{G}\left(x_j^i, x_j^{i-1}\right)}{\omega}\right)^2 & V_j^i \neq 0 \\ 0 & V_j^i = 0 \end{cases} \tag{5}$$

where κ_j is the degree of self-confidence of the agent about her own opinion. $\bar{E}_j$ is a normalized mean error measure taken over the agent historic performance. Ω_γ is the level of mastery of all the agents in the group γ. $\mathcal{G}(X, Y)$ is the fuzzy Gower similarity [3] between the fuzzy triplet X and the fuzzy triplet Y (see equation 9). X_j^i is the opinion given by the agent at the iteration i. $\omega \geq 1$ is an inertia parameter which regulates the agents opinions shifts.

$\bar{E}_j$ is defined as:

$$\bar{E}_j = \frac{1}{L}\sum_{l=1}^L \kappa_j^l \cdot \left(1 - \mathcal{G}\left(O^l, \hat{O}_j^l\right)\right) \cdot \xi_j^l \tag{6}$$

being L the number of decision-making exercises in which agent A_j has participated; O^l is the correct or consensual solution in the l-th decision-making exercise; $\hat{O}_j^l$ is the corresponding opinion given by the agent; κ_j^l is the self-conf dence provided by the agent about such opinion. The term ξ_j^l is a measure of the error the agent induced in in the n-th collective decision-making exercise and is given by

$$\xi_j^l = \begin{cases} \mathcal{G}(O^l, \hat{O}_{-j}^l) - \mathcal{G}(O^l, \hat{O}^l) & O^l \neq null \\ 1 & O^l = null \end{cases} \tag{7}$$

being $\hat{O}^l$ the collective decision yield in the aggregation process and $\hat{O}_{-j}^l$ the collective decision resulting from ignoring the opinion of agent A_j.

Ω_γ is computed adaptively: The initial value for each new group is assigned 'by design'. Then, this value is changed after each decision-making exercise, based on the average error committed by all members of the group, according the following relationship:

$$\Omega_\gamma = \hat{\Omega}_\gamma (1 + \bar{E}^{-\gamma} - \bar{E}^\gamma) \tag{8}$$

where $\hat{\Omega}_\gamma$ is the current value of Ω_γ, that is, the value used in the last decision-making exercise; $\bar{E}^{-\gamma}$ is the average error produced by all the participating in the exercise, except those belonging to the group γ and $\bar{E}^\gamma$ is the average error produced by agents belonging to the group γ in the exercise.

$\mathcal{G}(X, Y)$, the fuzzy Gower similarity measure is defined as [2]:

$$G_j^i = \frac{1}{3}\left(1 - |\mu_j^i - \mu_j^{i-1}| + g_c(X_j^i) + g_s(X_j^i)\right) \tag{9}$$

where

$$g_c(X_j^i) = \begin{cases} 1 & \alpha_j^i = \alpha_j^{i-1} \\ 0.5 & \mathcal{N}(\alpha_j^i, \alpha_j^{i-1}) \\ 0 & \text{Any other case} \end{cases} \tag{10}$$

and

$$g_s(X_j^i) = \begin{cases} 1 & \alpha_j^i = \alpha_j^{i-1} \text{ and } s_j^i = s_j^{i-1} \\ 0.5 & \mathcal{N}(\alpha_j^i, \alpha_j^{i-1}) \text{ and } x_j^i \mapsto \alpha_j^{i-1} \text{ and } x_j^{i-1} \mapsto \alpha_j^i \\ 0 & \text{Any other case} \end{cases} \tag{11}$$

3.2. Candidate solution

The solution proposal at iteration i, $O^{l(i)}$, is defined as:

$$O^{l(i)} = \left(\alpha_{I_{max}^{(i)}}^i, I_{max}^{(i)}, S_{max}^{(i)}\right) \tag{12}$$

being $\alpha^i_{I^{(i)}_{max}}$ the fuzzy set whose fuzzy aggregation index, $I^{(i)}_{max}$, got the highest value at iteration i and $S^{(i)}_{max}$ is chosen so the solution points to the fuzzy set whose fuzzy aggregation index obtained the second largest value.

3.4. *Iteration stability*

Given some tolerance ε, the condition for iteration stability is defined as:

$$g\left(O^{l(i)}, O^{l(i-1)}\right) \leq \varepsilon \tag{13}$$

4. Conclusions

In this paper we presented a new iterative method for group decision making called "moviQuest Decision Making" (MQDM). Individual opinions are integrated using a fuzzy aggregation algorithm. The MQDM algorithm takes into account aspects such as the status of the agent in the community, his record of accuracy in past decisions and their own declaration of competence on a given topic. Iterations allows to provide arguments for or against certain positions so that participants in the process may reconsider their views. To manage the impact of the opinions given by agents who may be changing their views between iterations, the method uses an inertia weight that can be adjusted to tolerate or restrict such variations.

References

1. de Albornoz, A. Inductive Reasoning and Reconstruction Analysis: Two Complementary Tools for Qualitative Fault Monitoring of Large-Scale Systems, Ph. D. Thesis, Universitat Politécnica de Catalunya (1996).
2. Herrera F, Herrera-Viedma E. Choice functions and mechanisms for linguistic preference relations. European Journal of Operational Research, 120: 144–161 (2000).
3. Herrera F, Herrera-Viedma E. Linguistic decision analysis: steps for solving decision problems under linguistic information. Fuzzy Sets and Systems, 115: 67–82 (2000).
4. Rodríguez, J. T., López, V., Gómez, D., Vitoriano, B. Montero, J., A computational definition of aggregation rules, Proceedings IEEE WCCI-FUZZIEEE'10 pp. 33 - 37 (2010)
5. Soto, R., Fuzzy Backpropagation Neural Networks for Nonstationary Data Prediction, Foundations of Fuzzy Logic and Soft Computing (LNAI 4529, P. Melin, O. Castillo, L.T. Aguilar, J. Kacprzyk y W. Pedrycz, Eds.) (2007).

6. Soto, R., Soto, A., Camalich, J.A., MQDM: A Method for Fuzzy Group Decision Making in Structured Social Networks. In: The 16th IASTED International Conference on Software Engineering and Application, SEA 2012 (2012).
7. Xu Z., Linguistic Aggregation Operators, Linguistic Decision Making. Theory and methods. Science Press, Beijing and Springer Berlin Heidelberg, ISBN: 978-3-642-29439-6, DOI: 10.1007/978-3-642-29440-2_2 pp 15-85 (2012).
8. Yager R R. Centered OWA operators. Soft Computing, 11: 631–639. (2007).
9. Yager R R. Time series smoothing and OWA aggregation. Technical Report# MII-2701, Machine Intelligence Institute, Iona College, New Rochelle, NY. (2007).
10. Zadeh L A, Kacprzyk J, eds. Computing with Words in Information/ Intelligent Systems 1: Foundations. Heidelberg: Physica-Verlag. (1999).
11. Zadeh L A, Kacprzyk J, eds. Computing with Words in Information/ Intelligent Systems 2: Applications. Heidelberg: Physica-Verlag. (1999).

A FUZZY LINGUISTIC DECISION TOOLS ENHANCEMENT SUITE TO SOLVE LINGUISTIC DECISION MAKING PROBLEMS

F.J. ESTRELLA*†, M. ESPINILLA, L. MARTÍNEZ

Department of Computer Science, University of Jaén, Campus Las Lagunillas s/n
Jaén, 23071, Spain

In linguistic decision making problems, the set of alternatives are assessed by means of linguistic terms, implying processes of Computing with Words (CWW). The 2-tuple linguistic model provides a computational model that offers linguistic results in the original linguistic domain in a precise way. Furthermore, this model has been extended to carry out processes of CWW in complex decision frameworks. Despite these advantages, this model and its extensions have not been developed in a software tool suite to facilitate the resolution of linguistic decision making problems. In this contribution, we present FLINTSTONES, a fuzzy linguistic decision tools enhancement suite to solve linguistic decision making problems based on the 2-tuple linguistic model and its extensions as well as the FLINTSTONES website.

Keywords: Decision Making; Linguistic Information.

1. Introduction

A decision making process is used to select the best alternative from a set of alternatives. This process can be decomposed into several steps (see Figure 1):

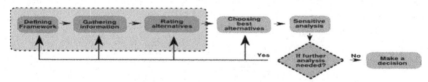

Figure 1: Decision resolution scheme

Generally, decision making problems are defined under uncertainty, which has a non-probabilistic nature, due to the fact that experts feel more comfortable providing their knowledge by using terms closer to human beings cognitive

* This paper has been partially supported by Projects TIN2012-31263 and AGR-6487
† estrella@ujaen.es

model. Fuzzy logic and fuzzy linguistic approach [10] provide tools to model and manage such an uncertainty by means of linguistic variables, improving the flexibility and offering reliability of the decision models in different fields [8,9].

The use of linguistic information involves processes of Computing with Words (CWW) in which the objects of computation are words or sentences from a natural language and results are also expressed in a linguistic expression domain. A computational scheme for CWW has been defined which includes a translation phase and a retranslation phase (see Figure 2).

Figure 2: CWW scheme

Usually, a lot of real world decision making problems are defined in complex and uncertain decision frameworks in which linguistic modeling is not enough, being necessary the use of numerical or interval domains (heterogeneous frameworks), multiple linguistic scales (multi-granular linguistic frameworks) or unbalanced linguistic scales (unbalanced linguistic frameworks). In [8,9] was shown that the 2-tuple linguistic model [4] is an excellent option to manage not only linguistic decision making problems but also complex decision problems due to the fact that it provides a flexible computational model that offers linguistic results in the original linguistic domain in a precise way and has been extended to carry out CWW processes in complex frameworks.

In the literature have been proposed several software tools to solve linguistic decision problems [7]. Nonetheless, there is not a software tools suite that implements the 2-tuple linguistic model and its extensions.

In this contribution, we present the architecture and functionality of FLINTSTONES, a fuzzy linguistic decision tools enhancement suite to solve linguistic decision making problems based on the 2-tuple linguistic model and its extension as well as the FLINTSTONES website.

This contribution is structured as follows: Section 2 reviews the theoretical fundamentals of 2-tuple linguistic model and its extensions. Section 3 presents FLINTSTONES architecture and functionality as well as its website. Finally, in Section 4, conclusions are drawn.

2. Preliminaries

In this section we review briefly some concepts about the 2-tuple linguistic model and its extensions.

The 2-tuple linguistic model was presented in [4] in order to represent the information by means of a 2-tuple, (s, α), where s is a linguistic term with a syntax and semantics, and $\alpha \in [-0.5, 0.5)$ is a numerical value that represents the *symbolic translation.* The 2-tuple linguistic model facilitates the CWW process by its computational model.

Sometimes, decision making problems are defined in complex frameworks and the 2-tuple linguistic model has been extended to carry out processes of CWW in the following complex decision frameworks:

- *Heterogeneous frameworks* in which assessments are expressed in different domains such as numerical, interval or linguistic. In [6] was proposed an extension to deal with this framework.

- *Multi-granular linguistic frameworks* in which the assessments are expressed in multiple linguistic scales. In [1], [2] and [5] were presented three different extensions to manage this framework.

- *Unbalanced linguistic frameworks* in which the assessments are expressed in an unbalanced linguistic scale, i.e., a scale with different number of labels on each side. In [3] was presented an extension to deal with this framework.

3. FLINTSTONES

This section introduces FLINTSTONES, a software tools suite to solve linguistic decision making problems based on the 2-tuple linguistic model and its extensions. To do so, we first present the architecture of the software suite, its functionality and, finally, the FLINTSTONES website.

3.1. *Architecture*

FLINTSTONES has been developed as an Eclipse Rich Client Platform (Eclipse RCP) application that is a platform for building and deploying rich client applications developed by IBM and maintained by Eclipse Community. The key value of Eclipse RCP is that allows to quickly developing professional applications with native look-and-feel on multiple platforms. An Eclipse RCP application consists of several *Eclipse components*, also called *plug-ins, bundles* or *OSGi components*. FLINTSTONES includes more than 15 components, which can be grouped into four basic types: i) libraries, ii) Graphical User Interface (GUI), iii) methods and iv) operators (see Figure 3a).

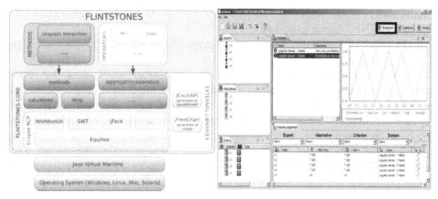

Figure 3: a) FLINTSTONES architecture   b) Framework

3.2. *Functionality*

FLINTSTONES is based on the main steps of decision resolution scheme that were shaded in Figure 1. In this section, we describe these three steps in detail.

The *framework* of the decision making problem is defined in Framework perspective (see Figure 3b). The set of alternatives and the set of criteria which characterize the alternatives are established and, finally, the group of experts that will evaluate the alternatives is fixed. Furthermore, the expression domains used to assess the alternatives are also defined. FLINTSTONES allows creating different expression domains (linguistic, numeric and interval), using wizards that guide the user through the process.

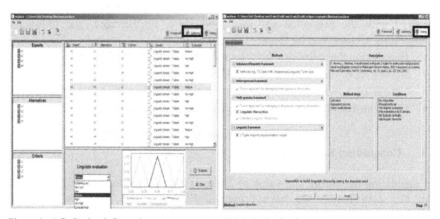

Figure 4: a) Gathering information   b) Method selection

In the step of *gathering information*, experts provide their assessments for each criterion of each alternative in the expression domains defined in the

380

framework. This stage is performed in the Gathering perspective of FLINTSTONES (see Figure 4a).

In order to facilitate the gather process, FLINTSTONES allows users to create Excel spreadsheets.

For *Rating* alternatives is computed the global assessment for each alternative using a solving process that implements the 2-tuple linguistic model or its extensions, depending on the defined decision making problem. The suite is able to indicate the most suitable extension to solve the decision making problem (see Figure 4b). When an extension cannot be employed for the current problem, the suite shows a message to the user that specifies the reason. The solving process follows a common schema (see Figure 2) with the following three processes. It is noteworthy that each extension carries out these steps in a particular way:

1. *Unification process.* If an extension is used, a translation process is needed to represent the gathered information into a unified domain.

2. *Aggregation process.* In this process, the information is aggregated, selecting aggregation operators, in order to obtain a global assessment for each alternative that summarizes its gathered information.

3. *Retranslation process.* If an extension is carried out, a retranslation process is conducted to express the global assessment for each alternative in a linguistic expression domain that can be easily interpreted by experts.

3.3. *FLINTSTONES website*

The website[‡] has been designed with the aim to publish all FLINTSTONES released versions and a repository of case studies with real datasets that can be solved with the presented software tools suite. Furthermore, the following interesting sections can be found in that website:

- *Description* that provides the theoretical foundations of FLINTSTONES.
- *Software tool* that offers FLINTSTONES released versions.
- *Case studies repository* with decision making problems to solve by the suite.
- *Video tutorials* that illustrate the functionality of our suite.

4. Concluding Remarks

Considering the merits and value of 2-tuple linguistic model and its extensions, in this contribution we have presented FLINSTONES, a fuzzy linguistic decision tools enhancement suite to solve linguistic decision making problems based on the 2-tuple linguistic model and its extensions. The proposed suite is a component-based application and its design is focused on reusability and the

---

‡ *http://sinbad2.ujaen.es/flintstones/*

inclusion of new features. The FLINTSTONES website includes a repository of case studies and datasets for different linguistic decision making problems in order to verify the performance of the software tools suite with real datasets and that allows making comparisons with either other proposals or problems.

References

1. M. Espinilla, J. Liu, L. Martínez. An extended hierarchical linguistic model for decision-making problems. Computational Intelligence, **27**, 489 (2011).
2. F. Herrera, E. Herrera-Viedma, L. Martínez. A Fusion Approach for Managing Multi-Granularity Linguistic Term Sets in Decision Making. Fuzzy Sets and Systems, **114**, 43 (2000).
3. F. Herrera, E. Herrera-Viedma, L. Martínez. A fuzzy linguistic methodology to deal with unbalanced linguistic term sets. IEEE Transactions on Fuzzy Systems **16**, 354 (2008).
4. F. Herrera, L. Martínez. A 2-tuple fuzzy linguistic representation model for computing with words. IEEE TFS **8**, 746 (2000).
5. F. Herrera, L. Martínez. A model based on linguistic 2-tuples for dealing with multigranularity hierarchical linguistic contexts in multiexpert decision-making. IEEE T SYST MAN CY C **31**, 227 (2001).
6. F. Herrera, L. Martínez, P.J. Sánchez. Managing non-homogeneous information in group decision making. European Journal of Operational Research **166**, 115 (2005).
7. Ishizaka, P. Nemery, Multi-criteria Decision Analysis: Methods and Software, Wiley, 2013
8. L. Martínez, F. Herrera. An overview on the 2-tuple linguistic model for Computing with Words in Decision Making: Extensions, applications and challenges. Information Sciences, **207**, 1 (2012).
9. R.M. Rodríguez, L. Martínez. An analysis of symbolic linguistics computing models in decision making. International Journal of General Systems, **42**, 121 (2013).
10. L.A. Zadeh. The concept of a linguistic variable and its applications to approximate reasoning. Information Sciences, Part I, II, III **8,8,9**, 199,301,43, (1975).

α -GROUP LOCK RESOLUTION PRINCIPLE BASED ON LATTICE-VALUED PROPOSITIONAL LOGIC $LP(X)$ *

HUA ZHU[1, 2], YANG XU[1], JIANBIN ZHAO[2]

Intelligent Control Center, Southwest Jiaotong University,
Chengdu 610031, China
School of Mathematics and Statistics, Zhengzhou University,
Zhengzhou 450001, China

α-resolution principle based on lattice-valued logic is focused on in this paper, which is a great extension of resolution principle based on classical logic. Concretely, based on α-Group resolution principle in lattice-valued logic, α-Group lock resolution principle is introduced, aiming to improve the efficiency of resolution and the ability of resolution. Then both the soundness and the completeness theorems of α-Group lock resolution principle are proved in lattice-valued propositional logic $LP(X)$. The example given in lattice-valued propositional logic $LP(X)$ illustrates that α-Group lock resolution method is, to some extent, more resolution efficiency than α-Group resolution method and more resolution ability than α-lock resolution method, which only permits binary resolution in lattice-valued logic. This work will provide theoretical foundations for the establishment of automated reasoning algorithm and the further applications of automated reasoning and decision making under uncertainty.

1. Introduction

Lattice-valued logic, as an important many-valued logic, is a great extension of the classical logic, which provides a useful tool for uncertain information processing [8]. In the real world, human knowledge includes lots of uncertainty, and sometimes one needs to deal with fuzzy and incomparable information. With these in mind, Xu proposed the concept of lattice implication algebra by combining algebraic lattice and implication algebra in 1993, which includes both comparable and incomparable elements [11, 16]. Many researchers have investigated this logical algebra [7, 5, 10, 22, 23, 24, 25]. Based on lattice implication algebra, lattice-valued propositional logic and lattice-valued first order logic are introduced and extensively investigated respectively [12, 14]. In 2000, α -resolution is proposed in lattice-valued propositional logic and lattice-valued first order logic, which is a great extension of Robinson's resolution

---

* This work is supported by the Natural Science Foundation of China (Grant No.61175055) and the Science and Technology Research Project of the Education Department of Henan Province (Grant No.13B110383). Email: zhuhua@zzu.edu.cn, xuyang@home.swjtu.edu.cn.

[13, 15], and α-resolution algorithms and applications based on automated reasoning have also been investigated [14, 17, 9, 6]. After that, some resolution strategies and resolution properties based on α-resolution have been proposed and further researched [1, 2, 18, 19, 20, 21].

Mainly inspired by α-Group resolution method in reference [19] and α-lock resolution method in reference [1], we introduce α-Group lock resolution method in lattice-valued propositional logic $LP(X)$, which can improve the resolution efficiency than α-Group resolution, and also can improve the resolution ability than α-lock resolution.

2. Preliminaries

By a lattice implication algebra [16] we mean a bounded lattice $(L,\vee,\wedge,O,I)$ with order-reversing involution ', in which I and O are the greatest and the smallest element of L respectively, and a binary operation $\rightarrow$ satisfying the follow axioms:

(I_1) $x \rightarrow (y \rightarrow z) = y \rightarrow (x \rightarrow z)$;

(I_2) $x \rightarrow x = I$;

(I_3) $x \rightarrow y = y' \rightarrow x'$;

(I_4) if $x \rightarrow y = y \rightarrow x = 1$, then $x = y$;

(I_5) $(x \rightarrow y) \rightarrow y = (y \rightarrow x) \rightarrow x$;

(L_1) $(x \vee y) \rightarrow z = (x \rightarrow z) \wedge (y \rightarrow z)$;

(L_2) $(x \wedge y) \rightarrow z = (x \rightarrow z) \vee (y \rightarrow z)$ for all $x, y, z \in L$.

In the following, unless otherwise stated, L always represents any given lattice implication algebra.

Example 2.1.[16] (Łukasiewicz implication algebra) Let L be a finite chain, $L = \{a_i | i \in \{1, 2, \cdots, n\}\}$ and $O = a_1 \le a_2 \le \cdots \le a_n = I$, define for any $a_i, a_j \in L$, $a_i \vee a_j = a_{\max\{i,j\}}$, $a_i \wedge a_j = a_{\min\{i,j\}}$, $(a_i)' = a_{n-i+1}$, $a_i \rightarrow a_j = a_{\min\{n-i+j,n\}}$.

Then $(L, \vee, \wedge, ', \rightarrow)$ is a lattice implication algebra, denoted by L_n.

Definition 2.1. [13] Let X be a set of propositional variables, $T = L \vee \{', \rightarrow\}$ a type with $ar(') = 1$, $ar(\rightarrow) = 2$ and $ar(a) = 0$ for every $a \in L$. The propositional algebra of the lattice-valued propositional calculus on the set X of propositional variables is the free T algebra on X and is denoted by $LP(X)$.

Definition 2.2.[13] A valuation of $LP(X)$ is a propositional algebra homomorphism $v : LP(X) \rightarrow L$.

Definition 2.3.[13] Let p be a logical formula of $LP(X)$, $\alpha \in L$.

(1). If there exists a valuation v of $LP(X)$ such that $v(p) \ge \alpha$, then p is satisfiable with truth value level α, in short, α-satisfiable;

(2). If $v(p) \ge \alpha$ for any valuation v of $LP(X)$, then p is called valid with truth value level α, in short, α-valid;

(3). If $v(p) \leq \alpha$ for any valuation v of $LP(X)$, then p is called false with truth value level α, in short, α-false.

Definition 2.4.[13] Let G, H be logical formulae of $LP(X)$, $\alpha \in L$.

(1). If $v(G) \leq v(H)$ for any valuation v of $LP(X)$, then we say that G is always less than H, which is denoted by $G \leq H$;

(2). If $H = \alpha$, we say that G is always less than α (or G is α-false), which is denoted by $G \leq \alpha$.

Definition 2.5.[13] A logical formula G of $LP(X)$ is called an extremely form, in short ESF, if a logical formula G^* obtained by deleting any constant or literal or implication term appearing in G is not equivalent to G.

Definition 2.6.[13] A logical formula G of $LP(X)$ is called an indecomposable extremely form, in short $IESF$, if

(1). G is an ESF containing connectives $\rightarrow$ and ' at most;

(2). For any logical formula H of $LP(X)$, if H is an ESF containing $\rightarrow$ and ' at most, where $\overline{LP(X)} = (LP(X)\big/_{\approx}, \vee, \wedge, ', \rightarrow, \overline{0}, \overline{1})$ is a lattice implication algebra and

$$LP(X)\big/_{\approx} = \{\overline{p} | p \in LP(X)\}, \quad \overline{p} = \{q | q \in LP(X), p \approx q\}.$$

Definition 2.7.[13] All the constants, literals and $IESFs$ in $LP(X)$ are called generalized literals.

Note 1: (1). A disjunction of finite generalized literals is called a generalized clause. A conjunction of finite generalized clauses is called a generalized conjunctive normal form ($GCNF$).

(2). Let $S = C_1 \wedge C_2 \wedge \cdots \wedge C_n$, always denoted by $S = \{C_1, C_2, \cdots, C_n\}$, where C_i is a generalized clause in $LP(X)$, $i \in \{1, 2, \cdots, n\}$, then S is a $GCNF$.

Definition 2.8. [3] Let C be a generalized clause in $LP(X)$, each occurrence of a generalized literal in C is assigned a positive integer in the lower left corner, this specific generalized clause C is called a lock generalized clause, and the positive integer in the generalized literal is called a lock index (the same generalized literals can be labeled different integer).

Definition 2.9.[19] Let $\alpha \in L$, and $C_i = p_{i1} \vee p_{i2} \vee \cdots \vee p_{im_i}$, $i \in \{1, 2, \cdots, m\}$, be generalized clauses of $LP(X)$, and $H_i = \{p_{i1}, p_{i2}, \cdots, p_{im_i}\}$ be the set of all generalized literals that occur in C_i.

If there exist generalized literals $x_i \in H_i$ such that $x_1 \wedge x_2 \wedge \cdots \wedge x_m \leq \alpha$, then $C_1(x_1 = \alpha) \vee C_2(x_2 = \alpha) \vee \cdots \vee C_m(x_m = \alpha)$ is called an α-Group resolvent of $C_1, C_2, \cdots, C_m$, which is denoted by $R_{m,\alpha}(C_1(x_1), C_2(x_2), \cdots, C_m(x_m))$, where $C_i(x_i = \alpha)$ means the generalized clause obtained by replacing x_i with α in C_i.

Theorem 2.1.[19](completeness) Suppose $S = \{C_1, C_2, \cdots, C_n\}$ be a $GCNF$ in $LP(X)$, $\alpha \in L$. If $S \leq \alpha$, then there exists an α-Group resolution deduction from S to $\alpha - \square$.

Note: $\alpha - \square$ represents α -empty clause.

For details of lattice implication algebra, lattice-valued logic based on lattice implication algebras, we refer to the references [16, 15, 12].

3. α -Group Lock Resolution Methods in *LP(X)*

Definition 3.1. Let $\alpha \in L$, $S = \{C_1, C_2, \cdots, C_m\}$ be a GCNF in $LP(X)$, where $C_i =_{j1} P_{i1} \vee_{j2} P_{i2} \vee \cdots \vee_{jk_i} P_{ik_i}$ is a lock generalized clause and $H_i = \{_{j1} P_{i1}, _{j2} P_{i2}, \cdots, _{jk_i} P_{ik_i}\}$ is the set of all lock generalized literals in C_i, $i \in \{1, 2, \cdots, m\}$. If there exist generalized literals $x_i \in H_i$ such that $x_1 \wedge x_2 \wedge \cdots \wedge x_m \leq \alpha$, where the index of x_i is the lowest indices of all lock generalized literals in H_i, then $C_1(x_1 = \alpha) \vee C_2(x_2 = \alpha) \vee \cdots \vee C_m(x_m = \alpha)$ is called an α -Group lock resolvent of $C_1, C_2, \cdots, C_m$, denoted by $R_{m,\alpha,L}(C_1(x_1), C_2(x_2), \cdots, C_m(x_m))$, where $C_i(x_i = \alpha)$ means the generalized clause obtained by replacing x_i with α in C_i and $(x_1, x_2, \cdots, x_m)$ is called an α -Group lock array.

Remark 3.1. By Definition 2.9 and Definition 3.1, an α -Group lock resolvent is easily proved to be an α -Group resolvent, that is $R_{m,\alpha,L}(C_1(x_1), C_2(x_2), \cdots, C_m(x_m))$ is a special case of $R_{m,\alpha}(C_1(x_1), C_2(x_2), \cdots, C_m(x_m))$. Hence by Definition 2.4,

$$R_{m,\alpha}(C_1(x_1), C_2(x_2), \cdots, C_m(x_m)) \leq R_{m,\alpha,L}(C_1(x_1), C_2(x_2), \cdots, C_m(x_m)).$$

Theorem 3.1. Let $C_i =_{j1} P_{i1} \vee_{j2} P_{i2} \vee \cdots \vee_{jk_i} P_{ik_i}$ be lock generalized clauses in *LP(X)*, $H_i = \{_{j1} P_{i1}, _{j2} P_{i2}, \cdots, _{jk_i} P_{ik_i}\}$ be the set of all lock generalized literals in C_i, $\alpha \in L$, $i \in \{1, 2, \cdots, m\}$. If there exist generalized literals $x_i \in H_i$ such that $x_1 \wedge x_2 \wedge \cdots \wedge x_m \leq \alpha$, where the index of x_i is the lowest indices of all lock generalized literals in H_i, then $C_1 \wedge C_2 \wedge \cdots \wedge C_m \leq R_{m,\alpha,L}(C_1(x_1), C_2(x_2), \cdots, C_m(x_m))$.

Proof. It can be obtained by theorem 4.1 of Reference [19] and Remark 3.1.

Definition 3.2. Suppose $\alpha \in L$, $S = \{C_1, C_2, \cdots, C_n\}$ be the set of lock generalized clauses in $LP(X)$, $H_i = \{_{j1} P_{i1}, _{j2} P_{i2}, \cdots, _{jk_i} P_{ik_i}\}$ is the set of all lock generalized literals in C_i, $i \in \{1, 2, \cdots, n\}$. $\omega = \{D_1, D_2, \cdots, D_t\}$ is called an α -Group lock resolution deduction from S to the lock generalized clause D_t, if

(1). $D_i \in S$ or

(2). there exist $r_1, r_2, \cdots, r_{k_i} < i$, such that $R_{m,\alpha,L}(C_1(x_1), C_2(x_2), \cdots, C_{r_{k_i}}(x_{r_{k_i}})) = D_i$, where the index of x_i is the lowest indices of all lock generalized literals in H_i.

Remark 3.2. If $D_t \leq \alpha$, then $\omega = \{D_1, D_2, \cdots, D_t\}$ is called an α -Group lock resolution deduction from S to $\alpha - \square$, or ω is an α -refutation of S.

Theorem 3.2. (Soundness) Suppose $\alpha \in L$, $S = \{C_1, C_2, \cdots, C_n\}$ be the set of lock generalized clauses in $LP(X)$, $\omega = \{D_1, D_2, \cdots, D_t\}$ is an α -Group lock resolution deduction from S to D_t. If $D_t \leq \alpha$, then $S \leq \alpha$.

Proof. By Theorem 3.1 and Definition 3.2, the conclusion holds obviously.

Theorem 3.3. (Completeness) Suppose $\alpha \in L$, $S = \{C_1, C_2, \cdots, C_n\}$ be the set of lock generalized clauses in $LP(X)$. If $S \leq \alpha$, then there exists an α-Group lock resolution deduction ω from S to $\alpha - \square$.

Proof. It can be proved by induction with the numbers of the difference between generalized literals and generalized clauses and Theorem 2.1.

Example 3.1. Let $S = \{_1(a_8 \to y) \vee_2 (x \to z)'{,}_3 (x \to y){,}_4 z' \vee_5 y'{,}_6 ((x \to y) \to z)\}$ be the set of lock generalized clauses in lattice-valued propositional logic $L_9P(X)$, $a_8 \in L_9$, $\alpha = a_6 \in L_9$. By computation, $S \leq \alpha$, and there exists an α - Group lock resolution deduction from S to $\alpha - \square$ by Theorem 3.3. We have the following α - Group lock resolution deduction ω^*:

(1) $_1(a_8 \to y) \vee_2 (x \to z)'$;

(2) $_3(x \to y)$;

(3) $_4 z' \vee_5 y'$;

(4) $_6((x \to y) \to z)$;

(5) $_5 y' \vee \alpha$ resolved by (2), (3) and (4);

(6) $_2(x \to z)' \vee \alpha$ (1) and (5);

(7) $\alpha - \square$ (2), (5) and (6).

Remark 3.2. There are only 3 α-Group lock resolvents, but 10 α-Group resolvents will be obtained to get $\alpha - \square$. On the other hand, there is no α-lock resolvent at first step, but there is surely an α-refutation of S, that is, α-Group lock resolution has more resolution ability than α-lock resolution.

4. Conclusions

α-lock resolution introduced in Reference [1], was limited to binary α-resolution, thus it would have less resolution ability than α-Group resolution which may permit more than two generalized clauses participating in every steps of the α-resolution deduction. In reference [19], α-Group resolution method was proposed to improve the resolution ability, but there may have many unnecessary resolvents during the process of α-Group resolution deduction. Aiming to enhance the resolution efficiency and resolution ability, we proposed α-Group lock resolution by adding some limits to the generalized literals without loss of the completeness. The proposed work will become the theoretical foundation to establish the resolution-based automated reasoning algorithms and tools with the goal to apply these in some practical fields such as expert system design, machine learning system design under uncertain environment and intelligent robot design, and so on.

References

[1] XingXing He, Yang Xu, Jun Liu, Da Ruan, α-lock resolution method for lattice-valued first-order logic, *Engineering applications of artificial intelligence*, 24(2011) 1274-1280.

[2] XingXing He, Yang Xu, Jun Liu, Shuwei Chen, On compatibilities of α-lock resolution method in linguistic truth-valued lattice-valued logic, *Soft Computing*, 16(4)(2012) 699-709.

[3] XingXing He, Jun Liu, Yang Xu, Luis Mart'ınez, Da Ruan, On α-satisfiability and its α-lock resolution in a finite lattice-valued propositional logic, *Logic Journal of IGPL*, 20(3)(2012) 579-588.

[4] X.H. Liu, Automated reasoning based on resolution methods, *Science Press, Beijing (in Chinese)*, 1994.

[5] Yonglin Liu, San-yang Liu, Yang Xu, et al, *ILI*-ideals and prime *LI*-ideals in lattice implication algebras, *Information Science*, (115)(2003) 157-175.

[6] Jun Liu, Da Ruan, Yang Xu, Zhengming Song, A resolution-like strategy based on a lattice-valued logic, *IEEE transactions on fuzzy systems*, 11(4)(2003) 560-567.

[7] Jiajun Lai, Yang Xu, Linguistic truth-valued lattice-valued propositional logic system *LP(X)* based on linguistic truth-valued lattice implication algebra, *Information Sciences*, (180)(2010) 1990-2002.

[8] M.L. Ginsberg, Multi-valued logics, *Readings in Nonmonotonic Reasoning, In Ginsberg, M.(ed.), Morgan-Kaufmann Pub.*, (1987) 251-255.

[9] Jun Ma,Wenjiang Li, Da Ruan, Yang Xu, Filter-based resolution principle for lattice propositional logic LP(X), *Information Science*, 177(4)(2007) 1046-1062.

[10] Xiaodong Pan, Yang Xu, Lattice implication ordered semigroups, *Information Science*, 178(2)(2008) 403-413.

[11] Yang Xu, Keyun Qin, Lattice-valued propositional logic (I), *Journal of Southwest Jiaotong University*, 1(2)(1993) 123-128.

[12] Yang Xu, Keyun Qin, Jun Liu, Zhenming Song, L-valued propositional logic $Lvpl$, *Information Science*, 114(1)(1999) 205-235.

[13] Yang Xu, Da Ruan, E.E. Kerre, Jun Liu, α-Resolution principle based on lattice-valued propositional logic LP(X), *Information Science*, 130(1-4)(2000) 195-223.

[14] Yang Xu, Jun Liu, Zhenming Song, Keyun Qin, On semantics of *L*-Valued first-order logic $Lvfl$, *International Journal of General System*, 29(1)(2000) 53-79.

[15] Yang Xu, Da Ruan, E.E. Kerre, Jun Liu, α-Resolution principle based on first-order lattice-valued logic LF(X), *Information Science*, 132(1-4)(2001) 221-239.

[16] Yang Xu, Da Ruan, Ke-yun Qin, et al., Lattice-valued logic: An Alternative Approach to treat Fuzziness and Incomparability, *Germany: Springer, Berlin*, 2003.

[17] Yang Xu, Jun Liu, Da Ruan, Tsu-Tian Lee, On the consistency of rule bases based on lattice-valued first-order logic LF(X), *International Journal of Intelligent Systems*, (21)(2006) 399-424.

[18] Yang Xu, Jun Liu, Da Ruan, Xiaobing Li, Determination of α-resolution in lattice-valued first-order logic LF(X), *Information Sciences*, (181)(2011) 1836-1862.

[19] Yang Xu, Jun Liu, Xiaomei Zhong, Shuwei Chen, Multiary α-Resolution Principle for a Lattice-Valued Logic, *IEEE Transactions on Fuzzy Systems*, 21(5)(2013) 898-912.

[20] Weitao Xu, Yang Xu, Resolution Determination of Generalized Literals in Linguistic Truth valued Lattice-valued Propositional Logic System, *Computer Science*, 40(2)(2013) 237-240.

[21] Xiaomei Zhong, Yang Xu, Jun Liu, Da Ruan, Shuwei Chen, General form of α-resolution based on linguistic truth-valued lattice-valued logic, *Soft Computing*, 6(2012) 1767-1781.

[22] Hua Zhu, Shuwei Chen, Jianbin Zhao, Multi-fold fuzzy positive implicative filter of residuated lattice implication algebras, *Journal of Zhengzhou University (Science Edition)*, 41(2)(2009) 19-23.

[23] Hua Zhu, Shuwei Chen, Jianbin Zhao, The Extended filter in lattice implication algebras, *Fuzzy Systems and Mathematics*, 25 (5)(2011) 50-53.

[24] Hua Zhu, Shuwei Chen, Jianbin Zhao, Yang Xu, Multi-fold Fuzzy Associative Filter of Residuated Lattice Implication Algebras, *The Journal of Fuzzy Mathematics*, 20(1)(2012) 211-216.

[25] Hua Zhu, Jianbin Zhao, Yang Xu, IFI-ideals of lattice implication algebras, *International Journal of Computational Intelligence Systems*, 6(6)(2013) 1002-1011.

FUZZY RELATIONAL EQUATIONS AND THE COVERING PROBLEM

Q.Q. XIONG*, Q.Y. SHU and X. P. WANG

*College of Mathematics and Software Science, Sichuan Normal University,
Chengdu, Sichuan 610066, People's Republic of China
* E-mail: xqq309@msn.com*

The work considers the problem of solving a system of fuzzy relational equations and introduces the concepts of characteristic matrix and attainable variables. It is proved that maximal solutions of the system correspond to irredundant coverings of characteristic matrix.

Keywords: Fuzzy relational equation; Maximal solutions; Covering problem; Irredundant covering

1. Introduction

Fuzzy relational equations play important roles in many applications, such as intelligence technology,[2] compression/decompression of images and videos[6,8] and fuzzy decision marking,[6] etc. The first paper of fuzzy relational equations was due to Sanchez,[9] where the max-min composition was adopted. Di Nola et al.[2] found that in fuzzy relational calculus and reasoning inf-α composition is better. Chen and Wang[1] provided a proof by transforming polynomially the minimum covering problem, which is a well known NP-hard problem, into the problem of solving a system of sup-min equations. In the covering problem, the goal is to find all irredundant coverings of a matrix. Markovskii[7] showed that solving fuzzy relational equations with max-product composition is closely related with the covering problem, which belongs to the category of NP-hard problems. Further, Markovskii proved that minimal solutions of system of equations with max-product composition correspond to irredundant coverings. Lin[4] extended Markovskii's work to fuzzy relational equations with max-Archimedean-t-norm composition. Further, Lin[5] investigated fuzzy relational equations with u-norm and transformed the problem of solving a system of fuzzy relational equations into covering problem. In 2012, Shieh[10] developed an efficient algorithms for finding minimal coverings. In fact, Lin[4,5] and Shieh[10] discussed the relations between the minimal solutions of the equations and the irredundant coverings. However, fuzzy relational equations with inf-implication composition have no minimal solutions, there are maximal solutions of the equations. In this paper, we discuss fuzzy relational equations with inf-implication composition on [0,1], in particular, the set of all maximal solutions, and transform the problem of solving fuzzy relational equations into a covering problem.

2. Preliminary

We are only interested in fuzzy relational equations which have the system-of-equation representation:

$$A \circ_{\mathcal{I}} X = B \text{ or } \inf_{j \in J} \mathcal{I}(a_{ij}, x_j) = b_i \text{ for all } i \in I, \tag{1}$$

where $a_{ij} \in [0,1]$, $b_i \in [0,1]$ for all $i \in I$, $j \in J$ and $\circ_{\mathcal{I}}$ denotes inf-implication composition. The equations are signed by system (1) whose solution set is defined by $\mathcal{X} = \{X = (x_j)_{j \in J} : A \circ_{\mathcal{I}} X = B\}$.

Definition 2.1. [11] (1) A binary operation $\mathcal{T}$ on L is called a pseudo-t-norm if it satisfies the following conditions:
(T_1) $\mathcal{T}(1,a) = a$ and $\mathcal{T}(0,a) = 0$ for all $a \in L$;
(T_2) $b \leqslant c \Rightarrow \mathcal{T}(a,b) \leqslant \mathcal{T}(a,c)$ for all $a,b,c \in L$.
  A pseudo-t-norm $\mathcal{T}$ on L is said to be infinitely $\vee$-distributive if it satisfies the following condition:
$(T_\vee)$ $a, b_j \in L$ $(j \in J) \Rightarrow \mathcal{T}(a, \bigvee_{j \in J} b_j) = \bigvee_{j \in J} \mathcal{T}(a, b_j)$.
(2) A binary operation $\mathcal{I}$ on L is called to be an implication if it satisfies the following conditions:
(I_1) $\mathcal{I}(0,0) = \mathcal{I}(1,1) = 1$ and $\mathcal{I}(1,0) = 0$;
(I_2) $b \leqslant c \Rightarrow \mathcal{I}(a,b) \leqslant \mathcal{I}(a,c)$ and $\mathcal{I}(b,a) \geqslant \mathcal{I}(c,a)$ for all $a,b,c \in L$.
  An implication $\mathcal{I}$ on L is said to satisfy the left neutrality property if $\mathcal{I}(1,b) = b$ for every $b \in [0,1]$.
  An implication $\mathcal{I}$ on L is said to be infinitely $\wedge$-distributive if it satisfies the following condition:
$(I_\wedge)$ $a, b_j \in L$ $(j \in J) \Rightarrow \mathcal{I}(a, \bigwedge_{j \in J} b_j) = \bigwedge_{j \in J} \mathcal{I}(a, b_j)$.

Definition 2.2. [11] Let φ be a mapping from $L \times L$ into L. Define $\mathcal{I}_\varphi$, $\mathcal{L}_\varphi$ as follows:
$$\mathcal{I}_\varphi(a,b) = \sup\{x \in L : \varphi(a,x) \leqslant b\} \text{ for all } a,b \in L,$$

$\mathcal{L}_\varphi(a, b) = \inf\{x \in L : \varphi(a, x) \geqslant b\}$ for all $a, b \in L$.
It is tacitly assumed that the least upper bound of the empty set is 0 and the largest lower bound of the empty set is 1.

From now on, we always assume that $\mathcal{T}$ is an infinitely $\vee$-distributive pseudo-t-norm and $\mathcal{I}$ is an infinitely $\wedge$-distributive implication with the neutrality property, and $\mathcal{T}(a, 0) = \mathcal{T}(0, a) = 0$, $\mathcal{I}(0, b) = \mathcal{I}(b, 1) = 1$, for all $a, b \in L$. Denote $X_* = (x_{j*})_{j \in J} \triangleq (\max_{i \in I} \mathcal{T}(a_{ij}, b_i))_{j \in J}$.

Lemma 2.1.[12] *System (1) is solvable if and only if X_* is a solution of system (1), and X_* is the smallest solution of system (1).*

3. Relation between maximal solutions and irredundant coverings

In this section, we first give the concepts of characteristic matrices and attainable variables. Further, some properties are described. The complete solution set $\mathscr{X} = \cup_{X^0 \in \mathscr{X}^0} [X_*, X^0]$, where $\mathscr{X}^0$ denotes the set of all maximal solutions of system (1). If $b_i = 1$ for all $i \in I$, then $\mathscr{X}^0 \triangleq \{(1, 1, \cdots, 1)'\}$. In the following, we may assume that there exists $i_0 \in I$ such that $b_{i_0} < 1$.

Example 3.1. Consider the following fuzzy relational equations with inf-$\mathcal{I}_{\mathcal{T}_L}$ composition $A \circ_{\mathcal{I}_{\mathcal{T}_L}} X = B$, where $A = \begin{pmatrix} 0.5\ 0.7\ 0.2\ 0.3\ 0.7\ 0.8 \\ 0.9\ 0.4\ 0.6\ 0.5\ 0.4\ 0.7 \\ 0.4\ 0.6\ 0.3\ 0.3\ 0.1\ 0.8 \\ 0.1\ 0.8\ 0.4\ 0.1\ 1.0\ 0.2 \\ 0.6\ 0.2\ 0.3\ 0.2\ 0.4\ 0.5 \end{pmatrix}$,

$B = (0.5\ 0.7\ 0.6\ 0.4\ 1)'$ and $\mathcal{I}_{\mathcal{T}_L}(x, y) = \min\{1, 1 - x + y\}$. It can be verified that the equation is solvable and the smallest solution is $X_* = (0.6, 0.2, 0.3, 0.2, 0.4, 0.5)'$.

Definition 3.1. For the smallest solution X_*, the characteristic matrix $\widetilde{Q} = (\widetilde{q}_{ij})_{m \times n}$ of the system (1) is defined as

$$\widetilde{q}_{ij} = \begin{cases} [x_{j*}, \mathcal{I}_{\mathcal{I}}(a_{ij}, b_i)], & \text{if } \mathcal{I}(a_{ij}, x_{j*}) = b_i, \\ \emptyset, & \text{otherwise.} \end{cases} \quad (3)$$

for all $i \in I$ and $j \in J$.

Lemma 3.1. *Let $X = (x_j)_{j \in J} \in \mathscr{X}$. If the component x_j satisfies $\mathcal{I}(a_{kj}, x_j) = b_k$ for some $k \in I$, then the corresponding component x_{j*} in smallest solution also satisfies $\mathcal{I}(a_{kj}, x_{j*}) = b_k$.*

Proof. By Definition 2.1, $\mathcal{I}(a_{kj}, x_{j*}) \leqslant \mathcal{I}(a_{kj}, x_j) = b_k$ since $X_* \leqslant X$. By $\inf_{j \in J} \mathcal{I}(a_{ij}, x_{j*}) = b_i$ for all $i \in I$, we have $\mathcal{I}(a_{ij}, x_{j*}) \geqslant b_i$ for all $i \in I$. Therefore, $\mathcal{I}(a_{kj}, x_{j*}) = b_k$. □

Definition 3.2. Let $X = (x_j)_{j \in J} \in L^n$. A variable x_j is called attainable if $\mathcal{I}(a_{ij}, x_j) = b_i$ holds for some $i \in I$; otherwise, x_j is called unattainable.

Definition 3.3. Let $a, b, c \in L$.
   (i) The implication $\mathcal{I}$ is said to satisfy the right cancelation law, if

$$\mathcal{I}(a, b) = \mathcal{I}(a, c) \text{ implies } a = 0 \text{ or } b = c. \tag{4}$$

   (ii) The implication $\mathcal{I}$ is said to satisfy the right conditional cancelation law, if

$$\mathcal{I}(a, b) = \mathcal{I}(a, c) < 1 \text{ implies } b = c. \tag{5}$$

Next, we have the following result.

Lemma 3.2. *Let $\mathcal{I}$ satisfy the right conditional cancelation law and its second partial mapping $\mathcal{I}(a, \cdot)$ be infinitely distributive. Then the equation $\mathcal{I}(a, x) = b$ with $b \in [0, 1)$ has a unique solution $\mathcal{I}_\mathcal{I}(a, b)$ and $\mathcal{I}_\mathcal{I}(a, b) \neq 1$.*

Lemma 3.3. *Let $\mathcal{I}$ satisfy the right conditional cancelation law, $0 \leqslant b_i < 1$ for all $i \in I$ and $X = (x_j)_{j \in J} \in \mathcal{X}$. If a component x_j is an attainable variable, then $x_j = x_{j*} < 1$.*

Proof. Since x_j is an attainable variable, therefore $\mathcal{I}(a_{ij}, x_j) = b_i$ holds for some $i \in I$. By Lemma 3.1, we have $\mathcal{I}(a_{ij}, x_j) = \mathcal{I}(a_{ij}, x_{j*}) = b_i$. Since $b_i < 1$ for all $i \in I$ and $\mathcal{I}$ satisfies the right conditional cancelation law, therefore $\mathcal{I}(a_{ij}, x_j) = b_i$ has a unique solution $x_j \in [0, 1)$ by Lemma 3.2. Thus $x_j = x_{j*} < 1$. □

By Lemma 3.3, we have the following results.

Lemma 3.4. *Let $X = (x_j)_{j \in J} \in \mathcal{X}^0$. If $x_j < 1$ for some $j \in J$, then $x_j = x_{j*}$.*

Lemma 3.5. *Let $0 \leqslant b_i < 1$ for all $i \in I$. Then a component x_j^0 is not an attainable variable if and only if $x_j^0 = 1$ for any $X^0 = (x_j^0)_{j \in J} \in \mathcal{X}^0$.*

Next, we transform the problem of finding all maximal solutions of system (1) into that of finding all irredundant coverings of the characteristic matrix of system (1). Denote $I(x_j) \triangleq \{i \in I : \mathcal{I}(a_{ij}, x_j) = b_i\}$.

Definition 3.4.[3] Let $\widetilde{Q}$ be a characteristic matrix of system (1).

i) A column j is said to cover a row i if $\widetilde{q}_{ij} \neq \emptyset$. A set of nonempty columns C forms a covering of $\widetilde{Q}$ if each row of $\widetilde{Q}$ is covered by some column in C.

ii) A column j in a covering C is called redundant if the set of columns $C\backslash\{j\}$ remains to be a covering of $\widetilde{Q}$. A covering C is irredundant if it has no redundant columns.

Let $C \in \Phi(\widetilde{Q})$. The mapping vector of C is denoted by $X^C = (x_j^c)_{j \in J}$ with

$$x_j^c = \begin{cases} 1, & \text{if } j \notin C, \\ x_{j*}, & \text{otherwise.} \end{cases} \tag{6}$$

Theorem 3.1. *If $\mathscr{X} \neq \emptyset$ and $b_i < 1$ for all $i \in I$, then there exists a one-to-one mapping between maximal solutions of system (1) and irredundant coverings.*

Proof. We prove it from the following three procedures.

First, we prove that if C is an irredundant covering, then $X^C \in \mathscr{X}^0$. Let C be an irredundant covering. Then $\cup_{j \in C} I(x_{j*}) = I$. Further, there exists $j \in J$ such that $\mathcal{I}(a_{ij}, x_{j*}) = b_i$ for each $i \in I$. By formula (6), we have that $\mathcal{I}(a_{ij}, x_j^c) = b_i$ for each $i \in I$. That is to say $X^C \in \mathscr{X}$. Next, we show that X^C is a maximal solution of system (1). Assume to the contrary that $X^C \notin \mathscr{X}^0$. There exists $k \in J$ such that $\mathcal{I}(a_{ik_i}, x_{k_i}) > b_i$ for every $i \in I$. By Lemma 3.4, we can define $X(k) = (x_j)_{j \in J}$ with

$$x_j = \begin{cases} 1, & \text{if } j = k, \\ x_j^c, & \text{otherwise.} \end{cases}$$

Therefore, we have $C\backslash\{k\}$ is a covering, which contradicts with that C is an irredundant covering. Hence $X^C \in \mathscr{X}^0$.

Second, we prove that if $X = (x_j)_{j \in J} \in \mathscr{X}^0$, then $J_c \triangleq \{j \in J : x_j < 1\}$ is an irredundant covering. By $X = (x_j)_{j \in J} \in \mathscr{X}^0$, then $\inf_{j \in J} \mathcal{I}(a_{ij}, x_j) = b_i$ for all $i \in I$. Hence, for each $i \in I$, there exists $j \in J_c$ such that $\mathcal{I}(a_{ij}, x_j) = b_i$. By Lemma 3.4, we have $\mathcal{I}(a_{ij}, x_{j*}) = b_i$. Therefore, $\cup_{j \in J_c} I(x_{j*}) = I$. By Definition 3.4, we have J_c is a covering. If $\cup_{j \in J_c\backslash\{j_0\}} I(x_{j*}) = I$ for some $j_0 \in J$, then for each $i \in I$, there exists $j \in J_c\backslash\{j_0\}$ such that $\mathcal{I}(a_{ij}, x_j) = \mathcal{I}(a_{ij}, x_{j*}) = b_i$. Define $X'(j_0) = (x_j')_{j \in J}$ with

$$x_j' = \begin{cases} 1, & \text{if } j = j_0, \\ x_j, & \text{otherwise.} \end{cases}$$

Obviously, $X'(j_0) \in \mathscr{X}$ and $X'(j_0) \geqslant X$ and $X'(j_0) \neq X$, which contradicts with that $X \in \mathscr{X}^0$. Therefore, J_c is an irredundant covering.

At last, we can construct a one-to-one mapping $f\colon C \to X^C$ with $x_j^c = x_{j*}$ for $j \in C$ and $x_{j*} = 1$ for $j \notin C$. Hence, there is a one-to-one mapping between maximal solutions of system (1) and irredundant coverings. $\square$

Acknowledgments

This was supported by National Natural Science Foundation of China (Nos. 11201325 and 11171242) and Sichuan Education Department Scientific Research Fund (No.13ZB0165).

References

1. L. Chen, P. P. Wang, Fuzzy relation equations (I): the general and specialized solving algorithms, Soft Computing 6 (2002) 428-435.
2. A. Di Nola, S. Sessa, W. Pedrycz, E. Sanchez, Fuzzy relation equations and their applications to knowledge engineering, Kluwer Academic Publishers, Dordrecht, 1989.
3. P. K. Li, S. C. Fang, On the resolution and optimization of a system of fuzzy relational equations with sup-T composition, Fuzzy Optimization and Decision Making, 7 (2008) 169-214.
4. J. L. Lin, On the relation between fuzzy max-Archimedean t-norm relational equations and the covering problem, Fuzzy Sets and Systems 160 (2009) 2328-2344.
5. J. L. Lin, Y. K. Wu, S. M. Guu, On fuzzy relational equations and the covering problem, Information Sciences 181 (2011) 2951-2963.
6. V. Loia, S. Sessa, Fuzzy relation equations for coding/decoding processes of images and videos. Information Sciences 171 (2005) 145-172.
7. A. V. Markovskii, On the relation between equations with max-product composition and the covering problem, Fuzzy Sets and Systems 153 (2005) 261-273.
8. H. Nobuhara, W. Pedrycz, S. Sessa, Hirota K., A motion compression/reconstruction method based on max t-norm composite fuzzy relational equations, Information Sciences 176 (2006) 2526-2552.
9. E. Sanchez, Resolution of composite fuzzy relation equations, Information and Control 30 (1976) 38-48.
10. B. S. Shieh, Solution to the covering problem, Information Sciences 222 (2013) 626-633.
11. Z. D. Wang, Y. D. Yu, Pseudo-t-norms and implication operations on a complete Brouwerian lattice. Fuzzy Sets and Systems 132 (2002) 113-124.
12. Q. Q. Xiong, X. P. Wang, Solution sets of inf-$\alpha_{\mathcal{T}}$ fuzzy relational equations on complete Brouwerian lattices, Information Sciences 177 (2007) 4757-4767.

THE INFLUENCE ON CLUSTERING RESULTS OF ELECTRICITY LOAD CURVES USING DIFFERENT CLUSTERING ALGORITHMS WITH DIFFERENT DATA NORMALIZATION METHODS *

TIEFENG ZHANG, MINGDI GU, FEI LV, AND RONG GU

School of Electrical and Electronic Engineering, North China Electric Power University, Baoding, China

To find the influence on clustering result of load curves using different clustering algorithms with different data normalization methods, seven data normalization methods are used with k-means, fuzzy c-means, SOM clustering algorithm for clustering load curves and their influences on the clustering results are analyzed in this paper, the matching relations between normalization methods and clustering algorithms are obtained. Numerical examples show data normalization methods have different influences on clustering results using the same clustering algorithm.

1. Introduction

Today, the main way of obtaining load pattern by analyzing load curves is using clustering techniques. The clustering process usually includes the following basic steps [1]: data selection, data cleaning, data preprocessing, load curve clustering, clustering analysis and feedback and customer classification and TLPs generation. A lot of literatures [2-5] about load curve clustering methods have been published in the past years, in contrast, there are few involving the influences of data preprocessing. The literature [6] studied five normalization methods with FCM in obtaining load pattern; the results indicted normalization method can influence the accuracy and efficiency of mining algorithms. So, the influence of data normalization method in obtaining load pattern should be investigated further.

In this paper, seven normalization methods are applied with three clustering methods. By experiment with 147 electricity customer's load curves, the influence of normalization method for each clustering method is analyzed.

This paper is organized as follows. Section 2 introduces data normalization methods and the clustering techniques used. Section 3 presents numerical

---

* This work is supported by the Fundamental Research Funds for Central University (No.11MG39).

examples and the clustering results and analysis. Finally, conclusions and future work are given in Section 4.

2. Data normalization methods and clustering techniques

Data preprocessing is an important step in the process of obtaining load pattern of electricity customers by clustering their typical load curves into several groups, where clustering load curves is based on the shape of a load curve but not by absolute MW values, so the data should be normalized, that is, scaled to a specific range such as [0.0, 1.0]. Normalization may improve the accuracy and efficiency of mining algorithms involving distance measurements [7]. There are many methods for data normalization, such as min-max normalization, z-score normalization, normalization by decimal scaling. In this paper, seven data normalization methods are used as follows.

1. Min-max Normalization

Suppose $x = (x_1, x_2, ..., x_m)$, min-max normalization maps a value x_k to $f(x_k)$ in the range [0, 1] by computing $f(x_k) = (x_k - x_{\min})/(x_{\max} - x_{\min})$ (1)

Where $x_{\max} = \max(x) = \max(x_1, x_2, ..., x_m)$, $x_{\min} = \min(x) = \min(x_1, x_2, ..., x_m)$

2. Mean-variance Normalization

Suppose $x = (x_1, x_2, ..., x_m)$, mean-variance normalization maps a value x_k to $f(x_k)$ in the range [-1, 1] by computing $f(x_k) = (x_k - x_{mean})/x_{var}$ (2)

Where $x_{mean} = mean(x) = mean(x_1, x_2, ..., x_m)$, $x_{var} = \text{var}(x) = \text{var}(x_1, x_2, ..., x_m)$

3. Sum Normalization

Suppose $x = (x_1, x_2, ..., x_m)$, sum normalization maps a value x_{ij} to x'_{ij} by

computing $x'_{ij} = x_{ij} / \sum_{i=1}^{m} x_{ij}$ (i = 1, 2, ..., m; j = 1, 2, ..., n) (3)

Where x'_{ij} satisfies $\sum_{i=1}^{m} x'_{ij} = 1$ ($j = 1, 2, ..., n$)

4. Z-score Normalization

In z-score normalization (or zero-mean normalization), the values for an attribute, A, are normalized based on the mean and standard deviation of A. A value x_{ij}, of A is normalized to x'_{ij} by computing

$$x'_{ij} = (x_{ij} - \bar{x}_j)/s_j \ (i = 1, 2, ..., m; j = 1, 2, ..., n)$$ (4)

The new value obtained by z-score normalization satisfies

$$\bar{x}_j' = \frac{1}{m}\sum_{i=1}^{m} x_{ij}' = 0 \quad , \quad s_j' = \sqrt{\frac{1}{m-1}\sum_{i=1}^{m}(x_{ij}' - \bar{x}_{ij}')^2} = 1$$

5. Maximum Normalization

Suppose $x = (x_1, x_2, ..., x_m)$, maximum normalization maps a value x_{ij} to x_{ij}'

by computing $\quad x_{ij}' = x_{ij} \Big/ \max_{i}\{x_{ij}\} \quad (i = 1, 2, ..., m; j = 1, 2, ..., n)$ (5)

For the new value, the maximum value is 1, other is less than 1.

6. Normalization by Decimal Scaling

Normalization by decimal scaling normalizes by moving the decimal point of values of attribute A. The number of decimal points moved depends on the maximum absolute value of A. A value x_{ij}, of A is normalized to x_{ij}' by

computing $\quad x_{ij}' = x_{ij} \Big/ 10^m \quad (i = 1, 2, ..., m; j = 1, 2, ..., n)$ (6)

Where m is the smallest integer such that $\max(|x_{ij}'|) < 1$.

7. Improved z-score Normalization

For a matrix formed by x_{ij}, its transposed matrix is processed by z-score normalization, after that, the processed matrix is transposed again to obtain the new matrix formed by x_{ij}', finally, a value x_{ij} of A is normalized to x_{ij}'.

Using Matlab tool, suppose x is the matrix formed by x_{ij}, y can be got from x_{ij}', the program will be y= z-score (x')' (where "'" means transposition).

For clustering techniques, the k-means [8], fuzzy c-means [9], and the SOM [10] algorithms are used to clustering load curves after data normalization and illustrated in detail in [1].

3. Experiments and analysis

3.1. *Data*

147 typical load curves from 147 customers are got after the data cleaning step.

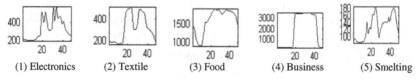

(1) Electronics   (2) Textile   (3) Food   (4) Business   (5) Smelting

Figure 1. The typical load curves of 5 classifications

These customers typically belong to 5 classifications in terms of industrial classification of national economic activities, their typical load curves of 5 classifications are shown in Figure 1(Vertical axis: load, unit: kW; horizontal axis: time, unit: 30-minute)

This set of data X including 147 load curves with 48 values has been formed in the original vector space. In order to assess the performance of each algorithm with different data normalizations, two indices are used. One is accuracy represented by the number of clustering error, the other is efficiency with the CPU time of algorithms.

3.2. Experiments of three clustering algorithms with seven data normalization methods

1. Experiment of k-means algorithms

After the data was preprocessed with seven data normalization methods separately, the load curves were clustered into 5 classifications by k-means algorithms, by comparison with the real classifications which the electricity customers belong to, the clustering results are shown in Table 1. In Table 1, Accuracy is computed by (the total number of load curves - the number of clustering error)/the total number of load curves.

From Table 1, we can see mean-variance normalization is the best methods when k-means algorithm is used to cluster the load curves.

2. Experiment of FCM

In the k-means experiment, we replaced k-means with FCM, the clustering results are shown in Table 2.

From Table 2, we can see sum normalization, maximum normalization and improved z-score normalization are the suitable methods in accuracy when FCM algorithm is used to cluster the load curves.

Table 1. The clustering results of K-means algorithms with seven data normalization methods

Normalization method	The number of clustering error	Accuracy (%)	The CPU time(s)
Min-max	40	72.8	0.174
z-score	37	74.9	0.719
Mean-variance	10	93.2	0.166
Decimal scaling	40	72.8	0.288
Sum	34	76.9	1.023
Maximum	33	77.6	0.514
Improved z-score	24	84	0.885

Table 2. The Clustering Results of FCM Algorithms with Seven Data Normalization Methods

Normalization method	The number of clustering error	Accuracy (%)	The CPU time(s)
Min-max	53	63.9	0.153
z-score	46	68.7	0.031
Mean-variance	37	74.8	0.005
Decimal scaling	48	67.3	0.238
Sum	5	96.6	0.018
Maximum	3	97.9	0.036
Improved z-score	6	96	0.542

3. Experiment of SOM algorithm

We replaced k-means with SOM, the clustering results are shown in Table 3.

From Table 3, we can see z-score normalization, maximum normalization and improved z-score normalization are the suitable methods when SOM algorithm is used to cluster the load curves.

4. Summary

In summary, we can pull above information together, the recommendation of the dada normalization methods for clustering algorithms is shown in Table 4.

Table 3. The clustering results of SOM algorithms with seven data normalization methods

Normalization method	The number of clustering error	Accuracy (%)	The CPU time(s)
Min-max	31	79.9	17.113
z-score	2	98.6	18.317
Mean-variance	60	59.2	16.316
Decimal scaling	33	77.6	16.968
Sum	48	67.4	17.452
Maximum	4	97.3	16.325
Improved z-score	2	98.6	19.895

Table 4.The recommendation of the data normalization methods for clustering algorithms

Normalization method	K-means	FCM	SOM
Min-max			
z-score			X
Mean-variance	X		
Decimal scaling			
Sum		X	
Maximum		X	X
Improved z-score		X	X

Note: The "x" means that this data normalization method is suitable for the clustering algorithm.

From Table 4, we can see that as follows:

- No one data normalization method is suitable for all clustering algorithm.
- Each clustering algorithm has one or more suitable data normalization methods;
- Min-max normalization and normalization by decimal scaling are not suitable for any clustering algorithm in this study.

4. Conclusions

To find the matching relations between data normalization and clustering algorithms, the influence of data normalization on the clustering results in using clustering algorithms to cluster load curves is studied in this paper, the result shows that data normalization is very important and will affect the clustering result in subsequent use of clustering algorithms for data processing results. That means it is very necessary to choose a suitable data normalization method before applying a clustering algorithm, it can improve the accuracy and efficiency of clustering algorithm.

The research conclusions of this paper are based on the data used and more experiments are expected to prove them and they are limited to the application of clustering algorithm to cluster load curves. For other field data with different features, the matching relations between data normalization methods and clustering algorithms may be different, similar experiments need to be done in order to avoid the data-dependent conclusion. In a sense, the authors initiate a discussion around the topic rather than intend to give conclusions.

Acknowledgment

This research was financially supported by the Fundamental Research Funds for Central University (No.11MG39).

References

1. T.F. Zhang, G.Q. Zhang, J. Lu, X.P. Feng, W.C. Yang. *A New Index and Classification Approach for Load Pattern Analysis of Large Electricity Customers, IEEE Transactions on Power System*, vol.27, Feb. 2012; 1, pp.153-160.
2. N. M. Kohan, M. P. Moghaddam, S. M. Bidaki, G. R. Yousefi. *Comparison of modified k-means and hierarchical algorithms in customers load curves clustering for designing suitable tariffs in electricity market, in Proc. 43rd International Universities Power Engineering Conference*, Padova, Italy. Sep. 2008, pp.1-5.
3. Z. Zakaria, K. L. Lo and M. H. Sohod. *Application of fuzzy clustering to determine electricity consumers' load profiles. in Proc, IEEE International Power and Energy Conference, Putra Jaya, Malaysia,* Nov. 2006, pp.99-103.
4. W.Y. Li, J.Q. Zhou, X.F. Xiong, J.P. Lu. *A statistic-fuzzy technique for clustering load curves, IEEE Transactions on Power Systems*, vol.22, May 2007; 2, pp.890-891.
5. S. V. Verdu, M. O. Garcia, C. Senabre, A. G. Marin, F. J. G. Franco. *Classification, filtering, and identification of electrical customer load patterns through the use of self-organizing maps, IEEE Transactions on Power Systems*, vol.21, Nov. 2006; 4, pp.1672-1682.
6. L.Q. Liu, Q.L. Ding, T.F. Zhang. *Data pretreatment method of fuzzy c-means clustering effects, Electric Power Science and Engineering*, vol.27, Aug. 2011; 8, pp.24-27.
7. J. Han, M. Kamber, *Data mining: concepts and techniques, 2nd edition, San. Francisco: Morgan Kaufmann Publishers,* 2006.
8. J.A. Hartigan, M.A. Wong. *Algorithm AS 136: a k-means clustering algorithm, Journal of the Royal Statistical Society Series C (Applied Statistics).* vol.28, Jan. 1979, 1, pp.100-108.
9. J.C. Bezdec, *Pattern recognition with fuzzy objective function algorithms, New York: Plenum Press,* 1981.
10. T. Kohonen, *Self-organized formation of topologically correct feature maps, Biological Cybernetics*, vol.43, Jan.1982; 1, pp.59-69.

A GLOBAL DISCRETIZATION METHOD BASED ON CLUSTERING AND ROUGH SET

HAIRUI LUO, JIANZHUO YAN, LIYING FANG, HUI WANG, XINQING SHI

College of Electronic Information and Control Engineering,
Beijing University of Technology
Beijing, 100124, China

Discretization is an important algorithm and considered to be a process of information generalization and data reduction. To avoid information loss and total number of cut point decrease after discretization of continuous attributes, based on multi-attribute discretization algorithm with good global clustering effects for selecting candidate cut points is proposed. The improved algorithm is combined with the advantages of clustering method and algorithm based on the importance of cut points, The experimental results show that the proposed algorithm can significantly decrease the number of discretization cut points and increase the predictive accuracy of the classifier than both.

1. Introduction

Rough sets theory is a useful technique to deal with discrete data, but actually most attributes of decision table are continuous [1], the effect of discretization of continuous attributes directly affects the learning process and the final outcome of learning. So, discretization of continuous attributes is critical.

The results of discretization depend on different discretization methods. Currently, there are many methods on discrete data, such as equidistant or equal frequency method, information entropy method, the method based on attribute importance, based on the importance of the cut point method, a method based on clustering and so on [2,3]. Equidistant or equal frequency methods are easy to use, but may lead to redundant discrete cut points, loss of information. The cut points importance-based and information entropy method are used widely approach [4,5].

This paper presents a global discrete algorithm based clustering, considering the distribution of data between the attribute and the importance of the cut points in the discrete process, allowing data to obtain a good global clustering effect to generate a minimum and the optimal set of cut points [6]. So we use rough reduction ideas to eliminate redundant cut point while ensuring the quality of approximate classification decision table.

2. Rough Set Theory and Discrete Description

2.1. *Information system*

According to rough sets theory, an information system is represented as follows: $S = (U, A, V, f)$, $A = C \cup D, C \cap D = \varnothing$,in which C represents a condition attributes set and D represents decision attributes set; $V = \bigcup V_r$ represents the domain of attributes value, in which V_r is the domain of the attribute $r \in A$; $f : U \times A \to V$ is the total decision function, the decision table is the tabular form of S.

2.2. *Approximations of sets*

$X \subseteq U$ and $R \subseteq C$, R -lower and the R -upper approximation of X respectively, the R-lower approximation objects is defined as :

$$R\_(X) = \{x \in U, [x]_R \subseteq X\} \tag{1}$$

The R -upper approximation objects is defined as:

$$R^-(x) = \{x \in U, [x]_R \cap X \neq \phi\} \tag{2}$$

Where $[x]_R$ is equivalence class of R containing elements $x \in U$.

2.3. *Rough classification*

With every subset $X \in U$, $R \subset X$, the coefficient

$$\gamma_P(X) = \frac{\sum_{i=1}^{n} card(\underline{R}X_i)}{card(U)} \tag{3}$$

is called the quality of approximation of classification X by set of attributes. We introduce it to verity the discretization effects.

2.4. *The description of discrete problem*

A cut points on a range V_a can be written as (a, c), where $a \in R$, c is a real number. The cut points collection $\{(a, c_1^a), (a, c_2^a), ..., (a, c_{k_a}^a)\}$ on the range $V_a = [l_a, r_a]$ defines a classification P_a on the V_a ,

$$P_a = \{[c_0^a, c_1^a), [c_1^a, c_2^a), ..., [c_{k_a}^a, c_{k_a+1}^a]\} \tag{4}$$

$$l_a = c_0^a < c_1^a < c_2^a < \ldots < c_{k_a}^a < c_{k_a+1}^a = r_a \tag{5}$$

$$V_a = [c_0^a, c_1^a) \cup [c_1^a, c_2^a) \cup \ldots \cup [c_{k_a}^a, c_{k_a+1}^a] \tag{6}$$

Therefore, any $P = \cup_{a \in R} P_a$ defines a new decision table $S^P = <U, R, V^P, f^P>$, the original information system is replaced by a new information system.

3. Discrete Algorithm Based on Clustering and Cut Points Importance Analysis

3.1. *The importance analysis of cut points*

The continuous set of attributes $C^* \subset C$ needed for discrete, which cut point denoted as Eq. (7):

$$Q = \bigcup_{ci \in c^*} \{c_i\} \times P_i = \bigcup_{ci \in c^*} \left\{ \left(c_i, c_i^0\right), \left(c_i, c_i^1\right), \left(c_i, c_i^2\right), \cdots \left(c_i, c_i^{ki}\right) \right\} \tag{7}$$

The number of instances can be distinguished from given cut points c_m^a to be defined as $W^X\left(c_m^a\right)$: where c_m^a is the m-th cut points on attribute a, $1 \le m \le n_a$, n_a is the number of cut points of attribute a.

$$l^X\left(c_m^a\right) = \sum_{j=1}^{r} l_j^X\left(c_m^a\right) = \left| \left\{ x \in X : a(x) < c_m^a \right\} \right| \tag{8}$$

$$r^X\left(c_m^a\right) = \sum_{j=1}^{r} r_j^X\left(c_m^a\right) = \left| \left\{ x \in X : a(x) > c_m^a \right\} \right| \tag{9}$$

So you can get:

$$W^X\left(c_m^a\right) = l^X\left(c_m^a\right) \cdot r^X\left(c_m^a\right) - \sum_{i=1}^{r} l_i^X\left(c_m^a\right) \cdot r_i^X\left(c_m^a\right) \tag{10}$$

The larger the $W^X\left(c_m^a\right)$ value, the higher importance of the cut points c_m^a.

3.2. *The ideas and steps of the proposed algorithm*

There are a lot of redundant cut point set after the cluster, so the need for the cut point selection process. Therefore, combining the merits of k-means clustering with the nature of rough sets theory, a global discretization algorithm based on clustering and rough sets theory is proposed.

In this algorithm, firstly, using k-mean method discrete each continuous attributes in the original decision system, getting an initial result, and then select the cut point according to cut point importance calculation, to get the best cut point of each attribute; secondly, introduce approximation quality of classification of rough set theory, to calculate the resulting approximate classification quality changes in the decision table, repeat the above steps until the results satisfy the discrete algorithm termination condition; finally, get discrete cut points of decision table to achieve discrete.

The algorithm is represented blow:

Input :Decision tables $S = (U, A, V, f)$

Output: The cut points set Ci of decision tables and decision table S' after discrete.

Step 1: $P = \varnothing$, $L = \{U\}$;

Step 2: Calculate the $\gamma_P(X)$ of decision table in the non-discrete case ;

Step3:Discrete the each condition attributes with a C-mean clustering method, to obtain a candidate set of cut points;

Step 4: For each $c \in C$, calculate the $W_P(C)$ value of the candidate cut point C of each attribute successively, select the maximum cut point C_{max} added in P, $P = P \cup \{C_{max}\}$; $C = C - \{C_{max}\}$;

Step 5: calculating the changing value of approximate classification quality $\gamma_P(X)$ of decision table after inserting cut points;

Step 6: If the approximate classification quality of the decision table reached a similar classification quality of the original table, and the equivalence class of each instance of the L have the same decision value, then go to step 7, otherwise go back to step 3;

Step 7: For cut point set in P, which is deleted do not affect the quality of approximate classification of decision table , then the cut point is redundant, which excluded;

Step 8: Algorithm terminates and outputs P and S', $S = S'$.

The ultimate objective is to make samples of same categories have highest similarity, while samples from different categories have the lowest similarity. K-means clustering is a kind of partition methods. One prerequisite of k-means clustering is that the clustering number should be pre-designated. This may affect the effectiveness of attribute reduction subsequently. For these reasons, two auxiliary statistics and variables are introduced to supervise the clustering results.

All continuous attributes discretization get a new decision-making system. Removing the conflicts rules in the new decision-making system to ensure the recognition accuracy of the system.

4. The Experimental Results and Analysis

The experiment using C4.5 classification to validate proposed discrete method in a number of large data sets. In contrast, discrete algorithm based on clustering method (denoted by A1), Heuristic algorithm based on the importance of cut points (represented by A2), proposed discrete algorithm with a combination of both algorithm (represented by A3). The number of conditions attributes after discrete is expressed as A-attributes. Firstly, discrete processing, then, attribute reduction and attribute value reduction so as to obtained inference rules, finally, use the knowledge gained to test classification accuracy on the test data. The experiment has proved that the method is effective in decision-making data analysis and extracting concise rules. It can also reduce the complexity of calculation.

Details of the UCI datasets are as follows:

Table 1. The data Features of UCI datasets.

ID	Dataset	samples	conditions attributes	decision attributes
1	iris	150	4	3
2	glass	214	10	7
3	wine	178	13	3
4	Heart	303	14	2

Comparison results are shown in Table 2:

Table 2. The results of three discrete algorithms.

Dataset	Classification Accuracy (C4.5)			A-attributes			Time(s)			Cut point amount		
	A1	A2	A3	A1	A2	A3	A1	A2	A3	A1	A2	A3
iris	94.3	93.2	94.4	3	3	3	1	2	2	6	5	5
glass	60.1	59.3	62.5	8	7	7	2	5	21	13	10	11
wine	91.4	89.5	93.7	12	10	8	1	1	14	11	9	9
Heart	75.8	74.9	79.4	9	9	8	1	2	8	7	5	5

As can be seen from table 2:

1. Discrete effects may be inversely proportional to computing time for an algorithms, the longer the calculation time of algorithm of discrete, the better discrete effect.
2. Due to fully considering the classification accuracy and cut points importance, A3 has less the cut point amount on four data sets, but the computational cost is relatively larger. Also, the calculated time of A3 on the corresponding data set are higher than the other algorithms on the

respective data sets, is able to generate optimal classification accuracy while minimizing the number of discrete intervals.

3. We can see that, when the number of objects and the number of the conditions attribute data set unchanged, the more the classification decision value, the more cut points, the lower the classification accuracy, the longer the calculation time.

5. Conclusion and Future Work

Experimental results show that the algorithm can effectively select important candidate cut points, greatly reduced the number of candidate cut points, reducing the complexity of the algorithms and the improving the classification accuracy.

The key of the discrete algorithm lies in how to obtain the optimal division, in short, try to satisfy the discrete simplicity, consistency (approximate quality of classification) and accuracy. The accuracy and adaptability of the refined rules will be verified, and the operating efficiency of the algorithm and optimization of rules repository will be studied in the further so as to use this method to a wide range of areas.

References

1. Pawlak Z. Rough sets [J]. Int J of Computer and Information Science, 11(5): 341-356(1982).
2. L. Shen, H. Tay. A discretization method for rough sets theory. Intelligent Data Analysis, 5(5) : 431-438(2001)
3. E. Xu, G. Xue Dong, C. Yi, et al. Clustering Algorithm Based on Rough Set[J]. Computer Engineering, 33(4):14-16(2007).
4. Z. Qing Hui, M. Xiao Dong, L. Yi, et al. A global discretization algorithm based on hierarchical method[J]. Microcomputer Information, 25(5-3):213-215(2009).
5. L. Ye Zheng, J. Ning, J. Yuan Hun. Study on comparison of discretization algorithms of continuous attributes[J]. Application Research of Computers, 24(9): 28-33(2007).
6. X. Xin Jian, M. Stolle. An algorithm of discretization of continuous attributes in rough sets based on cluster[J]. Journal of Zhejiang University of Science and Technolog ,15(3):154-157(2009).
7. H. Min .A Global Discretization and Attribute Reduction Algorithm based on K-means Clustering and Rough Sets Theory. International Symposium on Knowledge Acquisition and Modeling, (2009).

DETECTION OF WEB SERVER SECURITY PROBLEMS USING SELF ORGANIZING MAPS

GRZEGORZ KOŁACZEK, TOMASZ KUZEMKO

Wroclaw University of Technology, Wybrzeze Wyspianskiego 27 str.
50-370 Wroclaw, Poland

The paper presents the novel approach to detection of some types of network attacks using web server logs. As the web server log files are just collections of strings describing users' requests to the server, the method of conversion informative part of the requests to numerical values has been proposed. The vector of values obtained as the result of web server log file processing is then used as the input to Self-Organizing Map (SOM) network. Finally, the SOM network has been trained to detect SQL injections and brute force password guessing attack. The method has been validated using the data obtained from a real data center.

1. Introduction

The security breaches are very frequent events in worldwide computer network environment which are related not only to big enterprises and the most popular web servers. Each day, there are hundreds of new attacks which are performed using newly discovered vulnerabilities and new types of malware and hacking tools. Because the hacking tools are widely available and also there are many tools which automate the computer system exploitation every Internet user should be prepared not only to protect himself/herself but also it is important to detect if the applied security countermeasures have not been broken [6].

Classical protective mechanisms as firewalls, antivirus systems etc. must be combined with intrusion detection and prevention systems (IDS/IPS). Because of rapid changes in protection systems as well as in attack methods, the companies developing IDS/IPS solutions started to combine typical signature based solutions with methods related to soft computing (e.g neural networks, Support Vector Machines, etc.).

The purpose of research presented in the article is a presentation of a new method of computer system security related events detection and evaluation in an implemented system using real world data sets. The main element of the proposed solution is based on artificial neuron network which processes the complex data sets characterizing web server user's behavior. The data sets are derived from the web server status logs and the neural network type is Self Organizing Map (SOM).

1.1. *Related Works*

There are several works which present the usability of SOM networks to solve the problem of security breaches in computer networks [1-5]. In most cases the SOM networks are used to process the numerical data sets. This means that there is no need to preprocess data before the SOM can be applied. For example, in [3], the network traffic analyzer has been presented. For each ISO/OSI network layer a separate SOM network has been trained. The final decision about security related event detection comes from the additional SOM network which is responsible for combining pieces of information coming from the all network layers. The similar, multilayer SOM approach has been presented in papers [2,3,7]. The authors proposed the application of the specialized SOM networks for processing the selected groups of features describing the system behavior. These networks constitute the first layer of the analysis. Then, the SOM from the second layer combines the data from the first stage of data processing and produces the final decision about system security. Next element which has been derived from the previous researches is the sliding window for SOM networks training. However, to the authors' best knowledge there are no publications considering the application of SOM networks to the web server log analysis.

The rest of the paper is organized as follows. The next section presents the background of the log analysis problem and defines the detection method of attacks on web server. In the section 3 the experimental evaluation of the proposed method has been presented. The last section contains conclusions and describes future works.

2. Server Log Analysis

The main directions in research related to web servers security incident detection are related to the network traffic and server log analysis [6,7]. As each HTTP request to the web server can be recorded in server's access log file it becomes a natural source of the information about the server healthiness. The correct user request as well as the invalid or related to attacks against server will be present at access log. Then, the logs can be analyzed and symptoms of the security incidents can be recognized. Due to log file size it cannot be analyzed thoroughly by system administrator. So, some additional tools supporting the system administrator should be provided. The final solution must be a compromise between computational complexity, detection precision and speed.

The proposed method is offline processing of the recorded user activity available in web server log files. This assumption gives greater possibility for data preprocessing optimization. It also is more flexible and easy to be applied in real web server environment.

The main steps of the web server incident detection method are as follows:

- log file preprocessing including:
  - o sorting the data by IP address and time stamp
  - o features selection
  - o transformation of selected features into numerical values
  - o encoding sequence number (in learning phase only)
  - o encoding the number of event/attack class (in learning class only)
  - o saving the data into CSV file
- training the SOM network (in learning phase only)
- attack detection in preprocessed log file

2.1. Data Preprocessing

The original web server log file must be preprocessed because it does not contain the numerical values required as the input to SOM network. Log file should be preprocessed to extract the most informative part of the record. The general idea of HTTP request/response interpretation has been presented in Figure 1. The string representing particular request is divided into a few separate pars which are interpreted by so called "extraction modules".

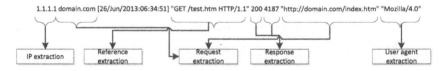

Figure 1 Log record interpretation

The most important operations performed during features extraction phase include: identification and numerical representation of the continent related to IP address, representation of HTTP method and version as a binary vector, calculation of the URL request depth, calculation of the no alphanumerical characters number in the request, hash value calculation from the file extension, change of user-agent name into corresponding ID value, etc. After this phase the vector of numerical values describing the recorded in log file request is passed to the next module.

2.2. Network Training

To be able to use the system for the detection of attacks, it is necessary to train SOM network on the training data containing information about the class of the event. This phase is crucial, because the system is able to identify only those attacks that learned to recognize.

The training data must possess information about the class of the event. For example, normal traffic can be assigned to the class of *normal*, while attacks classes with names which correspond names of attacks like: *sqlinjection*, *pathtraversal* and so on. Label with name of the class should be added to each record of access logs used to train the system. It should apply the following format [CLASS], where CLASS is the name of the class to which is assigned to the record. Label in this form should be appended the end of each row.

The detection system is multi-layered SOM network. Multilayer network consists of multiple layers of standard Kohonen network. Each of them is trained to determine the similarity of the analyzed record to the characteristics of a single attack category. At the input of the network is presented a single data sample. It was isolated three groups of features: *Request*, *Response*, and *Referer*. For each group there is a separate network layer Kohonen.

2.3. Attacks Detection

Trained Kohonen network system is ready to perform the classification of unknown earlier records of account access logs. For this purpose, it is necessary to convert logs into a metrics number. The neuron whose weight vector is most similar to the input is called the best matching unit (BMU). BMU of the sample is calculated by finding the node with the minimum distance to it. Distance sample to a node is calculated as the sum of the partial-weighted distances for each layers. Weight for each layer is defined as a parameter before network training. The classification is made on the basis of class BMU given sample. In the training phase to each node is assigned one class. This information is used in step of anomaly detection to determine previously unknown class of the sample. After finding the BMU for a given sample the information on the BMU class is determined. The class name is returned as the final decision on the classification.

3. Experimental Results

The full set of access log contains more than 600 thousand records from the server of one hosting company. For the experiment was selected subset comprising the first 10000 records. As a result of the classification procedure performed by the expert two different types of attacks have been identified: SQL injection and brute force password scan. Together with the normal requests the three classes of network traffic has been defined.

The implemented method using SOM networks allows setting the values of the following parameters in the detection algorithm: set of log features defining the SOM dimensions, the sliding window size, number of rows and columns of SOM network, gridtype, weights of features, training ration and number of iterations. In performed experiments the correlation of the algorithm parameter value and the detection precision (eq. 1) has been investigated.

$$precision = \frac{\sum diag(M_{conf})}{\sum(M_{conf})} \tag{1}$$

where M_{conf} is a confusion matrix.

The results for the default values of algorithm parameters has been presented in Table 1 and Figure 2.

Table 1 Confusion matrix for the default parameters algorithm

	Bruteforce	Normal	Sqlinjection
Bruteforce	41	47	0
Normal	27	4955	1
Sqlinjection	0	15	58
Precision	98,25%		

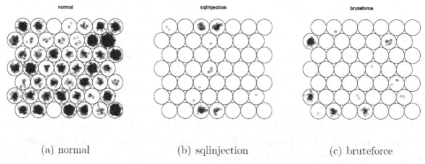

(a) normal   (b) sqlinjection   (c) bruteforce

Figure 2 Mapping for each class of attack to the default SOM parameter values

4. Conclusions

Application of soft computing methods to recognition of attack against web server extends the possibilities of the security incident detection. Also previously unknown attacks can be detected only if they are described by similar set of features. The proposed method uses SOM networks for event type classification where events are defined by the records in web server log files. The approach defines also the method of transformation of log files records into corresponding numerical vectors which can be processed by SOM network.

Finally, the several experiments on real data sets have been performed. The results of the experiments are promising for security incidents detection precision. The average detection precision for the proposed method is about 98%.

Further work will focus on improving the rate of attacks detection. Despite the achievement of high values of precision indicator, the number of correctly detected brute force attacks are relatively low. This is widely known problem in computer attack detection where the number of normal events is much greater than the number of events related to attacks. The next steps will be dedicated to the improvement of learning phase to provide the better brute force attack recognition.

References

1. P. Lichodzijewski,et.al. Host-based intrusion detection using self-organizing maps. Neural Networks, 2002. IJCNN '02. pp. 1714–1719. 2002.
2. Heywood M.I. Dynamic intrusion detection using self-organizing maps, 2002
3. C. Rhodes et.al., Multiple self-organizing maps for intrusion detection. W Proceedings of the 23rd National Information Systems Security Conference. 2000.
4. Stevanovic, D., Vlajic, N., & An, A. (2013). Detection of malicious and non-malicious website visitors using unsupervised neural network learning. Applied Soft Computing, 13(1), 698-708
5. Burdka Łukasz, Niżałowska Katarzyna, Adamski Michał, Kołaczek Grzegorz SOM-based system for anomaly detection in network traffic / Łukasz Burdka [i in.]. - W: Information systems architecture and technology : network architecture and applications [Dokument elektroniczny] / eds. Adam Grzech [i in.]. Wrocław : Oficyna Wydawnicza Politechniki Wrocławskiej, 2013. s. 97-106,
6. Kołaczek Grzegorz Multi-agent platform for security level evaluation of information and communication services / Grzegorz Kolaczek. - W: Advanced methods for computational collective intelligence / Ngoc Thanh Nguyen [i in.] (eds.). Berlin ; Heidelberg : Springer, cop. 2013. s. 107-116
7. Kolaczek, G., Juszczyszyn, K. (2012). Traffic pattern analysis for distributed anomaly detection. Parallel Processing and Applied Mathematics, 648-657.

A NEW CONCEPT OF FUZZY IMAGE SEGMENTATION

D. GÓMEZ[1] E. ZARRAZOLA[2] J.YÁÑEZ[3] J.T.RODRÍGUEZ[3] and J. MONTERO[3]

[1] Facultad de Estudios Estadísticos,
Universidad Complutense de Madrid, 28040-Madrid, Spain.
*E-mail: dagomez@estad.ucm.es, www.ucm.es

[2] Instituto de Matemáticas,
Universidad de Antioquia, Colombia.
*E-mail: edwzar@matematicas.udea.edu.co, www.udea.edu.co

[3] Facultad de Matemáticas,
Universidad Complutense de Madrid, 28040-Madrid, Spain.
*E-mail {jayage,jtrodrig,monty }@ucm.es, www.ucm.es

A crisp image segmentation can be characterized in terms of the set of edges that separates the adjacent regions of the segmentation. Based on these edges, an alternative way to define a fuzzy image segmentation is introduced in this paper. In this sense, the notion of fuzzy image segmentation is characterized by means of a fuzzy set over the set of edges, which could in this way be understood as the fuzzy boundary of the image. Also, an algorithm to construct this fuzzy boundary is provided based on the relations that exist between the fuzzy boundary set problem and the (crisp) hierarchical image segmentation problem. Finally, some computational experiences have been included in order to show the fuzzy boundaries of some digital images.

Keywords: Image Processing; Hierarchical Cluster; Fuzzy Sets.

1. Introduction

Given an image in which some objects of interest must be detected, an appropriate technique to carry out this detection is segmentation, which produces a partition of the pixels in regions;[9] these regions are delimited by their boundaries and these boundaries not always are *crisply* defined. Fuzzy approaches are very popular methods for crisp image segmentation due to the fact that they are able to model in a better way the noise of the image or the fuzzy nature of the objects. Nevertheless, few efforts has been dedicated to extend the concept of crisp image segmentation into a fuzzy framework, which cannot be confused with the concept of (crisp) image segmentation obtained through a fuzzy-based technique (see[1,2,7]), or with some other authors that try to measure some concepts as connectivity, area or perimeter in a fuzzy way for crisp partitions (see[1,6,8]).

Generally speaking, a fuzzy image segmentation should be a set of fuzzy regions $R_1, \ldots, R_k$ of the image. In order to differentiate this definition from a standard fuzzy classification, we should impose some covering, connectivity and redundancy properties on the fuzzy regions $R_1, \ldots, R_k$ in order to have a suitable fuzzy image segmentation output. How to define a fuzzy image segmentation, or equivalently what are the characteristics a fuzzy classification of the nodes should satisfy to constitute a suitable fuzzy image segmentation, is a question that is not addressed in this work, but that should be explored in the future.

In this paper, however, we present an alternative way to define the concept of fuzzy image segmentation (that is not clearly defined or does not have a fully-accepted definition) based on the fact that a crisp image segmentation can be characterized in terms of the set of edges that separate the adjacent regions of the segmentation. Taking into account that there exist a bijection between the classical definition of crisp image segmentation (i.e., a partition of the set of nodes into connected regions) and the set of edges that connects two nodes of different regions (i.e. the boundary edges set), in this paper we introduce an alternative way to define the concept of fuzzy image segmentation. As it happens in the crisp case, here we propose a definition of fuzzy image segmentation by means of a fuzzy set over the set of edges, which therefore could be understood as the fuzzy boundary of the image.

Once an alternative concept of fuzzy image segmentation is provided, in order to construct the fuzzy boundary set here we establish some relations that exist between fuzzy image segmentation problems and the hierarchical segmentation problems. The hierarchical algorithm used in this approach was proposed in[5] and extended in.[3]

2. The Segmented Image

A digital image I is considered as a graph whose nodes are the pixels. Formally, let $V = \{P_1, P_2, \ldots, P_n\}$ be the finite set of pixels of the image. Let $E = \{\{P_a, P_b\} \mid P_a, P_b \in V\}$ be the set of non-ordered pairs of neighbor pixels: if two pixels $P_a, P_b \in V$ are neighbor or adjacent ones, then there exists an edge $e_{ab} = \{P_a, P_b\} \in E$; otherwise, $\{P_a, P_b\} \notin E$. Although other topologies could be considered, in this work we assume that a pixel is linked with just four neighbors: up, down, left and right.

Hence, we define a graph $G = (V, E)$ that shows the neighboring relations between the pixels of the image.

Given $e_{ab} = \{P_a, P_b\} \in E$, i.e. given an edge joining two adjacent pixels P_a and P_b, let $d_{ab} \geq 0$ be the degree of dissimilarity between these pixels: the greater d_{ab} is, the more dissimilar P_a and P_b are. Let $D = \{d_{ab} \mid e_{ab} \in E\}$ be the set of all dissimilarities. This measure is defined taking into account the specific problem and the characteristics of the elements considered. Its construction and properties are beyond the objectives of this paper.

In this way, the available information on a digital image I can therefore be summarized by the network

$$N(I) = \{ \, G = (V, E); \, D \, \}. \tag{1}$$

Definition 2.1. Given an image I modeled as a network $N(I) = \{ \, G; \, D \, \}$, the set $S = \{R_1, \ldots, R_r\}$, where $R_i \subset V$ for all $i \in \{1, \ldots, r\}$ is a segmentation of the image I if and only if the following holds:

(1) Non Overlapping regions: $R_i \cap R_j = \emptyset$ for all $i \neq j$.
(2) Covering (all the pixels are covered by the regions): $\bigcup_{i=1}^{r} R_i = V$.
(3) Connectivity: for all i, the subgraph $(R_i, E_{|R_i})$ is a connected graph.

With the above definition, all pixels belonging to a region are graph-connected. Obviously, two different and not adjacent regions can share the same characteristics (in terms of the dissimilarity distance d); in this case, these regions will belong to the same class after a classification procedure is applied on the segmented image.

In a digital image I, modeled as a network $N(I) = (G, D)$, a segmented image can be also defined by the boundaries of its regions. These boundaries are characterized by the edges $F \subset E$ linking pixels belonging to different and adjacent regions. It is easy to prove the following property: *Given the segmentation $S = \{R_1, \ldots, R_r\}$ of the image I, each subset $R_i \subset V$ is a maximal connected component of the partial graph $G_F = (V, E - F)$.*

Associated to this concept of segmented image, a crisp membership function $\mu : E \longrightarrow \{0, 1\}$ is defined in such a way that $\mu(e) = 1(0)$ if and only if $e \in (\notin)F$.

In order to visualize the segmented image I through the network $N(I)$, the endpoints of the edges in F are colored as white and the other nodes are colored as black.

Remark 2.1. We can notice that the edge detection problem is different from the segmentation problem, since the solution of the former problem not necessarily divides the image into homogeneous regions. That is, it is possible to pass in a direct way from an image segmentation solution into an edge detection solution, but the opposite is not always true.

3. The Fuzzy Image Segmentation Problem

Image segmentation usually assumes that an image can be broken into homogeneous regions. However, it does not allow us to distinguish whether some of these regions are more different among them than from the other ones. At this respect, human segmentation is a useful technique, as it allows separating those strongly different adjacent regions with a more solid white line than those slightly different regions. Therefore, it seems reasonable to define in a formal way the concept of fuzzy segmentation, based on the equivalent concept of boundaries $F \subset E$ of the regions.

Definition 3.1. Given an image I and its network $N(I)$, the fuzzy set $\widetilde{F} = \{(e, \mu_F(e)), \ e \in E\}$ produces a fuzzy image segmentation if and only if for all $\alpha \in [0, 1]$ the crisp set $F(\alpha) = \{e \in E$ such that $\mu_F(e) \geq \alpha\}$ is the associated subset of boundary edges of a (crisp) image segmentation.

4. From Hierarchical Segmentation to Fuzzy Segmentation

In this section we present a general procedure to build a fuzzy image segmentation (i.e. the membership function μ_F of the set of links) from a hierarchical image segmentation. In order to illustrate this procedure, we need to define some concepts first.

Definition 4.1. Given an image I, its associated network $N(I)$, and two partitions $\mathcal{P}$ and $\mathcal{Q}$ of the set of pixels V, it is said that $\mathcal{P}$ is *finer* than $\mathcal{Q}$ (and we will denote it by $\mathcal{P} \widetilde{\subseteq} \mathcal{Q}$) if for all $A \in \mathcal{P}$, there exist $B \in \mathcal{Q}$ such that $A \subseteq B$.

Definition 4.2. Given an image I and its network $N(I)$, the set $\mathcal{D} = (\mathcal{S}^0, \mathcal{S}^1, \mathcal{S}^2, \ldots, \mathcal{S}^h)$ is a hierarchical image segmentation of I when the following holds:

- There are two trivial partitions: the first $(\mathcal{S}^0)$, with one cluster containing all the pixels, and the last one, which has all pixels as singleton clusters $(\mathcal{S}^h = \{\{v\}, v \in V\}.)$
- $|\mathcal{S}^t| > |\mathcal{S}^{t-1}|$ for all $t = 1, \ldots, h$ (i.e., in each iteration we increase the number of regions in the image segmentation).
- $\mathcal{S}^t \widetilde{\subseteq} \mathcal{S}^{t-1}$ for all $t = 1, \ldots, h$.

In the same way that a segmentation is characterized by a subset of edges $F \subset E$ and the connected components of the partial graph $G_F = (V, F)$, a hierarchical segmentation can be defined by the family $\mathcal{F} = \{F^0, \ldots, F^h\}$ of subsets $F^t \subset E$, which produces a hierarchical partition if and only if the following holds:

- For all $t \in \{0, 1, \ldots, h\}$ $F^t \subset E$ produces an image segmentation S^t.
- The sequence of image segmentations $\{S^0, \ldots, S^h\}$ produced by the sequence $\{F^0, \ldots, F^h\}$ is a hierarchical segmentation of $N(I)$.

As a logical consequence, that the following property can be proven to hold: $F^0 = \emptyset \subset F^1 \subset \ldots \subset F^h = E$. Given a hierarchical image segmentation, let $\mu^t : E \longrightarrow \{0, 1\}$ be the membership function of any boundary set $F^t \subset E$; then the fuzzy segmentation produced by the fuzzy set $\widetilde{F}$ can be defined (it is not the only way, though) as:

$$\mu_F(e) = \sum_{t=0}^{h} w_t \mu^t(e) \qquad \forall e \in E \qquad w_t \geq 0 \forall t \quad and \quad \sum_t w_t = 1$$

for a given sequence of weights $w = (w_1, \ldots, w_h)$.

5. Computational Experiences and Final Remarks

In order to illustrate the concepts introduced in this paper, four images from the Berkeley Data Base have been analyzed. A Hierarchical Segmentation Algorithm, developed by the authors ([4]), has been used with the following parameters: $h = 80$ and $w_t = 1/81$. In Figure 1, the original images and a possible visualization associated with each fuzzy segmented image are depicted. Let us note that it is possible to visualize a fuzzy segmented image through a graduation of color of the endpoints of the edges $e \in E$, proportional to the membership functions $\mu_F(e)$: the greater this value, the bigger the white intensity of the endpoints of the edge. In this sense, the fuzzy set $\widetilde{F}$ defines in a natural way a *fuzzy boundary*.

To visualize the fuzzy boundary, we have assigned to each pixel a degree of intensity obtained as the maximum of its edges' fuzzy boundary membership degrees. How to transform the output of a fuzzy image segmentation process into the output of a fuzzy edge detection process is not a trivial question, and should be explored in a future. In this sense, let us note that the previous computational experiences have been introduced only to illustrate the fuzzy boundary of the objects, and obviously cannot be compared (in a fair way) with other well-known edge detection algorithms, as

Fig. 1.   Some fuzzy segmented images

Robert's, Prewitt's or Sobel's, for different reasons (basically, the outputs are different: fuzzy versus crisp, despite the problems they address are quite different).

References

1. I. Bloch. Fuzzy connectivity and mathematical morphology. *Pattern Recognition*, 14:483488, 1993.
2. H. Bustince, V. Mohedano, E. Barrenechea, and M. Pagola. Definition and construction of fuzzy di-subsethood measures. *Information Sciences*, 176(21):3190–3231, 2006.
3. D. Gómez, J. Montero, and J. Yáñez. A coloring algorithm for image classification. *Information Sciences*, 176(3645-3657), 2006.
4. D. Gómez, J. Montero, and J. Yáñez. A divide-link algorithm based on fuzzy similarity for clustering networks. *International Conference on Intelligent Systems Design and Applications, ISDA*, pages 1247–1252, 2011.
5. D. Gómez, J. Montero, J. Yáñez, and C. Poidomani. A graph coloring algorithm approach for image segmentation. *Omega*, 35:173–183, 2007.
6. A. Rosenfeld. The fuzzy geometry of image subsets. *Patt*, 2:311–317, 1991.
7. N. Senthilkumaran and R. Rajesh. Edge detection techniques for image segmentation a survey of soft computing approaches. *International Journal of Recent Trends in Engineering*, 1(2):250–254, 2009.
8. J.K. Udupa and S. Samarasekera. Fuzzy connectedness and object definition: Theory, algorithms, and applications in image segmentation. *GRAPHICAL MODELS AND IMAGE PROCESSING*, 58:246–261, 1996.
9. Y. J. Zhang. *Image Segmentation.* Science Plublisher, Beijing. China, 2001.

HISTOGRAM EQUALIZATION BASED ON THE FUZZY LOCAL FITTINGNESS

MARCO A. GARCÍA

City, State ZIP/Zone, Country CITIS, Universidad Autónoma del Estado de Hidalgo,
Mineral de la Reforma, Hidalgo, 42090, México

CHERIF BEN-YOUSSEF

DEPI, Instituto Tecnológico de Cancún, Av. Kabah km. 3
Cancún, Quintana Roo, 77500, México

RAMÓN SOTO C.

ECA, Universidad de Sonora, Blvd. Transversal y Rosales
Hermosillo, Sonora, 83000, México

Histogram modification techniques are an important tool for image enhancement. However, the efficiency of most of these techniques is limited due to the lack of mechanisms to differentiate between pixels that have the same intensity but belong to regions which are semantically distinct. In this paper, a method for histogram equalization, able to selectively modify each pixel in a digital image based on the context established by its neighboring pixels is proposed. This method emulates the decision–making process used by living organisms to recognize patterns, as described by the Gestalt theory.

1. Introduction

The mechanisms by which human beings and other living organisms make decisions to recognize patterns has been of great interest in diverse fields of computer science, such as cybernetics, pattern recognition, machine learning and soft computing. The goal of researchers in these areas is to develop algorithms that emulate the natural skills of living beings to make decisions and apply them to automated pattern recognition tasks.

An interesting approach to describe human perception mechanisms and an attractive source for the development of soft computing metaphors may consist in the use of the Gestalt theory [1, 2]. According to the Gestalt psychology, people perceive the world by organizing individual objects into groups that convey richer information than that provided by the isolated objects. The way a person decides how to perform such an organization is based on basic principles such as proximity, similarity and continuity.

Different authors have shown interest in exploiting local information around each pixel in a digital image to reduce the effect of noise and other distortions produced by the processes of capture and digitization as well as to capture global behaviors. Reed and Wechsler [2] used local information and gestalt principles for texture segmentation and object grouping. Soto and Clemente [3] introduced a method for automatic thresholding and segmentation of digital images using a fuzzy measure of busyness. In this approach, each pixel was classified either as background or as a figure depending on how well it is integrated in its neighborhood. Kootstra *et al.* [4] presented an image segmentation method based on clustering of neighboring pixels, called superpixels. The authors grouped pixels with similar colors in the reduced color space of a low-resolution version of the image. Clusters were successively refined using higher resolutions versions. Subsequently, small clusters (less than 50 pixels) were binded to the neighboring superpixels having the closest color. Kunpeng *et al.* [5] presented an edge detection method that uses information from the neighborhood of a pixel to determine whether the pixel belongs to the contour of the object or is considered as noise. Such discrimination of pixels belonging to the contour is based on the distribution of the 8-neighbors of the feature pixel.

In this paper we present a method for histogram equalization, able to selectively modify each pixel in a digital image depending on the context established by its neighboring pixels. The presented technique has been tested on a wide variety of images. However, due to space constraints, only results obtained on two images are presented: a scanning electron micrograph of penicillium mold producing spore (Figure 3) and a Moon photograph (Figure 4).

2. Histogram Equalization

Histogram equalization is a method used to increase the contrast of a digital image by applying a gray level transform which re-assigns intensity values of the pixels in the input image to obtain an image with intensity values equally distributed. This technique is effective in details enhancement and in the correction of non-linear effects such as those introduced by a digitizer system [6].

Let $\mathbf{I}$ be a digital image of $n = \text{M} \times \text{N}$ pixels, L the length of the range of available intensity values in the image and n_i the number of occurrences of intensity level i. The relative frequency of pixels with intensity value i in the image, f_i, is given by:

$$f_i = \frac{n_i}{n} \tag{1}$$

The purpose of histogram equalization is to 'flatten' the histogram in a way that all the relative frequencies in the new histogram have the same value $\bar{f}$:

$$\bar{f} = \frac{n}{L}, \forall\, i \in [0, L-1] \tag{2}$$

In order to reduce or increase the relative frequency of pixels at each intensity level, so that the desired frequency value for all intensities is obtained, it is necessary to split some groups of pixels with the same intensity into two subgroups with different intensities, as outlined in Figure 1. Because the standard equalization technique carries on the same processing to all pixels with a given intensity level, the resulting histogram is usually not "flat" and corresponds to only an approximation to the desired histogram.

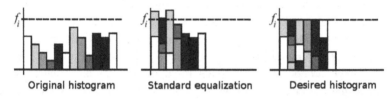

Original histogram   Standard equalization   Desired histogram

Figure 1. Standard equalization versus desired output for a fictitious histogram.

3. Fuzziness in an Image

Pixels in an image can be seen as belonging to several fuzzy subsets, defined by the image intensity levels [7]. The membership of each pixel with intensity value $i_{m,n}$ in the fuzzy set corresponding to the intensity value b, depends on the distance between $i_{m,n}$ and b, and the specific shape chosen for the fuzzy set.

The shape for the membership function is chosen as a pair of increasing/decreasing logistical curves. The membership of a given pixel (m, n) with an intensity value $i_{m,n}$ in the fuzzy set β corresponding to the intensity value b, is calculated by Eq. (3).

$$\mu_\beta(x) = \begin{cases} 0 & i_{m,n} \le a_d \\ 2[(a_d - i_{m,n})/(b - a_d)]^2 & a_d < i_{m,n} \le b_d \\ 1 - 2[(b - i_{m,n})/(b - a_d)]^2 & b_d < i_{m,n} \le b_u \\ 2[(a_u - i_{m,n})/(a_u - b)]^2 & b_u < i_{m,n} \le a_u \\ 0 & i_{m,n} > a_u \end{cases} \tag{3}$$

$\Omega = a_u - a_d$ is defined as the support of the fuzzy set and $\Delta = b_u - b_d$ as the set bandwidth.

4. Fuzzy Local Fittingness

Histogram equalization can be improved by using a criterion for discriminating between pixels having the same intensity value. We introduce the Fuzzy local fittingness (FLF) to describe how well each pixel in an image is integrated into its neighboring.

The FLF for pixel (m, n) with intensity $i_{m,n}$ is given by:

$$\phi(m, n) = \mu_{\beta_{m,n}}(m, n) \tag{4}$$

where $\beta_{m,n}$ is a fuzzy set defined by Eq. (1), with the reference value b given by:

$$b = \frac{1}{8}\big(i_{m-1,n-1} + i_{m,n-1} + i_{m+1,n-1} + i_{m-1,n} + i_{m+1,n} + i_{m-1,n+1} + i_{m,n+1} + i_{m+1,n+1}\big) \tag{5}$$

b is chosen as the mean intensity value over the 8- neighbors of the pixel (m, n). As it can be inferred from Eq. (4), $\phi(m, n) = 1$ for pixels surrounded by pixels with the same intensity value $i_{m,n}$ and $\phi(m, n) = 0$ for pixels with intensity 'very different' from the intensity of its neighbors ($|b - i_{m,n}| > \Delta$).

5. Local Histogram Equalization

The fuzzy local fittingness, $\phi(m, n)$ provides a measure of how much a given pixel (m, n) belongs to the (fuzzy) set of pixels having a value of intensity distinctive of the region where it is located. With this measure as a discriminant, it is now possible to selectively modify the pixels having the same intensity in order to have the right number of pixels in each set. Local histogram equalization is achieved by selective modification of the intensity of each pixel of the image, as sketched in the flow diagram in Figure 2.

6. Results

Figures 3 and 4 show the result of local histogram equalization on two test images. In both cases, the left column (a) shows the original image, the central column (b) shows the result of the histogram equalization with the conventional technique and the right column (c) shows the result obtained by applying the local histogram equalization technique to the test images. From Figure 3, it can be seen that while the standard histogram equalization technique emphasized the features of the watermark, it also causes a loss of definition in the features of the hyphae and spores of *Penicillium*. Local histogram equalization, on the other hand, allowed to emphasize the features of the fungus as those of the watermark. Similar results are obtained for the picture of the moon, as can be seen in Figure 4.

422

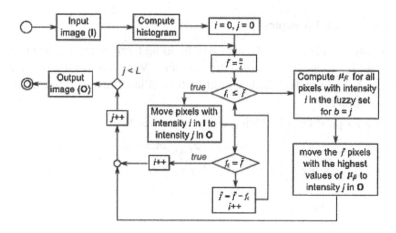

Figure 2. Local histogram equalization (LHE) algorithm.

Figure 3. Testing of LHE algorithm on a scanning electron micrograph of penicillium mould.

Figure 4. Testing of LHE algorithm on a Moon photograph.

7. Conclusions

In this paper, a method for histogram equalization based on local information has been presented. The concept of fuzzy local fittingness (FLF) is introduced as a way for discriminating between pixels having the same intensity value. Thanks to this ability to discriminate between apparently identical pixels, but which belong to different global features in the scene, is possible to make a good approximation to a specific distribution of intensity values. Although the method has been illustrated for the equalization of the histogram, its generalization to arbitrary histogram specification is straightforward. The results obtained from the tests carried out show that local histogram equalization allows to preserve valuable information in subsequent analysis steps.

References

1. Max Wertheimer. Laws of Organization in Perceptual Forms. In Source Book of Gestalt Psychology, Willis D. Ellis (Ed.). Harcourt, Brace and Co, (1938).
2. T.R. Reed, H. Wechsler. Segmentation of textured images and Gestalt organization using spatial/spatial-frequency representations. IEEE Transactions on Pattern Analysis and Machine Intelligence. Volume: 12, Issue: 1, (1990).
3. R. Soto C., and M.A. Clemente S. Thresholding and Segmentation of Images Using a Fuzzy Measure of Busyness. Joint International Conference of Information Sciences, (1997).
4. G. Kootstra, N. Bergström and D. Kragic. Fast and automatic detection and segmentation of unknown objects, in Proceedings of the IEEE-RAS International Conference on Humanoid Robots, Humanoids 2010, (2010.)
5. L. Kunpeng, W. Sunan, C. Naijian and D. Hongyu. Contour feature detection based on Gestalt rule and maximum entropy of neighborhood. IEEE Conference on Robotics Automation and Mechatronics, RAM, (2010).
6. T. Arici, S. Dikbas. A Histogram Modification Framework and Its Application for Image Contrast Enhancement. IEEE Transactions on Image Processing, Vol. 18, No. 9, (2009).
7. S.K. Pal, A. Rosenfeld. Image enhancement and thresholding by optimization of fuzzy compactness. Pattern Recogn. Lett. 7, 2, (1988).

DESIGN OF INTELLIGENT CONTROL FOR HVAC SYSTEM USING FUZZY LOGIC

ANDREAS MUÑOZ

Automatics and Systems Department, UNED
28040-Madrid, Spain

MATILDE SANTOS, VICTORIA LÓPEZ

Computer Sciences, Universidad Complutense de Madrid
28040-Madrid, Spain

HVAC (Heating, Ventilation and Air Conditioning) systems are important subsystems in buildings and it is necessary to control them in order to improve energetic efficiency. Conventional control systems have been used over the past years for controlling these systems with successful results. But classical control requires analytic models and HVAC are too complex processes to be mathematically represented. In this paper an approach based on fuzzy logic is proposed. The fuzzy control does not require the mathematical model and is able to incorporate the knowledge of an expert. Simulation results prove the feasibility of this solution.

1. Introduction

Heating, Ventilation and Air Conditioning (HVAC) systems are one of the most important subsystems in buildings [1]. Besides, those systems represent the major source of energy consumption in buildings, almost 50% [2]. Because of that, the development of effective control systems for HVAC is a crucial task.

Different control strategies have been applied to this system, being conventional PID control one of the most extended one [3]. But these control approaches require a mathematical model of the system that may become too complex to be calculated. Furthermore, these systems are usually non-linear and even time-variant, and classical control is not suitable.

On the other hand, intelligent control –control based on soft computing techniques- has been proved as an efficient way of developing non-linear controllers that are able to include expert knowledge and to control complex processes [4].

In this work, HVAC control problem is faced following [5]. In that paper, authors deals with the control problem of a HVAC 4x4 as a centralized experimental system for heating, cooling and air conditioning of four rooms at the same time. The main problem they found was the difficulty of obtaining the transfer function of the process, mainly due to the interaction between air flows of different rooms. They had to assume some strong simplifications to obtain the model and the computational cost was very high.

In our work a similar control system is designed but using intelligent techniques as an alternative to conventional ones. The aim is to prove that intelligent control makes easier the development of the control and the obtained results are similar.

Fuzzy logic has been chosen as it does not require previous data of the process. Besides, knowledge about the process is available. Therefore, this intelligent technique allows us a simple and direct approach to the problem.

2. Description of the Scenario

Figure 1 shows the scenario we are working with. It consists of four rooms.

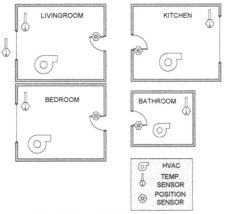

Figure 1. Scenario of the HVAC system

The values of the input variables are measured from the different sensors distributed along the scenario. Some preprocessing of the signals such as noise removing is included to improve the control. The main variable to be controlled is the temperature of each room. To find the best place to place the temperature sensors is not a trivial task. An analysis of the indoor temperature distribution was performed and the conclusion is that this distribution varies strongly depending on the HVAC system used [5]. In our case it is assumed that the sensor is located in the best position as shown in Figure 1.

Other variables to take into account are the air flow between rooms and the external temperature. The air flow is caused by the difference of temperature if the door is open or not. If the door is open, the air will flow to the other rooms, causing a loss of conditioning in that room. This fact, difficult to deal with conventional methods, is represented in the rules set of the fuzzy logic control. The measurement of this variable includes the position of the sensor.

There are some works on the impact of the window in the overall temperature of a room; the conclusions indicate a high influence on the final temperature of the room [6]. So the external temperature has been included except in internal rooms such as the bathroom (see Figure 1).

3. Design of the Fuzzy Logic Controller

The goal of the intelligent control is to keep the temperature at a desired value and to get this temperature in the smallest possible time.

Fuzzy logic approaches human thinking in a natural language. The design of a fuzzy control system relies on two modules: the definition of the membership functions for each input and output variable, and the rules that connect the antecedents with the consequents [7].

3.1. Membership Functions

The input variables of the HVAC system are: the four room temperatures, the position of the doors of each room and the external temperature.

For the temperature, five fuzzy sets are defined: "very cold", "cold", "average", "hot" and "very hot" (Figure 2, left). But we are not going to work with the raw data from the sensors. The input variables are the error, defined as the difference between the real temperature and the desired one. This allows us to make the universe of discourse independent of the average temperature that can be different for each room. The range considered is [-10, +10] ºC for the indoors temperatures and [-20, +20] ºC for the external one. For the latter, three fuzzy set: "cold", "average", "hot", were defined (Figure 2, right). Uniformly distributed triangular or trapezoidal membership functions were used as it is a common practice in control problem due to the simplicity of calculations.

Three different positions are considered for the door: "close", "half open" and "open". Gaussian curves were used to define the three fuzzy sets in the domain between 1 and 100 (percentage of opening) (Figure 3, left).

Finally, the output of the fuzzy controller is the control variable of the HVAC. There are different types of HVACs, in our case we are going to use an air conditioned system, so the output will be the increment or decrement of the output temperature of the HVAC. We labeled the three possible values as "cooler", "temperate" and "hotter", between [-5, +5] °C (Figure 3, right).

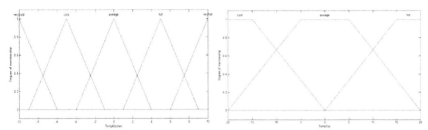

Figure 2. Membership functions for indoors temperature (left) and external temperature (right)

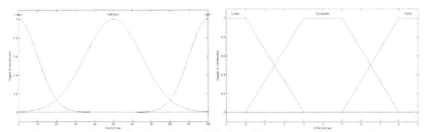

Figure 3. Membership functions for one of the doors (left) and HVAC of a room (right)

3.2. Set of Rules

The relationship between the input variables and the output is represented by if-then rules. As we assume that the air flow between rooms depends on the position of the door of each room, four independent controllers have been designed, one for each HVAC room. Table 1 shows the rules for one the HVAC as an example. The bathroom, without windows, is not affected by the external temperature and the rules are slightly different.

The fuzzy have been weighted according to the influence of that particular rule on the output. For example, if the actual temperature of the room is the main cause of variations in the output, the weight is set to 1. On the other side, the variations caused by the air flow due to open doors has a limited relevance, so the weight of the rules was set to 0.2 and 0.4, depending on the percentage of the door opening. The last three rules were generated to simulate the influence of the external temperature in the result.

4. Discussion of the Results

To test the behavior of the controller, the temperature of the room has been varied along its range. A fixed opening position of the door is supposed. Three different external temperatures are considered: the two extremes and one in the middle (-20, 0, 20) °C. Figure 4 (left) shows the results.

Table 1. Fuzzy rules of the HVAC of one room.

TmpIn	TmpOut	Door	HVAC	Weight
		HVAC Kitchen		
VeryCold			Hotter	1
Cold	Cold		Hotter	1
Cold	Not Cold		Medium	1
Average			Medium	1
Hot	Not Hot		Medium	1
Hot	Hot		Cooler	1
VeryHot			Cooler	1
VeryCold		Half	Hotter	0.2
Cold		Half	Hotter	0.2
Average	Cold	Half	Hotter	0.2
Average	Hot	Half	Cooler	0.2
Hot		Half	Cooler	0.2
VeryHot		Half	Cooler	0.2
VeryCold		Open	Hotter	0.4
Cold		Open	Hotter	0.4
Average	Cold	Open	Hotter	0.4
Average	Hot	Open	Cooler	0.4
Hot		Open	Cooler	0.4
VeryHot		Open	Cooler	0.4
	Cold		Hotter	0.2
	Average		Temperate	0.2
	Hot		Cooler	0.2

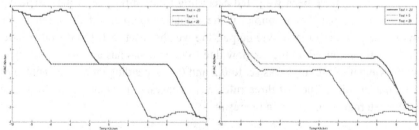

Figure 4. System output for three different external temperatures (left) and including the last three rules (right)

It can be noticed in Figure 4 (left) how difficult to distinguish the three functions is because of the low impact of the external temperature according to the rules. To take into account its effect, the last three rules of Table 1 were included. Figure 4 (right) shows how the profile changes. The curves seem to be stepped due to the limited precision of the output variable of the fuzzy controller. In a commercial air conditioner system is impossible to set an accurate temperature as set-point.

Finally, the effect of an open door (air flow) on the output is shown in Figure 5. As expected, the variability of the temperature is not big.

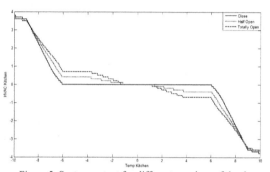

Figure 5. System output for different openings of the door

5. Conclusions and Future Work

In this work, fuzzy logic has been proved as a useful technique to design a control strategy for the HVAC problem in an easy and direct way. Knowledge has been incorporated in the definition of the rules. Simulations show how this intelligent technique gives good results.

Further work includes the possibility of working with hybrid controller, merging classical PID regulators and fuzzy logic, to improve the efficiency of the control solution.

References

1. M. Trčka, J.L.M. Hensen, *Automation in Construction* **19.2,** 93 (2010).
2. L. Pérez-Lombard, J. Ortiz, C. Pout. *Energy and buildings* **40.3,** 394 (2008).
3. Q. Bi, et al. *Control Engineering Practice* **8.6,** 633 (2000).
4. M. Santos, *Rev. Iberoam. Automatica Inf. Ind.* **8.4,** 283 (2011).
5. J. Garrido, F. Vázquez, F. Morilla. *J. Process Control* **22.6,** 1044 (2012)
6. C.P. Underwood. Routledge (2002).
7. J. Jantzen, John Wiley & Sons (2013).

USE OF GENETIC ALGORITHMS FOR UNMANNED AERIAL SYSTEMS PATH PLANNING

PABLO GARCÍA AUÑÓN

System Engineering and Automatic Control, UNED
c/ Juan del Rosal s/n, 28040-Madrid, Spain

MATILDE SANTOS PEÑAS

Computer Sciences, University Complutense of Madrid
C/ Profesor García Santesmases s/n, 28040-Madrid, Spain

This paper shows a comparison of different methods based on genetic algorithms in order to find a computational cost efficient path planning strategy for unmanned aerial systems (UAS). For that purpose, two different population generations and three crossover operators are proposed, comparing the computational time they require and the paths found. Results prove that it is possible to design a reliable and fast evolutive algorithm, capable of finding a sub-optimal solution without too high computational cost for a complex problem such as minimizing the path between two points for rotorcrafts.

1. Introduction

Finding the best trajectory (path planning) between two points has become an important issue for autonomous aerial systems (UAS) [1]. Artificial intelligence techniques have shown good results to solve this issue in different environments. For example neural networks, although they may become very large if complexity of the environment increases or changes; probabilistic methods such as the ant colony, which may find global optimums but needs much time to converge and is quite sensitive to the initialization; genetic algorithms (GA) and other evolutionary strategies, etc. Skeleton methods, Dijkstra's algorithm and the potential field approach, have also been used to solve this problem [2].

In this paper the goal is to find a sub-optimal path between two points using different evolutive algorithms and comparing them in terms of computational cost and solution given. The path planning problem is aimed to be applied to UAS (Unmanned Aerial System), particularly rotorcrafts.

Combining two different population generation strategies and three crossover operators [7], a total of 6 methods will be compared.

2. Population Generation

2.1. *Random Generation*

The first method considered to generate the initial population is *Random Generation*. Given a *Np* number of points between the initial point, P_A, and the final point, P_B, N_p-2 points will be randomly generated inside an ellipse whose focuses are the points P_A and P_B, with an eccentricity of 0.5 and a parameter, $a = |\overline{P_A P_B}|$, being the points far away from P_A and P_B not considered. The obtained points on the *x-y* surface are sorted regarding the proximity to P_A. The *z* coordinate (height) is chosen to keep the UAS above the terrain.

2.2. *Heuristic Generation*

The second method consists of generating an indeterminate number of points by some heuristics rules. In this case the rules take into account the distance and angle of the path in order to generate the next point to a P_i, likely closer to the final P_B in the *x-y* plane.

3. Crossover and Mutation Methods

Once the initial population is generated, the fitness function is defined as the inverted of the energy needed to travel through the path. Individuals with a fitness value lower than 0.2 are eliminated and the rest are matched using the roulette system, without repeating any pair. After the crossover, the new members are again evaluated and the new generation is created choosing the best *N* members between the new generation and the old one.

3.1. *Chain of Genes Crossover*

The probability of crossover P_c is set to 0.8 and then two points of the gene chain are randomly chosen, P_1 and P_2. That section of the chain is interchanged between the two individuals, creating two new offspring. A mutation is applied to each gene of each new individual with a probability of $1/N_p$.

3.2. *Single Gene Crossover*

The crossover operator is applied to each gene independently, with a probability of 0.3. The position of the points is interchanged between the two individuals. Standard mutation is applied afterwards.

3.3. *Paths Based on Bezier Curves*

The paths are generated using Bezier curves [4], so the chromosomes are the position of the control points of the curves. This way we get smooth curves between two points. Two crossover methods are applied: the single gene crossover (section 3.2), with $Pc = 0.6$, and the Double Directional Alpha (DDA) method as described in [5] but in a simplified way.

Two mutation operators are proposed: the standard mutation and the so called Vibrational Mutation [5] with $P_M = 0.2$.

4. Application to Path Planning

Table 1 summarizes the 6 methods presented, where P-P means point to point curve; Bez, Bezier curves; Ran., random generation; Heu., heuristic generation; Simp., simple mutation; Vibra., vibrational mutation.

Table 1. Summary of the proposed methods to be compared.

Method		1.1	1.2	2.1	2.2	3.1	3.2
Curve		P-P	P-P	P-P	P-P	Bez.	Bez.
Population		Ran.	Ran.	Heu.	Heu.	Ran.	Ran.
Crossover	Type	Chain	Single	Chain	Single	Single	DDA
	Pc	0.8	0.6	0.8	0.6	0.3	0.6
Mutation	Type	Simp.	Simp.	Simp.	Simp.	Simp.	Vibra.
	Pc	$1/N_p$	$1/N_p$	$1/N_p$	$1/N_p$	$1/N_p$	0.2

The fitness function is based on the energy needed to travel along the path given by (1) and the fitness function by (2):

$$E(i) = \begin{cases} \sum_{j=1}^{N_p-1} R_j \cdot \left[\cos(\varphi_j) + 2.5 \frac{1 - \cos(\varphi_j)}{1 + \cos(\varphi_j)} \right] & \text{if } \varphi_j \geq 0 \\ \sum_{j=1}^{N_p-1} R_j \cdot \left[\cos(\varphi_j) - 0.5 \frac{1 - \cos(\varphi_j)}{1 + \cos(\varphi_j)} \right] & \text{if } \varphi_j < 0 \end{cases} \quad (1)$$

$$e_i = \frac{1/E_i}{\max_i(\frac{1}{E_i})} \quad (2)$$

where φ_j is the climbing angle between the points j and $j+1$ of the path and R_j is the distance traveled between these two points. A penalty in the energy will be assumed in case the path runs into the ground (3), where a is a coefficient high enough (here assumed as 20) and l is the length of the path inside the ground.

$$E_{pi} = E_i \cdot a \cdot l \tag{3}$$

The GA will stop when during 3 consecutive generations the reduction of the energy necessary to travel is lower that 5%.

5. Results and Discussion

The energy value of reference, called E_S, is the energy to travel between the initial and the final points in a straight line, following the shape of the land. Three different lands are considered and five pairs of random initial and final points are generated for each one. The size of the initial population was set to N = 10, 20, 40, 60 and 80. Different number of waypoints in the path was considered: $Np = 4, 6, 8, 10$ and 12.

An average of the dimensionless energy needed for each method, for all the points and lands considered, is calculated:

$$Ef_i'(N, N_p) = \frac{1}{3 \cdot 5} \sum_{t=1}^{3} \sum_{p=1}^{5} \frac{E_s(t,p)}{E_i(t,p)} \tag{4}$$

where Ef'_i and E_i are the efficiency and the energy of the method i, respectively. Computational time (t) is also included as follows,

$$Ef_i(N, N_p) = Ef'_i(N, N_p) \cdot a_t \quad \text{where} \quad a_t = \begin{cases} 1 & if \ t \le 5s \\ (5/t)^2 & if \ t > 5s \end{cases} \tag{5}$$

Figure 1 (left) shows, for N=60 and Np=8, the number of generation required for each method vs. Energy. Methods 3.1 and 3.2 fall rapidly after 3 iterations, while the other methods do the same but slower, given less efficient solutions in that case.

The obtained paths depend on the size of the population N and the number of points N_p in the path. Figure 1 (right) shows, as an example, how the energy varies with N for different N_p for the method 2.1. The paths became better with larger number of individuals, while larger N_p than 8 produces worse results. That happens because the paths become too complicated when using more intermediate points and the methods cannot find better solutions; however, Methods 3.1 and 3.2 showed less differences for large N_p, but still worse.

As an example, Figure 2 presents the paths found. At first glance, Method 3.1 seems to provide the best solution, while Methods 3.2 and 1.2 seem to be the worst. N and N_p have been chosen so that the best solutions are achieved for each method between these two points.

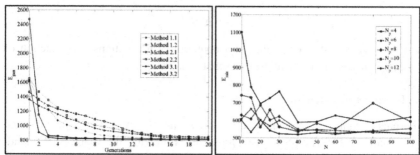

Figure 1. Number of generations required for each method to achieve the same average energy (left); Variation of the minimum energy using Method 2.1 as a function of N and Np (right).

The results are summarized in Table 2 (left side), where the energy is an average of the 5 initial and final points in the three lands proposed.

Table 2: Efficiency of each method for all cases. Case of Figure for Methods 2.1, 3.1 and 3.2.

Method	1.1	1.2	2.1	2.2	3.1	3.2	2.1	3.1	3.2
N	80	80	60	60	10	10	60	40	60
N_p	4	4	4	4	4	4	4	4	4
Energy	-	-	-	-	-	-	639	615	748
Time (s)	-	-	-	-	-	-	1.0	16	29
Efficiency	1,532	1,520	1,542	1,542	1,362	1,409	2,074	0,210	0,053

The best methods are Method 2.1 and 2.2 (heuristics population generation), which need a medium number of individuals and fewer waypoints. Methods 1.1 and 1.2 reach also good results, needing bigger size population. The Methods 3.1 and 3.2 reach lower values with the lowest values of N and Np. This happens because the higher N, the better the solution, but it requires higher computing times and then the factor at (5) reduces drastically the efficiency.

On the right side of Table 2 the energy needed for the path of Figure 2 is presented for Methods 2.1, 3.1 and 3.2 with the best combination of N and Np in terms of energy needed. Method 3.1 achieves a good path in this case, but it also needs much more time. The Method 2.1 provides also good solutions, but with computing times much smaller. This is because Methods 3.1 and 3.2 first check whether the path goes into the ground, requiring small discretization and therefore more computational operations.

On the other hand, the crossover and the mutation are not as simple as in the other methods, which also demands more time. Method 3.2 does not achieve results as good as it was shown in [4]. Maybe the trajectories are not complicated enough to use all the potential of this method, or the parameters used are not sufficiently well tuned.

In any case, the resulting trajectories when using Bezier curves are smoother and in some cases need lower energies, but a deeper study of the energies shows that those two methods do not achieve generally the best results.

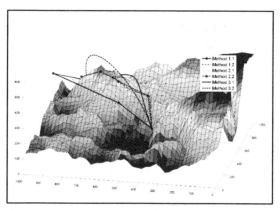

Figure 2. Paths obtained for each method for type of land 3 between two random points.

6. Conclusions and Future Work

In this paper, it has been proved that genetic algorithms can be successfully used for aerial path planning, having been presented six different methods to be compared.

As future work, the energy equation, i.e. the fitness function, should be reviewed, since it seems that there are not big differences in the energy needed for different paths, although graphically some solutions are much better.

References

1. G. Pajares et al. *Rev. Iber. Autom. Inf. Ind.* **5.1** 83 (2008).
2. B.M. Sathyaraj et al. *Fuzzy Optim. Decision Making* **7.3** 257 (2008).
3. D. Whitley. *Inf. Soft. Techn*, **43.14** 817 (2001).
4. Y.V. Pehlivanoglu, O. Baysal and A. Hacioglu, A. *Aircr Eng Aerosp Tec.* **79.4**, 352 (2007).
5. A. Hacioglu and I. Özkol. *Aircr Eng Aerosp Tec.*, **74.3**, 228 (2002).

IMAGE STABILIZATION SYSTEM BASED ON MINIMIZATION FRAME DIFFERENCES BY A FUZZY LOGIC SUPERVISOR

DAVID REOLID ROLDÁN

Complutense University of Madrid, C/ Profesor García Santesmases s/n
28040 Madrid, Spain

MATILDE SANTOS, VICTORIA LÓPEZ

Complutense University of Madrid, C/ Profesor García Santesmases s/n
28040 Madrid, Spain

This article presents, in contrast to more complex usual options, a simple and low computational cost solution for image stabilization. The solution is based on the minimization of frame differences and the use of a fuzzy logic supervisor. The fuzzy logic supervisor is designed as a control system for the stabilization to avoid undesired compensations. An analysis of the performance and viability of the system has been carried out and the results of this fuzzy approach are encouraging.

1. Introduction

Video sequences are often shaky and contain undesirable jitter due to undesired camera motions during video captures. Image stabilization has taken a key role in video quality by preventing these vibrations during its capture or in post-processing.

One aspect that most stabilization solutions have in common is the use of complex and computational demanding techniques for the motion estimation and stabilization. Although different approaches have been studied, they all tend to estimate motion based on the changing position of a group of selected subjects like SIFT interest points [1], edge patterns [5] or simple areas of pixels (blocks) of the frame. On top of the computational cost needed to track subjects, additional processing is needed to improve accuracy. Kalman filtering [4, 9] and DFT filtering [7] are commonly used, making the resulted solution even a little more complex.

Opposed to those approaches, the main goal of the proposed solution is its simplicity that makes viable its integration into ad-hoc systems with limited capacity (like embedded or portable systems), in order to increase their image quality without the necessity of post-processing.

To reduce the complexity of the proposed solution some concessions have been made. Instead of using invariant features as in the other solutions, only frame differences are used, making the approach more vulnerable to high contrast repetitive patterns and to large number of moving objects situations. Additionally, as part of this first approach, only two-axis stabilization has been implemented and its actual real use would be limited to fixed camera situations affected by vibrations or small movements (like the ones generated by the wind and earth movements).

2. Methodology

Most image stabilization systems can be divided into three modules: motion estimation, detection of unwanted movements and motion compensation; or two modules considering the last two part of a unique motion correction system. The proposed solution is based on this last architecture and is composed of only two modules for motion estimation and compensation supervising, being this last one based on a fuzzy logic control system in charge of correcting the necessary compensation.

2.1. Motion Estimation

Motion calculation is performed using two independent differences analysis. The first one obtains the differences between the current frame and the previous N frames (taking N = 2 for this study) in the defined search area. The second analysis tool calculates just the differences between the search area of the last frame and the same area of a set of M frames, representing the current frame with a movement vector applied to (X,Y) axis (Fig. 1). The following vectors compound the set of M movements applied to the frame in this study: (3,0), (3,3), (0,3), (-3.3), (-3,0), (-3,-3), (0.-3), (3,-3).

2.1.1. Search Area

The search area is defined as the difference between the original video sequence and the stabilized output sequence. It consists of the surrounding area of the original one. If no movement compensation is applied to the cropped output sequence then it is in the middle (centered). Corners are also excluded from calculations and not taken into consideration (Fig. 1).

438

Figure 1. Original sequence versus search area with a movement detection mask applied.

2.1.2. Calculation of Frame Differences and Motion Data

The two differences calculation explained in the previous subsection is carried out in a simple way by calculating the difference of the grey level for each pixel. Only differences that surpass a minimum threshold are considered to be significant and are marked as part of a movement area.

Pixel differences between current frame and previous N frames are taken as variability data. The calculated movement areas for each of the movement vectors are compared, and the one that minimizes the number of pixels is taken as the motion estimation vector.

3. Fuzzy Logic Supervisor

In order to make up for the simple motion estimation technique, a supervisor has been added to include the possibility of analyzing each motion situation and then to make the final decision on the motion compensation needed. This supervisor will make a decision whether apply any compensation or if motion estimation vector must be softened or just be applied as it is.

To keep computational costs to a minimum, and to keep knowledge representation simple and close to reality, a fuzzy logic system [6, 8] has been chosen to implement this supervisor. Implementation has been done with the software tool jFuzzyLogic [2, 3].

3.1. Input/output Variables

Input variables of the solution viability are called: is_success and variability. They will provide, respectively, an index of the stabilization success degree and the amount of movement/changes among last frames.

The input variable *is_success* is obtained as the proportion between the number of movement area pixels of the stabilized frame and the current frame without motion compensation. It will take a value in the range (0,1), where a 0 value means a perfect motion compensation and 1 means no improvement (Figure 2, left).

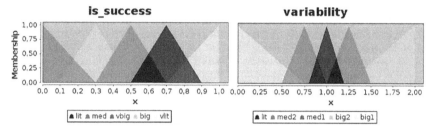

Figure 2. Membership functions and fuzzy sets for is_success and variability input variables.

Variability is calculated as the ratio between the changes between the current frame with the previous one and the differences between the current frame and the second previous frames. It will have a value near 1 when movements/changes between frames are consistent, and it will take a value far from 1 when the variability is larger (Figure 2, right).

For each input variable five fuzzy sets and their membership functions have been defined in their corresponding universe of discourse (Fig. 2).

In order to keep the model as simple as possible there will be only one output variable called: isCompensation. It will be used as an adjustment coefficient for the motion compensation vector. Two fuzzy sets have been defined for this variable: none and reduce (which will, respectively, not affect the motion compensation vector or reduce its effect) (Fig. 3). Its output value will be in the (0,1) range.

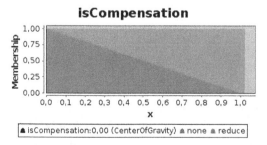

Figure 3. Fuzzy output variable isCompensation description.

440

3.2. *Rule Set*

To test the fuzzy supervisor system, the following rule set was defined to detect voluntary panning situations. The first two rules identify good stabilization results with little variability and therefore they force no intervention, while the rest reduce the compensation.

IF is_success IS vbig THEN isCompensation IS none
IF is_success IS big AND variability IS lit THEN isCompensation IS none
IF is_success IS med AND variability IS lit THEN isCompensation IS reduce
IF is_success IS lit AND variability IS lit THEN isCompensation IS reduce
IF is_success IS vlit AND variability IS lit THEN isCompensation IS reduce
IF variability IS med1 OR variability IS med2 THEN isCompensation IS reduce
IF variability IS big1 OR variability IS big2 THEN isCompensation IS reduce

4. Results

In order to test how the fuzzy system performs a video sequence with horizontal panning from side to side was captured.

During the simulation three cases were considered: an output frame with no motion compensation (just cropped), an output frame stabilized using the motion compensation vector without the supervision of the fuzzy logic control system, and an output frame stabilized and under the intelligent supervisor control. For each frame of the sequence, a measure of the difference in pixels between the output frame and the previous one was obtained.

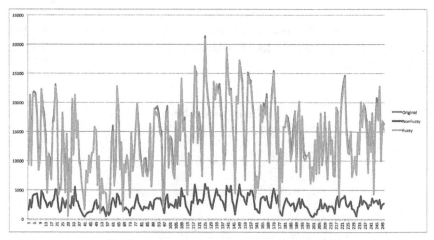

Figure 4. Differences between current frame and the previous one.

In Figure 4 the results of the three measures taken during the test for each frame can be observed: without compensation (blue line), without supervisor (red line), and with the fuzzy supervised stabilization (green line).

As it can be seen, the fuzzy logic supervisor, as expected, blocks almost completely the stabilization of images, taking place only in a few moments in which the differences between frames are smaller.

It can be appreciated the changes of the direction of the movement (the difference between frames decreases). There are also some situations where the stabilized image (without the fuzzy supervisor) cannot recover from the difference with the original frame. This situation can be unavoidable during the changes of direction when a large number of pixels have been changed.

5. Conclusions and Future Work

The fuzzy system selects a good motion compensation vector for the frame that is being stabilized based on the minimization of changes, offering at the same time a high level control layer which is able to detect specific situations and modify the motion compensation vector as specified in the fuzzy logic system.

It also proves that situations were a smart control is needed do exist, and a simple but intelligent solution based on fuzzy logic is able to provide a viable image stabilization system with a low computational cost.

References

1. S. Battiato, G. Gallo, G. Puglisi and S. Scellato, *IS&T/SPIE Electronic Imaging*, 72500T (2009).
2. P. Cingolani and J. Alcalá-Fdez. *Int. J. Computational Intelligence Systems* **6.1** 61 (2013).
3. P. Cingolani and J. Alcala-Fdez *FUZZ-IEEE Int. Conf.* (2012)
4. N. Kyriakoulis, A. Gasteratos and A. Amanatiadis. *VISAPP* **2** 469-475 (2008).
5. J.K. Paik, Y.C. Park and D.W. Kim, *IEEE Trans Consumer Electronics*, **38,3** (1992).
6. W. Pedrycz, *Fuzzy sets and fuzzy systems, Research Studies Press, England* (1993).
7. F. Vella, A. Castorina, M. Mancuso and G. Messina. *IEEE Trans Consumer Electronics* **48(3)**, 796-801 (2002).
8. L. Zadeh, *Computer*, **21(4),** 83-93 (1998).
9. O. Kwon, J. Shin and J. Paik, *Image Analysis and Recognition* 141 Springer (2005)

FUEL FUZZY CONTROL IN AN AIRCRAFT: A FIRST APPROACH

ELIAS PLAZA ALONSO

Universidad Nacional de Educación a Distancia
Madrid, Spain

MATILDE SANTOS PEÑAS

Computer Architecture and Automatic Control, Computer Science
Universidad Complutense, C/ Profesor García Santesmases sn
Madrid, Spain

This paper presents an intelligent approach to the design and simulation of a conventional civil aircraft fuel system using fuzzy logic. The development is focused on the center of gravity balance problem in a plane, i.e., fuel re-distribution between several tanks during a complete operation (ground and flight). Additionally, the controller must guarantee the fuel feeding to the engines and allows the tanks refueling. Due to the problem characteristics we have selected fuzzy technique in order to design a controller with the appropriate features to accomplish all requirements. To make it more efficient, the rule base is reduced to simplify the design problem without loss of generality. Simulation results are encouraging.

1. Introduction

The aircraft (a/c) balance is essential to ensure its stability, especially along the longitudinal axis where if the a/c center of gravity (CoG) is located behind the a/c aerodynamic center (point where all aerodynamic forces have their action center), the aircraft becomes unstable. On the other hand, if the CoG is located too ahead then the a/c loses maneuverability ([1, 8]).

Therefore, there is a small margin where the CoG can be located to ensure a trade-off between inherent stability and maneuverability, known as Static Margin (SM) (Figure 1, left). It is also important for the CoG in lateral axis to be located as close as possible to the a/c plane of symmetry in order to avoid asymmetries in the control surfaces and/or in the engines thrust, even lateral-directional instability. Therefore positioning the CoG in the aircraft is one of the most important tasks during the design phase.

Hence there is a new problem: if the aircraft were a constant-mass solid, we could carry out a "static" design; but the a/c fuel is variable because of the initial feeding and, more important, because obviously it is consumed along the flight. Even more, the fuel can represent 24% of total weight and for structural reasons, it is impossible to keep all fuel inside only one tank.

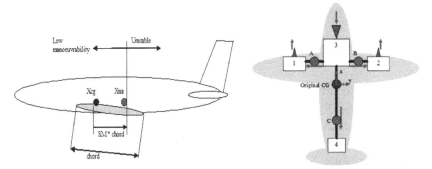

Figure 1. Left: Aircraft Longitudinal Center of Gravity (Xcg) and Aircraft Aerodynamic Center (Xna). Right: Placement of tanks and pump equipments.

Therefore, we must design a control system which allows to move fuel between the tanks in order to keep the CoG inside the stability and maneuverability margins.

This system is multivariable (MIMO) and non-linear, and it is difficult to be modeled and controlled by analytic techniques. In fact, the total mass dynamics is unknown and changeable. That is why fuzzy logic has been chosen as a tool which is able to deal with the uncertainty of the variables.

2. System Description

We consider the typical conventional plane system fitted with two engines (i.e.: Airbus A320, Boeing B737, or similar [3]). In this particular case, the system consists of four fuel tanks: two tanks placed in wings (tanks "1" and "2"), one central tank ("3"), and one tank located in a/c tail (tank "4") (Figure 1, right). The tanks are connected by pipes that link: tanks "1" – "3", "2" – "3", and "4" – "3". Each pipe has a pumps/valves equipment that can move the fuel in both directions or maintain the pipe closed. Then we have three pumps groups: A (between "1" and "3"), B (between "2" and "3"), and C (between "4" and "3"). In addiction the central tank ("3") is provided with a fuel charge inlet, and each wing tank ("1", "2") is provided with a fuel injection to one engine.

We are going to assume the following. Pressure losses in pipes and tanks inlets are negligible; the fuel is considered as an incompressible fluid; each tank has been designed to maintain its CoG constant. Finally, initial system components distribution has been performed to locate CoG at the optimal position respect to the static margin of stability.

2.1. *Equations and Variables*

The Mass Flow Balance Differential equations are the main ones (1).

$$\frac{dm_1}{dt} = G_A - G_{E1} \quad , \quad \frac{dm_2}{dt} = G_B - G_{E2} \quad , \quad \frac{dm_3}{dt} = -G_A - G_B - G_C + G_F \quad , \quad \frac{dm_4}{dt} = G_C$$

(1)

Where m_i refers to respective tank mass; G_A, G_B, G_C refer to respective pipe mass flow rates; G_{E1} and G_{E2} refer to each engine injection mass flow rate; and G_F refers to fuel charge inlet mass flow rate. The mass flow rates G_{E1}, G_{E2} and G_F are the consumptions laws of engines and the refueling law, and depend on the a/c performance. So they are an input to our design problem.

Solving those equations we obtain the fuel mass in each tank and then we can estimate the CoG variation using the centroid equation (2):

$$X_{cg} = \frac{\sum_i X_i \cdot m_i}{\sum_i m_i} \qquad Y_{cg} = \frac{\sum_i Y_i \cdot m_i}{\sum_i m_i}$$

(2)

Where X_{cg} is the longitudinal component of CoG while Y_{cg} is the lateral one. Each couple X_i, Y_i is each tank CoG position.

In order to simulate the aircraft, the reference system is shown in Figure 1, right, where dotted arrows indicate positive sense of geometry reference system. Solid arrows indicate positive sense of mass flow rates.

3. Fuzzy Control System

The controller decides the pumps state according to the CoG coordinates and the actual mass of each tank, ensuring CoG is inside stability margins. Therefore the control variables are G_A, G_B, and G_C. The state or decision variables are m_1, m_2, m_3, m_4, X_{cg} and Y_{cg}. The variables have been normalized to the range [-1, 1] except for the fuel mass which normalized range is [0, 1].

The characteristics of the fuzzy system are the following ([2, 4, 5, 7]): Mamdani-type with centroid defuzzyfication method and minimum for the implication.

In general, it is assumed that a conventional aircraft must have a SM between 10% and 20%. We are going to suppose the SM design value of 15% when a/c is in Zero Fuel Weight. Therefore, the allowed variation around the design value will be +/- 5%. Then, the critical values of Xcg have been calculated according to SM definition ([1, 8]) represented in Figure 1, left.

The fuzzy sets defined for the Xcg variable are: Acceptable (A), Positive Acceptable (PA), Negative Acceptable (NA), Positive Unacceptable (PU) and Negative Unacceptable (NU) (Figure 2, left). For the CoG lateral component we have defined the linguistic variables (A, PA, NA, PU, NU) (Figure 2, right).

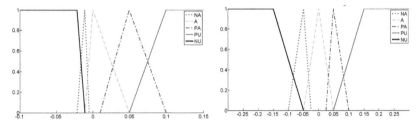

Figure 2. Left: Membership functions for Xcg. Right: Membership functions for Ycg. Note: The real range is [-1, 1] but it has been reduced for clarity.

The linguistic variables of Fuel mass in tanks 1 and 2 are: Normal (NO), Full (FU), In Reserve (RE). The membership functions are trapezoidal ones. For Fuel mass in tanks 3 and 4 it is not necessary to prevent tanks from being empty, so the linguistic variables are: Normal (NO) and Full (FU).

For each pump group, we define the linguistic variables: Closed (CL), Positive Flow (PF), and Negative Flow (NF). Obviously, closed correspond to no flow inside the pipe. The membership functions of these variables are triangular in the middle and trapezoidal at the ends.

For this problem we should define a very large number of rules. In order to reduce the rules base we have used the knowledge of the physic behaviour of the system. For example, it is impossible Y_{cg} to be Positive with m_1 being Normal and m_2 being In Reserve. And rules which have as input different values of Y_{cg} are equals for all possible values of m_3 and m_4 with a particular value set of the remained inputs. Therefore, the reduce rule base is presented in Table 1.

4. Simulations and Results

We have carried out the designed system implementation using *Matlab®* and *Simulink®* [6] software.

The flight history, that is, the refueling and consumption operations performed, is shown in Figure 3. It consists in a take-off (maximum consumption), an engine failure during climbing (asymmetric consumption) and an emergency landing (low consumption).

Table 1. Reduced Rule Base.

IF	THEN
Xcg is PU, & Tank.4 is not FU	Pump.C is PF
Xcg is NU, & Tank.3 is not FU	Pump.C is NF
Xcg is PA, & Tank.1 is not FU	Pump.A is PF
Xcg is PA, & Tank.2 is not FU	Pump.B is PF
Xcg is NA, & Tank.3 is not FU	Pump.A is NF & Pump.B is NF
Xcg is A, & Ycg is A, & Tank.1 is NO, &	Pump.A is CL & Pump.B is CL &
Tank.2 is NO, & Tank.3 is NO, & Tank.4 is NO	Pump.C is CL
Tank.1 is RE	Pump.A is PF
Tank.2 is RE	Pump.B is PF
Ycg is PU, & Tank.1 is not FU	Pump.A is PF
Ycg is PU, & Tank.2 is not RE, & Tank.3 is not FU	Pump.B is NF
Ycg is PA, & Tank.1 is not FU	Pump.A is PF
Ycg is NU, & Dep2 is not FU	Pump.B is PF
Ycg is NU, & Tank.1 is not RE, & Tank.3 is not FU	Pump.A is NF
Ycg is NA, & Tank.2 is not FU	Pump.B is PF

Figure 4, left, shows how the longitudinal CoG is outside the stability margin at first. Before starting the take off (at 150 seconds approximately), the longitudinal CoG component is inside the SM (SM is +/-19 cm). From here, the pumping to/from tank 4 finishes because of saving energy reasons according to design criteria. Analyzing lateral CoG component (figure 4, right) we can observe it is always located inside valid margin (defined as +/- 34 cm).

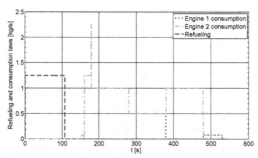

Figure 3. Flight history: refueling and consumption laws.

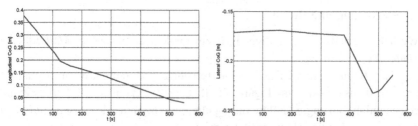

Figure 4. Left: Longitudinal CoG evolution. Right: Lateral CoG evolution.

Figure 5, left, shows the fuel consumption. Fuel flow to/from tanks 1 and 2 is the same at first. However, when engine 1 failure occurs (asymmetric consumption), there is a different fuel flow to/from tanks 1 and 2 to prevent lateral CoG unbalance. I.e.: pump A stops moving flow to tank 1 while pump B increases the flow to tank 2 because lateral CoG component began to move towards tank 1 when engine 1 consumption drops (Figure 5, right).

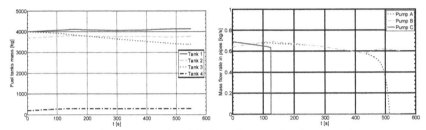

Figure 5. Left: Fuel mass tanks. Right: Mass flow rate of each pump equipment.

5. Conclusions and Future Work

In this paper we have designed and simulated a fuzzy control for a non-linear MIMO system, the balance of the fuel mass in an aircraft. The results show that the fuzzy system maintains CoG inside stability and maneuverability margins. Indeed, we have achieved all design criteria: *fuel system stability, aircraft longitudinal and lateral stability, aircraft performance stability,* and *energy optimization*. Also, the proposed control could help to simplify the payload distribution procedure.

However, if we had used a complete rules base, the solution stability may have improved. And we could see if there is any improvement if we introduce more linguistic values in mass flow rate of each pump.

References

1. B. N. Pamadi, AIAA Education Series, EEUU (2004).
2. D. G. Schwartz et al. *Proceedings of the IEEE* **82.4** (1994).
3. http://www.airbus.com/aircraftfamilies/
4. J. Jantzen, Tech. Report 98-E 864 Denmark (1998).
5. J. Jantzen, Tech. Report 98-E 868, Denmark (1998).
6. Matlab and Simulink, SW Package, R2007b, MathWorks, MA, (2007).
7. Santos, M. (2011). *Rev. Iberoam. Automática Inf. Ind.* **8.4**, 283 (2011)
8. F.P. Warren F, *Mechanics of Flight*, John Wiley & Sons, EEUU (2010).

FUZZY LOGIC VS ANALYTIC CONTROLLERS
ON A NON-LINEAR SYSTEM

E. ARANDA*, M. GUINALDO AND S.DORMIDO

*Department of Computer Science and Automatic Control,
Spanish University of Distance Education (UNED),
Juan del Rosal 16, 28040 Madrid, Spain*

M. SANTOS

*Department of Computer Architecture and Systems Engineering,
Complutense University
C/ Profesor Garca Santesmases s/n., 28040 Madrid, Spain*

In this paper, an intelligent control of the rotary inverted pendulum by fuzzy logic is presented. Specifically, the design consists of a Takagi-Sugeno fuzzy model to approximate the non-linear system to a succession of points where a linear system is described. A feedback gain is obtained that allows the stabilization of the inverted pendulum in a higher attractor than in the case of analytic Full State Feedback controller or Linear Quadratic Regulator.

1. Introduction

The control of the inverted pendulum and, in particular, of a Furuta pendulum (proposed by Furuta et al.[1]) has been studied by many authors[2-4] and it is a common example in Control Theory. The strong non-linearity multi-output system and, therefore, the difficulty and complexity of the control design, has made the inverted pendulum an interesting case of study that has been used as a benchmark to compare different control strategies.[5,6] In particular, the rotary inverted pendulum deployed by Quanser[7] consists of a motor which has a rotary arm attached that can move free 360°. The pendulum is connected at the end of the rotary arm (see Figure 1) and it can oscillate freely and perpendicularly to the rotary arm.

Generally, the control of the inverted pendulum consists of two steps:

---

*This work was supported in part by the Spanish Ministry of Economy and Competitiveness under the project DPI2012-31303.

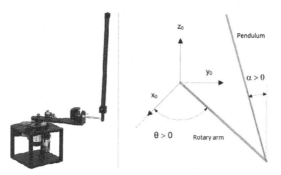

Fig. 1. Prototype by Quanser of the rotary inverted pendulum (left), and diagram of the rotary inverted pendulum (right).

The control used to swing up the pendulum up to positions close to the unstable equilibrium point ($\alpha = 0^o$ in Figure 1), and the control to stabilize the pendulum at this point. In this paper we focus on the stabilization control. This control is normally addressed linearizing around the unstable equilibrium point and obtaining a gain for this now linear system. Some methods that have used this linearization are Full State Feedback (FSF) or Linear Quadratic Regulator (LQR), as in Kumar et al.[8] However these methods work only near the linearization position. For this reason, it is interesting to search new control strategies for the stabilization of the pendulum even when the initial conditions are far from the unstable equilibrium point.

In this regard Takagi-Sugeno fuzzy controllers come on the scene.[9] In particular, we use the control presented in Farius et al.,[10] where a fuzzy model is developed and a control based on LQR is designed.

With this aim in mind, the paper is divided into 6 sections. In Section 2 the dynamics of the rotary inverted pendulum and how we obtain a model from the Lagrangian of the system is explained. In Section 3 the different control methods (FSF, LQR and Takagi-Sugeno fuzzy) are described. Finally in Section 4 a comparative between the proposed controllers is illustrated through simulations of the whole non-linear model. Section 5 provides the main conclusions of the paper.

2. Model of the Rotary Inverted Pendulum

In this section the theoretical model of the rotary inverted pendulum is described. The system is shown in Figure 1.b, where θ is the angle that the rotary arm forms with the X axis and α is the angle that the pendulum forms with the vertical axis.

The motion equations of the inverted pendulum can be derived from the Euler-Lagrange method using the Euler-Lagrange equation

$$\frac{\partial^2 L}{\partial t \partial \dot{q}_i} - \frac{\partial L}{\partial q_i} = 0, \tag{1}$$

where q_i are the generalized coordinates of the system$((q_i \ q_2) = (\theta \ \alpha))$.

If the dynamical equations that result from (1) are solved for the angles accelerations, it yields

$$\ddot{\theta} = \frac{h_3 \cos \alpha h_2 0.5 \sin 2\alpha \dot{\theta}^2 - B_P \dot{\alpha} + h_5 \sin \alpha - h_4(\dot{\theta}(B_R + h_2 \dot{\alpha} \sin 2\alpha) - \tau + h_3 \dot{\alpha}^2 \sin \alpha)}{H} \tag{2}$$

$$\ddot{\alpha} = \frac{(h_2 \sin^2 \alpha + h_1)(h_2 0.5 \sin 2\alpha \dot{\theta}^2 - B_P \dot{\alpha} + h_5 \sin \alpha) - h_3 \cos \alpha(\dot{\theta}(B_R + h_2 \dot{\alpha} \sin 2\alpha) - \tau + h_3 \dot{\alpha}^2 \sin \alpha)}{H}, \tag{3}$$

where $h_1 = J_R + m_P L_R^2$, $h_2 = \frac{m_P L_P^2}{4}$, $h_3 = \frac{m_P L_P L_R}{4}$, $h_4 = J_P + h_2$, $h_5 = \frac{m_P L_P g}{2}$, $h_6 = m_R L_R$, $H = h_1 h_4 + h_2 h_4 \sin^2 \alpha - h_3^2 \cos^2 \alpha$, and the meaning of the rest of the parameters can be found in.[7,11]

The following change of variables is performed so that the number of future rules in the fuzzy control can be reduced:[10]

$$z_1 = \frac{\sin \alpha}{\alpha}, \quad z_2 = \cos \alpha, \quad z_3 = \dot{\theta} \cos \alpha \sin \alpha, \quad z_4 = \dot{\alpha} \sin \alpha.$$

Therefore, a model of the form $\dot{x} = A(z)x + B(z)u$ is obtained, where $x^T = (\theta \ \alpha \ \dot{\theta} \ \dot{\alpha})$, $z^T = (z_1 \ z_2 \ z_3 \ z_4)$, and the coefficients of $A(z) = (a_{ij}(z))$ and $B(z) = (b_{ij}(z))$ can be derived strightforward from (2)-(3).

3. Control Algorithms

3.1. *Full State Feedback (FSF)*

We linearize (2)-(3) using a first order Taylor approach at the point $x_0^T = (0 \ 0 \ 0 \ 0)$. As a result, we obtain a linear system $\dot{x} = Ax + Bu$, where

$$A = \begin{pmatrix} 0 & 0 & 1 & 0 \\ 0 & 0 & 0 & 1 \\ 0 & 80.3 & -45.8 & -0.93 \\ 0 & 122 & -44.1 & -1.40 \end{pmatrix}, \quad B = \begin{pmatrix} 0 \\ 0 \\ 83.4 \\ 80.3 \end{pmatrix}, \quad u = -Kx.$$

According to the Quanser specifications,[7] the poles $p = (-40 \ -30 \ -2.80 \pm 2.86i)$ provide a damping ratio $\zeta = 0.7$ and natural frequency $\omega_n = 4$ rad/s, so that the feedback gain is $K_{FSF} = (-5.26 \ 28.16 \ -2.76 \ 3.22)$.

3.2. *Linear Quadratic Regulator (LQR)*

LQR technique is an optimal control technique which consists of minimizing the cost function $J = \int_0^\infty x^T(t)Qx(t) + u^T(t)Ru(t)dt$, and the feedback gain is given by $K = R^{-1}B^T P$, where P is the unique positive defined solution of the algebraic Ricatti's equation $A^T P + PA - PBR^{-1}B^T P + Q = 0$. We follow the same criterion as in[10] in the choice of Q and R, which corresponds to those that will be used in subsection 3.3. As a result, the feedback gain for the LQR controller is $K_{LQR} = (-3.162 \quad 56.49 \quad -4.77 \quad 8.08)$.

3.3. *Control based on Takagi-Sugeno Fuzzy Model*

The fuzzy model proposed by Takagi and Sugeno[12] is described by means of a succession of IF-THEN rules, each of them expresses the local dynamic by a linear system.[13,14] The output of the fuzzy model for any x is $\dot{x} = -\frac{\sum_{j=1}^n w_j f_j(x)}{\sum_{j=1}^n w_j}$, where $w_j = M_1^j \cdots M_n^j$, being M_i^j the membership functions and $f_i(x)$ the consequent of each rule.[12]

For the generation of the fuzzy model, it is necessary to write the variables z_i in terms of the membership functions M_i^j as $z_i = M_i \max(z_i) + \bar{M}_i \min(z_i)$, where $\max(z_i)$ and $\min(z_i)$ are the maximum and minimum value, respectively, the variable z_i can reach. For instance, $\max(z_1) = \max(z_2) = 1, \min(z_1) = 0.9003, \min(z_2) = 0.7071, \max(z_3) = -\min(z_3) = 6, \max(z_4) = -\min(z_4) = 4.2426$. Moreover, $M_i + \bar{M}_i = 1$ must hold, M_i is 0 if $z_i < \min(z_i)$ and is 1 if $z_i > \max(z_i)$ (and the opposite for $\bar{M}_i$).

Hence, 16 rules can be established and 16 A matrices and 16 B matrices with constant elements are obtained. That is, a fuzzy technique is applied in order to obtain 16 linear systems and their 16 corresponding feedback gains. As a result, after a defuzzification process, the gain K applied to the non-linear system can be computed from

$$u(t) = -\frac{\sum_{j=1}^{16} w_j K_j x(t))}{\sum_{j=1}^{16} w_j} = -K_{FZ}x(t), \tag{4}$$

where $w_1 = \bar{M}_1\bar{M}_2\bar{M}_3\bar{M}_4, w_2 = \bar{M}_1\bar{M}_2\bar{M}_3 M_4, \ldots, w_{16} = M_1 M_2 M_3 M_4$.

So that using the LQR design explained in Subsection 3.2 and the same matrices Q and R, we compute 16 K_i gains for the 16 states defined by (A_i, B_i), and using (4), the gain K_{FZ} is $K_{FZ} = (-3.16 \quad 100.5 \quad -4.28 \quad 26.74)$.

4. Experimental Results

In order to test and compare these controllers, we simulate the non-linear model described in Section 2. For each design of the controllers in Section 3,

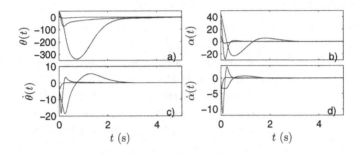

Fig. 2. (Solid line) FSF with initial α of 10°. (Dotted line) LQR control with initial α of 36°. (Dashdot line) Fuzzy control with initial α of 45°.

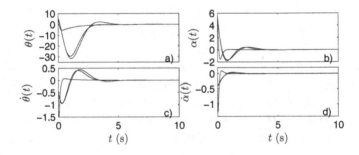

Fig. 3. (Solid line) FSF, (dotted line) LQR control, (dashdotted line) Fuzzy control with initial α of 6°.

the evolution of $\theta, \dot{\theta}, \alpha, \dot{\alpha}$, and the applied voltage are represented. Figure 2 illustrates the behavior of the system when the initial conditions are such that α takes the largest value so that the system is stabilized. In the case of the fuzzy controller, this angle is approximately 45°. For full state feedback is 20°, and for LQR is 36°. Furthermore a comparison for the same initial conditions with $\alpha = 6^o$ is carried out (see Figure 3). Observe how the fuzzy control developed presents a similar response to the FSF control, while LQR control results more abrupt. The applied control signal for the two situations described above is depicted in Figure 4.

5. Conclusions and Future Work

In this paper we have compared three control strategies applied to the rotary inverted pendulum: full state feedback, a LQR controller, and a LQR controller with a fuzzy model of the pendulum. Each design has been

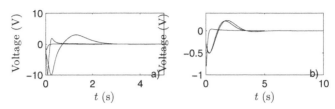

Fig. 4. (Solid line) FSF, (dotted line) LQR control, (dashdotted line) Fuzzy control. Control signal for the state in a) Figure 2 and b) Figure 3.

compared using a simulation of the non-linear model. From the simulation results, we can conclude that the attractor of the fuzzy system is considerably higher than in FSF control or LQR control. These results present great applicability if we deal with more complex systems, like the double rotary inverted pendulum. With the same initial conditions, the LQR control reaches the equilibrium point faster and with lower overshoot.

Future works include the application of these designs to the real system and the design of these controllers for the double rotary inverted pendulum.

References

1. K. Furuta, M. Yamakita and S. Kobayashi, *Journal of Systems and Control Engineering* **206**, 263 (1992).
2. K. Astrom and K. Furuta, *Automatica* **36**, 278 (2000).
3. F. Leung, L. Wong and P. Tam, *Electronics Letters* **32**, 1683 (1996).
4. J. Zhao and M. W. Spong, *Automatica* **37**, 1941 (2001).
5. J. Acosta, J. Aracil and F. Gordillo, *Control and intel. systems* **29**, 101 (2001).
6. K. Barya, S. Tiwari and R. Jha, Comparison of lqr and robust controllers for stabilizing inverted pendulum system, in *IEEE International Conference on Communication Control and Computing Technologies*, 2010.
7. Q. Inc., *SRV02 Rotary Pendulum User Manual.*, tech. rep., Quanser (2010).
8. P. Kumar, O. Mehrotra and J. Mahto, *International Journal of Research in Engineering and Technology* **1**, 532 (2012).
9. M. Santos, *Revista Iberoamericana de Automatica Inf. Ind* **8**, 283 (2011).
10. M. Fairus, Z. Mohamed and N. Ahmad, Fuzzy modeling and control of rotary inverted pendulum system using lqr technique, in *5th International Conference on Mechatronics*, 2013.
11. Q. Inc., *SRV02 User Manual*, tech. rep., Quanser (2009).
12. T. Takagi and M. Sugeno, *IEEE Transactions on Systems, Man and Cybernetics* **15**, 116 (1985).
13. K. Mehran, *Takagi-Sugeno Fuzzy Modeling for Process Control*, tech. rep., Newcastle University (2008).
14. M. Santos, J. de la Cruz and S. Dormido, Between fuzzy-pid and pid-conventional controllers: a good choice, in *IEEE NAFIPS*, 1996.

FROM SEMANTIC FUZZY 2-TUPLES TO LINGUISTICS: A SEMANTIC PARTITION

M.-A. ABCHIR

Deveryware, 43, rue Taitbout, Paris, 75009, France
E-mail: mohammed-amine.abchir@deveryware.com

I. TRUCK*

CHArt – EA4004, University Paris 8,
2 rue de la Liberté, Saint-Denis, 93526, France
* E-mail: isis.truck@univ-paris8.fr

This paper is a continuation of previous works on the semantic 2-tuples model, a representation model to deal with unbalanced linguistic terms sets. We propose to study how our semantic 2-tuples can help language processing since they offer a fuzzy semantic interpretation of words describing imprecise data. Thus, we propose two measures to catch the semantics of a set of words. We show the relevance of the measures in a use case where a lexicon has to be enriched.

Keywords: Linguistic fuzzy 2-tuples; Semantic 2-tuples; Semantic partition.

1. Introduction

Being able to handle imprecision and uncertainty is a crucial issue in many domains such as decision-making. Since decades, many researchers have stressed on this subject: as a leader, Zadeh and his followers have focused on the fuzzy sets and the fuzzy logic.[1-4] Other kinds of fuzzy models have emerged in the recent past, which allow users to express the results in the same set of values throughout the computations.[5-8] These models are called the *2-tuple* models. In this paper, we are interested in the partitions obtained with such models. Do they always reflect the reality? Do they take into account the semantics of the terms they are supposed to represent?

First, we review some of the 2-tuple models then we explain our proposal: to generate a partition that takes into account the semantics of the terms. We finally conclude this study with some future works.

2. State of the art

The fuzzy linguistic 2-tuple model considers a pair (s, α) composed of a linguistic term s and its symbolic translation α ($\alpha \in [-.5, .5[$) to express the uncertainty of the term.[5] The key idea is to consider always a same linguistic term set (*at the beginning*, *during* and *at the end of* the process) in order to give the user a final result expressed in its own term set. Thanks to the α translation, there should be no loss of information: when intermediate results don't exactly add up, the symbolic translation is used to support the difference between the real result and the closest term s. By default, all α are equal to zero. If α is positive, s is reinforced, else it is weakened. For instance, if s means "high", then $(s, .37)$ may mean "more than high". There are a comparison, a negation and several aggregation operators.

An improvement of this model has been proposed[7] where data may not be uniformly distributed on their axis. In that case, Herrera *et al.* define hierarchies to express the granularity at each level. Once the partitioning done (through an algorithm), a term is expressed by **one or two** levels of the same linguistic hierarchy. When there are two hierarchies, it means that a certain hierarchy (*e.g* with 3 labels) is used to the left of the term, and another hierarchy (*e.g* with 9 labels) is used to the right of the term. In this example, it would mean that there is more precision on the right of the term than of the left.

Recently, we have proposed a semantic 2-tuple model to permit to express data, even when they are *very* unbalanced.[9,10] In our proposal, a term can have a hierarchy with *e.g.* only 3 labels to the left and a hierarchy with 17 labels to the right, if needed. So the partitioning phase implies a list of semantic pairs (s, v) as input, where s is the linguistic term and v its associated position on the axis. We then proposed an algorithm to automatically place the terms while keeping the advantages of the 2-tuple model, knowing each position in advance.

3. A semantic partition

However, during the partitioning phase, it may happen that one of the v positions on the axis is not known. In our previous works, this case lead us to propose a balanced term sets, *i.e.* all the terms were placed symmetrically on their axis. Now, we propose an improvement: use the semantic relations between terms to organise them on the axis.

3.1. *Resemblance rate between two terms*

Let $S = S_1 \cup S_2$ be the set of terms used by experts to define a given notion. S_1 (S_2 respectively) contains terms that are synonymous amongst themselves but terms from S_1 are antonymous with terms from S_2 (and vice-versa).

Let L_i (L_j respectively) be the list of synonyms for term s_i (s_j respectively). L_i, L_j permit to enrich the lexicon and are obtained thanks to a French dictionary (http://www.crisco.unicaen.fr/des/) that is known to be exhaustive and particularly appreciated: the dictionary contains about 50,000 words with about 200,000 synonyms and the site averages over 200,000 hits (queries) per day and is accessed by 40,000 users every day[a].

The strength of the semantic link between two terms $s_i, s_j \in S_k$ ($k = \{1,2\}$) is called the *resemblance rate* between those terms and is denoted r_{ij}. It is computed through the resemblance function R defined as: $R(s_i, s_j) = r_{ij} = \dfrac{\nu_{ij}}{\nu_i}$ where ν_{ij} is the number of common synonyms between s_i and s_j, and ν_i is the total number of synonyms of s_i, *i.e.* $\nu_i = |L_i|$. The resemblance rate r_{ij} complies with several interesting properties, such as positivity, reflexivity, noncommutativity, existence, existence of a null value, existence of a maximal value (*i.e.* 1).

Thanks to this resemblance rate we propose a tentative quantification of the synonymy between two terms. Of course, the quantification is subjective (because no standard metrics stands) and directly related to the dictionary used. The more the resemblance rate between two terms, the closer the terms. And conversely. r_{ij} permits to propose a **semantic partition** of the linguistic terms. The procedure is the following:

- Let $S = \{s_1, s_2, \ldots, s_i, \ldots, s_n\}$ be a set of n linguistic terms, synonymous amongst themselves;
- For each s_i, we retrieve the list of its m_i synonyms;
- Each r_{ij} is computed between each pair of terms (s_i, s_j) from S;
- The results are stored in a $n \times n$ matrix denoted $M_R(S)$ composed of resemblance rates r_{11} to r_{nn}. Let us recall that M_R has no reason to be a symmetric matrix because r_{ij} is noncommutative.

3.2. *Term position and order*

The resemblance matrix permits to establish a relative positioning of the terms, *i.e.* the resemblance rates are considered as *distances* between terms. However, $M_R(S)$ is not such as to build the partition because we know the distances but not the term *positions*.

---

[a]See this article extracted from a French newspaper: http://rue89.nouvelobs.com/ 2012/10/28/qui-se-cache-derriere-le-dictionnaire-des-synonymes-de-caen-236552

Let us now take the following example (in French). The set S expresses the notion of distance (far, far away, a long way away, distant, remotely, etc.): $S = \{$loin, lointain, éloigné, distant$\}$. We obtain the following resemblance matrix:

$$M_R(S) = \begin{pmatrix} 1 & 0.1 & 0.2 & 0.1 \\ 0.2 & 1 & 0.4 & 0.2 \\ 0.2 & 0.4 & 1 & 0.3 \\ 0.1 & 0.2 & 0.2 & 1 \end{pmatrix}$$

The resulting partition is **not unique** and depends upon the first selected term. Of course, this is an issue that has to be addressed. Thus we are now interested in the **order** of the terms. First, it has to be given by the expert. Second, by looking at elementary mechanics and dynamics, there is an analogy between the placement of the terms on the axis, on the one hand, and the spring-mass systems, on the second hand. Indeed, a spring-mass system is composed of several masses linked together by horizontal springs (see figure 1 [b]). $x_1(t)$ and $x_2(t)$, the positions of the masses at time t, move significantly or not, under forces $F_1(t)$, $F_2(t)$ and $F_3(t)$ applied to the masses and due to the retraction forces of the three springs.

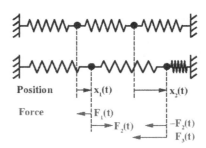

Fig. 1.   Spring-mass system.

By analogy, **terms** would be the **masses**, **semantic relations** between terms would be the **springs** and the **force** of these relations would be the **rigidity** of the springs. Thus, the closer the terms semantically (which corresponds to a high rigidity), the smaller the distance between them. And conversely. Several constraints have to be fullfilled to guarantee a coherent partitioning:

---

[b]source: http://www.iecn.u-nancy.fr

- the order of the terms is maintained;
- the first and the last terms in the subset don't change their positions. This permits to guarantee the minimum and maximum values of the universe. Going back to the spring-mass system analogy, those terms are considered as fixed elements — walls typically;
- the resemblance rate is only computed *between two successive terms*. The order being maintained, computing *all* the resemblance rates becomes useless.

3.3. Use case

To illustrate the computation of the resemblance rates, let us take a simple use case with three consecutive terms in French: $S = \{adjacent, proche, avoisinant\}$. The translation in English would be: $S = \{adjacent, close, neighbouring\}$. Table 1 shows the list of French synonyms that are common to at least two successive terms in S. In English, the table would contain terms like: beside, contiguous, nearby, next, touching, adjoining, etc.

Table 1. A comparative study of the lists of synonyms for three French terms.

adjacent	proche	avoisinant
-	adjacent*	adjacent
avoisinant	avoisinant*	-
attenant	attenant	attenant
-	circonvoisin	circonvoisin
contigu	contigu	contigu
-	environnant	environnant
joignant	joignant	-
limitrophe	limitrophe	limitrophe
prochain	prochain	prochain
proche*	-	proche*
riverain	riverain	riverain
voisin	voisin	voisin

According to the study, there are 8 common synonyms between terms *adjacent* and *proche* and 9 common synonyms between *proche* and *avoisinant*. One particular case has been marked with an asterisk: this case occurs when one of the studied term appears in the list of synonyms of another term and conversely. For instance, the number of synonyms between *adjacent* and *proche* is 8** because *adjacent* appears in the list of *proche* **and** *proche* appears **also** in the list of *adjacent*. The asterisk corresponds to a bonus point, so the total score is 10 in this case. Regarding the pair *proche* and *avoisinant*, the total score is 11 (9**). As we keep the original order of the terms and as *adjacent* and *avoisinant* are considered as the "walls" in the spring-mass system analogy, only the position of *proche* shall change.

We can now consider the three following *semantic pairs*: $(adjacent, \mathsf{v}_1)$, $(proche, \mathsf{v}_2)$ and $(avoisinant, \mathsf{v}_3)$. The total semantic distance is $10+11=21$. So the new position of *proche* is $\mathsf{v}_2 = \frac{8^{**} \times (\mathsf{v}_3 - \mathsf{v}_1)}{8^{**} + 9^{**}} = \frac{10 \ (\mathsf{v}_3 - \mathsf{v}_1)}{21}$.

The computation of all the **positions** v can easily be generalised as

$$\mathsf{v}_i = \frac{r_{(i-1)i} \times (\mathsf{v}_k - \mathsf{v}_1)}{\sum_{j=1}^{k-1} r_{j(j+1)}} \quad \text{where } S = \{s_1, s_2, \ldots, s_k\} \text{ and } i = \{2, 3, \ldots, k-1\}.$$

4. Conclusions

In this paper we have proposed a new partition: a **semantic way** to determine the positions of linguistic terms on the axis. This technique to obtain the partition is useful when the expert cannot define the terms precisely, *i.e.* he can only give a list of ordered terms. In that case, terms are first placed symmetrically on their axis, then the final positions are obtained through the computation of resemblance rates and term positions introduced in this paper. At the end, we obtain a partition that can take into account the real significance of the linguistic terms.

Further works will focus on *semantic modifiers*, *i.e.* on semantic adverbs, intensifiers, adjectives, etc. that should be applied on terms.

References

1. L. A. Zadeh, *Information Control* **8**, 338 (1965).
2. R. E. Bellman and L. A. Zadeh, *Management Science* **17**, 141 (1970).
3. R. R. Yager, *Fuzzy sets and systems* **1**, 87 (1978).
4. L. A. Zadeh, *IEEE Trans. on Fuzzy Systems* **4**, 103 (1996).
5. F. Herrera and L. Martínez, *IEEE Trans. Fuzzy Systems* **8**, 746 (2000).
6. F. Herrera, E. Herrera-Viedma and L. Martínez, A Hierarchical Ordinal Model for Managing Unbalanced Linguistic Term Sets Based on the Linguistic 2-Tuple Model, in *EUROFUSE Workshop on Preference Modelling and Applications*, 2001.
7. F. Herrera, E. Herrera-Viedma and L. Martínez, *Fuzzy Systems, IEEE Transactions on* **16**, 354 (2008).
8. J.-H. Wang and J. Hao, *Fuzzy Systems, IEEE Transactions on* **14**, 435 (2006).
9. M.-A. Abchir, I. Truck and A. Pappa, Dealing with Natural Language Interfaces in a Geolocation Context, in *The 10th International FLINS Conference on Computational Intelligence in Decision and Control*, (Istanbul, 2012).
10. M.-A. Abchir and I. Truck, *Kybernetika* **49**, 164 (2013).

ANALYSING SPANISH DAILY ENERGY DEMAND BY PROGRAMMING A GRAPHICAL IMPLEMENTATION WITH R

JOSE MANUEL VELASCO, BEATRIZ GONZÁLEZ-PÉREZ, GUADALUPE MIÑANA AND VICTORIA LÓPEZ

Complutense University of Madrid, Spain
* E-mail: mvelascc@ucm.es
https://www.ucm.es/english

RAQUEL CARO

Pontificia Comillas Universty of Madrid ICAI, Spain
http://www.upcomillas.es

The Iberian Electricity Market (MIBEL) is organized as a sequence of markets. Hourly marginal prices are obtained at the intersection of supply and demand curves. The price of electricity in the MIBEL is very changeable and the demand is a key variable for forecasting its final value for the 24 hours of the next day. Many different graphical techniques are proposed and implemented with R in order to explore, visualize and understand the behaviour of demand curves in the daily market along the time. This paper provides a graphical analysis by means of an easily reproducible and exportable automatization with R, a free software environment for statistical computing and graphics. Mibel 2011 and 2012 data are used for ilustrations. The results show the importance of the calendar effect, seasonality and trend as principal factors to take into account for posterior fases: modeling and forecasting.

Keywords: Electricity markets, time series analysis, R

1. Introduction

Electricity is the main energy source of society as we know it today and can not be stored. This is the reason why the power consumption must be equal to the amount of energy generated. All sectors depend on it so deeply.

Since 1998, the Spanish and Portuguese Administrations in response to deregulation began to share a common path in building the Iberian Electricity Market (MIBEL),[1] created in 2009. This cooperation has been very successful, not only to Iberian level, but also on a European scale. Other European countries have created similar markets. MIBEL organiza-

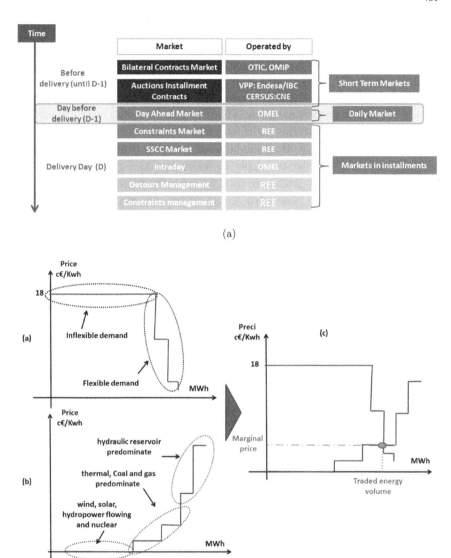

Fig. 1. a) Time Frame for MIBEL Operations. b) Schematic representation of the Hour price setting evaluation in the Mibel's Day-ahead Market

tion is a sequence of markets, see figure 1. In Spain, the daily market covers about 65% of the energy traded, derivatives energy and bi-lateral contracts cover the other 35%. Hourly marginal prices are obtained at the intersection of supply and demand curves, see figure 2. In the MIBEL framework, consumers and traders may negotiate their electricity. This reflects the need to find good models and forecast methods.

The price of electricity in the MIBEL is very changeable. This creates a lot of uncertainty and risk in market actors. Due to continuous changes in demand and marginal price adjustment, buyers and sellers can not know in advance the evolution of prices. This feature led some grand consumers to prefer Derivatives Market or Bilateral contracts to minimize risks and guarantee a stable price. Risk management in electrical prices search for the best contract in order to supply to consumers and guarantee profit to producers. The market prices are used as reference to set Derivatives and Bilateral Contracts. So, generators, grand consumers and electrical traders, always try to find the best solution. Domestic consumers must get there electricity by electrical traders.

Our interest is to study of this uncertainty. The aim of this work is to develop a graphical analysis of the variables involved in the Spanish Energy Market and provide to users, that could be interested in participating in that market, better knowledge of the schedule in order to evaluate, safely, different scenarios that provide information during strategies designing processes (short, mid and long term). Large industrial consumers use this information to design strategies for optimizing its production capacity and improving their production costs. The availability of such tools may extend traders activities and increasing the number of agents that participate in such markets.[5]

The rest of the paper is organized as follows. Section 2 describes a set of variables that are involved in the spanish electric market. Section 3 explains all the R packages that we have used and the results that we have obtained. Conclusions and Future work is summarized in section 4.

2. Day Ahead Market Variables

In this section we define the variables that influence the Daily Market in the value of the marginal price of electricity. This market begins with the information demand forecasting and wind power generation, hourly. These variables have represented as follows: D_i = Power demand in h_i, VH_i = Wind energy generated in h_i, h_i = time of day, $i = 0, \ldots, 23$. On the other hand, we have the outputs of the Daily Market. These are price marginal electricity and the total traded volume of energy and technology per hour (we have not considered all available technologies, only the most important). These variables we have shown the following way: VT_i = Total volume of negotiated energy in h_i, VH_i = Volume of energy hydraulic negotiated in

h_i, VN_i = Volume of energy nuclear negotiated in h_i, VFG_i = Volume of fuel and gas negotiated in h_i, VCI_i = Volume of Charcoal of import negotiated in h_i, VCC_i = Volume of energy of Combined Cycle negotiated in h_i, VRE_i = Volume of energy of special regime negotiated in h_i, PME_i = Marginal Price Electrical in h_i. To analyze the effect calendar in electricity demand, and therefore the price, we defined the following variables: D_i = day of the week, $i = 1, \ldots, 7$, $D_L = \{0, 1\}$(working, nonworking), M_i = months of the year, $i = 1, \ldots, 12$, S $= \{0, 1, 2, 3\}$(Winter, Spring, Summer, Autumn). It has also created a database format. csv with the inputs and outputs of the Daily Market of the years 2011 and 2012 and first quarter of 2013, and note that there is a day with 23 hours and a day with 25 hours.

3. Exploratory Analysis with R

This paper presents an exploratory analysis of the energy demand data for the years 2011 and 2012. These data are published by MIBEL and are available for consumers. The goal is to visually, classify and summarize the information contained in the data file. This study is necessary as a first step before we can model and predict the price time series. A total of around 150 graphs were generated by means of seven scripts implemented with R^2 and subsequently analyzed. Below is a selection of the total presented.

In figure 2a , we show the monthly density and box plots[4] for the monthly distribution of the energy demand. We can note a higher demand for the first two mounths of the year. Furthermore, the boxplots show the hourly distribution have a long low tail. These boxplots also are interesting because we can conclude that we need to study separately the nightly hours from the daily hours. At the same time, figure 2b shows a correlation plot of the price versus the total demand. We can find clear distribution of patterns based on months. For instance, during the summer months, the price dont drop to zero while during winter months, it is a frequent situation.

Figures 3a and 3b are the autocorrelation function and the partial autocorrelation function[6] of the hourly energy demand data during the whole period of the study from zero to forty-eight lag. After these figures we can conclude: there is a strong correlation of each hour with the previous day hour and there are trend and daily seasonality.

4. Conclusions and Future Work

Once data are available to be forecasted, the next step is to select a model for forecasting. The purpose of this work is to show as statistical and graphic

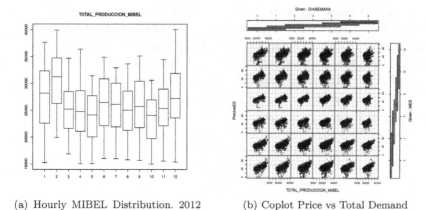

(a) Hourly MIBEL Distribution. 2012 year.

(b) Coplot Price vs Total Demand

Fig. 2.   Hourly Energy demand and CoPlot Graph

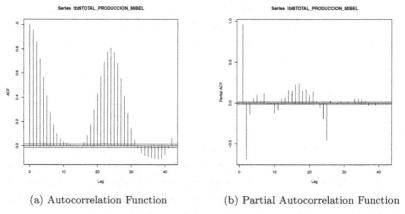

(a) Autocorrelation Function

(b) Partial Autocorrelation Function

Fig. 3.   ACF and PACF Functions

techniques may be useful to the analyst in the selection process. The best place to start with any time series forecasting analysis is to graph sequence plots of the time series to be forecasted. A sequence plot is a graph of the data series values against time. The purpose of the sequence plot is to give the analyst a visual impression of the nature of the time series. This visual impression should suggest to the analyst whether there are certain behavioral components present within the time series.

A study over approximatelly 150 graphics implemented with R is developed. Graphics suggest that the series must be modeled by taking into account stational, trend and cyclical components. Several methods of time series forecasting are available in the literature. A first approximation is a time series forecasting of marginal price by using Holt-Winters[7] exponential smoothing. This method is used to model univariate series when the data shows trend and seasonality. Figures also suggest relationships between the output variable and one or more input variables. For instance, demand or techhological effect over the marginal price and wind generation influence. Furthermore, the series can be partitioned into subsets for studying the calendar effect due to the summer season or winter specifications. The presence/absence of such components can help the analyst in selecting the model with the potential to produce the best forecasts. After selecting a model, the next step is its specification.

Acknowledgment

The authors would like to thank the colaboration, suggenstions and expertise in Spanish Electricity Market of Jesús Gil and Hugo Marrão (Ekergy Software, S.L. Madrid, Spain)

References

1. www.omelholding.es. February 2014.
2. www.r-project.org. February 2014.
3. http://www.seio2013.com. February 2014.
4. W. N. VENABLES AND B. D. RIPLEY, Modern Applied Statistics with S *Springer. ISBN 0-387-95457-0, 2002.*
5. W. REINISCH, T. TEZUKA, Market power and trading strategies on the electricity market: a market design view *IEEE Transactions on Power Systems In Power Systems, IEEE Transactions on, Vol. 21, No. 3. (August 2006), pp. 1180-1190,ISSN :0885-8950*
6. ROBERT H. SHUMWAY, DAVID S. STOFFER, Time Series Analysis and Its Applications With R Examples *ISBN: 978-1-4419-7864-6 (Print) 978-1-4419-7865-3 (Online)*
7. PETER KENNEDY, JAN KMENTA, ZARYLBEK I. KUDABAEV, ET AL. EDITED BY MIODRAG LOVRIC, Exponential and Holt-Winters Smoothing *International Encyclopedia of Statistical Science In International Encyclopedia of Statistical Science (2011), pp. 488-490*
8. AGGARWAL, S. K., SAINI, L. M. y KUMAR, A., Electricity price forecasting in deregulated markets: A review and evaluation, *Electrical Power and Energy Systems*, **31**, pags. 13-22, 2009.

POST-PROCESSING EXPRESSIVE RENDERING EFFECTS FOR VISUAL DEFICIENCY

C. Sauvaget[1] and M. Magdics[2] and R. J. Garcia[2] and M. Sbert[2]

Universitat de Girona, Girona, Spain
[1] *E-mail: catherine.sauvaget@gmail.com*
[2] *E-mail:magdics,rgarcia,mateu@ima.udg.edu*

Visual accessibility appears not to be the essential priority of artists when they produce an artwork. However, they do not choose colors randomly but depending on the message they want to deliver, which can be partially or entirely misunderstood by people with vision problems. This paper proposes to study the possibility of using expressive post-processing effects which can be applied on any kind of 2D image sequence and which allow to improve image perception for many kinds of visual impairments.

Keywords: Expressive Rendering; Accessibility; Visual Impairment.

1. Introduction

Images surround us. Their goal is to transmit information which can be emotional or informational. Realistic images often contain too many details disrupting the message to be delivered. Thus, artists often simplify images highlighting information using stylization. In computer graphics it is called expressive rendering or NPR (Non-Photorealistic Rendering).

The relation linking the 3D scene and the dual nature of 2D picture (both flat and representing 3D objects) is intricate due to the complexity of the human visual system.[1] Thus, our idea consists in optimizing the image for the viewer's needs. This is the reason why games, software interfaces and even TV broadcast should allow users to attempt different stylizations and adjust their preferences to satisfy their requirements. Nowadays, most game engines support post-processing effects, turning screen space methods into a cheap and powerful tool for stylization of games, but despite the great diversity of effects developed by researchers, game engines contain almost no screen space NPR effects. NPR is also used in video-games to help the user to perceive interesting objects or danger. Such effects can serve other purposes than entertainment like alleviating visual impairments and our understanding of human perception may help in achieving this goal.

This work addresses the topic of seamless integration of styles using expressive post-processing methods to help people with visual impairment by gathering a collection of screen space stylization methods and applying it to any kind of video or image stream. Our effects have been applied to existing video-games created with a well-known game engine, Unity.[2] Using post-processing effects implies that their inclusion into an existing game requires negligible effort.

2. Visual impairement

This section presents visual impairments that can be alleviated using NPR.

2.1. *Color vision deficiency*

This problem is an inability or a decreased ability to see certain colors or to perceive color differences, leading to different perceptions.

- Monochromacy: people see in grey level due to a lack of cones.
- Dichromacy: color vision defect where one of the 3 colors (RGB) detected by the 3 types of cones does not function properly or not at all. People without red retinal photoreceptors are called protanopes. Deuteranopes do not have green retinal photoreceptors. Tritanopes are rare, they do not pocess blue retinal receptors.

2.2. *Amblyopia*

The stereoscopic vision is the perception of the same image by two different sensors: our eyes. These images are perceived from a slightly different angle allowing our brain to reconstruct a complex information: depth perception.

People born with Amblyopia use other visual benchmarks to estimate distances, such as object position at different depths. Distances are better apprehended when the object is moving: filling a glass can be tricky.

2.3. *Photophobia*

The human visual perception system functions well in a high dynamic range of light conditions, from moonlight to the brightest sunshine. However, people suffering from photophobia are intolerant to ordinary bright light.

Glare can affect our ability to see clearly. It may occur when a light source is too strong for our eyes like when coming from dark we enter a bright room. Glare resulting from extreme bright light can also reduce our visual performance. Caused by eye diseases, it may occur at an ordinary light intensity level as well. With age, some eye problems may happen and the eye structure becomes less clear. The most common example is a cataract: the light is scattered making things unclear and blurred. Its thickness impacts on the blur importance. Other kinds of glare causes also exist (macular degeneration (AMD), uveitis, ocular albinism or corneal problems). The most obvious way to cope with glare is to limit the amount of light entering the eye. Tinted and polarized lenses help to minimise it. Light activated sunglasses which get darker in brighter conditions are also a solution. How to minimize visual impairment with NPR? We propose to study briefly how artists use perception.

3. How art uses perception

Artists use stylization to highlight information they want to deliver. They do not choose the style randomly but they use the human perception and a specific stylization to convey the desired message.[3] Nowadays, artistic effects are widely used in movies and video games but are not used to help people with visual impairments. Hereafter, we present the three principal characteristics we perceive and what type of information they convey.

Contours are abrupt changes of light intensity level and are the base of our visual perception.[4–6] When contours are not drawn, our visual system tends to imagine them to dissociate the different objects observed. Contours serve two main goals: they are, by themselves capable of depicting abstracted objects that our brain can recognize and they aid our perception process by enhancing details (e.g. silhouettes or texture lines) on images with great diversity in color and texture. Additionally, artists use the decreasing thickness of contours at the background to emphasize depth.

Light is often used by artists to create the illusion of depth. Following specific stylizations, it may be a great help in understanding scene geometry and produce different depth sensations.[7]

Colors also permit to create depth. Artists use the detail level and the desaturation of colors to depict depth.

4. Implementation framework

Our effects are created as post-processing running on the graphic hardware and in image space, in order to provide easy portability and fast applicability to different graphic engines and architectures. We have integrated them into the Unity game engine.[8] In previous work, we showed that such effects are capable of real-time performance and thus we can process the rendered image stream on-the-fly; details are given in.[9] The effects have been packed into a coherent library (a.k.a. *unitypackage*), which can be imported into other Unity projects.

5. NPR effects for visual impairment

We propose a set of screen space methods to modify the style of the rendered image stream which implies real-time rates and temporal coherence.

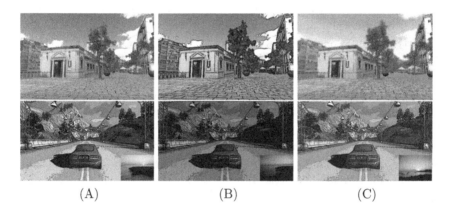

(A)   (B)   (C)

Fig. 1.   Example effects. Upper row: (A) Original image with photo-realistic rendering, (B) Edge enhancement, (C) Depth illusion using desaturation and image simplification based on depth. Lower row: color stylization by example in the Unity Car Tutorial.

5.1. *Edge enhancement*

In order to better distinguish different objects in images and to locate them in the scene, we propose to use edge enhancement.

There are two main approaches for edge extraction. The first class of methods tries to mimic artists: lines follow object silhouettes. The second follows a perceptual viewpoint: the sensitivity of our eyes to abrupt changes in light intensity, utilizing classic edge detection methods of image processing that search for pixels of high gradient magnitude. The former approach depicts shapes better but forfeits texture information while standard edge detection methods provide a less clean representation of shape contours, but preserve texture details. Their combination preserves only the benefits.[10] It can help Amblyopia and color deficiency that may lead to merge different objects.

Among the edge detection methods, variations of the *Difference of Gaussian* filter, which has a biological relevance by providing a model to the activation mechanism to certain retinal cells,[11] allow to control edge thickness. We adopted the separable, flow-based implementation proposed by Kyprianidis et al.[12] and the extension proposed by Winnemöller.[13]

As artists do, we can decrease thickness following depth, also helping to locate an object in the scene for Amblyopia.

5.2. Abstraction level following depth

We reduce the scene complexity using depth by changing the main components of a style: color and texture.

Artists often use less saturated colors to distract viewer's attention from less important parts of images.[14] Saturation can be modified by converting the pixel color into HSL or HSV. Fragments farther or closer from the focus point (alterable in our implementation) are desaturated, based on a linear distance from this point. We use an exponential correction with user specified exponent to control how fast saturation changes with depth.

Background is often smoothed in artistic depictions due to lower importance of background objects. Depth-based parametrization of texture simplification filters[15,16] can produce higher abstraction level for the background objects.

5.3. Color palette modification by example

This technique may be used for daltonism using images with adapted colors depending on the color vision deficiency.

Automatic *color style transfer* methods allow to specify example images for color palette adjustment to obtain a similar color histogram. The average and variance of the color input distribution are adapted to the image. Different color spaces[17,18] may be used to compute average and variance to get slightly different results. Pyramid reduction techniques are commonly used for computing the average and variance in parallel.[19]

6. Conclusion

We have proposed NPR effects that can be used to help people with visual impairment. Using vision and perception knowledge permits to understand how we can help people. Visual impairments and NPR techniques have been linked. Results show that NPR has a visual impact on the targeted visual problems. In future work, we plan to adapt more NPR techniques and to present a user study for each technique and impairment.

References

1. F. Durand, An invitation to discuss computer depiction, in *Proceedings of the 2nd international symposium on Non-photorealistic animation and rendering*, NPAR '02 (ACM, New York, NY, USA, 2002).
2. Unity Demo Projects, Unity (2013), http://unity3d.com/learn.
3. S. McCloud, *Understanding Comics the invisible art* (Harper Paperbacks, 1994).
4. D. Marr and E. Hildreth, *Proceedings of the Royal Society of London Series B* **207**, 187 (1980).
5. J. Koenderink, *Perception* **13**, 321 (1984).
6. S. E. Palmer, *Vision science: photons to phenomenology* (MIT Press, Cambridge, Mass., 1999).
7. G. Roig, *Peindre la lumière*, oskar éditions edn. (Guides Oskar, 2010).
8. U. Technologies, Unity (2013), http://unity3d.com.
9. M. Magdics, C. Sauvaget, R. Garcia and M. Sbert, Post-processing NPR effects for video games, in *12th ACM International Conference on Virtual Reality Continuum and Its Applications in Industry: VRCAI 2013*, 2013.
10. N. Redmond and J. Dingliana, A hybrid approach to real-time abstraction, in *Proceedings of Eurographics Ireland, 2009*, 2009.
11. R. A. Young, *Spatial Vision* , 273 (1987).
12. J. E. Kyprianidis and J. Döllner, Image abstraction by structure adaptive filtering, in *Proc. EG UK Theory and Practice of Computer Graphics*, 2008.
13. H. Winnemöller, Xdog: advanced image stylization with extended difference-of-gaussians., in *NPAR*, eds. J. P. Collomosse, P. Asente and S. N. Spencer (ACM, 2011).
14. N. Redmond and J. Dingliana, Influencing user attention using real-time stylised rendering, in *EG UK Theory and Practice of Computer Graphics, Cardiff University,, United Kingdom, 2009. Proceedings*, eds. W. Tang and J. P. Collomosse (Eurographics Association, 2009).
15. H. Winnemöller, S. C. Olsen and B. Gooch, *ACM Trans. Graph.* **25**, 1221(jul 2006).
16. C. Tomasi and R. Manduchi, Bilateral filtering for gray and color images, in *Proceedings of the Sixth International Conference on Computer Vision*, ICCV '98 (IEEE Computer Society, Washington, DC, USA, 1998).
17. E. Reinhard, M. Ashikhmin, B. Gooch and P. Shirley, *IEEE Comput. Graph. Appl.* **21**, 34(sep 2001).
18. H. Zhao, X. Jin, J. Shen and F. Wei, Real-time photo style transfer, in *CAD/Graphics*, 2009.
19. L. Szirmay-Kalos, L. Szécsi and M. Sbert, *GPU-Based Techniques for Global Illumination Effects*Synthesis Lectures on Computer Graphics and Animation, Synthesis Lectures on Computer Graphics and Animation (Morgan & Claypool Publishers, 2008).

TOWARD A POLISH INTELLIGENT VIRTUAL TUTOR: AN OVERVIEW OF EXISTING WORK

I. TRUCK*

CHArt – EA4004, University Paris 8,
2 rue de la Liberté,
Saint-Denis, 93526, France
* E-mail: isis.truck@univ-paris8.fr

M. DURAND and M. WATOREK

UMR 7023 — Structures Formelles du Langage
59/61 rue Pouchet,
Paris, 75017, France

In this paper, we lay the groundwork for future research about a Polish intelligent tutor that would be able to teach learners for only a 14-hour-lesson, giving them the A1 level of the Common European Framework of Reference. The design and the implementation of the future software will be guided by linguists and psycholinguists.

Keywords: Intelligent Tutoring Systems; Polish language; learner model; machine learning; human-machine interface.

1. Introduction

The problem of learning new languages as a foreign language has received much attention for decades. An old dream is to be able to conceive a generic method that would permit people to learn a foreign language (at least the basics of hearing and speaking language) in only a few hours. Moreover this method would be available anywhere, anytime and for everybody, *i.e.* it should be cheap and online (no need to have a real teacher in front of you).

Thus several solutions have been proposed either through books, interactive language learning software, and also on-line courses (*e.g.* Assimil, babbel.com, BYKI (Before You Know It), e-Polish, EuroTalk, Pimsleur, Pronunciator.com, Reise Know-How, Rosetta Stone, etc.). All these methods can help but they are essentially deductive logic, they do not really focus on language theory or anything that leads to a person being able to compose his own dialogue in just hours. That is why, from a psycholinguistic point of view, they are not satisfactory. In fact, despite decades of research, very little is known about the first acquisition stages when people learn a second language, which is nonetheless crucial to the implementation of a language self-study program.

In this paper, we are interested in giving thought about a program to learn Polish as a second language, taking into account the acquisitional progress (stages of acquisition) of the learner, the language representations, the learning and teaching strategies, and being able to give him a satisfactory level in a short period of time. Section 2 reviews some related works and, in particular, VILLA project that we are relying upon. Then we introduce in Section 3 the ITS (Intelligent Tutoring Systems) that provide immediate and customized feedback to learners, especially those with tutorial dialogue in natural language. Starting from an ITS and the VILLA project, we explain our seven-step-work plan in Section 4 as a basis to begin the modelling and then the implementation of the software. We conclude with a few observations in Section 5.

2. The VILLA project

Research on language acquisition usually tries to focus on three main objectives: observing the acquisitional progress from a zero level of knowledge to understand which stages are the first in language acquisition;[1] studying the processing (by the learner) of the input (*i.e.* what is given to the learner) in several domains such as perception, understanding, grammatical analysis and production, because the input influences a lot the way the learner makes the language his own;[2] studying the role played by previous knowledge in the way the input is processed by the learner because the mother tongue as well as language-specific and communication-specific universal principles play a great role.[3,4]

That way a project named VILLA (*Varieties of Initial Learners in Language Acquisition*) has been proposed recently (2011–2014) and has made a significant contribution[5] to the following issues:

- To know the skills of the learners regarding perception, understanding and production in a new foreign language after a 14-hour-lesson (14 hours was the — rather short — length chosen for the experiments);
- To know the role played by the learner mother tongue as well as by other foreign languages learnt before. To know the role played by extra-linguistic knowledge;

- To know the role played by the input, for instance the frequency of the items from the input, as well as the lexical transparency[a] of them. To know the role played by the metacommunication or the paralinguistic signs, such as gestures, context, etc.;
- To know how the learners' skills evolve during the lessons (and more generally during the 14-hour-lesson), in particular to understand if the focus on the semantic considerations evolves compared to the focus on the structural considerations;
- To understand the impact of the way to explain the foreign language (lessons focusing on *meaning* vs. lessons focusing on *form*).

More precisely, during the VILLA project, learners were given a Polish induction course (a 14-hour course) given by a native speaker. The methodology used is mainly based on a communicative approach: the linguistic contents are introduced depending on different communication situations. However, some principles are not related to the framework of the so-called communicative approach. For instance, the input is only monolingual and the teacher **doesn't use the learners' mother tongue at all**. Practically speaking, a large experiment has been performed in five countries (Germany, Great Britain, Italy, the Netherlands and France): two distincts groups (from 14 to 20 learners in each one) with the same profile (same age, same education level, same kind of studies, etc.) have received a certain course. Indeed, there were two kinds of courses, depending on the amount of metalinguistic explanations given for each lesson. One kind was a meaning-based course and the other one was a form-based course, knowing that the content has been the same.

Our idea is to use this work to propose a software that would implement these kinds of courses, without the need of a real teacher. To do so, in order to keep the oral and the interaction, it is necessary to use first an avatar with a voice system. These kinds of "talking heads" are called *Intelligent Tutoring Systems*.

3. Intelligent Tutoring Systems

The Intelligent Tutoring Systems (ITS) are systems that aim at understanding automatically and dynamically the learner's speech in natural language, in order to propose a learning by dialoguing.[6] Several ITS exist in

---

[a]The lexical transparency corresponds to properties a word from a given language must fulfill in order to be considered as potentially understandable to a non-native speaker

the literature[7] but all of them have the following properties: Virtual tutor: 3D avatar and speech synthesis; Documents showing; Interactive learning (question/answer); Dialogue planning; Expert model; Natural Language Processing: speech act classifier and morphosyntaxic analysis; Latent Semantic Analysis.

One of them is more interesting for us: GnuTutor[8] an open-source C# version of AutoTutor[9] ITS that teaches people by having a conversation with them. AutoTutor is proposed without knowledge but its domains can be developed very quickly. Four separate modules are needed: the tagger (morphosyntactic analysis), the speech act classifier (to retrieve the learner's intentions), the dialogue planning and the corpus in the foreign language.

A session is held in seven steps: (i) a short presentation of the lesson; (ii) a general question; (iii) a first answer; (iv) feedback and healing; (v) other answers — go to (iv) if necessary; (vi) dropout or completion; (vii) evaluate the comprehensive understanding of the learner counting the loops (iv) and (v) — go to (i) if necessary.

Figure 1 shows a screenshot of GnuTutor. Left, a customisable talking head with gestures and synthesized speech is interacting with the learner. Below is the text area with the written dialogue (it permits to obtain the dialogue history) and right are the areas with the log files (cosine computations between given and expected answers, etc.).

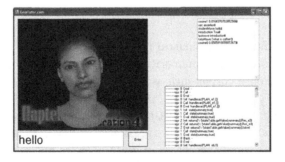

Fig. 1.   GnuTutor by Graesser *et al.*: An open-source intelligent tutoring system.

GnuTutor is based on rhetorical structure theory that permits the machine to interpret the intention of the learner. It consists of a dialogue system planning implemented in Prolog for the tutor's movements, a rule-based tagging, an expert model to compare given and expected answers by latent semantic analysis, and an interface with a talking head (speech synthesis) with writing tools.

Let us now explain our work plan to conceive and model our software.

4. Work plan

First of all, the teaching method we want to implement is both oral and written. The learning is determined by the immersion in the language, the repetition and the interaction between, on the one hand, the teacher and the learner and between two learners, on the other hand. This first learning step should permit the learner to segment language, to infer the basics regarding tagging in Polish (grammatical gender and logical construction on the phrases), to have a basic vocabulary and to be able to construct a discourse. Secondly, it is necessary to use solutions such as ITS because they offer an animated agent for educational purpose with a vocal avatar. Besides, the specifications of the software we want to implement are the following: (i) Monolingual (only Polish); (ii) Communicative approach; (iii) Teacher-learner **and** learner-learner interactions; (iv) Control of the inputs; (v) Meaning-based vs. Form-based courses; (vi) Interactive dialogue; (vii) Immediate feedback; (viii) No explicit correction of errors.

Starting from a version of the GnuTutor, we now propose the following work plan:

- Add a Polish speech synthesis;
- Add a virtual actor: a virtual learner for the learner-learner interaction;
- Add a **fuzzy comparison module for the audio signal** to take into account the pronunciation of the learners;
- Use a Polish corpus such as IPI Pan[b] for the latent semantic analysis;
- Dialogue planning: add a scheme of what is asked and what is expected by the learner (the Polish lessons). Depending on the (fuzzy) resemblance between given answers and the implemented expert system, provide feedbacks and healings for the learner in order to reach the completion of the lesson;
- Improvement of the speech act classifier in order to take into account the Polish;
- Improve the tagger used which is the Brill tagger[10] because for Polish, its performance is only 89.2% compared to 95.5% obtained for

---

[b]http://korpus.pl/index.php?lang=en

English.[11] There are several potential solutions, such as multi-pass tagging, generalized transformation templates, lexical transformation templates, and even fuzzy tagging that should be investigated.

5. Conclusions

In this paper we have reviewed several existing works for a starting project: propose a software to permit learners reach the A1 level of the Common European Framework of Reference for Languages in Polish in only a 14 hour lesson. We showed that the Intelligent Tutoring Systems are the most adapted for our needs: in particular GnuTutor is an open source ITS that proposes a 3D talking head that can be customized quite easily. We defined a seven-step work plan to improve GnuTutor in order to obtain a smart virtual Polish tutor. Future works are the implementation of it.

References

1. R. Rast, *Foreign language input: Initial processing* (Multilingual Matters, 2008).
2. M. Tomasello, *Constructing a language: A usage-based theory of language acquisition* (Harvard University Press, 2003).
3. J. Giacobbe, *Acquisition d'une langue étrangère: Cognition et interaction: études sur le développement du langage chez l'adulte* (Éd. du Centre National de la Recherche Scientifique, 1992).
4. W. Klein, *Trends in Linguistic Studies and Monographs* **133**, 81 (2001).
5. R. Rast, C. Dimroth and M. Watorek, *Discours, acquisition et didactique des langues, les termes d'un dialogue* **Collection Universités, série Sciences du Langage**, 71 (2011).
6. D. Sleeman and J. S. Brown, *Intelligent Tutoring Systems* (London: Academic Press, 1982).
7. P. Brusilovsky, E. Schwarz and G. Weber, Elm-art: An intelligent tutoring system on world wide web, in *Intelligent Tutoring Systems*, eds. C. Frasson, G. Gauthier and A. Lesgold, Lecture Notes in Computer Science, Vol. 1086 (Springer Berlin Heidelberg, 1996) pp. 261–269.
8. A. M. Olney, Gnututor: An open source intelligent tutoring system based on autotutor., in *AAAI Fall Symposium: Cognitive and Metacognitive Educational Systems*, (AAAI, 2009).
9. A. C. Graesser, P. Chipman, B. C. Haynes and A. Olney, *IEEE Trans. Education* **48**, 612 (2005).
10. E. Brill, A simple rule-based part of speech tagger, in *ANLP*, (ANLP, 1992).
11. S. Acedanski and K. Goluchowski, A Morphosyntactic Rule-Based Brill Tagger for Polish, in *Recent Advances in Intelligent Information Systems*, (Academic Publishing House EXIT, Kraków, Poland, June 2009).

PROPOSAL FOR A SEMANTIC ANNOTATION OF GRAPHICAL DOCUMENTS

I. TRUCK* and D. ARCHAMBAULT

CHArt – EA4004, University Paris 8,
2 rue de la Liberté,
Saint-Denis, 93526, France
* E-mail: isis.truck@univ-paris8.fr

L. LEGER and F. FENOUILLET

CHArt – EA4004, University Paris Ouest,
200 Avenue de la République
Nanterre, 92000, France

M. MURATET and C. MOREAU and G. GABRIEL and A. TROMEUR

Grhapes – EA7287, INS HEA
60 Avenue des Landes
Suresnes, 92150, France

This paper aims at giving thoughts about a proposal of a smart annotation regarding graphical documents. This research is dedicated to people with special needs, especially to blind or visually-impaired people. The idea is to propose a software that can annotate graphs with semantic descriptors (*i.e.* sentences) automatically.

Keywords: semantic annotation; blind people; graphical documents; accessibility.

1. Introduction

The Digital Revolution has been changing our habits for decades and is not only changing the research in computer science but also mathematics, psychology, sociology, etc. What is called the "big data" is forcing us to imagine new ways of storing and processing these massive digital informations, to extract relevant features among them, to generate statistical and summary reports, etc.

Thus, among all these generated reports are a lot of graphical displays such as statistical charts or diagrams, bar charts, etc. to indicate a trend, alert opinion to situations, provide relevant indicators, or simply to provide reporting. With the speed with which these graphical documents are produced, we are more or more swamped beneath those graphical reports, which are usually computer-generated and thus, they are often not explained nor annotated (manually or automatically). That is why a new problem araises for blind or visually-impaired people: how to read and interpret those reports if no textual annotation is available and if the only available information is "hidden" in the graph itself?

We all know that accessibility to documents is still unresolved because many documents have to be interpreted by assistants or specialists to be understandable by blind people. This paper is thus a proposal for contributing to this issue. First, we describe the project partners that are computer scientists, psychologists and disability experts. Section 3 goes deeper in details and explains the work plan while Section 4 concludes this study.

2. Project partners

To carry out such a project, several partners are needed: (i) computer scientists with a great expertise in image processing, in natural language processing and in imprecise knowledge for the semantic annotation in natural language; (ii) psychologists with a great expertise in visual perception, from visual informations to impression formation to be able to construct the meaning of the image and to formalize the content; (iii) experts in visual impairment in order to propose a well perceived annotation with the right number of details, for example.

The partners are the following. First, CHArt laboratory from Paris 8 University includes experts in disability and particularly in helping people to become self-reliant. The project should be based on an ongoing work that recognizes automatically the captions, the shaded areas, etc. in the graphical documents, including maps, in order to generate tactile graphs easily printable with specialty printers. For example, Figure 1 shows, left, a pie chart explaining the different types of reaction people usually have when they find a coin on the pavement: either they try to pick up the coin, or they try to kick it, or they have a look on it without taking it, or they put their foot on it to pick it up. Right of the figure is the same pie chart translated in Braille automatically, ready to be relief printed. This work[1] will be a starting-point to analyse semantically and linguistically the graphs.

Moreover, CHArt – Paris 8 has also a great expertise in natural language processing and representation of approximate data[2,3] that will be essential to express linguistically the descriptions, commentaries or annotations of the graphs.

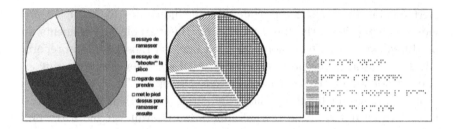

Fig. 1. Left, a simple pie chart (in French), right, the same chart in Braille.

The second partner is CHArt laboratory from Paris Ouest University that includes experts in eye tracking methods. One of the topics developed by this team is about the intensity of attention paid by humans when they are looking at a scene (a text, a picture, a Web site, whatever).[4] In our project, the aim is to track the eye movements on the image (the screen) to be able to **guide** the textual and semantic description. Indeed, even if the perception for blind people issue is a topic on its own, in our case, it seems relevant to be guided by the perception of sighted people to explain the blind people what is to be seen in the graphical document. Starting from the analysis of the eye movements, it is possible to identify the most interesting zones as well as their visualisation **order** and so, to know what parts of the graph may give some sense to the image, even if they are not put into words explicitly by the observers.[5]

The last partner is the French national institute for research on the education of disabled children and adapted teaching (INS HEA). INS HEA will permit to conduct experiments with disabled people. Since many years, the INS HEA does research on suited documents for visual impaired[6,7] and in particular on the adaptation of geographic maps in relief based on the simplification on contour lines, shapes and colors, a wisely choice of the title position. We will use this well-known expertise in the maps for our project, since maps are a kind a graphical document.

3. Toward a semantic annotation of graphical documents

3.1. *Example of a smart automatic annotation*

To illustrate our proposal, we now take an example with Figure 2 which shows an example of a pie chart explaining some predictions about the fields where future jobs will take place.

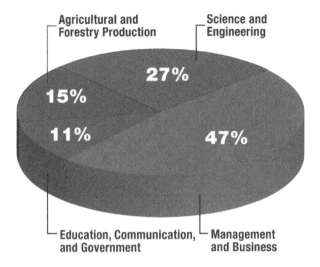

Fig. 2. A 2010 study showing the fields of predictive job opportunities for 2010–2015.

The annotation in this case would be something like: "**according to the USDA study in 2010, almost half the jobs will be in Management and Business; one third, more or less, will be in Science and Engineering and the rest in Agriculture, Education or other fields**". In this example, we can see that the linguistic summary takes into account the quantity of percentage points, as well as the meaning of the information contained (*e.g.* agriculture).

3.2. *Work plan*

The planned schedule is the following: we plan a 24-month-project in five lots and seven work packages (WP), see Figure 3. Some WP will be done in parallel to save time.

- Lot #1 (6 months): WP1 (Document): State of the art about automatic extraction of captions and graphical zones in images (diagrams, statistical charts, etc.) and state of the art on eye-tracking when people look at this kind of graphical documents, and choice of a dataset to work with (a dataset of all kinds of graphs we want to address);
- Lot #2 (4 months): WP2 (Software): Development of textual descriptors (XML files) to detail the contents of the images, start-

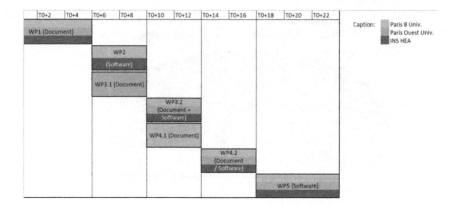

Fig. 3.   The planned schedule for our project.

ing from the existing works (pattern recognition, optical character recognition, etc.). Advice and expertise provided by INS HEA;

- Lot #3 (8 months) : WP3.1 (Document): Eye-tracking and experiments on a series of test images from the dataset (cf. WP1); WP3.2 (Document + Software): Development of *declarations* (descriptors or declarative files) in XML of all the typical eye movements in the images. Advice and expertise provided by INS HEA;
- Lot #4 (8 months) : WP4.1 (Document): Transform the descriptors from WP2 into sentences (or pseudo-sentences), *i.e.* represent the approximations, the semantics, establish summaries, etc. (Natural language processing using abstract grammars, Tree Adjoining Grammars, etc.); WP4.2 (Document/Software): First version of the software using WP3.2 as a guidance through the XML files for the description of the image. First experiments with blind people.
- Lot #5 (6 months): WP5 (Software): Final version and experiments. The software will take as input a graphical document and will give as output a semantic and linguistic description of the graph. The output will be an XML file in addition to a display output (for the control). The XML output file will be readable by a screen reader directly.

4. Conclusions

In this paper we have presented a new research that we are beginning about a semantic annotation system for graphical documents to improve the accessibility of visual-impaired people. The team is composed of three laboratories and the work is divided into 5 lots and 7 work packages. Future work is to implement the whole annotation system.

References

1. Y. Chen and J. Lopez-Krahe, Shape Recognition, Image Analysis and Artificial Vision for Blind People Using Mainstream Devices, in *The 5th International Congress on Design, Research Networks and Technology for all*, (Madrid, 2013).
2. M.-A. Abchir, I. Truck and A. Pappa, Fuzzy semantics in closed domain question answering, in *Decision Aid Models for Disaster Management and Emergencies*, eds. B. Vitoriano, J. Montero and D. Ruan, Atlantis Computational Intelligence Systems, Vol. 7 (Atlantis Press/Springer, 2013) pp. 171–188.
3. I. Truck and M.-A. Abchir, *International Journal of Intelligent Systems (Special Issue)* **to appear** (2014), Wiley.
4. L. Léger and E. Chauvet, Quand Canari amorce Jaune: effet sur l'orientation attentionnelle, in *The 55th Congress of the Société Française de Psychologie*, (Lyon, 2013).
5. J.-M. Henderson, *TRENDS in Cognitive Sciences* **7**, 498 (2003).
6. M. Lesage and A. Tromeur, *La nouvelle revue de l'adaptation et de la scolarisation - Scolariser les élèves déficients visuels aujourd'hui* (2006).
7. M. Bris and G. Gabriel, Lecture du dessin en relief, conception du Tact 2 Voice, in *Journée d'études du Groupement des Intellectuels Aveugles et Amblyopes*, (Paris, 2013).

PART 5

INTELLIGENT SYSTEMS AND KNOWLEDGE ENGINEERING

CORRELATION ANALYSIS OF PERFORMANCE METRICS FOR CLASSIFIER

Yangming Zhou

Ningbo Institute of Technology, Zhejiang University,
Ningbo, Zhejiang Province 315100, China
Department of Control Science and Engineering, Zhejiang University
Hangzhou, Zhejiang Province 310027, China
E-mail: ym_zhou@zju.edu.cn

Yangguang Liu*

Ningbo Institute of Technology, Zhejiang University,
Ningbo, Zhejiang Province 315100, China
* E-mail: ygliu@acm.org

The correct selection of performance metrics is one of the most key issues in evaluating classifier's performance. Although many performance metrics have been proposed and used in machine learning community, there is not any common conclusions among practitioners regarding which metric to choose for evaluating a classifier's performance. In this paper, we attempt to investigate the potential relationship among some common used performance metrics. Based on definitions, We first classify seven most widely performance metrics into three groups, namely threshold metrics, rank metrics, and probability metrics. Then, we focus on using Pearson linear correlation and Spearman rank correlation to investigate the relationship among these metrics. Experimental results show the reasonableness of classifying seven common used metrics into three groups. This can be useful for helping practitioners enhance understanding about the different relationships and groupings among the performance metrics.

Keywords: Classification; Performance metrics; Correlation analysis.

1. Introduction

One of the key issues in evaluating and selecting classifier is to choose several suitable metrics to measure the classifier performance. A number of performance metrics have been proposed for this purpose in different application scenarios. For example, accuracy is typically used to measure the percentage of correctly classified test instance. It is so far the primary metric for assessing classifier performance;[1,2] precision and recall metrics are widely applied in information retrieval;[3] medical decision making community prefers the area under the receiver operating characteristic (ROC) curves (i.e., AUC).[4] It is not a uncommon situation, where a classifier performs well on one performance metric but badly on others. For example, boosted trees and SVM classifiers achieve good performance on classification accuracy, while they obtain poor performance on root mean square error.[5]

Generally, a common practice is to choose performance metrics depending on the practical requirements of specific applications. For example, neural network typically optimise squared error, thus the metric of root mean square error can better reflect the actual performance of a classifier than other metrics. However, in some case specific criteria are unknown in advance, practitioners tend to select several measures from widely adopted ones, such as classification accuracy, kappa statistic, F-measure and AUC, for evaluating a new classifier.[6] Additionally, most metrics are derived by calculating the confusion matrix of the classifier. It could be very reasonable to think that some of such performance metrics are closely related, which may cause redundancy on measuring the performance of classifiers. On the other hand, it is difficult for practitioners to derive exact conclusion when two metrics provide conflicting results.

There are some previous studies that compare and analyse the relationship between the metrics. Caruana et al. analyse the behaviour of the multiple metrics against multiple supervised learning algorithms and the relationship between metrics by using multi-dimensional scaling and correlation.[5] Seliya et al. apply factors analysis to investigate the relationships among classifiers'performance space which is characterized by 22 metrics.[7] Ferri et al. explore the relationships among 18 different performance metrics in multiple different scenarios, identifying clusters and relationships between metrics.[8] However, the result of clustering among the performance metrics is not obvious. In addition, some commonly-used performance metrics are not included, such as the area under the precision and recall curve.

This study focuses on using Pearson linear correlation and Spearman rank correlation to investigate the relationships among some special popular performance metrics. By the definitions and the experiments, a clear taxonomy of these metrics has been given, namely threshold metrics, rank metrics, and probability metrics. Then, we use correlation analysis to measure the correlations of these metrics. Experimental results confirm that metrics inside the same group have high correlation, and metrics from different groups have low correlation. This may provide practitioners with a more profound understanding of the performance metrics.

2. Performance Metrics

In this section, we describe seven common performance metrics in data analytic domains. Based on the definitions of evaluation metrics, we preliminarily divide these seven metrics into three groups:

Threshold metrics, which are sensitive to thresholds, including accuracy, F-measure and kappa statistic. These metrics do not care about how close the prediction value to true value is, but only care about whether the predicted value is above or below a threshold value.

Rank metrics, which measure how well a model ranks the positive instances above the negative instances. This category metric mainly include the area under ROC curves (i.e., AUC) and PR curves (i.e., AUPRC). AUC and AUPRC have been widely used in information retrieval. These metrics can be viewed as a summary of the performance of a model across all possible thresholds.

Probability metrics, which measure the deviation between the predicted value and the truth value. Such metrics we study here are mean absolute error and root mean squared error, which neither directly compare the results with a threshold value, nor directly compare the instances' order with one another. These metrics are widely used in regression problems, especially for assessing the reliability of the classifiers.

3. Experimental Settings

In this section, we briefly introduce the algorithms, data sets, as well as the specific experimental procedures, respectively. The experiments run on Weka 3.7.6 [a]. Eight well-known classification models are used, including Artificial Neural Network, C4.5 (J48), k-Nearest Neighbours (kNN), Logistic Regression, Naive Bayes, Random Forest, Bagging with 25 J48 trees, AdaBoost with 25 J48 trees. Referring to,[9] we can see more details about these classifiers and their WEKA implementations. We use 18 binary data sets from Weka website, as shown in Table 1.

In the experiments, all the results are derived by stratified 10 fold cross-validations, and the default parameters are used. Two common correlation analysis methods, i.e.,Pearson linear correlation[10]and Spearman rank correlation,[11] are used in the experiments. To facilitate the calculations, we work with 1-RMSE and 1-MAE.

---

[a]http://www.cs.waikato.ac.nz/ml/weka/index.html

Table 1. Data sets and their properties

data set	#instance	#features	% min - % max
Colic	368	22	36.96-63.04
Credit-rating	690	15	44.50-55.50
Heart-disease	303	13	45.54-54.46
Heart-statlog	270	13	44.45-55.55
Hepatitis	155	19	20.65-79.35
House-voting	435	16	38.62-61.38
Ionosphere	351	34	35.90-64.10
Kr-vs-kp	3196	36	47.78-52.22
Monks1	556	6	50.00-50.00
Monks2	601	6	24.28-75.72
Monks3	554	6	48.01-51.99
Mushroom	8124	22	48.20-51.80
Optdigits	5620	64	49.79-50.21
Sick	3772	29	6.12-93.87
Sonar	208	60	46.63-53.37
Spambase	4601	57	39.40-60.60
Spectf	80	44	50.00-50.00
Tic-tac-toe	958	8	34.66-65.34

4. Results

In this section, we present some interesting findings from the analysis of Pearson linear correlation and Spearman rank correlation between metrics.

Firstly, Table 2 shows the correlation matrix for House-voting problem, in which the results are obtained based on kNN classification algorithm. From the table, we have the following observations:(1) For Spearman rank correlation, the correlation of any two metrics from the same group is very big, i.e., 0.82 for probability metrics, 0.92 for rank metrics, and 0.92 to 1.0 for threshold metrics. (2) For Pearson linear correlation, the correlation is 0.91 for probability metrics, 0.95 for rank metrics, and 0.99 to 1.0 for threshold metrics. In contrast, the correlation of metrics from different groups is not so high as the correlations of metrics from the same group. That is, for Spearman rank correlation, any inter-group correlation is between 0.22 to 0.65, i.e., from 0.22 to 0.37 between threshold and rank metrics, 0.35 to 0.55 between rank and probability metrics, and 0.42 to 0.65 between threshold and probability metrics; whereas for Pearson correlation, we can obtain similar results.

From above results, we can draw the conclusion that metrics from the same group are closely associated with each other, and comparatively metrics from different groups are not so closely related. Secondly, to investigate

Table 2. Pearson (bottom-left) and Spearman (top-right) correlation coefficients for House-voting dataset based on kNN algorithm (Intra-group correlation in bold)

| | Threshold metrics | | | Probability metrics | | Rank metrics | |
	ACC	KAP	FSC	1-MAE	1-RMSE	AUC	AUPRC
ACC		**1.0**	**0.93**	0.65	0.58	0.32	0.22
KAP	1.0		**0.92**	0.62	0.57	0.37	0.27
FSC	1.0	0.99		0.63	0.42	0.27	0.22
1-MAE	0.65	0.65	0.63		**0.82**	0.50	0.35
1-RMSE	0.59	0.61	0.57	**0.91**		0.55	0.47
AUC	0.18	0.18	0.17	0.49	0.39		**0.92**
AUPRC	0.19	0.19	0.19	0.37	0.31	**0.95**	

Table 3. Pearson (bottom-left) and Spearman (top-right) correlation coefficients for all datasets (Intra-group correlation in bold)

| | Threshold metrics | | | Probability metrics | | Rank metrics | |
	ACC	KAP	FSC	1-MAE	1-RMSE	AUC	AUPRC
ACC		**0.94**	**0.91**	0.63	0.59	0.28	0.26
KAP	**0.96**		**0.90**	0.60	0.57	0.29	0.26
FSC	0.94	0.94		0.60	0.55	0.29	0.26
1-MAE	0.67	0.63	0.63		**0.77**	0.46	0.41
1-RMSE	0.63	0.61	0.58	**0.79**		0.43	0.39
AUC	0.30	0.29	0.29	0.47	0.45		**0.85**
AUPRC	0.26	0.26	0.26	0.42	0.40	**0.89**	

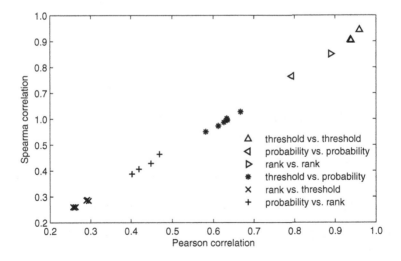

Fig. 1. The distribution of correlations between seven common performance metrics.

the adaptability of our grouping of metrics, we compute the correlation of performance metrics on each dataset, i.e., the correlation of the 8 models for one datasets, and give the average of 18 correlation matrix, as shown in Table 3. Compared with Table 2, there are some changes in the correlation values, i.e., the intra-group correlation become smaller. A clearer description can be found in Figure 1, i.e., there is a strong correlation (greater than 0.77) between the performance metrics in the same groups and a low correlation (less than 0.67) of metrics from different groups. The experimental results verify the reasonableness of the classification of performance metrics in the previous.

4.1. *Conclusions and Future Work*

In this paper, we have intensively studied the relationship across seven widely adopted performance metrics for binary classification. All metrics within a given group are highly correlated but less correlated with metrics from different groups. This finding provides practitioners with a better understanding about the relationships among these common metrics. In the future, an interesting and challenging direction is to investigate an all-in-one metric that can perform the functions of all three groups of metrics.

Acknowledgment

This work was supported by the Zhejiang Provincial Natural Science Foundation of China (No.Y1101202) and the Ningbo Natural Science Foundation of China (No.2012A610018).

References

1. A. Ben-David, *Eng. Appl. of AI* **20**, 875 (2007).
2. J. Huang and C. X. Ling, *IEEE Trans. Knowl. Data Eng.* **17**, 299 (2005).
3. R. Baeza-Yates, B. Ribeiro-Neto *et al.*, *Modern information retrieval* 1999.
4. T. A. Lasko, J. G. Bhagwat, K. H. Zou and L. Ohno-Machado, *Journal of Biomedical Informatics* **38**, 404 (2005).
5. R. Caruana and A. Niculescu-Mizil (2004).
6. M. Sokolova, N. Japkowicz and S. Szpakowicz (2006).
7. N. Seliya, T. M. Khoshgoftaar and J. V. Hulse, A study on the relationships of classifier performance metrics, in *ICTAI*, 2009.
8. C. Ferri, J. Hernández-Orallo and R. Modroiu, *Pattern Recognition Letters* **30**, 27 (2009).
9. T. Ngo, *ACM SIGSOFT Software Engineering Notes* **36**, 51 (2011).
10. P. Ahlgren, B. Jarneving and R. Rousseau, *JASIST* **54**, 550 (2003).
11. M. Kendall and J. D. Gibbons, *Rank Correlation Methods*, 5 edn. 1990.

ARTIFICIAL DEVELOPMENT AND EVOLUTION OF ARTIFICIAL NEURAL NETWORKS USING PARAMETRIC L-SYSTEMS WITH MEMORY[*]

LIDIO MAURO LIMA DE CAMPOS

*Programa de Pós Graduação em Engenharia Elétrica, Universidade Federal do Pará,
Rua Augusto Corrêa, 01- Guamá, Belém, Pará, CEP 66075-100, Brasil*

ROBERTO CÉLIO LIMÃO DE OLIVEIRA

*Faculdade de Engenharia de Computação, Universidade Federal do Pará, Rua Augusto
Corrêa, 01- Guamá, Caixa Postal 479, Belém, Pará, CEP 66075-100, Brasil*

The Development of Neuro-Evolutives (NEAs) Algorithms, designed specifically for evolving Artificial Neural Networks (ANNs) architectures, has aroused the interest of many researchers in the last twenty-five years. This paper shows that a direction to be followed in the development of NEAs more biologically plausible is to evolve ANNs through artificial development models. Whereas the analogous biological process should be viewed as a process of organization carried out by genetic information encoded in DNA and when followed will generate the final shape of the organs, including the brain. This research develops a biologically inspired methodology for automatic design of ANNs. With this goal using an artificial development system based on a parametric Lindenmayer with memory (allowing to incorporate aspects of organization, geometry and repetition of patterns in obtaining the topologies of neural networks), integrated to a Genetic Algorithm (GA) which simulates artificial evolution, allowing generate architectures of ANNs direct and recurrent with optimal number of neurons and appropriate topology. The technique was tested on XOR problem and in Classification Problem, some advantages of the proposed methodology is that it increases the level of implicit parallelism of Genetic Algorithm (GA) and seems to be capable to generate satisfactory neural architectures, reducing the project cost and increasing the performance of the obtained ANN.

1. Introduction

Currently, there are several methods for automatic design of neural networks. The earliest methods used direct encoding [2, 3], these methods have scalability problems, a low level of biological plausibility, and furthermore, most are only able to generate direct topologies. In response to these limitations, other researchers have evolved indirectly encoded ANNs [1, 4, 6, 7, 8 and 9], which

---

[*] This work is supported by Universidade Federal do Pará.

means that they evolve a compressed description of the ANN rather than the ANN itself, these methodologies are more biologically plausible, because in the biological genetic encoding the mapping between genotype and phenotype is indirect.

Our approach includes improvements to our previous proposal [4], first the chromosome used by the GA in our research has a variable length from 122 to 300 bits, in contrast to previous that has a fixed length of 1024 bits, due this our current approach evolve to a compressed description of the ANN that reduces the search space of the GA and enables to generate more complex, direct, recurrent and multilayer networks, than the previous one [4]. Furthermore reduces the scalability problem of other methodologies [2, 3]. Second our L-Rules presented in section 3.1 allows generate ANN architectures, without requiring additional configuration of substrates for each particular type of problem, as required by the methodologies [5, 7], our model automates this process. Our L-System generates recursive branches in the artificial development process, which is biologically plausible.

Usually in the problems of local search where the GAs are employed, a bit string is called a chromosome, each bit is a gene and a gene set represent the parameters of a function to be optimized. However, in our research with the goal of making genetic algorithms closer to biological processes, in the encoding scheme adopted, the genes encode a recipe that will drive the stages of development, and this genetic information is passed on to their offspring's by evolutionary processes acting on genes over generations.

The section 2 describes state of art, section 3 describes a new methodology of automatic design of ANN, in section 4 the experiments are discussed and finally in section 5 the conclusions and directions for future research are presented.

2. State of the Art

A method inspired by L-Systems that takes a slightly more biological approach was produced by Lee, Kong and Sim [6]. Similar to biological DNA, information is coded using the symbols A, G, T and C. A sequence of three of these symbols is known as a codon. The sequence of codons between these delimiters is translated into a production rule for developing a neural controller. A similar idea [4] using binary strings also exists in which the process of reading and translating bits can be repeated from different bits in the string to produce different production rules.

In HyperNEAT, the CPPN(Compositional Patten Producing Networks) is used to generate a neural network, the same is an abstraction of development. For instance, [5] have shown that the objective of this coding is to allow patterns of regularities with symmetry, repetition, and repetition can be represented as networks of simple functions. The nodes of the phenotypic network are laid out on a substrate, i.e., a grid, such that each has a position. [7] presents a methodology for Automatic design of ANNs which uses a set of advanced techniques in neuroevolution into a new method called ES-HyperNEAT (Evolvable- Substrate HyperNEAT).

The ES-HyperNEAT is an improvement over HyperNEAT [5]. While the location of the hidden nodes in the substrate, had to be decided by the designer on the original HyperNEAT. ES-HyperNEAT showed that the decision might in fact be automated. In the HyperNEAT CPPN encodes an infinite number of weights within the Hypercube, from which a subset should be chosen to be incorporated into the ANN. [7] Consider other important information is the density of nodes from which an additional increase of the same does not offer any advantage. For more details about state of art, query the authors' research [8].

3. A Biologically Inspired Methodology for ANN Design

This section continues to describe and explore a methodology that incorporates aspects of biological plausibility and can be seen as a growth model based on a parametric L-Systems with memory, that tries to mimic the natural process of nervous system growing and the Genetic Algorithm (GA) that mimic the evolution process that evolves and optimizes the nervous system architecture suited for an specific task.

3.1. *Neural Network Codification with L-System*

Our model explores aspects of regularity, organization and geometry. The architecture of an ANN is defined as the directed graph representing the connectivity of the network. Each node represents a neuron and each directed edge represents a weighted connection from one neuron to another. The L-System proposed in this research allows generate direct and recurrent connections with ramifications. The same can be described as grammar $G=\{\Sigma,\Pi,\alpha\}$, where the alphabet is $\Sigma =\{.,f,F(rand(\Theta),rand(l)),l,*,[,],B\}$ the productions L-rules (Π) are described in Figure 2 , the axiom $\alpha = .$ is the start point where the process of development begins, where "**f**" means drawing a provisional neuron and "**F**" draw a connection between neurons with angle (Θ) and length "**l**", "**[**" means storing the current state of the development and "**]**" recovery the current state, "**n**" means turning a provisional neuron into permanent. The third rule is divided into six others. Figure 3 illustrates an example of the construction process of one branche of an ANN, starting from input neurons to the hidden layer and from the hidden layer to the output layer.

3.2. *Rules Extraction with Genetic Algorithms and Fitness Evaluation of the Neural Network Structure*

In our work we try to model the "constructive" approach found in the evolutionary process. Here, L-rules are extracted automatically by the GA in order to control the number of firing times, i.e. times we can apply each rule. The algorithm tries to mimic the process of decoding the genetic formula that is encoded in DNA and when decoded will conduct the process of neurons development. It is known that in the development of a tree, plant or neuron, each one has its own "genetic formula". That is also true for the biological genes, which only begin to have some meaning when translated, by the |protein synthesis in growth rules for a developing embryo. Here we described only the principal idea of the algorithm used for rules extraction, which was inspired on protein synthesis. As we want to find optimized neural structures capable to solve a given problem, the fitness function adopted, equation 1, considers a minimum number of: Mean Square Error (RMSE) + hidden neurons (NCIH).

$$Fitness = 1/(RMSE + NCIH) \tag{1}$$

4. Experiments

The GA used the following parameters: the length of the chromosomes was variable from 122 to 300 bits, these binary strings will be used in the process of reading and translating bits that can be repeated from different bits in the string to produce different production rules. The initial population was variable from 30 to 100, the number of generations was variable from 30 to 100, and the crossover rate was (c.rate=0.6) being adopted (number of genes/36) points of cuts on chromosome randomly chosen, the mutation rate was (m.rate=0.1). The parameters used by ANNs were : learning rate α_o=0.9, α_t=$\alpha_{(t-1)}$/(1+t/ρ), t=1,..,ρ where α is the learning rate, t(epoch) and ρ(maximum epochs=90000).

The model of artificial development produces genotypic representations ("strings") that are mapped onto RNAs architectures. After the obtained neural networks are trained and calculated the fitness of each one, the individuals are sorted and selected for application of genetic operators. It was used tournament selection operator because this operator is well suited for parallel genetic algorithm, after these steps, a new population is obtained. The previous steps are repeated a number "n" of generations.

On 10 runs, the best experiment shows that the ADBPANN system finds a structure for XOR in 28 generations, on average a solution network had 2.65 hidden nodes. The best network that was found for a desired RMSE (*root-mean-square error*)<=ξ1 , ξ1=0.0001 has the following specifications (neurons in the input layer, neurons in the intermediate layer, neurons in the output layer) = (2, 4, 1) and the lowest network (2, 2, 1), in the tests of generalization the mean square error of the ANN was RMSE=0.000037376. Figure 1 shows the best and mean fitness obtained in a simulation where the convergence of GA was in 100 generations. On 100 runs, NEAT system [2] finds a structure for XOR in an average of 32 generations (4,755 networks evaluated). On average a solution network had 2.35 hidden nodes.

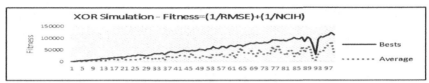

Figure 1. Bets and Average Fitness for XOR.

The second experiment have used a training set of class-labeled tuples randomly selected from the AllElectronics customer database (the data are adapted from [10]). The database describes attributes of the customers, such as their id, age, income, occupation, and credit rating. The customers can be classified as to whether or not they have purchased a computer at *AllElectronics*. Table 1 presents a sample of the training set. The lowest network found that simulated the problem has the following specifications (4, 4, 1). The RMSE for the generalization tests was 0.00115 and for validation tests was 0.00019.

RULE 1 - R_1	$S \longrightarrow .$ (axiom)
RULE 2 - R_2	$. \longrightarrow (f) n - (f \ f \dots f)n$; where $n =$ **numbers of neurons of the input layer**
RULE 3 - R_3	$f \longrightarrow [f^{(3.1)} / f \ F (\text{rand} (\ominus)^{(3.2)}) , \text{rand} (l)) f / f \ F(\text{rand} (\ominus)^{(3.3)}, \text{rand} (l)) / n^{(3.4)} / f^{(3.5)} / fB^{(3.6)}$
RULE 4 - R_4	$[\longrightarrow [F(\text{rand} (\ominus)), \text{rand} (l)) f \ ]$
RULE 5 - R_5	$f \longrightarrow f *$

Figure 2. Production Rules of L-System

5. Conclusions

Our results prove that our approach reduces the problem of scalability because the reduced size of the chromosome that used only 122 bits. In the methods of direct encoding the size grows quadratically in relation to the number of neurons of the network. In conclusion, our approach solves the two problems presented previously without trouble and in doing so keeps the topology small. We are improving our previous methodology [4], in the section 1 we discussed some improvements made, especially in terms of biological plausibility. Our results prove that our approach reduces the problem of scalability because the reduced size of the chromosome that used only 122 bits. In the methods of direct encoding the size grows quadratically in relation to the number of neurons of the network. In conclusion, our approach solves the two problems presented previously without trouble and in doing so keeps the topology small. We are improving our previous methodology [4], in the section 1 we discussed some improvements made, especially in terms of biological plausibility.

Table 1.Class-labeled training tuples from AllElectronics customer database

RID	Age	Income	Students	Credit-Rating	Buys-computer
1	Youth	High	No	Fair	No
2	Youth	High	No	Excellent	No
3	Middle-aged	High	No	Fair	Yes
4	Senior	Medium	No	Fair	Yes
5	Senior	Low	Yes	Fair	Yes
6	Senior	Low	Yes	Excellent	No
7	Middle-aged	Low	Yes	Excellent	Yes
8	Youth	Medium	No	Fair	No
9	Youth	Low	Yes	Fair	Yes
10	Senior	Medium	Yes	Fair	Yes
11	Youth	Medium	Yes	Excellent	Yes
12	Middle-aged	Medium	No	Excellent	Yes
13	Middle-aged	High	Yes	Fair	Yes
14	Senior	Medium	No	Excellent	No

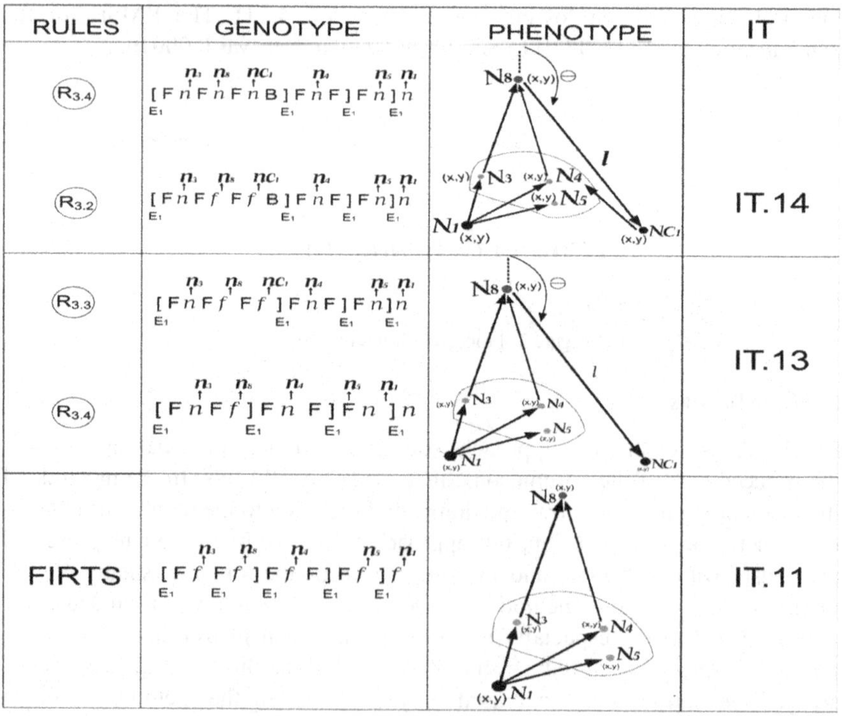

RULES	GENOTYPE	PHENOTYPE	IT
$R_{3.4}$	$[F n F n F n B] F n F] F n] n$		
$R_{3.2}$	$[F n F f \; F f \; B] F n F] F n] n$		IT.14
$R_{3.3}$	$[F n F f \; F f \;] F n F] F n] n$		IT.13
$R_{3.4}$	$[F n F f] F n \; F] F n \;] n$		
FIRTS	$[F f \; F f \;] F f \; F] F f \;] f$		IT.11

Figure 3. Construction Process of an iterated ANN, starting from the input to the output layer.

The next improvements will be: possibilities of obtaining partially connected networks and connections between non-adjacent layers, ability to generate recurrent networks or multilayer networks. Furthermore obtaining RNAs that incorporate aspects of biological plausibility, for example the use of Hebbian learning.

References

1. Townsend, J., Keedwell, E., and Galton, A. (2013). Artificial development of biologically plausible neural-symbolic networks. Cognitive Computation, 1(1)
2. Stanley, K. O. and Miikkulainen, R. (2002). Evolving neural networks through augmenting topologies. Evolutionary Computation, 10:2002.
3. Miller, G. F., Tood, P. M., and Hedge, S. U. (1989). Designing neural networks using genetic algorithms. In Proceedings of International on Genetic Algorithms and their Applications, pages 379–384.
4. De Campos, L. M. L., Roisenberg, M., and de Oliveira, R. C. L. (2011). Automatic design of Neural Networks with L-Systems and genetic algorithms - A biologically inspired methodology. In International Joint Conference Neural Networks, pages 1199–1206.
5. Gauci, J. and Stanley, K. O. (2010). Autonomous Evolution of Topographic Regularities in Artificial Neural Networks. Neural Computation, 22: 1860–1898.
6. Lee, D. W. and Seo, S. W. (2007). Evolvable neural network based on developmental models for mobile robot navigation. In International Journal of Fuzzy Logic and Intelligent Systems, vol.7, No.3, pages 176–181. IEEE.
7. Risi, S. and Stanley, K. O. (2012). An Enhanced Hypercube-Based Encoding for Evolving the Placement, Density, and Connectivity of Neurons. Artificial Life, Early Access:1–33.
8. De CAMPOS, L.M.L; Oliveira, R.C.L. (2013). A Comparative Analysis of Methodologies for Automatic Design of Artificial Neural Networks from the Beginnings until Today. In: Proceedings of 1st BRICS Countries Congress (BRICS-CCI) and 11th Brazilian Congress (CBIC) on Computational Intelligence, v. 1. p. 1-8.
9. Prusinkiewicz, P. and Runions, A. (2012). Computational models of plant development and form. New Phytologist, 193(3):549–569.

A FRAMEWORK FOR OVERLAPPING CLUSTERING[*]

QI ZHANG

*School of Information Science & Technology, Southwest Jiaotong University,
Chengdu, 610031, China*

YAN YANG[†]

*School of Information Science & Technology, Southwest Jiaotong University,
Chengdu, 610031, China*

HONGJUN WANG

*School of Information Science & Technology, Southwest Jiaotong University,
Chengdu, 610031, China*

FEI TENG

*School of Information Science & Technology, Southwest Jiaotong University,
Chengdu, 610031, China*

Nowadays, many real world datasets are inherently overlapping clusters, and it is also a critical problem for the clustering analysis techniques to partition partially overlapping clusters. In this paper we propose a framework for overlapping clustering, and it consists of clustering, selecting and aggregation. In the clustering part, all kinds of clustering algorithms are suitable. In the selecting part, we propose a method called ConSim (confusion-similarity) to select some overlapping clusters. In the aggregation part, the selected clusters will be blended, and the overlapping objects will be found out. The framework is more flexible and powerful and it is demonstrated effective through experiments on datasets.

1. Introduction

Clustering is a methodology to divide a dataset into a set of clusters so that the data objects belong to the same cluster are similar and objects from different clusters are dissimilar. In general, most clustering methods divide the objects

---

[*] This work is supported by the National Science Foundation of China (Nos. 61170111, 61134002, 61202043) and the Research Fund of Traction Power State Key Laboratory, Southwest Jiaotong University (No. 2012TPL_T15).

[†] corresponding author: yyang@swjtu.edu.cn

into non-overlapping regions, but in a variety of important applications, overlapping clustering wherein some items are allowed to be members of two or more discovered clusters is more appropriate. For example, in the field of document clustering, some documents may contain multiple relevant topics [1]. And overlapping clustering is also important in biological data such as several metabolic pathways for one gene [2].

In this paper, we propose a framework for overlapping clustering. It consists of three parts. In the clustering part, all kinds of clustering algorithms can be used to find the property of clusters. And in the selecting part, some methods are used to find the clusters which may have overlapping objects. In the last part, the overlapping clusters will be aggregated so that the overlapping data objects can be assigned.

2. Related Work

The first overlapping clustering method (ADCLUS) was presented by Shepard and Arabie in 1979 [3]. In the fuzzy logic community, an object is allowed to be assigned to multiple sets [4]. One of the earlier works on overlapping clustering techniques was presented in reference [5]. It is appropriate to assign genes to multiple overlapping clusters when clustering micro-array gene expression data [6, 7]. Several methods for obtaining overlapping gene clusters, including gene shaving [8] and mean square residue bi-clustering [9] have been proposed. Banerjee et al [11] interpreted an overlapping clustering model proposed by Segal et al [10]. Heller et al developed a new model for overlapping clusters based on a principled statistical framework [12]. Fu et al presented Multiplicative Mixture Models (MMMs) as an appropriate framework for overlapping clustering [13]. Airel et al proposed a new graph-based algorithm for overlapping clustering [14].

3. Overlapping Clustering Framework

The framework is shown in Figure 1. We note that the framework consists of three parts: clustering, selecting and aggregation.

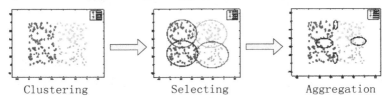

Clustering   Selecting   Aggregation

Figure 1. Framework of Overlapping Clustering.

From Figure 1, we noted that the data is divided into four clusters as shown in Clustering, and the some clusters which maybe overlapping are selected as shown in Selecting, and finally four overlapping clusters are found out as shown in Aggregation.

3.1. Clustering

Assume a set of n data points $\{X_i\}_{i=1}^n$ in M^d represented by matrix $X_{n \times m}$. Any kinds of clustering algorithms can be chosen to find out the clusters prototype. The overlapping items may occur at some clusters' edges when the prototype is not so good. In other words, the centers of the output clusters are far from the real centers, the overlapping clusters may be deviated. In brief, in this part we try to find a good prototype clusters that indicate the data points' distributions in dataset well. The clustering prototype is output as $\{\pi_i\}_{i=1}^n$, where π_i represents clusters i.

3.2. Selecting

The selecting part aims at finding out which clusters may have common overlapping items. Let π_i be a cluster vectors, a measure of separation between clusters is as follow.

$$M_{i,j} = \| A_i - A_j \|_q = \sqrt[q]{\sum_{k=1}^n | a_{k,i} - a_{k,j} |^q} \tag{1}$$

where A_i is the center of π_i. $a_{k,i}$ is the kth element of A_i, and there are n such elements in A, for it is an n dimensional center, where k is indexes of the data's features. Moreover, the scatter of a cluster is defined as follows

$$\text{var } Sim(\pi_i, \pi_j) = \frac{D(\pi_i) + D(\pi_j)}{M_{i,j}(\pi_i, \pi_j)} \tag{2}$$

where π_i and π_j are clusters i and j. $D(\pi_i)$ and $D(\pi_j)$ are the variance of cluster i and cluster which describe the scatter of clusters. Assume there two clusters, if the intra-cluster is sparser and the centers of cluster are closer, the clusters may have common overlapping items and the value of var $Sim()$ will be higher. Entropy also could represent the scatter of a cluster as below

$$\text{entr} Sim(\pi_i, \pi_j) = \frac{H(\pi_i) + H(\pi_j)}{M_{i,j}(\pi_i, \pi_j)} \tag{3}$$

where π_i and π_j are clusters i and j. $H(\pi_i)$ and $H(\pi_j)$ are the entropy of clusters i and clusters j. The formulas (2) and (3) combine into formula (4)

$$ConSim(\pi_i, \pi_j) = (C(\pi_i) + C(\pi_j)) \times Sim(\pi_i, \pi_j) \tag{4}$$

where $C(\pi_i)$ represents the sparse level of cluster i, and $Sim(\pi_i, \pi_j)$ means the similarity of cluster i and cluster j.

It is difficult for us to determine whether the clusters are overlapping or not when the values of the formula (4) are close to each other. We then consider about the radius and directions of a cluster. Here the radius varies with the directions shown in Figure2.

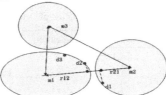

Figure 2 the radius of clusters

Using Cosine law, the radius will be calculated by formula (5) shows.

$$r_{ij} = \max(|\alpha| \times \cos(\theta)) = \max(\frac{\alpha}{|\alpha|} \cdot \beta) \tag{5}$$

where $\cos(\theta) = <\alpha \cdot \beta>/|\alpha||\beta|$, α is vector m_{ij}, β is vector m_{id_j}. d_j is the cth data object of cluster i. On different directions, there is some different radius for each cluster. On a certain direction, radius is the maximum value of a data projection. We constructed a weight by radius, and the radius could cover the shortage of the formula (4). The weight is calculated as follow

$$weight_{ij} = \frac{r_{ij} + r_{ji}}{|m_{ij}|} \tag{6}$$

Where r_{ij} is the radius of cluster i (j) directing to cluster j (i), and m_{ij} is the distance of the centers between cluster i and cluster j. if the weight is more than 1, it implies that the clusters have overlapping data. Finally a complete formula is obtained as follow:

$$ConSim(\pi_i, \pi_j) = (C(\pi_i) + C(\pi_j)) \times Sim(\pi_i, \pi_j) \times weight_{ij} \tag{7}.$$

3.3. Aggregation

In Aggregation part, the membership matrix is used to merge the clusters that selected before. The membership is calculated as follow:

$$u_{ij} = \left[\sum_{k=1}^{c} (\frac{d_{ij}}{d_{kj}})^{2/(g-1)} \right]^{-1} \tag{8}$$

where d_{ij} is the distance between cluster i and cluster j, and $g \in [1, \infty)$ is a weight factor.

4. Experiment Evaluation

4.1. *Dataset*

We conduct the experiments on UCI datasets and MoviesLens datasets. The description of datasets is shown in Table 1.

Table 1. Description of Datasets

DataSets	Source	Dimension	Instance	Class
Glass	UCI	9	214	6
Iris	UCI	4	150	3
Wine	UCI	13	178	3
Wave	UCI	40	5000	3
Mov_aat	MoviesLens	2791	358	3
Mov_acf	MoviesLens	2791	365	3
Mov_cfw	MovieLens	2791	206	3

4.2. *Results*

We compare three clustering algorithms: K-means clustering algorithm [KM], Fuzzy-K-means clustering algorithm [FCM]and our overlapping framework [OFW]. Here an external criterion NMI[15] and a relative criterion Ocq[16] are used to compare different clustering methods. Table 2 reports the Ocq and NMI on datasets.

Table 2. Ocq and NMI on Datasets

Dataset	KM		FCM		OFW	
	Ocq	NMI	Ocq	NMI	Ocq	NMI
Glass	**0.6209**	0.4412	0.5703	0.4502	0.4703	**0.4821**
Iris	**0.4966**	0.8179	0.4959	0.8211	0.4854	**0.8877**
Wine	**0.8166**	0.6841	0.8168	0.6838	0.8114	**0.7128**
Wave	**0.5954**	0.3606	0.5896	0.3645	0.5760	**0.3812**
Mov_aat	0.7848	0.4321	**0.7851**	0.4332	0.7821	**0.4432**
Mov_acf	0.7551	0.4034	**0.7577**	0.4072	0.7494	**0.4205**
Mov_cfw	**0.7179**	0.3912	0.7096	0.4003	0.7088	**0.4157**

From Table 2, it is noted that KM and FCM perform better than OFW on Ocq. The OFW makes the centers of clusters move to nearer each other, and it also increases the distances of the intra-cluster. This phenomenon is due to the fact that OFW finds the overlapping items, so it doesn't mean that the OFW performance is not good. OFW performs better than KM and FCM on NMI, because more objects are assigned correctly.

5. Conclusion

Overlapping clustering allows that the data objects can belong to multiple clusters, but the traditional algorithm cannot. This paper proposes a framework for overlapping clustering. The framework is flexible and powerful, because it could discover the overlapping clusters using any existed clustering algorithm. It also assigns the overlapping data objects to multiple clusters and finds out the overlapping clusters and their overlapping objects.

References

1. M. Sahami, M. Hearst, and E. Saund, *ICML-96*, **Cf**435-443 (1996).
2. S. C. Madeira and A. L. Oliveira, *IEEE Trans. CBB,* **Cf1(1)**:24-25 (2004).
3. R. N. Shepard and P. Arabie, *Psyc. Rev.* **Cf86(2)**:87-123 (1979).
4. J. C. Bezdek and S. K. Pal, **Cf**267. New York: *IEEE Press* (1992).
5. W. T. McCormick, P. J. Schweitzer, and T. W. White, *Operations Research,* **Cf20(5)**:993-1009 (1972).
6. A. Battle, E. Segal and D. Koller, *Journal of Computational Biology,* **Cf12(7)**:909-927 (2005).
7. E. Srikant and R. Agrawal, *VLDB-95,* **Cf**407-419 (1995).
8. T. Hastie, R. Tibshirani, M. B. Eisen, A. Alizadeh, R. Levy, L. Staudt, W. C. Chan, D. Botstein, and P. Brown, *Genome Biology,* **Cf1(2)**:1-3 (2000).
9. Y. Cheng and G. M. Church, *ICMB,* **Cf**93-103 (2000).
10. E. Segal, A. Battle and D. Koller, *In Proc. of the Pacific Symposium on Biocomputing,* **Cf**89-100 (2003).
11. A. Banerjee, C. Krumpelman, J. Ghosh, S. Basu and R. J. Mooney, *ACM SIGKDD KDD,* **Cf**532-537 (2005).
12. K. A. Heller and Z. Ghahramani, *In Intl. Conf. on Artificial Intelligence and Statistics,* **Cf**187-194 (2007).
13. Q. Fu and A. Banerjee, *ICDM,* **Cf**791-796 (2008).
14. Airel P. S., J. F. M. Trinidad, J. A. C. Ochoa and J. E. M. Pagola, *Neurocomputing,* **Cf**234-247 (2013).
15. Lancichinetti A, Fortunato S and Kertsz J, *New Journal of Physics,* **Cf11(3)** (2009).
16. Y. Yang, F. Jin and K. Mohamed, *Application Research of Computers,* **Cf25(6)**:1630-1632 (2008).

TEXT CO-CLUSTERING USING MATRIX BLOCK AND CORRELATION COEFFICIENT[*]

CHAOYANG CHUN

School of Information Science & Technology, Southwest Jiaotong University, Chengdu, 610031, P.R China

YAN YANG[†]

School of Information Science & Technology, Southwest Jiaotong University, Chengdu, 610031, P.R China

HUIJIA TANG

School of Information Science & Technology, Southwest Jiaotong University, Chengdu, 610031, P.R China

Co-clustering is an unsupervised machine learning technique, and it simultaneously clusters rows and columns for the input data matrix. In text co-clustering, the input data matrix is a high dimension and sparse matrix, and the traditional co-clustering ignores the similarity between word and word, and the similarity between text and word. In this work, we propose a text co-clustering using matrix block and correlation coefficient. In the first step, the matrix block and correlation coefficient are used to reduce dimension, and the relevant feature terms are merged as a hybrid feature term. In the second step, the text terms are clustered using K-means algorithm. And in the last step, the hybrid feature terms and text terms are iteratively clustered by the adjusting algorithms. Experimental results show that our algorithm is effective for a high dimension and sparse text matrix.

1. Introduction

Co-clustering has received a significant amount of attention as an important problem in many applications. It simultaneously clusters objects and features, for example it simultaneously finds and links partitions on both row and column dimension in a data matrix [1]. An example of co-clustering may be drawn from DNA microarray analysis, rows of DNA microarray matrix are patients with various diseases and other conditions, and columns are various genes. It is to

---

[*] This work is supported by the National Science Foundation of China (Nos.61170111, 61003142 and 61134002) and the Research Fund of Traction Power Key Laboratory, Southwest Jiaotong University (No.2012-TPL_T15)

[†] yyang@swjtu.edu.cn

extract combinations of genes with regard to patients which suggest possible genetic sources of diseases. There are many approaches for co-clustering, Chen et al. built concepts for AI Agents using information theoretic co-clustering [2]. Ding et al. presented orthogonal nonnegative matrix tri-factorizations for co-clustering data matrix [3]. Ling et al. studied Bayesian approach for co-clustering by utilizing correspondence analysis algorithms to process matrix decomposition [4]. Li et al. developed a hierarchical co-clustering algorithm to cluster different types of data [5].

In this paper, first of all, we use matrix block and correlation coefficient methods to find the most relevant feature terms and merge them as a hybrid feature term. Then we cluster on the text terms by K-means algorithm. After that the adjusting algorithms are used to simultaneously clustering text terms and hybrid feature terms according to the results of K-means algorithm.

The rest of this paper is organized as follows: Section 2 presents the text co-clustering. Section 3 discusses the matrix block and correlation coefficient methods. Section 4 describes how to use the adjusting algorithms to simultaneously clustering text and hybrid feature terms. Section 5 brings the experiment results and evaluations. Finally, section 6 summarizes our work.

2. Related work

Recently more and more texts can be obtained in the network, clustering is widely applied to text clustering. Text clustering organizes larges of texts into coherent clusters, in the same cluster texts are similar to each other while texts are dissimilar in different clusters [6].

Most text clustering algorithms ignore the similarity between word and word, and the similarity between text and word. To further enhance text clustering performance, there have also been some efforts on text co-clustering. Huang et al. presented a semi-supervised hierarchical text co-clustering algorithm. In the hierarchical co-clustering process, the semantic information was used to measure similarity. Text and feature simultaneously were used as leaf nodes, so feature clustering results were contained in text clustering results [7]. Song et al. proposed a constrained text co-clustering based on information-theoretic [8]. Yang et al. proposed a new heuristic semi-supervised fuzzy co-clustering algorithm for clustering large Web texts [9].

3. Feature preprocessing

3.1. *Text expression*

In general, the texts are represented by a vector space model (VSM), and the basic idea of VSM is that a text corresponds to a vector consisting of non-negative values on each dimension [10]. Suppose an input data matrix consists of m rows and n columns, the data matrix is shown as Eq. (1), each row d_i indicates a text term, each column t_j indicates a feature term, x_{ij} is the weight of feature term t_j in text d_i, and calculated by *tfidf*, shown as Eq. (2),

$$X_{m \times n} = \begin{matrix} & t_1 & t_2 & \cdots & t_n \\ d_1 \\ d_2 \\ \vdots \\ d_m \end{matrix} \begin{bmatrix} x_{11} & x_{12} & \cdots & x_{1n} \\ x_{21} & x_{22} & \cdots & x_{23} \\ \vdots & \vdots & \vdots & \vdots \\ x_{m1} & x_{m2} & \cdots & x_{mn} \end{bmatrix}. \tag{1}$$

$$tfidf(d_i, t_j) = tf(d_i, t_j) \cdot \log_2 \frac{m}{df(t_j)}. \tag{2}$$

Where $tf(d_i, t_j)$ is the feature term frequency of feature term t_j in the text term d_i, $df(t_j)$ is all the text numbers of feature term t_j contained in the text set.

3.2. *Matrix block and correlation coefficient*

It is difficult to cluster all feature terms, so the feature terms clustering usually contains a phase of dimensionality reduction. In recent years many methods of feature reduction were proposed, such as information gain, expected cross entropy, mutual information and so on. Most of these methods need to input the number of feature terms clusters in advance. But in experiment we may not easily get the number of feature terms clusters.

We proposed correlation coefficient to describe the relationship between two feature vectors. The correlation coefficient not only expresses the clustering contribution degree of a feature vector, but also describes the similarity between features. The correlation coefficient of feature term t_a and t_b is defined as

$$\rho_{t_a t_b} = \frac{Cov(t_a, t_b)}{\sqrt{D(t_a)D(t_b)}}. \tag{3}$$

$$Cov(t_a, t_b) = \sum_i^m \sum_j^m [x_{ia} - E(t_a)][x_{jb} - E(t_b)]p_{ij}. \tag{4}$$

where $D(t_a)$ is the variance of feature term t_a, $Cov(t_a, t_b)$ is the covariance of t_a and t_b. If $|\rho_{t_a t_b}| > 0.95$, t_a and t_b are correlation, we can use Eq. (5) to merge t_a and t_b. For example, if $|\rho_{economy, financial}| = 0.96$, economy and financial are correlation and merged as a hybrid feature. We calculate correlation coefficient for each column, shown as Eq. (6). After that, we select the largest $|\rho_{t_i t_j}|$ for each row, and merge the two feature terms t_i and t_j using Eq. (5).

$$lx_{ij} = \frac{x_{ia} + x_{ib}}{2}. \tag{5}$$

$$|\rho_{t_i t_j}| = \begin{bmatrix} |\rho_{t_1 t_1}| & |\rho_{t_1 t_2}| & |\rho_{t_1 t_3}| & \cdots & |\rho_{t_1 t_n}| \\ |\rho_{t_2 t_1}| & |\rho_{t_2 t_2}| & |\rho_{t_2 t_3}| & \cdots & |\rho_{t_2 t_n}| \\ |\rho_{t_3 t_1}| & |\rho_{t_3 t_2}| & |\rho_{t_3 t_3}| & \cdots & |\rho_{t_3 t_n}| \\ \vdots & \vdots & \vdots & & \vdots \\ |\rho_{t_n t_1}| & |\rho_{t_n t_2}| & |\rho_{t_n t_3}| & \cdots & |\rho_{t_n t_n}| \end{bmatrix}. \tag{6}$$

If we only merge the most relevant two columns, maybe a few columns are merged. In this work, we use matrix block and correlation coefficient methods to select feature terms and reduce the number of column. We divided the data matrix into several small matrices. In experiment, the number of matrix block will be discussed. For example, we divided a data matrix into three small matrices,

$$X_{m \times n} = \begin{bmatrix} x_{11} & x_{12} & \cdots & x_{1i} & x_{1j} & x_{1j+1} & \cdots & x_{1k} & x_{1p} & x_{1p+1} & \cdots & x_{1n} \\ x_{21} & x_{22} & \cdots & x_{2i} & x_{2j} & x_{2j+1} & \cdots & x_{2k} & x_{2p} & x_{2p+1} & \cdots & x_{2n} \\ \vdots & \vdots & \vdots & \vdots & \vdots & \vdots & \vdots & \vdots & \vdots & \vdots & \vdots & \vdots \\ x_{m1} & x_{m2} & \cdots & x_{mi} & x_{mj} & x_{mj+1} & \cdots & x_{mk} & x_{mp} & x_{mp+1} & \cdots & x_{mn} \end{bmatrix}. \tag{7}$$

where $0 < i < n, i < k < n, j = i+1, p = k+1$

In each small matrix, the number of column is reduced, we merge the processed small matrices into a matrix and correlation coefficient method is used again. The number of column is greatly reduced and a merged column may be contains more than two columns.

4. Simultaneous clustering

The adjusting algorithms are used to guide simultaneously clustering text terms and feature terms. The higher the similarity between two feature terms are, the larger weight sum they have in the same text set. For example, given a disjoint text terms clusters $D_1, ..., D_k$, k is the number of text clusters, the corresponding feature terms clusters $T_1, ..., T_k$ may be get as

$$T_m = \left\{ t_i : \sum_{j \in D_m} \frac{x_{ij}}{M} >= \sum_{j \in D_l} \frac{x_{ij}}{L}, \forall l = 1, ..., k \right\}. \tag{8}$$

where M, L is the number of texts in D_m and D_l respectively. t_i belongs to the feature term clustering T_m only when its weight sum in the text terms clustering D_m is greater than its weight sum in any other text terms clustering.

At the same time, the text terms clusters may be determined according to the result of feature terms clustering. $D_1, ..., D_k$ may be calculated by

$$D_m = \left\{ d_j : \sum_{i \in T_m} \frac{x_{ij}}{M} \succ= \sum_{i \in T_l} \frac{x_{ij}}{L}, \forall l = 1, \ldots, k \right\}. \tag{9}$$

Where M, L is the number of feature terms in T_m and T_l respectively. The adjusting algorithms iteratively clustering hybrid feature and text until the results are no longer change. In our co-clustering algorithm, we not only consider the similarity between texts, but also the similarity between text and hybrid feature. The number of text clusters and hybrid feature clusters are the same and a hybrid feature cluster correspondences a text cluster, the hybrid feature cluster is the topic of the text cluster, so it is good to find a topic for a text cluster.

5. Experiment analysis

In experiment, dataset1, 2 and3 are supplied by Institute of Noetics and Wisdom, Southwest Jiaotong University [11] and dataset4 is standard text categorization collection Reuters-21578 [12]. Dataset1 has 3000 texts and 10000 dimensions for each text; dataset2 has 300 texts and 4198 dimensions for each text; dataset3 has 500 texts and 5413 dimensions for each text. Reuters-21578 is a collection of texts that appeared on Reuters newswire in 1987. We randomly selected 1000 texts of 8 classes, and removed corresponding zero column to get dataset4, so dataset4 is a 1000×5846 data matrix.

We compared the result of the hierarchical [7] and information theoretic [4] co-clustering with our improved algorithm in Figure 1.

From the Figure1, it is observed that the quality of co-clustering was influenced by the number of the divided data matrix. When the number is 40, the F-measure is the best. Feature extraction reduces the feature dimensions but maybe changes the original characteristics of feature terms. It is said that F-measure does not increase with the number of divided data matrix enlarges.

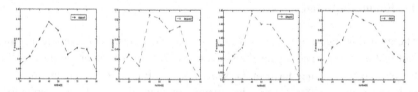

Figure 1. F-measure changing along with different number of the divided data matrix

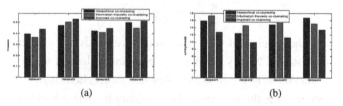

(a)   (b)

Figure 2. F-measure and running times on datasets

Each experiment was run 10 times. The average F-measure [9] and running time along with $n=40$ comparisons are shown in Figure 2 (a) and (b) respectively.

From the Figure 2(a) we noted that the proposed algorithm is better than the hierarchical and information theoretic co-clustering. The text matrix is a high dimension and sparse matrix, the correlation coefficient roughly find the relevant feature items and reduce the dimension. Feature clustering simultaneously guided text clustering, so it improves the performance of co-clustering. From the Figure 2(b), it is clear that the running time of the proposed algorithm is less than that of the hierarchical and information theoretic co-clustering. The greater the dimension is, the longer running time of the hierarchical and information theoretic co-clustering. In the divided matrices, the total calculation time of correlation coefficient is less than the original matrix.

6. Conclusion

In this work, we propose a text co-clustering algorithm. Firstly, the correlation coefficient is used to calculate the similarity of feature terms and merge them, which not only reduce dimension but also need not to give the number of feature terms clustering in advance. Secondly, the matrix block method improves the clustering efficiency. Experiment results show that the proposed algorithm improves the performance of co-clustering and reduces the running times.

References

1. X. Shi, W. Fan and S. Philip, *ICDM*. 1043 (2010).
2. J. R. Chen, *IEEE IS*. 355 (2010).
3. C. Ding, T. Li, W. Peng and H. Park, *ACM SIGKDD*. 126 (2006).
4. Y. Ling and C. Ye, *APCIP*. 201 (2009).
5. J. Li and T. Li, *SIGIR*. 861 (2010).
6. K. Hanmouda and M. Kamel, *IEEE Trans. KDE*. **Cf16(10),** 1270 (2004).
7. F. Huang, Y. Yang, T. Li, J. Zhang, T. Rutagisire, and A. Mahmood, *JRS, LNAI7414*. 310 (2012).
8. Y. Song, S. Pan, S. Liu, F. Wei, X. Michelle, and W. Qian, *IEEE Trans.KDE*. 1 (2012).
9. Y. Yang, L. Chen, and W. Tjhi, *FSS*. **Cf215(8),** 74 (2013).
10. Y. Yang, M. Kamel, and F. Jin, *WTRD*. 100 (2005).
11. http://www.yebol.com.cn.
12. http://www.daviddlewis.com/resources/testcollection/reuters21578.

EDUVISOR – DATA INTEGRATION SYSTEM FOR EDUCATION

JER LANG HONG

*School of Computing and IT, Taylor's University, Subang
Jaya, Malaysia*

There are many university websites on internet. These websites can be considered as
external information resources on the internet that academic institutions or students can use
this external resources in order to improve their decision making process. It is therefore,
very important and critical that the information of these external resources can be acquired
precisely and on time. Most university web sites provide data in a semi-structured form on
the internet. The combination of semi-structured data from different sources on the internet
often fails because of syntactic and semantic differences. The access, retrieval and
utilization of information from the different websites impose a need for the data to be
integrated. Integration of web data is a complex process because of the heterogeneity nature
of web data and thus needs some kind of a web data integration system. There are many
types of heterogeneity and differences among university websites that makes data
integration a difficult process (e.g., different data model, different syntax and semantics in
schema and data instance level among web sources). In this paper, we recommend a system
architecture for web data integration focusing on resolving the problems of semantic
heterogeneity between university websites. We propose an ontology-based approach as a
solution for the reconciliation of semantic conflicts between websites of universities and
then develop a prototype of the proposed system for universities.

Keywords: Academic institution website, Web data integration, Semantic conflict

1. Introduction

The web is the platform for information publishing; it is the biggest resource of
in-formation of any type. There are a lot of academic institution websites on
internet that contain valuable data that academic institutions can use to improve
their decision making process. It is therefore, very important and critical that this
information be complete, precise and can be acquired on time [5]. It is also vital
that such external information be systematically managed and utilized for users.
The solution to the mentioned problem is a web data integration system.
External information can be extracted from university websites and utilized for
users through a web data integration system. The access, retrieval and utilization

of information from the different websites impose a need for the data to be integrated. There are many types of heterogeneity and differences among university websites that make a combined effort to access data from different sources on the internet difficult and error-prone [6], [3].

In the extraction and integration of data of university websites we need to resolve heterogeneity conflicts between their data. There are different views about classification of Heterogeneity conflicts. The heterogeneity conflicts can be classified according to the following abstraction levels [3], [7]:

- Data Value Conflicts: Data value conflicts are those conflicts that arise at the instance level. They are related to the representation or the interpretation of the data values. Examples of these conflicts are discrepancies of type, unit, precision and allowed values (e.g. "kg" and "gram" or "$" and "dollar").

- Schema Conflicts: Schema conflicts are due to different alternatives provided by one data model to develop schemas for the same reality. For example, what is mod-eled as an attribute in one relational schema may be modeled as an entity in another relational schema for the same application domain (e.g. "Author" as attribute for the entity "book" and "author" as an entity that has a relationship with "book"). Another example two sources may use different names to represent the same concept (e.g. "price" and "cost") , or the same name to represent different concepts , or two differ-ent ways, for conveying the same information(e.g. "data of birth" and "age").

- Data Model Conflicts: Data model conflicts occur when databases use different data models, e.g., one database designed according to the relational model, and another one object-oriented. Conflicts in each level can be categorized into two categories:

- Syntactic Conflicts: Syntactic conflicts refer to discrepancies in the representation of data (e.g. "1/23" and "1.23" or "price=23$" and "price: 23$").

- Semantic Conflicts: Semantic conflicts refer to disagreement about the meaning, interpretation use of the same or related data (e.g. "staff" and "employee").

The major aim of our work is to give a solution for resolving heterogeneity conflicts mentioned above whiting university websites in a web data integration process. For this purpose we first recommend an approach and architecture for web data integration system and subsequently develop a prototype of our web data integration system in domain of universities.

2. Related Work

This section introduces some of the major projects that focus on web data extraction and integration. We categorize studied projects to ontology-based and non onto-logical web data integration system. Our focus is further on ontology-based projects for resolving semantic conflicts.

2.1. *Ontology-based web data integration projects*

The following projects use ontologies for resolving of semantic conflicts between web data sources. We briefly explain them in the next subsections.

1. COIN. The COIN [4] project presents a suitable architecture for semantic interoperability between distributed information sources. A context interchange (COIN) mediator is an automated reasoning engine to assist an organization in resolving semantic conflicts between its own receiver's context and the contexts of data sources. Context mediator resolve semantic conflicts among information sources through comparison of contexts associated with the in-formation sources. The COIN framework uses a data model and logical language to define the domain model of the application and the contexts. The domain model has the role of the ontology in the COIN-framework. Context mediator in Coin-architecture performs the process of rewriting queries posed in the receiver's context into a set of mediated queries where all potential conflicts are explicitly resolved.

2. MOMIS. MOMIS (Mediator Environment for Multiple Information Sources) [2] is one approach to the integration and query of semi-structured and structured heterogeneous data sources. The goal of MOMIS is to define a global schema that allows uniform and transparent access to the data stored in a set of semantically heterogeneous sources. MOMIS creates a global virtual view (GVV) of information sources, independent of their location or their data's heterogeneity.

3. KRAFT. The KRAFT (Knowledge Reuse And Fusion/Transformation) system [8] is a research prototype which is being developed collaboratively with BT by three UK universities - Aberdeen, Cardiff and Liverpool - for combining and transforming constraint based knowledge. The KRAFT architecture is designed to support knowledge fusion from distributed, heterogeneous databases and knowledge bases [8]. KRAFT is a project for the integration of heterogeneous information, using ontologies to resolve semantics problems. They extract the vocabulary of the community and the definition of terms from documents existing in an application domain.

4. SIMS. SIMS [1] is a system that exploits a semantic model of a domain to integrate the information from various information sources. SIMS uses a model from an application domain that includes a hierarchical terminological knowledge. The application model plays the role of a global

ontology in SIMS. SIMS uses a model from each information source that must be described for this system by relating the objects of each source to the global domain model. The relationships clarify the semantics of the source objects and help to find semantically corresponding (similar in meaning) objects. SIMS uses Loom as a knowledge representation language to describe the domain model and contents of the information sources.

3. Proposed Solution

To fully integrate the education advisor system, we need to develop a complete sys-tem which can be separated into several fundamental steps. Detail of these steps is described below:

1. Searching for education related information through the use of crawler

To search and located the desired information, we use Google API and per-form a specialized search using a specific search query which will return search results relevant to education information. Once search results are obtained from the Google search engine, we filtered them out using a set of heuristic rules. We repeat this step for Yahoo and Bing search engines, using their provided search API.

2. Extraction of education related information

Extracting relevant information from a web page where the layout and structure are of diverse format is a non trivial task. Fortunately, with the advancement of computing resources, and the wide availability of ontologies tools, it becomes possible to extract relevant information from web page using their semantic properties regardless of their structure and layout. To achieve this, we did a thorough study on several state of the art ontology tools. We found that CYC ontology is robust and covers a wide range of knowledge, however it is not suitable for our research due to its slow speed. Further observations led us to the well known and publicly available ontology tool WordNet. We found that WordNet provides a wide range of functionalities in their lexical database. Furthermore, several versions of Word-Net exist where upper ontology support is provided in their implementation. WordNet can also be implemented on various platforms, and it is also easily extensible in different environments. Finally, the processing of WordNet operation is reasonably fast, which is important for our system which relies on huge and highly dynamic data.

To locate the relevant information from the web page, we use HTML Parser to parse through the HTML page and obtained the DOM Tree. Once the DOM Tree is created, we traverse through the DOM Tree using depth first search. We create a list of keywords related to education information such as courses, departments, and universities. When a text node is encountered, its content is tokenized into a list of words which are separated by spaces. Irrelevant characters such as ', ; are removed from these words, and words are then converted to their root words using stemmers. Then, we match the words with the education information keywords we have created. We use WordNet similarity check to determine whether two words are related or not. For example, the words "School", and "Department" are nearly identical, hence WordNet similarity check will eventually detect and match them correctly.

Once the relevant keywords are identified, we use VIPS segmentation techniques to determine regions and have them extracted out accordingly. This procedure is repeated for the rest of the web pages.

3. Formatting of education related information

Using the previous segments, we can then format the data and have them presented in tabular form. We remove irrelevant content in segments by checking for irregularities in HTML structure and content. We pay more attention to the starting and ending of each content, where content such as bar, and navigation usually exists. We further use WordNet similarity check to remove content which is irrelevant to education information. After that, we parse through the segments and identify similar keywords within segments. Data with similar semantic properties are identified and grouped into similar category. For example, the keywords "School", and "Department" are semantically related and as such, they should be grouped into similar category. A label is chosen from the keywords that matched each category.

4. Analysis of education related information

Once formatting and tabulating of information is completed, we can then use the available data for further analysis. We assigned specific labels and tags to each category so that future users can easily identify and search for data which is relevant to their query. Labels and tags are assigned based on a number of criteria, such as number of occurrences of the keywords, number of keywords with the highest similarity in terms of semantic relatedness, and keywords which appear the most in the segments.

5. Development of decision support rules

Once the data is labeled and tagged, we develop a system which provides an intuitive interface for the users to browse, navigate, and search for information. A general interface is provided where users are able to enter a specific search query to obtain the information. A more specific search interface is provided where users are able to search for their information based on specific criteria, such as "Year", and "Range of Tuition Fees". A design of the user interface is made to be as simple as possible and user friendly.

4. Conclusions

In this paper, we have developed an education based search engine for users to locate their course on interest. Our system provides an intuitive interface for the users to locate their desire information. To make our system fast and efficient, our system is supported by background updating of data, where the crawler will search through the web and perform the necessary updates. Unlike existing decision support system, our system is capable to search through a wide range of education information regardless of their structure and layout. We hope to extend our system to support other type of data in the near future, such as stock exchange, airline booking, and financial data.

References

1. Arens, Y., Ciiee, Y., Knoblock, A. (1997). SIMS: Integrating Heterogeneous, Distributed Information Sources. Proceedings of the 1997 ONDCP/CTAC International Technology Symposium. Office of National Drug Control Policy, Executive Office of the President. Chicago, IL. August 18-21, 1997.
2. Beneventano, D., Bergamaschi, S., Guerra, F. and Vincini. M. (2004). The MOMIS Methodology for Integrating Heterogeneous Data Sources, IFIP World Computer Congress. Toulouse France, 22-27 August 2004.
3. Fensel, D. 2001: Ontologies: A Silver Bullet for Knowledge Management and Electronic Commerce. Springer-Verlag.
4. Goh, C. H., Bressan, S., Madnick, S. and Siegel, M. (1999). Context interchange New features and formalisms for the intelligent integration of information. ACM Transaction on Information Systems, vol. 17, no. 3, pages 270–293.
5. Heflin, J., and Hendler, J., 2000: Semantic interoperability on the web. In Extreme Markup Languages 2000.http://www.cs.umd.edu/projects/plus/ SHOE/pubs/extreme2000 .pdf.
6. Kashyap, V., and Sheth, A. 1998: Semantic heterogeneity in global information systems: The role of metadata, context and ontologies. In Papazoglou, M. P. and Schlageter, G., editors, Cooperative Information Systems: Current Trends and Directions, pages 139–178.Academic Press Ltd.
7. Ram S., Park, J. 2004: Semantic Conflict Resolution Ontology (SCROL): An Ontology for Detecting and Resolving Data and Schema-Level Semantic Conflicts, IEEE Transactions on Knowledge and Data Engineering, v.16 n.2, p.189-202.
8. Visser, P. R., Jones, D. M., Beer, M., Bench-Capon, T., Diaz B. and Shave, M. (2000). *KRAFT: An Agent Architecture for Knowledge Fusion.* International Journal on Intelligent Cooperative Information Systems (IJCIS). http://www.csd.abdn.ac.uk/research/kraft.html

A NOVEL FRAMEWORK FOR VALIDATING DYNAMIC WEB APPLICATIONS WITH MULTI LANGUAGE INTEGRATION ACROSS DIFFERENT PLATFORMS

CHEE SHEEN CHAN

*School of Computing and IT, Taylor's University, Subang
Jaya, Malaysia*

JER LANG HONG

*School of Computing and IT, Taylor's University, Subang
Jaya, Malaysia*

Most of the dynamic web applications generates HTML web documents that are deemed invalid as they do not adhere to the HTML standards defined under the World Wide Consortium (W3C). Though state-of-the-art web browsers are capable of rendering malformed HTML documents by correcting these errors discretely, most of the time such incidents poses compatibility issues which causes performance degradation for some applications. Various validation tools have been developed and are widely available across the Internet to address the mentioned issue, however, these tools only worked well for static web applications since it doesn't address the aggressive nature of dynamic web applications. Furthermore, validation tools targeting dynamic web applications available currently employ a static technique which is impossible in examining every single execution route possible. To resolve such issue, we have presented a novel framework for validating dynamic web applications through a set of heuristic rules which takes into consideration the syntax of several well-known server side languages such as PHP, Java EE and ASP.NET. As an extension to that paper, we now introduces a path finding and cross platform tools to validate HTML tags based on the server side language flow of execution.

Keywords: Validation, HTML, Web Technologies.

1. Introduction

The World Wide Web (WWW) was introduced by Sir Tim Bernes-Lee as a heterogeneous system that is capable of linking various browsers and servers developed by a wide range of software vendors. To assure the development of high-quality and robust web applications within the WWW environment, W3C has laid out a set of standards in which web developers should follow while coding their web applications. As a matter of fact, high quality web applications are typically developed by adhering to a number of criterions suggested by W3C with markup validity being the top in the list. Markup validity refers to the official DTD for HTML 4.01 or XHTML 1.0 of web documents in HTML as well as other client-side markup web languages with respect to their respective grammar, vocabulary and syntactical rules. There are a number of validation tools provided by W3C as well as other external parties which are widely available over the Internet to validate HTML documents such as W3C markup validation service, which verifies well-formedness of HTML and XHTML documents, grammar, syntax, spelling as well as proofreading.

It is apparent that dynamic web applications are gradually replacing static HTML due to the potential benefits it has to offer in the future. Since the web documents are generated at run time by these scripts running on a web server such as PHP, ASP.NET, Java EE and etc, it poses multiple challenges to web developers to ensure its validity. Although state-of-the-art web browsers in the market such as Internet Explorer, Google Chrome, Mozilla Firefox and etc. mostly comes with the capability of parsing and rendering malformed HTML web documents, there exists certain bugs or defects which are present in web applications that cannot be identified easily due to the dynamic nature of server-side programming. Checking for HTML validation errors during the development stage has been proven to be one of the methods on which the effort of identifying bugs and defects could be minimized. A large number of web professionals admitted that HTML validation errors are the first thing they cheek whenever they run into scripting or web styling bug based on a survey conducted by W3C [1].

There are a collection of validation tools which caters for dynamic web applications, however these tools can only perform static analysis on the HTML web documents that are being generated on the fly which doesn't take into consideration of the defects that are 'hidden' within the web application. In actual fact, every single execution route within the dynamic web application needs to be validated in an ideal environment in order to guarantee that valid HTML documents could be generated because most of the time, these 'hidden' defects are responsible for generating these malformed HTML documents.

Prior to this paper, we have introduced a novel framework which utilizes an aggregation of heuristic rules to validate dynamic web applications. The framework proposed is implementable by PHP, Java EE and ASP.NET which act as the stepping stone to a more sophisticated dynamic web validation. And in this paper, our goal is to detect the most crucial part in dynamic web validation, which is the execution path generated by server side scripts. Checking and determining the flow of execution is a non-trivial task due to the highly dynamic and unpredictable codes generated and written by the developers. Fortunately, it is possible to determine the flow of execution as languages written in PHP, Java EE, and ASP.NET come with well-defined libraries, and well developed programming syntaxes.

2. Related Work

Several former work on web application testing concentrated on static web pages as well as the non-closely structure control flow between them, where a handful of them focused on server-side scripts. Unfortunately, these works are not appropriate for testing malformed HTML web pages that are being generated on the fly because they do not address the dynamic issues of web applications [7]. Due to this reason, languages under consideration of this paper: PHP, ASP.NET and J2EE are distinctive as compared to previous researches due to its dynamic nature. Kung et. al. [2][3] developed a test enumeration algorithm based on several models which encompasses Object Relation Diagrams, Object State Diagrams, Script Cluster Diagram as well as a Page Navigation Diagram of the application under investigation. Fisher et. al. [6] demonstrates methodologies which attempt to extract the application behavior using client side information. A form of dynamic analysis, in which direct requests are forwarded to the applications and inferences regarding its interface can be acquired by examining responses can be used in distinguishing interfaces of web applications.

Ricca and Tonella [4] introduce a methodology to examine static web pages through the utilization of UML models of web applications. Web application is perceived as an instance of the UML model because it does not encompasses any dynamic perspective of web applications. There exists a contradiction within its claim of guaranteeing coverage of "all paths in a web application" because the information regarding the links composed on the fly prohibits the paths that are being covered. Elbuam et. al. [8] uses several techniques to aggregate user session data while users are operating web applications to facilitate testing those applications from a functional perspective. Their results has proven that more effective test suites can be generated from user session data as compared to those produced by white-box techniques. Lee and Offutt [9] illustrate a system that generates test cases by using a form of mutation analysis. Their focus was about validation of the reliability of data interaction among web-based software components. Benedikt et. al [5] presented VeriWeb for testing dynamic web pages without human intervention by examining sequences of links in web applications by analyzing sequence of actions non-deterministically. A human tester pre-populate the user profiles with values where users would possibly supply such that these name-value pairs furnished by the human tester will then be used by VeriWeb to provide data to forms.

3. Problem Formulation

The architecture of dynamic web applications are different and a lot more complex as compared to static web pages because it consists of more than the front end graphical user interface that users see. Most of the time, dynamic web applications are functioning in a non-clustered asynchronous environment, making the quality of web applications a multidimensional attribute. Without a shadow of doubt, various aspects of web applications needs to be addressed in the process of improving its quality, for instance accessibility, derivation of appropriate models, evaluation of multilingual positioning as well as reorganization. However, the gist of this paper is the quality of web applications in terms of validity (adherence to official DTD for HTML 4.01 or XHTML 1.0 set by W3C) of HTML documents generated by these web applications.

4. Motivation

Prior to this paper, we have introduced a novel framework which utilizes an aggregation of heuristic rules to validate dynamic web applications. The framework proposed is implementable by PHP, Java EE and ASP.NET which act as the stepping stone to a more sophisticated dynamic web validation. Since mobile devices are progressively being used as a tool for browsing the internet, there exists an increased necessity in validating the HTML web documents generated on the fly against the official DTD for HTML 4.01 or XHTML 1.0 set by W3C because it is the fundamental step in ensuring compatibility across various devices and web browsers. Furthermore, browsers process valid sites faster than invalid ones although they are equipped with modules that correct markup errors. And last but not least, we are the first to extend from the novel validation framework in our previous paper.

5. Proposed Solution

5.1. *UniConstruct*

In UniConstruct, we first parse through the server side scripts and then construct a list of commands which could potentially interpreted by the server side scripts. Special attention is given to commands which print out HTML Tags. Commands which called an external library are ruled out from the list as these commands do not contribute to the HTML Tag creation, which is crucial for HTML

Validation. The same applies for class creation, and exit statements. Commands which are given due consideration are such as logical statements (they could potentially determine the output of server side scripts when executed), print statements, echo statements, and method calls. Every valuable commands interpreted by the server side scripts leading to HTML Tag creation are stored in a list. In this list, special labels are given to each command, where a command can be method call, print statements, logical operator, nested loops, and reference to other objects.

Since server side scripts are written and implemented differently across languages, we need to carefully examine them and determine which languages are they implemented in. PHP language is widely used and simple, however they are not type safe. For this reason, a conversion tool is implemented to convert variables to their associated type. Due considerations are given to include statements and PHP class which can be encapsulated within other PHP class. For the case of Java EE, there are two types of files which could generate HTML Tags, they are JSP and Servlets. In the case of JSP, we implement a tool for handling HTML Tags and JSP Tags. Mapping between JSP codes and HTML Tags are carried out in JSP pages. Since JSP codes are highly dynamic, we determine the possibilities of HTML codes generated by the JSP codes. For the static HTML codes in JSP, we append them to the generated JSP codes so that we can determine the expected output. In the case of Servlets, we need to carefully examine the flow of execution of logical operator that could lead to println statements, particularly statements which print out HTML tags. As in ASP.NET codes, we develop a tool which could potentially handle the various languages supported such as C, C++, VB, and C#. Similar conventions to that of Java are applied to these languages. Since languages such as C# are the logical codes in ASP.NET, we need to convert the output of these languages to the output in ASP pages. We use the same convention in JSP for this conversion.

5.2. UniFlow

In UniFlow, we check for the flow of execution path. From the list created in the previous section, we first called the server side scripts using predefined parameters, and then we determine the flow of execution based on these parameters. The parameters entered could lead us to certain state, which generates a set of HTML codes. Using the generated HTML codes, we can then validate them to check their conformance to HTML syntaxes. Since server side scripts are highly dynamic, we test our approach by providing a list of parameters, and then we validate the output of the generated HTML codes. To cover the validation test as much as possible, we determine the lower and upper bound of each parameter. Then, we randomly select a parameter within the range to test the validation. The test is repeated for the remaining scripts.

6. Conclusions

We proposed a novel framework for validating dynamic server side scripts. To the best of our knowledge, our framework is the first to validate such scripts across multiple platforms. Validating server scripts is a non trivial task due to the highly dynamic codes generated server side language. We are able to validate server side scripts across multiple platforms using flow check and path execution of the implemented languages. Validating server side scripts is important as it allows compatibility across different browsers and faster processing when the browsers render the pages. Our tool is certainly useful for future validator tool design.

References

1. "Why Validate," http://validator.w3.org/docs/why.html, W3C.
2. D. Kung, C. H. Liu, P. Hsia. A model-based approach for testing Web applications. Proceedings of 12th International Conference on Software Engineering and Knowledge Engineering (2000).
3. D. Kung, C. H. Liu, P. Hsia. An object-oriented Web test model for testing Web applications. Proceedings of IEEE 24th Annual International Computer Software and Applications Conference (2000).
4. F. Ricca, P. Tonella, "Analysis and testing of web applications," International Conference on Software Engineering (2001).
5. M. Benedikt, J. Freire, and P. Godefroid, "VeriWeb: Automatically testing dynamic Web sites," *Proc. Int'l Conf. World Wide Web* (2002).
6. M. Fisher, S. G. Elbaum, and G. Rothermel, "Dynamic characterization of Web application interfaces," *Proc. Int'l Conf. FundamentalApproaches to Software Eng.* (2007).
7. Rick Hower. Web site test tools and site management tools. Software QA and Testing Resource Center. Available: http://www.softwareqatest.com/qatweb1.html.
8. S. Elbaum, S. Karre, G. Rothermel, M. Fisher, "Leveraging user session data to support Web application testing," Proceedings IEEE Transaction on Software Engineering, vol. 31. no. 3 (2005).
9. Suet Chun Lee, Jeff Offutt. Generating test cases for XML-based Web component interactions using mutation analysis. Proceedings of the 12th International Symposium on Software Reliability Engineering (2001).

MULTI-FOLLOWER TRI-LEVEL DECISION MAKING WITH UNCOOPERATIVE FOLLOWERS

JIALIN HAN[1,2], JIE LU[2], GUANGQUAN ZHANG[2], SHUYUAN MA[1]

[1]*Industrial and Systems Engineering Laboratory, School of Mechanical Engineering, Beijing Institute of Technology, China*
[2]*Decision Systems and e-Service Intelligence Laboratory, Center for Quantum Computation & Intelligent Systems, Faculty of Engineering and Information Technology, University of Technology, Sydney, Australia*

Multi-follower tri-level (MFTL) decision making addresses compromises among three interacting decision units within a hierarchical system of which multiple followers are involved in two lower-level units. The leader's decision is affected not only by reactions of the followers but also by various relationships among them. The uncooperative relationship is the most basic situation in MFTL decision cases where multiple followers at the same level make individual decisions without any information exchange or share among them. To support such a MFTL decision, this paper firstly proposes a general model for the decision problem and then develops an extreme-point search algorithm based on bi-level Kth-Best approach to solve the model. Finally, a numerical experiment illustrates the decision model and procedures of the extreme-point search algorithm.

1. Introduction

Tri-level decision making (also known as tri-level programming) can be considered as solving two optimization problems in sequence within a three-level hierarchical system where the constraint region of the first is implicitly determined by the solution to the second that is a bi-level programming problem. This category of decision making often appears in many decentralized management problems with decision processes in a hierarchy in real world [1, 2]. Decision entities allocated at the three hierarchical levels are respectively termed as the top-level leader, the middle-level follower and the bottom-level follower. Their decision processes are interactive until they achieve equilibrium in the vertical structure.

Tri-level decision making has been attracting increasing research on models [3, 4], solution concepts [3, 4], solution algorithms [3-5] and applications [6, 7]. However, the research has been limited to that one single decision entity is allocated at each level. Actually, multiple followers are often involved at the middle and bottom levels of a tri-level decision case called multi-follower tri-level (MFTL) decision making [8]. In this instance, the leader's decision is affected not only by reactions of multiple followers at both lower levels but also by various relationships among multiple followers at the same level. Tri-level decision making with such different relationships is needed to describe and solve by individual decision models and solution algorithms. However, investigates on hierarchical decision making with multiple followers have been centered on bi-level hierarchy [9-11] while nearly no research on MFTL decision making has been proposed except few brief programming models [8, 12]. Therefore, the research on MFTL decision making involving models, solution algorithms and applications should be further explored.

Within the framework of MFTL decision making, the uncooperative relationship is the most basic situation where multiple followers at the same level make their respective and individual decisions without any information exchange or share. This situation is very popular in a hierarchical organization involving competitive and uncooperative decision entities. Therefore, contributions of this paper aim to establish a general decision model and develop an available solution algorithm to describe and solve the uncooperative MFTL decision problem. More specifically, we firstly propose a linear MFTL decision model with the uncooperative relationship among both the middle-level followers and the bottom-level followers. To find a solution to the model, an extreme-point search algorithm based on bi-level Kth-Best approach [13] is developed. Finally, a numerical experiment is adopted to illustrate the MFTL decision model and procedures of the algorithm.

2. An Uncooperative MFTL Decision Model

For $x \in X \in R^k$, $y_i \in Y_i \subset R^{k_i}$, $z_{ij} \in Z_{ij} \subset R^{k_{ij}}$, $F: X \times Y_1 \times \cdots \times Y_n \times Z_1 \times \cdots \times Z_{1m_1} \times \cdots \times Z_{nm_n} \to R^1$, $f_i^{(2)}: X \times Y_i \times Z_{i1} \times \cdots \times Z_{im_i} \to R^1$, $f_{ij}^{(3)}: X \times Y_i \times Z_{ij} \to R^1$, $j = 1,2,\cdots,m_i$, $i = 1,2,\cdots,n$, an uncooperative MFTL decision model in a linear version in which one leader, n middle-level followers and m_i bottom-level followers attached to the ith middle-level follower are involved is defined as follows:

$$\min_{x \in X} F(x, y_1, \cdots, y_n, z_{11}, \cdots, z_{1m_1}, \cdots, z_{n1}, \cdots, z_{nm_n}) = cx + \sum_{i=1}^{n} d_i y_i + \sum_{i=1}^{n} \sum_{j=1}^{m_i} e_{ij} z_{ij} \tag{1a}$$

$$\text{s.t.} \quad Ax + \sum_{i=1}^{n} B_i y_i + \sum_{i=1}^{n} \sum_{j=1}^{m_i} C_{ij} z_{ij} \le b, \tag{1b}$$

where $(y_i, z_{i1}, \cdots, z_{im_i})$ $(i = 1,2,\cdots,n)$ solves the ith middle-level follower's and its bottom-level followers' problems (1c-1f):

$$\min_{y_i \in Y_i} f_i^{(2)}(x, y_i, z_{i1}, \cdots, z_{im_i}) = c_i x + g_i y_i + \sum_{j=1}^{m_i} h_{ij} z_{ij} \tag{1c}$$

$$\text{s.t. } A_i x + D_i y_i + \sum_{j=1}^{m_i} E_{ij} z_{ij} \le b_i, \tag{1d}$$

where z_{ij} $(j=1,2,\cdots,m_i)$ solves the ith middle-level follower's jth bottom-level follower's problem (1e-1f):

$$\min_{z_{ij} \in Z_{ij}} f_{ij}^{(3)}(x, y_i, z_{ij}) = c_{ij} x + p_{ij} y_i + q_{ij} z_{ij} \tag{1e}$$

$$\text{s.t. } A_{ij} x + P_{ij} y_i + Q_{ij} z_{ij} \le b_{ij}, \tag{1f}$$

where $c, c_i, c_{ij} \in R^k$, $d_i, g_i, p_{ij} \in R^{k_i}$, $e_{ij}, h_{ij}, q_{ij} \in R^{k_{ij}}$, $A \in R^{s \times k}$, $A_i \in R^{s_i \times k}$, $A_{ij} \in R^{s_{ij} \times k}$,

$B_i \in R^{s \times k_i}$, $D_i \in R^{s_i \times k_i}$, $P_{ij} \in R^{s_{ij} \times k_i}$, $C_{ij} \in R^{s \times k_{ij}}$, $E_{ij} \in R^{s_i \times k_{ij}}$, $Q_{ij} \in R^{s_{ij} \times k_{ij}}$, $b \in R^s$, $b_i \in R^{s_i}$,

, $b_{ij} \in R^{s_{ij}}$ for $j=1,2,\cdots,m_i, i=1,2,\cdots,n$.

3. An Extreme-point Search Algorithm

According to theoretical properties of multi-follower bi-level (MFBL) programming proposed by Calvete and Gale [9], we have the following theorem about MFTL decision making.

Theorem 1 The uncooperative MFTL decision problem (1) is equivalent to the MFTL decision problem (2) involving one leader, n middle-level followers and one single bottom-level follower attached to each middle-level follower:

$$\min_{x} F(x, y_1, \cdots, y_n, z_{11}, \cdots, z_{1m_1}, \cdots, z_{n1}, \cdots, z_{nm_n}) = cx + \sum_{i=1}^{n} d_i y_i + \sum_{i=1}^{n} \sum_{j=1}^{m_i} e_{ij} z_{ij} \tag{2a}$$

$$\text{s.t. } Ax + \sum_{i=1}^{n} B_i y_i + \sum_{i=1}^{n} \sum_{j=1}^{m_i} C_{ij} z_{ij} \le b, \tag{2b}$$

where $(y_i, z_{i1}, \cdots, z_{im_i})$ $(i=1,2,\cdots,n)$ solves the ith middle-level follower's and its bottom-level followers' problems (2c-2f):

$$\min_{y_i} f_i^{(2)}(x, y_i, z_{i1}, \cdots, z_{im_i}) = c_i x + g_i y_i + \sum_{j=1}^{m_i} h_{ij} z_{ij} \tag{2c}$$

$$\text{s.t. } A_i x + D_i y_i + \sum_{j=1}^{m_i} E_{ij} z_{ij} \le b_i, \tag{2d}$$

where $(z_{i1}, \cdots, z_{im_i})$ solves the ith middle-level follower's bottom-level follower's problem (2e-2f):

$$\min_{z_{i1}, \cdots, z_{im_i}} f_i^{(3)}(x, y_i, z_{i1}, \cdots, z_{im_i}) = \sum_{j=1}^{m_i} (c_{ij} x + p_{ij} y_i + q_{ij} z_{ij}) \tag{2e}$$

$$\text{s.t. } A_{ij} x + P_{ij} y_i + Q_{ij} z_{ij} \le b_{ij}, j=1,2,\cdots,m_i. \tag{2f}$$

The extreme-point search algorithm

Step 1: Set $k=1$, adopt the simplex method to obtain the optimal solution $(x^1, y_1^1, \cdots, y_n^1, z_{11}^1, \cdots, z_{1m_1}^1, \cdots, z_{n1}^1, \cdots, z_{nm_n}^1)$ to the linear programming problem

$\{\min_x F(x, y_1, \cdots, y_n, z_{11}, \cdots, z_{1m_1}, \cdots, z_{n1}, \cdots, z_{nm_n}) : (x, y_1, \cdots, y_n, z_{11}, \cdots, z_{1m_1}, \cdots, z_{n1}, \cdots, z_{nm_n}) \in S\}.$

Let $W = \{(x^1, y_1^1, \cdots, y_n^1, z_{11}^1, \cdots, z_{1m_1}^1, \cdots, z_{n1}^1, \cdots, z_{nm_n}^1)\}$ and $T = \varnothing$. Set $i=1$ and go to Step 2.

Step 2: Put $x = x^k$, and adopt the bi-level Kth-Best approach [13] to solve the ith bi-level decision problem (2c-2f) and obtain the optimal solution $(\hat{y}_i, \hat{z}_{i1}, \cdots, \hat{z}_{im_i})$.
Then go to Step 3.

Step 3: If $(\hat{y}_i, \hat{z}_{i1}, \cdots, \hat{z}_{im_i}) \neq (y_i^k, z_{i1}^k, \cdots, z_{im_i}^k)$, go to Step 4. If $(\hat{y}_i, \hat{z}_{i1}, \cdots, \hat{z}_{im_i}) = (y_i^k, z_{i1}^k, \cdots, z_{im_i}^k)$ and $i \neq n$, set $i=i+1$ and go to Step 2. If $(\hat{y}_i, \hat{z}_{i1}, \cdots, \hat{z}_{im_i}) = (y_i^k, z_{i1}^k, \cdots, z_{im_i}^k)$ and $i = n$, stop and $(x^k, y_1^k, \cdots, y_n^k, z_{11}^k, \cdots, z_{1m_1}^k, \cdots, z_{n1}^k, \cdots, z_{nm_n}^k)$ is the optimal solution to the decision problems (2) and (1), and $K^* = k$.

Step 4: Let W_k denote the set of adjacent extreme points of $(x^k, y_1^k, \cdots, y_n^k, z_{11}^k, \cdots, z_{1m_1}^k, \cdots, z_{n1}^k, \cdots, z_{nm_n}^k)$ such that $(x, y_1, \cdots, y_n, z_{11}, \cdots, z_{1m_1}, \cdots, z_{n1}, \cdots, z_{nm_n}) \in W_k$
implies $cx + \sum_{i=1}^{n} d_i y_i + \sum_{i=1}^{n}\sum_{j=1}^{m_i} e_{ij} z_{ij} \geq cx^k + \sum_{i=1}^{n} d_i y_i^k + \sum_{i=1}^{n}\sum_{j=1}^{m_i} e_{ij} z_{ij}^k$. Let $T = T \cup \{(x^k, y_1^k, \cdots, y_n^k, z_{11}^k, \cdots, z_{1m_1}^k, \cdots, z_{n1}^k, \cdots, z_{nm_n}^k)\}$ and $W = (W \cup W_k) \setminus T$. Go to Step 5.

Step 5: Set $k=k+1$ and choose $(x^k, y_1^k, \cdots, y_n^k, z_{11}^k, \cdots, z_{1m_1}^k, \cdots, z_{n1}^k, \cdots, z_{nm_n}^k)$ such that $cx^k + \sum_{i=1}^{n} d_i y_i^k + \sum_{i=1}^{n}\sum_{j=1}^{m_i} e_{ij} z_{ij}^k = \min\{cx + \sum_{i=1}^{n} d_i y_i + \sum_{i=1}^{n}\sum_{j=1}^{m_i} e_{ij} z_{ij} : (x, y_1, \cdots, y_n, z_{11}, \cdots, z_{1m_1}, \cdots, z_{n1}, \cdots, z_{nm_n}) \in W\}$. Set $i=1$ and go to Step 2.

4. A Numerical Experiment

For $X = \{x : x \geq 0\}$, $Y_i = \{y_i : y_i \geq 0\}$, $Z_{ij} = \{z_{ij} : z_{ij} \geq 0\}$, $j = 1, 2, \cdots, m_i$, $i = 1, 2$, $m_1 = m_2 = 2$,

$\min_{x \in X} F(x, y_1, y_2, z_{11}, z_{12}, z_{21}, z_{22}) = -x + y_1 - 2y_2 + 2z_{11} + z_{12} - z_{21} - 3z_{22}$
s.t. $x + y_1 + y_2 + z_{11} + 2z_{12} + 2z_{21} + z_{22} \geq 9$,
$x \leq 1$,

$\left\{\begin{array}{l}\min_{y_1 \in Y_1} f_1^{(2)}(x, y_1, z_{11}, z_{12}) = x - y_1 + z_{11} + z_{12} \\ \text{s.t. } 2x + y_1 + z_{11} + z_{12} \geq 8, \\ \quad\quad y_1 \leq 1, \\ \left\{\begin{array}{l}\min_{z_{11} \in Z_{11}} f_{11}^{(3)}(x, y_1, z_{11}) = x + y_1 + 2z_{11} \\ \text{s.t. } x + y_1 + z_{11} \geq 4, \\ \quad\quad z_{11} \leq 3, \\ \min_{z_{12} \in Z_{12}} f_{12}^{(3)}(x, y_1, y_0, z_{12}) = 2x + y_1 + z_{12} \\ \text{s.t. } x + y_1 + z_{12} \geq 5, \\ \quad\quad x + z_{12} \leq 4, \end{array}\right.\end{array}\right.$

$\left\{\begin{array}{l}\min_{y_2 \in Y_2} f_2^{(2)}(x, y_2, z_{21}, z_{22}) = x + 2y_2 + z_{21} + z_{22} \\ \text{s.t. } x + y_2 + z_{21} + z_{22} \geq 4, \\ \quad\quad y_2 \leq 1, \\ \left\{\begin{array}{l}\min_{z_{21} \in Z_{21}} f_{21}^{(3)}(x, y_2, z_{21}) = x + y_2 + 3z_{21} \\ \text{s.t. } x + y_2 + z_{21} \geq 2.5, \\ \quad\quad z_{21} \leq 1, \\ \min_{z_{22} \in Z_{22}} f_{22}^{(3)}(x, y_2, z_{21}) = x + 2y_2 + 2z_{22} \\ \text{s.t. } x + y_2 + z_{22} \geq 3, \\ \quad\quad z_{22} \leq 2. \end{array}\right.\end{array}\right.$

We adopt the extreme-point search algorithm to solve the MFTL decision problem and the detailed computing process is showed as Table 1.

Table 1 The detailed computing process by the extreme-point search algorithm

Iteration k	$s^k = (x^k, y_1^k, y_2^k, z_{11}^k, z_{12}^k, z_{21}^k, z_{22}^k)$	W_k	T	W
1	(1,1,1,2,3,1,2)	{(1,1,1,2,3,1,1), (0.5,1,1,2.5,3.5,1,2), (1,1,0.5,2,3,1,2), (1,1,1,2,3,0.5,2)}	$\{s^1\}$	W_1
2	(1,1,1,2,3,0.5,2)	{(1,1,1,2,3,0.5,1.5)}	$\{s^1, s^2\}$	$(W \cup W_2) \setminus T$
3	(1,1,0.5,2,3,1,2)	{(1,1,0.5,2,3,1,1.5)}	$\{s^1, s^2, s^3\}$	$(W \cup W_3) \setminus T$
4	(0.5,1,1,2.5,3.5,1,2)	{(0.5,1,1,2.5,3.5,1,1.5)}	$\{s^1, s^2, s^3, s^4\}$	$(W \cup W_4) \setminus T$
5	(1,1,1,2,3,0.5,1.5)	$\varnothing$	$\{s^1, s^2, s^3, s^4, s^5\}$	$(W \cup W_5) \setminus T$
6	(1,1,0.5,2,3,1,1.5)			

Table 1 presents the set W_k of adjacent extreme points of each vertex s_k after each iteration k. T represents the set of extreme points that have been searched in the past iterations while W is the set of extreme points that are needed to verify whether the optimal solution or not in the following iterations. We finally get the optimal solution through six iterations. In iteration 6, $(x^6, y_1^6, y_2^6, z_{11}^6, z_{12}^6, z_{21}^6, z_{22}^6) = (1,1,0.5,2,3,1,1.5)$ is the optimal solution to the uncooperative MFTL decision problem and the objective function values of all decision entities are $F = 0.5$, $f_1^{(2)} = 5$, $f_2^{(2)} = 4.5$, $f_{11}^{(3)} = 6$, $f_{12}^{(3)} = 6$, $f_{21}^{(3)} = 4.5$, $f_{22}^{(3)} = 5$. It is noticeable that $W_5 = \varnothing$ in Table 1 does not mean adjacent extreme points of $(x^5, y_1^5, y_2^5, z_{11}^5, z_{12}^5, z_{21}^5, z_{22}^5)$ do not exist but implies its adjacent extreme points have been found in previous iterations and have been involved in W.

5. Conclusions

In a MFTL decision problem, various relationships among multiple followers at the same level would generate different decision processes. To support MFTL decision in an uncooperative situation, this paper firstly proposes a general decision model in a linear version. To find an optimal solution to the model, it then develops an extreme-point search algorithm based on bi-level Kth-Best approach [13]. Finally, a numerical experiment is adopted to illustrate the model and algorithm, which shows that the algorithm provides an available way in solving the proposed uncooperative MFTL decision problem. Our further research is to explore other relationships, such as cooperative and reference-uncooperative situations [8], among multiple followers and applications of MFTL decision making in real world.

References

1. X. Xu, Z. Meng, and R. Shen, A tri-level programming model based on Conditional Value-at-Risk for three-stage supply chain management, Computers & Industrial Engineering, 66, 470-475 (2013).
2. N. Alguacil, A. Delgadillo, and J. M. Arroyo, A trilevel programming approach for electric grid defense planning, Computers & Operations Research, 41, 282-290 (2014).
3. J. F. Bard, An investigation of the linear three level programming problem, IEEE Transactions on Systems, Man, and Cybernetics, SMC-14, 711-717 (1984).
4. G. Zhang, J. Lu, J. Montero, and Y. Zeng, Model, solution concept, and Kth-best algorithm for linear trilevel programming, Information Sciences, 180, 481-492 (2010).
5. D. J. White, Penalty function approach to linear trilevel programming, Journal of Optimization Theory and Applications, 93, 183-197 (1997).
6. A. Street, A. Moreira, and J. M. Arroyo, Energy and reserve scheduling under a joint generation and transmission security criterion: An adjustable robust optimization approach, IEEE Transactions on Power Systems, 29, 3-14 (2013).
7. Y. Yao, T. Edmunds, D. Papageorgiou, and R. Alvarez, Trilevel optimization in power network defense, IEEE Transactions on Systems, Man, and Cybernetics, 37, 712-718 (2007).
8. J. Lu, G. Zhang, J. Montero, and L. Garmendia, Multifollower trilevel decision making models and system, IEEE Transactions on Industrial Informatics, 8, 974-985 (2012).
9. H. I. Calvete and C. Galé, Linear bilevel multi-follower programming with independent followers, Journal of Global Optimization, 39, 409-417 (2007).
10. B. Liu, Stackelberg-Nash equilibrium for multilevel programming with multiple followers using genetic algorithms, Computers & Mathematics with Applications, 36, 79-89 (1998).
11. J. Lu, C. Shi, and G. Zhang, On bilevel multi-follower decision making: General framework and solutions, Information Sciences, 176, 1607-1627 (2006).
12. S. Hsu-Shih, L. Young-Jou, and E. S. Lee, Fuzzy approach for multi-level programming problems, Computers & Operations Research, 23, 73-91 (1996).
13. J. F. Bard, Practical Bilevel Optimization: Algorithms and Applications. Dordrecht: Kluwer Academic Publishers, 195-204 (1998).

A FUZZY SNS COMMUNITY CENTRALITY ANALYSIS METHOD AND A CASE STUDY ON *REN REN NET* IN CHINA*

ZI LU[1], QIULUAN ZHANG[1], DIANSHUANG WU[2], FANG GAO[1]

[1]*School of Tourism, Hebei Normal University, Shijiazhuang, Hebei 050024, P.R. China*
[2]*Decision Systems & e-Service Intelligence Lab, Centre for Quantum Computation & Intelligent Systems, Faculty of Engineering and Information Technology, University of Technology, Sydney, Australia*

Social networking services (SNS) have had a rapid development. To explore the interpersonal node spatial distribution characteristics in SNS community, a fuzzy SNS community centrality analysis method is proposed, which combines graph-theory with related fuzzy approaches. A case study on two types of topic groups in *Ren Ren Net* is conducted. The study finds that centralization characteristics exist in the interpersonal node spatial distribution in SNS community and present significant difference among groups of different relation types. The findings can directly support the SNS management and development.

1. Introduction

Social networking services (SNS) have been developed rapidly and many SNS communities have been constructed, which attracts great attention from researchers. Some SNS community theoretical analysis has been done. For example, Abbasi et al. [1] developed a theoretical model based on social network theories and analytical methods, using measures from social network analysis. Recently, SNS community researches began to focus on the spatial characteristic. The methods to analyze the SNS community include graph-theory method, matrix method, social metrology method, algebraic method, etc. Among these methods, the graph-theory method is suitable for describing the relations in groups and expressing the structure characteristics of network intuitively. So far, in geographic fields, the graph-theory method has been used in many aspects [2, 3]. Lu and Wang [4] applied two methods, namely, information entropy and degree distribution to study the interpersonal node spatial distribution characteristics of SNS community.

With the in-depth research into the nature of online networking community, it is found that the relation between actors in social network is fuzzy, and the relationship between actors could not be simply divided into binary relation --

* The work presented in this paper was supported by the National Natural Science Foundation of China (Grant No.41271142).

"Yes (1)" and "No (0)". Hence, Nair and Sarasamma [5] proposed the definition of fuzzy social networks. They took the nodes and edges in fuzzy graphs as actors and the relation between actors in social networks respectively, and took that fuzzy social network as a result of giving practical meanings to the fuzzy graph. Ciric and Bogdanovic [6] defined social network as a fuzzy relational structure. They pointed out that the social network is a special case of fuzzy social network. Although social networks have been widely studied, and fuzzy social network has been proposed [7], research on SNS is limited, and there is no report about the application developments of fuzzy social network analysis in interpersonal node relation [8, 9].

This paper proposes a fuzzy SNS community centrality analysis method, which combines graph-theory method with fuzzy approaches. A case study on *Ren Ren Net* is conducted based on the proposed method. The structural features of the SNS community and the distribution of interpersonal nodes are analyzed. It is a significant exploration to use fuzzy approaches in SNS community analysis and study spatial pattern of community members and their communications, which expands SNS community research methods and improves the applications and research of SNS community spatial structure. The research findings in this study can support information management in electronic era, and can also help local governments to make decisions on the development of e-industry.

The rest of the paper is organized as follows. The fuzzy SNS community centrality analysis method is described in Section 2. In Section 3, a case study is conducted and illustrates the application of the proposed method. A set of conclusions are presented in Section 4.

2. Fuzzy SNS Community Centrality Analysis Method

This section will first give some important concepts of fuzzy SNS community, and then present the fuzzy SNS community centrality analysis method.

2.1. *Basic Concepts of Fuzzy SNS Community*

Definition 1. Fuzzy SNS community can be defined as a fuzzy relational structure $\tilde{G} = (V, \tilde{E})$, where $V = (v_1, v_2, ..., v_n)$ is a non-empty set of actors, $\tilde{E} = \sum_{i=1}^{n} \sum_{j=1}^{n} \tilde{E}(e_{ij}) / e_{ij}$ is the fuzzy relation on V.

Definition 2. The fuzzy node degree of a node v_i is the sum of membership degrees of the edges that attach to v_i, denoted as: $\tilde{d}(v_i) = \sum_{j=1}^{n} e_{ij}$. The average node degree of the fuzzy social network is: $\bar{\tilde{d}} = \sum_{i=1}^{n} \tilde{d}(v_i) / n$, where n is the number of nodes. The fuzzy node degree is also known as the connectivity, which indicates the influence and significance of an individual. The greater the degree is, the greater the influence is.

Definition 3. The scale of a fuzzy SNS community refers to the number of actors in it. The scale affects the relation complexity between actors in a fuzzy SNS community. The larger scale means more members, thus more complex of their relationship structure.

2.2. Fuzzy Condensation Degree and Fuzzy Cluster Coefficient

Definition 4. The fuzzy condensation degree (FCD) of a node v_i is defined as

$$\bar{cd}(v_i) = (\sum_{j=1}^{n} e_{ij}(\sum_{j=1}^{n} e_{ij} - 1))/(2 \cdot \tilde{d}(v_i)),$$ where n is the number of nodes.

FCD is a positive evaluation index of the importance of a node, which can be used to analyze the centrality characteristic in SNS community interpersonal node distribution.

To measure the centralized degree of interpersonal node distribution in the cyberspace, a fuzzy geographic concentration index $\tilde{G}$ is defined as $\tilde{G} = 100\sqrt{\sum_{i=1}^{n} (\bar{cd}(v_i)/T)^2}$, where n is the number of nodes, T is the sum of all the nodes' fuzzy condensation degree. When $\tilde{G}$ is close to 100, the interpersonal node distribution will present a centralized state.

Definition 5. The fuzzy cluster coefficient (FCC) of a node v_i is defined as $\tilde{c}(v_i) = 2\lambda(v_i)/\sum_{j-1}^{n} e_{ij}(\sum_{j-1}^{n} e_{ij} - 1)$, where $\lambda(v_i)$ is the number of triangle formed by the two nodes connected with V_i. The closer is $\tilde{c}(v_i)$ to 1, the greater is the collectivization degree of local network spatial structure entered by this node.

3. A Case Study on *Ren Ren Net*

3.1. Data Source

Two typical types of groups in *Ren Ren Net*, learning relation group, which is a network for teachers and students with original relationship, and topic interest group, which is a network for common interests and hobbies, are chosen as research objects. Specifically, a discussion section of university life theme: Love in East China Normal University, and a discussion section of online game theme: The List, were selected. The data of two topic groups in each section was collected. "The back door of East China Normal University is gone, gloomy", which got 12957 browses and 796 replies, represented by $I_①$, and "photograph on campus", which got 7793 browses and 518 replies, represented by $I_②$, were chosen in Love in East China Normal University section. "How to exchange the ingot?", which got 3557 browses and 429 replies, represented by $II_①$, and "How to upgrade rooms?", which got 2983 browses and 372 replies, represented by $II_②$, were chosen in The List section. To clearly reveal the SNS community interpersonal node spatial relationship, nodes were used to represent the city that an individual lives in.

3.2. Data Processing

The FCD and FCC of each node in the topic groups were calculated, which are shown in Figure 1 and Figure 2.

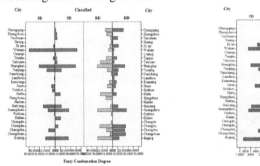

Figure 1. Calculation results of each node's FCD   Figure 2. Calculation results of each node's FCC

The rank linear regression analysis was conducted. The results are shown in Table 1. The interpersonal node spatial distribution of the four topic groups are shown in Figure 3.

Table 1. The rank linear regression analysis results of each level node's FCD

FCD rank	Fitting equation	Related coefficient
The first rank	lnP(k)=1.719-0.037lnk	0.956
The second rank	lnP(k)=1.491-0.013nk	0.971
The third rank	lnP(k)=1.247-0.014lnk	0.958
The fourth rank	lnP(k)=0.941-0.017lnk	0.964

3.3. Result Analysis

Based on previous analysis, FCD reflects the centrality characteristic of nodes in the network. The first and second rank FCD is taken as the strong FCD, and the corresponding node is the central node. In Figure 3, there are three central nodes in $I_①$ and $I_②$ and six central nodes in $II_①$ and $II_②$ respectively. The SNS community interpersonal node spatial distribution presents the multi-centers feature. The interpersonal node spatial distributions of different groups present different centrality characteristics. In the learning relation group $I_①$ and $I_②$, central nodes present relative concentration and significant local cluster characteristic, which are surrounded by other nodes. It shows local centralization

534

characteristic restricted by learning relation and the specific location. By contrast, in the topic interest group II① and II②, central nodes show scattered feature in distribution without the restriction of specific location.

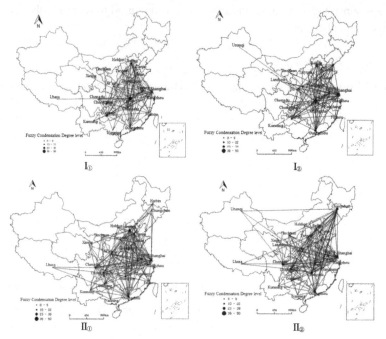

Figure 3. The interpersonal node spatial distribution of topic group friends in *Ren Ren Net*

The average FCC of I①, I②, II① and II② are 0.356, 0.352, 0.179 and 0.205 respectively, which proves that interpersonal nodes in learning relation groups present stronger collectivization degree and a prominent mono-center feature, while that in topic interest groups present weaker collectivization degree.

The fuzzy geographic concentration index of I①, I②, II① and II② are 38.37, 35.19, 25.24, and 26.28, which clearly shows that there is a multi-centers trend on SNS community interpersonal node spatial distribution, and the centralization characteristics of groups with different relation types are significantly different. Node spatial distribution of the topic interest groups spreads evenly, and possesses more central nodes. Conversely, there is a relative centralized trend on the node spatial distribution of learning relation groups. The assembled area may be the group formation location in virtual or real, or the developed area.

4. Conclusion

This paper proposes a fuzzy SNS community centrality analysis method by combing the graph-theory method with fuzzy approaches. Fuzzy condensation degree (FCD), fuzzy geographic concentration index, and fuzzy cluster coefficient (FCC) are defined to analyze the fuzzy SNS community. A case study on two types of topic groups in *Ren Ren Net* is conducted. The results show that: 1) the SNS community interpersonal node spatial distribution presents the multi-centers feature; 2) the interpersonal node spatial distributions of different groups present different centrality characteristics; 3) interpersonal nodes in learning relation groups present stronger collectivization degree and a prominent mono-center feature, while that in topic interest groups present weaker collectivization degree; 4) the centralization characteristics of groups with different relation types are significantly different; 5) interpersonal nodes distribution in the virtual community is influenced by the reality to some extent. The cognition on the assembled development rules and interaction rules of topic groups in a certain region can provide some guidance for public opinion spread and business operation.

References

1. Abbasi, A., Altmann, J., Hossain, L. (2011). Identifying the effects of co-authorship networks on the performance of scholars: A correlation and regression analysis of performance measures and social network analysis measures. *Journal of Informetrics*, 5(4), 594-607.
2. Liu, H.Y., Wei, L.L., Zhang, J. (2012). The research on the characteristics of network structure of area tourist flows based on the tourism routine. *Human Geography*, 27(4), 131-136.
3. Wang, Y.M., Ma, Y.F., Wang, M.X. (2012). Network structure of multicity inbound tourists to China. *Process in Geography*, 31(4), 518-526.
4. Lu, Z., Wang, W.T. (2011). The spatial distribution characteristics of interpersonal node in social networking services community and the analysis of geopolitical factors. *Scientific Geographica Sinica*, 31(11), 1293-1300.
5. Nair, P.S., Sarasamma, S.T. (2007). Data mining through fuzzy social network analysis. *Proceedings of the 26th Annual Meeting of the North American Fuzzy Information Processing Society*, San Diego, CA. 251-255.
6. Ignjatovic, J., Ciric, M., Bogdanovic, S. (2010). On the greatest solutions to weakly linear systems of fuzzy relation inequalities and equations. *Fuzzy Sets and Systems*, 161(24), 3081-3113.
7. Tseng, M.L. (2010). Implementation and performance evaluation using the fuzzy network balanced scorecard. *Computers & Education*, 55, 188-201.
8. Lu, Z., Lu, J., Zhang, C. (2002). Website development and evaluation in the Chinese tourism industry. *Networks and Communication Studies*, 16(3-4), 191-208.
9. Lu, J., Tang, S., McCullough, G. (2001). An assessment for internet-based electronic commerce development in businesses of New Zealand. *Electronic Markets*, 11(2), 107-115.

MANUFACTURE'S LOGISTICS OUTSOURING DECISION RESEARCH BASED ON FREE-RIDER[1]

GUO QIANG, JIANG MIN

(School of Economics and management, Southwest Jiaotong University, NO.111 of the North Second Ring Road , Chengdu City, Sichuan Province, Chengdu 610031 China)

This paper studies manufacturer's logistics outsourcing decision in double channel supply chain. We respectively establish without free-rider manufacturers logistics outsourcing, logistics self-management and situation with free-rider of logistics outsourcing and self-management .And further we analyze the logistics outsourcing and self-management critical point. This paper mainly discusses market share and the cost of logistics system's influence on the manufacturer's logistics outsourcing decision-making The results show that: manufacturer logistics outsourcing decision largely depends on the cost of logistics system; manufacturers and retailers exists both competition and cooperation relationship in the double channel of the supply chain, considering free-rider factors will change the point of manufacturers logistics outsourcing decision.

1. Introduction

With the development of ecommerce, enterprise sales model has changed. Double channel mode as a kind commercial mode both including traditional and modern commercial characteristics, more and more enterprises attention and favor. Haier in store and online direct marketing, to better meet the needs of different types of customer needs. Logistics decision is the important strategic question of enterprise, the same as the traditional supply chain, "also faces the problem of logistics outsourcing decision-making double channels" manufacturers sell their products on the internet. If the manufacturer Logistics Good service can not only increase sales but also increase their brand awareness, and logistics do not will not only lead to the decline in sales will affect brand. On the logistics outsourcing theory, the existing research is rich. Eisenhardt[1], Logan[2] use the principal - agent theory study logistics outsourcing motivations. Earl[3] points out that outsourcing will reduce the enterprise's logistics innovation ability, cannot keep up with the changing needs of customers. Bartholomew[4] in the study pointed out that, in

---

[1] This work is supported by The National Natural Science Fund (71340009); the fundamental research funds for the Central Universities Fund (SWJTU12CX122); Sichuan Provincial Department of science and technology project(2013ZR0038)

addition to pay for third party outsourcing of logistics costs, including many hidden costs such as communication cost. Menon[5], Qureshi[6] believes that in the third party logistics service provider selection should consider the both subjective factors and objective   factors. Peng Benhong, Sun Shaorong[7], Bai Xiaojuan, Wang Yaoqiu[8] and so on study possible risks in logistics outsourcing. Zhang Xuhui[9] consider the information asymmetry in the process of logistics outsourcing, establishes the game model of the cooperation. Liu Xiaoqun, Lai Yining[10] analysis the reason of logistics outsourcing including logistics information technology development , market pressure. Shuai Bin,Sun Zhaoyuan[11] study critical point of manufacturing enterprises logistics outsourcing. But almost all lack the consideration of double channel manufacturer logistics outsourcing, with the prevalence of double channel, it is necessary to consider dual channel manufacturer logistics outsourcing.

With the appearance of dual channel, free riding emerge as the same time in the supply chain, free riding phenomenon was first proposed by the USA economists Manke Olson, its basic meaning is not pay cost and enjoy other benefits. Free riding phenomenon often occurs in the dual channel supply chain, for example (consumers and then orders, in the Internet in the store trying on clothes after this is network built entity shop lift) manufacturers because of the increase of a service to increase their brand awareness, the retailer may therefore increase sales, but retailers do not pay the corresponding cost throughout the process and, thus it is called free riding phenomenon. Telser[12] is the first scholar studying on the free rider, he thought the fierce market competition may enable businesses enthusiasm to provide pre-sale information services down. Zhang Haoyu, Feng Nanping[13]studied strength hitchhike behavior for supply chain decision and state. Cao Lei, Zhang Zigang[14]studied the effects of information free riding on channels in the article. Singley and Williams[15] studied the relationship between the price difference and free riding behavior. Antia[16]pointed out that if the customer different sensitive degree of the service, the overall demand for channel will be different. Previous research on the free riding situation mainly focus on the information provided, after sale service and other aspects of free riding behavior. Then the logistics outsourcing in double channel will produce free riding phenomenon? Double channel manufacturer when to make the choice of logistics self-supporting or outsourcing? On the other hand, free riding phenomenon will have an impact on the logistics outsourcing decision-making? These are the issues needed to be studied further.

This paper mainly studies on the problem of manufacturers logistics outsourcing in dual channel supply chain, and discusses free riding effects on logistics outsourcing selection. The conclusion will provide advice to manufacturers on logistics decision to better their decision-making.

2. Problem Description

In this study, the assumption is made that a manufacturer, a retailer, a third party logistics operators in a supply chain system. Manufacturers only produce a product, the product can be wholesale to retailers or their direct sell online in two ways, for wholesale to retailers, manufacturers do not need to assume the logistics; logistics for direct marketing products, manufacturers have self and outsourcing two choices. Choose self-logistics, logistics cost includes 3 parts: (1) the cost of self-built logistics team $ak(1-r)$, (2) each unit with variable cost occurs c_1, (3)operating logistic cost $0.5v_1s^2$, logistics outsourcing, directly for each product payment to the third party logistics operators u, logistics operation business includes the cost of each unit with variable cost c_2, the cost of logistics operation team $0.5v_2s^2$. The following parameters:

r: market share of the retail $1-r$: market share of the manufacturers direct sales a: for the total market capacity w: the wholesale price for manufacturers to retailers P_1: Retailers selling prices P_2: manufacturers direct sales prices b: service demand coefficient y: competitor price impact coefficient c_2:a single variable cost of third party logistics service u:for the costs of manufacturers each product to logistics companies e:free-riding coefficient c_1: single variable costs for manufacturers self-logistics service $0.5v_1s^2$: manufacturers self-logistics operational cost $0.5v_2s^2$: the operation cost of logistics service of third party logistics operators s: the logistics service level $ak(1-r)$: the manufacturers to self-built logistics system cost.

It is assumed that the logistics operator's team system has been built, so regardless of the team's expenses. No rider considering the logistics, logistics outsourcing without riding, riding logistics self-supporting, hitchhiking logistics outsourcing in four cases, through revenue size comparison make outsourcing decision.

3 Solving the Model

3. 1. *No free riding self- logistics situation*

No freeriding circumstances, manufacturers choose self-logistics service, freeriding phenomenon does not exist in the supply chain. The demand function of retailer and manufacturer respectively D_1, D_2:

$$D_1 = ra - p_1 + yp_2 \tag{1}$$

$$D_2 = a(1-r) - p_2 + yp_1 + bs \tag{2}$$

Retailers' profit function is : $R = (p_1 - w)(ra - p_1 + yp_2)$

Manufacturers benefit function is :

$$M = w(ra - p_1 + yp_2) + [(p_2 - c_1)(a(1-r) - p_2 + yp_1 + bs) - \frac{1}{2}v_1 s^2 - ka(1-r)] \tag{3}$$

We get retailers' profit : $R = \frac{1}{16}(yc_1 + ra)^2 \tag{4}$

Manufacturers benefit is : $M = \frac{1}{8}\frac{G_1 + G_2}{2v_1 y^2 + b^2 - 2v_1} - ka(1-r) \tag{5}$

$G_1 = -2v_1 c_1^2 y^4 - 4c_1 rav_1 y^3 + c_1^2 b^2 y^2 - 8ac_1 v_1 y^2 - 2v_1 r^2 a^2 y^2 + 6v_1 c_1^2 y^2 + 8rac_1 v_1 y^2 + b^2 a^2 r^2 + 8rv_1 a^2$

$G_2 = -8v_1 ra^2 y + 4c_1 v_1 ray + 8r^2 a^2 v_1 y + 2c_1 rab^2 y - 6v_1 r^2 a^2 - 8rac_1 v_1 - 4v_1 a^2 - 4v_1 c^2 + 8ac_1 v_1$

3.2. No free riding logistics outsourcing situation

Manufacturers choose logistics outsourcing , free riding does not exist in the supply chain.

Retailers' demand function is : $D_1 = ra - p_1 + yp_2 \tag{6}$

Manufacturers demand function is : $D_2 = a(1-r) - p_2 + yp_1 + bs \tag{7}$

The logistics business profit function is :

$$L = (u - c_2)(a(1-r) - p_2 + yp_1 + bs) - \frac{v_2 s^2}{2} \tag{8}$$

Solved as before, we get retailers' profit :

$$R = \frac{1}{4}\frac{\left(y^2 v_2 + b^2 - v_2\right)^2 \left(rab^2 + yc_2 b^2 + yv_2 ra - av_2 r - yv_2 a\right)^2}{\left(4v_2 y^2 b^2 + 2b^4 + 2v_2^2 - 3v_2^2 y^2 - 4v_2 b^2 + y^4 v_2^2\right)^2} \tag{9}$$

Manufacturers benefit is : $M = \frac{N_1^2}{4N_2} \tag{10}$

$N_1 = rab^2 + yc_2 b^2 + yrav_2 - arv_2 - yav_2$
$N_2 = 4y^2 b^2 v_2 + 2b^4 + 2v_2^2 - 3v_2^2 y^2 - 4v_2 b^2 + y^4 v_2^2$

The logistics business benefit:

$$L = -\frac{1}{2}\frac{(G_3 + G_4)(G_5 + G_6)}{\left(v_2^2 y^4 + 4v_2 y^2 b^2 - 3v_2^2 y^2 + 2v_2^2 - 4v_2 b^2 + 2b^4\right)^2} \tag{11}$$

$G_3 = v_2(v_2 c_2 vy^4 + v_2 ray^3 - 2 v_2 ray^2 + 2c_2 b^2 y^2 + 2v_2 ay^2 - 3c_2 v_2 y^2)$
$G_4 = v_2(-v_2 ray + 2rayb^2 - 2rab^2 + 2av_2 r + 2b^2 a + 2c_2 v_2 - 2av_2 - 2c_2 b^2)$
$G_5 = b^2(c_2 v_2 y^4 + v_2 ray^3 - 3 v_2 ray^2 + 3v_2 ay^2 + b^2 c_2 y^2 - 3c_2 v_2 y^2 + b^2 ray)$
$G_6 = b^2(-2rab^2 + 2av_2 r + 2b^2 a + 2c_2 v_2 - 2av_2 - 2b^2 c_2)$

We have got the benefit in both no free riding self- logistics situation and no free riding logistics outsourcing situation. $k = \dfrac{(G_1+G_2)N_2 - 2N_1^{\,2}(2v_1y^2+b^2-2v_1)}{8a(1-r)N_2(2v_1y^2+b^2-2v_1)}$ manufacturers choose outsourcing and private income equality, when k is greater than the critical value, the manufacturer outsourcing benefits are greater than the self return, should choose the logistics outsourcing, if less than this critical value, should choose the logistics self.

3.3. *Free riding self- logistics situation*

Free riding exists in the supply chain; Manufacturers choose self-logistics.as for free riding, retailers' demand function increase *es*

Retailers' demand function is : $D_1 = ra - p_1 + yp_2 + es$ $\qquad\qquad$ (12)

Manufacturers demand function is : $D_2 = a(1-r) - p_2 + yp_1 + bs$ (13)

We get retailers' profit :

$$(14)$$

$$R = \frac{1}{4}\frac{(H_1+H_2)^2}{\left(-4v_1+e^2+4eby+e^2y^2+2b^2+4y^2v_1\right)^2}$$

$H_1 = ebra + rab^2 + ec_1b - eba - 2v_1ra$

$H_2 = 2v_1y^3 + 2rav_1y^2 + ebc_1y^2 + raye^2 + ebray - 2v_1c_1y + c_1yb^2 - aye^2 + c_1ye^2$

Manufacturers benefit :

$$(15)$$

$$M = \frac{1}{4}\frac{H_3+H_4+H_5+H_6+H_7}{\left(-4v_1+e^2+4eby+e^2y^2+2b^2+4y^2v_1\right)^2} - ka(1-r)$$

$H_3 = -2c_1^{\,2}v_1y^4 - 4ac_1rv_1y^3 - 2v_1a^2r^2y^2 + b^2c_1^{\,2}y^2 + 6v_1c_1^{\,2}y^2 - 8ac_1v_1y^2$

$H_4 = 8ac_1rv_1y^2 + 2ebyc_1^{\,2} + 8v_1ya^2r^2 + 4ac_1rv_1y - 8rv_1ya^2 - 2eac_1by$

$H_5 = 2rac_1yb^2 + 2erac_1by - 2bera^2 + c_1^{\,2}e^2 - 8ac_1rv_1 + 2ber^2a^2 + b^2e^2a^2$

$H_6 = -2ac_1e^2 + -2ac_1re^2 - 6v_1a^2r^2 - 2re^2a^2 + 8ac_1v_1 + r^2e^2a^2 + 8rv_1a^2$

$H_7 = 2erac_1b + e^2a^2 - 4v_1c_1^{\,2} - 4v_1a^2$

3.4. *Free riding logistics outsourcing situation*

Free riding exists in the supply chain, Manufacturers choose logistics outsourcing.

Retailers' demand function is : $D_1 = ra - p_1 + yp_2 + es$ $\qquad\qquad$ (16)

Manufacturers demand function is: $D_2 = a(1-r) - p_2 + yp_1 + bs$ $\qquad\qquad$ (17)

The logistics business profit function is :

$$L = (u - c_2)(a(1-r) - p_2 + yp_1 + bs) - \frac{v_2s^2}{2}$$ $\qquad\qquad$ (18)

Solved as before 。
The logistics business benefit ：

$$L = -\frac{1}{2} \frac{K_1(K_2 + K_3 + K_4 + K_5)(K_6 + K_7 + K_8 + K_9 + K_{10} + K_{11})}{(K_{12} + K_{13})^2} \tag{19}$$

$K_1 = v_2(ey + 2b)$

$K_2 = c_2 e^2 y^4 + 2c_2 v_2 y^4 + rae^2 y^3 + 2rav_2 y^3 + 4ec_2 by^3 - 4rav_2 y^2$

$K_3 = 4av_2 y^2 - c_2 e^2 y^2 + 4c_2 b^2 y^2 + 4ebray^2 + 2ae^2 y^2 - 2rae^2 y^2$

$K_4 = -6c_2 v_2 y^2 + 4b^2 ray - 4ec_2 by + 6eaby + e^2 ray - 6ebray$

$K_5 = -2rav_2 y + 4c_2 v_2 - 4c_2 b^2 - 4av_2 + 2ebra + 4rav_2 - 4rab^2 + 4ab^2$

$K_6 = 2c_2 v_2 ey^5 + c_2 e^3 y^5 + 6c_2 e^2 by^4 + 4c_2 v_2 by^4 + 2rav_2 ey^4 + rae^3 y^4 - c_2 e^3 y^3 + 10c_2 eb^2 y^3$

$K_7 = 2ae^3 y^3 - 6v_2 ec_2 y^3 + 6brae^2 y^3 + 4rav_2 by^3 - 2rae^3 y^3 - 4rav_2 ey^3 + 4av_2 ey^3$

$K_8 = -12c_2 v_2 by^2 - 10c_2 be^2 y^2 - 12brae^2 y^2 + 12av_2 by^2 + 12aby^2 e^2 - 2rav_2 ey^2$

$K_9 = 4c_2 b^3 y^2 + rae^3 y^2 + 10erab^2 y^2 - 12rav_2 by^2 + 20b^2 aey + 4vec_2 y + 2aye^3$

$K_{10} = 2rabye^2 - 20c_2 eyb^2 - 2raye^3 - 20raeyb^2 + 4rayb^3 - 2c_2 ye^3 - 4brae^2 + 8av_2 b - 8rab^3$

$K_{11} = 8rav_2 b + 8c_2 v_2 b + 4erav_2 + 4bae^2 + 8ab^3 - 8c_2 b^3 - 4bc_2 e^2$

$K_{12} = y^2 e^4 + y^4 e^4 + 8be^3 y^3 + 4ybe^3 + 4v_2 y^4 e^2 - 4v_2 y^2 e^2 + 22y^2 b^2 e^2 + 4b^2 e^2 - 16v_2 ybe$

$K_{13} = 24yeb^3 + 16v_2 bey^3 + 8b^4 + 8v_2{}^4 - 12y^2 v_2{}^2 + 16y^2 b^2 + 4y^4 v_2{}^2 - 16v_2 b^2$

we get retailers' profit ：

$$R = \frac{1}{4} \frac{U_1(U_2 + U_3)^2}{(U_4 + U_5)^2} \tag{20}$$

$U_1 = (-2v_2 + 3yeb + 2b^2 + 2v_2 y^2 + y^2 e^2)^2$

$U_2 = 2c_2 yb^2 + 2rab^2 - 2eba + 2brae + ybrae + 2ec_2 b + bey^2 c_2$

$U_3 = -2yav_2 + c_2 ye^2 - yae^2 - 2rav_2 + yrae^2 + 2yrav_2$

$U_4 = y^2 e^4 + y^4 e^4 + 8be^3 y^3 + 4ybe^3 + 4v_2 y^4 e^2 - 4v_2 y^2 e^2 + 22y^2 b^2 e^2 + 4b^2 e^2 - 16v_2 ybe$

$U_5 = 24yeb^3 + 16v_2 bey^3 + 8b^4 + 8v_2{}^4 - 12y^2 v_2{}^2 + 16y^2 b^2 + 4y^4 v_2{}^2 - 16v_2 b^2$

Manufacturers benefit is ：

$$M = \frac{1}{4} \frac{(U_6 + U_7)^2}{(U_8 + U_9)} \tag{21}$$

$U_6 = bec_2 y^2 + 2c_2 yb^2 - aye^2 - 2av_2 y + ebray + raye^2 + c_2 ye^2$

$U_7 = 2rav_2 y + 2rab^2 - 2eba + 2ec_2 b - 2rav_2 + 2ebra$

$U_8 = y^2 e^4 + y^4 e^4 + 8be^3 y^3 + 4ybe^3 + 4v_2 y^4 e^2 - 4v_2 y^2 e^2 + 22y^2 b^2 e^2 + 4b^2 e^2 - 16v_2 ybe$

$U_9 = 24yeb^3 + 16v_2 bey^3 + 8b^4 + 8v_2{}^4 - 12y^2 v_2{}^2 + 16y^2 b^2 + 4y^4 v_2{}^2 - 16v_2 b^2$

We have got the benefit in both free riding self- logistics situation and free riding logistics outsourcing situation, we can get conclusions as follows:

$$k = \frac{1}{4} \frac{(H_3 + H_4 + H_5 + H_6 + H_7)(U_8 + U_9) - (-4v_1 + e^2 + 4eby + e^2 y^2 + 2b^2 + 4y^2 v_1)^2 (U_6 + U_7)^2}{a(1-r)(-4v_1 + e^2 + 4eby + e^2 y^2 + 2b^2 + 4y^2 v_1)^2 (U_8 + U_9)}$$

manufacturers choose outsourcing and private income equality, when k is greater than the critical value, the manufacturer outsourcing benefits are greater than the self return, should choose the logistics outsourcing, if less than this critical value, should choose the logistics self.

4. Example Analysis

When $a = 100, y = 0.8, c_1 = 4, b = 0.8, v_1 = 3, e = 0.2, r = 0.6, c_2 = 5, v_2 = 4, k = 70$

we can get these as follows:

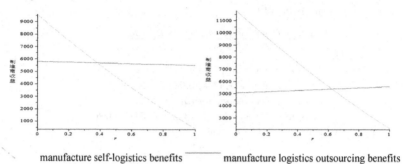

manufacture self-logistics benefits ——— manufacture logistics outsourcing benefits

Fig. 1 no free riding situation relationship
between manufacturer's benefit and retailer
market share

Fig 2 free riding situation relationship
between manufacturer's benefit and retailer
market share

As you can see from figure 1, with the change of the market share, the income of the manufacturer in logistics outsourcing and self-logistics alternating leading, it suggests that the market share of the manufacturer (1-r) will have an impact on their own logistics decision. And if the manufacturer's market shares more should take self-logistics. Manufacturers in the market share more than 0.617 should choose the logistics.

Free riding situation, with the changes in market share, the income of the manufacturer leading alternately in logistics outsourcing and self-logistics, this shows that the market share of the manufacturer will have an impact on their logistics decision. Manufacturers in the market share of more than 0.377 should choose self-logistics, compared to the first case, free riding considerations make manufacturers market share critical point of logistics decision becomes small. Manufacturers change with the share of retailer's market share , this does not meet the general situation, but retailers and manufacturers in a dual channel supply chain both have competition and cooperation relationship, when manufacturers direct sales per unit profits as direct wholesale to retailers, he is more willing to place the product directly to wholesale to retailers variable assembly, retailer market share to the income of the manufacturer is bigger.

5. Conclusion

This article conducts the research on the manufacturers' logistics outsourcing problem in dual channel supply chain, and considering the effect of free riding on whole supply chain and outsourcing and decision making. The study found 1.When there is no free riding situation,

$$k = \frac{(G_1 + G_2)N_2 - 2N_1^2(2v_1y^2 + b^2 - 2v_1)}{8a(1-r)N_2(2v_1y^2 + b^2 - 2v_1)}$$

is the critical point whether

outsourcing, when K is greater than the critical value, should choose logistics outsourcing, when K is less than the critical value should be the choice of logistics self-supporting. 2. When there is free riding

$$k = \frac{1}{4} \frac{(H_3 + H_4 + H_5 + H_6 + H_7)(U_8 + U_9) - \left(-4v_1 + e^2 + 4eby + e^2 y^2 + 2b^2 + 4y^2 v_1\right)^2 (U_6 + U_7)^2}{a(1-r)\left(-4v_1 + e^2 + 4eby + e^2 y^2 + 2b^2 + 4y^2 v_1\right)^2 (U_8 + U_9)}$$

is the critical point is outsourcing, when k is equal to the critical value, the manufacturer of logistics outsourcing and private income equality. When K is greater than the critical value, manufacturers choose logistics outsourcing. When the K is less than the critical value, will choose the logistics self. 3. Free riding consideration will enable manufacturers' logistics decision change. 4. In a dual channel supply chain manufacturers and retailers both cooperate and compete, when the manufacturer directly sale profits not as the profits to retailers, manufacturers are more willing to place the product directly to retailers, they reflect the cooperation, the other situations reflects the competitive relations, both strive to expand their the size of the market so as to increase their income.5.Market share will influence the outsourcing decision.6.Logistics outsourcing decision is affected by many factors, manufacturers need to consider when making decisions on the global.

References

1. Eisenhardt, *KM,Academy of Management*. **57-74**,14(1989).
2. Logan, May S, *International Journal of Logistics Management*. **21-32** 2(2000).
3. Earl, M.J, *Sloan Management Review*. **26-32**,3(1996).
4. Barthelemy, *Sloan Management Review*.**60-69**,3 (2001).
5. Menon M K, McGinnis M A and Ackerman K B, *Journal of Business Logistics*. **121-136**,19(1998).
6. Qureshi M N, Kumar D and Kumar P.*Asia Pacific Journal of Marketing and Logistics*. **227-249**,20(2008).
7. Peng Benhong and Sun Shaorong, *Science & Technology Progress and Policy*. **129-131**, 24 (2007).
8. Bai Xiaojuan and Wang Yaoqiu. *Transportation*. **54-56**,11(2009).
9. Zhang Xufei. *Journal of Chongqing Jianzhu University*.**132-135**,29(2007).
10. Liu Xiaoqun and Lai Yining, *Journal of Hanzhou University of Commerce*. **27-29**,3(2004).
11. Shuai Bin and Sun Chaoyuan, *Journal of Southwest Jiaotong University*.**296-299**,3 (2006) .
12. Telser L G, *Journal of Law and Economics*. **86-105**,3(1960).
13. Zhang Haoyu and Feng Nanping, *Value Engineering*. **1-2**, 17(2011).
14. Cao Lei and Zhang Zigang, *Journal of Intelligence*.**180-184**,28(2009).
15. Singley R ,*Marketing Theory Practice*, **64-74**,32(1995).
16. Antia K D, *MIT Sloan Management Rev*. **63-69**, 46(2004).

TRAINING STRATEGY TO IMPROVE THE EFFICIENCY OF AN INTELLIGENT DETECTION SYSTEM[*]

CÉSAR GUEVARA

Dept. Computer Architecture And Automatic Control, School of Computing Sciences,
Complutense University Of Madrid,
C/ Profesor García Santesmases S/N
28040-Madrid, Spain

MATILDE SANTOS

Dept. Computer Architecture And Automatic Control, School of Computing Sciences,
Complutense University Of Madrid, C/ Profesor García Santesmases S/N
28040-Madrid, Spain

VICTORIA LÓPEZ

Dept. Computer Architecture And Automatic Control, School of Computing Sciences,
Complutense University Of Madrid, C/ Profesor García Santesmases S/N
28040-Madrid, Spain

Detection systems of computer accesses are essential for information security. In this article we propose a classification system that combines two intelligent algorithms: Supervised Classification Systems, UCS, and Decision Trees, C4.5. The experiments were carried out using a dataset provided by Amazon, the Kaggle challenge. The system has been trained by dividing the dataset into subgroup. This training strategy has resulted more efficient than if the whole database is used as an only set. Results prove that the use of the proposed detection system provides higher classification accuracy and reduces the percentage of false positives in comparison to other classification techniques.

1. Introduction

The security problem of data loss in information systems is important and concerns public and private companies worldwide[1]. This problem occurs when employees make incorrect use of the access to a resource because they steal confidential information or perform operations they are not allowed to.

The leakage of confidential information is one of the greatest threats for any country. It is necessary to develop efficiency methods to prevent these attacks

---

[*] This work has been partially supported by Government of the Republic of Ecuador.

[2, 3]. But the problem is complex because it involves the creation of a behavioral profile of each employee, and this profile changes dynamically. Furthermore, it can be uncertain at some stages. Therefore the application of intelligent techniques has been proved to be very useful for dealing with these problems[4].

Some of the most used methods for dealing with this problem are classification techniques[5]. Although there are many intrusion detection systems, it is still an open issue because the number of false positives when detecting fraud is usually high. The detection system proposed in this paper is based on two classification methodologies: Decision Trees (C4.5) [6], and Supervised Classification Systems (UCS) [7]. It has resulted more accurate than their application separately.

Moreover, to improve the efficiency of this detection system, this work proposes a learning strategy that consists of dividing the training set into subgroups. These subgroups are formed according to some attributes that provide relevant information for the classification.

The database used for testing this proposal is the Amazon dataset Kaggle Challenge, which contains accesses of employees of that company during the period of 2010 and 2011. The data consists of real, historical data [8]. Users were allowed or denied access to the different system resources manually.

The goal of this work is to generate an automatic method that analyzes the data in order to predict the rejection or acceptance of the accesses to the system resources by an employee.

2. Materials and Methods

Figure 1 shows the process followed for the classification of accesses to the computer system resources. The process initiates with the information about the users' accesses that is pre-processed (discretization, normalization). Then, the now refined datasets are divided into groups according to some relevant attributes. This is done by using filters and wrappers. The classifier is generated by combining decision trees C4.5 Supervised Classification Systems. This classifier is applied to each of the groups of the dataset. Finally an error function has been defined to evaluate and validate the classifier.

546

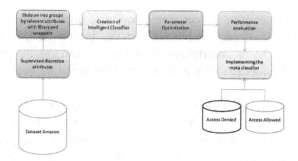

Figure 1. Accesses Classifier System.

2.1. *Dataset Kaggel Amazon*

The data consists of real, historical data collected in 2010 and 2011. The employees were allowed or denied access manually. We have used 32,769 records for training and 58,921 for tests. The operations are described by 10 attributes such as: time (day, hour), action (allowed, 0, or denied, 1), resource (file accessed), role of the user, department, etc.

The pre-processing consists of eliminating redundancy, noise, etc. using filters and wrappers [9].

3. Generation of an Intelligent Detection System

The intelligent detection system has been generating combining Decision Trees C4.5, and Supervised Classification System UCS, which uses genetic algorithms to create classification rules. These techniques were selected after applying several ones because these gave the best results with the dataset of Amazon.

3.1. *Division of Data for Training*

First of all, in order to eliminate redundancy and noise, the analysis tool Wakaito Environment for Knowledge Analysis (WEKA) [10] was used. Then the dataset was divided regarding the most relevant attributes.

To find the correlation between the attributes we applied a wrapper [11]. After that, the Gain Ranking Filter showed that the most significant one in terms of discrimination was resource. That is, the resource the user accesses is the attribute that most influence on the final value the attribute Action (denied or allowed access).

Therefore, the registers that correspond to allowed accesses were sorted out in descending order according to the resource. They were divided into 15 groups. All the denied accesses were added to each group (Figure 2).

RESOURCE	MGR_ID	ROLE_ROLLUP_1	ROLE_ROLLUP_2	ROLE_DEPTNAME	ROLE_FAMILY_DESC	ROLE_TITLE	ROLE_CODE	ROLE_FAMILY	ACTION
13878	54258	117890	118102	117878	117879	117905	117880	290919	0
19723	54762	117951	117952	118008	117879	118536	117880	308574	0
20284	60823	118953	118954	117941	117886	117879	117880	19721	0
27416	50601	117916	117917	117941	117886	118321	117880	290919	0
36646	27873	117978	117979	117884	117886	119323	117880	19793	0
37732	65460	118079	118080	117878	118177	118568	117880	19721	0
37734	119058	118079	118080	117878	118177	118980	117880	118295	0
38480	51382	118079	118080	117878	118177	126820	117880	118638	0
42085	59000	118181	118182	117941	117897	128230	117880	4673	0
64721	50589	118079	118080	117878	121386	117879	117880	19721	0
3853	20560	117876	117877	117878	117879	118784	117880	290919	1
20279	17695	117890	117891	117878	117879	119093	117880	119095	1
25330	19702	118269	118270	117878	117879	120773	117880	118960	1
33642	13196	117951	117952	117941	117897	119962	117880	118205	1
36674	14633	118106	118107	117884	117886	118321	117880	290919	1
78766	56683	118079	118080	117878	304519	117885	117880	117887	1
79228	13400	117983	117984	117878	117879	118321	117880	290919	1
81480	96704	117910	117911	117894	117886	128230	117880	118704	1

Access Denied, Allowed Access

Figure 2. Division of Amazon dataset into sub groups.

3.2. Selection of the Classification Techniques

Once the dataset is divided into sub groups, different classification techniques are applied to this data and evaluated. Table 2 summarizes the performance on each of the methodologies that have been tried on the Amazon dataset. The best results are reached with the decision trees C4.5 and the UCS, which give a percentage of right classification of 98.3 % and 97.6 %, respectively.

Table 2. Classification Techniques Accuracy for each of the subgroups of the dataset.

DATASET	ACCURACY						
	ID3	XCS	BAYES Net	RNM	C4.5	UCS	SVM
D1	0.970	0.950	0.969	0.974	0.982	0.981	0.950
D2	0.978	0.945	0.981	0.952	0.988	0.981	0.927
D3	0.994	0.956	0.992	0.972	0.997	0.994	0.920
D4	0.976	0.869	0.961	0.972	0.985	0.981	0.896
D5	0.963	0.912	0.928	0.948	0.973	0.967	0.780
D6	0.969	0.951	0.974	0.973	0.983	0.974	0.765
D7	0.967	0.950	0.965	0.939	0.976	0.973	0.691
D8	0.976	0.913	0.921	0.890	0.990	0.974	0.784
D9	0.968	0.886	0.975	0.923	0.982	0.975	0.797
D10	0.976	0.838	0.975	0.901	0.982	0.974	0.795
D11	0.963	0.910	0.964	0.922	0.971	0.973	0.884
D12	0.982	0.897	0.984	0.924	0.990	0.977	0.884
D13	0.975	0.972	0.956	0.924	0.979	0.972	0.654
D14	0.967	0.944	0.979	0.926	0.983	0.977	0.654
D15	0.973	0.927	0.978	0.926	0.981	0.976	0.654
AVERAGE	0.973	0.921	0.967	0.938	0.983	0.976	0.802

3.3. Generating the Detection System

The detection system combines the outputs of the classifiers C4.5 and UCS. But then the results given for each of these techniques is weighted and introduced in a rule base system. Figure 3 shows the model of the final classifier and its respective tools and modules.

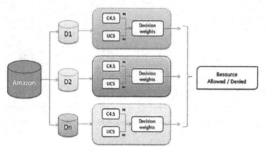

Figure 3. Design of the intelligent detection system.

The final detection system applies a rule given by (1) to weight the answers obtained by the two classification techniques over each subgroup, being R1 the tree C4.5 and R2 the UCS. Different weights were tried but theses ones give the best results. They are related to the efficiency of each technique.

$$Result = \frac{3R1}{5} + \frac{2R2}{5}$$

(1)

4. Experiment Results

The detection system was applied to the Amazon dataset. The results prove an accuracy of 0.984 in training and 0.981 in the tests. The KEEL (Knowledge Extraction bases on Evolutionary Learning) [12] tool for training and testing classification techniques are used. Table 3 shows the percentage of hits in comparison to other techniques.

Table 3. Comparison of the classification algorithms with the dataset Amazon.

	ACCURACY	
ALGORITHM	**TRAIN**	**TEST**
Meta Classifier System UCS and C4.5	0.984	0.981
Naive Bayes	0.912	0.901
UCS	0.949	0.939
XCS	0.942	0.936
Multilayer perceptron	0.942	0.94
J48	0.945	0.941

5. Conclusions

In this paper we have proposed an intelligent decision system that allows us to detect intrusions in information systems.

This intelligent classifier combines some techniques, in our case, decision trees and UCS, as it has been proved that the fusion of these strategies improves the accuracy of the classifier in comparison to the application of different techniques but separately.

On the other hand, in order to train the system we have divided the data set intro subgroups, regarding some relevant attribute. Then we have added all the cases of intrusions in each group. This strategy improves the efficiency of the classifier.

Simulation results show how the system reaches a high percentage of hits in the classification of accesses.

Future work includes obtaining a dynamic profile of the behaviour of the user. Furthermore, this profile should change in an adaptive way with the performance of the users.

References

1. S. Liu and K. Rick, IT prof. 12.2 (2010): 10-13.

2. C. Phua ,V. Lee, K. Smith, and R. Gayler, arXiv preprint arXiv:1009.6119, (2010).

3. G. Lawton, Computer 41.9 (2008): 14-17.

4. C. Guevara, M. Santos and J. A. Martín H, ISKE 2013.

5. V. Jaiganesh , S. Mangayarkarasi and P. Sumathi, ijarcce,vol, 2, 1629-1635, (2013).

6. K. Polat and S. Günes, Expert Syst. Appli., 36(2), 1587-1592,(2009).

7. E. Bernadó-Mansilla and J. M. Garrell-Guiu, Evol. compu, 11(3), 209-238, (2003).

8. Kaggel - Amazon.com, http://www.kaggle.com/c/amazon-employee-access-challenge

9. M. Kantardzic, Data mining,book,(2011).

10. WEKA: http://www.cs.waikato.ac.nz/ml/weka/

11. M. Gutlein, E. Frank, M. Hall, and A. Karwath, IEEE Symp., (pp. 332-339), (2009).

12. KEEL: http://sci2s.ugr.es/keel/index.php

A NOVEL WEIGHTING METHOD FOR ONLINE ENSEMBLE LEARNING WITH THE PRESENCE OF CONCEPT DRIFT

ANJIN LIU, GUANGQUAN ZHANG, JIE LU

Decision Systems & E-Service Intelligence Research Laboratory,
Center for Quantum Computing and Intelligent System,
School of Software, Faculty of Engineering and Information Technology,
University of Technology Sydney, Australia

Ensemble of classifiers is a very popular method for online and incremental learning in non-stationary environment, as it improves the accuracy of single classifiers and is able to recover from drifting concept without explicit drift detection. However, current ensemble weighing methods do not consider the relationship between a test instance and each ensemble member's training domain. As a result, a locally correct ensemble member may be reduced weight unfairly because that its prediction result of an out of domain test instance is wrong. These inaccuracies will increases when there is a significant concept change. In this paper, therefore, we proposed a fuzzy online ensemble weighting method which takes the consideration of the degree of membership of each instance in each ensemble member and a modified majority voting method to improve the ability of ensembles on handling online classification tasks with concept drift.

1. Introduction

In the past few years, a growing number of applications demand online machine learning algorithms for tackling the problems caused by that training data are available continuously in time with changing concept. For example, personal assistance applications deal with information filtering, macroeconomic forecasts, bankruptcy prediction or individual credit scoring [1]. These real-world applications require incremental learning processes to deal with their continuous coming data and take the concept drift into account.

The term *concept* refers to the whole distribution of the problem in a certain point in time [2]. *Concept drift* is caused by the changes of the feature space, the distribution or the reoccurrence of past concepts [3]. It will lead to the predictions of well-trained classifiers become less accurate as time passes. Recently, Minku, et al. [4] proposed that concept drift can be categorized into 14 types based on the drifting speed, severity, predictability, frequency and recurrence. In the real-world applications, the types of concept drift are varied and mixed. This issue has made concept drift even difficult to be solved.

Presently, classifier ensemble is the most popular mechanism for handling non-stationary data streams [5-9]. Since a classifier ensemble is a set of weak classifiers, it can easily adapt to changes by modifying each member or adjusting their influence by changing their weights. Various ensemble member replacement and weighting methods have been applied for refining or removing knowledge of past target concepts of data stream. The existing online ensemble learning methods only give a limited attention to their weights adjustment methods. Many online ensemble learning methods still operate with the offline ensemble weighting method, which is reducing the weights by a predefined constant parameter $\beta \in [0, 1]$ [6]. The offline ensemble weighing methods can not reflect the drifting of concept and they cannot help ensembles recover from concept drift quickly. Therefore, the aim of this study is to propose an fuzzy online ensemble weighting method to add a degree of membership of each instance in each ensemble members to support the weighting and the majority voting processes. As a result, only the genuinely affected ensemble members' weights will be modified.

The main contribution of this paper is that we propose a novel weighting method for online ensemble learning with concept drift. The organization of this paper is as follow: In the next section, we survey the most popular online ensemble methods which are designed for handling online classification tasks with the presence of concept drift. Section 3 presents the difference between online and offline ensemble weighting methods, and proposes a novel online ensemble weighting method to improve the performance of online ensembles. Section 4 concludes the paper and discusses some future works.

2. Related Works

In machine learning, many ensemble algorithms have been developed to solve the problem of data stream classification with concept drift, as ensemble does not require explicit drift detection (A comprehensive study of concept drift handling approaches with explicit drift detection can be found at [10]). The Streaming Ensemble Algorithm (SEA) maintains a fixed-size collection of classifiers, each built from a batch of training examples [5]. SEA uses new arrived batch of examples to build new base classifiers and replaces the poor performance one if the number of base classifier reached the capacity. The adjustment of ensemble members is only based on their performance on the current batch of examples and there is no comment about the weighting methods used in this paper. Dynamic weighted majority (DWM) is another ensemble method specifically designed for handling concept drift [6]. In this method, weighted experts are dynamically created and removed in response to changes in classifier accuracy. DWM applies four techniques for coping with concept drift: trains each component in an online way, assigns a weight to each component, removing/adding components as required. A weighing method that decrease incorrect predictions by a predefined parameter $\beta \in [0, 1]$, which usually is 0.5, has been applied. Elwell and Polikar presented an ensemble-based batch learning algorithm for non-stationary environments (Learn++.NSE) which uses weighted majority voting [7]. For each incoming dataset D^t they build an independent base classifier h_t. The new classifier h_t will focus on previously misclassified data. After that, weights are assigned to each ensemble members based on their performance and the time step they were built. The final classification result is determined by weighted majority voting of all base classifiers. Learn++.NSE is a good example of online ensemble weighting with consideration of time constrains. It considered the difference between training domain and testing domain which caused by time shift. However, its weighting method still may not be able to reflect the change of data distribution. Diversity for dealing with drifts (DDD) used four different diversity ensembles to handle concept drift [8]. DDD start with drift detection and then take the advantage of that different diversities perform differently in different concept drift stage. Their experiment result shows that high diversity can help to reduce the initial increase in error caused by a drift, but does not provide a faster recovery from drifts in long term [8]. As this paper is focus on the impact of ensemble diversity, there are only limited comments about ensemble weighting methods. The weighting method they used is highly depends on the ensemble learning algorithm they choose.

In these algorithms, only limited attention was given to online ensemble weighing with concept drift. As online ensembles have to adjust weights continuously and may encounter concept drift, the weight of a well-trained classifier in old concept might be reduced unfairly because of an out training domain test instance. Therefore, conventional ensemble weighting is no longer appropriate for online ensembles.

3. A Novel Fuzzy Online Ensemble Weighting Method

This section proposes a novel ensemble weighting method for handling online data stream learning with the presence of concept drift. Section 3.1 presents the limitations of conventional ensemble weighing method for handling online data stream ensemble learning. Section 3.2 gives the description of the proposed algorithm.

3.1. *Limitations of Conventional Ensemble Weighting*

The reason why conventional weighting methods is not appropriate for handling concept drift can be illustrated in Figure 1.

In Figure 1, the two big circles represent the training domain of ensemble member A (built at t_1) and B (built at t_2). The points with different shapes (triangle, circle, and rectangle) stand for different data points with different labels. The dotted lines represent the hyperplane of the classifier which separate different labels. The empty points x_1, x_2 represent next coming test instances at t_3, t_4. In this situation, A will predict x_2 as "Circle" and B will predict x_1 as "Circle". As both of them output incorrect results, conventional weighting methods will decrease both of their weights. If instances like x_1 and x_2 come in time sequence repeatedly (gradual drift), the weights of A and B will be inaccurate and unstable.

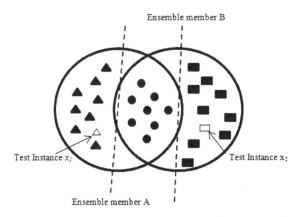

Figure1. A demonstration of the problem of conventional weighting method handling concept drift

In ensemble learning, the weights is aim to reflect the importance of an ensemble member and assist majority voting to achieve a better result. Therefore, adjusting weights appropriately is crucial to online ensembles. Especially in online data stream learning with concept drift, where new ensemble members may have much different training domain than old ensemble members.

3.2. *Fuzzy Ensemble Weighting Description*

The basic idea of our method is to only punish or reward the responsible ensemble members, but not the one whose training domain does not cover the test instance. Meanwhile, we can use this method to identify if a new test instance is in a new concept (unlearned instance) by measuring the similarity between it and each training datasets.

The description of fuzzy online ensemble weighting with concept drift is as follow:

Fuzzy online ensemble weighting with concept drift (c, D, θ, γ, β)

  $c \in N^*$: number of classes, $c \geq 2$

  D : degree of membership, $0 \leq D \leq 1$

  θ : threshold for ignoring experts

γ : threshold for concept drift, $0 \le \gamma \le c$

β : conventional weights adjustment parameter $0 \le \beta \le 1$

1: Divide training dataset into c sub training datasets

2: **For each** training dataset:

3:     Build a classifier

4:     Assign an initial weight w_i

5: **For each** test instance T:

6:     **For each** ensemble member e

7:         Calculate the degree of membership D_{ti} = MAX(similarity of T in e)

8:         Count, $num_{Dti<\theta\ Dti}$,the number of ensemble member $D_{ti} < \theta$

9:     **If** $num_{Dti<\theta\ Dti} < \gamma$

10:         Replace the lowest accurate ensemble members

11:     **Else**

12:         Adjust weights based on prediction result

13:         **If** $D_{ti} < \theta$, $w_i = w_i$ **Else**, $w_i = w_i D_{ti}\beta$

    Majority voting

1:     **For each** prediction label calculate $w_f = MAX(\sum_{i=0}^{k} w_i D_{ti})$

2:     **Return** the prediction label with the biggest w_f

4. Conclusion and Further Study

In this paper, we present a novel weighting method to improve the ability of online ensembles for handling concept drift. The new proposed weighting method assigns a degree of membership of each instance in each base classifier to improve the weights rewarding and punishing strategy. Also, whenever a new test instance comes, the degree of membership will be taken into consideration for the majority voting.

The proposed weighting method improved the ability of conventional ensemble weighing method on handling online data stream learning with concept drift. As it simply multiplied a degree of membership when changing weights, it can be used with other conventional weighting methods at the same time.

In the future, an experiment study needs to be conducted to support our proposed method. Moreover, it is necessary to extend our method on linguistic/ unstructured training datasets.

Acknowledgments

This work is supported by the Australian Research Council (ARC) under discovery grant DP110103733.

References

1. I. Zliobaite, "Learning under concept drift: an overview," Overview", Technical report, Vilnius University, related areas, applications Subjects: Artificial Intelligence (2009).
2. N. Lu, J. Lu, and G. Zhang, 'Case-Base Maintenance for Concept Drift', International Conference on Information Systems, Issue 72: Proceedings of the International Conference on Information Systems, WASET, Penang, Malaysia, pp. 333-340, (2012)
3. A. Tsymbal, "The problem of concept drift: definitions and related work," *Computer Science Department, Trinity College Dublin* (2004).
4. L. L. Minku, A. P. White, and Y. Xin, "The Impact of Diversity on Online Ensemble Learning in the Presence of Concept Drift," *IEEE Transactions on Knowledge and Data Engineering,* vol. 22, pp. 730-742 (2010).
5. W. N. Street and Y. Kim, "A streaming ensemble algorithm (SEA) for large-scale classification," presented at the Proceedings of the seventh ACM SIGKDD international conference on Knowledge discovery and data mining, San Francisco, California (2001).
6. J. Z. Kolter and M. A. Maloof, "Dynamic weighted majority: An ensemble method for drifting concepts," *The Journal of Machine Learning Research,* vol. 8, pp. 2755-2790 (2007).
7. R. Elwell and R. Polikar, "Incremental learning of concept drift in nonstationary environments," *IEEE Trans Neural Netw,* vol. 22, pp. 1517-31 (Oct 2011).
8. L. L. Minku and Y. Xin, "DDD: A New Ensemble Approach for Dealing with Concept Drift," *Knowledge and Data Engineering, IEEE Transactions on,* vol. 24, pp. 619-633 (2012).
9. D. M. Farid, L. Zhang, A. Hossain, C. M. Rahman, R. Strachan, G. Sexton, and K. Dahal, "An adaptive ensemble classifier for mining concept drifting data streams," *Expert Systems with Applications,* vol. 40, pp. 5895-5906 (2013).
10. N. Lu, G. Zhang, and J. Lu, "Concept drift detection via competence models," *Artificial Intelligence,* vol. 209, pp. 11-28, 4 (2014).

A MODIFIED LEARN++.NSE ALGORITHM FOR DEALING WITH CONCEPT DRIFT

FAN DONG[†*], JIE LU[*], GUANGQUAN ZHANG[*], KAN LI[†]

[†]*School of Computer, Beijing Institute of Technology, Beijing, 100081, P. R. China*
[*]*Decision Systems & E-Service Intelligence Research (DeSI) Laboratory,*
Center for Quantum Computing and Intelligent System (QCIS),
Faculty of Engineering and Information Technology,
University of Technology, Sydney, NSW 2007 Australia

Concept drift is a very pervasive phenomenon in real world applications. By virtue of variety change types of concept drift, it makes more difficult for learning algorithm to track the concept drift very closely. Learn++.NSE is an incremental ensemble learner without any assumption on change type of concept drift. Even though it has good performance on handling concept drift, but it costs high computation and needs more time to recover from accuracy drop. This paper proposed a modified Learn++.NSE algorithm. During learning instances in data stream, our algorithm first identifies where and when drift happened, then uses instances accumulated by drift detection method to create a new base classifier, and finally organized all existing classifiers based on Learn++.NSE weighting mechanism to update ensemble learner. This modified algorithm can reduce high computation cost without any performance drop and improve the accuracy recover speed when drift happened.

1. Introduction

Concept drift refers to a change in class definitions and a change in underlying data distribution. Data in the non-stationary environments always involve with concept drift, which is a very pervasive phenomenon in real world data-stream applications, such as intrusion detection in telecommunications, email spam filtering and credit card fraud. Learning from such non-stationary environment becomes an indispensable problem to apply machine-learning techniques on real world application. Normally, the change type of concept drift can be normally divided into three categories: sudden drift, gradual drift and reoccur contexts. While Minku, White and Yao [1] presented another drifts categorization based on multiple criteria – drift speed, severity, predictability, frequency and recurrence. In most of real world applications, data is organized in the form of data-stream, in which the nature or rate of drift is various and convoluted [2]. It makes more challenge to learning knowledge from data involving concept drift.

According to a literature review [3], the approaches that deal with concept drift can be divided into two groups: trigger based or evolving. Trigger based approaches focus on when a drift happened. After a drift is detected, there is a mechanism that indicates learner updating for adapting current data environment. Then, the learner will reset and retrain its model by using recently instances that can reflect current data distribution. Drift detection method is usually conducted by statistical theory that monitors the underlying data distribution [4, 5] or the outputs (error) of learners [6, 7]. Evolving approaches can adapt to non-stationary environment without indicating any drift occur point explicitly. Ensemble, which is the most popular evolving technique for reacting concept drift, usually use majority weighting strategies for combining several base classifiers to make a final decision [8, 9]. However these algorithms above usually have a restrictive assumption that there is no reoccurring drift in the data stream.

Learn++.NSE [10] is an incremental ensemble algorithm that assumes data batches are incrementally arrived. Its distinctively weighting strategy and base classifiers association mechanism can track concept drift without any assumption on change type of drift. However, compared with other learning algorithm, Learn++.NSE can react concept drift well with sophisticated weighting strategies, this ensemble algorithm has limitations of high computation costs and significant accuracy drop after drift occurred.

Motivated by these issues above, we propose a modified Learn++.NSE algorithm for dealing with concept drift. Our modification is that integrating drift detection method into Learn++.NSE. By monitoring distance-error-rate of the ensemble learner (Early Drift Detection Method), our modified algorithm has ability of indicating where and when drift happened, so that we can create a new base classifier on demand. At last, we use weighting mechanism of Learn++.NSE to make finally decision. The main contributions of this paper are: 1) maintaining good performance with less computation costs on handling concept drift problem 2) improving the accuracy recover speed when drift happened.

This paper is organized as follows. Section 2 discusses related works including the Learn++.NSE algorithm. Section 3 proposes a modified Learn++.NSE algorithm. Section 4 presents the conclusion, with a discussion of future work.

2. Related Works

2.1. *The Problem of Concept Drift*

The data involving concept drift, compared to data under stationary environment, is extended with time dimension. Learner dealing with concept drift problem must have an assumption that is uncertainty about the future [3]. A sequence data $X_1, X_2, \cdots, X_n$ ($X \in \mathfrak{R}^p$ is a vector in p − dimensional feature space), observed from stationary environment with corresponding class label $y \in \mathfrak{R}^1$, could be used for prediction unlabeled data X_{n+1} by using Bayesian posterior probability of a class, $P(y|X) = P(X|y)P(y)/P(X)$. While concept drift can be formally defined as data collected from unstable environment in which the underlying posterior probability changes as time shift, i.e., $P_t(y|X) \neq P_{t+1}(y|X)$ [10].

2.2. *EDDM: Early Drift Detection Method*

EDDM [7], inspired by Drift Detection Method (DDM) [6], is a drift detection method that monitors the online error-rate of the learning algorithm. Different with DDM, this method considers the distance between two errors classification, which can improve the ability of identifying slow gradual concept drift. This method adopt that a significant decrease in the distance suggests that a drift may occurred. It calculates the average distance between two errors (p_i') and its standard deviation (s_i'). In addition, it obtains p_{max}' and s_{max}' when $p_i' + 2 \cdot s_i'$ reaches its maximum value. This method defines two thresholds α for the warning level and β for the drift level. If $(p_i' + 2 \cdot s_i')/(p_{max}' + 2 \cdot s_{max}') < \alpha$, the instances will be cached in advanced of a possible change of context. When $(p_i' + 2 \cdot s_i')/(p_{max}' + 2 \cdot s_{max}') < \beta$, the new model is learnt using the instances cached since the warning level triggered, and then p_{max}' and s_{max}' are reset.

2.3. *Learn++.NSE Algorithm*

Learn++.NSE [10] is an incremental learning algorithm for non-stationary environments. Learn++.NSE is a passive ensemble learner that pays no attention to when the drift happened. It assumes that data are incremental received in batches. For each incoming data batch, this algorithm creates a new classifier, and then adjusts each existing classifier weighting based on its time-adjusted accuracy on latest data batch. The final classification decision is determined by weighted majority voting of all base classifiers. This algorithm can track the concept drift closely without any assumption on change type of concept drift.

3. The Modified Learn++.NSE Algorithm

Even though Learn++.NSE algorithm has good performance on dealing variety change type of concept drift, it still has limitations. One of limitation is Learn++.NSE algorithm has no explicitly drift detection, which results that it has a significant accuracy drop after a drift happened. For Learn++.NSE algorithm is a batch ensemble learner, another limitation is that its learning performance will highly depend on the training examples in every coming data batch.

Considering the limitation of Learn++.NSE, we proposes a modified Learn++.NSE algorithm which integrating drift detection method to maintain learning performance of dealing concept drift without too much computation costs. Because of Learn++.NSE already has a sophisticated weighting strategy to deal with various types of concept drift, we decide to use a simple and effective drift detection method, EDDM, incorporating with Learn++.NSE. We assume that the instances arrive one at one time. Learner must predict the label of new instance when it arrived. Once the prediction has been made, learner can access the true label of instance and utilize it to update the learning model. The pseudocode of algorithm is as follow:

[Modified Learn++.NSE Algorithm]

Initialization:

- Training data $\{X_t \in \mathfrak{R}^p, y_t \in \mathfrak{R}^1 = \{1, \cdots, c\}\}, t = 1, \cdots, m$
- Supervised learning algorithm Base Classifier C
- Sigmoid parameters a (slope) and b (inflection point)
- Drift detection thresholds α (warning level) and β (drift level)

1: Call Base Classifier with training data,

   obtain $C_j: X \rightarrow y, W_j^k = 1$, where $j = 1, k = 1$

2: $buf \leftarrow$ empty //buffer that stores instances involving possible drift

3: Ensemble learner $H^k \leftarrow C_1$ with W_1^1, where $k = 1$

4: **while true do**

5:    $X_i \leftarrow$ the latest instance

6:    $y'_i \leftarrow$ get prediction $H^k(X_i)$ by using Weighted Majority

7:    drift $\leftarrow$ DriftDection$(y'_i, y_i, \alpha, \beta)$

8:    **if** drift == warning level **then**

9:      cache X_i into buf

10:   **else** drift == drift level **then**

11:     $j = j + 1, k = k + 1$

12:     call **Base Classifier** with each $X_l \in buf$, obtain C_j

13:     $E^k \leftarrow$ compute error of the current ensemble on each $X_l \in buf$, where the error is $H^{k-1}(X_l) \neq y_l$

14:     use E^k to update and normalize instance weights D^k

15:     use D^k evaluate all existing classifier $C_1, \cdots, C_j$ normalized error θ_j^k on each instances in the buf

16:     $\bar{\theta}_j^k$ ←apply sigmoidal weights ω_j^k to normalized classifier errors θ_j^k

17:     calculate each classifier $C_1, \cdots, C_j$ voting weights W_j^k by log-normalized reciprocals of the adjusted normalized error $\bar{\theta}_j^k$

18:     construct a new ensemble H^k with classifier $C_1, \cdots, C_j$ and corresponding voting weights W_j^k

19:     buf ← empty //reset the buffer

20: **end if**

21: **end while**

The core idea of modified Learn++.NSE algorithm is using drift detection method to indicate when a drift happened and accumulate relevant instances involving concept drift. The drift detecting method we used is EDDM. It is possible that replacing with other drift detection method. After drift has occurred, we use stored instances to obtain a new base classifier, adjust all existing classifiers' voting weights and update existing ensemble learner. The voting weights adjustment strategy from line 13 to line 17 are inherited from Learn++.NSE.

Compared with original Learn++.NSE algorithm, our modified algorithm has advantage in learning time. The learning time for Learn++.NSE increase linearly since a new base classifier will be created as new batch data arrived, and then adjust weights of all existing base classifier to update ensemble learner. If the learning time is increase linearly, it must take too much time to learn knowledge when the learner has been running for a long time. Moreover, it may waste too much computation resource for a period of data stream without drift. Our modified algorithm only creates new base classifier and adjusts weights when a drift is detected, it will reduces high computation costs and learning time.

Learn++.NSE algorithm assumes that data are incremental arrived in batch. For Learn++.NSE can only update its model when next training instances of data batch arrived, this assumption leads that accuracy drop of learner will be seriously when a drift happened in data batch since many instances are misclassified. By processing instance once a time with drift detection method, our algorithm can identify drift without any delay, and update learner quickly with instances that contains a possible change of context. Our modified Learn++.NSE algorithm can track concept drift timely with less misclassification.

4. Conclusion and Future Work

We present a modified Learn++.NSE algorithm for dealing with concept drift. The novelty of the algorithm is eliminating the limitations of Learn++.NSE algorithm, which are has no explicitly drift detection and only deal with data arrived in batch. Our modified Learn++.NSE algorithm can maintain good performance on handling concept drift with less computation costs, and shortening the recover time of accuracy drop when drift happened. In the future, an empirical study will be made to prove our proposed algorithm is effective, and diversity adjustment mechanism could be incorporated into our algorithm.

Acknowledgments

This work is supported by the Australian Research Council (ARC) under discovery grant DP140101366.

References

1. Minku, L.L., A.P. White, and Y. Xin, *The Impact of Diversity on Online Ensemble Learning in the Presence of Concept Drift.* Knowledge and Data Engineering, IEEE Transactions on, 2010. **22**(5): p. 730-742.
2. Tsymbal, A., *The problem of concept drift: definitions and related work.* 2004, Computer Science Department, Trinity College Dublin, Ireland.
3. Zliobaite, I., *Learning under concept drift: an overview.* 2009, Faculty of Mathematics and Informatics, Vilnius University, Vilnius, Lithuania.
4. Lu, N., G. Zhang, and J. Lu, *Concept drift detection via competence models.* Artificial Intelligence, 2014. **209**(0): p. 11-28.
5. Bifet, A. and R. Gavalda. *Learning from Time-Changing Data with Adaptive Windowing.* in *In Proceedings of the Seventh SIAM International Conference on Data Mining (SDM'07).* 2007. Minneapolis, MN, USA: SIAM.
6. Gama, J., et al., *Learning with drift detection*, in *Advances in Artificial Intelligence–SBIA 2004.* 2004, Springer. p. 286-295.
7. Baena-García, M., et al., *Early drift detection method.* 2006.
8. Chen, S. and H. He, *Towards incremental learning of nonstationary imbalanced data stream: a multiple selectively recursive approach.* Evolving Systems, 2011. **2**(1): p. 35-50.
9. Ditzler, G. and R. Polikar, *Incremental learning of concept drift from streaming imbalanced data.* IEEE Transactions on Knowledge and Data Engineering, 2013. **25**(10): p. 2283-2301.
10. Elwell, R. and R. Polikar, *Incremental learning of concept drift in nonstationary environments.* IEEE Transactions on Neural Networks, 2011. **22**(10): p. 1517-1531.

IMPROVING GROUP RECOMMENDATION WITH OUTLIER DATA FILTERING

Jorge Castro, Manuel J. Barranco and Luis Martínez

Universidad de Jaén, Campus Las Lagunillas, 23071, Jaén
{jcastro,barranco,martin}@ujaen,es

Keywords: Group recommendation; Heterogeneous groups; Disagreement.

New trends in recommender systems face new challenges as group recommendation, in which users give their preferences over items and the system provides recommendations for a group of known users. In certain types of groups, it often occurs that several members do not agree on their preferences over some items so their inclusion in the group recommender system (GRS) may mislead the recommendation results. In this contribution a technique to detect and filter conflictive ratings before their use in the recommendation process is proposed and then its performance evaluated by using a well known recommendation dataset. The results show that rating filtering leads to improvements on GRSs performance.

1. Introduction

A recommender system[1] (RS) is a tool that helps users on situations where an overwhelming amount of choices exists and there is no possibility of examining all of them to pick the best one in a reasonable time. Hereby, a RS tries to filter the possible choices by using a set of items for which customer already tried and provided his/her preference about them, trying to predict the best items fitting his/her current needs.

There exist many recommendation techniques,[2] but a simple, effective and widespread technique is collaborative filtering with k-nearest neighbors (kNN-CF). In kNN-CF the recommendations are computed by finding similar users (neighborhood) to the target user and combine their ratings to compute a prediction for the items that the target user did not experience yet, then the top-n items are recommended (see Fig. 1).

Among the new trends in RS,[2] such as context awareness, multiple dimensions recomendations, natural noise, etc; we focus our research on group recommender systems[3] (GRS) which look for suitable recommendations for groups of users (related or not). Usually GRSs suggest products whose purchase or use have a social component to be enjoyed by several people together, such as watch a movie,[1] listen to music[4] or travelling.[5]

Group recommendations are specially challenging in random groups whose members could have different opinions/preferences over the products. This contribution proposes a group recommender technique that pre-filters conflictive opinions in the group for improving group satisfaction regarding the recommendations.

The contribution is structured as follows: section 2 reviews concepts on GRS, section 3 describes the proposed technique for GRS, section 4 shows a case study and section 5 concludes the contribution.

2. Group recommender systems

This section explains the basic concepts on GRS, describing the inputs and basic techniques for group recommendation. Most of RSs use three types of information: users' data ($U = \{u_1, \ldots, u_n\}$), products' data ($I = \{i_1, \ldots, i_m\}$) and users' ratings over the products, to describe how satisfied is a user regarding a particular item ($R \subseteq U \times I \to D$, D rating domain).

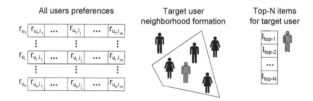

Fig. 1. Single user recommendation kNN-CF.

RSs try to predict ratings for unrated items to perform recommendation using these data. GRS extends RS such that, instead of recommending to one user, recommendations are targeted to groups of users ($G = \{m_1, \ldots, m_r\} \subseteq U$). There exists different modes of group recommendation, such as recommending groups to a user for joining[6] or finding the most suitable group of users for a target item,[7] but we focus on recommending items to a target group of users. Formally, group recommendation consists on finding the item (or set of items) that maximizes the rating prediction for the group of users:

$$GroupRecommendation(I, G) = \arg \max_{i_j \in I}[Prediction(i_j, G)] \qquad (1)$$

There are two basic tecnhiques[8] for GRS: (i) *model aggregation*,[4] which consists on aggregating individual ratings of each member to compute an aggregated group rating profile and perform individual recommendation for this *pseudo-user*; and (ii) *prediction aggregation*,[1,9,10] which computes the list of recommendations for each member and aggregates them into a single group recommendation list (see Fig. 2).

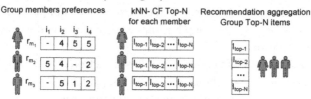

Fig. 2.   Group recommendation with prediction aggregation.

Both techniques can aggregate information about a particular item, in which one or several members of the group fully disagreed. In this situation, the group's recommendations are biased negatively.

3. Filtering dissagreements in group recommender systems

In this section, a novel GRS technique is introduced, which filters out items with a high level of disagreement among group members to avoid the biased recommendations aforementioned. Therefore, the application of a filtering process to eliminate disagreement on members ratings might help to improve the recommendation process.

Even though there are different situations for disagreements this contribution, due to page limit, is focused on the following situation: *groups whose members agreed in most product ratings but disagreed in a small set of items*. In this situation the use of data about disagreed items can highly vary the recommendations.

The proposed method is structured in two phases:

(1) The dissagreement of each member rating (see Equation 2) is computed.

$$Disagreement(r_{u,i}) = |\overline{\{R_{G-\{u\},i}\}} - r_{u,i}|, \ u \in G \qquad (2)$$

where $r_{u,i}$ is the rating of user u over item i, $R_{G-\{u\},i}$ is the set of ratings from group G members over the same item i without $r_{u,i}$.

(2) Members ratings with dissagreement greater than certain threshold μ are removed from the data used afterwards to compute the group recommendations.

Several special cases should be considered in this situation:

(a) Items rated by $g \le n$ members: they should not be filtered out. This case is shown in Fig. 3, i_1.

(b) Items with fully disagreement of all members: all their ratings over the same item can be removed (remove item from group data) or keep an aggregated rating for the item. This is controlled by parameter Keep One Rating (KR). This case is shown in Fig. 3, i_3.

(c) Avoid group data deletion: a Maximum Percentage of Deletions (MPD) should be fixed or avoid this technique in datasets whose members are totally different.

Therefore, the proposed technique avoids controversial items, specially when KR parameter is set to $false$. This way, the filtering technique may reduce item coverage in order to gain prediction accuracy.

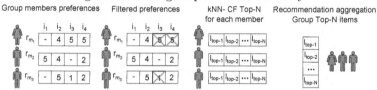

Fig. 3.   Group recommendation with prediction aggregation and filtering.

4. Evaluation and results

To validate the proposed method, memory based kNN-CF algorithm with prediction aggregation using least misery[1] is taken as baseline technique and is compared with different configurations for the proposed method.

GroupLens Research[a] in University of Minnesota provides a number of datasets for RS in the movies domain. In this experiment, ml-100k is used. For our purposes, it is needed to have information about groups of users, which MovieLens dataset does not provide. The group formation technique used selects random groups of a fixed number of members and the group sizes evaluated are 3, 5, 7 and 9. Hold-out validation scheme has been applied with 20%test, performing 100 independent executions. On each execution, 100 different groups were generated.

The proposed technique has four parameters:

(1) n: minimum members rating an item, $n = 1$ is used.
(2) MPD: ensure sufficient information for the GRS, $MPD = 80\%$ is used.
(3) μ: maximum disagreement value of ratings mantained, $\mu = \{1.0, 2.0, 3.0\}$ are tested.

---

[a]http://grouplens.org/

(4) *KR*: to decide what to do in special case 2: *true* to use an aggregated rating, *false* to remove all item ratings. Both cases tested.

The evaluation measure applied is MAE, to measure prediction error. The described experiment was executed in AMD Opteron 6272 with 16GB RAM. It took 8h 58m and its CPU process time was 7d 9h 18m.

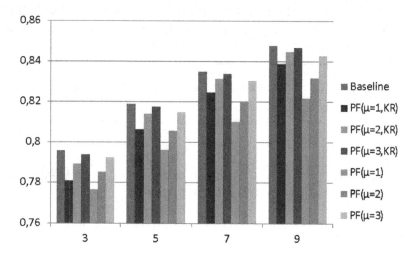

Fig. 4.   Mean Average Error by group sizes.

In terms of algorithm performance, Fig. 4 shows the different configurations MAE by group size. As it shows, the proposed technique improves the baseline results for all parameter combinations.

Regarding the disagrement threshold, the smaller μ the better prediction (error decreases). This shows that as the filtering technique is applied in a stronger way (allows less disagreement, hence it deletes more ratings), the error decreases. Given that the experiment has been carried out with $\mu =\{1.0, 2.0, 3.0\}$ and the best prediction error is with $\mu = 1.0$, further experimentation is needed to determine if there is a value for μ between 0 and 1.0 that improves the results.

Looking at the results over different values for KR parameter, we can affirm that keeping a rating of movies on which there is no consensus is bad for the technique performance. Therefore, if an item is too controversial for the group, is better to remove all members ratings about it and perform group recommendation without it.

The proposed technique improves the baseline results for all group sizes, being $\mu = 1.0$ and $KR = false$ the best configuration for the tried group sizes, so filtering outlier ratings is a technique to consider in GRSs.

5. Conclusions

In this work, a filtering technique for group recommender systems is defined. This filtering process deletes users' ratings when members of the group do not agree on its preference. Therefore the proposed filtering process keeps ratings whose preferences agreed by the group and removes those ones with high disagreement. This technique has been compared with the baseline technique and shows improvements, which shows that disagreement ratings deletion improves recommendations results.

Acknowledgments

This work is partially supported by the Research Project TIN2012-31263, P10-AGR-6581, UJA2011/12/23 and ERDF funds.

References

1. M. O'Connor, D. Cosley, J. A. Konstan and J. Riedl, Polylens: a recommender system for groups of users, in *Proceedings ECSCW'01*, 2001.
2. F. Ricci, L. Rokach and B. Shapira, Introduction to recommender systems handbook, in *Recommender Systems Handbook*, (Springer, 2011) pp. 1–35.
3. J. Masthoff, Group recommender systems: Combining individual models, in *Recommender Systems Handbook*, (Springer, 2011) pp. 677–702.
4. J. F. McCarthy and T. D. Anagnost, Musicfx: an arbiter of group preferences for computer supported collaborative workouts, in *Proc. of CSCW '98*, (ACM, 1998).
5. L. Ardissono, A. Goy, G. Petrone, M. Segnan and P. Torasso, Intrigue: personalized recommendation of tourist attractions for desktop and hand held devices, in *Applied Artificial Intelligence, Vol 17 (8-9)*, (Taylor & Francis, 2003) pp. 687–714.
6. K. Myszkorowski and D. Zakrzewska, Using fuzzy logic for recommending groups in e-learning systems, in *Computational Collective Intelligence. Technologies and Applications*, (Springer, 2013) pp. 671–680.
7. N. Zheng and H. Bao, Flickr group recommendation based on user-generated tags and social relations via topic model, in *Advances in Neural Networks–ISNN 2013*, (Springer, 2013) pp. 514–523.
8. I. Cantador and P. Castells, Group recommender systems: New perspectives in the social web, in *Recommender Systems for the Social Web*, (Springer, 2012) pp. 139–157.
9. R. Meena and K. Bharadwaj, Group recommender system based on rank aggregation an evolutionary approach, in *Mining Intelligence and Knowledge Exploration*, (Springer International Publishing, 2013) pp. 663–676.
10. Y. Song, Z. Hu, H. Liu, Y. Shi and H. Tian, A novel group recommendation algorithm with collaborative filtering, in *International Conference on Social Computing (SocialCom) 2013*, Sept 2013.

GENETIC ALGORITHM BASED INSTANCE SELECTION FOR NEAREST NEIGHBOR RULE

Hua Zhao* and Keyun Qin

School of Mathematics, Southwest JiaoTong University, Chengdu 610031, China
* E-mail: zzh8008@gmail.com

Instance selection is an important pre-processing step in pattern recognition and machine learning. In this paper, we propose a novel instance selection method based on genetic algorithm for nearest neighbor (AGAIS_NN), which compose of three main parts: elitist strategy, adaptive probabilities of crossover and mutation, and fitness function. To validate the proposed algorithm, we compare AGAIS_NN with other classical instance selection methods. The experimental results show that our proposal is more effective and useful than other approaches.

Keywords: Instance selection; Nearest neighbor rule; Genetic algorithm.

1. Introduction

The nearest neighbor (NN) rule, originally proposed by Cover and Hart, is one of the most well known classifiers and has been applied to many classification tasks. However, it is noted that NN suffers from some drawbacks. It requires a large memory space as the entire training data set has to be stored, and it has high computational complexity, namely, each test pattern has to be compared with every training pattern. To alleviate these drawbacks, instance (prototypes) selection are widely discussed. The objection of instance selection (IS) is to reduce the size of training data as well as to improve performance of classification task.

Genetic algorithms have been used recently for instance selection and a great deal of progress has been made. The main advantages of genetic instance selection are better instance reduction rates, higher classification accuracy, and models that are easier to interpret.[1] García[2] proposed a model of evolutionary algorithm that incorporates an ad hoc local search specifically designed for optimizing the properties of prototype selection problem with the aim of tacking the scaling up problem. To perform feature and instance selection in nearest neighbor classification, Derrac[3] introduced an evolutionary model, which is based on cooperative coevolution. In,[1] an empirical study of the performance of four representative EA models has been carried out. The four models are CHC Adaptive Search Algorithm (CHC), Steady-State genetic algorithm (SSGA), generational genetic algorithm (GGA) and population-based incremental learning (PBIL). The experimental results show that the evolutionary instance selection algorithms consistently outperform the nonevolutionary ones. Furthermore, a hybrid genetic approach is proposed to instance selection. This method can simultaneously treat the double problem of editing instance patterns and selecting features as a single optimization problem, and aims at providing a better level of information. By comparing to the other approaches, the usefulness of the method is demonstrated with artificial and real data.

In this paper, we propose an adaptive genetic algorithm (AGAIS_NN) to deal with instance selection for NN. AGAIS_NN compose of three key parts: elitist strategy, adaptive probabilities of crossover and mutation, and fitness function. Elitist strategy is used to select the best chromosome, and adaptive probabilities of crossover and mutation be employed to improve the convergence speed. More importantly, fitness function is determined by misclassified rate and present rate.

The rest of the paper is organized as follows: Section describes the proposed algorithm. Experiment results and analysis are described in Section and some conclusions are draw in Section .

2. Instance selection via genetic algorithm

(1) Population initialization

The representation of the chromosome in GAIS is usually a string of binary values (0 or 1). The gene of chromosome is 1, if its corresponding instance is included in the subset of training set, or 0 if this instance is not contained in the training set. In this paper, we sort the instances of training set from smallest to largest and guarantee that each gene's corresponding instance is smaller than the prior gene's and larger than the posterior gene's.

(2) Adaptive probabilities of crossover and mutation

The crossover rate and mutation rate in our study are determined by following.

$$P_c = \begin{cases} \frac{\lambda_1(f_{max}-f')}{(f_{max}-\overline{f})}, & f' \geq \overline{f}; \\ \lambda_1, & f' < \overline{f}. \end{cases} \tag{1}$$

and

$$P_m = \begin{cases} \frac{\lambda_2(f_{max}-f)}{(f_{max}-\overline{f})}, & f \geq \overline{f}; \\ \lambda_2, & f < \overline{f}. \end{cases} \qquad (2)$$

where $f_{\max}$ is the maximum fitness of chromosomes in the population; $\overline{f}$ denotes the average fitness of all chromosomes in the population; f' is the larger fitness value of the chromosomes to be crossed; f is the fitness value of the chromosome to be mutated. Moreover, λ_1 and λ_2 are two constants and $\lambda_1 = 1$ and $\lambda_2 = 0.5$.

(3) Fitness function

Each one of the chromosomes in the population is evaluated according to a fitness function, which is composed by two parts: $gain\_red$ and $rate\_red$. $gain\_red$ can reflect the classification rate of instance subset and $rate\_red$ represents the rate of instances occur in a chromosome.

$$fitness(S) = \alpha \times gain\_red + (1 - \alpha) \times rate\_red \qquad (3)$$

where

$$gain\_red = (1 - \frac{gain}{|T|}) \qquad (4)$$

and

$$rate\_red = (\frac{|T| - |S|}{|T|}) \qquad (5)$$

$|T|$ denotes the numbers of training set, while $|S|$ means the size of instance subset. In other words, $|S| = |\{g_i \in S | g_i = 1\}|$.

The aim of the fitness function is to minimize the misclassification rate and minimize the number of instances obtained. Specially, $gain$ is an index, which can reflect the importance of instances for classification task. Concretely, as to $g_i \in S$, $gain = 1$ if the nearest neighbor of g_i is classified by instance subset updated when g_i is removed (namely $g_i = 0$), while $gain = 0$ if it is classified correctly. The more fitness value of a chromosome, the corresponding instance subset is more relevant to classification. The pseudocode of fitness function is described in Algorithm 2.1.

In Algorithm 2.1, we denote by $NN(g_i, S)$ the NN of g_i in S. Then, g_i^- and g_i^+ represent, respectively, the prior gene of g_i and the posterior gene of g_i. $L(*)$ denotes class label of $*$.

Then, a flow chart of AGAIS_NN is shonw in Figure.1.

Algorithm 2.1 The pseudocode of fitness function

Input: A chromosome $S = \{g_1, g_2, \cdots, g_n\}$, $\alpha = 0.5$;
Output: $fitness(S)$;
1: $gain = 0$;
2: **for** each $g_i \in \{u \in S | u = 0\}$;
3: **if** $(L(g_i) = L(NN(g_i, S)))$
4:    **if** $(L(g_i^-) = L(NN(g_i^-, S))$ and $L(g_i^+) = L(NN(g_i^+, S))and$ $L(g_i^-) \neq L(g_i^+)$
5:      $gain = gain + 1$;
6:    **else**
7:      $gain = gain + 0$;
8: **else**
9:    $gain = gain + 0$;
10: **end**
11:   compute $fitness(S) = \alpha \times (1 - \frac{gain}{|T|}) + (1 - \alpha) \times (\frac{|T| - |S|}{|T|})$
12: **return** $fitness(S)$.

---

3. Experiment

The data sets used in experiment are from the machine learning data repository, University of California at Irvine.[4] These data sets involves fields including biomedical, environment, financial and business. The details of these data sets are characterized in Table 1.

Table 1.   The data sets excerpted from the UCI machine learning repository

	Data sets	Instances	Numerical	Category	Class
1	Heart1	270	7	6	2
2	Liver	345	5	1	2
3	Teaching	151	1	4	5
4	Method	1473	2	7	3
5	Chess1	28056	3	3	18
6	Cancer	569	30	0	2
7	Bench	208	60	0	2
8	Ecoli	336	7	0	8
9	Image	210	19	0	7
10	Ionosphere	351	34	0	2
11	Parkinsons	195	22	0	3
12	Wine	178	13	0	3

To test the usefulness of AGAIS_NN, we compare the proposed algorithm with some classical instance selection techniques: NN,[5] CNN,[6] CHC[1] and SSMA.[2] The classification accuracies and reduction rates of four techniques are presented in Table 2, in which R denotes the reduction rate and

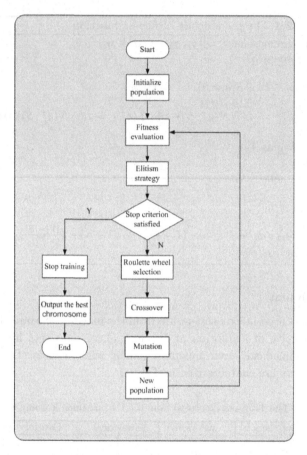

Fig. 1. Flowchart of instance selection via GA (AGAIS_NN)

the highest accuracy values are depicted by bold type.

From the results presented in Table 2, we can observe that the classification accuracies of the proposed algorithm outperforms other algorithms. However, the reduce rates are lower than others in the most of cases. With the above experimental analysis, we can obtain the following conclusions: AGAIS_NN is able to find the useful instances and more effective than the other algorithms.

4. Conclusion

This paper presented a new method to select instance from the training set, called adaptive genetic algorithm for instance selection (AGAIS_NN),

Table 2. Comparison of classification accuracy and reduction rate between AGAIS_NN and other learning algorithms

Data sets	CNN	R	CHC	R	SSMA	R	AGAIS_NN	R
Heart1	83.18	88.26	84.16	88.11	87.42	82.19	**89.11**	79.67
Liver	71.46	85.19	72.53	82.62	78.96	79.55	**80.71**	76.13
Teaching	82.99	88.90	83.84	88.13	84.08	87.33	**85.69**	81.94
Method	65.90	91.47	65.84	90.14	66.45	89.22	**67.15**	83.12
Chess1	**75.57**	88.78	72.36	94.36	73.27	92.19	74.26	91.20
Cancer	93.40	81.49	92.97	87.61	**95.93**	82.66	95.32	83.91
Bench	87.41	78.47	90.17	77.43	90.92	76.52	**91.62**	75.91
Ecoil	65.29	90.14	65.93	89.65	66.31	88.27	**67.26**	86.64
Image	78.50	90.42	80.81	91.25	81.28	89.64	**81.95**	89.11
Ionosphere	83.99	87.36	92.25	84.91	95.62	85.72	**97.42**	78.37
Parkinsons	75.31	64.84	83.42	62.56	86.45	63.14	**89.32**	61.49
Wine	84.85	67.18	85.54	66.57	88.05	64.92	**91.51**	60.42

which is based on genetic algorithm. The experimental results demonstrate the validity of the new proposed method.

Acknowledgements

This work has been supported by the National Natural Science Foundation of China (Grant Nos. 61175044 and 61175055) and the Fundamental Research Funds for the Central Universities of China (Grant No. SWJTU11ZT29).

References

1. J. R. Cano, F. Herrera and M. Lozano, *IEEE Tran. Evo. Com.* .
2. S. García, J. R. Cano and F. Herrera, *Pat. Rec.* **41**, 2693 (2008).
3. J. Derrac, S. García and F. Herrera, *Pat. Rec.* **43**, 2082 (2010).
4. UCI, machine learning data repository (1997), http://archive.ics.uci.edu/ml/datasets.html.
5. T. Cover and P. Hart, *IEEE Trans. Inf. Theo.* **13**, 21 (1967).
6. P. Hart, *IEEE Trans. Inf. Theo.* **14**, 515 (1968).

PRIORITIZATION OF URBAN TRANSFORMATION PROJECTS IN ISTANBUL USING MULTIATTRIBUTE HESITANT FUZZY LINGUISTIC TERM SETS

Basar Oztaysi, Sezi Cevik Onar and Cengiz Kahraman

Industrial Engineering Department, Istanbul Technical University, Macka 34367, Istanbul / Turkey

Hesitant fuzzy sets are used to handle the situations where a set of values are possible in defining membership functions. In urban transformation problems usually there are multiple actors with different perspectives and they represent hesitant evaluations on subjective criteria. Hesitant fuzzy linguistic term sets (HFLTS) enable aggregating the different linguistic evaluations of different actors without loss of information. This paper proposes a hierarchical multiattribute method based on hesitant fuzzy linguistic term sets for prioritizing the urban transformation projects in Istanbul.

1. Introduction

Designing the cities based on different aspects and more over planning the urban transformation process is one of the biggest challenges for the authorities that develop and execute urban plans. In order to achieve sustainable urban development the decision makers should consider several complex factors such as environmental, social, economic factors. Prioritizing the urban transformation projects is among the most crucial decisions that should be given related with urban transformation since usually there are limited resources. Unfortunately this prioritization process involves many complex factors with several decision makers such as politicians, urban planners etc. involving in the decision making process (Lefebvre, 1998). Usually these decision makers reflect different perspectives which make the problem even more complex. In literature there are only few studies that try to enhance urban transformation planning process and most of the studies mainly try to find the project that should be applied in a given territory. For instance Lami and Vitti (2011) utilized Quality Function Deployment and Analytic Network Process methods for evaluating the urban development projects for a predefined region in France. Similarly Ferri and Maturo (2013) select alternative projects for a defined region in Italy via ANP. But usually within cities there are several problematic areas that should be considered and prioritizing these areas are very important since it directly affects the city (Blecic et al., 2008).

The prioritization problem is more important for rapidly changing cities such as Istanbul since the prioritization defines the direction of the change. The high level of change causes problems such as population increase due to rural-to-urban migration which causes low standard living spaces with limited social services and green area usage and illegal rent usage on land belonging to others without permission. Moreover the hazard due to natural invents increases in such cities due to overcrowding and faulty buildings with inadequate infrastructures. An appropriate prioritization may limit these problems. But the prioritization of urban transformation projects is hard since it involves subjective criteria and multiple actors with different perspectives. Our paper proposes a hierarchical HFLTS method for overcoming this problem. The rest of the paper is organized as follows. Section 2 introduces urban transformation projects in Istanbul. Section 3 gives the steps of the proposed multi-attribute HFLTS Method. Section 4 includes the application of the method to urban transformation projects in Istanbul. The final section, gives conclusions and recommendations for further research.

2. Urban Transformation Projects in Istanbul

Istanbul, which is the largest and the most populous city in Turkey, is having a significant urban transformation. In the 1980s, urban development became a key source for national and international capital accumulation, seen in large-scale real estate projects in and around the city, such as gated communities, finance, real estate and insurance sector business centers, shopping malls, and various tourist attractions. The large-scale development projects necessitated vast tracts of land, something lacking in Istanbul's centre, and thus in order to overcome the obstructions of inner-city Istanbul, developers took to land reclamation in the suburbs and countryside, areas subsequently scarred by construction projects.

The projects, which are more directly related to Istanbul's urban transformation are Galata Port, Balat, Esenler and, Tarlabaşı.

With urban transformation in Istanbul, commercial and collective interests naturally collide. In a city like Istanbul, where trade and industry have moved into the suburbs, vast built-up city-center areas have become available and inevitably elicit huge financial appetites. It is seen that all transformation projects even in different places in Turkey, generally have one type and the same solutions. The economic, social, and cultural factors are not considered and the focus is to simply transform the physical. Urban planners argue that places produced by the transformation process are unfamiliar with the spirit and region of the city.

3. Multi-attribute HFLTS Method

The steps of our method are given in Figure 1. In order to deal with hierarchical structure of the urban transformation problem, our proposed method extends Rodriguez et al., (2013)'s study. The detailed steps can be found in our other paper presented at FLINS 2014 (Kahraman et al, 2014).

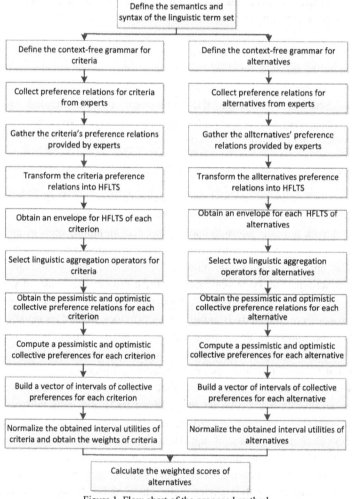

Figure 1. Flow chart of the proposed method

4. Prioritization of Urban Transformation Projects in Istanbul

The hierarchy of prioritizing urban transformation projects in Istanbul is given in Figure 2.

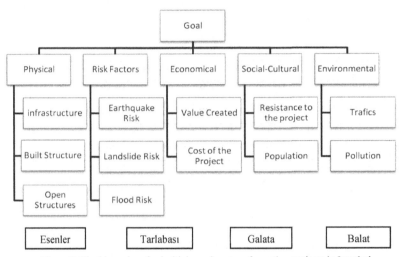

Figure 2. The hierarchy of prioritizing urban transformation projects in Istanbul

Three experts evaluated the criteria and alternatives of urban transformation projects in Istanbul. The weights of the main criteria and sub-criteria are given in Tables 1-6.

Table 1. Weights of the main criteria with respect to Goal

Criteria	Linguistic intervals	Interval Utilities	Midpoints	Weights
Physical	[(m,-.33),(vh,-.25)]	[2.67,4.75]	3.71	0.25
Risk	[(vh,-.34),(a,-.42)]	[4.66,5.58]	5.12	0.35
Economical	[(n,.17),(l,-.25)]	[0.17,1.75]	0.96	0.07
Social-Cultural	[(n,-.0),(vl,.42)]	[0,1.42]	14.67	0.05
Environmental	[(m,.34),(vh,-.0)]	[3.34,5]	4.17	0.28

Table 2. Weights of the criteria with respect to *Physical*

Criteria	Linguistic intervals	Interval Utilities	Midpoints	Weights
Infrastructure	[(l,.16),(h,-.17)]	[2.16,3.83]	2.995	0.32
Building	[(m,.34),(a,-.50)]	[3.34,5.5]	4.42	0.47
Open	[(vl,.34),(m,-.16)]	[1.34,2.84]	2.09	0.22

Table 3. Weights of the criteria with respect to *Risk Factor*

Criteria	Linguistic intervals	Interval Utilities	Midpoints	Weights
Earthquake	[(m,.34),(h,.50)]	[3.34,4.5]	3.92	0.53
Landslide	[(vl,.33),(m,.16)]	[1.33,3.16]	2.245	0.30
Flood	[(n,.34),(l,.17)]	[0.34,2.17]	1.255	0.17

Table 4. Weights of the criteria with respect to *Economical*

Criteria	Linguistic intervals	Interval Utilities	Midpoints	Weights
Value created	[(m,.33),(vh,.33)]	[3.33,5.33]	4.33	0.77
Cost	[(n,.33),(l,.33)]	[0.33,2.33]	1.33	0.23

Table 5. Weights of the criteria with respect to *Social-Cultural*

Criteria	Linguistic intervals	Interval Utilities	Midpoints	Weights
Resistance	[(n,-.0),(l,-.0)]	[0,2]	1	0.16
Population	[(vh,-.33),(a,-.0)]	[4.67,6]	5.335	0.84

Table 6. Weights of the criteria with respect to *Environmental*

Criteria	Linguistic intervals	Interval Utilities	Midpoints	Weights
Traffics	[(m,-.0),(vh,.33)]	[3,5.33]	4.165	0.74
Pollution	[(vl,-.33),(l,.33)]	[0.67,2.33]	1.5	0.26

The global weights of the criteria and the scores of the alternatives for each criterion are given in Table 7. Based on these weights and scores the weighted scores of the alternatives are calculated. According to these results the order is obtained as follows Esenler > Tarlabaşı > Balat > Galata.

5. Conclusion and Further Research

HFLTS are very successful in aggregating different opinions of different experts. The proposed method is original since it provides a multiattribute and hierarchical point of view to the problem. The main approach in our proposed method is rather similar to the hierarchical approach in Analytic Hierarchy Process method. The main difference is in the construction of pairwise comparison matrices and in the combination of the different evaluation. The performance of the mentioned methods can be compared.

Table 7. Calculation of global alternative weights

Main & Sub-criteria		Criteria Weight	Sub-criteria Weight	Sub-Criteria Global Weight	Evaluations of the Alternative			
C1	Physical	0.25			Esenler	Tarlabaşı	Galata	Balat
C11	Infrastructure		0.32	0.080	0.429	0.319	0.190	0.062
C12	Building		0.46	0.115	0.320	0.454	0.072	0.155
C13	Open		0.22	0.055	0.494	0.183	0.100	0.223
C2	Risk	0.35						
C21	Earthquake		0.53	0.186	0.428	0.161	0.102	0.310
C22	Landslide		0.30	0.105	0.662	0.134	0.070	0.134
C23	Flood		0.17	0.060	0.477	0.150	0.080	0.293
C3	Economical	0.07						
C31	Value created		0.77	0.054	0.039	0.277	0.413	0.271
C32	Cost		0.23	0.016	0.101	0.233	0.459	0.207
C4	Social-Cultural	0.05						
C41	Resistence		0.16	0.008	0.087	0.239	0.247	0.427
C42	Population		0.84	0.042	0.159	0.375	0.380	0.087
C5	Environmental	0.28						
C51	Traffics		0.74	0.207	0.085	0.439	0.288	0.189
C52	Pollution		0.26	0.073	0.455	0.188	0.080	0.277
	Global Alternative Weights:				0.337	0.281	0.173	0.208

References

Ivan Blecic, Arnaldo Cecchini, Clara Pusceddu Constructing strategies in strategic planning: a decision support evaluation model Oper Res Int J (2008) 8:153–166

Lefebvre C (1998) Metropolitan government and governance in western countries, a critical review. Int Urban Reg Res 22(1)

Barbara Ferri and Antonio Maturo Decisional models for a holistic perspective of Risk in urban regeneration projects. A case Study in pescara (Italy) International Journal of Risk Theory, Vol 3(no.1), 2013 (37-53)

Isabella M Lami and Elena L Vitti A combination of Quality Function Deployment and Analytic Network Process to evaluate urban redevelopment projects: An application to the Belle de Mai – La Friche of Marseille, France Journal of Applied Operational Research (2011) 3(1), 2–12.

Kahraman C., Oztaysi B., Cevik Onar S. (2014), A Multicriteria Supplier Selection Model Using Hesitant Fuzzy Linguistic Term Sets, FLINS 2014 Proceedings.

Rosa M. Rodriguez, Luis Martinez, Francisco Herrera A group decision making model dealing with comparative linguistic expressions based on hesitant fuzzy linguistic term sets. Information Sciences 241 (2013) 28–42.

A PARALLEL APPROACH FOR COMPUTING APPROXIMATIONS OF DOMINANCE-BASED ROUGH SETS APPROACH

SHAOYONG LI, TIANRUI LI * and HONGMEI CHEN

School of Information Science and Technology, Southwest Jiaotong University,
Chengdu, 610031, China
E-mail: meterer@163.com
{trli, hmchen}@swjtu.edu.cn

Computation of approximation in Dominance-based Rough Sets Approach (DRSA) is a necessary step for multi-criteria decision analysis and other related works. This paper presents a parallel approach for computing approximations of DRSA. Its feasibility is validated by a numerical example in this paper.

Keywords: Rough sets; Parallel computing; Dominance relation; Multi-core.

1. Introduction

Dominance-based Rough Set Approach (DRSA)[1] proposed by Greco et al. is a way to solve multi-criteria decision analysis problems, which had been successfully applied in many fields.[2] Parallelization of algorithms is a feasible way to speed up the computational process. In rough sets based knowledge acquisition, Zhang et al. proposed a parallel algorithm for computing approximations of rough sets under the indiscernible relation.[3] Then they compared the parallel algorithms of computing approximations of rough sets on different MapReduce runtime systems.[4] Computation of approximations in DRSA is an important step for solving multi-criteria decision analysis problems. The real-time problems often face with comparatively large data, then the improvement of computational efficiency is urgent to decision makers. Since the person computer with a multi-cores processor is very popular, the study of parallel computing approximations of DRSA on person computers with multi-core processors may contribute to improve the efficiency of decision making. To our knowledge, there is not a parallel algo-

---

*Corresponding author.

rithm for computing approximations of DRSA on multi-core environments. In this paper, we investigate the strategy how to parallelize the procedure of computing approximations of DRSA with multi-core processors.

The remainder of this paper is organized as follows. We present basic notions of DRSA in Section 2. We introduce a parallel approach for computing approximations of DRSA on multi-core environments in Section 3. In Section 4, a numerical example is used to validate the feasibility. This paper ends with conclusions and further research topics in Section 5.

2. Preliminaries

In this section, we briefly review some concepts, notations and properties of DRSA[1].

An information system is a four-tuple $S = (U, A, V, f)$, where U is a non-empty finite set of objects, called the universe. $A = C \cup \{d\}$. C is a non-empty finite set of condition attributes, and d is a decision attribute. V is regarded as the domain of all attributes. $f : U \times A \to V$ is an information function such that $f(x, a) \in V_a$, $\forall a \in A$ and $x \in U$, where V_a is the domain of attribute a.

In DRSA, the universe U is divided by the decision attribute d into a family of decision classes with preference-ordered. Let $\mathbf{Cl} = \{Cl_n, n \in T\}$, $T = \{1, \cdots, t\}$, be a collection of decision classes. $\forall r, s \in T$ such that $r > s$, the objects from Cl_r are preferred to the objects from Cl_s.

The concepts to be approximated in DRSA are upward unions and downward unions of decision classes such that $Cl_n^{\geq} = \bigcup_{s \geq n} Cl_s$, $Cl_n^{\leq} = \bigcup_{s \leq n} Cl_s$, $\forall n, s \in T$. Notice that $Cl_1^{\geq} = Cl_t^{\leq} = U$, $Cl_t^{\geq} = Cl_t$ and $Cl_1^{\leq} = Cl_1$.

D_P is a dominance relation on the universe U with respect to P, where

$$D_P = \{(x, y) \in U \times U | f(x, a) \geq f(y, a), \forall a \in P\}.$$

For any object $x \in U$, there are two sets of it as follows:

- A set of objects dominating x, called P-dominating set, $D_P^+(x) = \{y \in U | y D_P x\}$;
- A set of objects dominated by x, called P-dominated set, $D_P^-(x) = \{y \in U | x D_P y\}$.

P-dominating set and P-dominated set are the granule of knowledge in DRSA.

Definition 2.1. For $P \subseteq C$, $n \in T$, the lower and upper approximations of $Cl_n^\geq$ are defined as:

$$\underline{P}(Cl_n^\geq) = \{x \in U : D_P^+(x) \subseteq Cl_n^\geq\} \tag{1}$$

$$\overline{P}(Cl_n^\geq) = \{x \in U : D_P^-(x) \cap Cl_n^\geq \neq \emptyset\} \tag{2}$$

The lower and upper approximations of $Cl_n^\leq$ are defined as:

$$\underline{P}(Cl_n^\leq) = \{x \in U : D_P^-(x) \subseteq Cl_n^\leq\} \tag{3}$$

$$\overline{P}(Cl_n^\leq) = \{x \in U : D_P^+(x) \cap Cl_n^\leq \neq \emptyset\} \tag{4}$$

3. Parallel strategy of computing approximations of DRSA on the multi-core environment

In order to improve the efficiency of computing approximations of DRSA, we discuss a parallel strategy on multi-core environments. Assumed that an information system may be divided into many subsystems. Let $S = \bigcup_{i=1}^m S_i$, where $S_i = (U_i, A, V, f)$ called a subsystem of information system S and satisfies the following items.

(i) $U = \bigcup_{i=1}^m U_i$;

(ii) If $i \neq j$, then $U_i \cap U_j = \emptyset$.

In our previous work, a character variant

$$r^a(x, y) = \begin{cases} 1, & f(x, a) \geq f(y, a) \\ 0, & f(x, a) < f(y, a) \end{cases} \tag{5}$$

was defined to present the preference relation between x and y with respect to the attribute a^5. For $P \subseteq C$, $\phi^P(x, y) = \sum_{a \in P} r^a(x, y)$ is used to indicate the dominance relation between x and y with respect to the attribute set P. If $\phi^P(x, y) = |P|$, then x dominates y. Hence, the definition of the dominating and dominated sets is written as

$$D_P^+(x) = \{y \in U | \phi^P(y, x) = |P|\} \tag{6}$$

$$D_P^-(x) = \{y \in U | \phi^P(x, y) = |P|\} \tag{7}$$

Since that the universe can be divided into many subsystems, computation of the dominance relation on U can be assembled by many parallel procedures of computing its subsets.

Proposition 3.1. *Let* $D_P^{i,j} = \{(x, y) \in U_i \times U_j | \phi^P(x, y) = |P|\}$ *be the subset of the dominance relation, then* $D_P = \bigcup_{i=1, j=1}^{m,m} D_P^{i,j}$.

Proposition 3.2. *Let* $D_P^+(x)^i = \{y \in U_i | \phi^P(y,x) = |P|\}$ *and* $D_P^-(x)^i = \{y \in U_i | \phi^P(x,y) = |P|\}$ *be subsets* $D_P^+(x)$ *and* $D_P^-(x)$, *respectively. Then we have* $D_P^+(x) = \bigcup_{i=1}^m D_P^+(x)^i$ *and* $D_P^-(x) = \bigcup_{i=1}^m D_P^-(x)^i$.

Proposition 3.3. *Let* $Cl_n^{\geq i} = \{x \in U_i | f(x,d) \geq d_n\}$ *and* $Cl_n^{\leq i} = \{x \in U_i | f(x,d) \leq d_n\}$ *be subsets of* $Cl_n^\geq$ *and* $Cl_n^\leq$, *respectively. Then we have* $Cl_n^\geq = \bigcup_{i=1}^m Cl_n^{\geq i}$ *and* $Cl_n^\leq = \bigcup_{i=1}^m Cl_n^{\leq i}$.

Proposition 3.4. *Let* $\underline{P}(Cl_n^{\geq i})^j = \{x \in U_j | D_P^+(x)^i \subseteq Cl_n^{\geq i}\}$ *and* $\underline{P}(Cl_n^{\leq i})^j = \{x \in U_j | D_P^-(x)^i \subseteq Cl_n^{\leq i}\}$ *be subsets of* $\underline{P}(Cl_n^\geq)$ *and* $\underline{P}(Cl_n^\leq)$ *on subsystem* U_j. *Then we have* $\underline{P}(Cl_n^\geq) = \bigcup_{j=1}^m [\bigcap_{i=1}^m \underline{P}(Cl_n^{\geq i})^j]$ *and* $\underline{P}(Cl_n^\leq) = \bigcup_{j=1}^m [\bigcap_{i=1}^m \underline{P}(Cl_n^{\leq i})^j]$.

Proposition 3.5. *Let* $\overline{P}(Cl_n^{\geq i})^j = \{x \in U_j | D_P^-(x)^i \cap Cl_n^{\geq i} \neq \emptyset\}$ *and* $\overline{P}(Cl_n^{\leq i})^j = \{x \in U_j | D_P^+(x)^i \cap Cl_n^{\leq i} \neq \emptyset\}$ *be subsets of* $\underline{P}(Cl_n^\geq)$ *and* $\underline{P}(Cl_n^\leq)$ *on subsystem* U_j. *Then we have* $\overline{P}(Cl_n^\geq) = \bigcup_{i=1,j=1}^{m,m} \overline{P}(Cl_n^{\geq i})^j$ *and* $\overline{P}(Cl_n^\leq) = \bigcup_{i=1,j=1}^{m,m} \overline{P}(Cl_n^{\leq i})^j$.

4. A numerical illustration

Example 4.1. Table 1 is an information system, four sub-tables of it are listed in Table 2. Let $P = \{a_1, a_2, a_3\}$.

Table 1: An information system

U	a_1	a_2	a_3	d	U	a_1	a_2	a_3	d
x_1	2	1	3	1	x_7	3	1	2	3
x_2	2	1	2	2	x_8	2	2	2	2
x_3	3	1	1	2	x_9	2	3	1	3
x_4	2	3	1	1	x_{10}	2	3	3	3
x_5	1	2	3	1	x_{11}	1	1	2	1
x_6	2	2	1	2	x_{12}	2	2	2	2

Since the information system is divided into four subsystems, there are sixteen parallel procedures for computing subsets of the dominance relation, P-dominating and P-dominated sets, upward and downward unions, and approximations.

For U_i and U_j, $i, j = 1, 2, 3, 4$, when $i = 1$ and $j = 1$, we can get the following results.

Table 2: Four sub-tables of Table 1

(a) Sub-table 1

U_1	a_1	a_2	a_3	d
x_1	2	1	3	1
x_2	2	1	2	2
x_3	3	1	1	2

(b) Sub-table 2

U_2	a_1	a_2	a_3	d
x_4	2	3	1	1
x_5	1	2	3	1
x_6	2	2	1	2

(c) Sub-table 3

U_3	a_1	a_2	a_3	d
x_7	3	1	2	3
x_8	2	2	2	2
x_9	2	3	1	3

(d) Sub-table 4

U_4	a_1	a_2	a_3	d
x_{10}	2	3	3	3
x_{11}	1	1	2	1
x_{12}	2	2	2	2

The subset of the dominance relation on universe U_1

$$D_P^{1,1} = \{(x_1, x_1), (x_1, x_2), (x_2, x_2), (x_3, x_3)\}.$$

The subsets of P-dominating and P-dominated sets of objects in U_1

$$D_P^+(x_1)^1 = \{x_1\}, \quad D_P^+(x_2)^1 = \{x_1, x_2\}, \quad D_P^+(x_3)^1 = \{x_3\},$$
$$D_P^-(x_1)^1 = \{x_1, x_2\}, \quad D_P^-(x_2)^1 = \{x_2\}, \quad D_P^-(x_3)^1 = \{x_3\}.$$

The subsets of upward and downward unions of decision classes

$$Cl_{\bar{1}}^{\geq^1} = U_1, \quad Cl_{\bar{2}}^{\geq^1} = \{x_2, x_3\}, \quad Cl_{\bar{3}}^{\geq^1} = \emptyset,$$
$$Cl_{\bar{1}}^{\leq^1} = \{x_1\}, \quad Cl_{\bar{2}}^{\leq^1} = U_1, \quad Cl_{\bar{3}}^{\leq^1} = U_1.$$

The subsets of approximations

$$\underline{P}(Cl_{\bar{1}}^{\geq^1})^1 = U_1, \quad \underline{P}(Cl_{\bar{2}}^{\geq^1})^1 = \{x_3\}, \quad \underline{P}(Cl_{\bar{3}}^{\geq^1})^1 = \emptyset,$$
$$\overline{P}(Cl_{\bar{1}}^{\geq^1})^1 = U_1, \quad \overline{P}(Cl_{\bar{2}}^{\geq^1})^1 = U_1, \quad \overline{P}(Cl_{\bar{3}}^{\geq^1})^1 = \emptyset,$$
$$\underline{P}(Cl_{\bar{1}}^{\leq^1})^1 = \emptyset, \quad \underline{P}(Cl_{\bar{2}}^{\leq^1})^1 = U_1, \quad \underline{P}(Cl_{\bar{3}}^{\leq^1})^1 = U_1,$$
$$\overline{P}(Cl_{\bar{1}}^{\leq^1})^1 = \{x_1, x_2\}, \quad \overline{P}(Cl_{\bar{2}}^{\leq^1})^1 = U_1, \quad \overline{P}(Cl_{\bar{3}}^{\leq^1})^1 = U_1.$$

Analogously, we can also obtain the subsets of approximations on other cases.

By Propositions 3.4 and 3.5, we can get the lower and upper approximation sets for upward and downward unions of decision classes on U as follows:

$$\underline{P}(Cl_{\bar{1}}^{\geq}) = U, \quad \underline{P}(Cl_{\bar{2}}^{\geq}) = \{x_3, x_7, x_8, x_{10}, x_{12}\}, \quad \underline{P}(Cl_{\bar{3}}^{\geq}) = \{x_7, x_{10}\},$$
$$\underline{P}(Cl_{\bar{1}}^{\leq}) = \{x_5, x_{11}\}, \underline{P}(Cl_{\bar{2}}^{\leq}) = \{x_1, x_5, x_8, x_{11}, x_{12}\}, \quad \underline{P}(Cl_{\bar{3}}^{\leq}) = U,$$

$\overline{P}(Cl_1^{\geq}) = U$, $\overline{P}(Cl_2^{\geq}) = \{x_1, x_2, x_3, x_4, x_6, x_7, x_8, x_9, x_{10}, x_{12}\}$, $\overline{P}(Cl_3^{\geq}) = \{x_2, x_3, x_4, x_6, x_7, x_9, x_{10}\}$, $\overline{P}(Cl_1^{\leq}) = \{x_1, x_2, x_4, x_5, x_6, x_9, x_{11}\}$, $\overline{P}(Cl_2^{\leq}) = \{x_1, x_2, x_3, x_4, x_5, x_6, x_8, x_9, x_{11}, x_{12}\}$, $\overline{P}(Cl_3^{\leq}) = U$.

From this example, one can see the parallel approach is feasible to compute approximations of DRSA.

5. Conclusions and future works

It is necessary for decision makers in this big data era to improve the performance of algorithms for computing approximations of DRSA. Parallel computing has been proved as a suitable way to reduce the computational time. In this paper, we proposed a parallel approach for computing approximations of DRSA on multi-core environments and validated the feasibility by a numerical illustration. In the future, we will develop a parallel algorithm based on this approach and evaluate the performance of computing approximations of DRSA on public benchmark datasets.

Acknowledgements

This work is supported by the National Science Foundation of China (Nos. 61175047, 61100117, 71201133) and NSAF (No. U1230117).

References

1. S. Greco, B. Matarazzo and R. Slowinski, *European Journal of Operational Research* **129**, 1 (2001).
2. Z. Pawlak and A. Skowron, *Information Sciences* **177**, 28 (2007).
3. J. Zhang, T. Li and D. Ruan, *Information Sciences* **194**, 209 (2012).
4. J. Zhang, J. Wong, T. Li and Y. Pan, *International Journal of Approximate Reasoning* **55**, 896 (2014).
5. S. Li, T. Li and D. Liu, *Knowledge-Based Systems* **40**, 17 (2013).

PART 6

UNCERTAINTY MODELING

AN INFORMATION SYSTEM SECURITY EVALUATION METHOD OF BUSINESS OPERATION TARGETING THE SERVICE COMPOSITION[*]

DAN-CHEN WANG

Intelligent Control Development Center, Southwest Jiao tong University, 610031, Chengdu, Sichuan, China
Sichuan Information Security Testing Evaluation Center, 610017 Chengdu, Sichuan, China

YANG XU

Intelligent Control Development Center, Southwest Jiao tong University, 610031, Chengdu, Sichuan, China

WEI PU

Sichuan Information Security Testing Evaluation Center, 610017 Chengdu, Sichuan, China

Seeing the business flows of service composition as the research object, this paper aims at bringing the security service provided by security components that deployed by system into composition service. Its major focus is in the premise of ensuring the accuracy of system business, to formulate the security efficiency that transitional operation composition of security service identifies system business, and to put forward a safeguard approach that reasonably restructure the security components targeting the security service which dissatisfies system requirements. By producing an appropriate redundant path of component service based on the existing execution records and logical structure, this approach will help reach the safeguard goals of business operation security in information system.

1. Introduction

Normally, the security operation of system operation mainly conducts security function measurement focusing on the security equipment deployed, concludes specific safeguard measures[1], and the security protection of business flows is realized by making static verification with credibility to the input/output of data flows and by processing analysis with credibility based on the networked

[*] This work is supported by National Science Foundation of China (Grant No.61175055), Sichuan Key Technology Research and Development Program (Grant No.2011FZ0051), Radio Administration Bureau of MIIT of China(Grant No.[2011]146), China Institution of Communications (Grant No.[2011]051).

software[2]. However, the methods mentioned above are difficult to be adapted to the security protection requirements of multi-service system. For example, plenty of service compositions are being operated in the financial system. According to the requirements of the terminal user, the structure of flows is evolved dynamically and transferred to a new structure, but the business flows have the characteristics of continuous execution and relative-independence. Hence, the structural transfer of business flows becomes an important factor for security protection of system operation.

This paper focuses mainly on the operational security of structural transfer of business flow targeting the service composition. Bring the security service provided by security equipment to the service composition, in order to systematic assessment operational security. To construct a redundant path by using transitional operation set of security service so as to identify the transfer path with the maximum frequency of execution and the service sets that do not satisfy the expected indexes of security protection.

2. The transitional operation set of security service in the business of service composition

In light of the dynamic characteristic of service composition flows, Petri net is adopted to describe the workflow net (Abb. WF-net)[3]. Transition indicates service, place indicates the condition that transition is triggered, and flow relationship indicates the logical and structural relationship among transitions. Also, the dynamic changes of the token place describe the state of workflow net.

Definition 1 (workflow net). $WFN = (P, T, F)$ is called the workflow net, and it satisfies conditions below:

(1)   Exists an initial place $i \in P$, which makes $^*i = \phi$;

(2)   Exists a terminal place $o \in P$, which makes $o^* = \phi$;

(3)   Every node $x \in P \cup T$ is set in the path from i to o.

Definition 2(colored workflow net of security strategy). A colored workflow net of security strategy is a multi-component system: $SCWFN = \{\Sigma, P, T, F, C, S, i, o, M_0\}$, and in this system:

(1) Σ is a nonempty finite set, which is called the colored set;

(2) P is the nonempty finite set of place;

(3) T is the nonempty finite set of transition;

(4) F is the logical and structural relationship among transitions;

(5) $C : (P \cup T) \rightarrow \Sigma$, which is the colored function;

(6) $S : (P \cup T) \rightarrow \Sigma$, which is the security strategy function, and it satisfies

$$\forall t \in T, \forall col \in C(\bullet t): Type(S(t,col)) = c \land Type(Var(S(t,col))) \subseteq \Sigma \bigcup T$$
$$\forall t \in T, \forall col \notin C(\bullet t): S(t,col) = 0$$

In actual workflows, a majority of initiated security strategy services are in the condition of waiting for being processed, rather than being processed. Therefore, a service scene is required to show this condition. The common workflow modes that based on conditions are deferred choice and milestone. An evolved operation set based on the service composition of security strategy is given to testify the rationality of workflows after the transitions of business flows.

Definition 3 (added operation of security service). Seeing

$SCWFN_1 = (\Sigma, P_1, T_1, F_1, C_1, S_1, i_1, o_1, M_{01})$ and $SCWFN_2 = (\Sigma, P_2, T_2, F_2, C_2, S_2, i_2, o_2, M_{02})$

as two business workflows containing different security strategies, and

$P_1 \bigcap P_2 = \varnothing, T_1 \bigcap T_2 = \varnothing, F_1 \bigcap F_2 = \varnothing, S_1 \bigcap S_2 = \varnothing$, seeing $SCWFN = \{\Sigma, P, T, F, C, S, i_1, o_2, M_0\}$ is a

workflow net which is required by adding $SCWFN_2$ to $SCWFN_1$. Therein to,

$P = (P_1 \setminus \{o_1\}) \cup P_2, T = T_1 \cup T_2, S = S_1 \cup S_2 \quad F = \{(x,y) \in F_1 | y \neq o_1\} \cup \{(x,i_2) \in T_2 \times P_1 | (x,o_1) \in F_1\} \cup F_2$.

Similarly, the cancelling operation of security service is the counter-operation of the adding operation.

Definition 4 (substitution of security service). Seeing $SCWFN_1 = (\Sigma, P_1, T_1, F_1, C_1, S_1, i_1, o_1, M_{01})$ as a rational subnet of a workflow net $SCWFN = \{\Sigma, P, T, F, C, S, i, o, M_0\}$, and $SCWFN_2 = (\Sigma, P_2, T_2, F_2, C_2, S_2, i_2, o_2, M_{02})$ is a workflow net contains different security strategies. Also, $P_1 \bigcap P_2 = \varnothing$, $T_1 \bigcap T_2 = \varnothing, F_1 \bigcap F_2 = \varnothing, S_1 \bigcap S_2 = \varnothing$, By making a substitution from $SCWFN_1$ to $SCWFN_2$ gains $SCWFN' = \{\Sigma, P', T', F', C', S', i', o', M_0'\}$ as a workflow net. Among which, $P' = (P \setminus P_1) \cup P_2, T' = (T \setminus T_1) \cup T_2, F' = (F \setminus F_1) \cup F_2 \cup F'$ satisfies

$$F' = \{(x,i_2) \in P \times T_2 | (x,i_1) \in F_1\} \cup \{(o_2, y) \in T_2 \times P | (o_1, y) \in F_1\}.$$

Definition 5 (order adjustment of security service).

$SCWFN_1 = (\Sigma, P_1, T_1, F_1, C_1, S_1, i_1, o_1, M_{01})$ and $SCWFN_2 = (\Sigma, P_2, T_2, F_2, C_2, S_2, i_2, o_2, M_{02})$

combined into $SCWFN = \{\Sigma, P, T, F, C, S, i, o, M_0\}$ according to sequence,

$$P = P_1 \cup P_2, T = T_1 \cup T_2, F = F_1 \cup F_2, S = S_1 \cup S_2, i = i_1, o_1 = i_2, o = o_2.$$

(1) The concurrent adjustments of security strategy:

$SCWFN_\parallel = (\Sigma, P_\parallel, T_\parallel, F_\parallel, C_\parallel, S_\parallel, i_\parallel, o_\parallel, M_{0\parallel})$ is gained from $SCWFN_1$ and

$SCWFN_2$ though concurrent adjustment in sequence, where, $P_\parallel = P \cup \{i_\parallel, o_\parallel\}$,

$T_\parallel = T \cup \{t^{split}, t^{join}\}$, $S_\parallel = S_1 \cup S_2, F_\parallel = F \cup \{\langle i_\parallel, t^{split} \rangle, \langle t^{split}, i_1 \rangle, \langle t^{split}, i_2 \rangle, \langle o_1, t^{join} \rangle, \langle o_2, t^{join} \rangle, \langle t^{join}, o_\parallel \rangle\}$.

(2) The selected adjustments of security strategy:

$SCWFN_+ = (\Sigma, P_+, T_+, F_+, C_+, S_+, i_+, o_+, M_{0+})$ is gained from $SCWFN_1$ and $SCWFN_2$ though selected adjustment in sequence, $P_+ = (P \setminus \{i_x, i_y, o_x, o_y\}) \cup \{i_+, o_+\}, T_+ = T, S_+ = S$

$F_+ = \{(p,q) \in F | p \neq i_1, i_2 \wedge q \neq o_1, o_2\} \cup \{(p, o_+) | (p, o_1) \in F_1 \vee (p, o_2) \in F_2\}$

Testifying the accuracy of business flow structure of security strategy and other service composition is a vital criterion. The accuracy of flow structure after transition can demonstrate that the security strategies enable to serve business work, and to complete the work accurately.

Definition 6 (an accurate workflow net of service composition). Assuming that a workflow net of service composition $SCWFN = \{\Sigma, P, T, F, C, S, i, o, M_0\}$ is rational of meeting business needs and it satisfies the conditions below:

(1) $\forall M(M_0 \xrightarrow{*} M) \Rightarrow (M \xrightarrow{*} M_{end})$;

(2) $\forall M(M_0 \xrightarrow{*} M \wedge M \geq M_{end}) \Rightarrow (M = M_{end})$;

(3) $\forall t \in T \exists M, M' s.t. M_0 \xrightarrow{*} M \xrightarrow{t} M'$.

The formulas above illustrate that it can always reach to the terminal condition from the initial condition. Also, when a token is put in a place, all the other places are empty, stipulating that no dead transition is existed.

3. A security evaluation method of business operation in information system targeting the service composition.

3.1. *An analysis of business security measure effectiveness*

Definition 7 (transition path). For an accurate workflow net of service composition $SCWFN = \{\Sigma, P, T, F, C, S, i, o, M_0\}$, the transition sequence from the initial condition M_0 to the terminal condition M_{end} is called as a transition path of this workflow net, and noted as tp and $tp \in T^*$, The set of $SCWFN$ all the transition path is called as the log of this workflow, which noted as L.

By analyzing the execution records of security strategy of service composition, the business path tp whose execution rate of security strategy is in maximum and the component service set S which does not reach the expected security indexes are gained. Based on the analysis of tp, weights are assigned in light of security attributes to the initiated security strategy. The confidentiality, integrality, and availability are noted as W_C, W_I, W_A respectively, and $W_C + W_I + W_A = 1$. The access control permission of business flows for every business subject is noted as P_i, and its impact factors are noted as W_{Ci}, W_{Ii}, W_{Ai},

$\sum_{i=1}^{n} W_{Ci} = 1, \sum_{i=1}^{n} W_{Ii} = 1, \sum_{i=1}^{n} W_{Ai} = 1$. Seeing the success rate of vulnerability of business flows for every business subject as Pr, and the security measure effectiveness of the present operation business is E.

3.2. *The transition process of business flows*

Definition 8 (transition relationships) Seeing L as the log of workflow net $SCWFN = \{\Sigma, P, T, F, C, S, i, o, M_0\}$, and $a, b \in T$ are the two transitions of this workflow net.

(1) For a transition path $tp = t_1 t_2 \cdots t_n \in L$, if $t_i = a, t_j = b, j \geq i+1$, then call a on tp as the precursor of b ;

(2) For transition paths tp, $tp' \in L$, if $a >_{tp} b, b >_{tp'} a$, then call a and b on L as a concurrency relation;

(3) For a random transition path $tp \in L$, if there exists $a \not>_{tp} b, b \not>_{tp} a$ when tp includes transitions a and b simultaneously then call a and b on L as a selected relation.

The basic transition sequence ts is gained from the business flow path tp whose execution rate of security strategy is in maximum and the component service set S which does not reach the expected security indexes. However, this transition path includes not only the unexpected transitions, but also the necessary tp transitions. If constructing a business sub-workflow net of service composition directly from the basic transition, the accuracy of business function is damaged. Therefore, the core of processing is to see the basic transition ts as the basis, and to solve a minimum transition sequence ts' .To extend by comparing the relationship between the two adjacent transitions in the basic transition sequence, and to obtain a ts' after a well-organized extension. In the end, a business workflow net of service composition which maximizes the security strategy based on the accurate business function is gained.

4. Method demonstration

There contain four steps: (1) To require the historical execution records L, finding out the transition path tp whose execution rate of security strategy is in maximum and the component service composition S that do not reach the expected security indexes; (2) To evaluate the security attribute of security strategy, and to calculate the security measure effectiveness E of business composition; (3) If the security measure effectiveness E cannot satisfy the business security requirements, to generate a redundant path from the basic transition sequence, and though transitional operation set of security service to the redundant path and a sub-business flow which belongs to the original service composition; (4) When the flow structure is confirmed, to reselect a security component service by making use of the project method.

5. Conclusion

This paper mainly discusses a security evaluation method of business operation in information system targeting the service composition. In order to ensure the operation security of evaluation system, firstly, to bring the security service into business composition service which is provided by security components, and to construct a transition operation set of security service so as to guarantee the rationality of flows after the business transition operation; secondly, to calculate the business security measure effectiveness by analyzing the transition path and to compare the safeguard requirements, so as to evaluate the security condition of system business operation. Meanwhile, in light of the security service which does not satisfy the business requirements, to generate an appropriate component redundant path according to the existing execution records of service composition and the logical structure, and to re-choose the security component service based on the planning method. At last, to demonstrate the steps of this method.

References

[1] Danchen Wang, Yang Xu, An Information system security dynamic assessment method using stochastic petri net based on business flow. Proceedings of 2013 International Conference on Machine Learning and Cybernetics. 2013 (4):1818–1823.

[2] Chen HW, Wang J, Dong W. High confidence software engineering technologies. Chinese Journal of Electronics, 2013,31(12A): 1933-1938.

[3] von de Aalst WMP, von Hee K. Workflow Management Models, Methods, and Systems. Cambridge: The MIT Press, 2002.

[4] WU Di, FENG Deng-Guo, LIAN Yi-Feng, CHEN Kai,. Efficiency Evaluation Model of System Security Measures in the Given Vulnerabilities Set, Journal of Software,2012,23(7):1880–1898.

[5] Elahi G, Yu E, Zannone N. A vulnerability-centric requirements engineering framework: Analyzing security attacks, countermeasures, and requirements based on vulnerabilities. Requirements Engineering, 2010,15(1):41–62.

A SEARCH METHOD FOR FEASIBLE NEIGHBORHOODS OF INTELLIGENT CAR BASED ON NEIGHBORHOOD SYSTEMS *

HAILIANG ZHAO

*School of Mathematics, Southwest Jiaotong University,
Chengdu, Sichuan 610031, China*

The control methods based on neighborhood systems can break down a dynamic and complex control process into a series of static and simple ones. They are available approaches for the control of automatic driving. According to a car's orientation relative to road, a neighborhood system for intelligent cars is presented in this paper. Methods to select some feasible neighborhoods for an automatic driving car are discussed, which are built by considering the changes of road edges and the relative speed to the front of cars or obstacles. All the methods are designed depending on data from available sensors of angle and distance. Each of the feasible neighborhoods could reflect some changes of the environment factors, so that it can be used to fuzzy predictive control. The effectiveness of the presented methods is simulated with a full size car on road.

1. Introduction

In order to imitate the dynamic decision and action mode of intelligent creatures, in reference [1], we present a dynamic decision and control model based on neighborhood systems [2]. Whose main idea is to break down a decision-making process that is dynamic and complex from a macro point of view, into a series of static and simple decision-making processes from a microscopic point of view. Theoretical analysis and simulation results show that the method is effective to intelligent movement objects such as robot, intelligent driving systems etc. Obviously, if the feasible neighborhoods are obtained by considering some changes of the environment factors, then the neighborhoods could be used to fuzzy predictive control and get better control performance. However, how to find a feasible neighborhood that can reflect the comprehensive changes of environmental factors with time have not been discussed in reference [1]. In fact, an experienced driver can make a car run fast and smoothly, since he is able to use of much predictive information to select a neighborhood of the car as a feasible neighborhood. The information includes the changes of road edges, the

* This work was supported by the National Natural Science Foundation of China (No. 61175044)

relative speed to the front and back of cars and the color's time of the traffic light insight, etc. Therefore, to select a feasible neighborhood with predictive information is important to a control method based on neighborhood systems.

Based on the above analysis, this paper suggests an actual method to find feasible neighborhoods for automatic driving cars running on roads. In the method, the tangent direction of road edge and the relative speed to the front of car are taken into account. Simulation results show that the selected feasible neighborhoods are more approximate to skill driver's selection than that by the method in reference [6].

2. Basic concepts and terminology conventions

For explicity, some important terms are cited as follows. All of the terms that appear in this section and its explanations can be found in reference [1].

Definition 2.1 (Neighborhood system[2-3]) Let X be the universe of discourse and x be an object in X. A neighborhood of x is a non-empty subset of X. A neighborhood system of an object x, denoted by $NS(x)$, is a maximal family of neighborhoods of x.

Using neighborhood we are able to easily express a region near a point x. Fig. 1 shows an example for a car's neighborhoods as running in trees and buildings.

System observation variables: All the system parameters that can be measured by instruments are called system observation variables[4-5]. A point in the universe of the system observation variables is called a **system state**.

Control algorithm and **control system**[4-5]: Assume that the mapping f : $I \times X \to U$ such that $\forall (t, x) \in I \times X$,

$$(t, x) \mapsto u = c(t, x) \qquad (1)$$

Call c a control algorithm or control function. Where $I \subseteq [0, +\infty)$ is an interval with a finite or infinite right endpoint. $X \subseteq R^n$ is the universe of the system observation variables and U is the universe of control variables. Let the capital letter C denote the set consists of all control algorithm.

Definition 2.2 (State track [4-5]) Every control algorithm can make the system state response over time, which can be expressed as curves over time. The curves are called the track of the system state generated by control algorithm c. Call it as state track for simply.

We write $x(t;c) = (x_1(t;c), \cdots, x_n(t;c))$ express the track curves generated by the control algorithm c. Let $\{x(t;c); x_0, T\}$ denote the track of system state in time interval $[t_0, t_0 + T]$ with initial state x_0. Obviously, we have

$$\{x(t;c); x_0, T\} = \{ x(t;c) | x(t_0) = x_0, t_0 \leq t \leq t_0 + T \} \qquad (2)$$

For simplicity, write $\Gamma(x_0)=\{\ \{x(t;c);\ x_0,T\}|T>0,c\in C\}$. This is, let $\Gamma(x_0)$ denote the set of all tracks of system state with initial state x_0. If we do not emphasis control algorithm c, write $\{x(t;c);x_0,T\}$ as $\{x(t);x_0,T\}$ for short.

Definition 2.3 (Feasible neighborhood) Assume $Q(x_0,T)$ is a bounded open region of the universe of the observation variables. If $\forall z\in Q(x_0,T)$, $\exists$ $\{x(t);x_0,T\}\in\Gamma(x_0)$ such that $z\in\{x(t);x_0,T\}$ and $\{x(t);x_0,T\}\subseteq Q(x_0,T)$, then call $Q(x_0,T)$ a feasible neighborhood of state x_0, while T is called holding time of the feasible neighborhood. A set contains all feasible neighborhood of state x_0 is called the feasible neighborhood system of x_0, denoted by $FNS(x_0)$, that is,

$FNS(x_0)=\{\ Q(x_0,T)\ |\ T\in(0,+\infty),\ Q(x_0,T)$ is a feasible neighborhood of $x_0\}$

Definition 2.4 (Sufficient neighborhood) Call a sufficient neighborhood of state x_0 with respect to time T if all state tracks from x_0 are contained in $E(x_0,T)$, i.e. $\{\{x(t);x_0,\tau\}|\tau\le T\}\subseteq E(x_0,T)$.

From the definition we can see that any region contained a sufficient feasible neighborhood is also a large sufficient region that the object can not get out of it in time interval T. Obviously, to make a decision based on the minimal sufficient range is a good choice.

Definition 2.5 (Differential neighborhood) Assume $B(t)$ is the boundary of a neighborhood at time t. When t has a increment Δt, the neighborhood boundaries have to get a change ΔB. The neighborhood with boundary $B(t)+\Delta B$ is called Differential neighborhood of the original neighborhood.

Since the change of neighborhood is taken into count in a short period, differential neighborhood is more adequate to predictive control.

Figure 1. A car's neighborhoods with different shapes as running in trees and buildings

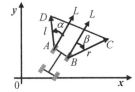

Figure 2. Diagrammatic sketch Detection parameters and $S(\alpha,l;\beta,r)$

3. Trapezoid neighborhood systems of a car

When a car runs on the roads, there are varieties of neighborhoods around it. What kind of feasible neighborhoods is suitable to fuzzy control must be considered in control methods based on neighborhood systems [1]. We assume that all data about the obstacles around the car can be obtained with sensors. The data should include the distance between the car and the edges of road, the relative speed to the cars in front of it. For ease of representation and computation, by definition 2.3 we can select trapezoid neighborhoods to serve as

598

the feasible neighborhoods of a car. As shown in Fig. 2, let α, β be the angles between the detection vectors **AD, BC** and longitudinal direction **L** of the car, respectively, and we take α,β positive in anti-clockwise rotation from L. We denote the length of **AD** and **BC** simply by l and r, and the trapezoid with four vertexes A,B,C,D by $S(\alpha,l;\beta,r)$, respectively. Since a car's the maximum steer angle is usually less than $\pi/4$, we can assume α, $\beta \in [-\pi/4,\pi/4]$, and use $l(\alpha)$ and $r(\beta)$ denote the distance to the obstacle being detected in the directions characterized by α or β respectively. If there are no obstacles or road edge being detected then the length of corresponding detection vector will be infinite, so $l(\alpha)=\infty$, or $r(\beta) =\infty$. We can regard a detection vector as infinite when they are large than a large enough value M. say $M= 120m$.

3.1. The car's orientation relative to road

Without loss of generality, we assume the following conditions about a road.

(1) The edges of the two sides of road are continuous and can be detected. The edges and obstacles can be distinguished by the car.

(2) The distance from the front left corner of a car to any point at the left edge of road is less than that from the front right corner of a car

(3) The car can only move forward along the road, or the car always knows which direction is forward. For simplicity, the angle between the car's longitudinal direction and the tangent of road is less than $\pi/2$.

(4) Along any ray direction, only the nearest obstacle point to the car can be detected.

For example, if the road has a left turn in front of the car, the last or the furthest point at the left edge of road is just the tangent point from the view of the front left corner of a car.

According to the orientation of a car in road, it can be divided into three kinds of situations as shown in Fig.3. Let θ denote the angle between the longitudinal direction L of a car and tangent direction T of the road, then we have $\theta_1 <0$, $\theta_2>0$ and $\theta_3=0$ in Fig.3, respectively. Obviously, the feasible neighborhoods are closely associated with θ.

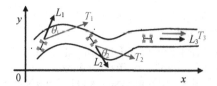 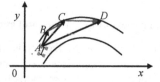

Figure 3. Three cases of the angles between longitudinal direction and tangent direction

Figure 4. Right-hand bend recognition by cross product of vectors

3.2. *Building model of feasible neighborhood without obstacles*

Notice that an intelligent car should be capable of real-time evaluation of the degree of bending road in order to find a predictive feasible neighborhood. By using the cross product of vector and the symbols marked in Fig.4, let A, B and C are three detection points in sequence of along the road edge, and

$$\Delta = \begin{vmatrix} c_x - b_x & c_y - b_y \\ d_x - c_x & d_y - c_y \end{vmatrix} \tag{3}$$

Obviously, the segment of road in front of the car is right-hand bend, left-hand bend and straight if and only if $\Delta<0$, $\Delta>0$ and $\Delta=0$, respectively. Where, (a_x,a_y), (b_x,b_y) and (c_x,c_y) are the coordinates of point A, B and C, respectively. Therefore, we can take Δ as a discriminant of bending road.

A trapezoid feasible neighborhood $S(\alpha,l;\beta,r)$ and a predictive one $S'(\alpha,l;\beta,r)$ can be obtained by the rules as follows.
(1) if $\theta<0$, then $S(\alpha,l;\beta,r)= S(0,l(0);-\pi/4, l(0))$, $S'(\alpha,l;\beta,r)= S(-\delta,l(-\delta);-\pi/4, l(-\delta))$.
(2) if $\theta>0$, then $S(\alpha,l;\beta,r)= S(\pi/4,r(0);0, r(0))$, $S'(\alpha,l;\beta,r)= S(\pi/4,r(\delta);\delta, r(\delta))$.
(3) if $\theta=0$, then $S(\alpha,l;\beta,r)= S(0,\infty;0, \infty)$.
Where, $\delta\leq\pi/4$ is a safety angle depending on the longitudinal velocity of the car, and can be taken a small positive constant for absolute safety, say $\pi/36$.

3.3. *Building model of feasible neighborhood with obstacles*

Due to the page limit, we only give a brief description on how to get a satisfactory trapezoid feasible neighborhood with obstacles on the road. All of the symbols below are shown just as in Figure 5. That BC and FG are the minimum distance from the obstacle to the left and right edges of road, respectively. If only one of the two distances is large than car's width AE, then we take the feasible neighborhood in the large side. Otherwise, calculating the absolute value of vector product $|BC{\times}CD|$ and $|FG{\times}FH|$, take the feasible neighborhood in the large side as below.

$$S(\alpha,l;\beta,r)= \begin{cases} S(\frac{\pi}{4},d_{\min};0,d_{\min}) & \text{if } |BC \times CD| \geq |FG \times FH| \\ S(0,d_{\min};\frac{\pi}{4},d_{\min}) & \text{if } |BC \times CD| < |FG \times FH| \end{cases} \tag{4}$$

Where, $d_{min}=\min\{l(\alpha){\wedge}r(\beta), \alpha,\beta \in[-\pi/4,\pi/4]\}$. In the case as Fig 5, the satisfactory feasible neighborhood is the trapezoid $AEMN$, and $AN=EM= d_{min}$, i.e. the minimum distance from the car to the obstacle.

If the obstacle is substituted by a mobile vehicle, it should be consider the differential neighborhoods and is omitted due to the page limit.

4. Simulation results and conclusions

The feasible trapezoid neighborhoods in Fig.6 are the simulation results with a car which has length 1.82m and width 4.747m on a road with a width of 5m. It

600

can be seen that the results are better than that of [6]. The trapezoid feasible neighborhoods are different at different places in the road, and are just like some choices by a skilled driver in real time. Therefore, the feasible neighborhoods search method should be available for the fuzzy predictive control in automatic driving.

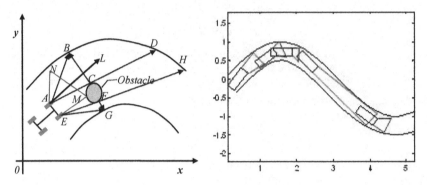

Figure 5. A feasible neighborhood with obstacles in road

Figure 6. A full-size car's feasible neighborhoods at different places in road

References

[1] Hailiang Zhao, A Dynamic Optimization Decision and Control Model Based on Neighborhood Systems, Proceedings of 2013 6rd International Congress on Image and Signal Processing, Dec. 16-18, 2013, Hangzhou, China, pp1319-1324.

[2] T.Y. Lin, Granular computing on binary relations I: data mining and neighborhood systems, in: L. Polkowski, A. Skowron (Eds.), Rough Sets in Knowledge Discovery 1, Methodology and Applications, Physica-Verlag, Heidelberg, 1998, pp. 286–318.

[3] Y.Y.Yao, Neighborhood systems and approximate retrieval Information Sciences 176, 2006, pp. 3431–3452

[4] Hailiang Zhao, Tsu-Tian Lee, "Research on multiobjective optimization control for unknown nonlinear systems," Proceedings of IEEE 2003 International Conference on Fuzzy Systems, St. Louis, MO, USA, May 25-28, 2003. pp.402-406.

[5] Hailiang Zhao, Tsu-Tian Lee, "Monotone inertial system model for unknown nonlinear systems," Proc. IEEE International Conference On Systems, Man & Cybernetics, October 5-8, 2003, pp.3542-3547.

[6] XIONG Sheng-hua, ZHAO Hai-liang, "Simulations on the movement of intelligent vehicle based on rectangular safe neighborhood," Application Research of Computers, Vol.30 No.12 Dec. 2013 pp.3593-3596 (in Chinese)

A HYBRID DEA-FUZZY METHOD FOR
RISK ASSESSMENT IN VIRTUAL ORGANIZATIONS

Fernanda Sales Bittencourt de LEMOS, Rafael Giordano VIEIRA,

Adriano FIORESE and Omir Correia Alves JUNIOR

Department of Computer Science, Santa Catarina State University,
R. Paulo Malschitzki, Joinville, Brazil
* E-mail: dcc6fsbl@joinville.udesc.br
www.cct.udesc.br

The Virtual Organization (VO) concept has emerged as one of the most promising forms of collaboration among companies by providing a way of sharing their costs, benefits and risks, in order to attend particular demands. Although these advantages, VOs face several risks that need to be identified, measured, and mitigated through a well defined process. In this way, this paper proposes a hybrid DEA-Fuzzy method for analyzing risk in VO formation. This method assesses the level of risk present in a set of previously selected Service Providers (SPs) using Key Performance Indicators (KPIs), providing a way to helping decide on the VO formation.

Keywords: DEA, Fuzzy Logic, Risk Analysis, Virtual Organizations

1. Introduction

Nowadays, small and medium enterprises (also called SMEs) need to specialize themselves and collaborate in order to increase their value and compete in the global market. The concept of Virtual Organization (VO)[1] emerges from this scenario, where autonomous, heterogeneous and usually geographically dispersed companies can collaborate to form a dynamic alliance, in order to attend to certain demands, sharing costs, benefits and risks, acting as one single enterprise.[2]

Regarding this work, a VO is composed of Service Providers (SPs)[3] that have previously agreed to collaborate in a mutual goal, also referred to as Collaboration Opportunity (CO).[4] In spite of some benefits, VOs have to face higher risks than other general forms of organization that, in part, come from the increasing sharing of responsibilities among companies and the dynamic nature of their relationships.[5,6] Faults in some SPs can affect other partners and lead the given VO to fail in its goals.[6] Therefore, it is very important to measure the risk of each SP, and consequently to the overall VO, for further decision-making.

In this sense, this paper complements the proposal of Ref. 7, proposing a new method to evaluate the risk in VO formation process, given a set of pre-selected SPs, taking into account its Key Performance Indicators (KPIs). For this purpose, the proposed method makes use of Data Envelopment Analysis (DEA)[8] and Fuzzy Sets Theory (FST).[9]

The rest of this paper is organized as follows: Section 2 presents related work. Section 3 specifies the proposed risk analysis method. Finally, Section 4 concludes and discusses future works.

2. Related Work

In the state of the art review, some works related to risk analysis using a wide range of strategies have been identified. Ref. 10 presents a survey mainly focusing on fuzzy risk assessment approaches in projects as a whole. In Ref. 11, the authors considered the fuzzy features and the project organization mode of VOs to propose Multi Strategy Multi Choice (MSMC) risk programming models. Specifically in the VO context, Ref 12 proposes an ETA-FTA based method to measure the risk in VO formation process.

Unlike the Ref. 12, the relative efficiency obtained by DEA allows to know whether there is better SPs that could be selected instead of what was selected for a given service, which may be useful in decision making. Moreover, this paper takes into account the impact of each service on the overall VO risk, which is suitable in real circumstances, where VO partners are often heterogeneous and have different priorities.

Regarding to the classical main phases of a VO lifecycle (creation, operation, evolution and dissolution phases),[4] this paper focuses specifically on Partner's Search and Selection step, which is part of the creation phase. However, sources of risks should be identified and risks measured having in mind the whole VO lifecycle.[13] There are four main sources of risks regarding VOs: trust, communication, collaboration and commitment.[5] In this work, they are modeled as KPIs, and their values are calculated and provided accordingly Ref. 7.

3. The Hybrid DEA-Fuzzy Method

In general, this method aims to measure the risk of n SPs to form a VO, basing on their individual risk levels. The individual risk calculation initiates with DEA,[8] that is a nonparametric programming approach for measuring and evaluating the relative efficiency of a set of units with similar attributes. In this context, the term "efficiency" is related to the unit ability to produce the maximum outputs using the minimal inputs, i.e., to maximize the ratio output/input.[14] Therefore, since the efficiency of an SP is related to the risk of unfulfilling the VO requirements, it is necessary to view the problem in terms of inputs and outputs as to make possible the risk measurement.

3.1. *Calculating DEA input/output values*

The process for calculating the inputs of each SP is carried out by repeated calculations of linear regressions, as seen in Figure 3.1. More specifically, for each KPI, is calculated a linear regression for the first participation in a VO, to estimate the value of the second, and then for the first two, to estimate the value of the third, and so until the $m - 1$ participations, where is estimated the value of the last participation. The procedures for obtaining the input and output values will be presented as follows:

Let $K = \{K_1, K_2, K_3, K_4\}$ the set of KPIs earlier mentioned (trust, communication, collaboration and commitment), respectively. Let also $H_{ki} = \{h_1, h_2, ..., h_m\}$ the set of historical (real) values and $X_{ki} = \{x_2, ..., x_m\}$ the set of estimated values of the KPI i for the SP k on the m past VOs.

Equation 1 presents the average of estimated values, which are calculated by the linear regressions, i.e., the average of all dotted bar values shown in Figure 1:

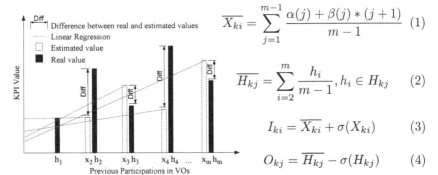

$$\overline{X_{ki}} = \sum_{j=1}^{m-1} \frac{\alpha(j) + \beta(j) * (j+1)}{m-1} \quad (1)$$

$$\overline{H_{kj}} = \sum_{i=2}^{m} \frac{h_i}{m-1}, h_i \in H_{kj} \quad (2)$$

$$I_{ki} = \overline{X_{ki}} + \sigma(X_{ki}) \quad (3)$$

$$O_{kj} = \overline{H_{kj}} - \sigma(H_{kj}) \quad (4)$$

Fig. 1: Calculating the input values of a given SP using its historical values.

where $\alpha(j)$ and $\beta(j)$ are, respectively, the slope and linear coefficient of the j_{th} past participation of the SP k in a given VO for the KPI i. Next, the calculation of the output values is done through averaging all the historical (real) values from the second participation forward, as in the Equation 2.

It is also worth to consider the real and estimated variations for the historical values of a given SP. These variations are represented by the standard deviations of the two averages (estimated and real), and acts over the input and output values as a factor for increasing or decreasing the efficiency of an SP, as seen in Equations 3 and 4, respectively.

In fact, this process is based on a difference between the real value of the KPIs on previous SP's participations in VOs and its estimated values, as seen in Figure 1. Therefore, the more the estimated values are higher than the real ones, the riskier are the SP. At the same time, the more variation has in a given historical series, the more risky are the SP too. Since obtained, the input and output values are applied to the DEA method to calculate the SPs' efficiency, whose process will be explained in the following.

3.2. Evaluating efficiencies with DEA

The DEA model named BCC[15] was designed to measure the relative efficiency of units with variable returns to scale, i.e., units whose the increase in their inputs does not result in a proportional change in the outputs. For this reason, the BCC is a suitable model for the problem in question, and can be represented by Linear Programming (LP), as shown in P.1:

$$\min z = \sum_{i=1}^{r} v_i I_{oi} + v_* \tag{5}$$

$$\text{s.t.} \sum_{j=1}^{s} \mu_j O_{oj} = 1 \tag{6}$$

(P.1)

$$\sum_{i=1}^{r} v_i I_{ki} - \sum_{j=1}^{s} \mu_j O_{kj} + v_* \geq 0, k = 1, ..., N_o \tag{7}$$

$$v_i, \mu_j \geq 0, v_* \in R$$

where I_{ki} and O_{kj} are the input i and output j of the SP k, respectively, and v_i and μ_j are the weights; v_* is a real scale factor; N_o is the number of SPs that offer the same service as the SP o. Since calculated the weights, Equation 8 results the efficiency of the SP o.

$$Eff_o = \frac{\sum_{j=1}^{s} u_j O_{oj}}{\sum_{i=1}^{r} v_i I_{oi} + v_*} \tag{8}$$

3.3. Fuzzy approach

The Fuzzy Sets Theory (FST)[9] is specially helpful when involving human assessment, which is the case of risk management, where humans usually evaluate the risk by using linguistic expressions like "high" or "low".[16] Further, in the VO environment, humans judge the performance of their partners. Hence, this work uses FST to measure the risk of a VO failure due to a particular SP. This analysis take into account two factors: 1) *efficiency of the SP*; 2) *the impact of an isolated failure of the service on the failure of the whole VO*. The first factor is obtained by DEA on the previous step. Nevertheless, it is a human VO manager the responsible for determine the another factor, being another reason to use FST. The triangular shape, which is commonly used in membership functions,[16] is used in this work to all fuzzy sets and is presented in the Figure 2.

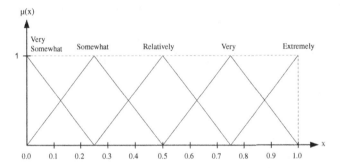

Fig. 2: Membership function for all the fuzzy sets.

For a given collaboration opportunity that a VO responds, the failure of a service can be more harmful to overall VO operation than others. In this way, the more critical is a service, the less its provider can run the risk of failing. Otherwise, the greater the risk of compromising the entire VO. These relations between the factors must be translated into IF-THEN Fuzzy Rules, which along with fuzzy sets, forms the knowledge base of the inferencing system.[17] For example, *"IF service is extremely important AND the provider is relatively efficient THEN the VO is very risky"*. The Table 1 presents a possible set of rules that comprises the causal relations between the factors, where each acronym corresponds to a fuzzy set. The *"E"* suffix means *"Efficient"*, *"I"* means *"Important"* and *"R"* means *"Risky"*, and the prefix *"E"* means *"Extremely"*, *"V"* means *"Very"* , *"R"* means *" Relatively"*, *"S"* means *"Somewhat"* and *"VS"* means *"Very Somewhat"*.

Hence, given the SPs' efficiency obtained by DEA and the importance

Table 1: Fuzzy rules showing the influence of the relation between efficiency of an SP and the importance of its service over the VO risk as a whole.

Service Importance	Provider Efficiency				
	Extremely (EE)	Very (VE)	Relatively (RE)	Somewhat (SE)	V. Somewhat (VSE)
Extremely (EI)	RR	VR	VR	ER	ER
Very (VI)	SR	RR	VR	VR	ER
Relatively (RI)	SR	SR	RR	VR	VR
Somewhat (SI)	VSR	SR	SR	RR	VR
V. Somewhat (VSI)	VSR	VSR	SR	SR	RR

of services on the CO accomplishment, the fuzzy inferencing process (Fuzzification → Inference → Deffuzification)[17] must be carried out n times, and for each run, the outcome of the process is the risk R_i of the VO fails due to a failure of the SP i. The defuzzification process is based on the well-known Center of Gravity (COG) method. Finally, the VO global risk, i.e., the risk of the VO failing, is calculated by averaging R_i for $i = 1, ..., n$.

4. Conclusion

In general, risk analysis has become an inherent problem in Virtual Organization (VO) formation since bad choices can lead to impairment as a whole. Therefore, the definition of strategies for risk assessment are key to ensure the success of the VO. In this way, the main contribution of this paper is a hybrid DEA-Fuzzy method to measure the risk of a set of Service Providers (SPs) to compose a VO.

One of the main contributions of the proposed method it is the relative efficiency calculated by DEA. With this, it is possible to compare a given preselected SP with all the others nonselected SPs of the same service, which allows to know whether, among all the others possibilities of partners, it is a good choice or not. This is interesting because a selected SP with low efficiency can still be the best available, being its discard useless. Moreover, this proposal enables to prioritize the services according to their real importance for the VO success, being advantageous the use of FST, which supports the handling of imprecise data given by humans (e.g. partners and VO managers). In real circumstances, experts can modify the fuzzy rules to fit them the VO interests. The method to input and output determination that considers the variation of the SPs' historical data comprises another contribution of this work. In this way, the risk of a provider is related not only to its performance level, but also to its predictability.

As a future work, the method will be tested in near-real scenarios in order to compare it with other methods that have the same goal. Moreover, it is intended to test different fuzzy rules.

Acknowledgements

The authors would like to thank our colleague professor R. S. Parpinelli, member of Computer Science Department at UDESC, who contributed with valuable comments to this research.

References

1. A. Mowshowitz, *Communications of the ACM* **40**, 30 (1997).
2. L. M. Camarinha-Matos and H. Afsarmanesh, *International Journal of Production Research* **46**, 2453 (2008).
3. S. Dustdar and W. Schreiner, *Intenational Journal of Web Grid Services* **1**, 1 (2005).
4. L. M. Camarinha-Matos and H. Afsarmanesh, *Journal of Intelligent Manufacturing* **16**, 439 (2005).
5. M. Alawamleh and K. Popplewell, Risk sources identification in virtual organisation, in *Enterprise Interoperability IV*, (Springer London, 2010) pp. 265–277.
6. M. Grabowski and K. H. Roberts, *Journal of Computer-Mediated Communication* **3**, 704 (1998).
7. O. C. A. Junior and R. J. Rabelo, *International Journal of Networking and Virtual Organisations* **12**, 149 (2013).
8. A. Charnes, W. Cooper and E. Rhodes, *European Journal of Operational Research* **2**, 429 (1978).
9. L. A. Zadeh, *Information and control* **8**, 338 (1965).
10. P. Rezakhani, *Slovak Journal of Civil Engineering* **20**, 35 (2012).
11. L. Fei and L. Zhixue, A fuzzy comprehensive evaluation for risk of virtual enterprise, in *10th International Conference on Internet Technology and Applications*, (Corfu, Greece, 2010).
12. O. C. A. Junior, R. Rabelo, R. G. Vieira and A. Fiorese, A risk analysis method for selecting logistic partners to compose virtual organizations, in *14th Working Conference on Virtual Enterprises*, (Dresden, Germany, 2013).
13. D. Vose, *Risk analysis: a quantitative guide* (John Wiley & Sons, New Jersey, USA, 2008).
14. W. W. Cooper, L. M. Seiford and K. Tone, *Introduction to data envelopment analysis and its uses: with DEA-solver software and references* (Springer, 2005).
15. R. D. Banker, A. Charnes and W. W. Cooper, *Management science* **30**, 1078 (1984).
16. I. Dikmen, M. T. Birgonul and S. Han, *International Journal of Project Management* **25**, 494 (2007).
17. A. P. Engelbrecht, *Computational intelligence: an introduction* (John Wiley & Sons, 2007).

AN ONLINE DESIGN OF EXPERIMENTS FOR OPTIMIZING HUMAN PERCEPTION ON VIRTUAL GARMENTS

XIAO CHEN, XIANYI ZENG, LUDOVIC KOEHL

GEMTEX Laboratory, ENSAIT, University of Lille 1
2 allée Louise et Victor Champier, 50056 Roubaix Cedex 1 France

JULIE BOULENGUEZ-PHIPPEN

GEMTEX Laboratory, HEI, University of Lille 1
13 rue de Toul, 59046 Lille

In virtual reality-based 3D garment design, one important issue is to minimize the perceptual gap between real and virtual products in their static and dynamic representations so that they can be considered as the same by both designers and consumers. In this paper, we present a new method of online experimental design for quickly controlling human perception on virtual garments towards real products within a very few number of sensory tests. For each real product, this method uses the uniform design to generate the initial virtual fabrics then the principle of online active learning to sequentially create new virtual samples according to the evaluated similarity degrees of previous samples related to the real product. The proposed design of experiments will permit to identify the optimal values of the design parameters corresponding to the desired fabric. The criterion of data sensitivity is used to determine the most relevant design parameter on which we will enhance searches in the following step.

1. Introduction

Currently, 3D virtual garment design using specific CAD software has attracted attention of a great number of textile/garment companies. Virtual garment design can be considered as an optimal combination of designers, computer technology and animation technology, permitting to realize and validate design ideas and principles within a very short time [1].

A garment CAD software is usually built from a model whose input parameters are composed of a number of optical and mechanical properties measured on real fabrics, called design parameters. There generally exists a perceptual gap between virtual and real products for both designers and consumers. In this context, characterization and optimization of human perception on virtual garments with different styles and fabric materials have become a very important issue for the success of new garment design. They will permit to determine how far a virtual product is from its reality and how to adjust the software parameters to acquire perceptual effects similar to the real product within a limited number of tests. Designers wish to identify the technical properties of fabric samples according to the comparison between virtual and real products without performing expensive and time-consuming mechanical measurements.

As the similarity between virtual and real products is evaluated by human evaluators, the selection of an optimal design of experiments minimizing the number of tests becomes very important. The existing designs of experiments like orthogonal design [2] are mostly static and offline methods and the selection of new samples is independent of the previous evaluation results. In this context, online active learning seems to be an appropriate technique for solving this problem. In an online active learning algorithm, the learner encounters the data points sequentially, and at each instant, the model has to decide whether to query the current point and update the hypothesis. Viewed as an online active learning method, stochastic learning automata have been used for solving complex function optimization problems by successively computing the optimal action corresponding to the biggest value of the estimates of reward probabilities [3, 4].

Compared with the existing online active learning methods optimizing complex functions, the context of our study is different in the following aspects: 1) Our objective is to optimize the human perception-based similarity degree of virtual products related to a real product and then the required accuracy is relatively lower; 2) The number of concerned factors (parameters of the software generating virtual products) is very important; 3) The number of allowed learning data is even more limited and then the application of a stochastic optimization method is less practical.

In this paper, we proposed a new online active learning method for quickly and successively controlling human perception on virtual products towards the real product. First, it utilizes the uniform design [5] for acquiring the initial virtual fabrics. Next, according to the evaluated similarity degrees of previous virtual samples related to the real product, we sequentially generate new samples. At each step of this procedure, the new samples are generated by enhancing searches on the most relevant garment design parameter, identified by the fuzzy logic-based data sensitivity criterion [6] of the design parameters. This procedure will permit us to identify through a very limited sensory tests the optimal values of the garment design parameters, which constitute the inputs to the garment CAD software and generate a virtual garment very close to the real one in both static and dynamic visual representations.

2. Similarity of virtual and real fabrics

2.1. *Generation of virtual fabrics*

In our approach, Clos3D, a well-known commercialized 3D garment CAD software system, is selected for quickly simulating garments for both static and dynamic effects (see Figure 1).

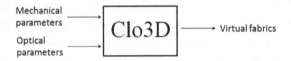

Figure 1. A scheme of the Clo3D software for generating virtual fabrics

In order to realize virtual fabrics using the Clo3D software, two categories of fabric design parameters, i.e. optical and mechanical parameters, are required as inputs. The optical parameters include texture picture, color, brilliance, and transparence while the mechanical ones are composed of fabric stretch resistance, shear resistance, basic mass and others. For simplicity, we only study the effects of fabric mechanical parameters on human perception on virtual fabrics.

2.2. *Sensory experiment for evaluating similarity degree*

A sensory experiment is carried out in order to find the optimal combination of the mechanical inputs related to the real fabric draping. A panel of 10 persons is recruited for evaluating 19 fabric samples. For each fabric, both real and virtual fabric draping at different views are put together (See Figure 2).

Figure 2. One example for comparing the real and virtual fabric draping.

The panellists are first invited to evaluate the similarity degree between the real and virtual fabric draping for each combination of parameters obtained from the developed online design of experiments by selecting one score from 0 to 4. These scores are interpreted as follows: 0-very similar, 1-a little different, 2-different, 3-very different and 4-extremely different. The above procedure is repeated for all the 19 fabrics. Finally, all the scores are collected for each fabric. Using the same evaluation scores, the panellists also evaluate the similarity degrees of the dynamic effects of virtual fabrics, generated by the garment CAD software, related to the real ones taken in a video. For each fabric sample, the overall similarity degree is the weighted average of the evaluation scores given by all the panellists for its static and dynamic effects. According to our experience, we give more important weights to static effects.

3. Development of the online design experiment

3.1. *Uniform design*

The proposed online design experiment first utilizes the uniform design [5] to generate the initial values of the garment design parameters and the corresponding virtual samples. The uniform design is a classical method of fractional factorial design. Its principle is described below.

Suppose there are m design parameters, and n tests are to be conducted. Without loss of generality, assume that the experimental domain is the unit cube $C^m = [0, 1]^m$; then a design consists of n points in C^m. We want these points to be uniformly scattered over C^m. A measure of uniformity called discrepancy is adopted in order to choose n points with the smallest discrepancy. The resulting design is called a uniform design.

Compared with the well-known orthogonal design, the uniform design is less accurate but requires fewer tests. In practice, the uniform design has been proved to be more efficient when the design parameters have many levels and the general number of tests is more strictly controlled. Therefore, it is more adapted to our context in which 7 design parameters have continuous values and the total number of allowed tests is very small. The uniform design is used to generate 11 initial virtual fabrics corresponding to different combinations of levels of the 7 design parameters ($n=11$). For each virtual fabric, its similarity degree related to the real one is evaluated by several evaluators using the scores defined in Section 2.2.

3.2. *The proposed method of online active learning*

Based on the evaluation results on the initial virtual fabrics, we carry out an iterative procedure in which the fuzzy sensitivity criterion [6] of the design parameters is used to find the most relevant design parameter. The detailed description is given below.

Let $D=\{D_1, ..., D_m\}$ be the set of all the m design parameters served as inputs to the garment CAD software, $P=\{P_1, ..., P_n\}$ the set of the n combinations of levels of the design parameters generated in the previous steps, and $SD=\{SD_1, ..., SDS_n\}$ the set of overall evaluated similarity degrees corresponding to the $P_1, ..., P_n$. We first identify the two best data P_a and P_b so that $SD_a<SD_b<SD_i$ for all $i\in\{1, ..., n\}$ and $i\neq a$ and $i\neq b$. Next, we compute the sensitivity criteria $Sens_1, ..., Sens_m$ for all the m design parameters and select the most sensitive design parameter D_r from all the feasible solutions, namely the design parameters that have not been searched. We carry out new searches in the neighboring region of P_a along the axis D_r with the step length $SL=max\{SL_{min}, |P_a(D_r)-P_b(D_r)|/2\}$. SL_{min} is the predefined smallest step length. Two new data (combinations of levels of the design parameters) are generated as follows: $P_{n+1}=(P_a(D_1) ... P_a(D_{r-1}) P_a(D_r)-SL\ P_a(D_{r+1}) ... P_a(D_m))$ and $P_{n+2}=(P_a(D_1) ... P_a(D_{r-1})\ P_a(D_r)+SL\ P_a(D_{r+1}) ... P_a(D_m))$. The evaluated similarity degrees of the corresponding virtual fabrics are denoted as SD_{n+1} and SD_{n+2}. We compute the rates of variation caused by these new data related to the previous data P_a as follows: $R_1=|SD_a-SD_{n+1}|/SD_a$, $R_2=|SD_a-SD_{n+2}|/SD_a$. If all these rates of variation are smaller than a predefined threshold e, we stop searches on the axis D_r and select another feasible design parameter. In this case, D_r will become infeasible and no more searches will be done on it. Otherwise, we continue new searches on D_r. This procedure is repeated until the rates of variation for all the design parameters are smaller than e or the number of tests reaches its predefined limit.

4. Results of the experiments

In order to validate the proposed method, we generate the virtual fabric draping using the optimal values of the design parameters identified by 4 different methods, i.e. classical orthogonal design, classical uniform design, learning automata, and the proposed method.

Table 1. Comparison of the experimental results between the 4 methods for design of experiments.

Selected method	Orthogonal design	Uniform design	Learning automata	The proposed method
Number of tests	27	25	31	26
Similarity of the final virtual fabric	1.3 (static)/1.4 (dynamic)	0.9 (static)/1.8 (dynamic)	0.8 (static) /1.3 (dynamic)	0.5 (static) /1 (dynamic)

In these experiments, we control the total number of tests to be around 30. Therefore, in the orthogonal design, we use a table of 7 design parameters, 3 levels and 27 tests. In the uniform design, we use a table of 7 design parameters, 25 levels and 25 tests. The two other methods utilize the uniform design for obtaining the 11 initial tests and then recursively generate 15 or 20 tests with online active learning. The corresponding results are shown in Table 1.

From the previous results we can find that within a very limited number of tests, the proposed online active learning method leads to the best performance. Also, compared with the learning automata, the proposed method converges more quickly to its stable value. In fact, its final similarity degrees show that the corresponding virtual fabric is very close to the real product in both static and dynamic representations.

5. Conclusion

This paper presents an online active learning-based method for quickly identifying the appropriate values of the design parameters for generating a virtual fabric draping very close to the real product. This method has been shown more efficient than the other online active learning methods in terms of number of tests, convergence speed and final accuracy. It can also be applied to optimize other complex functions in which the number of levels of input variables is more important and the number of tests is more strictly controlled.

References

1. P. Volino and N.M. Thalmann, *Virtual Clothing Theory and Practices*. Ed. Springer-Verlag (2000).
2. I.N. Vuchkov and L.N. Boyadjieva, *Quality Improvement with Design of Experiments: A Response Surface Approach*. Kluwer Academic Publishers. Dorderecht (2001).
3. S. Chakraborty, V. Balasubramanian and S. Panchanathan, Generalized Batch mode active learning for face-based biometric recognition, *Pattern Recognition*. 46 pp.497-508 (2013).
4. Q.H. Wu and H.L. Liao, Function optimization by learning automata, *Information Sciences*. 220 pp.379-398 (2013).
5. K.T. Fang, W.C. Shiu and J.X. Pan, Uniform designs based on Latin squares, *Statistica Sinica*. 9 pp.905-912 (1999).
6. X. Deng, X. Zeng, P. Vroman and L. Koehl, Selection of relevant variables for industrial process modelling by combining experimental data sensitivity and human knowledge, *Engineering Applications of Artificial Intelligence*. 23 n°8 pp.1368-1379 (2010).

A STUDY ON AFTER-TEMPORAL ASSOCIATION BETWEEN ONLINE SEARCH VOLUME AND STOCK PRICE WITH AN INTELLIGENT ATARII METHOD[*]

CHANGYU WANG, QIANG WEI[†], XUNHUA GUO, GUOQING CHEN

School of Economics and Management, Tsinghua University
Beijing 100084, China

Existing research shows significant associations between online search volume and stock price on market level. Due to the individuality of each stock and limited attention of investors, how to effectively discover the association between search volume and the price on individual stock level is worth studying. This paper investigates the association pattern between search volume variation and stock price variation on individual stock level, and designs a so-called ATARII method, which can effectively discover qualified association rules between search volume and stock price in an after-temporal manner. Furthermore, real world data experiments are conducted on China's A-share stock market. Based on the discovered after-temporal associations, a new trading strategy is designed, i.e., ATARII-Trading, which obtains best cumulative return, significantly outperforming market level trading strategy, buy-and-hold strategy and random strategy as well as A-share 300 index.

1. Introduction

Nowadays, Internet users highly frequently interact with search engines with their intents, attentions, interests, etc., forming an important resource of swarm/collective intelligence, which has been widely recognized by many business sectors. Particularly, search engine is one of the most important portal through which stock market investors acquire useful information related to the stocks they pay attention to, especially for retail investors [1, 2, 3]. For instance, hundreds of thousands of search queries on Google or Baidu take the stock IDs or quotes as keywords, e.g., "AAPL" (Apple), "00941" (Petro China), etc. The queries reflect Internet users' investing/trading attentions, further associating the stock price variation, which has been demonstrated by many existing research, i.e., search volume variation on a stock is highly associated with the stock's price

[*] The work was partly supported by the MOE Project of Key Research Institute of Humanities and Social Sciences at Universities(12JJD630001), the National Natural Science Foundation of China (71110107027/71372044), and Tsinghua University Initiative Scientific Research Program (20101081741).

[†] Corresponding author. Email: weiq@sem.tsinghua.edu.cn

variation [4, 5, 6, 7, 8, 9]. Thereafter, search volume could be deemed as a novel and agile index, which help investors not only better understand the dynamics of stock market and but design better trading strategy to gain abnormal return.

More research reveal tight associations between search volume and stock market. Da et al. indicated that search volume significantly positively impacted retail investors' trading volume [4], which is also validated by [10] on German stock market. Joseph et al. discovered that the search volumes of querying stock IDs can forecast the trading volumes and designed a long-short trading strategy to gain abnormal return [5]. Preis et al. found the search volume of "debt" on Google is highly associated with the stock market variation and design a corresponding trading strategy to gain high return [11]. More research have been conducted and significant associations between market index, e.g., DAX, CAC40, DOW, FTSE, S&P, and related search volumes, are found [9, 12].

Nevertheless, the studies in this field are still emerging and need to be further explored. First, the above studies mainly focus on the associations on market level, which to some extent neglect the association between a stock price and its search volume on individual stock level, lacking of practical trading significance. Second, the above studies are model-oriented, i.e., a statistical pattern on concrete stock/index should be constructed before empirical analysis, which is just to verify limited perceived associations and possibly ignore novel associations. Finally, the above association discovery methods are not automatic, which cannot be easily applied to design programmatic trading strategy.

This paper will investigates the association pattern in an after-temporal manner between search volume and stock price on individual stock level (Section 2) and designs an intelligent method, called ATARII (Section 3). Furthermore, a programmatic trading strategy is designed based on the ATARII method and its outperformance will be verified by the real world experiments on China's A-share stock market (Section 4). Concluding remarks will be given in Section 5.

2. After-Temporal Association Rule

Data from search engine and stock market are of important temporal nature. Generally speaking, there are 13 major temporal association, i.e., after/before, during, equal, overlap, etc [13]. To analyze the association between search volume and stock price, or concretely, to forecast stock's closing price variation based on search volume variation, the *after-temporal* pattern is of concern and considered.

For simplicity, for a stock, an after-temporal association rule could be denoted as $v \rightarrow^{[t1, t2]} p$, where v and p are two events, $v \in V$ and $p \in P$, $[t_1, t_2]$ is a duration period, where $t_2 \geq t_1 \geq 0$. Moreover, V and P are two different group of events, i.e., $V = \{v^+, v^-\}$, where v^+ represents the increase of the stock's search volume and v^- represents the decrease, $P = \{p^+, p^-\}$, where p^+ represents the increase of the stock's closing price and p^- represents the decrease. Thus $v \to^{[t_1, t_2]} p$ means event p will happen in $[t_1, t_2]$ after event v. For example, for a stock APPL, an after-temporal association rule could be "*if the search volume of stock APPL decreases, then the closing price of APPL will increase in* [4, 5] *days*".

In order to discover the after-temporal association rules, the original data from search engine and stock market should be pre-processed and transformed. For simplicity, given a original dataset T containing all the stocks' search volume and closing price with time labels, T could be transformed into a new dataset, denoted as D, in which each record could be denoted as a triple (v, p, t), where $v \in V, p \in P$ and t is the corresponding time lag between v and p.

Similar to association rule, the degree of support could be defined as follows:

$$Dsupport\left(v \to^{[t_1, t_2]} p\right) = \frac{\|v \cup_{[t_1, t_2]} p\|}{|D|} \tag{1}$$

where $v \cup_{[t_1, t_2]} p$ represents the records in the data set D containing events v and p after $[t_1, t_2]$ period, and $\|*\|$ represents the cardinality. Moreover, the degree of confidence could be defined as follows:

$$Dconfidence\left(v \to^{[t_1, t_2]} p\right) = \frac{Dsupport(v \to^{[t_1, t_2]} p)}{\|v\|} \tag{2}$$

Surely, given the thresholds α and β ($0 < \alpha, \beta < 1$), only the rule with large-enough degrees of support and confidence will be regarded as qualified. For the after-temporal association rule mining, a classical method, namely ATAR [14], could be used. However, the performance of ATAR could be further improved.

First of all, many uninteresting associations which are regarded redundant could be obtained. Therefore, a Lift measure is defined in the same manner in [15] to evaluate the interestingness of a rule. Clearly, only the rule with Lift value more than 1 are interesting and need to be considered.

$$Lift\left(v \to^{[t_1, t_2]} p\right) = \frac{Dconfidence(v \to^{[t_1, t_2]} p)}{\|p\|} \tag{3}$$

Second, two properties could be further derived to improve the performance. **Property 1**: Given $Dsupport(v \to^{[t_3, t_4]} p)$, for any time period $[t_1, t_2]$ containing $[t_3, t_4]$, i.e., $t_1 \le t_3 \le t_4 \le t_2$, $Dsupport(v \to^{[t_1, t_2]} p) \ge Dsupport(v \to^{[t_3, t_4]} p)$ holds.

Moreover, if both $Dsupport(v \to^{[t_1, t_2]} p) \ge \alpha$ and $Dsupport(v \to^{[t_3, t_4]} p) \ge \alpha$, then $v \to^{[t_3, t_4]} p$ could be regarded as redundant rule with respect to $v \to^{[t_1, t_2]} p$, since $v \to^{[t_1, t_2]} p$ covers the information of $v \to^{[t_3, t_4]} p$.

Property 2: An after-temporal rule $v \to^{[t_1, t_2]} p$ is not redundant, if and only if

(1) $\forall$ t_3 and t_4, where $t_1 \leq t_3 \leq t_4 \leq t_2$, $Dsupport(v \rightarrow^{[t_3,\ t_4]} p) \geq \alpha$, and,

(2) $\forall$ t_5 and t_6, where $t_5 \leq t_1 \leq t_2 \leq t_6$, $\exists$ t_7 and t_8, where $t_5 \leq t_7 \leq t_8 \leq t_6$, $Dsupport(v \rightarrow^{[t_7,\ t_8]} p) < \alpha$.

3. The ATARII Method

Due to space limitation, Figure 1 shows the algorithmic structure of ATARII method.

Input:
FTDB;   // Search Volume Dataset
LTDB;   // Stock Closing Price Dataset
t_0, t_0';   // Maximal Period Duration
Min_support;   // Minimal Threshold of Degree of Support
Min_confidence;   // Minimal Threshold of Degree of Confidence
Output:
ATARset = $\varnothing$;   // Initialize the Set of After-Temporal Association Rules
1. *Rset = GenDelayTDB(LTDB, t_0, t_0')*;
2. *F1set = GenF1(FTDB, Min_support)*;
3. *L1set = GenL1(Rset, Min_support)*;
4. *FL2set = GenFL2(FTDB, Rset, F1set, L1set, Min_support)*;
5. *ATARset = GenATAR(FTDB, Rset, FL2set, Min_confidence)*;

Figure 1. The algorithmic structure of ATARII method.

4. Experiments and Analysis

In order to show the outperformance of the proposed ATARII method, real world data experiments are conducted, and a trading strategy based on ATARII method, i.e., ATARII-trading, is applied to compare with other strategies.

The experimental data contains two parts, i.e., 1,654 China's A-share stocks' price data (obtained from Wind Financial database) and Baidu search volume data (obtained from http://index.baidu.com), in the period of 2011/01/01 to 2013/06/30. More specifically, the data in 2011/01/01 to 2012/12/31 are used as training data, while the data in 2013/01/01 to 2013/06/30 are used as test data.

Before conducting the ATARII method, a classical empirical model [6, 11] on market level is adopted to validate the effectiveness of the data and could be used to design a market level trading strategy for comparison. Panel regression results verify that search volume positively correlates to the return of stock. Then, based on the derived market level pattern, a corresponding trading strategy could be designed, i.e., if the search volume of current stock ID/quote is low, then buy in; otherwise sell out, denoted as Market-trading strategy. After applying the strategy on test data, it could be found that Market-trading strategy retrieved a cumulative return -0.8403%, significantly outperforming buy-and-hold strategy (-2.7313%), random strategy (-3.7004%) and A-share 300 Index strategy (-13.0378%), revealing that search volume do provide insightful intelligence for forecast stock price variation. However, since the Market-trading strategy ignores the differentiation and individuality of each stock and applies a unified trading strategy on all stocks, it is expected that an appropriate individual stock level trading strategy, i.e., ATARII-trading, can further promote the performance by applying specific association on each corresponding stock.

Therefore, the ATARII method was conducted with $\alpha = 0.20$, $\beta = 0.60$ and minimal Lift = 1. Finally 2,070 qualified association rules are discovered related with 1,509 stocks. After applying a programmatic ATARII-trading strategy with discovered association for each stock, the cumulative return of ATARII-trading is increased remarkably to 5.0401%. Figure 2 shows the cumulative returns of the 5 strategies, i.e., ATARII trading, Market level trading, buy-and-hold, random and the A-share 300 Index. Undoubtedly, the ATARII-trading strategy significantly outperforms others, showing its advantage.

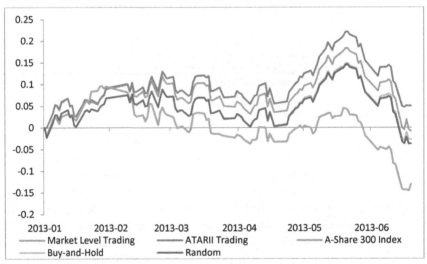

Figure 2. Cumulative Returns of ATARII Trading Strategy and other 4 Strategies

5. Conclusion

Search volume data of stocks' ID/quotes show tight associations with the stock prices, which is valuable for analysis to help investor better trade. Moreover, compared with existing market level analysis methods, individual stock level association can provide more differentiate and customized trading strategy, which can further improve the trading performance, e.g., return. This paper proposed a new intelligent method, called ATARII, which can effectively discover after-temporal association rules between search volume variations and stock price variations, further leading to design a better trading strategy, i.e., ATARII-trading. Real world data experiments on China's A-share stock market sufficiently verify the outperformance of the ATARII method, showing significantly better cumulative returns than those of the market level trading strategy, buy-and-hold strategy, random strategy as well as the A-share 300 index strategy.

References

1. Statistical Yearbook, China Security Registration Clearing Company, 2012.
2. Structural and Behavioral Analysis of Investors in Shenzhen Stock Market, Shenzhen Security Exchange Investor Training Center, 2013.
3. Shanghai Security Exchange Statistical Yearbook, Shanghai Security Exchange, 2012.
4. Da Z, Engelberg J, Gao P. In search of attention. The Journal of Finance, 2011, 66(5):1461-1499.
5. Joseph K, Babajide Wintoki M, Zhang Z. Forecasting abnormal stock returns and trading volume using investor sentiment: Evidence from online search. International Journal of Forecasting, 2011, 27(4):1116-1127.
6. Barber B M, Odean T. All that glitters: The effect of attention and news on the buying behavior of individual and institutional investors. Review of Financial Studies, 2008, 21(2):785-818.
7. Qingjin Yu, Bing Zhang, Investors' Limited Attention and Stock's Return – An Empirical Study on Baidu Index as an Attention Measure. Journal of Finance Research, 2012(08):152-165.
8. Mishkin F. The economics of money, banking, and financial markets[M]. Pearson education, 2007.
9. Dimpfl T, Jank S. Can internet search queries help to predict stock market volatility? CFR working paper, 2011.
10. Bank M, Larch M, Peter G. Google search volume and its influence on liquidity and returns of German stocks. Financial markets and portfolio management, 2011, 25(3):239-264.
11. Preis T, Moat H S, Stanley H E. Quantifying trading behavior in financial markets using Google Trends. Scientific reports, 2013,3.
12. Dzielinski M. Measuring economic uncertainty and its impact on the stock market[J]. Finance Research Letters, 2012,9(3):167-175.
13. Allen J F. Maintaining knowledge about temporal intervals. Communications of the ACM, 1983, 26(11):832-843.
14. Li Zhang, Guoqing Chen, Tom Brijs, Xing Zhang, Discovering During-Temporal Patterns (DTPs) in Large Temporal Databases, Volume 34, Issue 2, 2008, pp. 1178-1189.
15. PN Tan, V Kumar, J Srivastava, Selecting the Right Interestingness Measure for Association Patterns, Proceedings of the 8th ACM SIGKDD, 2002, pp. 32-41.

INTRODUCTION OF NEW FUZZY METHODS IN CREDIT RISK MANAGEMENT

MILAN MRKALJ

Faculty of organizational sciences, University of Belgrade, Jove Ilica 154
Belgrade, Serbia

The main goal of this paper is to expose the possibilities for applying of the new fuzzy methods for the evaluational modeling of credit risk, which is in its nature a composite quantity, and as such could be conveniently modeled through Interpolative Boolean Algebra. This approach to modeling allows expressing intensity measures of single components/properties of credit risk, as much as complex logical constructions made of basic components and their logical interactions, which altogether increases the possibilities of consistent mathematical articulation of the problem of aggregation of multicriterial aspects of credit risk into a single representative parameter.

Keywords: Credit risk modeling, fuzzy methods, Interpolative Boolean Algebra.

1. Introduction

Credit risk or risk of default is a specific type of risk that is associated with financial investments – putting money into assets with expectation of return.

It consists of the degree of uncertainity that investment will return, that it will return completely and that it will return with expected timing. This risk is reduced to its minimum if the investment is in government bonds or bank depostis guaranteed by government.

Credit risk is the primary risk that is related to the business of commercial banks. Risk control in the banking business has a social significance. Disturbances in the banking sector have a bad impact on the entire economy and can have significant impact on social processes. From the point of economic development and in terms of the profitability of banks, the question is how big banking placements can be and how much risk is acceptable, without endangering safety of obligation of debt servicing performance.

Credit risk is observed at the level of individual credit line - the risk of a single transaction or grouped – as portfolio credit risk. In order to establish a relationship between the total risk exposure and bank capital, which is the last "line of defense" of solvency, G7 countries promoted the Basel standards.

Each of the modes of view of the credit risk concept has a common property: the measure of credit risk is a quantity, and for its expression, a composite model is required with complex immanent structure, as a result of multi-criterial nature of the concept of credit risk.

For such quantity to be expressed with unique scalar measure (from this scalar measure a linear order of these quantities can be established), it's needed to aggregate single partial demand measures (attributes) through a model such that the preferrence or the decision maker and/or evaluator could be expressed/articulated by math language.

Few distinct models exist for this purpose. One of the potentially good and not often used aproach is math modeling with Interpolativne Boolean algebra [2], due to the fact that this algebra provides a wide range of possibilities for mathematical articulation of the complex and composite nature of the concept of credit risk in the sense of the possibility of combining the individual requests/ criteria, as well as their logic interactions.

2. A short review of existing solutions for credit risk modeling

There are various ways of mathematical articulation of credit risk measures with its subcomponents. Significant progress in this area is certainly the introduction of the concept of fuzzy set for verbal score expressing in a mathematically convenient way. Fuzzy set is a better carrier of information about an object (the intensity of a property of the object), as compared to an ordinary scalar numeric data. In [1] the importance of recognizing the "fuzzy" nature of the credit rating evaluation (higher rating => less risk) is pointed out. Evaluation criteria are modeled as a hierarchical structure of decision making process, and as *aggregation technique, fuzzy integrals* have been used.

Exactly on this stage (chosing an aggregation technique), the possibility of using Interpolative Boolean algebra is opened [2], with its advanced capabilities for better mathematical expression of preferences of the assessor/decision maker.

There are different approaches for creating decision support software in the area of credit risk assessment. One of the methods is the use of artificial neural networks. In [3], a problem is indicated; the users of decision support systems hesitate to use a system based on neural networks, because they do not have the intuitive insight into the mechanisms of functioning of the tool. Also, the process of selecting an adequate neural network is shown, and then a validation is carried out over the specific real data from various sources. The results of this study show encouragingly high degree of confidence for that method.

One of the tools is *machine learning* method for classification and regression analysis - SVM (Support Vector Machine), based on the theory of statistical learning. In [4] a "fuzzyfied" version of this method is presented. The main "fuzzy" improvement of this method is in the use of fuzzy set concept which allocates importance measures to the individual data in order to reduce the influence of the "noise" immanent in the data, which hinders the training of classification vector machines.

In [5], fuzzy quantification theory usage is presented in order to improve the classical multivariate analysis.

Given the relatively sparse interpretability of artificial intelligence methods (neural networks) and little intuitive insight into the mechanisms of their work, a study [6] is done, aimed for improving the understanding of neural network for the purpose of credit risk analysis. A comparative analysis (done on actual data) of the two models - artificial neural networks and vector machines (Support Vector Machine) was carried out. It was established that the reliability of the both methods was approximately equal, while the understanding of the measures of relative importance of the input variables was increased.

3. New fuzzy methods – applicability to the domain of credit risk

Conventional aggregation tools are often inadequate due to limitations in the form of inability to elegantly and consistently use logic interactions between attributes/criteria. Improvement of the models via using advanced methods of logical aggregation significantly expands the possibilities of adapting the model to specific needs. This is especially true if complex logic functions are included where non-trivial complex attributes/criteria emerge. The new approach treats the logical functions (partial aggregation requirements) as a generalized Boolean polynomial, which processes the values in the real unit the interval [0, 1]. Aggregation (in general) is a generalized pseudo-logical function [2]. This approach may, for example, improve an aggregation technique used in [1].

Credit risk can be assessed primarily, ie. as "absolute" by using a model technically similar to the model presented in [7]. Definition of the criteria is first to do, simple or complex (logical interaction over the set of the primary/base attributes) which are to be expressed with measures adequate for input of the model (normalization process of inputs), and their "weight", ie. measures relevance/importance. In this way a fixed mathematical model is made that gives the result according to preferences of the decision maker.

Another way is a "relative" (secondary) assessment of credit risk. In this case, the concept of the secondary similarity measures shown in [8] may be applied. The primary evaluation model generates referent "prototypes", while the secondary evaluation model determines the measure of similarity with some of the prototypes from the "knowledge base" obtained from primary model output (or elsewhere). For secondary evaluation of credit risk, it is important to note that data for reference are needed.

The computing of partial similarity measures [8] is a trivial task for the evaluator, because referent data exists. The comparation of partial similarity measures is done in one-dimensional space of values for each single attribute, so the expert knowledge is not needed (unlike the "absolute" - primary evaluation).

4. Conclusion

The importance of adequate modeling of credit risk and its evaluation through the model is closely related to performance of the creditors who are placing their investment. This paper provides an overview of the better known and significant methods for evaluating credit risk and points out the possibilities of improving the existing fuzzy method.

Relatively new, and so far little used method of logical aggregation, the Interpolative Boolean algebra [2] has the potential to contribute in this area, especially in methods where there is room for improvement of aggregation techniques, which is often the main "hub" of the model, and is crucial for the adequacy and validity of the model.

In this way, new studies may be done that could result in emerging of new models tested via comparative analysis. Hybrid models could be made, simultaneously using multiple techniques.

References

1. Liang-Hsuan Chen, Tai-Wei Chiou, A fuzzy creditrating approach for commercial loans: a Taiwan case, Omega, Int. J. Mgmt. Sci. 27 (1999) 407-419
2. Radojević D., Logical Aggregation Based on Interpolative Realization of Boolean Algebra, Eusflat Conf. (1) (2007) pages 119-126.
3. Shorouq Fathi Eletter, Saad Ghaleb Yaseen and Ghaleb Awad Elrefae, Neuro-Based Artificial Intelligence Model for Loan Decisions, American Journal of Economics and Business Administration 2(1): 27-34, (2010).
4. Yanyou Hao, Zhongxian Chi, Deqin Yan, and Xun Yue, An Improved Fuzzy Support Vector Machine for Credit Rating, fskd, vol. 1, pp.603-607, Fourth International Conference on Fuzzy Systems and Knowledge Discovery (FSKD 2007) Vol.1, 2007.
5. Antonio Carlos Pinto Dias Alves, Fuzzy Models in Credit Risk Analysis,

Perception-based Data Mining and Decision Making in Economics and Finance Studies in Computational Intelligence, 2007, Volume 36/2007, 353-367

6. Zan Huang, Hsinchun Chen, Chia-Jung Hsu, Wun-Hwa Chen, Soushan Wu, Credit rating analysis with support vector machines and neural networks: a market comparative study, Decision Support Systems 37 (2004) 543–558

7. Mrkalj Milan, Model za anticipaciju cena nekretnina zasnovan na konceptu ZOS i LA, Info M, no. 28, (2008), pages 35-43 (in Serbian)

8. Mrkalj Milan, Agregirane mere sličnosti i njihova primena u teoriji odlučivanja i upravljanju kvalitetom, SYM-OP-IS conference (2009), pages 369-370 (in Serbian)

A HEURISTIC MODEL OF PARTIAL INTERDICTION MEDIAN PROBLEM FOR MULTI-SOURCING SUPPLY SYSTEMS

SHAOHUI ZHANG,

School of Automation Science and Electrical Engineering,
Beihang University Beijing, China

ZHENG ZHENG

School of Automation Science and Electrical Engineering,
Beihang University Beijing, China
Key Laboratory for Science and Technology of National Defense Beijing,

China

XIAOYI ZHANG

School of Automation Science and Electrical Engineering,
Beihang University Beijing, China

YUENI ZHU

School of Automation Science and Electrical Engineering,
Beihang University Beijing, China

This paper discusses the partial r-interdiction median problem for multi-sourcing supply systems (PRIM-MS). Compared with r-interdiction median problem (RIM), PRIM-MS mainly has three characteristics: (1) Limited capacity for each facility; (2) Partial interdiction; (3) Multi-sourcing property for supply systems. PRIM-MS falls into bilevel programming in the form of leader-follower decisions, where the attacker tries to degrade system performance the most by determining offensive resources invested while the user rebuilds supply-demand relationship to reduce the influences by interdiction. In this paper, we model the problem as a single level heuristic model based on two heuristic strategies. Experiments are carried out to testify the effectiveness of the heuristic model.

Keywords: partial interdiction; heuristic strategies; multi-sourcing supply systems;

1. Introduction

Critical infrastructure undertakes the important responsibility of supplying essential goods or service and are more vulnerable to various disruptions in modern society [1,2]. As important components in supply systems, facilities are subject to intentional attacks, e.g. military actions, terrorist attacks and sabotage, which can cause catastrophic results [3,4]. Therefore, it is recognized that identifying or fortifying critical facilities is a necessary and important task [5]. The r-interdiction median problem (RIM) was firstly introduced in [6] to identify critical facilities whose failures can result in the worst-case sum of weighted distances among customers and facilities after interdiction. The basic assumptions that RIM model relies on are as follows:

1. The capacity of any facility is without upper bound;

2. Complete interdiction is carried out, which assumes a facility loses all its capacity upon interdiction.

3. Each demand can only be served by its closest available facility.

Subsequently, some researchers [7, 8, 9, 10,11, 12] start to focus on at least one of the three assumptions in facility interdiction problem for diverse applications. In this paper, we explore the models and solutions for a new RIM problem, which mainly has three characteristics compared with the original RIM: (1) Limited capacity for each facility; (2) Partial interdiction; (3) Multi-sourcing property for supply systems. The three characteristics correspond to the three assumptions above one by one. We call the new problem as partial r-interdiction median problems for multi-sourcing supply systems (PRIM-MS in short). PRIM-MS is in the form of the *leader-follower* hierarchical decisions [13], where the attacker (the *leader*) makes interdiction strategies to cause the biggest damage to the system and reassignment is performed by the user (the *follower*) to minimize the system operation cost after interdiction. Because solving bilevel programming falls into the class of NP-hard problem even though all variables involved are continuous [10], two heuristic strategies are developed to formulate the bilevel problem into a single-level heuristic model. Experiments are conducted to verify the effectiveness of the heuristic model.

2. A Heuristic Model for PRIM-MS Problem

In order to solve PRIM-MS, we develop two heuristic strategies as follows.

Strategy 1: For each demand node, it is inclined to be supplied by the facility which is closer to it.

Strategy 2: For each facility, it tends to supply the demand nodes which are closer to it.

Based on the two heuristic strategies, a heuristic model is presented below.

Parameters:

p number of facilities

n number of demand nodes

r relative amount of attacking resources

i index representing places of demand

a_i measure of demand at demand node i

j index representing service facilities

d_{ij} measure of distance between facility j and demand i

c_j the capacity of facility j

ϑ a penalty paid for each unit demand that is not served by any facility

N the set representing all demand nodes

F the set representing the existing facilities

T_{ij} $\{\, k \mid k \in F,\ k \neq j \text{ and } d_{ik} > d_{ij} \,\}$, the set of facilities the distances from which to demand node i are farther than that from facility j

A_{ij} $\{\, u \mid u \in N,\ u \neq i \text{ and } d_{uk} > d_{ij} \,\}$, the set of demand nodes the distances from which to facility j are farther than that from demand node i

Decision variables:

s_j the relative amount of offensive resources invested to facility j

x_{ij} demand fraction of node i served by facility j after interdiction

u_i demand fraction of node i which is not served after interdiction

y_{ij} if facility j has remaining capacity after supplying demand node i, $y_{ij}=1$; otherwise, $y_{ij}=0$.

The heuristic model of PRIM-MS is as follows:

$$Max_x\left(\sum_{i\in N}\sum_{j\in F} x_{ij}d_{ij} + \vartheta \sum_{i\in N} u_i\right) \tag{1}$$

$$\text{s.t. } \sum_{j\in F} s_j \leq r \tag{2}$$

$$0 \leq s_j \leq 1, \forall j \in F \tag{3}$$

$$\sum_{j\in F} x_{ij} + u_i \geq a_i, \forall i \in N \tag{4}$$

$$x_{ij} \geq 0, \forall i \in N, \forall j \in F \tag{5}$$

$$u_i \geq 0, \forall i \in N \tag{6}$$

$$\cdot y_{ij} \geq \frac{(1-s_j)c_j - \sum_{u \in N \setminus A_{ij}} x_{uj}}{c_j}, \forall i \in N, \forall j \in F \tag{7}$$

$$\sum_{k \in T_{ij}} x_{ik} + u_i \leq (1 - y_{ij})a_i \tag{8}$$

$$\sum_{u \in A_{ij}} x_{uj} \leq y_{ij} * \sum_{i \in N} a_i, \forall i \in N, \forall j \in F \tag{9}$$

$$y_{ij} \in \{0,1\}, \forall i \in N, \forall j \in F \tag{10}$$

Formulation (1) expresses the objective function of the interdiction problem. Constraints (2) can be viewed as the budget limit of interdiction. Without loss of generality, we assume that full capacity of different facilities consumes equal units of offensive resources. Therefore, parameter r can represent the relative amount of offensive resources. Constraints (4) claim that requirements of each demand node must be satisfied, no matter which facilities supply it.. Constraints (7) express the auxiliary variable y_{ij} that has value 1 if facility j has remaining capacity after serving demand node i, and 0 otherwise. Constraints (8) realize Strategy 1, which show the preferences of demand nodes to select their respective suppliers. Constraints (9) realize Strategy 2 to ensure that each facility serves closer demands within their respective capacity. Constraints (3),(5),(6),(10) are variables

3. Experiments

Our experiments are conducted on Swain data set, which is a data set used widely in the literature related with interdiction model [6,8]. Swain data set constructs a problem with 55 demand points and 55 potential facility sites in addition to the demand and distance information. All results displayed were run on a PC with an Intel, 2.4GHz processor and 4GB of RAM.

In our experiments, we assume that facilities in the initial configuration are located at the optimal sites identified by having solved the p-median problem. Since Swain data set does not contain information about facility capacities, we adopt the capacity generation methods in [9], i.e. facility capacity equals to

$$\sum_i a_i / ((1 - \varepsilon) * p) \tag{11}$$

where ε is a constant on behalf of the built-in idle capacity percentage under normal conditions. In this way, $\sum_j c_j \geq \sum_i a_i$ is guaranteed. Penalty factor ϑ in objective functions is designed to be ten times the maximal distance between demand nodes and facilities.

In order to observe the effectiveness of the heuristic model, we generate randomly 1500 instances. Considering the size of Swain data set (55 nodes), the number of facilities p ranges from 5 to 10. Relative attacking resources r cannot exceed p considering optimization conditions. Capacity redundancy ε (denoted in (11)) ranges from 0 to 0.4. We compute the reallocation results by CPLEX given interdiction decisions results of the heuristic model. Furthermore, the percentage gap between the two objective values is used to measure the effectiveness. We divide the interval of the percentage gap into four ranges denoted as g1, g2, g3, g4 and show the results of each range in Figure1. The ranges are less than 2%, from 2% to 5%, from 5% to 10% and more than 10% respectively.

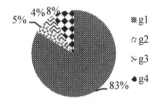

Figure 1. The effectiveness heuristic model

From Figure1, we can observe that the instances whose percentage gaps are less than 2% account for 83% of total instances. Only 8% of instances obtain worse results whose percentage gaps exceed 10%. Therefore, the heuristic model can solve effectively most PRIM-MS problems.

4. Conclusions

In this paper, we introduce a revised r-interdiction median problem called PRIM-MS, which has three characteristics, i.e. limited facility capacity, partial interdiction and multi-sourcing delivery strategy. We introduce a heuristic model of PRIM-MS and verify its effectiveness for solving PRIM-MS.

Further researches on PRIM-MS need be conducted from the aspects of models and solutions. On the other hand, comparisons with other facility interdiction problem need to be done to explore the respective changes brought by the three characteristics.

References

1. X.Y. Zhang, Z. Zheng, Y.N. Zhu and K.Y. Cai, C&OR **43**,137 (2014).
2. N. Alguacil, A. Delgadillo and M. Arroyo, C&OR **41**, 282 (2014).
3. H. R. Medal, E. A. Pohl, and M. D. Rossetti, A Multi-objective Integrated Facility Location-Hardening Model: Analyzing the Pre-and Post-Disruption Tradeoff. Eur. J. Oper. Res (2014) (in press).
4. X.W. Qin, X. Liu, and L.X. Tang, Comput. Ind. Eng.**65**, 614(2013).
5. A. T. Murray, GeoJournal **78**, 209(2013).
6. R.L. Church, M.P. Scaparra and R.S. Middleton, Annals of the Association of Association of American Geographers **94**, 491(2004).
7. D. Aksen., N. Piyade, and N.Aras, Cent Eur J Oper Res.**18**, 269 (2010).
8. Y.N. Zhu, Z. Zheng, X.Y. Zhang and K.Y. Cai, Leader-follower hierachical decision model for critical infrastructure protection and its solving algorithm. Systems Engineering-Theory & Practice (in Chinese, in press).
9. M. P. Scaparra and R. Church, IRSR **35**, 188 (2012).
10. M. P. Scaparra and R. L. Church, C&OR **35**, 1905 (2008).
11. D. Aksen, S. Şengül Akca, and N. Aras, C&OR **41**, 346 (2014).
12. F. Liberatore, M.P. Scaparra and M.S. Daskin, Omega **40**, 21(2012).
13. Z. H. Sheng, *The theory of leader-follower hierarchical decision-Stackelberg problem* (Science Press, Beijing, 1988).

SELECTING RELEVANT PARAMETERS OF A TEXTILE PROCESS USING FUZZY SENSITIVITY AND OWA OPERATORS

IMED FEKI [*] & FAOUZI MSAHLI

*Etude des Systèmes Industriels et des Energies Renouvelables (ESIER),
Ecole Nationale d'Ingénieurs de Monastir, Av. Ibn Jazzar 5019 Monastir, Tunisia.*

XIANYI ZENG & LUDOVIC KOEHL

*Laboratoire GE.M.TEX., Ecole Nationale Supérieure des Arts et Industries textiles,
2 allée Louise et Victor Champier 59056 Roubaix, France*

Selection of relevant parameters from a high dimensional process operation setting space is a problem frequently encountered in industrial process modelling. This paper presents a method for selecting the most relevant fabric mechanical parameters for each sensory quality feature. The proposed relevancy criterion has been developed using two approaches. The first utilizes a fuzzy sensitivity criterion by exploiting from experimental data the relationship between mechanical parameters and all the sensory quality features for each evaluator. Next an OWA aggregation procedure is applied to aggregate the ranking lists provided by different evaluators. In the second approach, a panel of experts provides their ranking lists of mechanical features according to their professional knowledge. Also by applying OWA, the data sensitivity-based ranking list and the knowledge-based ranking list are combined to determine the final ranking list and the final relevant mechanical parameters for a given sensory quality feature.

1. Introduction

In textile industry, the desired fabric quality can be either assessed by experts or measured using laboratory devices. However, for the sake of production stability and cost optimization, it is preferable to use mechanical parameters to characterize the fabric quality because the expert's availability cannot always be guaranteed. In practice, as the number of mechanical parameters measured on fabrics is very big, it is necessary to select those which are the most relevant or sensitive to consumer's perception, namely human sensory quality. In general, this selection can be realized by exploiting the relationship between the mechanical parameters (input variables) and each sensory quality feature (output

---

[*] Correspondent author
Email : fekiimed@yahoo.fr

variable). In general, the selection of relevant parameters constitutes the first step in the modeling of a complex industrial process.

Selection of relevant variables has been widely studied in pattern recognition, system modeling and data mining. Most of the existing methods utilize the supervised learning strategy, i.e. the objective of selection is to improve the classification accuracy or class label predictive accuracy of data samples. Several well-known methods are the decision-tree method, the nearest-neighbor method and the mutual information measure based method [1]. Recently some new variable selection methods have been developed using fuzzy techniques, e.g. a modified fuzzy decision trees with supervision [2]. A method of variable selection combining experimental data sensitivity and human knowledge has been developed in our previous approaches [3]. It is efficient to rank all the input variables according to their sensitivity to an output variable with few numbers of experimental data. Some data aggregation methods such as the Kendall criterion (1962) and Ordered Weighted Averaging (OWA) [4] are also efficient for ranking variables.

In our approach, we apply both fuzzy sensitivity proposed in [3] and the OWA method to achieve a more robust and more efficient ranking list of mechanical variables with respect to a given sensory feature. Two panels of evaluators have been used. The first panel, consisting of 6 general evaluators, classifies 41 fabric samples according to their sensitivity to the predefined sensory features such as *smooth*, *elastic*, *wrinkle*, and *soft*. The second panel is composed of 8 experts who master professional knowledge in textile metrology and mechanical fabric features. The data sensitivity-based ranking list and the knowledge-based ranking list are then combined in order to form an overall aggregated ranking list of mechanical parameters.

2. Selection of relevant variables for mechanical denim fabric features

The proposed relevant variable selection system is composed of several functional blocks. More details are given below.

2.1. *FS: the fuzzy sensitivity criterion*

The principle of the fuzzy sensitivity criterion is to build a fuzzy model *FIS1* in which the input data variation Δx (distance between two normalized vectors of mechanical parameters) and the output data variation Δy (distance between two normalized values of one specific sensory feature) are taken as two input variables, respectively, and the general sensitivity *FS* as output variable. Evidently, *FS* is a function of Δx and Δy, denoted as $FS=FIS1(\Delta x, \Delta y)$. This fuzzy model includes an interface of fuzzification, a base of fuzzy rules, an inference mechanism and an interface of defuzzification.

The fuzzification procedure aims to uniformly partition each of the two input variables into three fuzzy values: *Small* (S), *Medium* (M) and *Big* (B). The output variable varies from 0 to 1 and also fuzzified into three fuzzy values: *Small* (S), *Medium* (M) and *Big* (B) (illustrated in Figure 1).

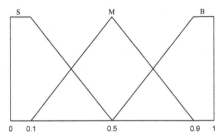

Figure 1. Fuzzy values for each input and output data variable in *FIS1* model

According to the experience of control quality operators on the relationship between mechanical parameters and sensory features, a set of fuzzy rules are defined by experts (See Table 1). Mamdani's fuzzy inference method is then used for aggregating these fuzzy rules and obtaining defuzzified output values, i.e. the sensitivity criterion.

Table 1. Fuzzy rules of fuzzy sensitivity criterion

FS	and	Δy		
		Small	*Medium*	*Big*
	Small	*Small*	*Big*	*Big*
Δx	*Medium*	*Small*	*Medium*	*Big*
	Big	*Small*	*Small*	*Medium*

Given a specific sensory feature y_β, for any pair of data samples $(X_i, y_{i\beta})$ and $(X_j, y_{j\beta})$ denoted as (i, j), the input data variation $d(X_i, X_j)$ and the output data variation $d(y_{i\beta}, y_{j\beta})$ are calculated. The corresponding sensitivity in the data pair (i, j) related to y_β, is calculated by $FS_\beta (i,j)=FIS1(d(X_i, X_j), d(y_{i\beta}, y_{j\beta}))$. $FS_\beta(i,j)$ can be considered as a measure of information content of all the input variables in the pair (i,j) related to the output y_β.

When removing x_k from the whole set of mechanical parameters, the sensitivity of the remaining mechanical parameters in the data pair (i, j) related to the output y_β can be calculated by

$$\Delta FS_{k,\beta} (i,j)=FIS1(\Delta d_k(X_i, X_j), d(y_{i\beta}, y_{j\beta})) \tag{1}$$

where $\Delta d_k(X_i, X_j)=d(X_i, X_j)- d_k(X_i, X_j)$

The general fuzzy sensitivity criterion $FS_{k,\beta}$ for all the pairs of data sample when removing the mechanical parameter x_k is defined by

$$FS_{k,\beta} = 1/\sum_{i=1}^{m}\sum_{j=i+1}^{m}\Delta FS_{k,\beta}(i,j) \tag{2}$$

Clearly, when $FS_{k,\beta} < FS_{p,\beta}$ for all $p\neq k$, then the removed mechanical parameter x_k is considered as the most insensitive among all variables.

The FS criterion $FS_{k,\beta}$ is normalized in [0,1]. In this way, the closer the value of $FS_{k,\beta}$ is to 1, the more the input variable x_k is sensitive to the output variable y_β. The closer the value of $FS_{k,\beta}$ is to 0, the more the input variable x_k is insensitive to the output variable y_β.

2.2. OWA1: Aggregating ranking lists of different evaluators

By applying the fuzzy sensitivity criterion (FIS1), we obtain a ranking list of mechanical features for each sensory feature and each evaluator. However, the evaluation data provided by different evaluators are often different due to their personalized experience and perception. In this context, their ranking lists of mechanical parameters, calculated from FIS1, are quite different. OWA has been used for aggregating all these ranking lists in order to obtain more robust and relevant results related to individual ones (OWA1 model).

Before aggregating the individual ranking lists of m mechanical parameters (the highest rank is m and the lowest 1) provided by n evaluators (Panel 1), we use the Regular Increasing Monotone (RIM) linguistic quantifier of OWA and the corresponding weight definition [4] to set up the formula of the weights. We obtain $w_i=(i/n)^{\alpha}-((i-1)/n)^{\alpha}$. The coefficient α can be determined as follows.

If we wish to select the N_s most relevant mechanical parameters from the OWA results, their aggregated ranks should be from m to $m-N_s+1$. The aggregation for n evaluators is performed according to the following principle: if k evaluators ($k\leq n$) agree to take one mechanical parameter as one of the p most relevant ones (i.e. its individual rank is between m and $m-p+1$), then its aggregated rank for all the n evaluators should be at least $m-N_s+1$.

We suppose that a specific mechanical parameter is selected by the aggregation. By applying OWA to its ranks given by all the n evaluators, denoted as $a_1,...,a_n$, and the previous aggregation principle and weight definition, we have

$$F_\alpha(a_1,a_2,......,a_n) = \sum_{i=1}^{n}b_iw_i \geq (m-p+1)\sum_{i=1}^{k}w_i + \sum_{i=k+1}^{n}w_i = (m-p)\left(\frac{k}{n}\right)^{\alpha}+1 \tag{3}$$

where b_i is the ith largest of $a_1,...,a_n$.

As the minimal condition for being selected corresponds to the aggregated rank $m-N_s+1$, we have

$$(m-p)\left(\frac{k}{n}\right)^{\alpha}+1 = m - N_s + 1 \tag{4}$$

The coefficient α can be calculated from the previous equation.

2.3. *OWA2: Aggregating human knowledge experts using OWA operator weights*

To confirm and validate the previous ranking list generated by the fuzzy sensitivity criterion and OWA using experimental data, eight experts (Panel 2) have been invited to evaluate the relevancy of each mechanical parameter to a specific sensory feature using their professional knowledge. The evaluation scores take values from {0, 1, 2, 3} where 3 stands for *relevant*, 2 *moderate relevant*, 1 *little relevant* and 0 means *no relation*. The aggregation of these ranking results given by the 8 experts is also performed using OWA (OWA2 model). The procedure of weight computation is the same as that of Section 2.2.

2.4. *OWA3: Aggregation of mechanical features rankings for each sensory parameter by OWA1 and OWA2*

After obtaining the aggregated ranking lists using the OWA1 and OWA2 models, we further aggregate them to form the final ranking list of mechanical parameters for each specific sensory feature. The sensitivity of experimental data, perceptual divergence of human evaluators, as well as expert's professional knowledge are all taken into account in this final ranking list.

3. Experimental results and analysis

The proposed relevant parameter selection method has been applied to a denim fabric washing process for obtaining 41 various fabric samples. From 20 ($m=20$) mechanical parameters measured on fabrics, We wish to determine the most relevant ones for a set of sensory quality features, including *smooth, fluffy, full, supple, elastic, wrinkle, soft, cold,* and *sliding*. Panel 1 is composed of 6 evaluators ($n=6$) for evaluating sensory quality features according to their perception.

Using OWA1, we wish to select 6 relevant parameters ($N_s=6$) from the top 4 individual relevant parameters ($p=4$) provided by two-third of evaluators ($k=4$). The identified value of $\alpha=0.33$ and the RIM linguistic quantifier-based weights for all the sensory descriptors are shown in Table 2.

Table 2. Aggregation weights for OWA1

	w_1	w_2	w_3	w_4	w_5	w_6	$\Sigma\, w_i$
Smooth	0.554	0.142	0.099	0.079	0.067	0.058	1.000
Fluffy	0.589	0.151	0.106	0.084	0.071	0	1.000
Full	0.633	0.162	0.114	0.090	0	0	1.000
Supple	0.589	0.151	0.106	0.084	0.071	0	1.000
Elastic	0.589	0.151	0.106	0.084	0.071	0	1.000
Wrinkle	0.633	0.162	0.114	0.090	0	0	1.000
Soft	0.633	0.162	0.114	0.090	0	0	1.000
Cold	1.000	0	0	0	0	0	1.000
Sliding	1.000	0	0	0	0	0	1.000

By using the same principle to OWA2, we obtain the weights of aggregation for all the sensory features and the 8 experts as follows.

$$(0.533\ 0.124\ 0.086\ 0.068\ 0.057\ 0.049\ 0.044\ 0.040)$$

By applying the same principle to OWA3, we obtain the weights combining the data sensitivity and human knowledge-based ranking lists for all the sensory features: *(0.526 0.474)*. From our experiments we find that these two ranking lists are strongly correlated and the relevant mechanical parameters selected from the aggregated ranking list is more robust and efficient than those generated from individual ranking lists.

4. Conclusion

This paper presents a method of selecting mechanical parameters related to a specific sensory quality feature. This proposed method integrates the data sensitivity criterion and human professional knowledge by using the techniques of fuzzy logic and OWA operators. More robust relevant parameters can be selected by aggregating ranking lists generated from various information sources.

References

1. H. Liu, J. Sun, L. Liu and H. Zhang. *Pattern Recognition*, **42 (7)**, 1330 (2009).
2. P.C. Chang, C.Y. Fan and W.Y. Dzan. *Expert Syst. Appl.*, **37(1)**, 214 (2010).
3. X. Deng, X. Zeng, P. Vroman and L. Koehl. *Eng. Appl. Artif. Intel.*, **23(8)**, 1368 (2010).
4. I. Palomares. *6th International Summer School on Aggregation Operators - AGOP 2011*, 125-130 (2011).

PART 7

INTELLIGENT INFORMATION PROCESSING

GMAPREDUCE: A SELF-ADAPTION MAPREDUCE FRAMEWORK BASED ON GRANULAR COMPUTING*

Junbo Zhang, Tianrui Li, Fei Teng, Chuan Luo

School of Information Science and Technology,
Southwest Jiaotong University, Chengdu 610031, China
E-mail: {jbzhang,luochuan}@my.swjtu.edu.cn, {trli, fteng}@swjtu.edu.cn

In this paper, we propose a self-adaption MapReduce framework based on granular computing (GrC), named gMapReduce. In the MapReduce model, the input data is partitioned into many data blocks which is the key step for the following parallel processing. The number of data blocks depends on the size of the block. It means the block size will affect the total running time. According to the proposed gMapReduce model, we design two algorithms, naive and advanced, for finding the appropriate granule. Both two algorithms can find the appropriate size of data block, thereby accelerating the running process effectively.

Keywords: Granular Computing; MapReduce; Hadoop; Cloud Computing.

1. Introduction

Granular computing (GrC) emerges as a new and rapidly growing paradigm of information processing, and has received much attention in recent years. GrC is an umbrella term to cover any methodologies, theories, techniques, and tools that make use of information granules in complex problem solving.[1] MapReduce, by Google, is a scalable and fault-tolerant data processing tool that enables to process a vast amount of data in parallel with many low-end computing nodes.[2,3] Hadoop is one of the most popular MapReduce runtime system.[4]

In MapReduce, the input data is partitioned into many data blocks which is the key step for the following parallel processing. We desire to

---

*This work is supported by the National Science Foundation of China (Nos. 60873108, 61175047, 61100117, 61202043), and NSAF (No. U1230117). the Fundamental Research Funds for the Central Universities (No. SWJTU12CX098), the Science and Technology Planning Project of Sichuan Province (No. 2012RZ0009), China, and the Fostering Foundation for the Excellent Ph.D. Dissertation of Southwest Jiaotong University 2012.

know how the block size affects the running time. We only change the block size and keep other arguments constant. The running time varies with the variation of block size as shown in Figure 2(a). From the point of GrC, the *block size* can be viewed as a *granule*. It performs the best when the block size is 32MB. The number of blocks is equal to the size of input data divided by the size of the block. It means that the smaller size, the more blocks. There are 493 and 2 blocks when the block size is equal to 1MB and 256MB, respectively. When there are more blocks, it would increase the I/O time because the cluster processes more times repeatedly. Conversely, the working slots in the cluster would be idle when there are fewer blocks. In this experiment, 14 map slots are idle when the block size equals to 256MB.

1.1. *Problem description*

Before describing the problem, we first give the following notation.

Notation:

D: input data;

F: specific function, *e.g.*, WordCount;

P: computing resource, *e.g.*, working slots in Map phase;

$G = \{g_1, g_2, \cdots, g_n\}$: a finite set of granules;

i: granule index;

T: the function of running time.

Given the input data D, the specific function F, the working cores P, and a finite set of granules $G = \{g_1, g_2, \cdots, g_n\}$, it aims to find the appropriate granule $g_\kappa \in G$ so as to minimize the running time:

$$\arg \min_{g_\kappa} T(D, F, P, g_\kappa) \qquad (1)$$

Example 1.1. The example in Section 1.1 can be described as: D is the input data, whose size is 493MB; F is the specific function, *i.e.*, WordCount in Hadoop; P is the computing resource, *i.e.*, working slots in Map phase $P = 16$; $G = \{1MB, 2MB, ..., 256MB\}$. According to Figure 2(a), we find the appropriate granule $g_\kappa = 32MB$.

2. A GrC-based MapReduce Framework

2.1. *The MapReduce model*

The MapReduce model always includes the following stages: (1) Map phase; (2) Sort/Shuffle phase; (3) Reduce phase.

Definition 2.1. In MapReduce, the total running time is denoted as

$$T_{all} = T_m + T_r + T_o \tag{2}$$

where T_m is the running time in Map phase; T_r is the running time in Reduce phase; T_o is the running time in other phases, *e.g.*, sort/shuffle, pass intermediate data, output result.

2.2. *The gMapReduce model*

In this subsection, we give a GrC-based MapReduce framework, called gMapReduce, as shown in Figure 1.

The difference between the gMapReduce model and MapReduce is the size of the data block. As we know, in MapReduce, the block size is set by user, which is always static, fixed and experience-based. However, the idle resource of the running cluster varies with time. The fixed block size can not match the cluster perfectly. Therefore, we propose the gMapReduce model, which can give a dynamic and learning-based block size.

The gMapReduce model includes the following steps:
(1) Sample the data with different granules;
(2) Upload the data blocks;
(3) Start MapReduce Jobs for each block;
(4) Record the running time of each Job;
(5) Select the appropriate granule which satisfies the objective function.

Here, the objective function is the total running time. Assume that the granule g_i is selected and the corresponding running time is t_i. Hence, the number of total blocks is $nb_i = \left\lceil \frac{D}{g_i} \right\rceil$. Assume that p cores are idle in the cluster. Then, the repeat times is $\left\lceil \frac{nb_i}{p} \right\rceil$. Therefore, the estimated time is $et_i = t_i \times \left\lceil \frac{nb_i}{p} \right\rceil$. The granule g_κ will be selected which satisfies $et_\kappa = \min_{g_i \in G}\{et_i\}$. The detailed algorithm is outlined in Algorithm 1.

Algorithm 1 is a naive greedy algorithm for finding the appropriate granule. When we compare the estimated time and the actual time, the result is not ideal. The main reason is that it does not consider the initial time of the Job. Hence, we design an advanced greedy algorithm for finding the appropriate granule. Before it, we present the new definition of the total runtime as follows.

Definition 2.2. In MapReduce, the total running time is denoted as

$$T_{all} = T_i + T_m + T_r + T_o \tag{3}$$

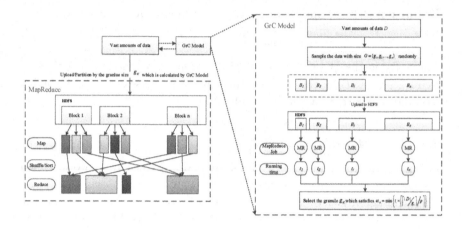

Fig. 1.   The gMapReduce model

where T_i is the initialization time; T_m is the running time in Map phase; T_r is the running time in Reduce phase; T_o is the running time in other phases, *e.g.*, sort/shuffle, pass intermediate data, output result.

Algorithm 1: A naive greedy algorithm

Input: $G = \{g_1, g_2, \cdots, g_n\}$; D; p.
Output: The appropriate granule: g_κ

1 **begin**
2   **for** $g_i \in G$ **do**
3        $B_i = S(D, g_i)$; //   Sample the data with size g_i from D
4        $t_i = \text{RunJob}(B_i)$; //   Record the running time of B_i
5        $nb_i = \left\lceil \frac{|D|}{g_i} \right\rceil$; //   Compute the number of blocks
6        $et_i = t_i \times \left\lceil \frac{nb_i}{p} \right\rceil$; //   Estimated time when partitioning data with g_i
7   **Select** the granule g_κ which satisfies $et_\kappa = \min\limits_{g_i \in G}\{et_i\}$;
8   **Output** g_κ.

Algorithm 2 first tests the initialization time of the Job. To test the initialization time, a Job with empty input data set is submitted to the cluster, then the running time is recorded. The following steps but the function of the estimated time are the same with Algorithm 1. The function of the estimated time is changed to $(t_i - t_\emptyset) \times \left\lceil \frac{nb_i}{p} \right\rceil + t_\emptyset$, where $t_\emptyset$ is the initialization time of the Job.

Algorithm 2: An advanced greedy algorithm

Input: $G = \{g_1, g_2, \cdots, g_n\}$; D; p.
Output: The appropriate granule: g_κ

1 **begin**
2   Let $B_\emptyset = \emptyset$; // Set the data $B_\emptyset$ with empty set
3      $t_\emptyset = \text{RunJob}(B_\emptyset)$;
4   **for** $g_i \in G$ **do**
5          $B_i = S(D, g_i)$; // Sample the data with size g_i from D
6          $t_i = \text{RunJob}(B_i)$; // Record the running time of B_i
7          $nb_i = \left\lceil \frac{|D|}{g_i} \right\rceil$; // Compute the number of blocks
8          $et_i^A = (t_i - t_\emptyset) \times \left\lceil \frac{nb_i}{p} \right\rceil + t_\emptyset$; // Estimated time
9   **Select** the granule g_κ which satisfies $et_\kappa = \min_{g_i \in G} \{et_i^A\}$;
10   **Output** g_κ.

---

3. Experimental Analysis

To test the proposed algorithms, the experiments are carried out on two different Hadoop clusters, which are outlined in Table 1.

Table 1. The description of the clusters

	Small cluster	Large cluster
Hadoop version	1.0.1	1.0.1
JDK version	1.7.0_5	1.7.0_5
Operating system	Ubuntu 12.04	CentOS 6.2
CPU	Inter(R) Core(TM) i7-2670QM	AMD Opteron(TM) Processor 2376
Clock frequency	2.20GHz	2.3GHz
Total working cores	4	32
Total Map slots	2	16
Total Reduce slots	2	16

We set the set of granules $G = \{1, 2, 4, 8, 16, 32, 64\}$ with the unit MB. Table 2 shows the estimated time of two algorithms on both clusters. In the small cluster, both two algorithms find the appropriate granule is 64MB. However, in the large cluster, they find the appropriate granule is 32MB. It shows that different clusters have different appropriate granules as different software and hardware configurations.

To verify the difference between Algorithms 1 and 2, we give a comparison of actual running time and estimated time of Algorithms 1 and 2 in the large cluster as shown in Figure 2(b). It is obvious to show that the curve of the estimated time of Algorithm 2 is close to that of actual running time. Therefore, Algorithm 2 has better estimate than Algorithm 1.

Table 2. Estimated Time

	Small cluster				Large cluster		
g_i	t_i	et_i	et_i^A	g_i	t_i	et_i	et_i^A
1	28	6916	1996	1	27	837	237
2	27	3321	881	2	26	416	116
4	30	1860	640	4	26	208	68
8	26	806	206	8	29	116	56
16	29	464	164	16	34	68	48
32	39	312	172	32	41	__41__	__41__
64	49	__196__	__136__	64	55	55	55

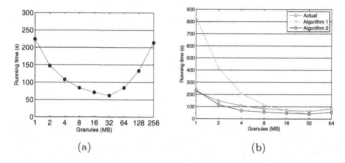

(a)   (b)

Fig. 2.   (a) Running time with different granules (block sizes). (b)A comparison of actual running time and estimated time of Algorithms 1 and 2.

4. Conclusion

In this paper, we proposed the gMapReduce model and designed two algorithms for finding the appropriate granule. Both algorithms can find the appropriate block size, and the advanced algorithm has better performance than the naive one, thereby accelerating the running process effectively. However, there still exist two problems. One is how to give the set of granules. In this paper, we present a simple set of granules in our experiments. Another is how to estimate the running time exactly. We will research on these two aspects in the future.

References

1. J. Yao, A. Vasilakos and W. Pedrycz, *Systems, Man, and Cybernetics, Part C: Applications and Reviews, IEEE Transactions on* **PP**, 1 (2013).
2. J. Dean and S. Ghemawat, *Communications of the ACM* **51**, 107(January 2008).
3. K.-H. Lee, Y.-J. Lee, H. Choi, Y. D. Chung and B. Moon, *SIGMOD Rec.* **40**, 11(January 2012).
4. T. White, *Hadoop: The Definitive Guide*, 2nd edn. (O'Reilly Media / Yahoo Press, 2010).

COMPARING THE PERFORMANCE OF RBFN NETWORKS BASED SOFTWARE EFFORT ESTIMATION MODELS

ALI IDRI AND WAFA EL BOUKILI

Software Project Management Reseach Team, Mohammed V Souissi University, Morocco
wafa.elboukili@gmail.com, idri@ensias.ma

ABDELALI ZAKRANI

ENSAM, Hassan II – Mohammedia University, Casablanca, Morocco
zakrani@gmail.com

This paper investigates the use of RBF neural networks for software effort estimation. The focus of this study is on the design of these networks, especially their middle layer composed of receptive fields, using the Self Organizing Maps (SOM). An evaluation of the accuracy of effort estimation models that use either an RBFN construction-based on SOM, C-means or APC-III, is hence presented. This study uses the Tukutuku dataset.

1. Introduction

Techniques for estimating software development effort may be divided into two major categories [1]: Parametric models, which are derived from the statistical or numerical analysis of historical projects data [2], and non-parametric models, which are based on a set of artificial intelligence techniques such as artificial neural networks [3,4], case-based reasoning [5], and decision trees [6]. This paper focuses on non-parametric software effort estimation models based on Radial Basis Function Neural Networks.

An RBF neural network may be used for software effort estimation because it can approximate any regular function. It is a special two-layer network with a nonlinear hidden layer and a linear output layer. An important issue in the RBF neural modeling is to determine the number of the hidden nodes and their adjustable parameters including the centers and the width σ which has a substantial influence on the RBFN networks performance. This study uses the SOM to define the hidden layer parameters and compares the results obtained with those when using two other clustering techniques APC-III and C-means.

In our earlier studies, three clustering techniques, APC-III, C-means and Fuzzy C-means were empirically evaluated to design the middle layer of RBFN for software effort estimation [7]. This paper evaluates and compares, on the

Tukutuku database, the accuracy of effort estimates generated by an RBFN construction-based on SOM with an RBFN construction-based either on APC-III or C-means. More specifically, the following research question was investigated: Will an RBFN construction-based on SOM performs much better, in term of MMRE and Pred, than that of an RBFN construction-based on C-means or APC-III?

The remainder of the paper is organized as follows. Section 2 describes the Tukutuku dataset and the evaluation criteria used in this study. Section 3 illustrates how SOM is incorporated in the construction of the hidden layer of the RBFN networks. Section 4 discusses the results of this study. Finally, Section 5 holds up conclusions and overview of future work.

2. Data Description and Evaluation Criteria

2.1. *Database Description*

The Tukutuku database contains data of 53 Web projects [8]. Each project is described using 9 numerical variables such as the number of html or shtml files used and the number of media files and team experience. Examples of web project attributes of the Tukutuku dataset are given in Table 1.

Table 1 - Software attributes for the web dataset.

Attribute	Description
Webpages	Number of web pages in the application
Textpages	Number of text pages in the application(text page has 600 words)
Img	Total number of images
Anim	Number of animations in the application
Audio/video	Number of audio/video files in the application

2.2. *Evaluation Criteria of Prediction Accuracy*

The following criteria to assess and compare the performance of effort estimation models were used [9]. A common criterion for the evaluation of cost estimation model is the magnitude of relative error (MRE) given by:

$$\text{MRE}_j = \left| \frac{\text{Effort}_{\text{actual},j} - \text{Effort}_{\text{estimated},j}}{\text{Effort}_{\text{actual},j}} \right| \tag{1}$$

The MRE values are calculated for each project in the dataset, while mean magnitude of relative error (MMRE) computes the average of MRE over N projects. Prediction at Level q, Pred(q) is a measure of what proportion of the predicted values have MRE less or equal than to a given value q:

$$pred(q) = \frac{k}{N} \qquad (2)$$

where q is the given value, k is the number of projects with MRE less or equal to q, and N is the total number of projects in the dataset. This paper used Pred(25) because it's commonly used in the software effort prediction literature [9].

3. RBFN Networks Construction

RBFN networks have been investigated in software effort estimation due to the simplicity of their training phase. Indeed, a possible learning algorithm for RBFN consists in a determination of the number of neurons in input/hidden layers and a computation of centers c_j, widths σ_j and weights β_j. Figure 1 illustrates a possible RBFN architecture configured for software effort estimation.

The number of neurons in input layer is the number of the attributes describing the historical software projects in the used dataset. Therefore, 9 is the number of input neurons when applying the RBFN to Tukutuku dataset. The number of hidden neurons is determined by the number of clusters (c) assigned by the APC-III, C-means or SOM algorithms. The SOM clustering technique is briefly presented in the following section.

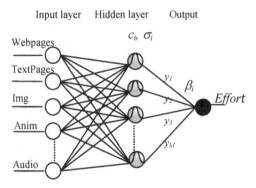

Figure 1. An RBFN network architecture for software development effort estimation.

3.1. *Self-Organizing Maps for Designing RBFN Networks*

SOM, originally proposed by Kohonen [10,11], consists of neurons organized on low-dimensional grid (most commonly 2D). Each neuron is represented by p-dimensional weights vector $W=[w_1,...,w_p]$, where p is equal to the dimension of the input vectors. For each input vector, the most responsive neuron is located (Best Matching Unit). The weights of the BMU neuron and those of its neighborhood are adapted to reduce their distances to the current input vector. Figure 2 illustrates a possible SOM architecture configured for clustering web projects of the Tukutuku dataset. After training the BMU neurons, their weight vectors are transmitted to the centers of hidden neurons of RBFN.

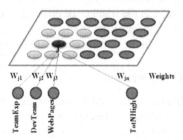

Figure 2. An example of Self Organizing Maps architecture for clustering the web projects

The outline of the SOM algorithm can be stated as follows:

Input:
- Map of units u_i with randomly selected weights vectors w_i

- Training projects $P=\{p_j\}$

- A neighborhood kernel function is defined by Eq. (3) where d_{ij} is the map distance between units u_i and u_j, and r(t) is the neighborhood radius:

$$h_{ij} = e^{\left(\frac{-d_{ij}^2}{2r(t)^2}\right)} \tag{3}$$

Loop over time steps t, until convergence:

1. Determine the index c of best matching unit u_c (Eq. (4)) for each data item p_j.

$$\|p_j - w_c\| = \min\{\|p_j - w_i\|\} \tag{4}$$

$\|.\|$ denote Euclidean distance.

2. Update each model w_i using Eq. (5) to better fit the data items assigned to it and the data in its neighborhood:

$$w_i(t+1) = \frac{\sum_k h_{ic(k)}(t).p_k}{\sum_k h_{ic(k)}(t)} \tag{5}$$

3. Update (decrease) neighborhood radius r(t)

Radius is monotonically decreasing function of t, The mathematical form of r(t) is not crucial, as long as its value is fairly large in the beginning of the training;

4. Overview of Empirical Results

This section presents and compares the results obtained when we apply the RBFN construction-based on APC-III, C-means and SOM to the Tukutuku database. The calculations were achieved over two software prototypes. The first prototype implements the clustering algorithms APC-III, C-means and SOM, providing clusters and their centers from Tukutuku dataset. The second prototype implements an effort estimation model based on an RBFN architecture where the middle layer parameters were determined by the first software prototype. The APC-III, C-means and RBFN are developed with the C programming language whereas the SOM is implemented with the Matlab SOM Toolbox software package under a Microsoft Windows PC environment.

To measure the coherence of clusters in the case of SOM, the quantization error (QE) is used, which is the average distance between each project and weights of its BMU neuron. The criterion of good mapping is low quantization error. Figure 3 illustrates the relationship between the quantization error of SOM and the number of clusters. It is noticed that the error decreases slowly and stabilizes when the number of class is 45.

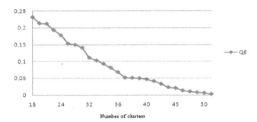

Figure 3. Relationship between the quantization error of SOM and the number of clusters

Figure 4-a illustrates the relationship between the estimates accuracy of RBFN and the number of clusters c generated with SOM. We can notice that the accuracy, in terms of Pred(25) and MMRE, is acceptable when c is higher than 45. Otherwise if c is less than 45, the RBFN generates inaccurate estimates. The aim is to reduce the number of clusters and keep estimates accuracy acceptable (Pred(25) is around or higher than 70%, MMRE is around or less than 30%).

Figure 4-b compares the Pred(25) of the RBFN using the C-means, APC-III and SOM. It can be noticed that the accuracy of the RBFN based on C-means is better than accuracy of the RBFN based either on SOM or APC-III, especially when decreasing the number of cluster c.

5. Conclusion

This paper compared the accuracy of RBFN construction-based on SOM, C-means and APC-III. This comparison is based on a web hypermedia applications dataset that contains 53 software projects. We used the entire dataset to train and to test the designed RBFN. We have found that the RBFN designed with the C-means algorithm performs better, in terms of cost estimates accuracy, than the RBFN designed with the APC-III or SOM algorithms.

650

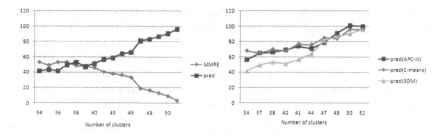

Figure 4. (a) Accuracy in terms of Pred(25) and MMRE of RBFN using SOM. (b) Accuracy comparison in terms of Pred(25) of RBFN using SOM, APC-III or C-means.

References

1. M. Jørgensen, M. Shepperd. "A *systematic review of software development cost estimation. Studies*". *IEEE Trans. Softw. Eng.* 33, 1 (2007).

2. B.W. Boehm, "*Software Engineering Economics*," Prentice-Hall(1981).

3. G. R. Finnie, G. Witting, and J.M. Desharnais. "*A Comparison of Software Effort Estimation Techniques: Using Function Points with Neural Networks, Case-Based Reasoning and Regression Models*", *J. Syst. Software*, vol. 39, no. 3, pp. 281-289 (1997).

4. A. Idri, A. Hassani and A. Abran. "*Assessing Software Cost Estimation Models Based on RBF Neural Networks*", 25th International Conference on Software Engineering and Knowledge Engineering, SEKE, 27-29 June, Boston, ISSN 2325-9000, pp. 483-487, (2013)

5. M. Shepperd and C. Schofield. "*Estimating Software Project Effort Using Analogie,*" IEEE Trans. Softw. Eng., vol. 23, no. 12, pp. 736-747 (1997).

6. R. W. Selby and A. A. Porter. "*Learning from examples: generation and evaluation of decision trees for software resource analysis*". IEEE Trans. Softw. Eng., vol. 14, no. 12, pp. 1743-1757 (1988).

7. A. Idri, A. Zakrani, and A. Zahi. "*Design of Radial Basis Function Neural Networks for Software Effort Estimation,*" in Int. J. of Computer Science Issues (IJCSI), vol. 7, Issue 4, no 3, pp. 21-31 (2010).

8. B. Kitchenham, E. Mendes. "*A Comparison of Cross-company and Within company Effort Estimation Models for Web Applications*" ,in Proc. of EASE, 47-55 (2004)

9. B. A. Kitchenham, L. M. Pickard, S. G. MacDonell and M. J. Shepperd. "*What accuracy statistics really measure*", Software, IEE Proceedings - , vol. 148, no. 3, pp. 81-85 (2001).

10. T. Kohonen. "*The self-organizing map*". Proc. of the IEEE, vol. 78, no 9, pp. 1464-1480 (1990).

11. T. Kohonen, "*Essentials of the self-organizing map*", Neural Networks, Vol 37, pp. 52-65, ISSN 0893-6080 (2013). Networks, Vol 37, pp. 52-65, ISSN 0893-6080 (2013).

EXTENDED APPROACH FOR EVOLVING NEO-FUZZY NEURAL WITH ADAPTIVE FEATURE SELECTION

A. M. SILVA$^{\diamond *}$, W. M. CAMINHAS*, A. P. LEMOS* and F. GOMIDE†

$^\diamond$ *Federal Center of Technological Education of Minas Gerais*
* *Graduate Program in Electrical Engineering, Federal University of Minas Gerais*
† *School of Electrical and Computer Engineering, University of Campinas*
E-mail: alissonmarques, caminhas, andrepl @cpdee.ufmb.br,
gomide@dca.fee.unicamp.br

This paper introduces an evolving neo-fuzzy neural network with adaptive feature selection approach in which *candidate* models with larger and smaller number of input variables than the *current* model are developed concurrently. The best amongst the *current* and *candidate* models is chosen at each step. The approach uses an incremental learning algorithm to simultaneously update the weights, to select the input variables, and evolve the network structure. Computational experiments concerning identification of a nonlinear process is performed to evaluate the method and to compare its performance against alternative evolving models. The results show that the extended evolving neo-fuzzy neural network with adaptive feature selection approach achieves higher or as high performance as alternatives evolving modeling methods.

Keywords: Evolving Neural Fuzzy Network, Feature Selection, Neo-Fuzzy Neuron

1. Introduction

This paper introduces a new approach for evolving fuzzy system with adaptive feature selection using the neo-fuzzy neuron (NFN).[1] The approach extends the eNFN-AFS approach suggested in.[2] In eNFN-AFS, whenever data is input, the connection weights of the neural network and the parameters of the membership functions may be modified, new membership functions can be either added or deleted, and input variables added or deleted. Granulation of the input variables domains, and computation of the degree of activation of the membership functions are done only once at each step. There is a unique set of membership functions for each input variable.

In the approach developed in this paper the neural network structure of distinct neural models called *current* and *candidate* models evolve individually and concurrently. Unlike eNFN-AFS, granulation of the input variables domains and computation of the activation degrees in X-eNFN-AFS is done at each time step for the *current* and *candidate* models. The network structure of the X-eNFN-AFS evolves by adding or deleting input variables, membership functions, and adapting the parameters and weights of the neural network.

2. Extended Evolving Neural Fuzzy Network with Adaptive Feature Selection - X-eNFN-AFS

The X-eNFN-AFS is an evolving neuro-fuzzy network with adaptive feature selection that uses an incremental, one pass learning algorithm. All computations are done recursively and there is no need to store past data. The algorithm for X-eNFN-AFS can be summarized as follows.

Step 1: Select the Initial Input Variables and Choose the *Current* and the *Candidate* Models - Selection considers the *current* model and two *candidate* models. The first *candidate* model includes new variables in the *current* model. The X-eNFN-AFS attempts to replace the *current* by the more complex model if the neural network modeling performance increases. The second *candidate* model has fewer input variables than the *current* model. The idea is to replace the *current* by a simpler model if modeling performance improves. Let n be the overall number of input variables and a be the number of input variables of the *current* model. Thus, we can choose any of the remaining $(n - a)$ variables and add it in the *current* model to assemble a *candidate* model with $(a + 1)$ input variables. On the contrary, any of the a variables of the *current* model can be deleted to provide a simpler *candidate* model with $(a - 1)$ input variables.

Step 2: Initialization of the Membership Functions - We use triangular and complementary membership functions to uniformly granulate the domain of each of the input variable. The resulting partition will be called *uniform partition* for short. Initially, *current* and *candidate* models start with two functions for each input variable only. The modal values of the initial membership functions are $b_{i1} = min_{x_i}$ and $b_{i2} = max_{x_i}$, where i indexes the input variable, min_{x_i} is the lower bound, and max_{x_i} the upper bound of the respective domains. Steps 1 and 2 are performed only once and starts the X-eNFN-AFS learning and adaptation.

Step 3: Model Output - The output $\hat{y}_t$ at step t is the sum of individual outputs y_{ti} of the *current* model, i.e., $\hat{y}_t = \sum_{i=1}^{a} y_{ti}$. The domain of each input variable x_{ti} is granulated into m_i membership functions. Because partitions are uniform, at most two are active for a given input x_{ti}.

The individual outputs y_{ti} are computed for active membership functions only: $y_{ti} = \mu_{A_{ik_i}}(x_{ti})q_{ik_i} + \mu_{A_{ik_i+1}}(x_{ti})q_{ik_i+1}$, where k_i and $k_i + 1$ indexes the active membership functions.

Step 4: Update Network Weights - Only the weights corresponding to the active membership functions at t are updated using $q_{ik_i} = q_{ik_i} - \alpha_t(y_t - \hat{y}_t)\mu_{ik_i}(x_{ti})$ for each input x_{ti}. y_t is the desired output, $\hat{y}_t$ the network output, and $\alpha_t = 1/(\sum_{i=1}^{n} \mu_{ik_i}(x_{ti})^2 + \mu_{ik_i+1}(x_{ti})^2)$. Steps 3 and 4 are performed for *current* and all *candidate* models.

Step 5: Adaptive Feature Selection - Feature selection is performed using a statistical test. The statistics are based on a modification of the F test.[3] The F test statistics used to evaluate the larger *candidate* model is $F_{inc} = ((RSS_a - RSS_c)(s_c - p_c))/(RSS_c(s_c - s_a + p_a - p_c))$ and the one to evaluate the smaller *candidate* model is $F_{exc} = ((RSS_a - RSS_c)(s_c - p_c))/(RSS_c(s_c - s_a + p_c - p_a))$, where s_a and s_c are the number of samples used to estimate the parameters of the *current* and the *candidate* models, RSS_a and RSS_c are the sum of squared residuals, and p_a and p_c are the number of model parameters. The F_{inc} and F_{exc} statistics requires p_value to be found for both *candidate* models. The *candidate* with the smallest p_value replaces the *current* model only if its p_value is smaller than a significance level γ divided by the number of tests λ, where λ is $(n - a)$ for F_{inc} and a for F_{exc}.

Step 6: Creation of the Membership Functions - Membership functions are created using the following recursive procedure. Given the input x_t, compute the mean value of the global modeling error $\hat{\mu}_{m_t}$ by $\hat{\mu}_{m_{t-1}} - \beta(\hat{\mu}_{m_{t-1}} - (\hat{y}_t - y_t))$ and the corresponding variance $\hat{\sigma}_{m_t}^2$ by $(1 - \beta)(\hat{\sigma}_{m_{t-1}}^2 + \beta(\hat{\mu}_{m_t} - (\hat{y}_t - y_t))^2)$, where β is the learning rate. Find the most active membership function (b_i^*) and compute the local mean error $\hat{\mu}_{b_{ti}}$ using $\hat{\mu}_{b_{t-1i}} - \beta(\hat{\mu}_{b_{t-1i}} - e_t)$. If $\hat{\mu}_{b_{ti}} > \hat{\mu}_{m_t} + \hat{\sigma}_{m_t}^2$ and $dist > \tau$ then a new membership function is created. Here $dist$ is the distance between the modal value of the new membership function created and the modal values of its adjacent membership functions. τ is $(max_{x_i} - min_{x_i})/\eta$, and η is a parameter used to compute the smallest distance allowed. The new membership function requires updating the granulation of the *i-th* input variable domain as follows: If $b_i^* \neq 1$ and $b_i^* < m_i$, then b_i^* is replaced by two membership functions whose modal values are $new\_b_1 = b_{ib_i^*-1} + dist$ and $new\_b_2 = b_{ib_i^*-1} + 2 * dist$; If $b_i^* = 1$, then a new membership function is created and its modal value is $new\_b = b_{ib_i^*} + dist$; If $b_i^* = m_i$, then a new membership function is created and inserted with modal value given by $new\_b = b_{ib_i^*} - dist$.

Step 7: Elimination of the Membership Functions - The procedure to eliminate membership functions uses the idea of age.[4] Here, age is the number of steps during which a membership function has been inactive. The procedure is as follows. For each input variable i, find b_i^-, the index of the least active membership function enabled by x_{ti}. If $age_{b_i^-} > \omega$ and $m_i > 2$ then b_i^- is excluded. ω is an age threshold. Elimination of a membership function requires updating the granulation of the i-th input variable domain. Steps 6 and 7 are performed for the *current* and *candidate* models.

3. Computational Results

The evaluation of the X-eNFN-AFS was performed using a nonlinear system identification problem. The results are compared with six evolving systems: DENFIS,[5] eNFN,[6] eNFN-AFS,[2] eTS,[7] NFN-AFS[8] and xTS.[9] The nonlinear system to be identified is $y_t = ((y_{t-1}y_{t-2}(y_{t-1} - 0.5))/(1 + (y_{t-1})^2 + (y_{n-2})^2)) + u_{t-1}$, where $u_t = sin(2\pi t/25)$, and $y_0 = y_1 = 0$. The aim is to use the model to predict the output y_t using past input and outputs. We assume that the model has the following form $\hat{y}_t = f(y_{t-1}, y_{t-2}, u_{t-1})$ where $\hat{y}_t$ is the predicted output at t. The overall number of variables is 3, the cardinality of $y_{t-1}, y_{t-2}, u_{t-1}$.

The experiments use 5200 samples, 50% of the samples for modeling and the remaining 50% to evaluate the model performance. The evaluation scheme adopted in this paper was suggested in.[6] The best values of model parameters are found by exhaustive search. The error measure adopted is the *RMSE* (Root Mean Squared Error).

The parameters of the algorithms were chosen as follows: DENFIS ($dthr = 0.07$, $mofn = 3$); eNFN ($\beta = 0.01$, $w = 100$, $\eta = 10$); eNFN-AFS ($\beta = 0.01$, $w = 100$, $\lambda = 0.01$, $\eta = 10$); eTS ($r = 0.06$, $\Omega = 550$); NFN-AFS ($m = 4$, $\beta = 0.01$, $\lambda = 0.01$); X-eNFN-AFS ($\beta = 0.01$, $w = 100$, $\lambda = 0.01$, $\eta = 10$); xTS ($\Omega = 650$). The eNFN-AFS, NFN-AFS and X-eNFN-AFS start using y_{t-1} as input variable only while DENFIS, eNFN, eTS e xTS start with and keep all three inputs during all steps.

The adaptive input selection mechanism of eNFN-AFS and X-eNFN-AFS selected y_{t-1} and y_{t-2} as input variable, and NFN-AFS uses all three inputs. Figure 1a shows how the structure of the X-eNFN-AFS evolves depicting the number of input variables and membership functions after each data sample is input. Notice in Figure 1a that the X-eNFN-AFS network starts with one input variable and two membership functions. The input selection mechanism adds a second input variable at $t = 66$ and keeps it up to the end of the simulation period. The number of membership functions also changes. X-eNFN-AFS starts with two and ends with 19 membership functions. Figure 1b illustrates the actual and the output predicted by X-eNFN-AFS during the first 500 samples. Looking at figures 1a and 1b we can see that the adaptation of X-eNFN-AFS significantly improves modeling performance.

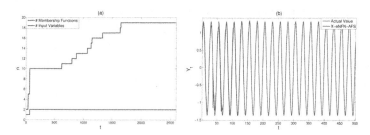

Figure 1.   (a) X-eNFN-AFS model adaptation, (b) Model output.

Table 1 shows the *RMSE* values and the number of rules/neurons produced by the evolving modeling methods. It suggests that the X-eNFN-AFS performs better than the DENFIS, eNFN-AFS, eTS, NFN-AFS and xTS, and worse RMSE terms than the eNFN. The results achieved by DENFIS, eNFN, eNFN-AFS, NFN-AFS and X-eNFN-AFS are comparable, and are better than the eTS and xTS by an order of magnitude.

Table 1.   Performance Evaluation.

Model	Rules	RMSE
DENFIS	10	0.0530
eNFN	28	0.0473
eNFN-AFS	09	0.0667
eTS	07	0.7994
NFN-AFS	12	0.0524
X-eNFN-AFS	19	0.0506
xTS	05	0.7990

4. Conclusion

This paper has suggested a new approach for adaptive modeling using neo-fuzzy neural networks called X-eNFN-AFS. The learning algorithm of X-eNFN-AFS continuously updates the weights, adds, deletes or keeps input variables and membership functions the same. The X-eNFN-AFS approach adapts a *current* and *candidate* models of distinct complexity individually. The approach was evaluated using a nonlinear system identification example. Simulation results suggest that the X-eNFN-AFS has a comparable or better performance than alternative evolving models as a result of its adaptive feature selection of the learning algorithm. The approach seems to be particularly useful in situations in which little or no a priori knowledge/data of the system to be modeled is available. Future work shall address techniques to analyze the interdependence between input variables, to extend X-eNFN-AFS to handle MIMO systems, and to investigate mechanisms to reduce the complexity of the input variable selection algorithm.

Acknowledgement

The authors acknowledge the support Brazilian Ministry of Education (CAPES), the Brazilian National Research Council (CNPq), and the Research Foundation of the State of Minas Gerais (FAPEMIG) for their support. The last author also thanks CNPq for grant 304596/2009-4.

References

1. T. Yamakawa, E. Uchino, T. Miki and H. Kusabagi, A neo fuzzy neuron and its applications to system identification and predictions to system behavior, in Proc. Int. Conf. on Fuzzy Logic and Neural Networks, 1992.
2. A. Silva, W. Caminhas, A. Lemos and F. Gomide, Evolving neo-fuzzy neural network with adaptive feature selection, in Proc. BRICS-CCI , 2013.
3. D. Potts and C. Sammut, Incremental Learning of Linear Model Trees, in Machine Learning , 5 (2004).
4. E. Lughofer and P. Angelov, Handling drifts and shifts in on-line data streams with evolving fuzzy systems, in Applied Soft Computing , 2057 (2011).
5. N. Kasabov and Q. Song, DENFIS: Dynamic Evolving Neural-Fuzzy Inf. System and Its Applic. for Time-Series Prediction, in Fuzzy Systems , 144 (2002).
6. A. Silva, W. Caminhas, A. Lemos and F. Gomide, A fast learning algorithm for evolving neo-fuzzy neuron, in Applied Soft Computing , 194 (2014).
7. P. Angelov and D. Filev, An approach to online identification of Takagi-Sugeno fuzzy models, in IEEE Trans. SMC , 484 (2004).
8. A. Silva, W. Caminhas, A. Lemos and F. Gomide, Evolving neural fuzzy network with adaptive feature selection, in Proc. ICMLA, 2012.
9. P. Angelov and X. Zhou, Evolving fuzzy systems from data streams in real-time, in Proc. ISEFS, 2006.

USER DEMAND-DRIVEN PATENT TOPIC CLASSIFICATION USING MACHINE LEARNING TECHNIQUES

Fujin Zhu[†], Xuefeng Wang, Donghua Zhu

School of Management and Economy, Beijing Institute of Technology
Beijing, 100081, China
[†]E-mail: zinfuture1991@gmail.com

Yuqin Liu

Academic of Printing and Packaging Industrial and Technology, Beijing Institute of
Graphic Communication, Beijing 100038, China
E-mail: liuyuqin2004@126.com

Traditional patent classification schemes, which are mainly based on either IPC or UPC, are too complicated and general to meet the needs of specific industries. The paper proposes a dynamic classification method, the "user demand-driven patent topic classification", aiming to a specific industry or technology area. In the paper, classification topics of the method are grouped into technical topic, application topic and application-technical mixed topic. Automatic process of the method using machine learning techniques is presented as well. A case study on the technology area of system on a chip (SoC) is conducted using machine learning techniques, validating the feasibility of the method. The experiment results demonstrate that automatic patent topic classification based on the combination of patents' metadata and citation information can obtain perfect performance with a greatly simplified document preprocessing.

Keywords: User demand-driven; Patent topic classification; Machine learning; Document representation; SoC

1. Introduction

The issue of automatic patent classification has received increasing academic attention and has become an area of increased focus [1-8]. Current schemes of patent classification can be categorized into two categories: (i) technology-dependent schemes such as the International Patent Code (IPC) or the United States Patent Code (UPC) for patent application, examination and searching [2, 4, 8]; (ii) TRIZ-based scheme for the demand of TRIZ users [5, 7]. The first

[†] Work partially supported by the General Program of National Natural Science Foundation of China (Grant No.71373019) and the National Key Technology R&D Program (Grant No. 2013BAH20F01).

kind of schemes is too complex and hard to comprehend. A lot of fuzzy terminologies exist in traditional patent classification systems, making it more difficult to understand. Moreover, the result of the analysis by current classifications is insufficient to reflect the technological niche of a company and mis-categorization results in further difficulties for patent management. In addition, traditional patent classification systems are static systems, which mean they do not evolve with the development of technology [3].

In general, traditional patent classifications are based on a fixed framework, which is either a general technology hierarchy of all fields or the 40 TRIZ Inventive Principles. These schemes of patent classification are static and too general to meet the demands of specific industries. In this paper, we propose a dynamic and more industry specific methodology, the user demand-driven patent topic classification aiming to a specific industry, to overcome the disadvantages of traditional approaches.

This paper mainly focuses on three issues: (i) proposing the new method of "user demand-driven patent topic classification" and summarizing its classification topics; (ii) to illustrate automatic process of the new method using machine learning techniques and verify its feasibility; (iii) comparing the performance of various document presentation based on different sections of a patent and to figure out the ideal document presentations for the special method.

2. Methodology

2.1. *Patent topic classification*

When enterprises are carrying out R&D planning, patents may need to be categorized by their technical domains, applications, or functions. Since user's demand varies, a user demand-driven patent topic classification system is necessary. Classification topics are mainly grouped into three categories:

(i) Classify by Technical Topic: Technical topics of a patent care about technology innovations or breakthroughs it brings, but not areas it can be applied to. Taking the IPC as an example, current patent classification approaches are generally based on technical topic.

(ii) Classify by Application Topic: In contrary to technical topic, application topic cares about the application areas of a patent. Although patent documents, especially patents for invention, are focused on new technologies, patent analysts may be curious about where they can be used when doing R&D planning in an organization.

(iii) Classify by Application-Technical Mixed Topic: We got two observations from our past patent topic classification practices. First, it is sometimes very difficult to distinguish "technical topic" from "application topic", terminologies like "communication" can refer to both communication technology and communication application; Second, a great number of patent topic classification demands focus on both of them, analysts care about not only the technical topic, but also application areas of a patent.

2.2. Classification process

The process of the user demand-driven patent topic classification aided by machine learning techniques is illustrated as figure 1.

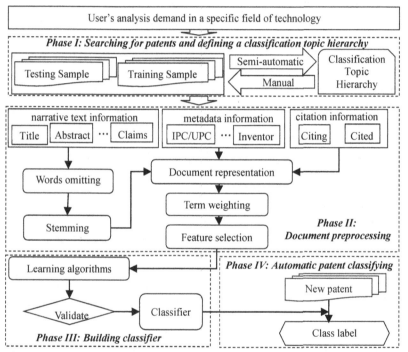

Fig. 1. Automatic classification processes of user demand-driven patent topic classification using machine learning techniques.

Phase I: Searching for patents and defining a classification topic hierarchy. As a dynamic approach to conduct more detailed patent classification of a specific technology area, the first task is to analyze the patent mining objective and possible requirements to collect raw patents and define an analysis-oriented classification topic hierarchy of the target technology field. With the help of techniques such as topic modeling [9] and text clustering, it becomes a semi-automatic task for domain experts to build the topic hierarchy. The last step of phase one is to manually build a suitable size of sample, which is of significance to build and validate a classifier in the third phase.

Phase II: Document preprocessing. Preprocessing of patent documents includes document representation, word segmentation, stop words omitting using a stop words dictionary, word stemming, feature selection and word/term weighting. In the paper, information of a patent document is divided into narrative text information, metadata information, and citation information. Narrative text information includes title, abstract and claims etc. of a patent document. Metadata information mainly includes the patent code, IPC codes, application date and inventor, etc. Citation information refers to the cited patents and citing patents of a patent document.

Phase III: Building classifier. After preprocessing of the sample patents, training process is conducted using different kind of classification algorithms. Classifiers are validated and compared by testing dataset afterwards.

Phase IV: Automatic patent classifying. In this phase, automatic classification of new patents using one of the satisfying classifiers above is conducted. Each patent is labeled by at least one of the classification topics. The issue of multi-label classification will be discussed in the following.

2.3. *Multi-label classification*

Multi-label classification is the task of assigning an object simultaneously to one or multiple classes. It is quite common in patent classification. Techniques and innovations in a patent can be used in many different applications; therefore, multi-label classification occurs widely in patent topic classification proposed in this paper. In the paper, MODEL-x proposed by Shen [10] is a reasonable choice to train our dataset in the case study section. Using MODEL-x, we train a binary classifier and analyze the performance of each class.

3. Case Study

3.1. *Data and experiment*

3.1.1. *Requirement analysis and data collection*

A system on a chip or system on chip (SoC or SOC) is an integrated circuit (IC) that integrates all components of a computer or other electronic system into a single chip. We have been working on a project to analyze SoC technology. According to the project's tech-mining requirement, we mainly focus on three parts of the SoC technology: SoC on digital television, Soc on personal mobile terminal, and the adaptive multimode RF SoC. An application-technical mixed topic hierarchy is built with the help of a team of SoC experts. The topic hierarchy has four layers and 201 leaves in total. Meanwhile, a number of 14414 patents relate to the SoC technology is collected from USPTO Patent Full-Text and Image Database, filed from 1976 to 2010. Our team of SoC experts manually classifies all the 14414 patents. Each patent document is labeled by 1 to 3 different categories. In our dataset, some classes have very little documents classified to them while others have a relatively huge amount. We just choose classes with more than 85 patent documents to conduct the experiment. After filtering, 28 classes covering 8316 documents are chosen at last.

3.1.2. Document preprocessing

After removing stop word in each document, word stemming is performed using the Porter stemmer. Term weighting is performed at word and code (e.g. the UPC code and reference patent number of a patent document) level by calculating the term frequency and inverse document frequency (TF-IDF) [11] of each attribute. We choose Title, Abstract, Claims, IPC, UPC, Reference and different combinations of them as the representation of a patent document to do experiments. Information Gain (IG) [12] is chosen to do feature selection.

3.1.3. Classifier building and validation

Three classical machine learning techniques, i.e. decision tree (DT), Naïve Bayes (NB), and support vector machine (SVM), are adopted to build classifiers. 10 fold cross validation is adopted to validate the quality of these algorithms. Performance of classifiers is measured using accuracy and average F1 values.

3.2. Result and analysis

Table 1 lists the classification performances based on single sections. Table 2 lists the classification performances based on different combinations of Title (T), Abstract (A), UPC (U), IPC (I), and Reference (R). It is obvious that satisfactory performances can be easily obtained using the combination of different sections as the document representation.

Table 1. Classification performances based on single sections of a patent document using three different machine learning algorithms.

		Title	Abstract	Claims	IPC	UPC	Reference
DT	accuracy	65.033%	84.012%	60.507%	46.97%	37.209%	5.565%
	average F1	0.65	0.84	0.603	0.507	0.396	0.046
NB	accuracy	66.570%	84.427%	67.110%	49.959%	40.449%	7.890%
	average F1	0.667	0.844	0.669	0.541	0.433	0.075
SVM	accuracy	67.857%	88.538%	70.474%	48.505%	39.161%	7.600%
	average F1	0.678	0.885	0.705	0.527	0.423	0.075

Table 2. Classification performances based on different combinations of a patent document sections using three different machine learning algorithms.

		T+A	T+U	T+I	T+R	A+I	A+U	A+R	U+R	I+R
DT	accuracy	98.677%	99.951%	100.0%	99.951%	100.0%	99.902%	100.0%	100.0%	100.0%
	average F1	0.978	1	1	1	1	0.999	1	1	1
NB	accuracy	100.0%	99.959%	100.0%	100.0%	100.0%	99.902%	100.0%	100.0%	100.0%
	average F1	1	1	1	1	1	0.999	1	1	1
SVM	accuracy	100.0%	99.959%	100.0%	100.0%	100.0%	100.0%	100.0%	100.0%	100.0%
	average F1	1	1	1	1	1	1	1	1	1

Table 3 lists the performance for classifying patents based on (i) IPC+ Reference and (ii) UPC+ Reference using NB, which is the best performed algorithm for metadata information and citation information. The table indicates that the more attribute number is, the higher average accuracy and F1 value are. Average F1 values are bigger than 0.8 when attribute number is more than 60.

Table 3. Average F1 value for different attribute number when classifying patents based on (i) IPC+ Reference (I+R) and (ii) UPC+ Reference (U+R) using Naïve Bayes.

NB		30	40	50	60	70	80	90	100	150
I+R	accuracy	57.018%	71.179%	71.179%	81.894%	85.465%	89.037%	92.608%	92.608%	100.0%
	average F1	0.55	0.695	0.695	0.807	0.846	0.885	0.925	0.925	1
U+R	accuracy	56.312%	70.598%	84.302%	85.797%	92.691%	96.263%	100.000%	100.00%	100.0%
	average F1	0.541	0.686	0.836	0.85	0.924	0.962	1	1	1

The experiment indicates that patent topic classification performs really poorly when using a single section of metadata information or citation information. But perfect performances are obtained when the document representation is based on the combinations of any two kinds of narrative text information, metadata information and citation information. Considering the merits of metadata and citation information of a patent described earlier, we draw a conclusion that using the combination of metadata information and citation information as the document representation, can not only improve the classification performance greatly, but also simplify the process of document preprocessing, improving the efficiency of classification.

4. Conclusion

The method proposed in the paper is a supplementary to traditional schemes of patent classification. Patents are classified according to a predefined hierarchy of technical topic, application topic or application-technical mixed topic. Automatic process of the method using machine learning techniques consists of four phases. A case study on SoC technology using DT, NB and SVM validates the feasibility of the method. From the experiment, we draw a conclusion that properly using the combination of narrative text information, metadata information and citation information as the document representation, can improve the classification performance greatly. The experiment result also demonstrate that automatic patent topic classification based on the combination of metadata information, namely IPC or UPC code, and citation information can not only obtain perfect performance, the process of document preprocessing can also be simplified greatly.

References

1. Montecchi T, Russo D and Liu Y, *Adv Eng Inform.* **C27**, 335 (2013).
2. Chen Y L and Chang Y C, *Inform Process Manag.* **C48**, 1017 (2012).
3. Lai K K and Wu S J, *Inform Process Manag.* **C41**, 313 (2005).
4. Fall C J, Törcsvári A, Fiévet P and Karetka G, *Expert Syst Appl.* **C26**, 269 (2004).
5. Loh H T, He C and Shen L, *World Patent Information*, **Cf28**, 6 (2006).
6. Tikk D, Biró G and Törcsvári A, *Emerging Technologies of Text Mining: Techniques and Applications. Idea Group Inc*, (2007).
7. Cong H and Tong L H, *Expert Syst Appl*, **C34**, 788 (2008).
8. Fall C J, Törcsvári A, Benzineb K, et al. ACM SIGIR Forum. (2003).
9. Griffiths T and Steyvers M. *P Natl A Sci*, **C101**, 5228 (2004).
10. Shen X, Boutell M, Luo J, and Brown C. *Electronic Imaging 2004. International Society for Optics and Photonics*. DOI 10.1117/12.523428.
11. Salton, Gerard, and Christopher Buckley, *Inform Process Manag.* **C24**, 513. (1988).
12. Yang Y and Pedersen J O. *ICML*. **Cf97**, 412 (1997).

OPENING AND CLOSING FROM IDEMPOTENT DILATIONS*

Nicolás Madrid[1] & Irina Perfilieva[2]

Institute for Research and Applications of Fuzzy Modeling,
University of Ostrava. Czech Republic.
[1] *nicolas.madrid@osu.cz*   [2] *irina.perfilieva@osu.cz*

In this paper we present a study aimed to define general openings and closing as specific morphological filters.[1] Specifically, we study how much openings and closing we can be define just by using idempotent dilations and erosions.

Keywords: Mathematical morphology, Openings, Closings

1. Introduction

The notions of opening and closing were introduced at first in the framework of topological spaces, later extended to the lattice of parts of a set and finally to complete lattices (for further details we refer to [2, Chapter V]). One of the most known ways to define openings and closings is by using morphological operators. Perhaps is due to the fact that, as Serra showed in [3, Chapter 1], every opening and closing can be generated by combining morphological *erosions* and *dilations*.

However, although specific studies of openings and closings has been done,[4] for the best of our knowledge none of them are aimed to find a minimal sets of dilations and erosions to generate all openings and closings. For example, it is well known that every bijective dilation and its respective erosion by adjointness[a] defines the same opening and closing: the identity. Finding a minimal set of dilations holding extra-properties and capable of generating the set of openings and closing is really useful from a theoretical point of view. In this paper we study the set of openings that can be generated by considering just idempotent dilations.

---

*This work was supported by the European Regional Development Fund projects CZ.1.05/1.1.00/02.0070 and CZ.1.07/2.3.00/30.0010
[a]see Section 2,Theorem 2.3

The structure of the paper is given as follows. In Section 2 we present the notions and theorems we use to prove our results. Subsequently, in Section 3 we show our main results. Finally in Section 4 we present conclusions and future works.

2. Preliminaries

The notions of opening and closing[2,4] are defined as follows.

Definition 2.1. Let L be a complete lattice and let $\psi\colon L \to L$ a mapping. We say that ψ is:

- *monotonic* if $x \le y$ implies $\psi(x) \le \psi(y)$ for all $x, y \in L$.
- *idempotent* if $\psi(\psi(x)) = \psi(x)$ for all $x \in L$.
- *extensive* if $x \le \psi(x)$ for all $x \in L$.
- *anti-extensive* $x \ge \psi(x)$ for all $x \in L$.
- an *opening* if it is monotonic, idempotent and anti-extensive.
- a *closing* if it is monotonic, idempotent and extensive.

Hereafter we use the greek letters α and γ to denote opening and closings respectively. Note that the set of openings (resp. closings) is a lattice structure with respect to the point-wise ordering induced by L. Moreover, one of the most important properties of the lattice of openings is that it is isomorphic to the lattice of subsets of L closed by supremum.[3,4] Let us recall that a subset $X \subseteq L$ is closed by supremum (resp. by infimum) if for all family of elements $Y \subseteq X$ we have $\sup Y \in X$ (resp. $\inf Y \in X$). Such isomorphism is giving by means of the set of invariance.

Definition 2.2. Given a mapping $\psi\colon L \to L$ the set of invariance of ψ is defined as $Inv(\psi) = \{x \in L \mid \psi(x) = x\}$.

Theorem 2.1.[4] *The set of invariance of every opening (resp. closing) is closed by supremum (resp. infimum). Conversely, given two sets $A, B \subseteq L$ closed by supremum and infimum respectively, the mappings $\alpha_A, \gamma_B\colon L \to L$ defined by $\alpha_A(x) = \sup\{y \in A \mid y \le x\}$ and $\gamma_B(x) = \inf\{y \in B \mid x \le y\}$ are the only opening and only closing respectively such that $Inv(\alpha) = A$ and $Inv(\beta) = B$.*

Perhaps one of the most known ways to define openings and closings is by using morphological operators. Specifically, opening and closing can be obtained just by combining morphological *erosions* and *dilations*.

Definition 2.3. [4] Let $(L_1, \le_1)$ and $(L_2, \le)$ be two complete lattices. A mapping $\varepsilon\colon L_1 \to L_2$ is called an erosion if for all $X \subseteq L_1$ we have

$\varepsilon(\inf X) = \inf_{x \in X} \varepsilon(x)$. Respectively, a mapping $\delta \colon L_2 \to L_1$ is called a dilation if for all $Y \subseteq L_2$ we have: $\delta(\sup Y) = \sup_{y \in Y} \delta(y)$

So, roughly speaking, every erosion commutes with infimum and so does dilation with supremum. The notion of adjoint pair determines a pretty relation between erosions and dilations. Let us recall that a pair (ε, δ) of mappings $\varepsilon \colon L_1 \to L_2$ and $\delta \colon L_2 \to L_1$ between complete lattices form an adjoint pair if and only if for every $x \in L_1$ and $y \in L_2$ we have

$$y \leq \varepsilon(x) \quad \text{if and only if} \quad \delta(y) \leq x$$

The use of the same letters than in the Definitions 2.3 is not casual, since there exists a certain equivalence between both notions. On the one hand, if (ε, δ) is an adjoint pair, then, ε is an erosion and δ is a dilation. On the other hand, the converse can be written in the following sense:

Theorem 2.2. [4] *Let $\varepsilon \colon L_1 \to L_2$ be an erosion (resp. dilation $\delta \colon L_2 \to L_1$). Then there exists exactly one dilation $\delta_\varepsilon \colon L_2 \to L_1$ (resp. erosion $\varepsilon_\delta \colon L_1 \to L_2$) such that $(\varepsilon, \delta_\varepsilon)$ (resp. $(\varepsilon_\delta, \delta)$) forms an adjoint pair. Specifically, such a dilation (resp. erosion) can be determined by the expression:*

$$\delta_\varepsilon(y) = \inf\{z \in L_2 \mid y \leq \varepsilon(z)\}$$
$$\left(\text{resp. } \varepsilon_\delta(x) = \sup\{z \in L_1 \mid \delta(z) \leq x\} \right)$$

for every $y \in L_2$ (resp. for every $x \in L_1$).

The notation used in Theorem 2.2 is used hereafter. An interesting relationship between dilations, erosions, openings and closings is given by the following result. Let us recall that the image of a mapping $\psi \colon L_1 \to L_2$ is given by $Im(\psi) = \{\psi(x) \mid x \in L_1\} \subseteq L_2$.

Theorem 2.3. [4] *Let (ε, δ) be an adjoint pair, then $\delta \circ \epsilon$ is the unique opening such that $Inv(\delta \circ \epsilon) = Im(\delta)$ and $\epsilon \circ \delta$ is the unique closing such that $Inv(\epsilon \circ \delta) = Im(\epsilon)$.*

3. Generating Opening from Idempotent Dilations

In this section we deal with the following question: given an opening α, is there any *idempotent dilation* δ such that $\alpha = \delta \circ \epsilon_\delta$? The following result shows that on totally ordered lattices, the answer of such a question is yes.

Theorem 3.1. *Let L be a totally ordered lattice and let $\alpha \colon L \to L$ be an opening. Then, there exists an idempotent dilation $\delta \colon L \to L$ such that $\alpha = \delta \circ \epsilon_\delta$.*

Proof. Let us consider the mapping $\gamma(x) = \inf\{y \in Inv(\alpha) \mid x \leq y\}$ and let us show that $\delta \colon L \to L$, given by the expression:

$$\delta(x) = \begin{cases} \alpha(x) & \text{if } \gamma(x) \notin Inv(\alpha) \\ \gamma(x) & \text{if } \gamma(x) \in Inv(\alpha) \end{cases} \tag{1}$$

is the dilation verifying $\alpha = \delta \circ \epsilon_\delta$. Note, first of all, that if $x \in Inv(\alpha)$ then $\delta(x) = x$, since in such a case we always have $\gamma(x) = x$. Moreover, if $x \notin Inv(\alpha)$ then, we have either $\gamma(x) = x$ or $\gamma(x) \neq x$. In the first case we have that $\delta(x) = \alpha(x) \neq x$ and in the second case, since $\gamma(x) \neq x$ and $\alpha(x) \neq x$, $\delta(x) \neq x$ as well. So, if we prove that δ is a dilation, by applying Theorem 2.3 we would conclude the proof, since $Im(\delta) = Inv(\alpha)$.

To prove that δ is a dilation, we need to prove previously the monotonicity of δ. So let $x, y \in L$ such that $x \leq y$. If $\gamma(x) = \gamma(y)$ then there are not $z \in Inv(\alpha)$ such that $x < z < y$, therefore $\delta(x) = \delta(y)$. If $\gamma(x) < \gamma(y)$ then there are three straightforward cases, namely: $\gamma(x), \gamma(y) \in Inv(\alpha)$; $\gamma(x), \gamma(y) \notin Inv(\alpha)$; and $\gamma(x) \notin Inv(\alpha), \gamma(y) \in Inv(\alpha)$. If $\gamma(x) \in Inv(\alpha)$ and $\gamma(y) \notin Inv(\alpha)$, then, by definition of γ, there exists $z \in Inv(\alpha)$ such that $x \leq z < y$. That implies that $\delta(x) = \gamma(x) \leq z \leq \alpha(y) = \delta(y)$.

Let us prove now that δ is a dilation, that is, that for every $X \subseteq L$, we have $\sup_{x \in X} \delta(x) = \delta(\sup(X))$. Let us distinguish cases:

• Let us assume firstly that $\sup(x_i) \notin Inv(\alpha)$. Then, as $Inv(\alpha)$ is closed under supremum, there exists $Y \subseteq X$ such that $y \notin Inv(\alpha)$ for all $y \in Y$, $\sup Y = \sup X$ and verifying $[\inf Y, \sup Y] \cap Inv(\alpha) = \emptyset$. The equality $[\inf Y, \sup Y] \cap Inv(\alpha) = \emptyset$ implies that there exist $c \in L$ such $\delta(y) = c$ for all $y \in Y$ according to the definition given in equation (1). Note that $\delta(\sup X) = \delta(\sup Y) = c$ as well. Moreover, as L is totally ordered, δ monotonic and $\sup Y = \sup X$ we have $\sup_{y \in Y} \delta(y) = \sup_{x \in X} \delta(x)$. Hence $\delta(\sup X) = c = \sup_{y \in Y} \delta(y) = \sup_{x \in X} \delta(x)$

• Let us assume secondly that $\sup X \in Inv(\alpha)$ and that there exists $Y \subseteq X$ such that $y \in Inv(\alpha)$ for all $y \in Y$ and $\sup Y = \sup X$. So we have $\delta(\sup X) = \delta(\sup Y) = \sup_{y \in Y} y = \sup_{y \in Y} \delta(y) = \sup_{x \in X} \delta(x)$

• Finally, let us assume that $\sup(x_i) \in Inv(\alpha)$ but the previous case does not hold. Then there exists $Y \subseteq X$ such that $y \notin Inv(\alpha)$ for all $y \in Y$, $\sup Y = \sup X$ and verifying that the interval $(\inf Y, \sup Y)$ and $Inv(\alpha)$ are disjoint. The equality $(\inf Y, \sup Y) \cap Inv(\alpha) = \emptyset$ implies that $\delta(y) = \gamma(y) = \sup X$ for all $y \in Y$ according to the definition of δ and γ. Therefore $\delta(\sup X) = \delta(\sup Y) = \sup X = \sup_{y \in Y} \delta(y) = \sup_{x \in X} \delta(x)$ $\qquad\square$

Let us continue by exposing that, in general terms, no every opening can be obtained directly by means of idempotent dilations.

Example 3.1. Let us a consider the complete lattice given by the following Hasse diagram and the opening α defined below:

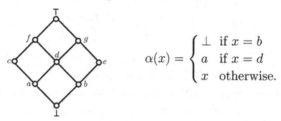

$$\alpha(x) = \begin{cases} \bot & \text{if } x = b \\ a & \text{if } x = d \\ x & \text{otherwise.} \end{cases}$$

Firstly, it is easy to check that α is actually an opening. Secondly, note that α is not a dilation, since $\alpha(\sup\{d,c\}) = \alpha(f) = f$ but $\sup\{\alpha(d),\alpha(c)\} = \sup\{a,c\} = c$. Finally, let us assume by reductio ad absurdum that there exists an idempotent dilation δ such that $\alpha = \delta \circ \epsilon_\delta$. Then, by Theorem 2.3, we know that $Im(\delta) = Inv(\alpha)$. Moreover, as δ is idempotent, $\delta(x) = x$ for all $x \in Inv(\alpha)$. Thus, on the one hand we have $\sup\{c,\delta(d)\} = \sup\{\delta(c),\delta(d)\} = \delta(\sup\{c,d\}) = \delta(f) = f$, and on the other hand $\sup\{e,\delta(d)\} - \sup\{\delta(e),\delta(d)\} = \delta(\sup\{e,d\}) = \delta(g) = g$. But the only element $x \in L$ such that $\sup(c,x) = f$ and $\sup(e,x) = g$ is $x = d$. So $\delta(d) = d$, which contradicts that $Im(\delta) = Inv(\alpha)$. Summarizing, there is not any idempotent dilation δ defined on L such that $\alpha = \delta \circ \epsilon_\delta$.

In the rest of this section we present some results establishing sufficient conditions to ensure that one opening can be obtained from an idempotent dilation. The first of them is given on the context of cartesian products of lattices. We use the notation $L^n = L \times .^{(n)}. \times L$.

Proposition 3.1. *Let L be a totally ordered lattice and let $\alpha_i \colon L \to L$ be an opening for each $i \in \{1, \ldots, n\}$. Then the opening $\alpha \colon L^n \to L^n$ given by*

$$\alpha(x_1, \ldots, x_n) = (\alpha_1(x_1), \ldots, \alpha_n(x_n))$$

can be obtained from a corresponding idempotent dilation $\delta \colon L^n \to L^n$ by $\alpha = \delta \circ \epsilon_\delta$.

Proof. The result can be obtained easily as a consequence of Theorem 3.1. □

The second result is given on the context of finite lattices.

Proposition 3.2. *Let α be an opening defined on a finite lattice L. If $Inv(\alpha)$ is closed by infimum then there exists an idempotent dilation $\delta \colon L \to L$ such that $\alpha = \delta \circ \epsilon_\delta$.*

Proof. Let us show that the mapping $\delta\colon L \to L$ determined by the expression $\delta(x) = \inf\{y \in Inv(\alpha) \mid y \geq x\}$ is an idempotent dilation $\delta\colon L \to L$ such that $\alpha = \delta \circ \epsilon_\delta$. Note that δ is the closing such that $Inv(\delta) = Inv(\alpha)$; so it is idempotent and $Im(\delta) = Inv(\alpha)$. Moreover, if we prove that δ is a dilation as well, by applying Theorem 2.3 we conclude the proof.

Note that, as L is finite, δ is a dilation if and only if $\delta(\sup\{x_1, x_2\}) = \sup\{\delta(x_1), \delta(x_2)\}$ for all $x_1, x_2 \in L$. So, let $x_1, x_2 \in L$ and let us show firstly that $\delta(\sup(x_1, x_2)) \leq \sup(\delta(x_1), \delta(x_2))$. As δ is a closing, we have $x_1 \leq \delta(x_1)$ and $x_2 \leq \delta(x_2)$. So $\sup\{x_1, x_2\} \leq \sup\{\delta(x_1), \delta(x_2)\}$. By using now that $Inv(\alpha)$ is closed by supremum and that $\delta(x_1), \delta(x_2) \in Inv(\alpha)$, we have that $\sup\{\delta(x_1), \delta(x_2)\} \in Inv(\alpha)$. Thus, by monotonicity of δ we obtain $\delta(\sup\{x_1, x_2\}) \leq \delta(\sup\{\delta(x_1), \delta(x_2)\}) = \sup\{\delta(x_1), \delta(x_2)\}$

Let us prove now that $\delta(\sup\{x_1, x_2\}) \geq \sup\{\delta(x_1), \delta(x_2)\}$. By definition of δ and finitude of L, we have that there exists $y_1, y_2 \in Inv(\alpha)$ such that $y_1 \geq x_1, y_2 \geq x_2, \delta(x_1) = y_1$ and $\delta(x_2) = y_2$. Then, as $\sup\{y_1, y_2\} \geq \sup\{x_1, x_2\}$ and $\sup\{y_1, y_2\} \in Inv(\alpha)$ we have $\delta(\sup\{x_1, x_2\}) = \inf\{y \in Inv(\alpha) \mid y \geq \sup\{x_1, x_2\}\} \leq \sup\{y_1, y_2\} = \sup\{\delta(x_1), \delta(x_2)\}$. □

4. Conclusions and Future Work

In this paper we have provided three theoretical results. The first of them shows that, in totally ordered lattices, every opening can be defined in terms of an idempotent dilation. The second and third give some condition to ensure that specific openings can be obtained form idempotent dilations. Moreover, all obtained results can be easily rewritten in terms of closings.

As a future work we want to obtain a subset of dilations, by imposing extra properties, able to define the set of openings on a lattice. Moreover, we want to apply that "hypothetical" result to compare the inverse F-transforms on a complete lattice[5] with its set of openings and closings.

References

1. G. G. Matheron, *Random sets and integral geometry*. Series in probability and mathematical statistics, Wiley,1975.
2. G. Birkhoff, *Lattice theory*, in Colloquium Publications, American Mathematical Society, (Third Edition), 1967.
3. J. Serra, *Image Analysis and Mathematical Morphology*, Academic Press, Inc., Orlando, FL, USA, 1988.
4. C. Ronse and H. J. A. M. Heijmans, *The algebraic basis of mathematical morphology* CVGIP: Image Understanding. **54**, 74 (1991).
5. I. Perfilieva, *Fuzzy transforms: Theory and applications*. Fuzzy Sets and Systems **157**, 993 (2006).

A ADJUSTMENT STRATEGY OF REGIONAL ENVIRONMENTAL QUALITY ASSESSMENT BASED ON GROUP DIFFERENCES[*]

BIN LUO

College of chemistry and environment protection , Southwest University for Nationalities, Chengdu, 610041, P.R.China

XIAOHONG LIU

College of Management, Southwest University for Nationalities, Chengdu, 610041, P.R.China

Environmental quality plays a very important role in the human survival and development, and therefore environmental quality assessment must be effectively carried out. The paper presents an adjustment regional environmental quality assessment based on differences of group bearing capacity, the strategy will help people to distinguish environmental quality real impacts on people and help people pay attention to and protect environment quality.

1. Introduction

Environmental protection is a global problem, natural disasters and human activities have caused serious damages to the environment, and there have been ten environmental problems that threaten to human. It is one of effective measures to further improve people's awareness of environmental quality in environmental protection. The OECD has done a lot of work to promote environmental education, so the United Nations Environment Program designated June fifth of each year as the world environment day in 1972. Over the past 40 years, various theme activities in the world environment day greatly promote the world environmental education and environmental protection. In some cases, the public do not care too much or believe in objective environment quality reports although quality reports have their objectivity and certain effects.

---

[*] This work is partially supported by State Bureau of Foreign Expert's Affairs project of China (grant No. 2013-12) and supported by grant 12XNZ007 of State Ethnic Affairs Commission of China, and supported by grant 2014XWD-S1202 of Southwest University for Nationalities.

This paper puts forward a kind of adjustment model for environmental quality assessment based on differences of the group bearing capacity so as to improve the effectiveness of the objective environment quality reports. First, this paper presents the basic concepts and the basic hypotheses. Second, in order to enhance the public awareness of environmental quality, it puts forward a forming process of environmental quality awareness. Third, the adjustment algorithm of the environmental quality assessment is established by the application of fuzzy comprehensive evaluation. Finally, it illustrates the application of the algorithm through an example.

2. Basic concepts and hypothesis

2.1. *Basic concepts*

The basic concepts relate to this paper are the group differences of environmental quality and adjustment of regional environmental quality assessment. Regarding this, the paper hereby specially makes the following explanations.

The environmental quality of group differences: It refers to the people's subjective perception of objective environmental quality. In a region (such as province, city, county, township and community etc), people have bearing capacity based on physical or psychological perception of environmental quality. Difference of capability to bear environmental quality leads to group bearing difference. Generally speaking, in a region, different types of environmental qualities show directly differences of group bearing capacity and finally reveal the degree of group's acceptance or rejection to objective environmental quality.

Adjustment of regional environmental quality assessment: It refers to the view of environmental quality assessment according to the idea of differences of group bearing capacity to environmental quality. It puts forward adjustment strategy of environmental quality reports because of differences of group bearing capacity in a region and adjusts the strategies of comprehensive factors.

2.2. *Basic hypothesis*

The paper mainly proposes two basic hypotheses about regional group division and adjustment results of regional environmental quality assessment.

Regional group division: suppose the total number in a region is N, different mark of environment capacity is ε, the number of group division is S_i or S_j ($i = 1,2,...,n$, $j = 1,2,...,n$) , group characteristics is $\|S_i\|$ and $\|S_j\|$ respectively.

$$(1) \bigcup_{i=1}^{n} S_i = N \; ; \; (2) \; S_i \bigcap S_j = \phi \; , \; i \neq j \; ; \; (3) \; \Big\| \|S_i\| - \|S_j\| \Big\| > \varepsilon \; , \; i \neq j$$

Adjustment results of regional environmental quality assessment: suppose the results of objective environment quality report in a region are A, the results of environmental quality adjustment in a region are B, adjustment strategy of difference of environmental bearing capability is λ,

$$(1) \; \lambda = f(\lambda_1, \; \lambda_2, \; ..., \; \lambda_n) = \lambda_1 \circ \lambda_2 \circ ... \circ \lambda_n \; ; \; (2) \; B = A \circ \lambda \; , \; \circ$$

synthetic operator.

3. A process of awareness of environmental quality

In this paper, the model of a forming process of awareness of environmental quality will be put forward to according to idea of differences of group bearing capacity to environmental quality, as shown in Figure 1.

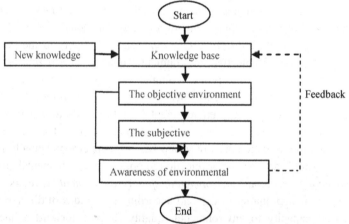

Figure 1   the model of a forming process of awareness of environmental quality

The terms shown in Figure 1 are as follows:

Knowledge database: it refers to database in which people save environmental information. Perceptual information of environmental quality has been formed on the basis of the people life experience or expertise. Environmental quality knowledge base which people own are the basis for carrying out the adjustment regional environmental quality assessment, environmental quality knowledge established by each group need be accumulated for a long time and constantly updated.

New knowledge: it is found by people in the process of their perception of environmental quality. With the improvement of people's living conditions, people wish to constantly improve environmental quality and new knowledge about environment is constantly emerging.

The objective environment: it exists objectively and does not change even if the crowd's environmental situation has been changed in the region, it presents regional environmental reports are issued by the relevant departments of the government or the authorized certification.

The subjective environment: it refers to different groups in the region are subjectively perceptive of environmental situations. Based on the objective environment, the sampling and calculation through different groups reflect perceptual results of environmental quality coming from different groups.

Awareness of environmental quality: it refers to the people's awareness of environmental quality in a region. Through the perception of the environment, people accept or reject the objective environment quality reports to some degree.

4. Algorithm of adjustment strategy of regional environmental quality assessment

In order to relatively effectively evaluate group awareness of the regional environmental quality, this paper suggests the two stage models of adjustment strategy of regional environmental quality assessment: evaluation of groups division **(S1)** and evaluation of adjustment strategy of environmental quality **(S2)**, as shown in Figure 2.

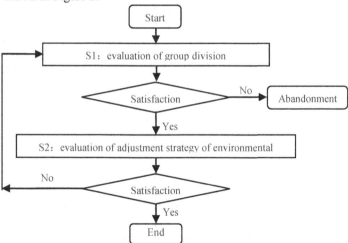

Figure 2   the algorithm flow of adjustment strategy of regional environmental quality assessment

The group division should synthesize each group property (such as constitution, sensitivity, vulnerability and sustainability etc) which should conform to hypothesis of the group division. According to the expert assessment of each property of group on satisfactory affiliation value (Li Kete five level scales: *very satisfactory, satisfactory, ordinary, dissatisfactory* and *very dissatisfactory*), group division results may be set up and take the aggregation operator calculation and determine evaluation results of the group division.

In algorithm of the adjustment strategy of regional environmental quality assessment, evaluation (**S1** evaluation) of group division is a necessary condition. If the evaluation results does not meet the requirements the group division should be given up, or it will directly affect the effectiveness of the strategy adjustment of regional environmental quality; after evaluating results meet the requirements, the second stage starts.

The second stage (**S2** evaluation): i.e. sufficient condition. It is necessary to comprehensively consider multi-factors of space, time, intensity and harm etc in the adjustment strategy of regional environment and some content boundaries of these multi-factors are not distinct. Therefore, adjustment strategy of regional environmental should synthesize strategies (such as space, time, intensity and harm). Similarly, each strategy should be consistent with hypothesis of adjustment results of the regional environmental quality assessment. According to the expert assessment of each strategy on satisfactory affiliation value (Li Kete five level scales: *very satisfactory, satisfactory, ordinary, dissatisfactory* and *very dissatisfactory*), adjustment strategy of regional environmental should be established and take the aggregation operator calculation and determine assessment results of environmental adjustment strategy.

In the algorithm of adjustment strategy of regional environmental quality assessment, evaluation of environmental adjustment strategy (**S2** evaluation) is a sufficient condition. If the evaluating results do not meet the requirements, return and readjust the **S1** evaluation; after the evaluating results meet the requirements, results of comprehensive adjustment strategy in the regional environmental quality assessment can be calculated.

5. A numerical example

We invite some experts in the field to evaluate group division in a regional and environmental assessment. If evaluation indexes of the first stage (S1) and the second stage (S2 evaluation) are four. The Li Kete five level scales is used as evaluation comments(very satisfactory, satisfactory, ordinary, dissatisfactory and very dissatisfactory) and get the fuzzy matrix of evaluation coefficient $\widetilde{T}(1)$ and $\widetilde{T}(2)$ on two stages after comprehensive expert opinion are obtained. If

$\alpha = 0.6$, the weight vector of each stage $W_{p1} = W_{P2} = (0.5 \; 0.5)$ respectively. Choose fuzzy set operator as $(.,+)$.

$$\widetilde{T}(1) = \begin{pmatrix} 0.65 & 0.35 & 0 & 0 & 0 \\ 0.65 & 0.35 & 0 & 0 & 0 \\ 0.7 & 0.3 & 0 & 0 & 0 \\ 0.7 & 0.3 & 0 & 0 & 0 \end{pmatrix} \qquad \widetilde{T}(2) = \begin{pmatrix} 0.7 & 0.3 & 0 & 0 & 0 \\ 0.7 & 0.3 & 0 & 0 & 0 \\ 0.8 & 0.2 & 0 & 0 & 0 \\ 0.8 & 0.2 & 0 & 0 & 0 \end{pmatrix}$$

$L(1) = (0.675 \quad 0.325 \quad 0 \quad 0 \quad 0)$, $b_{11} \geq \alpha = 0.6$, **S1** evaluation passes

$L(2) = (0.75 \quad 0.25 \quad 0 \quad 0 \quad 0)$, $b_{21} \geq \alpha = 0.6$, **S2** evaluation passes

$$\Delta = R \circ W = \begin{pmatrix} 0.6 & 0 & 0 & 0 & 0 \\ 0.6 & 0 & 0 & 0 & 0 \end{pmatrix} \circ (0.5 \quad 0.5) = (0.6 \quad 0 \quad 0 \quad 0 \quad 0)$$

According to the principle of maximum subordinate degree, the regional environmental adjustment strategy is relatively satisfactory

6. Conclusion

The key factors that people really pay attention to environmental quality are people's perception of the environmental quality. we put forward the model of regional environmental quality assessment based on the differences of groups to bear the environmental quality. Based on the objective environment quality reports and according to the difference of the group perception of environmental quality, it corrects the objective environment quality reports through the application of fuzzy comprehensive evaluation and improves the actual application effect of environmental quality assessment.

References

1. Brian M. Dpwd et al, Agricultural nonpoint source water pollution policy: the case of California's Central Coast. *Agriculture, Ecosystems and Environment*.128 (2008).
2. Shen Lei, Gao Li Managing energy and mineral resources development and pollution control coordinately in the western China, *China population resources environment*. 10,23(2013).
3. Zhou Shen Xian, The development course and result of environmental protection in China, *Environmental Protection*.14, 41(2013).
4. Han Dong Mei, Jin Su Qin, Analysis of Chinese agricultural and rural environmental protection policy, *Review of Economic Research*, 43(2013).

A FUZZY DOMAIN ADAPTATION METHOD BASED ON SELF-CONSTRUCTING FUZZY NEURAL NETWORK

PENG HAO* and GUANGQUAN ZHANG and VAHID BEHBOOD

*Centre for Quantum Computation and Intelligent Systems
Faculty of Engineering and Information Technology, University of Technology Sydeny,
Sydeny, NSW 2007, Austrialia*
** E-mail: Peng.Hao@student.uts.edu.au, Guangquan.Zhang@uts.edu.au,
Vahid.Behbood@uts.edu.au*

ZHENG ZHENG

*School of Automation Science and Electrical Engineering, Bei Hang University,
Beijing, 100191, China
E-mail: zhengz@buaa.edu.cn*

Domain adaptation addresses the problem of how to utilize a model trained in the source domain to make predictions for target domain when the distribution between two domains differs substantially and labeled data in target domain is costly to collect for retraining. Existed studies are incapable to handle the issue of information granularity, in this paper, we propose a new fuzzy domain adaptation method based on self-constructing fuzzy neural network. This approach models the transferred knowledge supporting the development of the current models granularly in the form of fuzzy sets and adapts the knowledge using fuzzy similarity measure to reduce prediction error in the target domain.

Keywords: Domain adaptation; Fuzzy Neural Network; Fuzzy Similarity.

1. Introduction

Traditional machine learning techniques have been proved to be effective when assuming the training and test data are sampled from the same distribution. However, this assumption does not hold in reality due to the quick change of external environment, which means that we can not make a direct use of out-dated model for a new task. Moreover, to gather enough manually labeled data for retraining a classifier is also a tough task in many practical applications, like computer vision,[1] object recognition,[2] natural language processing.[3] Domain adaptation seeks to solve the problem of generalizing a model trained in a previous domain (source domain) to perform predictions in a different but related domain (target domain) where we have little or no labeled data. Existed domain adaptation methods seek to solve this problem primarily in three ways: re-weighting source instances iteratively,[3] finding the common features shared between source and target domain,[4] or learning a new representation which is instrinsic in both domains.[1,5,6] Although many domain adaptation methods have been proposed, the performance is not yet acceptable. One key problem is lack of considering information granularity.[7,8] It is intuitively legitimate to anticipate that, while the models developed on the basis of the previously available experimental data produce numeric outcomes, the transferred knowledge supporting the development of the current models becomes granular (e.g., in the form of fuzzy sets) to capture the resemblance of the previously encountered environment with the current situations and account for differences. In this paper, in order to handle this key problem and take the information granularity into domain adaptation, we model the transferred knowledge granularly in the form of fuzzy sets and propose a new fuzzy domain adaptation method based on self-constructing fuzzy neural network.

The rest of this paper is organized as follows. Section 2 gives out necessary notations about domain adaptation and a brief introduction of self-constructing fuzzy neural network. In Section 3, we describe our proposed method. We summarize the paper and point out future study in Section 4.

2. Problem settings and notations

In this section, we introduce some notations for domain adaptation problem, then we briefly describe the components and functions of self-constructing fuzzy neural network.

2.1. *Notations*

Formally, let $D_s^l = \{(x_1^s, y_1^s), (x_2^s, y_2^s), \cdots, (x_{n_s}^s, y_{n_s}^s)\}$ denotes labeled source domain instances which are drawn from some distribution $P_s(x, y)$, where $x_i^s \in \chi^s \subset R^n$ represents a n dimensional feature vector developed from feature space χ^s and y_i^s is the corresponding label value from label space $Y = \{1, 2, \cdots, m\}$. Similarly, let $D_t^u = \{x_1^t, x_2^t, \cdots, x_{n_t}^t\}$ denotes unlabeled target domain dataset which is sampled from distributin $P_t(x, y)$, where $x_i^t \in \chi^t \subset R^n$. In the setting of domain adaptation, as the marginal distribution $P_s(\chi^s) \neq P_t(\chi^t)$, so that $P_s(x, y) \neq P_t(x, y)$. Regarding fuzzy domain adaptation, let $x_i^s \in \Lambda^s$ and $x_i^t \in \Lambda^t$, where $\Lambda^s = \{A_{ij}^s, i = 1, 2, \cdots, n, j = 1, 2, \cdots, r\}$ and $\Lambda^t = \{A_{ij}^t, i = 1, 2, \cdots, n, j = 1, 2, \cdots, r\}$ are the set of membership functions of fuzzy sets (clusters). n denotes the dimension of the data and r is the number of fuzzy sets generated in each dimension. So that fuzzy domain adaptation problem can be described as $\exists A_{ij}^s \in \Lambda^s$ and $A_{ij}^t \in \Lambda^t$, $A_{ij}^s \neq A_{ij}^t$. Our objective is to learn a classifier $f(x): \chi^t \rightarrow Y$ for unlabeled target domain data D_t^u by exploiting the knowledge of labeled source domain data D_s^l .

2.2. *Self-constructing fuzzy neural network*

Our method is based on self-constructing fuzzy neural network,[9] which contains five layers with n input nodes and one output node. The learned rules have the form

$$\textit{If } x_1 \textit{ is } A_{1k} \textit{ and } x_2 \textit{ is } A_{2k} \textit{ and } \cdots \textit{ and } x_n \textit{ is } A_{nk}$$
$$\textit{then } y \textit{ is } y_m \tag{1}$$

where A_{ik} is the kth fuzzy set generated by the ith dimensional variable of an input instance $\vec{x}$.

Layer1: Input layer. Each node represents one dimension of an input data.
Layer2: Fuzzification layer. In this layer, each node acts as a fuzzy set for one of the input variables in Layer1 based on the idea of clustering. Different fuzzy sets depict different rules, so the number of fuzzy sets formed by an input variable in Layer1 is equal to the number of fuzzy rules. Gaussian function is adopted to calculate the membership of an input variable belonging to a fuzzy set as follows:

$$A_{ik}(x_i) = exp\left\{ -\left(\frac{(x_i - \mu_{ik})^2}{\sigma_{ik}^2} \right) \right\} \tag{2}$$

where μ_{ik} and σ_{ik}^2 denotes the kth center and wideth of the fuzzy set respectively corresponding to the ith input variable x_i.
Layer3: Rule layer. Each node represents a fuzzy rule. The antecedent mathcing of a rule is expressed as:

$$E_k(\vec{x}) = \exp\left\{ \prod_{i=1}^{n} A_{ik}(x_i) \right\}, k = 1, 2, \cdots, r \tag{3}$$

where $E_k(\vec{x})$ denotes the firing strength of rule R_k when instance $\vec{x}$ is entered, and r is the total number of rule nodes.
Layer4: Defuzzification layer. There is only one node which sums up outputs from all the rule nodes and performs defizzification as follows:

$$y_m(\vec{x}) = \frac{\sum_{k=1}^{r} \omega_k E_k(\vec{x})}{\sum_{k=1}^{r} E_k(\vec{x})} \tag{4}$$

where ω_k denotes the kth connecting parameter and $y_m(\vec{x})$ is the output value based on the input instance $\vec{x}$. Generally, all the connecting parameters are selected randomly in the beginning.

Layer5: Output layer. There is only one label node in this layer which converts the output value in Layer4 to the label information. In binary classification problem, if $y_m(\vec{x}) \geq T_s$, where T_s controls the conversion degree, then the label node outputs "1" for the input data $\vec{x}$, otherwise outputs "0" instead.

3. Fuzzy domain adaptation based on self-constructing fuzzy neural network

The partition of input space determines the number of fuzzy rules generated. Each partition represents a specific rule and has a simple interpretation: it projects a Guassian function on each dimension and generates a cluster based on the center and variance of the Guassian function. As the source and target domain differ in distribution, the Guassion functions will be different. If the difference is essential, an additional cluster may need to be added to in the target domain and the output will be computed with existing similar clusters, because it is intuitive to believe that the more close of two instances mearsured in a Gaussian function the more similar they are in the knowledge representation. Our method can be accomplished in three steps as described below.

Step 1. Learning initial structure and connecting parameters

In this stage, we adopt the same structure and parameter learning method proposed in Ref. 9. Based on labeled source domain instances D_s^l, initial network structure can be formed in an unsupervised way and supervised gradient decent is applied with the loss function

$$F = \frac{1}{2} \sum_{j=1}^{n_s} (y_l^d(\vec{x}_j) - y_l(\vec{x}_j))^2 \tag{5}$$

to learn optimal connecting parameters for each initial rule node and to upgrade both center and wideth for each fuzzy set membership function. $y_l^d(\vec{x}_j)$ and $y_l(\vec{x}_j)$ denotes the desired and actual label of input instance $\vec{x}_j$, respectively.

Step 2. Adjusting the initial structure with target domain instances

Given a new input $\vec{x}_t$ in D_t^u, we can calculate the firing strength of this input to all existed rules in equation (3). If there is any a rule R_k that satisfies $E_k(\vec{x}_t) \geq T_D$, where T_D is a user defined threshold value, then the instance $\vec{x}_t$ can get the output variable through those fired rules associated with those corresponding connecting parameters in equation(4) and finally obtain the data label. If not, a new rule node R_{new} and n new fuzzy sets are added into the network, and the center and wideth of each new fuzzy set membership function is defined in Ref. 9 as following:

$$\mu_{(r+1)i} = \vec{x}_t^i, i = 1, \cdots, n \tag{6}$$

$$\sigma_{(r+1)i} = \frac{-1}{\beta}\left(\frac{1}{\ln arg \max\limits_{1 \le k \le r}(E_k(\vec{x}_t))}\right), i = 1, \cdots, n \tag{7}$$

where $\vec{x}_t^i$ is the ith dimensional variable of input data $\vec{x}_t$ and β controls the overlap degree between two fuzzy sets.

Step 3. Learning new connecting parameters

To learn the new connecting parameter for each newly generated rule node, we need to compare each new fuzzy set with all the existed ones. The fuzzy similarity measure in Ref. 9 is adopted:

$$S(A, B) = \frac{M \mid A \cap B \mid}{M \mid A \cup B \mid} = \frac{M \mid A \cap B \mid}{\sigma_1\sqrt{\pi} + \sigma_2\sqrt{\pi} - M \mid A \cap B \mid} \tag{8}$$

$$M \mid A \cap B \mid = \sum_{x \in U}(min[u_A(x), u_B(x)]) =$$
$$= \frac{1}{2}\frac{h^2[c_2 - c_1 + \sqrt{\pi}(\sigma_1 + \sigma_2)]}{\sqrt{\pi}(\sigma_1 + \sigma_2)} + \frac{1}{2}\frac{h^2[c_2 - c_1 + \sqrt{\pi}(\sigma_1 - \sigma_2)]}{\sqrt{\pi}(\sigma_2 - \sigma_1)} \tag{9}$$
$$+ \frac{1}{2}\frac{h^2[c_2 - c_1 - \sqrt{\pi}(\sigma_1 + \sigma_2)]}{\sqrt{\pi}(\sigma_1 - \sigma_2)}$$

where $S(A, B)$ represents the fuzzy similarity between two fuzzy sets A and B and $h(\cdot) = max\{0, \cdot\}$. Membership functions of two fuzzy sets A and B are $\mu_A(x) = exp\{-(x - c_1)^2/\sigma_1^2\}$ and $\mu_B(x) = exp\{-(x - c_2)^2/\sigma_2^2\}$, respectively, and we assume $c_1 \ge c_2$.

Ranking on the fuzzy similarity value, the most similar existed fuzzy set associated with the most similar existed fuzzy rule can be picked out. We then caculate average weight as the new connecting parameter in the formula below:

$$\omega_{new} = \frac{\sum_{i=1}^{n}(S(A_{ik}, A_{i-new}) \times \omega_k)}{\sum \omega_k} \tag{10}$$

where A_{i-new} and A_{ik} denotes, respectively, the new fuzzy set and the most similar existed fuzzy set generated by the new input variable $\vec{x}_t^i$, and ω_k is the corresponding rule node's connecting parameter.

After the new connecting parameter has been fixed, the output value for the new input instance $\vec{x}_t$ can be calculated in quation (4) based on the new network and the data label can be also obtained sequentially.

4. Conclusion and future work

Although there are tremendous studies in the field of domain adaptation, the role of information granularity is not yet investigated well. In this paper, a new fuzzy domain adaptation method based on self-constructing fuzzy neural network is proposed. It models the transferred knowledge from source domain to target domain in the form of fuzzy sets, and utilizes the fuzzy similarity measure to adapt knowledge for predicting target domain instances. Applying the proposed approach on the benchmark data sets, analysing experimental results and comparing with other domain adaptation mehods will be the next step in this study.

Acknowledgments

The work presented in this paper was supported by the Australian Research Council (DP 140101366) and China Scholarship Council (No. 201306020023).

References

1. B. Gong, Y. Shi, F. Sha and K. Grauman, Geodesic flow kernel for unsupervised domain adaptation, in *Computer Vision and Pattern Recognition, IEEE Conference on*, 2012.
2. R. Gopalan, R. Li and R. Chellappa, Domain adaptation for object recognition: An unsupervised approach, in *Computer Vision, IEEE International Conference on*, 2011.
3. J. Jiang and C. Zhai, Instance weighting for domain adaptation in nlp, in *Association for Computational Linguistics*, 2007.
4. M. Chen, K. Q. Weinberger and J. Blitzer, Co-training for domain adaptation, in *Advances in Neural Information Processing Systems 24*, eds. J. Shawe-Taylor, R. Zemel, P. Bartlett, F. Pereira and K. Weinberger 2011 pp. 2456–2464.
5. S. J. Pan, I. W. Tsang, J. T. Kwok and Q. Yang, *Neural Networks, IEEE Transactions on* **22**, 199 (2011).
6. M. Long, J. Wang, G. Ding, S. Pan and P. Yu, *Knowledge and Data Engineering, IEEE Transactions on* **PP**, 1 (2013).
7. V. Behbood, J. Lu and G. Zhang, *Industrial Informatics, IEEE Transactions on* **PP**, 1 (2013).
8. X. Yang, G. Zhang, J. Lu and J. Ma, *Fuzzy Systems, IEEE Transactions on* **19**, 105 (2011).
9. C.-T. Lin, C.-M. Yeh, S.-F. Liang, J.-F. Chung and N. Kumar, *Fuzzy Systems, IEEE Transactions on* **14**, 31 (2006).

AN APPROACH VIA FUZZY SETS THEORY FOR PREDATOR-PREY MODEL*

MAGDA DA SILVA PEIXOTO

Department of Physics, Chemistry and Mathematics, Federal University of São Carlos (UFSCar), Rodovia João Leme dos Santos, Km 110, Sorocaba. São Paulo, 18052-780, Brazil

LAÉCIO CARVALHO DE BARROS; RODNEY CARLOS BASSANEZY

Department of Applied Mathematics, State University of Campinas (UNICAMP), PO box: 6065, Campinas. São Paulo, 13083-859, Brazil

This paper describes a methodology based in Fuzzy Sets Theory to elaborate a model that studies the interaction between the prey, *Aphis glycines* (soybean aphids), and the predator, *Orius insidiosus*. The aim of this investigation has been to develop a simple and specific methodology to make a decision on the control of this prey.

1. Introduction

The soybean aphid, *Aphis glycines* (Hemiptera: Aphididae), is an invasive herbivore new to North America. It was first discovered in North America in Wisconsin in late July 2000 infesting soybean crop. Many natural enemies have been observed to attack this pest. Until this moment it was determined the economic damage threshold for the chemical control.

We considered in [1] a predator-prey fuzzy model to study the interaction between aphids and ladybugs and also a classical model of the Holling-Tanner type that was fitted and its parameters were found.

This current work describes a methodology based in Fuzzy Sets Theory to elaborate a model that studies the interaction of the prey, *Aphis glycines* (soybean aphids), and the predator, *Orius insidiosus* (Hemiptera: Anthocoridae). We intend to fit the phase-plane to a model of the type Lotka-Volterra. The aim of this investigation is to propose a specific methodology to make a decision on the control of this prey before it arrives in Brazil.

* This research is supported by CAPES

Brazil is the second exporter of soybean at present, after the USA and before Argentina. According to the Bureau of Agriculture of the USA, it has been estimated that Brazil will be the greatest exporter of soybean in 2023. Considering the economic importance of the soybean to Brazil, we need to be prepared for the effective proposals of the control and the combat to the soybean aphids before it did not arrive in our country yet.

2. Predation

Predation is an example of the interaction between two populations that result in negative effects on growth and on survival of a population and in positive or beneficial ones to another. A predator is an organism that hunts and kills other organisms (prey) for food [2].

The simplest differential equation model is known (like the model of interspecific competition) by the names of its originators: Lotka-Volterra. The Lotka-Volterra model is given by the equations:

$$\begin{cases} \dfrac{dx}{dt} = ax - bxy \\ \dfrac{dy}{dt} = -cy + dxy \end{cases} \tag{1}$$

where x and y represent prey and predator populations respectively, i.e.,
1- Preys grow in an unlimited way when predators do not keep them under control;
2- Predators depend on the presence of their prey to survive;
3- The rate of predation depends on the likelihood that a victim is encountered by a predator;
4- The growth rate of the predator population is proportional to food intake (rate of predation).

The net growth rate a of the prey population when predators are absent is a positive quantity (with dimensions of 1/time) in accordance with assumption 1. The net death rate c of the predators in the absence of prey follows from assumption 2. The term xy approximates the likelihood that an encounter will take place between predators and prey given that both species move about randomly and are uniformly distributed over their habitat. An encounter is assumed to decrease the prey population and increase the predator population by contributing to their growth. The ratio b/d is analogous to the efficiency of predation, that is, the efficiency of the converting a unit of prey into a unit of predator mass [3].

These hypotheses are illustrated in Figure 1.

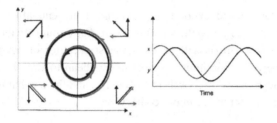

Figure 1. The Lotka-Volterra predator-prey model: the joint population moves with time from low predator-low prey, to low predator-high prey, to high predator-high prey, to high predator – low prey, and back to low predator – low prey. Source: [2].

According to the previous hypotheses, we have established fuzzy rule base.

3. The mathematical model

The soybean aphid, *A. glycines,* is serious pest of soybean throughout much of the North America [4]. Field studies have demonstrated that the insidious flower bug, *Orius insidiosus*, is an important predator of the soybean aphid [5]. This work describes a methodology based in Fuzzy Sets Theory to elaborate a model that studies the interaction of the prey, *A. glycines* (soybean aphids), and the predator, *Orius insidiosus* [6]. It has been proposed the use of a fuzzy rule-based system, instead of usual differential equations which characterize the classic deterministic models. Since there is not enough information derived from the experimental data that can be related to the phenomenon, it is difficult to express the variations as functions of the states. On the other hand, qualitative information from specialists allows to propose rules that relate (at least partially), the state variables, with their own variations.

Fuzzy Sets and Fuzzy Logic have become one of the emerging areas in contemporary technologies of information processing. Fuzzy Sets Theory was first developed by Zadeh [7] in the mid-1960s to represent uncertain and imprecise knowledge. It provides an approximate but effective means of describing the behavior of the system that is too complex, ill-defined, or not easily analyzed mathematically, and this is our case.

A fuzzy set is characterized by a membership function mapping the elements of a domain, space, or universe of discourse X to the unit interval [0,1]. That is, $\psi_A : X \to [0,1]$. Thus, a fuzzy set A in X may be represented as a set of ordered pairs of a generic element and its grade of membership: $A = \{(\psi_A(x)/x)/x \in X\}$. Clearly, a fuzzy set is a generation of the concept of a set whose membership function takes on only two values $\{0,1\}$, that is, the characteristic function of A, $\chi_A : X \to \{0,1\}$.

Fuzzy variables are processed using a fuzzy rule-based system. A general fuzzy rule-based system consists of four components: an input processor (fuzzification), a fuzzy rule base; a fuzzy inference method and an output processor (defuzzification). These components process real-valued inputs in order to provide real-valued outputs.

The fuzzification is the process in which the input values of the system are converted into appropriate fuzzy sets of their respective universes. It is a mapping of the dominion of the real numbers led to the fuzzy dominion [8].

The variables of the system are number of preys, number of the predators (input variables) and their variations (output variables). The fuzzy sets of the input variables are {*small, small medium, large medium, large*} and the fuzzy sets of the output variables are {*small positive, large positive, small negative, large negative*}.

The rule base characterizes the objectives and strategies used by specialists in the area through of a linguistic rule set. It is composed by a collection of fuzzy propositions of the form *if-then* [8].

Considering the phase plane (Figure 1), that is, the hypotheses of the Lotka-Volterra model, we have elaborated 16 rules of the form: "*If the number of aphids is small and the number of predator is small, then the variation of aphids is large positive and the variation of the predator is large negative; If the number of aphids is small and the number of predator is large, then the variation of aphids is large negative and the variation of predator is large negative*".

The fuzzy inference method performs an approximate reasoning using the compositional rule of inference. A particular form of fuzzy inference of interest here is the Mamdani method [9].

Finally, the result is fuzzy set (or several fuzzy sets). This fuzzy set is then converted into a single (crisp) value (or a vector of values) that, in some sense, is the best representative of the fuzzy set (or fuzzy sets). A typical defuzzification method, the one adopted in this paper, is center-of-gravity [9].

4. Results and conclusion

We have observed the variation of the number of the preys and the number of the predators in the numerical simulation. Let $x_0 = x(t_0)$ be an initial number of aphids and $y_0 = y(t_0)$ be an initial number of predators per plant (the input variables of the system). The system fuzzy produces $x'(t_0)$ and $y'(t_0)$ (the output variables of the system) by Euler's Method, that is, the number of preys and the number of predators are given by the formulas:

$$\begin{cases} x(t_{i+1}) = x(t_i) + hx'(t_i) \\ y(t_{i+1}) = y(t_i) + hy'(t_i) \end{cases} \tag{2}$$

where h is the increment and so on.

The phase plane by this fuzzy system (solid line) and the phase plane by the real data ([4];[5]) (dashed line) are illustrated in Figure 2.

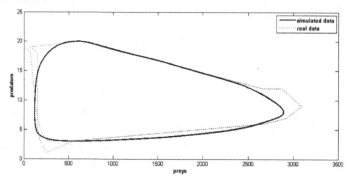

Figure 2. The phase plane by the fuzzy system and the phase plane by the real data with $x_0 = 74$ (the initial number of aphids) and $y_0 = 3$ (the initial number of predators).

In this way, the fuzzy system provides the phase plane that preserves the characteristics of the phase plane of the Lotka-Volterra model.

This study has suggested that the use of the Fuzzy Sets Theory in Ecology may represent the interaction among species in the environment where the available data are only qualitative. We have only used intuitive hypotheses of the dynamics of aphids-flower bug and the data from experts to elaborate the model without explicit differential equations.

We have considered the Fuzzy Sets Theory as a great contribution to the construction of mathematical models, mainly when parameters of the differential equations are not available.

We would like to highlight the advantages of using fuzzy rule-based models compared to the deterministic models:

▪ The input and output sets of fuzzy rule-based systems may be easily defined by experts, that is, specialists who may know when the population of a particular species is small, large and so forth of the predators population over time.

▪ We have used a rule base instead of systems given by equations, eliminating the difficulty of obtaining the parameters.

▪ Several differential equations parameters of the predator-prey type systems are not available.

▪ If it is necessary to know the parameters, they may be obtained through a curve fitting of the solution generated by the fuzzy model. That is, the parameters may be obtained through a curve fitting procedure from the solutions taken from the fuzzy rule-based model, i.e., it is imposed that the solution curve created by the fuzzy rule-based model be one solution to the deterministic system.

Acknowledgments

The first author acknowledges the Coordination for the Improvement of Higher Education Personnel (CAPES) and the second author acknowledges the National Council for Scientific and Technological Development (CNPq), process 305862/2013-8, for the financial support.

References

1. M. S. Peixoto, L. C. Barros, R. C. Bassanezi, Predator–prey fuzzy model, *Ecological Modelling*, 214, 39–44 (2008).
2. M. Begon, J. L. Harper and C. R. Townsend, Ecology: Individuals, Populations and Communities, Blackwell Scientific Publications (1990).
3. L. Edelstein-Keshet, Mathematical Models in Biology, Random House, NY (1988).
4. D. W. Ragsdale, B. P. McCornack, R. C. Venette, B. D. Potter, I. V. MacRae, E. W. Hodgson, M. E. O'Neal, K. D. Johnson, R. J. O'Neil, C. D. DiFonzo, T. E. Hunt, P. A. Glogoza, and E. M. Cullen. Müller and B. D. Serot, Economic Threshold for Soybean Aphid (Hemiptera: Aphididae), Journal of Economic Entomology 110, 1258-1267, (2007).
5. H. J. S. Yoo and R. J. O'Neil, Temporal relationships between the generalist predator, Orius insidiosus, and its two major prey in soybean, Biological Control 48, 168-180 (2009).
6. T. R. Brosius, L. G. Higley and T. E. Hun, Population Dynamics of Soybean Aphid and Biotic Mortality at the Edge of Its Range, Journal of Economic Entomology 100(4),1268-1275 (2007).
7. Zadeh, L.A. Fuzzy Sets. Informat. Control, 8, 338-353 (1965).
8. Klir, G.J.; Yuan,B.-Fuzzy Sets And Fuzzy Logic: Theory and Applications. Prentice Hall, N. Jersey (1995).
9. Pedrycs, W., Gomide, F., An Introduction to Fuzzy Sets: Analysis and Design, Massachusets Institute of Technology (1998).

LOGISTICS PERFORMANCE EVALUATION USING ANALYTICAL NEURAL NETWORK AND CUMULATIVE BELIEF DEGREES

ÖZGÜR KABAK

Industrial Engineering Department, Istanbul Technical University, Macka, Istanbul, 34357, Turkey

FÜSUN ÜLENGİN

Sabancı School of Management, Sabanci University, Orta Mah. Üniversite Cad. No: 27 Orhanli, Tuzla, Istanbul 34722, Turkey

ŞULE ÖNSEL EKİCİ

Industrial Engineering Department, Doğus University, Acibadem Zeamet Sok., Istanbul 34722, Turkey

Logistics plays a vital role in the economies. One of the attempt to measure logistics performance at national level is the Logistics Performance Index (LPI) published by the World Bank Group. In fact this study argues that there is a close relationship between global competitiveness level of a country and its logistics performance level. On this way, it aims to analyze the logistics competitiveness of a country from a national competitiveness perspective using an analytical neural network and cumulative belief degrees approach. LPI and World Economic Forum's competitiveness pillars are used for this purpose. The methodology is used to analyze the Turkey's logistics performance in order to develop suggestions for improving its current level.

1. Introduction

As the backbone of international trade, logistics encompasses freight transportation, warehousing, border clearance, payment systems and many other functions which are mostly performed by private service providers for private traders and owners of goods, however, it is also important for public policies of national governments and regional and international organizations (Arvis et al., 2012). The success in improving the logistics performance of a country is also highly dependent on the national competitiveness of that country. In fact, national competitiveness is generally defined as the set of institutions, policies and relevant factors that determine the level of productivity of a country (Artto, 1987).

Each year, selected organizations, such as the World Economic Forum (WEF) and the Institute for Management Development (IMD), apply several hundred objective and subjective indicators to assess the wealth created by the world's nations, and subsequently publish rankings of national competitiveness. These rankings serve as benchmark for policy-makers and other interested parties for judging the competitive success of their country within a global context. In fact several of these indicators have also an important impact on the performance of the logistics of the related country. Building infrastructure, developing regulatory regime for transport services, and designing and implementing efficient customs clearance procedures are just a few areas where government play an important role.

Logistics Performance Index (LPI), on the other hand, shows comparative performance of logistics in 155 countries and assesses performance flow of goods through country. The index is performed by the World Bank and the Turku School of Economics every two years since 2007 (Arvis et al, 2012). The index is directly influenced with the level of some of the indicators that shape the competition of a nation as a whole. Therefore, if it will be possible to highlight which of the WEF indicators have an important impact to improve the LPI of a country, this will provide an important road map for the government policy makers to find out to which of the indicators of the competitiveness of the country to focus on primarily in order to improve LPI rank of the country.

In parallel with these assertions, this study analyzes the relationship between logistics performance and competitiveness at national level. The aim is to develop a decision making tool to support the policy makers for their decisions to improve the logistics performance of Turkey. The WEF indicators for competitiveness of nations are considered as the fundamental source of criteria for the improvement of the logistics performance of the related nation. For this purpose the integration of the Artificial Neural Network (ANN) and a cumulative belief degree (CBD) approach are proposed for estimating relations between WEF indicators and LPI. By the use of this approach the LPI of a country can be analyzed based on the primary national competitiveness factors. Turkey is selected as a case study.

2. Proposed Methodology

Proposed methodology aims to find the relations between competitiveness of a country and logistics performance. For this aim WEF's twelve pillars and World Bank's LPI are used to represent the competitiveness and logistic performance, respectively (see Figure 1). In order to analyze with linguistic terms, LPI is represented by CBDs. Five-term linguistic term set is used for this purpose.

Figure 1. Proposed methodology

In LPI, the ratings are based on 6000 individual country assessments by almost 1000 international forwarders which rated the eight foreign countries their company serves most frequently. LPI takes into account customs, infrastructure, service quality, timeliness, international shipments, tracking and tracing as the key elements of logistics and compares these logistics profiles among 155 countries and rates them on a scale of 1 (worst) to 5(best) (Arvis et al, 2012).

Since 2005, the WEF has published global competitiveness reports for more than 100 countries on the basis of over 100 criteria. The WEF (2012) investigates 144 economies based on 111 indicators and classifies the indicators into twelve basic pillars. We used these twelve pillars to represent the country level indicators of the competitiveness (see Table 1).

Table 1. WEF's twelve pillars

ID	Pillar	ID	Pillar
1	Institutions	7	Labour Market Efficiency
2	Infrastructure	8	Financial Market Development
3	Macroeconomic Environment	9	Technological Readiness
4	Health and Primary Education	10	Market Size
5	Higher Education and Training	11	Business Sophistication
6	Goods Market Efficiency	12	Innovation

2.1. Cumulative Belief Degrees

Developed for evaluation of nuclear safeguards (Kabak and Ruan, 2011), CBD approach enables mathematical operations on the belief structures. In this study we used CBDs to represent LPI to reduce the quantitative uncertainty encountered in LPI by allowing fuzzy representations with linguistic terms. The basic use of CBD approach, similar to Kabak et al. (2013), is the quantification of causal relations. However instead of a regression based model, where the relations are assumed to be linear, ANN approach is used to estimate the relations.

In this study fuzzy linguistic terms are used to represent the information by the belief structure. The LPI is evaluated with a five-term set, $S = \{s_i\}$, $i \in \{0,...,4\}$, in which the following meanings to the terms are assigned. s_0: very low, s_1: low, s_2: medium, s_3: high, s_4: very high.

LPI is transformed to belief structures as the methodology defined in Kabak and Ruan (2011) and Kabak et al. (2013). The LPI of a country is a single value in 1-5 scale. However, the minimum and maximum scores of the countries are 1.61 and 4.19, respectively. Thus, the data were initially normalized in a 0–1 interval (the best score is 1 and the worst score is 0) based on minimum and maximum scores. Then, membership values of the normalized scores are calculated according to the fuzzy sets defined in Figure 2. These membership values constitute the belief degrees for each datum. For example, if the normalized score is 0.55, then the related belief structure is B(I) = {(s2, .8), (s3, .2)}.

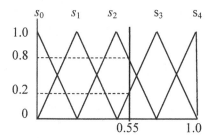

Figure 2. Fuzzy sets for transforming the data into a belief structure

2.2. Relations between WEF and LPI

In order to find the relations LPI and WEF, data of 124 countries from the reports of LPI 2007, 2010, and 2013 with WEF editions 2007, 2010, and 2013 are used.

ANN analysis which includes neural network training, testing, performance evaluation and comparison are conducted using MATLAB neural network tool box. The network defined is a two layer feed-forward network with sigmoid hidden neurons and linear outputs neurons. The first layer has 12 neurons as inputs each representing the related country's pillar scores. The number of output neurons is five, each representing the CBD values for LPIs of the countries.

Random data divisions have been used by Matlab in order to select the samples for the training. 70% of the samples have been used training data, 15% as validation data and the remaining 15% has been used as test data. Levenberg-Marquardt back-propagation method, which is one of the fastest back-propagation algorithm is used for training the ANN. It is robust and in many cases it finds solutions even if it starts far off from the final minimum. The number of hidden neurons to be used in the hidden layer is specified according to the suggestion of Masters (1993). Additionally, the ANN is run 10 times for each different number of hidden neurons. The analysis showed that the best performance values are obtained for 21 hidden neurons (Performances: test = 0.975, validation =: 0.944, train = 0.973). The activation function used for the hidden neurons is the type Tansig (hyperbolic tangent sigmoid transfer function). This best performing network is used to conduct detailed scenario analysis.

3. Scenario Analysis and Policy Suggestions

The resulting ANN model is used to conduct scenario analysis for Turkey. For this, we generate a number of results by simply increasing the values of each pillar by one for all different combinations of pillars. In this way, 2^{12} -1 (=4095) different scenarios are generated. Examples of the scenarios are given in Table 2. For instance in scenario 17, values of 1st and 5th pillars are increased by one, while the others remain the same. Scenario 0 represents Turkey's current situation.

Table 2. Examples of Scenarios for analyzing Turkey's Logistic performance

Pillars	Scenarios							
	0	1	17	185	436	1636	3934	4095
1	4.08	**5.08**	**5.08**	**5.08**	4.08	4.08	4.08	**5.08**
2	4.45	4.45	4.45	4.45	4.45	4.45	**5.45**	**5.45**
3	4.62	4.62	4.62	4.62	**5.62**	**5.62**	**5.62**	**5.62**
4	5.86	5.86	5.86	**6.86**	5.86	5.86	**6.86**	**6.86**
5	4.29	4.29	**5.29**	**5.29**	**5.29**	4.29	**5.29**	**5.29**
6	4.52	4.52	4.52	**5.52**	**5.52**	**5.52**	4.52	**5.52**
7	3.74	3.74	3.74	3.74	3.74	**4.74**	**4.74**	**4.74**
8	4.40	4.40	4.40	**5.40**	**5.40**	4.40	4.40	**5.40**
9	4.05	4.05	4.05	4.05	**5.05**	4.05	**5.05**	**5.05**
10	5.30	5.30	5.30	5.30	5.30	**6.30**	**6.30**	**6.30**
11	4.36	4.36	4.36	4.36	4.36	**5.36**	**5.36**	**5.36**
12	3.47	3.47	3.47	3.47	3.47	3.47	**4.47**	**4.47**
Estimated LPI values								
s_0 – very low	1.000	1.000	1.000	1.000	1.000	1.000	1.000	1.000
s_1 – low	0.976	0.973	0.992	1.000	1.000	1.000	0.966	0.919
s_2 – medium	0.976	0.870	0.954	0.970	1.000	1.000	0.966	0.919
s_3 – high	0.745	0.640	0.802	0.970	1.000	1.000	0.966	0.919
s_4 – very high	0.035	0.063	0.076	0.143	0.175	0.148	0.178	0.575
Aggregate	3.733	3.547	3.824	4.083	4.175	4.148	4.074	4.331

Estimated LPI values for the example scenarios are given the last six rows of Table 2. According to the results, for instance, if Turkey's level in pillars 1 and 5 are improved by one (scenario 17), the resulting CBD is $C(I_{17}) = \{(1, s_0), (.992, s_1)(.954, s_2), (.802, s_3), (.076, s_4), (.076, s_4)\}$. The sum of CBDs give an aggregate score for comparison purposes (see last row of Table 2).

In order to analyze the scenarios, they are grouped according to the number of improved pillars. For each group first three ranked scenarios with respect to aggregate score and s_4 level score are determined. Results fare presented in Table 3. From these result the following importance rankings of the pillars are derived:

Based on aggregate score: $9 - 6 - 11 - 10 - 12 - 1 - 8 - 2 - 3 - 7 - 5 - 4$

Based on s_4 level score: $9 - 11 - 6 - 10 - 12 - 1 - 8 - 2 - 5 - 4 - 7 - 3$

If the aim is to specify three most important pillars affecting logistic performance of Turkey, this analysis show that the Technological readiness (pillar 9), Goods market efficiency (pillar 6) and business sophistication (pillar 11) can be suggested. These three pillars are always in the list to be considered regardless of how many pillars will be taken into account.

Table 3. Set of Pillar(s) result with highest improvement

Number of pillars improved	Set of Pillar(s) result with highest improvement on aggregate score	Set of Pillar(s) result with highest improvement on s4 (Very High) level
1	{9}, {6}, {2}	{9}, {6}, {11}
2	{6, 9}, {6, 11}, {6, 10}	{9, 11}, {6, 9}, {1, 11},
3	{6, 9, 11}, {6, 9, 10}, {1, 6, 9}	{6, 9, 11}, {1, 6, 11}, {1, 9, 11},
4	{6, 9, 10, 11}, {6, 9, 11, 12}, {1, 6, 9, 11}	{6, 9, 10, 11}, {6, 9, 11, 12}, {1, 6, 9, 11}
5	{1, 6, 9, 11, 12}, {1, 6, 8, 9, 11}, {1, 3, 6, 9, 11}	{1, 6, 9, 11, 12}, {1, 6, 8, 9, 11}, {1, 6, 9, 10, 11}

4. Conclusions

In this study, a new hybrid methodology is proposed to analyze the relation between logistic performances of countries with their national competitiveness indicators. For this, the logistics performances of the countries are converted to CBD scores initially and an ANN model is used in order to quantify the relations. Finally a number of scenario analysis conducted to see the most important competitiveness factor affecting the logistics performance of the countries.

From the results of the scenario analysis technological readiness, goods market efficiency and business sophistication are found to have the highest importance on the level of LPI for Turkey.

References

1. J.-F. Arvis, M.A. Mustra, L. Ojala, B. Stepherd, D. Saslavsky, *Connecting to Compete: Trade Logistics in the Global Economy*, World Bank (2012)
2. E.W. Artto, *Management International Review*, **27**, 47-58 (1987)
3. WEF, *Global Competitiveness Report 2012-2013* (2012).
4. O. Kabak, D. Ruan, D., *IEEE Transactions on Knowledge and Data Engineering* **23**, 1441-1454 (2011)
5. O. Kabak, F. Ülengin, Ş. Önsel, Ö. Özaydin, E. Aktaş, *Knowledge-Based Systems*, DOI: 10.1016/j.knosys.2013.09.006 (2013)
6. T. Masters, *Practical Neural Network Recipes in C++*, Academic Press (1993)

BALLISTIC REACHING USING VISUOMOTOR MAPS IN A ROBOT MANIPULATOR FOR STARTING A VISUALLY GUIDED TASK

DANIEL FERNANDO TELLO GAMARRA

Department of Electrical Engineering Processing, Universidade Federal de Santa Maria, av. Roraima 1000- Santa Maria, Rio Grande do sul, 97105-900, Brazil

This paper describes a new way of constructing a visuomotor map that is applied in a manipulator robot to accomplish a ballistic reaching task. Ballistic reaching is employed to move the robot hand to a visible and optimal position, once the robot arrives to this position a visually guided task (visual servoing or a manipulation task) could be executed. The visuomotor map has been implemented using SOM neural networks in a simulated puma 560 robot. The visuomotor map deals with the visibility of the robot hand (end-effector) problem. So the robot can start with its end-effector in any random position of the workspace. A Cartesian controller triggered by a visuomotor map will find a suitable and visible position for the end-effector. Results and simulations are shown to demonstrate the applicability of our proposed model for a ballistic reaching task.

1. Introduction

Interaction of human beings with the environment involves the use of motor commands and perception, results of this interaction is embedded in visuomotor maps. Visuomotor maps are defined as a transformation from visual to motor coordinates [1]. The way in which visuomotor maps can represent these transformations are named internal models, as it has been suggested by recent findings in neuroscience [2]. In order to make artificial systems interact with the environment, roboticists have looked at biology and human development to mimic some solutions, based on the fact that biology have resolved this problem in a successful way; one of these solutions is the use of visuomotor maps. For instance, Kuperstein proposed a neural network model that achieves adaptive visual-motor coordination of a multijoint arm in simulation in [3]. Also, Gamarra proposed a visuomotor map embedded in a forward model using Fuzzy C means applied in a closed loop reaching task that is executed before visual servoing for a simulated robotic manipulator in [4]. Saegusa as well in [5], described a visuomotor correlation that allows a humanoid robot to define its own body through sensorimotor exploration following a developmental approach.

Two problems are addressed in this paper, the first one is, the application of a visuomotor map in a ballistic reaching task. A ballistic reaching task moves the robot end-effector to a desired position without using vision; a second problem, is the visuomotor map construction using SOM neural networks originated from recorded data of a robot manipulator. The remainder of the paper is as follows. The second section describes the algorithms used in this work; the third section shows the proposed architecture designed for the reaching task; in the fourth section the experimental platform setup is described; in the fifth section the motor babbling process is explained; in the sixth section the visuomotor map creation is detailed; the seventh section presents the results of the controller performance in a reaching task, finally, conclusions are discussed in the last section.

2. Theoretical Background

2.1. *Cartesian Space Control*

Based on the equations shown in Sanchez-Sanchez's paper in [6], the Cartesian controller is given by the equation:

$$\dot{q} = J^{-1}(q)(\dot{X} - \dot{X}_d)\lambda \tag{1}$$

Variable $\dot{X}$ represents the actual Cartesian position of the end-effector, $\dot{X}_d$ represents the Cartesian desired position, λ is the proportional gain controller , q is the joint variable, $(J^{-1}(q))$ is the inverse Jacobian matrix of the manipulator.

2.2. *SOM Neural Networks*

The Kohonen's self-organization map (SOM) is an unsupervised neural network that maps a set of n-dimensional vectors to a two dimensional topographic map. The algorithm description in this subsection is based on Zhang's paper [7], we assume a set of input vectors $x \in R_n$, and associate a weight vector $w_k \in R_n$, $k = 1,2,...,k$, with each of k neural nodes arranged in a regular two dimensional (rectangular) lattice. The initial values of the weights $w_k(t)$, computed at time t, may be randomly selected, each node of the network receives the same type of input vector and produces a single similarity value. The input record maps onto the best-matching (winning) node c, based on the largest similarity or the smallest distance. Each input vector is presented to the network, and an Euclidian distance between the input vector and each weight vector is computed, next, the winning node denoted by subscript c is determined, each new input vector adjusts the weight vector of the winning node along with those of its topological neighbors, the weight vectors are updated using the equation:

$$w_k(t+1) = w_k(t) + \alpha(t)h_{ck}(t)[x(t) - w_k(t)] \tag{2}$$

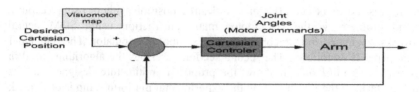

Figure. 1. Proposed architecture.

Parameter $\alpha(t)$ is the learning rate factor, and $h_{ck}(t)$ is the neighborhood function. The standard Gaussian neighborhood function could be used to define the neighborhood, as can be seen in the next equation:

$$h_{ck}(t) = \exp\left(-\|r_k - r_c\|/\delta^2(t)\right) \tag{3}$$

Where, r_k and r_c denote the coordinates of nodes k and c, respectively, on the two-dimensional lattice. Being δ of the neighborhood function.

3. Proposed Architecture Description

Figure 1 depicts the control architecture for the ballistic reaching proposed on this paper. The visuomotor map determines an initial waypoint position for the robot in which the hand is visible. The end-effector moves to this visible position using the Cartesian controller.

4. Experimental Platform Setup

The puma 560 robot manipulator was chosen for the simulations developed in this article. The simulations used the matlab robotics toolbox described in [8] and the epipolar geometry toolbox (EGT) created by Mariottini and referred in [9].

5. Motor Babbling

The process known as "motor babbling" in developmental robotics, is a process in which the robot manipulator moves randomly exploring its workspace. A manipulator puma 560 was created in the Matlab robotics toolbox and two fixed cameras are simulated in the Epipolar Geometry Toolbox.

The internal parameters for the two cameras are the same and are shown in Table 1. Both cameras have a rotation of -90 degrees with respect to x axis and are located at [0, -0.1, 0.8] and [0, 0.1, 0.8] in the world coordinates. The robot workspace was babbled in 36 stages. At the beginning of each stage the robojoint 0 is set to $10n$ degrees, where n is the stage number. Each stage is made of 60 babbling steps. The Cartesian position of the end effector, image features and joint coordinates of the robot are stored in this phase.

Table 1. Simulated cameras internal parameters

Parameter	Value
image pixel size	640*480
Orthogonality factor of the CCD image axes	1
Number of pixels per unit distance in image coordinates times the focal length	200

6. Visuomotor Map Creation

The visuomotor map was constructed using all the information recorded in the motor babbling phase. Before initializing to cluster the data, the image features information is analyzed in order to just use the Cartesian positions of the end-effector that are visible in both cameras. 120 visible points in which the end effector appears in both cameras from the original 760 sample points.

The 3D position data of the robot end-effector was clustered, for the clustering process we used the SOM neural network algorithm ([7]) from the matlab neural networks toolbox. Figure 2(a) shows the weight distribution of the network ordered in a two-dimensional grid, Figure 2(b) shows the resulting clusters A (X) is used in the figure to show the centroids of every cluster. The visuomotor map was utilized in the ballistic reaching phase. The parameters used for the clustering algorithm are: number of clusters = 6, maximum number of iterations = 500. Probably, the number of clusters could be optimized, but 6 is close to 4, that is referred in [10] as an optimized.

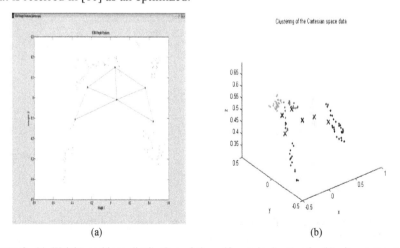

(a)   (b)

Figure 2. (a) Weight positions distribution of the self-organized network. (b) visuomotor map constructed with the 3D Cartesian position of the end effector. There are 6 clusters and the centers of the clusters are marked with a X.

7. Reaching Task

Different simulations were done to test the system architecture. In order to explain the results, one of the simulations performed by the robot will be described.

Initially, the robot end effector is in a random position. So we move the end effector to one of the visible positions encoded in the visuomotor map clusters. This is done following the next steps: a) compare the end-effector position with the positions of the clustered centroids in the Cartesian space; b) when we found the cluster centroid that is closest to the actual end-effector position, we look for a point in the clustered data that is close to this centroid. This step is necessary, because the cluster centroid could be a point in which we could have singularities. So by choosing a point in that cluster, we are sure that the chosen point is reachable and free of singularities in the workspace since it was reachable during the motor babbling phase; c) The end-effector is sent to that position using the Cartesian controller. For this trial the robot starts in the joint coordinates position of [-80, -1, -84, 0, 0, 0], Figure 3(a) shows the trajectory in the three dimensional space traversed by the puma 560 using the Cartesian controller and the visuomotor map. Figure 3(b) shows the error of the Cartesian controller; we can notice that approximately in less than 100 iterations the error converges.

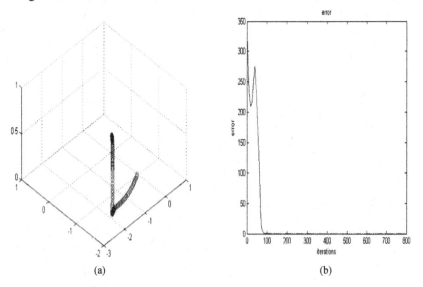

(a)   (b)

Figure 3. (a) Trajectories of the end-effector using the Cartesian and the visuomotor map. (b) Cartesian controller error.

8. Conclusions

The main discernible contributions proposed by the paper are the use of a visuomotor map to define a visible, suitable and free of singularities position that will be used for a Cartesian controller in a ballistic reaching task. It is important that the robot could reach a visible position, because we could start a more elaborated task, such as, manipulation, reaching guided by vision or planning using vision. Another contribution is.a new way of obtaining a visuomotor map constructed using self-organized neural networks with the data gathered from a babbling motor of the robotic manipulator workspace. Finally, the paper proposed a valid control architecture based on SOM networks for ballistic reaching.

References

1. P. Vetter, S.J. Goodbody and D. Wolpert, Evidence for an eye-centered spherical representation of the visuomotor map, *Journal of Neurophysiology*, vol. 81, pp. 935-939 (1999).
2. M. Kawato, Internal Models for Motor Control, *Curr Opin Neurobiol.*, vol. 9, pp. 718-727 (1999).
3. M. Kuperstein , Neural model of adaptive hand-eye coordination for single postures, *Science*, vol. 239, pp. 1308-1311(1988).
4. D. F. T. Gamarra and L.K. Pinpin, Forward Models Applied in Ballistic Reaching for Visual Servoing, Proceedings of the Second Brazilian Congress on Fuzzy Systems, Natal, Brazil, (2012).
5. R. Saegusa, G. Metta and G. Sandini, Body definition based on visuomotor correlation, *IEEE Transactions on Industrial Electronics*, vol. 59, 8, pp. 3199-3210, (2012).
6. P. Sanchez-Sanchez and F. Reyes-Cortes, A new Cartesian Controller for robot manipulator, Proceedings of the IEEE International Conferences on Intelligent Robots and Systemas – IROS, pp. 2059-2064, (2005) .
7. X.Y. Zhang, J.S. Chen, and J.K. Dong, Color Clustering using Self-Organizing Maps, in International Conference on Wavelet Analysis and Pattern Recognition, Beijing, China, (2007).
8. P.I. Corke, A robotic toolbox for matlab, *IEEE in Robotics and Automation Magazine*, vol. 3, 1, pp. 24-32 (1996).
9. G.L. Mariottini and D. Prattichizzo, EGT for multiple and visual servoing: robotics vision with pinhole and panoramic cameras, *IEEE in Robotics and Automation Magazine*, vol. 12, 4, pp. 26-39, (2005).
10. D. F. T. Gamarra, Forward Models with Cluster Validity Criteria Applied in Ballistic Reaching for Visual Servoing, *International Review on Modelling and Simulations*, vol. 6, N. 6, (2013).

SOME EXPERIMENTAL RESULTS IN CLASSIFICATION USING HYBRID FUZZY MORPHOLOGICAL/LINEAR PERCEPTRONS

Peter Sussner* and Felipe Roberto Bueno

Dept. of Applied Mathematics, IMECC, UNICAMP
Campinas, São Paulo, Brazil
*E-mails: * sussner@ime.unicamp.br, buenofelipe01@gmail.com*

Hybrid morphological/linear neural networks combine morphological with linear operators. In this paper, we introduce a feedforward artificial neural network representing a hybrid fuzzy morphological/linear perceptron called fuzzy dilation/erosion/linear perceptron (F-DELP). Following Pessoa's and Maragos' ideas, we apply an appropriate smoothing to overcome the non-differentiablity of the fuzzy dilation and erosion operators employed in the proposed F-DELP models. Then, training is achieved using a traditional backpropagation algorithm. Finally, we apply the F-DELP model to some well-known classification problems and compare the results with the ones produced by other classifiers.

Keywords: Fuzzy mathematical morphology; fuzzy morphological perceptron; hybrid fuzzy morphological/linear perceptron; classification.

1. Introduction

Morphological neural networks (MNNs)[1,2] first emerged in the 1990's. The original motivation for the development of MNNs can be found in the observation that the usual linear aggregation functions can be replaced by certain non-linear operations called "additive maximum" and "additive minimum" in a lattice algebra known as minimax algebra.[3] Since Davidson had previously shown that the classical approach towards gray-scale mathematical morphology can be embedded into minimax algebra,[4] that represents a subalgebra of image algebra, the resulting artificial neural network models were named morphological neural networks. According to a more general point of view, an MNN is defined as a type of artificial neural network that performs an operation of mathematical morphology at every node, possibly followed by the application of an activation function.

Morphological perceptrons (MPs) based on additive maximum/minimum operations were among the first MNN models to appear in the literature.[2] In recent years, morphological perceptrons were equipped with competitive hidden layer nodes and the morphological perceptron with competitive learning (MP/CL)[5] was proposed.

Hybrid models employing convex combinations of morphological, rank, and linear aggregation functions were first proposed by Pessoa & Maragos.[1] Later, some related models, that employ morphological and linear operations, found applications in both classification and financial time series prediction.[6]

In this paper, we introduce a hybrid fuzzy morphological/linear perceptrons that employs operators of fuzzy mathematical morphology (FMM), namely fuzzy erosion and fuzzy dilation. Recall that in FMM,[7] an erosion can be defined in terms of an infimum of implications and a dilation can be defined in terms of a supremum of conjunctions. Here, we construct fuzzy erosion and dilation operators by means of the implication and the t-norm of Lukasiewicz. We follow Pessoa's & Maragos' ideas for smoothing the infima corresponding to minima and the suprema corresponding to maxima. Training is performed using backpropagation. Moreover, the fact that nobody studied this hybrid model still motivated the writing of this paper.

The organization of the paper is as follows. First, we briefly review some basic concepts of FMM in Section 2. Then, Section 3 describes the proposed hybrid fuzzy morphological/linear perceptron called fuzzy dilation/erosion/linear perceptron (F-DELP) as well as the method that we chose for training this model. Section 4 compares the classification rates produced by the F-DELP model based on Lukasiewicz operators with the ones produced by a conventional MLP, the morphological/rank/linear neural network (MRL),[1] and the previous dilation/erosion/linear perceptron (DELP).[8] We finish with some concluding remarks.

2. Basic Concepts of Fuzzy Mathematical Morphology

In the early 1990's, Sinha & Dougherty observed that binary mathematical morphology (MM) can be extended to FMM by substituting the set-theoretic definitions of the elementary binary morphological operators with extended definitions using fuzzy set theory. Recall that binary images are represented as subsets of $\mathbb{R}^n$ or - equivalently - as functions $\mathbb{R}^n \to \{0, 1\}$.[9] Binary MM is concerned with the filtering and geometric analysis of binary images, i.e., sets, by means of other sets called structuring elements (SEs).

In FMM, the notion of fuzzy erosion of an image **a** by an SE **s** can be defined in terms of the degrees of inclusion of translated versions of **s** in **a**. Similarly, the notion of fuzzy dilation of an image **a** by an SE **s** can be defined in terms of the degrees of intersection of translated (and reflected) versions of **s** and **a**. De Baets presented a very general approach towards FMM which employs fuzzy inclusion measures given by infima of implications and fuzzy intersection measures given by suprema of conjuctions.[7]

Let $\mathcal{F}(\mathbf{X})$ denote the class of fuzzy sets on the universe $\mathbf{X}$. Mathematically speaking, $\mathcal{F}(\mathbf{X})$ can be viewed as the set of functions $\mathbf{a} : \mathbf{X} \to [0,1]$ and therefore we simply write $\mathbf{a}(\mathbf{x})$ instead of $\mu_{\mathbf{a}}(\mathbf{x})$. As usual in lattice theory, the symbol $\bigwedge$ denotes the infimum operator and the symbol $\bigvee$ denotes the supremum operator. The infimum of a finite number of elements of $[0,1]$ yields the minimum of these elements and the supremum of a finite number of elements of $[0,1]$ yields the maximum of these elements.

Definition 2.1. Let $\mathbf{a}, \mathbf{s} \in \mathcal{F}(\mathbf{X})$. Given a fuzzy implication I, such that $I(s, \cdot)$ commutes with the infimum for all $s \in [0,1]$, a fuzzy erosion of $\mathbf{a}$ by the SE $\mathbf{s}$ is defined as follows:

$$\mathcal{E}(\mathbf{a}, \mathbf{s})(\mathbf{x}) = Inc\,(\mathbf{s_x}, \mathbf{a}) = \bigwedge_{y \in \mathbf{X}} I\,(\mathbf{s_x}(\mathbf{y}), \mathbf{a}(\mathbf{y}))\,; \tag{1}$$

where $\mathbf{s_x}(\mathbf{y}) = \mathbf{s}(\mathbf{y} - \mathbf{x})$, $\forall \mathbf{y} \in \mathbf{X}$, is the translation of $\mathbf{s}$ by $\mathbf{x} \in \mathbf{X}$.

Definition 2.2. Let $\mathbf{a}, \mathbf{s} \in \mathcal{F}(\mathbf{X})$. Given a fuzzy conjunction C, such that $C(s, \cdot)$ commutes with the supremum for all $s \in [0,1]$, a fuzzy dilation of $\mathbf{a}$ by $\mathbf{s}$ is defined as follows:

$$\mathcal{D}(\mathbf{a}, \mathbf{s})(\mathbf{x}) = Sec\,(\bar{\mathbf{s}}_{\mathbf{x}}, \mathbf{a}) = \bigvee_{y \in \mathbf{X}} C\,(\bar{\mathbf{s}}_{\mathbf{x}}(\mathbf{y}), \mathbf{a}(\mathbf{y}))\,; \tag{2}$$

where $\bar{\mathbf{s}}_{\mathbf{x}}(\mathbf{y}) = \mathbf{s}(\mathbf{x} - \mathbf{y})$, $\forall \mathbf{y} \in \mathbf{X}$, is the reflection of $\mathbf{s_x}$ for all $\mathbf{x} \in \mathbf{X}$.

3. A Hybrid Fuzzy Morphological/Linear Perceptron

Let us introduce a hybrid morphological/linear neural network called fuzzy dilation/erosion/linear perceptron (F-DELP) which has a modular structure. Each module computes the following output y for an input $\mathbf{x} \in [0,1]^n$.

$$y = f(\lambda \alpha + (1 - \lambda)\beta), \tag{3}$$

$$\beta = \mathbf{x} \cdot \mathbf{p}^T = x_1 p_1 + x_2 p_2 + \cdots + x_n p_n, \tag{4}$$

$$\alpha = \theta \varphi + (1 - \theta)\omega, \tag{5}$$

$$\varphi = \delta_{\mathbf{a}}(\mathbf{x}) = \bigvee_{i=1}^{n} C(a_i, x_i), \tag{6}$$

$$\omega = \varepsilon_{\mathbf{b}}(\mathbf{x}) = \bigwedge_{i=1}^{n} I(b_i, x_i), \tag{7}$$

where f is an arbitrary activation function, $\lambda, \theta \in [0,1]$, and $\mathbf{a}, \mathbf{b}, \mathbf{p} \in [0,1]^n$. Note that Equations 6 and 7 correspond respectively to a fuzzy dilation by the SE $\mathbf{a}$ and a fuzzy erosion by the SE $\mathbf{b}$. Here, $\mathbf{x}$ plays the role of the image. Figure 1 depicts the topology of a single F-DELP module.

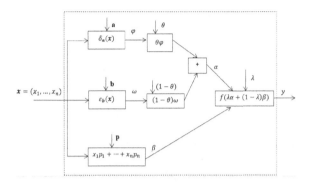

Fig. 1. Topology of an F-DELP Module.

Consider a training set of the form $\{(\mathbf{x}^1, \mathbf{y}^1), \ldots, (\mathbf{x}^P, \mathbf{y}^P)\}$. Observe that $\mathbf{y}^p$, where $p = 1, \ldots, P$, corresponds to the class label of $\mathbf{x}^p$ in classification problems. During the training phase, the weight vector $\mathbf{w} = (\mathbf{a}, \mathbf{b}, \mathbf{p}, \lambda, \theta)$ is iteratively adjusted according to an error criterion. Here, we employ the usual quadratic error function $E(w)$ that is given by $E(w) = \sum_{p=1}^{P} ||\mathbf{t}^p - \mathbf{y}^p||^2$, where $\mathbf{t}^p$ is the target for the input pattern $\mathbf{x}^p$. Note that the gradient of $E(\mathbf{w})$ is not guaranteed to exist since the partial derivatives $\frac{\partial \varphi}{\partial a_i}$ and $\frac{\partial \omega}{\partial b_i}$ are not guaranteed to exist due to the non-differentiability of the maximum and minimum operators in φ and ω. Since the maximum and minimum operators represent special cases of the rank operator, these non-differentiability issues can be overcome by substituting the rank function with the inner product of a smoothed rank indicator vector, that can be expressed in terms of a smoothed impulse function q_σ such as the one provided below, and the input vector.[1]

$$q_\sigma(x) = exp\left[-0.5\left(\frac{x}{\sigma}\right)^2\right]. \tag{8}$$

4. Experimental Results

In this section, we evaluate the classification performance of the F-DELP using 3 well-known datasets from the UCI machine learning repository:

(1) The *iris dataset* consisting of 50 samples from each of three species of Iris flowers. Each sample has four attributes. We partitioned the entire set into a training set consisting of the first 35 patterns of each class and a test set consisting of the remaining samples.

(2) The *image segmentation dataset* comprises 210 samples for training and 2100 samples for testing. These data have 19 continuous attributes.

(3) The *Wisconsin breast cancer dataset* has 569 instances (357 benign and 212 malignant) that are described in terms of 30 real-valued features.

For comparative purposes, we applied the following classifiers from the literature to the same problems: a multilayer perceptron (MLP) having sigmoid activation functions and a single hidden layer, the k-nearest neighbors (kNN) classifier,[10] a decision tree[11] whose criterion for choosing a split is given by Gini's diversity index, the MRL neural network,[1] and the previous DELP model that employs gray-scale dilations and erosions.[8]

The MLP models were trained using gradient descent with momentum and adaptive step backpropagation rule with learning rate $\eta = 10^{-4}$ and momentum factor $\alpha = 0.9$. For each of the three problems, we applied 10-fold cross-validation to determine the number of hidden neurons in $\{10, 20, 30\}$ (yielding 30 hidden neurons for the image segmentation dataset and 10 hidden neurons for the other two datasets) as well as the increase and decrease parameters $\rho_{inc} \in \{1.0, 1.1, 1.2\}$ and $\rho_{dec} \in \{0.5, 0.6, 0.7\}$. The parameter k of the kNN model was also determined individually for each problem using 10-fold cross-validation. As to the MRL, DELP, and F-DELP models, the number of modules was chosen to equal the number of neurons of the MLP models for each problem and training was performed using gradient descent with learning rate $\eta = 0.01$ and momentum factor $\nu = 0.8$. Training was stopped after reaching 10^4 iterations or a decrease in the $MSE \leq 10^{-6}$. The components of the parameters $\mathbf{a}, \mathbf{b}, \mathbf{p}, \lambda, \omega$ in the F-DELP model were randomly initialized in the range $[0, 1]$ and $\sigma = 0.05$ was chosen in Eq. 8. Since the fuzzy morphological operators in the F-DELP models require inputs and weights in $[0, 1]^n$, we normalized the training data within $[0.1, 0.9]^n$, thresholded the test data to lie in $[0, 1]^n$, and halved the step size whenever a step would lead to $\mathbf{a}$ or $\mathbf{b} \notin [0, 1]^n$.

Table 1 reveals that the F-DELP model achieved the highest classification rates in our simulations with the three aforementioned datasets.

5. Concluding Remarks

This paper presents a hybrid fuzzy morphological/linear perceptron called F-DELP. The F-DELP has a modular topology with each module computing a linear combination of linear and fuzzy morphological operators.

Table 1. Classification Rates.

Dataset	MLP	Decision tree	kNN	MRL	DELP	**F-DELP**
Iris	100.0	100.0	100.0	100.0	100.0	**100.0**
Image Seg.	93.62	90.29	80.48	93.62	93.29	**94.43**
Wisconsin	94.19	91.86	94.19	97.68	98.26	**98.84**

This fact appears to allow for a better fit to the training data than using traditional methods without causing overfitting. Due to the relationship of gray-scale and fuzzy MM,[12] the F-DELP can be viewed as a generalization of the previous DELP model. As is the case for the MRL neural network and the previous DELP model, training can be performed using a conventional backpropagation algorithm after smoothing the non-differentiable fuzzy morphological operators that occur in the F-DELP model. In some simulations using some well-known classification problems, an F-DELP model based on Lukasiewicz operators slightly outperformed MLP, decision tree, kNN, MRL and DELP in terms of classification rates.

References

1. L. F. C. Pessoa and P. Maragos, *Pattern Recognition* **33**, 945 (2000).
2. G. X. Ritter and P. Sussner, An introduction to morphological neural networks, in *Proceedings of the 13th International Conference on Pattern Recognition*, (Vienna, Austria, 1996).
3. R. Cuninghame-Green, *Minimax Algebra: Lecture Notes in Economics and Mathematical Systems 166* (Springer-Verlag, New York, 1979).
4. J. L. Davidson, Foundation and applications of lattice transforms in image processing, in *Advances in Electronics and Electron Physics*, ed. P. Hawkes (Academic Press, New York, NY, 1992) pp. 61–130.
5. P. Sussner and E. Esmi, *Information Sciences* **181**, 1929 (2011).
6. R. A. Araújo and T. A. E. Ferreira, *Inf. Sci.* **237**, 3(July 2013).
7. B. De Baets, Fuzzy morphology: A logical approach, in *Uncertainty Analysis in Engineering and Science: Fuzzy Logic, Statistics, and Neural Network Approach*, eds. B. M. Ayyub and M. M. Gupta (Kluwer Academic Publishers, Norwell, 1997) pp. 53–67.
8. R. de A. Araújo, A. L. I. Oliveira and S. R. L. Meira, *Learning and Nonlinear Models* **11**, 48 (2013).
9. D. Sinha and E. R. Dougherty, *J. Vis. Comun. Image Represent.* **3**, 286(September 1992).
10. L. Devroye, L. Gyorfi and G. A. Lugosi, *A Probabilistic Theory of Pattern Recognition* (Springer Verlag, Berlin-Heidelberg, 1996).
11. F. Esposito, D. Malebra and G. Semeraro, *IEEE Transactions on Pattern Analysis and Machine Intelligence* **19**, 476 (1997).
12. P. Sussner and M. E. Valle, *Journal of Mathematical Imaging and Vision* **32**, 139(October 2008).

INTELLIGENT SENSORY EVALUATION OF TOBACCO LEAF BASED ON NIRS

TING LIU

College of Information Science and Engineering, Ocean University of China, 23 Hong Kong East Road
Qingdao, 266071, China

NING YANG

New Star Computer Engineering Center, Ocean University of China, 23 Hong Kong East Road
Qingdao, 266071, China

ZHONGTAI LI

Department of Information and Network, Hongta Tobacco (Group) Co., Ltd, 118 Hongta Road
Yuxi, 653100, China

LINCHUN LI

Department of Information and Network, Hongta Tobacco (Group) Co., Ltd, 118 Hongta Road
Yuxi, 653100, China

Traditional tobacco intelligent sensory evaluation has no high accuracy due to the limitation of chemical components detection technologies. A new approach discussed in this paper utilizes the near-infrared spectroscopy (*NIRS*) to build the model of sensory quality instead of the analysis of chemical compositions. The results indicate that the *NIRS* models have greater ability to treat complex tobacco sensory analysis. The *NIRS* sensory evaluation which is fast, efficient and environmentally-friendly will become more prosperous in this field.

1. Introduction

Sensory evaluation is a measurement of the signals received via sensory organs [1]. Sensory quality of formulated products determines the usability of recipe-design [2]. Traditional approaches rely on professional panelists' senses such as sight, smell, taste and touch. Studies have been focused on human sensory evaluation in *silico* in the past few years [3-7], which built a model to compare chemical compositions with sensory quality. However, tobacco leaf, which consists of thousands of ingredients, cannot be detected completely and precisely because of the limitation of detection technologies, which will bring noise and error into sensory evaluation model. This work employs the near-infrared spectroscopy to build quantitative models of sensory quality evaluation.[*]

Near-infrared spectroscopy (*NIRS*) is a novel detection technology which is fast, efficient, environmentally-friendly. *NIRS* has been extensively used as the quality control tool in practice, such as petroleum, pharmaceutical, and tobacco industry. In tobacco industry, SHU Ru-xin *et al.* built a *NIR-PCA-SVM* model to identify the growth of flue-cured tobacco leaf [8]; WANG Jia-jun *et al.* used the *FT-NIR* technology to monitor the quality of cigarette blending process [9]; DENG Fa-da *et al.* used *NIRS* to characterize quality changes in tobacco during primary process [10]; ZHANG Ling-shuai *et al.* used *NIRS* to identify authentic and fake cigarettes with PCA and Mahalanobis-Distance [11]. Results from above mentioned studies have proved that the *NIRS* can be used to reveal the characteristics of the tobacco. However, these studies have been focused on quantitative analysis of chemical components or qualitative analysis of tobacco features.

Support vector machines (*SVM*) has been developed based on the small-sample learning theory and statistical learning theory [12-13]. As a method of machine learning, *SVM* is designed according to the solid theory, and is focused on the problem of small-sample learning. It has great capability of treating data samples with small size, high dimension and nonlinear distribution. Besides, *SVM* can reduce the influence of high noise due to the introduction of the ε-insensitive loss function.

This paper indicates the detailed description of tobacco-leaf simulation by using *NIRS* and *SVM*, which evaluates the sensory indicators such as Aroma-quality, thickness, stimulation, offensive-gas, strength and aftertaste.

2. Apparatus and Methods

2.1. *Apparatus*

FOSS NIRS DS2500 (Measurement-mode: diffuse reflection, Wavelength-range: 400-2500nm, Spectral-resolution: 0.5nm). Cyclone Sample Mill CSM-1 made by Beijing Industrial Technology Research Institute. PB303 Electronic Balance made by METTLER(Reciprocal sensibility: 0.001g).

[*] This work is supported by grant 12-4-1-9-gx of the Qingdao Science and Technology Plan Project.

2.2. Samples

A domestic tobacco enterprise supplied the samples of 269 tobacco leaves. The places of origins include Brazil(14), Zimbabwe(5), Yunnan(79), Fujian(29), Guangxi(13), Guizhou(37), Heilongjiang(13), Hubei(7), Hunan(22), Jiangxi(5), Shandong(13), Sichuan(29), and Chongqing(3).

2.3. Sample Treatment and Data Acquisition

Tobacco samples are dehydrated at 50°C for 10 minutes and then grounded through 60-mesh screen. 15g sifted tobacco powder is used for *NIR* spectrometric analysis, which is scanned via the wave length between 3800 and 10000 cm^{-1} with the resolution of 8 cm^{-1}.

Ten panelists from tobacco industry evaluate and grade the aroma-quality, thickness, stimulation, offensive-gas, strength, aftertaste of the tobacco leaf according to manufacturer's standards. Grading points are ranked from 1 to10 to assess the qualities of the samples. The points from the 10 experts are averaged with the same weights, which are listed in Table 1.

Table 1. The sensory qualities of the tobacco-leaf samples

ID	Aroma-quality	Thickness	Stimulation	Offensive-gas	Strength	Aftertaste
1	8	6.3	6.3	5.9	6.5	5.9
2	4	7	6.2	6.5	6	6.5
3	3	6.3	6.4	6.1	6.1	6
4	2	6.6	6.3	6.1	6	6.3
5	5	5	5.2	5.2	5.8	5.4
6	8	6.4	6.2	5.9	6	6.1
7	2	5.9	5.9	5.8	5.6	5.8
8	4	5.9	5.5	5.9	5.6	6
......						

3. Data Preprocess and Model

3.1. Data Preprocess

The preliminary *NIR* spectrometric data is pre-processed with the 1st-order derivative and Gaussian-filter smoothing [14, 15], and then is compressed with PCA in Matlab. During the compressing process, the contribution rate rises up to

88% when the number of chosen principle components was 10. The scatter diagram is plotted in a new feature space with the axes of the *PC1* and *PC2*, which is shown in Figure 1.

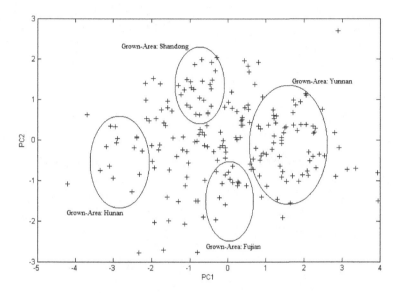

Figure1. The tobacco scatter diagram with PCA

The sensory qualities of tobacco leaf are as different as ecological conditions in growing area. As shown in Figure 1, *PC1* and *PC2* are able to distinguish the origins of tobacco leaves, for example, Yunnan, Hunan, Fujian and Shandong are well demonstrated. It is obvious that the principle components had great ability to characterize the tobacco sensory quality.

3.2. *SVM Model*

Considering the difference between the producing areas, 50 samples from different tobacco-leaf origins are selected to construct the test pool. The rest 219 samples are used for the modelling train pool. Based on the result of PCA, the first 10 principle components are chosen as the input-variables, and the output-variables are the sensory quality indicators.

The experiment adopts the *LS-SVM* (v1.8) algorithm of Matlab toolbox that was developed by J. A. K. Suykens[16]. In the process of *SVM* modeling, we chose RBF as kernel function and established models for different sensory quality indexes.

4. Results and Discussion

4.1. *Simulation of Train Samples*

The simulation of train samples reveals that the current model provides a good description of the data with good accuracies. And considering the generalization performance, the accuracy is not too high in order to avoid over-fitting the training set. The results for the train samples are illustrated in Figure 2.

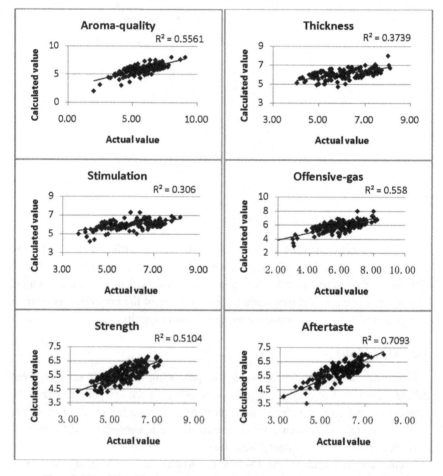

Figure 2. The relationships between calculated value and actual value of train samples

It can be seen from Figure 2 that relation between calculated values and experimental data shows linear trend. It proves that the models can simulate sensory qualities of train samples with good approximation. Moreover, margin of error indicates that the models are not over-fitted.

4.2. Prediction of Test Samples

The 50 testing samples are used to verify the models through the prediction errors, which analyzes generalization of models. The error function was:

$$\text{RMSE} = \sqrt{\frac{1}{n}\sum_i^n(\hat{y}_i - y_i)^2} \tag{1}$$

$\hat{y}_i$ - prediction value, y_i - actual value

The *RMSEs* of each sensory quality indicator are listed in Table 2.

Table 2. *RMSEs* of sensory quality prediction by *NIRS*

Aroma-quality	Thickness	Stimulation	Offensive-gas	Strength	Aftertaste
0.422	0.451	0.461	0.402	0.389	0.391

In Table 2, all the *RMSEs* of sensory quality indexes are below the scoring unit according to the national standard [17]. The training sensory panelists of tobacco enterprises can hardly differentiate samples as precisely as 0.5 in daily tobacco leaf evaluation. So the *RMSEs* of test samples are acceptable in practice.

In order to compare with the analysis of the chemical components, including total-sugar, total-nitrogen, nicotine, reducing-sugar, potassium, chlorine, protein. We established prediction models for sensory quality with the same algorithm and samples as *NIRS* simulation. The *RMSEs* of each sensory quality indicator is listed in Table 3.

Table 3. *RMSEs* of sensory quality prediction by Chemical components

Aroma-quality	Thickness	Stimulation	Offensive-gas	Strength	Aftertaste
0.831	0.763	0.456	0.739	0.353	0.833

Based on the *RMSEs* in Tables 2 and 3, the errors of the chemical components are larger than the ones from *NIRS*. The two indicators of stimulation and strngth have relative slight difference between predictions from the chemical components and *NIRS*. According to the previous empirical analysis, these two sense indicators should reveal a relatively thorough interpretation by using chemical components, such as nicotine, protein and other compounds containing nitrogen. Nevertheless, chemcial components associated with the other indicators cannot take enough information to bulid effective evaluation models. This experiment shows that the *NIRS* prediciton has greater capbility to deal with complex sensory evaluations.

4.3. *Discussion*

Near-infrared spectroscopy carries more information of tobacco sensory quality than the chemical components from traditional detection. From the result of simulation experiment, the *RMSEs* of sensory prediction are in the acceptable range of sensory experts who cannot even make such precise evaluation steadily. Besides, for some complex sensory indexes, such as aroma-quality, thickness and offensive-gas, *NIRS* prediction shows more processing capability than chemical components prediction. Due to it is fast, efficient and environmentally-friendly, the *NIRS* sensory evaluation is becoming more and more prosperous in the field of intelligent sensory evaluation.

References

1. ZENG Xian-yi, DING Yong-sheng. An Introduction to Intelligent Sensory Evaluation, Journal of Donghua University, Vol. 21, 2004, pp.1.
2. Alejandra M. Munoz. Sensory evaluation in quality control: an overview, new developments and future opportunities, Food Quality and Preference, 2002 (13), pp. 329–339.
3. YANG Ying-jun, et al. Application of Pattern Recognition Methods in Intelligent Food Sensory Evaluation, Food Science, 2007(28), pp. 573-577.
4. HU Jian-jun, et al. Grey Incidence Analysis on the Correlation between Main Chemical components and Sensory Quality of Flue-cured Tobacco, Tobacco Science & Technology, 2001(1), pp. 3-7.
5. John Blackman, et al. Examination of the Potential for Using Chemical Analysis as a Surrogate for Sensory Analysis, Analytica Chimica Acta, 2010(660), pp. 2-7.
6. DING Xiang-qian, YANG Ning, XIAO Xie-zhong. An intelligent Approach to Sensory Evaluation: LVQ Neural Network, Journal of Donghua University. 2004(21), pp. 40-42.
7. Ritaban Dutta, et al. Tea quality prediction using a tin oxide-based electronic nose: an artificial intelligence approach, Sensors and Actuators, 2003(B94). pp. 228-237.

8. SHU Ru-xin, et al. *NIR-PCA-SVM* Based Pattern Recognition of Growing Area of Flue-cured Tobacco, Tobacco Chemistry Vol. 292, 2011(11). pp. 50-57.

9. WANG Jia-jun, LI Juan. SIMCA Modeling Based on FT-NIR Analysis Technology and its Application in Quality Monitoring in Cigarette Blending Process, Manufacturing Technology, Vol. 248, 2008(3). pp. 5-9.

10. DENG Fa-da , et al. Using Near-infrared Spectroscopy to Characterize Quality Changes in Tobacco during Primary Processing, ActaTabacariaSinica, Vol. 17, 2011(2). pp. 42-49.

11. ZHANG Ling-shuai, et al. Identification of Authentic and Fake Cigarettes Using Near Infrared Spectroscopy Combined with Principal Component Analysis-Mahalanobis Distance, Spectroscopy and Spectral Analysis, Vol. 31, 2011(5). pp. 1254-1257.

12. C. Cortes and V N. Vapnik. Support-vector networks, Machine Learning, 1995(20). pp. 273-287.

13. B. Schölkopf, et al. New Support Vector Algorithms, Neural Computation, 2000(12). pp. 1207-1245

14. Aqil M, et al. Cortical brain imaging by adaptive filtering of *NIRS* signals, Neuroscience Letters, 2012, 514(1), pp. 35-41.

15. Young I T, van Vliet L J. Recursive implementation of the Gaussian filter, Signal processing, 1995, 44(2), pp. 139-151.

16. Information on http://www.esat.kuleuven.be/sista/lssvmlab/.

17. GB 5606.4-2005 in China. Cigarettes-Part 4: Technical requirements for sense evaluation, pp.2

LEARNING LOCALLY WEIGHTED BAYSIAN NETWORK FOR AUC RANKING

Qiong Wu[a,b], Lei Yuan[a], Zhihua Cai[b], and Qiong Gu[a]

[a] School of Mathematics and Computer Science,
Hubei University of Arts and Science, Xiangyang 441053, China
[b] Department of Computer Science,
China University of Geosciences Wuhan, 430074 China.

Learning the structure of a Bayesian network classifier (BNC) encodes conditional independence assumption between attributes. One major approach to mitigate BNCs's primary weakness (the attributes independence assumption) is the locally weighted approach. And this type of approach has been proved to achieve good performance for NB, a BNC with simple structure. However, we do not know whether or how effective it works for improving the performance of the complex BNCs. In this paper, we carry out an systematically experimental analysis to investigate the effectiveness of locally weighted method for complex BNCs measured by the area under the ROC curve ranking (AUC). Experiments on 36 benchmark data sets in Weka system demonstrate that although locally weighting significantly improve the performance of NB (a BNC with simple structure), it could not work well on BNCs with complex structures.

Keywords: Baysian Network; Locally Weighting; AUC; Classification.

1. Introduction

A Bayesian network (BN) consists of a set of local distributions under a structural model. In this paper, we assume that the $A_i, i = 1, 2, \cdots, n$, are n attributes. Each instance can be described by the tuple of attribute values $< a_1, a_2, \cdots, a_n >$, where a_n denotes the value of the nth attribute A_n. The most probable target value is described as ν_{MAP}, while C is a finite set building on every target value c_j. Typically, one set of training instances with class label is given, a classifier must be learned to predict the class distribution of an instance with its class label unknown. The classifier represented by Bayesian approach can be defined as:

$$c_{MAP} = \underset{c_j \in C}{\arg\max} \, P(c_j)P(a_1, a_2, \cdots, a_n \,|c_j) \tag{1}$$

It is easy to estimate $p(c_j)$, opposite to $P(a_1, a_2, \cdots, a_n \,|c_j)$.[1] Assume that all the attributes satisfy the attribute independence assumption, and then the probabilities of observing the conjunction are just the product of the probabilities for the individual attributes. This is the core concept of naive Bayes, simply NB. The details can be defined as:

$$c_{NB} = \arg\max_{c_j \in C} P(c_j) \prod_{i=1}^{n} P(a_i | c_j) \tag{2}$$

However, the attribute independence assumption made by naive Bayes harms its classification performance when it is violated in reality. In order to weak the attribute independence assumption of NB while at the same time retaining its simplicity and efficiency, researchers have proposed many effective methods[2-5] to further improve the performance of naive Bayes, such as *Structure Extension*, *Local Learning*, and *Attribute Weighting*.

The locally weighted method has been proved as a effect improvement for naive Bayes due to the studies in the previous works.[6-8] However, for the more complex BNC models, such as Tree Augmented Naive Bayes (TAN),[9] Averaged One-Dependence Estimators (AODE)[10] and Hidden Naive Bayes (HNB),[4] locally weighted learning is comparatively less explored. In this case, we could not make sure how much effect the locally weighting make exactly. Moreover, the accuracy is calculated by the percentage of successful predictions on domain specific problems.[11] Nevertheless, some real-world data mining applications require accurate rankings, not just only classification accuracy. Accordingly, in this paper, we analyze the performance of locally weighted complex BNCs (TAN, AODE and HNB) by using locally weighted learning method in.[8] Experiments and comparisons, on 36 UCI benchmark data sets demonstrate that the attribute weighted technologies just slightly outperforms unweighted complex BNCs on AUC, which means that the locally weighted do not work very well for the complex BNCs.

2. TAN: Tree Augmented Naive Bayes

Tree Augmented Naive Bayes (TAN) is a semi-naive Bayesian Learning method. It relaxes the naive Bayes attribute independence assumption by employing a tree structure, in which each attribute only depends on the class and one other attribute. TAN models are a resrticted family of Bayesian networks in which the class variable has no parents and each attribute has as parents the class variable and at most another attribute. The corresponding TAN classifier is defined as follows.

$$c_{TAN} = \arg\max_{c_j \in C} P(c_j) \prod_{i=1}^{n} P(a_i | p_{ai}, c_j) \tag{3}$$

Table 1. The detailed experimental results on AUC and standard deviation.

Data Sets	TAN	LWTAN	AODE	LWAODE	HNB	LWHNB
anneal	99.17±1.34	97.89±3.92	98.93±1.50	97.21±5.96	99.15±1.37	98.08±3.74
anneal.ORIG	96.73±6.07	94.89±7.33 *	97.29±3.93	94.82±7.26	97.87±3.27	96.18±7.68
audiology	83.59±1.47	83.79±1.58	83.81±1.48	83.61±1.60	84.08±1.48	83.80±1.57
autos	93.84±3.17	95.44±2.82 v	94.67±2.54	95.68±2.40	95.19±2.49	95.50±2.76
balance-scale	80.94±4.73	74.31±3.53 *	79.93±3.94	73.43±3.41 *	87.38±4.21	73.13±3.65 *
breast-cancer	65.36±10.84	64.05±10.64	71.18±10.03	64.15±10.27 *	66.69±10.61	66.53±9.20
breast-w	98.89±0.96	98.82±1.23	99.28±0.73	99.16±0.93	99.02±0.95	99.34±0.73 v
colic	85.58±6.24	84.71±6.97	86.79±6.08	84.53±6.81	86.73±6.09	86.31±6.01
colic.ORIG	72.02±8.41	75.47±8.99	82.22±7.24	76.02±8.87 *	83.70±5.62	78.35±7.79 *
credit-a	90.49±3.01	87.53±4.16 *	92.35±2.92	88.75±4.02 *	91.04±3.58	90.91±3.17
credit-g	77.10±4.88	72.48±4.77 *	79.68±4.14	73.50±4.75 *	79.65±4.42	75.89±4.10 *
diabetes	81.87±5.03	71.51±5.18 *	82.96±4.83	72.15±5.51 *	82.31±4.82	79.19±5.28 *
glass	80.10±5.91	82.85±6.25	83.60±5.64	84.60±5.95	88.37±4.57	86.28±5.41
heart-c	83.80±0.65	83.39±0.75 *	84.11±0.57	83.67±0.68 *	83.94±0.63	83.78±0.65
heart-h	83.71±0.54	83.58±0.75	83.97±0.54	83.69±0.72	83.79±0.59	83.79±0.64
heart-statlog	89.36±4.46	86.06±6.07	91.28±4.70	87.47±5.90 *	89.26±5.22	88.40±5.09
hepatitis	87.15±10.02	80.72±12.34	88.53±10.56	82.33±11.75 *	88.04±9.91	84.54±12.02
hypothyroid	86.67±7.28	79.98±8.77 *	87.34±7.23	80.33±8.87 *	88.77±6.29	84.12±7.94 *
ionosphere	98.05±2.42	96.25±2.92	97.57±2.23	96.90±2.33	98.19±1.95	97.47±2.16
iris	99.07±1.82	98.29±2.38	99.16±1.42	98.09±2.57	98.72±2.20	98.81±1.92
kr-vs-kp	98.26±0.62	99.18±0.45 v	97.44±0.75	99.29±0.41 v	98.21±0.56	99.62±0.32 v
labor	93.75±12.09	95.50±10.18	98.54±4.90	96.75±8.57	97.04±7.52	96.08±9.47
letter	98.10±0.33	97.54±0.47 *	98.40±0.28	98.02±0.45 *	98.89±0.20	98.79±0.27
lymph	93.61±4.58	93.72±4.23	95.03±4.35	93.97±4.30	94.82±4.27	94.63±4.32
mushroom	100.00±0.01	100.00±0.00	100.00±0.01	100.00±0.00	100.00±0.01	100.00±0.00
primary-tumor	84.59±2.32	81.33±3.11 *	85.72±2.07	81.47±2.88 *	85.86±2.12	83.98±2.42 *
segment	99.53±0.20	99.05±0.46 *	99.42±0.22	99.23±0.45	99.71±0.14	99.65±0.18
sick	98.08±1.21	97.61±2.04	97.09±1.69	97.70±2.00	98.24±1.22	98.91±0.86 v
sonar	83.79±8.35	87.12±7.38	90.01±6.77	91.28±6.34	90.15±6.63	91.58±6.37
soybean	99.94±0.08	99.73±0.30 *	99.91±0.09	99.75±0.26 *	99.96±0.05	99.89±0.10 *
splice	99.35±0.35	04.81±1.14 *	99.56±0.25	97.60±0.69 *	99.57±0.24	98.76±0.45 *
vehicle	90.76±2.01	85.79±2.80 *	89.91±2.03	86.93±2.38 *	90.73±2.00	88.81±2.13 *
vote	98.75±1.17	97.93±1.77	98.67±1.24	98.27±1.69	98.76±1.13	98.65±1.35
vowel	99.52±0.31	99.60±0.31	99.40±0.36	99.72±0.26 v	99.70±0.22	99.73±0.23
waveform-5000	92.85±2.12	84.06±3.17 *	96.70±1.27	87.83±2.76 *	96.63±1.31	92.02±2.35 *
zoo	99.01±1.44	99.02±1.48	99.07±1.43	99.07±1.43	99.26±1.11	99.12±1.30

v, * : statistically significant improvement or degradation with a 95% confidence level.

3. AODE: Averaged One-dependence Estimators

TAN has high computational complexity at training time. The determinant of its computational profile lead to the development of Averaged One-dependence Estimators, simply AODE.[10] In AODE, an aggregate of one-dependence classifiers are learned and the prediction is produced by averaging the predictions of all these qualified one-dependence classifiers. Except for having good classification performance, AODE retains the simplicity and direct theoretical foundation of naive Bayes without incurring the high time. The corresponding AODE classifier is defined as follows:

$$c_{AODE} = \arg\max_{c_j \in C} \left(\sum_{i=1}^{n} P(a_i, c_i) \prod_{j=1}^{n} P(a_j|a_i, c_j) \right) \qquad (4)$$

4. HNB: Hidden Naive Bayes

As discussed in previous sections, naive Bayes ignores attribute dependencies. On the other hand, although a Bayesian network can represent arbitrary attribute dependencies, it is intractable to learn it from data.[12] Thus, learning restricted structures, such as TAN, is more practical. However, only one parent is allowed for each attribute in TAN, even though several attributes might have the similar influence on it. The motivation of designing Hidden Naive Bayes (HNB) is to develop a new model that can avoid the intractable computational complexity for learning an optimal Bayesian network and still take the influences from all attributes into account. It represents an approximation of the joint distribution defined as follows.

$$c_{HNB} = \arg\max_{c_j \in C} P(c_j) \prod_{j=1}^{n} P(a_i \,|\, A_{hi}, c_j) \tag{5}$$

where

$$P(a_i | A_{hi}, c_j) = \sum_{j=1, j \neq i}^{n} w_{i,j} P(a_i | a_j, c_j) \tag{6}$$

where $w_{i,j}$ is the conditional weight contributed by attribute A_i and A_j. In HNB, attribute dependencies are actually represented by hidden parents of attributes. It can be viewed in such a way that a hidden parent A_{hi} is created for each attribute A_i. HNB should be an accurate model because of which can represent the influences on each attribute from all other attributes and assign higher weights to more importance attributes.

5. LW: Locally Weighting

The basic idea of the locally weighting approach is building a Bayesian network model on the neighbourhood of the test instance, instead of on the whole training data.[8] Local learning helps to mitigate the effects of attribute dependencies that may exist in the data as a whole and we expect this method to do well if there are no strong dependencies within the neighbourhood of the test instance.

The local learning approach is actually a kind of training data selection approach,[6] which helps to weaken the effects of attribute dependencies that may exist in the whole training data. As naive Bayes requires relatively little data for training, the neighbourhood can be kept small, thereby reducing the chance of encountering strong dependencies. Therefore, although the attribute conditional independence assumption of naive Bayes is always violated on the whole training data, it could be expected that the dependencies within the neighbourhood of the test instance is much weaker than that on the whole training data and thus the conditional independence assumptions required for naive Bayes are likely to be true.[13]

6. Experiments

6.1. *Experimental Settings*

In this section, we run our experiments under the framework of Weka[14] using 36 UCI data sets[15] to validate the effectiveness of our new algorithm. These data sets in format of *arff* are downloaded from the official website of Weka, which represent a wide range of domains. All reported results are based on 10 times 10-fold cross-validation[16] with AUC being used as the performance metric.

6.2. *Analysis of Locally Weighted BNCs*

Tables 1 reports the detailed results (AUC with the standard deviation) of BNCs (TAN, AODE and HNB) and locally weighted BNCs, respectively. In the table, the symbols v and $*$ represent statistically significant upgradation and degradation over the BNC with the p-value less than 0.05. Overall, the results can be summarized as: (1) Locally weighted TAN could not have significant superiority compared to TAN in AUC. Locally weighted TAN model LWTAN has inferior to TAN on AUC (2 wins and 14 losses); (2) LWAODE show worse performance on AUC (2 wins and 16 losses); and (3) LWHNB sightly fails than HNB in AUC (3 wins and 10 losses).

According, locally weighting could not achieve better performance on BNCs (TAN, AODE and HNB) with complex structure, but only works very well on BNC (NB) with simple structure. This is mainly attributed to the fact that for the complex BNCs, the reason why the corresponding BNCs can improve the their ranking performance in classification is mainly attributed to the structure not the locally weighting approach.

7. Conclusion and Future Work

In this paper, we first investigated the complex structure models for BNCs and their improvements, then carried out systematical experiments to analysis the effectiveness of the locally weighting strategies for complex BNCs focusing on Tree Augmented Naive Bayes (TAN), Averaged One-Dependence Estimators (AODE) and Hidden Naive Bayes (HNB). The systematic experiments and comparisons on 36 benchmark data sets on the AUC ranking performance showed that although locally weighting significantly improve the performance of NB (a BNC with simple structure), it could not work well on BNCs with complex structures.

8. Acknowledgments

This work was supported in part by the National Natural Science Foundation of China (61272296), and the Key Project of the Natural Science Foundation of Hubei Province, China (Grant No. 2013CFA004), and the Natural Science Foundation of Hubei Province of China (2012FFB01901), and the Educational Commission of Hubei Province of China (D20132601), and Xiangyang Science and Technology Development Funds.

References

1. J. Wu, Z. Cai and X. Zhu, Self-adaptive probability estimation for naive bayes classification, in *Proceedings of the International Joint Conference on Neural Networks*, (IEEE Publishers, Dallas, TX, USA, 2013).
2. J. Wu, Z. Cai, S. Zeng and X. Zhu, Artificial immune system for attribute weighted naive bayes classification, in *Proceedings of the International Joint Conference on Neural Networks*, (Dallas, TX, USA, 2013).
3. J. Wu and Z. Cai, *Journal of Intelligent Information Systems* , 1 (2013).
4. L. Jiang, H. Zhang and Z. Cai, *IEEE Trans. on Knowl. and Data Eng.* **21**, 1361 (2009).
5. J. Wu and Z. Cai, *Journal of Computational Information Systems* **7**, 1672 (2011).
6. L. Jiang, Z. Cai, H. Zhang and D. Wang, *J. Exp. Theor. Artif. Intell.* **25**, 273 (2013).
7. K. A. Umut Orhan and O. Comert, *Journal of New Results in Science.* , 71 (2012).
8. E. Frank, M. Hall and B. Pfahringer, Locally weighted naive bayes, in *UAI*, (San Francisco, CA, USA, 2003).
9. N. Friedman, D. Geiger and M. Goldszmidt, *Mach. Learn.* **29**, 131 (1997).
10. G. I. Webb, J. R. Boughton and Z. Wang, *Machine Learning* **58**, 5 (2005).
11. J. Wu, X. Zhu, C. Zhang and Z. Cai, Multi-instance multi-graph dual embedding learning, in *Data Mining (ICDM), 2013 IEEE 13th International Conference on*, (Dallas, Texas, USA, 2013).
12. H. Zhang, L. Jiang and J. Su, Hidden naive bayes, in *AAAI*, (AAAI Press, Pittsburgh, Pennsylvania, 2005).
13. L. Jiang, H. Zhang, Z. Cai and D. Wang, *Journal of Experimental and Theoretical Artificial Intelligence* **24**, 219 (2012).
14. I. H. Witten and E. Frank, *Data Mining: Practical Machine Learning Tools and Techniques*, 2nd edn. (Morgan Kaufmann Publishers, 2005).
15. K. Bache and M. Lichman, UCI machine learning repository (2013).
16. J. Wu, X. Zhu, C. Zhang and P. Yu, *Knowledge and Data Engineering, IEEE Transactions on* **PP**, 1 (2014).

F-TRANSFORM BASED ON GENERALIZED RESIDUATED LATTICES

Anand Pratap Singh* and S.P. Tiwari[†]

*Department of Applied Mathematics, Indian School of Mines,
Dhanbad, 826004, India*
* anandecc@gmail.com; [†] *sptiwarimaths@gmail.com*
www.ismdhanbad.ac.in

The main purpose of this research work is to introduce and study the concept of *F*-transform based on generalized residuated lattices.

Keywords: $F^\uparrow$-transform; $F^\downarrow$-transform; Generalized residuated lattices.

1. Introduction

F-transform, firstly proposed by Irina[11] has drawn the attention of a number of researchers due to its importance in fuzzy modelling (cf.,[1,9,10,14]). However, the fuzziness used in[11] is described by means of either ordinary fuzzy sets or residuated lattices. As in the literature, some other lattices, e.g., skew-residuated lattices and generalized residuated lattices have been proposed/considered by modifying residuation property or by considering non-commutativeness of conjunction and have been shown their own importance (cf.,[2]), these 'lattices' can apparently be used to introduce and study the theory of F-transform based on skew-residuated lattices/generalized residuated lattices. In this paper, we have initiated the study of *F*- transform based on generalized residuated lattices.

2. Preliminaries

The origins of residuation theory lie in the study of ideal lattices of rings in the 1930s. Ward and Dilworth investigated residuated lattices in a series of papers (cf.,[3,4,16–18]). Since that time, there have been substantial researches regarding some specific classes of residuated structures, such as (cf.,[5,7,8]). When we consider the conjunction to be non-commutative, the corresponding truth structures are weak-pseudo-BL-algebras[5] or pseudo-MTL-algebras[8] are the generalization of the generalized residuated lattices on $[0, 1]$ induced by left-continuous pseudo-t-norms.[5,6]

Definition 2.1.[15] A **generalized residuated lattice** is an algebra $(L, \wedge, \vee, \otimes, \rightarrow, \rightsquigarrow, 0, 1, T)$ such that the following conditions hold.

(i) $(L, \wedge, \vee, 0, 1)$ is a bounded lattice with the least element 0 and the greatest element 1;

(ii) $(L, \otimes, T)$ is a monoid;

(iii) For all a,b,c $\in L$ we have the following equivalence;
$a \otimes b \leq c$ iff $a \leq b \rightarrow c$ iff $b \leq a \rightsquigarrow c$
$\rightarrow$ and $\rightsquigarrow$ are called the left and right implication of $\otimes$, respectively.

A generalized residuated lattice $(L, \wedge, \vee, \otimes, \rightarrow, \rightsquigarrow, 0, 1, T)$ is said to be **commutative (resp. non-commutative)** if $\otimes$ is commutative (resp. non-commutative); **integral** if $T = 1$; and **complete** if the underlying lattice $(L, \wedge, \vee, \rightarrow, 0, 1)$ is complete.

Clearly, if $\otimes$ is commutative, then $\rightarrow = \rightsquigarrow$ holds. From now on, generalized residuated lattices are always referred to the integral generalized residuated lattices.

In,[15] it has been shown that, $b \otimes (b \rightarrow a) \leq a$ and $(b \rightsquigarrow a) \otimes b \leq a$ need not hold for all $a, b \in L$, when $\otimes$ is non-commutative. This is one of the way that how generalized residuated lattices differ from residuated lattices.

Lemma 2.1. *Let* $(L, \wedge, \vee, \otimes, \rightarrow, \rightsquigarrow, 0, 1)$ *be a generalized residuated lattice. Then the following hold for all* $a, b \in L$:

(1) $1 \rightarrow a = a$ *and* $1 \rightsquigarrow a = a$;

(2) $a \rightarrow a = 1$ *and* $a \rightsquigarrow a = 1$;

(3) $a \leq b$ *iff* $a \rightarrow b = 1$ *iff* $a \rightsquigarrow b = 1$;

(4) $a \otimes b \leq a \wedge b$;

(5) $a \leq b \rightarrow a$ *and* $a \leq b \rightsquigarrow a$;

(6) $b \rightarrow (a \otimes b) \leq a$ *and* $b \otimes (b \rightsquigarrow a) \leq a$.

We close this section by recalling the following concept of fuzzy partition introduced in[11]

Definition 2.2. Let $x_1 < ... < x_n$ be fixed nodes within $[a, b]$, such that $x_1 = a, x_n = b$ and $n \geq 2$. We say that fuzzy sets $A_1, ..., A_n$, identified with their membership functions $A_1(x), ..., A_n(x)$, defined on $[a, b]$, form a fuzzy partition of $[a, b]$ if they fulfill the following conditions for $k = 1, ..., n$:

(i) $A_k : [a, b] \rightarrow [0, 1], A_k(x_k) = 1$;

(ii) $A_k(x) = 0$ if $x \notin (x_{k-1}, x_{k+1})$ where for the uniformity of denotation, we put $x_0 = a$ and $x_{n+1} = b$;

(iii) $A_k(x)$ is continuous;

(iv) $A_k(x), k = 2, ..., n$, strictly increases on $[x_{k-1}, x_k]$ and $A_k(x), k = 1, ..., n-1$, strictly decreases on $[x_k, x_{k+1}]$;

(iv) for all $x \in [a, b]$

$$\sum_{k=1}^{n} A_k(x) = 1. \tag{1}$$

The membership functions $A_1, ..., A_n$, are called basic functions.

3. F-transform

In this section, we introduce the concept of direct $F^\uparrow$-transform and direct $F^\downarrow$-transform based on generalized residuated lattices. Throughout, we assume that for a fuzzy partition $A_1, ..., A_n, n \geq 2$ of $[0,1]$ and $\forall x \in [0,1] \exists i \in \{0, 1, ..., n\}$ such that $A_i(x) > 0$. We begin by introducing the following concept of $F^\uparrow$-transform.

Definition 3.1. Let f be a function defined at nodes $p_1, ..., p_l \in [0,1]$ and $A_1, ..., A_n, n < l$, be basic functions which form a fuzzy partition of $[0,1]$. We say that the n-tuple of real numbers $[F_1^\uparrow, F_2^\uparrow, ..., F_n^\uparrow]$ is a **left $F^\uparrow$-transform** of f w.r.t. $A_1, ..., A_n$, if

$$F_k^\uparrow = \bigvee_{j=1}^{l} (A_k(p_j) \otimes f(p_j)), \tag{2}$$

and respectively **right $F^\uparrow$-transform** if,

$$F_k^{*\uparrow} = \bigvee_{j=1}^{l} (f(p_j) \otimes A_k(p_j)). \tag{3}$$

We denote the left $F^\uparrow$-transform of f w.r.t. $A_1, ..., A_n$, by $F^\uparrow$ and write it as

$$F_n^\uparrow[f] = [F_1^\uparrow, F_2^\uparrow, ..., F_n^\uparrow].$$

The elements $F_1^\uparrow, F_2^\uparrow, ..., F_n^\uparrow$ are called components of the left $F^\uparrow$-transform. Similarly, the elements $F_1^{*\uparrow}, F_2^{*\uparrow}, ..., F_n^{*\uparrow}$ are called components of the right $F^\uparrow$-transform respectively.

The following shows that the $F^\uparrow$-transform satisfies linearity.

Proposition 3.1. *Let f and g be defined at nodes $p_1, ..., p_l \in [0, 1]$ and $A_1, ..., A_n, n < l$ be basic functions which form a fuzzy partition of $[0, 1]$. Then for given $\alpha, \beta \in [0, 1]$,*

$$F_n^{*\uparrow}[\alpha \otimes f \vee \beta \otimes g] = \alpha \otimes F_n^{*\uparrow}[f] \vee \beta \otimes F_n^{*\uparrow}[g], \qquad (4)$$

where on the right-hand side the operation $\vee$ is taken component-wise.

Corollary 3.1. *Let f and g be defined at nodes $p_1, ..., p_l \in [0, 1]$ and $A_1, ..., A_n, n < l$ be basic functions which form a fuzzy partition of $[0, 1]$. If $f \leq g$ then $F_n^{*\uparrow}[f] \leq F_n^{*\uparrow}[g]$, where the inequality $\leq$ between vectors is taken component wise.*

It has been proved in[11] that the components of the F-transform are weighted mean values of the given function, where the weights are given by the basic functions. A consequence for it in case of right $F^\uparrow$-transform is given below.

Proposition 3.2. *Let f be a function defined at nodes $p_1, ..., p_l \in [0, 1]$ and $A_1, ..., A_n, n < l$, be basic functions which form a fuzzy partition of $[0, 1]$. Then the kth component of the $F^{*\uparrow}$-transform is the least element of the following set:*

$$S_k = \{a \in [0, 1] | A_k(p_j) \leq (f(p_j) \to a) \text{ for all } j = 1, ..., l\}, \qquad (5)$$

where $k = 1, ..., n$.

Corollary 3.2. *Let the condition of above proposition be fulfilled. Then the kth component of the $F^{*\uparrow}$-transform is the least solution to the following equation with the unknown a:*

$$\bigwedge_{j=1}^{l} (f(p_j) \to (Ak(p_j) \to a)) = 1, \qquad (6)$$

where k= 1,...,n.

Similar to above, we now introduce the concept of $F^\downarrow$-transform.

Definition 3.2. Let f be a function defined at nodes $p_1, ..., p_l \in [0, 1]$ and $A_1, ..., A_n, n < l$, be basic functions which form a fuzzy partition of $[0, 1]$. We say that the n-tuple of real numbers $[F_1^\downarrow, F_2^\downarrow, ..., F_n^\downarrow]$ is a **left $F^\downarrow$-transform** of f w.r.t. $A_1, ..., A_n$, if

$$F_k^{\downarrow} = \bigwedge_{j=1}^{l} (A_k(p_j) \to f(p_j)), \tag{7}$$

and similarly the **right** $F^{\downarrow}$**-transform** is defined as:

$$F_k^{*\downarrow} = \bigwedge_{j=1}^{l} (A_k(p_j) \rightsquigarrow f(p_j)). \tag{8}$$

Denote the **right** $F^{\downarrow}$**-transform** of f w.r.t. $A_1, ..., A_n$, by $F_n^{*\downarrow}[f]$. Then we may write

$$F_n^{*\downarrow}[f] = [F_1^{*\downarrow}, F_2^{*\downarrow}, ..., F_n^{*\downarrow}].$$

The elements $F_1^{*\downarrow}..., F_n^{*\downarrow}$ are called components of the right $F^{\downarrow}$−transform.

Proposition 3.3. *Let f and g be defined at nodes $p_1, ..., p_l \in [0, 1]$ and $A_1, ..., A_n, n < l$, be functions. Then for arbitrary $\alpha, \beta \in [0, 1]$, the following equality holds.*

$$F_n^{*\downarrow}[(\alpha \to f) \wedge (\beta \to g)] = (\alpha \to F_n^{*\downarrow}[f]) \wedge (\beta \to F_n^{*\downarrow}[g]), \tag{9}$$

where on the right-hand side, the operation $\wedge$ is taken componentwise.

Corollary 3.3. *Let f and g be defined at nodes $p_1, ..., p_l \in [0, 1]$ and $A_1, ..., A_n, n < l$, be functions. If $f \leq g$ then $F_n^{*\downarrow}[f] \leq F_n^{*\downarrow}[g]$ where the inequality $\leq$ between vectors is taken component wise.*

Similar to the concept of $F^{\uparrow}$-transform, in case of the $F^{\downarrow}$-transform we have the following.

Proposition 3.4. *Let f be a function defined at nodes $p_1, ..., p_l \in [0, 1]$ and $A_1, ..., A_n, n < l$, be basic functions which form a fuzzy partition of $[0, 1]$. Then the kth component of the $F^{*\downarrow}$-transform is the greatest element of the following set .*

$$T_k = \{a \in [0, 1] | A_k(p_j) \leq (a \to f(p_j)) \text{ for all } j = 1, ..., l\}, \tag{10}$$

where $k = 1, ..., n$.

From the above, it is clear that the concept of inverse F-transform based on generalized residuated lattices can be introduced similarly. But, due to lack of space, we have not discussed here.

4. Conclusion

Chiefly inspired from,[11] in this paper, we have introduced the concept of F-transform based on generalized residuated lattices. Due to constraint, we have not provided the proofs of results. In near future, we will present the relationship between fuzzy rough set theory and the theory of F-transform.

References

1. B. Bede, I.J. Rudas, Approximation properties of fuzzy transforms, *Fuzzy Sets and Systems* **180** (2011) 20-40.
2. I. Chajda, J. Krnavek, Skew residuated lattices, *Fuzzy Sets and Systems*, **222** (2013) 78-83.
3. R.P. Dilworth, Abstract residuation over lattices, *Bulletin of the American Mathematical Society*, **44** (1938) 262-268.
4. R.P. Dilworth, Non-commutative residuated lattices, *Transactions of the American Mathematical Society*, **46** (1939) 426-444.
5. P. Flondor, G. Georgescu, A. Iorgulescu, Pseudo-t-norms and pseudo-BL algebras, *Soft Computing* **5** (2001) 355-371.
6. G. Georgescu, A. Popescu, Non-commutative fuzzy structures and pairs of weak negations, *Fuzzy Sets and Systems*, **143** (2004) 129-155.
7. P. Hajek, Metamathematics of Fuzzy Logic, *Kluwer Academic Publishers*, Boston, 1998.
8. P. Hajek, Observations on non-commutative fuzzy logic, *Soft Computing* **8** (2003) 38-43.
9. F. D. Martino, V. Loia, S Sessa, Fuzzy transforms method in prediction data analysis, *Fuzzy Sets and Systems*, **180** (2011) 146-163.
10. G. Patane, Fuzzy transform and least-squares approximation: Analogies, differences, and generalizations, *Fuzzy Sets and Systems*, **180** (2011) 41-54.
11. I. Perfilieva, Fuzzy transforms: Theory and applications, *Fuzzy Sets and Systems*, **157** (2006) 993-1023.
12. I. Perfilieva, Logical approximation, *Soft Computing*, **7** (2002) 73-78.
13. I. Perfilieva, Normal forms in BL-algebra of functions and their contribution to universal approximation, *Fuzzy Sets and Systems*, **143** (2004) 111-127.
14. L. Stefanini, F-transform with parametric generalized fuzzy partitions, *Fuzzy Sets and Systems*, **180** (2011) 98-120.
15. C.Y. Wang, B.Q. Hu, Fuzzy rough sets based on generalized residuated lattices, *Information Sciences*, **248** (2013) 31-49.
16. M. Ward, Residuation in structures over which a multiplication is defined, *Duke Mathematical Journal*, **3** (1937) 627-636.
17. M. Ward, Structure residuation, *The Annals of Mathematics*, **39** (1938) 558-568.
18. M. Ward, R.P. Dilworth, Residuated lattices, *Transactions of the American Mathematical Society*, **45** (1939) 335-354.

L-FUZZY ASSOCIATIVE MEMORIES WITH AN EMPHASIS ON INTERVAL-VALUED AND TYPE-2 FUZZY ASSOCIATIVE MEMORIES

Tiago Schuster* and Peter Sussner**

*Dept. of Applied Mathematics, IMECC, University of Campinas,
Campinas, So Paulo - Brazil
E-mail: schtiago@hotmail.com *
sussner@ime.unicamp.br ***

Keywords: Mathematical morphology, fuzzy systems and systems, associative memories, morphological neural networks, lattice computing, interval-valued fuzzy sets.

1. Summary

The last decade has witnessed the emergence of a variety of lattice computing approaches towards computational intelligence such as morphological neural networks[1,2] and fuzzy lattice reasoning/ neuro-computing models.[3] Here, the technical term "lattice" refers to a lattice in the mathematical sense of Birkhoff's seminal work.[4] Lattice theory grew out of Boolean algebra and has found a wide range of applications such as formal concept analysis, computational intelligence, fuzzy set theory, and mathematical morphology.[5] Recall that *mathematical morphology* (MM) is irrevocably linked to lattice theory since Serra established complete lattices as its appropriate theoretical framework.[6] Mathematical morphology on complete lattices represents the theoretical basis for a range of computational intelligence models known as morphological neural networks (MNNs) including gray-scale and *fuzzy morphological associative memories* (FMAMs).[7,8] In this context, recall that the class of fuzzy sets over a certain universe can be equipped with a partial ordering, giving rise to a complete lattice.

The advent of type-2 fuzzy systems suggests the development of type-2 FMAMs and in particular interval-valued (type-2) FMAMs. Recall that the classes of type-2 and interval-valued (as well as bipolar and intuitionistic) fuzzy sets together with different choices of partial orderings form classes of

L-fuzzy sets, where $\mathbb{L}$ denotes a complete lattice. For every complete lattice $\mathbb{L}$, approaches towards $\mathbb{L}$-fuzzy mathematical morphology ($\mathbb{L}$-FMM) arise by considering the complete lattice-ordered double semigroup (clodus) consisting of $\mathbb{L}$ together with a dilation and an erosion given respectively by an $\mathbb{L}$-fuzzy conjunction and an $\mathbb{L}$-fuzzy implication. The goal of this project is to devise $\mathbb{L}$-fuzzy morphological associative memories ($\mathbb{L}$-FMAMs) on the basis of $\mathbb{L}$-FMM. We will focus on developing (interval) type-2 FMAMs since type-2 fuzzy systems, in particular interval type-2 fuzzy systems, have found various applications in engineering, computing with words, and approximate reasoning.[9,10]

Thus far we have only introduced *interval-valued fuzzy morphological associative memories* IV-FMAMs based on representable conjunctions[11] and we have yet to analyze the properties of these particular IV-FMAMs as well as the ones of more general $\mathbb{L}$-FMAMs that we intend to introduce in the future. We applied the aforementioned IV-FMAM models in conjunction with the interval-valued subtractive clustering technique[12] and the Nie-Tan defuzzification method[13] to a time-series prediction problem in industry, namely the problem of forecasting the average monthly streamflow of a large hydroelectric plant located in southern Brazil,[14,15] in which case this approach scales linearly in comparison with our previous FMAM approach. In the near future, we will perform the clustering phase using clustering techniques for IV-fuzzy data such as dual centers fuzzy type-2 clustering and fuzzy type-2 c-ellipses clustering In addition, we intend to evaluate the validity of the resulting clusters using criteria that have recently appeared in the literature.[16]

In addition, our goals include the development of full type-2 fuzzy associative memories (T2-FAMs) as particular cases of $\mathbb{L}$-FMAMs and to employ these novel models together with full type-2 fuzzy clustering algorithms and validity indices in a number of applications such as the aforementioned streamflow prediction problem and a wind speed forecasting problem.[17] In addition, the zSlices method will be used to perform simulations.[18] We also intend to investigate the complexity issue of alternative design methods.

References

1. G. X. Ritter and G. Urcid, "A lattice matrix method for hyperspectral image unmixing," *Inf. Sci.*, vol. 181, pp. 1787–1803, 2011.
2. P. Sussner and E. Esmi, "Morphological perceptrons with competitive learning: Lattice-theoretical framework and constructive learning algorithm," *Information Sciences*, vol. 181, no. 10, pp. 1929–1950, 2011.
3. V. G. Kaburlasos, I. N. Athanasiadis, and P. A. Mitkas, "Fuzzy lattice reasoning (FLR) classifier and its application for ambient ozone estimation,"

International Journal of Approximate Reasoning, vol. 45, pp. 152–188, May 2007.

4. G. Birkhoff, *Lattice Theory*. Providence: American Mathematical Society, 3rd ed., 1993.

5. G. A. Grätzer, *General lattice theory*. Springer, 2003.

6. C. Ronse, "Why mathematical morphology needs complete lattices," *Signal Processing*, vol. 21, pp. 129–154, Oct. 1990.

7. P. Sussner and M. E. Valle, "Grayscale morphological associative memories," *IEEE Transactions on Neural Networks*, vol. 17, pp. 559–570, May 2006.

8. P. Sussner and M. E. Valle, "Fuzzy associative memories and their relationship to mathematical morphology," in *Handbook of Granular Computing* (W. Pedrycz, A. Skowron, and V. Kreinovich, eds.), ch. 33, New York: John Wiley and Sons, Inc., 2008.

9. H. Hagras and C. Wagner, "Introduction to interval type-2 fuzzy logic controllers - towards better uncertainty handling in real world applications," *The IEEE Systems, Man and Cybernetics eNewsletter*, 2009.

10. M. H. F. Zarandi, B. Rezaee, I. B. Türkşen, and E. Neshat, "A type-2 fuzzy rule-based expert system model for stock price analysis," *Expert Syst. Appl.*, vol. 36, no. 1, pp. 139–154, 2009.

11. G. Deschrijver and C. Cornelis, "Representability in interval-valued fuzzy set theory," *International Journal of Uncertainty, Fuzziness and Knowledge-Based Systems*, vol. 15, no. 3, pp. 345–361, 2007.

12. L. T. Ngo and B. H. Pham, "A type-2 fuzzy subtractive clustering," *Advances in Intelligent and Soft Computing*, vol. 125, pp. 395–402, 2012.

13. S. Greenfield and F. Chiclana, "Type-reduction of the discretised interval type-2 fuzzy set: What happens as discretisation becomes finer?," *IEEE Symposium on Advances in Type-2 Fuzzy Logic Systems (T2FUZZ), 2011*, pp. 102–109, Apr. 2011.

14. I. Luna, S. Soares, and R. Ballini, "An adaptive hybrid model for monthly streamflow forecasting," in *Proceedings of the IEEE International Conference on Fuzzy Systems*, (London, UK), pp. 1–6, July 2007.

15. M. E. Valle and P. Sussner, "Storage and recall capabilities of fuzzy morphological associative memories with adjunction-based learning," *Neural Networks*, vol. 24, pp. 75–90, Jan. 2011.

16. M. H. F. Zarandi and A. D. Torshizi, "A new validation criteria for type-2 fuzzy c-means and possibilistic c-means," *2012 Annual Meeting of the North American Fuzzy Information Processing Society (NAFIPS)*, pp. 1–6, Aug. 2012.

17. http://www.weatheroffice.gc.ca/canada_e.html, ed., *Canadian Weather Office*. 25-nov-2013.

18. C. Wagner and H. Hagras, "Toward general type-2 fuzzy logic systems based on zslices," *IEEE Transactions on Fuzzy Systems*, vol. 18, no. 4, pp. 637–660, 2012.

FUZZY MORPHOLOGICAL PERCEPTRONS AND HYBRID FUZZY MORPHOLOGICAL/LINEAR PERCEPTRONS

Felipe Roberto Bueno*   Peter Sussner (advisor)

Dept. of Applied Mathematics, IMECC, UNICAMP
Campinas, São Paulo, Brazil
*E-mails: * buenofelipe01@gmail.com, sussner@ime.unicamp.br*

SUMMARY

Morphological perceptrons (MPs) belong to the class of morphological neural networks (MNNs).[1–3] The latter represent a class of artificial neural networks that perform operations of mathematical morphology (MM) at every node, possibly followed by the application of an activation function.[4]

Recall that MM was conceived as a theory for processing and analyzing objects, i.e., images or signals, by means of other objects called "structuring elements". Although initially developed for binary image processing and later extended to gray-scale image processing, MM can be conducted very generally in a complete lattice setting.[5,6] Since the late 1990's, several researchers have started transferring operators, ideas, and concepts of MM into the area of computational intelligence and MNNs emerged as a new paradigm for computing with artificial neural networks.[1–3,7]

Originally, MNNs only employed certain operations of gray-scale MM, namely gray-scale erosion and dilation according to the umbra approach.[8] These operations can be expressed in terms of (additive maximum and additive minimum) matrix-vector products in minimax algebra.[9] Learning in morphological or hybrid morphological/linear neural networks[10] can be achieved using either specifically designed training algorithms[3] or general purpose training algorithms such as traditional non-linear optimization (after smoothing non-differentiable functions such as the maximum and minimum operator), extreme learning, or evolutionary algorithms.

Until now, MPs (with and without competitive learning) have mainly found applications in classification. For an m-class classification problem, the learning phases of MPs and morphological perceptrons with competitive learning (MP/CLs)[3] yield a function from the complete lattice $\mathbb{R}^n_{\pm\infty} = (\mathbb{R} \cup \{+\infty, -\infty\})^n$ to the complete lattice $\{0,1\}^n$. The resulting function $\mathbb{R}^n_{\pm\infty} \to \{0,1\}^n$ has a representation that is reminiscent of Banon & Barrera's decomposition of mappings between complete lattices.[11] Our goal is to generalize the training algorithms of MPs and MP/CLs to the fuzzy setting and to provide a relationship between the resulting function and Banon & Barrera's decomposition of mappings between complete lattices.[12] In this context, recall that the class of fuzzy sets over an arbitrary universe also constitutes a complete lattice.[13]

It was not until recently that operations of fuzzy MM[13] emerged as aggregation functions of MNNs. In this case, we speak of fuzzy MNNs. In particular, fuzzy morphological associative memories[7] were introduced as extensions of (gray-scale) morphological associative memories. This project focusses on fuzzy morphological perceptrons (FMPs) and hybrid fuzzy morphological / linear perceptrons (FMLPs), both of which have not yet been considered in the literature. We intend to apply FMPs as well as FMLPs to problems in classification and prediction and to compare their performances with the ones of MPs, hybrid morphological / linear perceptrons, and other competitive models from the literature.

Hybrid fuzzy morphological / linear perceptrons will initially be designed by generalizing existing morphological / linear perceptrons, i.e., FMLPs will be given by a convex combination of a fuzzy morphological part and a linear part. Moreover, FMLPs will be embedded into a new class of extensions of morphological/rank/linear neural networks[1] to the fuzzy domain. Time permitting, we will also investigate further extensions to more general types of complete lattices such as interval-valued fuzzy sets and type-2 fuzzy sets.

Keywords: *Morphological neural networks, morphological perceptrons, mathematical morphology, complete lattice, fuzzy set, fuzzy mathematical morphology, fuzzy morphological perceptron, hybrid fuzzy morphological / linear perceptron, classification, prediction.*

References

1. L. F. C. Pessoa and P. Maragos, *Pattern Recognition* **33**, 945 (2000).
2. G. X. Ritter and P. Sussner, An introduction to morphological neural net-

works, in *Proceedings of the 13th International Conference on Pattern Recognition*, (Vienna, Austria, 1996).

3. P. Sussner and E. Esmi, *Information Sciences* **181**, 1929 (2011).
4. P. Sussner and M. E. Valle, Fuzzy associative memories and their relationship to mathematical morphology, in *Handbook of Granular Computing*, eds. W. Pedrycz, A. Skowron and V. Kreinovich (John Wiley and Sons, Inc., New York, 2008)
5. H. Heijmans and C. Ronse, *Computer Vision, Graphics, and Image Processing* **50**, 245 (1990).
6. J. Serra, *Image Analysis and Mathematical Morphology, Volume 2: Theoretical Advances* (Academic Press, New York, 1988).
7. M. E. Valle and P. Sussner, *Neural Networks* **24**, 75 (2011).
8. S. R. Sternberg, *Computer Vision, Graphics and Image Processing* **35**, 333 (1986).
9. J. L. Davidson, Foundation and applications of lattice transforms in image processing, in *Advances in Electronics and Electron Physics*, ed. P. Hawkes (Academic Press, New York, NY, 1992) pp. 61–130.
10. R. A. Araújo and T. A. E. Ferreira, *Inf. Sci.* **237**, 3(July 2013).
11. G. J. F. Banon and J. Barrera, *Signal Processing* **30**, 299(February 1993).
12. P. Maragos, *Journal of Mathematical Imaging and Vision* **22**, 333(May 2005).
13. P. Sussner and M. E. Valle, *Journal of Mathematical Imaging and Vision* **32**, 139(October 2008).

AUTHOR INDEX

Special thanks go to Organizing Committee, Steering Committee and Scientific Committee for their invaluable contributions to this Conference.

ACKNOWLEDGEMENTS

Special thanks go to Organizing Committee, Steering Committee and Scientific Committee for their invaluable contributions to this Conference.

Honorary Chair:
Lotfi A. Zadeh (USA)

Founding Chair:
Da Ruan

Program Chairs:
Ronei M. Moraes (Brazil)
Jie Lu (Australia)

Program Co-Chairs:
Javier Montero (Spain)
Guoqing Chen (China)

Special Session Chairs:
Victoria López (Spain)
Yang Xu (China)

Poster Session Chairs:
Jun Liu (United Kingdom)
Guangquan Zhang (Australia)

Tutorials Chairs:
Luiz Martinez (Spain)

Award Chairs:
Etienne Kerre (Belgium)
Ronei M. Moraes (Brazil)

Publicity Chairs:
Tianrui Li (China)
Xianyi Zheng (France)

Cengiz Kahraman (Turkey)
Peijun Guo (Japan)

Organizing Chair:
Ronei M. Moraes (Brazil)

Organizing Co-Chair:
Liliane S. Machado (Brazil)

Local Organization Committee:
Benjamin R. C. Bedregal
Danielly C. S. C. Holmes
Elaine A. M. G. Soares
Frederico F. Ribeiro
Jodavid A. Ferreira
José T. D. Segundo
Laisa R. de Sá
Luana R. Almeida
Marcelo R. P. Ferreira
Regivan H. N. Santiago
Thaíse K. L. Costa
Tatiene C. Souza

Steering Committee:
Etienne Kerre (Chair, Belgium)
Cengiz Kahraman (Turkey)
Guoqing Chen (China)
Javier Montero (Spain)
Jie Lu (Australia)
Jun Liu (United Kingdom)
Luis Martinez (Spain)
Yang Xu (China)

X. Pan (China)
I. Pardines (Spain)
H. Peng (Australia)
S. Qiao (China)
K. Qin (China)
F. Ramezani (Australia)
J. Redmond (Spain)
M. Rocha (Brazil)
R. M. Rodríguez (Spain)
A. Sgora (Greece)
R. Soto (Spain)
T. Souza (Brazil)
K. M. Tay (China)
F. Teng (China)
A. C. Tolga (Turkey)
S. T. Vargas (Spain)

J. W. Vilanova (Mexico)
H. Wang (China)
W. Wang (China)
D. Wu (Australia)
J. Wu (Australia)
L. Xiaohong (China)
W. Xu (China)
J. Xuan (Australia)
C. Yáñez-Márquez (Spain)
A. Zeng (China)
N. Zeng (China)
M. Zhang (China)
Z. Zhang (China)
W. Zhao (China)
X. Zhong (China)
L. Zou (China)

Printed in the United States
By Bookmasters